Management

Management

Michael A. Hitt

J. Stewart Black

Lyman W. Porter

Pearson Education International

Editor in Chief: David Parker
Product Development Manager: Ashley Santora
Editorial Assistant: Elizabeth Davis
Marketing Assistant: Ian Gold
Senior Managing Editor: Judy Leale
Associate Managing Editor: Suzanne DeWorken
Production Project Manager: Carol Samet
Permissions Coordinator: Charles Morris
Senior Operations Specialist: Arnold Vila
Creative Director: Leslie Osher
Senior Art Director: Janet Slowik
Interior Design: Karen Quigley
Cover Design: Karen Quigley
Cover Illustration/Photo: Marc Bruce/Images.com
Illustration (Interior): ElectraGraphics, Inc.
Director, Image Resource Center: Melinda Reo
Manager, Rights and Permissions: Zina Arabia
Manager, Visual Research: Beth Brenzel
Manager, Cover Visual Research & Permissions: Karen Sanatar
Image Permission Coordinator: Richard Rodrigues
Photo Researcher: Rachel Lucas
Composition: GGS Book Services
Full-Service Project Management: GGS Book Services/Heidi Allgair
Printer/Binder: Quebecor/Versailles
Typeface: 10/12 pt Times Roman

Credits and acknowledgments borrowed from other sources and reproduced, with permission, in this textbook appear on page 551.

Pearson Education LTD., London
Pearson Education Singapore, Pte. Ltd
Pearson Education, Canada, Ltd
Pearson Education–Japan
Pearson Education Australia PTY, Limited
Pearson Education North Asia Ltd
Pearson Educación de Mexico, S.A. de C.V.
Pearson Education Malaysia, Pte. Ltd.
Pearson Education, Upper Saddle River, New Jersey

10 9 8 7 6 5 4 3 2 1
ISBN-13: 978-0-13-503276-3
ISBN-10: 0-13-503276-8

Brief Contents

Contents

Preface

What Makes This Book Unique?

One of our fundamental objectives as an author team was to create a textbook for students and instructors that was both relevant and rigorous. Despite the number of good textbooks on the market, many of them tend to lean in one of two directions: Some textbooks do a good job of presenting material and integrating research, but students struggle to make the connection between theory and practice. Other textbooks do a good job of relating the material to the real world, but they are not always based on the current research. Our experience in teaching students, talking with other instructors, and working with practicing managers led us to believe there was a need for a textbook that was both relevant and based on current research literature.

As an author team we are fortunate to have, collectively, nearly *100 years* of in-depth experience directly conducting research, reviewing articles, and studying management literature—particularly in the international sphere—and working with colleagues from a variety of different countries and cultures. The breadth and depth of our experience has helped us identify the key theories, concepts, and empirical findings that inform the practice of management in both domestic and global contexts.

We have also had a great number of opportunities over the years to teach many students, work with a large number of managers, and consult with various companies, all focused on the practice of management. Like our research, these experiences have taken place in a variety of places around the world. We have literally worked with managers from every part of the globe. We believe this experience has helped us understand the challenges that students of management face when it comes to relating theory to practice. As a consequence, we have worked hard to relate the findings from the current research to the implications they hold for practicing managers.

Why a New Edition?

The dual objectives of relevance and rigor were the basis of the first edition of *Management*, and they continue to be the basis for this second edition. However, as a team, we are great admirers and try to be good examples of the principle of continuous improvement. Toward this end, in this edition, we have made several changes that we believe enhance the book.

To make the connection between relevance and rigor more direct for students and instructors, we have added a new feature that appears at the beginning of each chapter, titled "Managerial Challenges from the Front Line." It includes a focused example of a managerial challenge faced by a real person. Several of these people are recent college graduates, and others are more experienced managers. The feature is designed to help students understand and relate the chapter content to managerial practice. We also provide a "Rest of the Story" feature at the end of the chapter that briefly describes how the manager resolved the challenge.

Because many undergraduates have not yet had extensive practical experience working in organizations, they are not always able to benefit from the self-insight and awareness that experience can provide. Yet, as we also know, much of a manager's approach to various managerial activities, such as decision making or communicating, are influenced by his or her own tendencies, orientations, and the like. As a consequence, we have added a new "Self-Assessment" feature at the end of each chapter to help students think about themselves and how their inclination or orientation relates to some of the material covered in the chapter.

Emphasizing the importance of relevance, we have updated all the "A Manager's Challenge" sections (real-life examples of challenges managers face) from the first edition of the book and inserted new ones in most of the chapters. In addition, we have added many other current managerial examples to the chapters. In order to emphasize the importance of current research and rigor, we have also added new, up-to-date content and current (2006 and 2007) references to the chapters.

This second edition is also now more concise, with 15 chapters. We made these revisions without sacrificing important content. In fact, we have added two new chapters, "International Management and Globalization" and "Operations Management," to this edition. We have also added an appendix titled "The History of Managerial Thought and Practice" for students who desire to learn more about the historical development of the management field. As a result, the second edition of *Management* now presents a comprehensive yet concise discussion of the important functions and activities of management.

Supplements to This Book

This second edition of *Management* has been designed specifically to support the instructor teaching the course and to be user friendly for students. The following support materials have been developed to accompany the second edition:

Instructor Resource Center

At www.prenhall.com/irc, instructors can access a variety of print, digital, and presentation resources available with this text in downloadable format. Registration is simple and gives you immediate access to new titles and new editions. As a registered faculty member, you can download resource files and receive immediate access and instructions for installing course management content on your campus server.

In case you ever need assistance, our dedicated technical support team is ready to help with the media supplements that accompany this text. Visit www.247.prenhall.com for answers to frequently asked questions and toll-free user support phone numbers.

The Instructor Resource Center provides the following electronic resources.

TEST BANK The test bank, authored by David Stuart, contains approximately 100 questions per chapter, including multiple-choice, true/false, short-answer, and scenario-based questions. Short-answer questions are questions that can be answered in one to five sentences. Scenario-based questions are essay-type questions developed around a short scenario.

In this edition, each question in the test bank contains a page reference and difficulty rating, and most include references to the chapter learning objectives to which they relate. In addition, the test bank incorporates the standards for education of the Association to Advance Collegiate Schools of Business (AACSB). For each question applicable to an AACSB standard, the related skill is noted.*

AACSB is a not-for-profit corporation of educational institutions, corporations, and other organizations devoted to the promotion and improvement of higher education in business administration and accounting. A collegiate institution offering degrees in business administration or accounting may volunteer for AACSB accreditation review. The AACSB makes initial accreditation decisions and conducts periodic reviews to promote continuous quality improvement in management education. Pearson Education is a proud member of the AACSB and is pleased to provide advice to help you apply AACSB learning standards.

One of the criteria for AACSB accreditation is the quality of the curriculum. Although no specific courses are required, the AACSB expects a curriculum to include learning

*Please note that some questions do not have learning objectives or AACSB topics indicated, as they are not always applicable.

experiences in a number of areas. To ensure that a curriculum meets the appropriate criteria, the AACSB has created the following six learning standards:

- Communication
- Ethical Reasoning
- Analytic Skills
- Use of Information Technology
- Multicultural and Diversity
- Reflective Thinking

Questions that test skills relevant to these standards are tagged with the appropriate standard. For example, a question testing the moral questions associated with externalities would receive the Ethical Reasoning tag.

Tagged questions help you measure whether students are grasping the course content that aligns with AACSB guidelines. In addition, the tagged questions may help to identify potential applications of these skills. This in turn may suggest enrichment activities or other educational experiences to help students achieve these goals.

This test bank is also available in a print version (ISBN 0-13-600741-4).

TESTGEN TEST GENERATOR SOFTWARE The easy-to-use TestGen software allows instructors to custom design, save, and generate classroom tests. Instructors can edit, add, or delete questions from the test bank; edit existing graphics and create new graphics; analyze test results; and organize a database of tests and student results. TestGen provides many flexible options for organizing and displaying tests, along with a search and sort feature.

POWERPOINTS Two PowerPoint packages developed by Susan Peterson of Scottsdale Community College are available for this textbook. The first is a fully developed set of instructor PowerPoints. The second is an enhanced, interactive version of the first, with video clips and Web links in each chapter. Both versions contain teaching notes. In addition to being available for download, the PowerPoints are also available on the Instructor Resource Center on CD-ROM (ISBN 0-13-600779-1).

INSTRUCTOR'S MANUAL Authored by Grace McLaughlin of the University of California, Irvine, the Instructor's Manual offers much more than just the traditional limited chapter outline and answers to the end-of-chapter materials. In addition to these basic items, you will find suggested teaching strategies for 45-, 90-, and 180-minute sessions; chapter coverage suggestions for semester- and quarter-length courses; and modular suggestions for courses focused on general management, strategy, and/or organizational behavior. The coverage for each chapter includes a variety of resources, such as exercises, critical thinking assignments, debate topics, and research assignments. Two appendixes contain complete PowerPoint slides and an in-depth video guide. The Instructor's Manual is also available in a print version (ISBN 0-13-600740-6).

FIGURES FROM THE TEXT All the figures from the textbook are available electronically for instructors to download, print, display in class, or use in customized materials.

Videos on DVD

The new DVD (ISBN 0-13-600780-5) accompanying this second edition of *Management* contains 12 video clips that highlight management issues at a variety of companies, including Patagonia, Swiss Army, Ernst & Young, the WNBA, The Golf Network, and more.

Student Web Site

The text's companion Web site, located at www.prenhall.com/hitt, features automatically graded, chapter-by-chapter quizzes students can take for practice as well as text-accompanying PowerPoint slides for easy student review. In addition, the slides can be conveniently printed three to a page for in-class note taking.

CourseSmart Textbooks Online

CourseSmart Textbooks Online is an exciting new choice for students looking to save money. As an alternative to purchasing the print textbook, students can subscribe to the same content online and save up to 50% off the suggested list price of the print text. With a CourseSmart eTextbook, students can search the text, make notes online, print out reading assignments that incorporate lecture notes, and bookmark important passages for later review. For more information, or to subscribe to the CourseSmart eTextbook, visit www.coursesmart.com.

Acknowledgments

We owe a debt of gratitude to David Parker, our editor, and the rest of the Prentice Hall team, including Kristen Varina, Carol Samet, and Charles Morris, for their efforts to support and help us develop and produce this edition. We also thank Amy Ray for her excellent support and editorial guidance. We owe special thanks to Grace McLaughlin and Melissa Luna for their efforts and research support for this edition. Grace also again did an excellent job in the development of the accompanying Instructor's Manual.

We extend a special thanks for the excellent feedback from reviewers, users, and focus group participants. These include:

David Albritton, Northern Arizona University

Forrest Aven, University of Houston–Downtown

Richard Babcock, University of San Francisco

Stacy Ball-Elias, Southwest Minnesota State University

Stephanie Bibb, Chicago State University

Gene Blackmun III, Rio Hondo College (FG)

Rochelle Brunson, Alvin Community College

Gary Bumgarner, Mountain Empire Community College

John Burns, North Harris Montgomery CC District–Tomball College (FG)

Barbara Carlin, University of Houston

Macgorine Cassell, Fairmount State University

Bruce Charnov, Hofstra University

Michael Drafke, College of DuPage

N. Mai Lai Eng, San Antonio College

Mary Fanning, College of Notre Dame of Maryland

Maruffi Fordham, Fordham University

Pat Hafford, Wentworth Institute

Gary Hensel, McHenry Country College

Tammy Hunt, University of North Carolina–Wilmington

Karen Jacobs, LeTourneau University

Connie James, Pepperdine University (FG)

James H. Kennedy, Angelina College (FG)

Jerry Kinard, Western Carolina University

Frank Krafka, St. Edward's University

Sal Kukalis, California State University, Long Beach

Leslie Ledger, Central Texas College (FG)

Lianlian Lin, California State Polytechnic University–Pomona (FG)

Tom Mahafey, Siena College

Mark Nagel, Normandale Community College

Abdul Qastin, Lakeland College

R. Nicholas Panepinto, Flagler College

Mark Poulos, St. Edward's University

Lois Shelton, Chapman University (FG)

Randi Sims, Nova Southeastern University

Tom Sy, California State University–Long Beach (FG)

Pat Tadlock, Horry-Georgetown Technical College

Spence Tower, Central Michigan University

Julia Underwood, Azusa Pacific University (FG)

David G. Vequist, University of the Incarnate Word

Bruce Walker, University of Louisiana–Monroe

Randy Westgren, University of Illinois, Urbana/Champaign

Johnnie Williams, Texas Southern University

Nancy Zimmerman, Community College Baltimore/Catonsville

Part One

Managing Ethically and Globally

1

The Nature of Management

Learning Objectives

After studying this chapter, you should be able to:

- Define the term *management*.
- Explain the major challenges with which managers must deal.
- Describe how historical research on management has contributed to the current practice of management.
- Identify and discuss the primary managerial functions.
- Explain the three general roles involved in managerial work and the specific roles within each.
- Explore and describe the three dimensions of managerial jobs.
- Discuss the primary skills required to be an effective manager.

Managerial Challenges from the Front Line

Name: Blaine Halvorson

Position: President and CEO, Junk Food

Alma mater: Montana State University (BA in Fine Arts/Graphic Design)

Outside work activities: Leisure time, travel, and painting (mainly pop art)

First job out of school: Designed clothes for rock bands and MTV while in college; post-college: worked for a short time at a Los Angeles apparel company followed by Planet Golf, where he oversaw the Japanese distribution of the company's products.

Hero: Jean-Michel Basquiat—I think that he is an amazing artist.

Motto to live by: Everyone should take a leap of faith once in their lives and see if they can do something great.

What drives me: The desire for accomplishment and to take something to the next level.

Management style: Not following a straight line—thinking outside of the box and having a tremendous drive.

Graphic designer Blaine Halvorson, along with his business partner Natalie Grof, are the founders of the multimillion-dollar clothing-design business Junk Food, Inc. They worked together at Planet Golf prior to starting their own company. They built the company from a two-person business operating out of an apartment into the world's largest licensing T-shirt manufacturer.

Halvorson experienced early success designing clothes, showing that he had talent and that there was a market for his ideas. He attended trade shows and received a lot of positive press. Then, he started receiving large orders for his designs. Unfortunately, he had no idea of how to mass produce his products. He couldn't meet the orders so he had to cancel them. He realized that he had to learn more about managing a business. However, he learned from his mistakes, and this helped him make Junk Food a success a few years later.

While working at Planet Golf, he was developing a business on the side that was the forerunner of Junk Food. After an investor bought Planet Golf, Halvorson sent him a new design and his idea for a different clothing line of T-shirts.

The owner of Planet Golf became an angel investor in Junk Food (a silent partner who provided money, but Halvorson and Grof managed the company). The basic idea for the company was to provide a different product customers valued. Halvorson and Grof built the brand name by using icons popular with people. Until then, licensing was only used for mass market merchandise, not "designer clothes," especially T-shirts. They started with names such as Twister, Candy Land, and My Little Pony. They then moved to other licensees, such as Sesame Street,

Rolling Stones, DC Comics, Looney Tunes. They developed a strong following for the Junk Food brand, and even the products have become collectables because of the Junk Food brand label. Now, the products are even sold in international markets.

To do what Halvorson did, build a successful company, requires a willingness to take risks and a desire to create something on your own. It also requires a significant amount of sacrifice, investing substantial amounts of time and effort to make the business work. It also took a significant amount of management skills. For example, Halvorson had to attract, hire, and manage a high-quality team of employees to make Junk Food a success. The business now has 45 employees. It also requires perseverance and knowing the market. He had to learn how to mass produce products and manage the business's cash flow, among other challenges. Halvorson describes the process as "moving in 50 different directions simultaneously and trying to solve 10 problems at the same time."

As described in the opening profile, Halvorson built a highly successful company. He did so by developing an idea for a different type of clothing design that customers valued. He is a creative and excellent designer, but his success was due to much more. For example, early in his career, he showed his talent for developing creative clothing designs that the market desired. However, he was unable to manufacture the products in the numbers necessary to fulfill the orders. Thus, after that time, he learned how to build and manage a business. He had to learn how to organize the company to design, manufacture, and distribute Junk Food's products. He had to hire and manage people to complete these tasks. And finally, he had to ensure that the company used resources efficiently to make a profit and ensure that the business was successful.

The profile on Halvorson shows that management is a challenging and necessary part of a successful business. It also depicts management as exciting and yet requiring a lot of hard work and dedication. In this chapter, we introduce the concept of management and show how it is done. We explore the challenges that managers face on a regular basis and the skills they must have to successfully handle them.

Now, we turn to a set of basic questions that are the focus for the remainder of Chapter 1: (1) What is management? (2) What are the primary challenges that managers face? (3) What do managers do? (4) What skills do managers need?

What Is Management?

To begin, we examine the concepts that form the base of this book.

Management is an activity or process. More specifically, **management** is the process of assembling and using sets of resources in a goal-directed manner to accomplish tasks in an organizational setting. This definition can be subdivided into its key parts:

management
the process of assembling and using sets of resources in a goal-directed manner to accomplish tasks in an organizational setting

1. Management is a process: It involves a series of activities and operations, such as planning, deciding, and evaluating.

2. Management involves assembling and using sets of resources: It is a process that brings together, and puts into use, a variety of resources: human, financial, material, and informational.
3. Management involves acting in a goal-directed manner to accomplish tasks: It is an activity with a purpose and direction. The purpose or direction may be that of the individual, the organization, or, usually, a combination of the two. It includes one's efforts to complete activities successfully and to achieve particular levels of desired results.
4. Management involves activities carried out in an organizational setting: It is a process undertaken in **organizations** by people with different functions intentionally structured and coordinated to achieve common purposes.

organizations
interconnected sets of individuals and groups who attempt to accomplish common goals through differentiated functions and their coordination

In addition to being "a process" or set of activities, management can also have several other meanings. The term sometimes designates a particular part of the organization: the set of individuals who carry out management activities. Thus, some may use the phrase "the *management* of IBM decided . . ." or "the management of University Hospital developed a new personnel policy . . . ." Often, when the term is used this way, it does not necessarily refer to all members of management but rather to those who occupy the highest-level positions within the organization (top management).

Another similar use of the term is to distinguish a category of people (that is, "management") from those who are members of collective bargaining units ("union" members or, more informally, "labor") or those who are not involved in specific managerial activities, whether or not they are union members ("nonmanagement employees" or "rank-and-file employees"). The term *member* refers to any person (any employee) in an organization without regard to that individual's place in the organization. In this book, we use the term *manager* to refer to anyone who has designated responsibilities for carrying out managerial activities, and *managing* to refer to the process of completing those activities.

However, *management* is too complex a concept for any one definition to capture accurately. Next, we explain several of the challenges with which managers must deal.

Managerial Challenges

Managers face a number of challenges on a regular basis. The nature of the environment in which managers operate requires that they manage change effectively. Managers are responsible for managing resources—financial, human, and otherwise. To ensure that their organization is competitive and survives in a rapidly changing environment, they must manage strategically. Because of the major changes occurring rapidly in the business world today, managers must be entrepreneurial and innovative. Essentially, they must continuously find ways to create more value for customers than do competitors. Managers' activities take place within organizations. Although managers are the primary "drivers" of their organizations, organizations put boundaries on what managers can and cannot do. We examine each of these challenges next.

Managing Change

Managing change is the most persistent, pervasive, and powerful challenge with which all managers have to deal, regardless of the organizations for which they work or where they're located. No matter how new or experienced managers are, they will be confronted with both the need for change and the opportunity to create change. Not making any changes is unlikely to be an option. As a Greek philosopher once wrote many centuries ago, "Change alone is unchanging,"[1] and that statement remains appropriate today.

Managing change is no simple task, especially because most people naturally resist change. Thus, managers must find ways to gain the employees' acceptance of change in order to implement it effectively. To gain acceptance, it is useful for managers to create "small wins." For example, the manager might implement the change in one smaller area and make it successful. This success then makes the change legitimate in the eyes of the employees.[2] Two of the major causes of change with which managers must deal are new technology and globalization.

TECHNOLOGY No managers in today's world can ignore the impact of technology and the way it affects their jobs and firms. Technology developments often force managers to make changes—whether they want to or not. The Internet is a case in point. The Internet has had far-reaching effects on how managers do their jobs.

The introduction of a new technology often leads to the development of new products and new processes for accomplishing tasks. The Internet has created many opportunities to market products differently, to reach distant markets, and to communicate internally and externally in more effective ways. Therefore, it has provided many opportunities for managers. Yet, they must identify these opportunities and find ways to exploit them. If they do not, competitors are likely to do so and take market share from them. Essentially, the Internet has increased the speed of change, the flow of information, the competitive reach into international markets, and the amount of competition in all markets.

Because the Internet provides information, it has served as a catalyst for the continued development of other technologies and information about them. It has placed an emphasis on the importance of knowledge and has increased the importance of human capital (the holder of the knowledge). It has helped many small and medium-sized firms to enter and compete in international markets, thereby enhancing globalization.[3]

GLOBALIZATION Globalization is the development and observation of the increasing international and cross-national nature of everything from politics to business. No longer can managers ignore what happens in the rest of the world because events in other countries tend to affect their organizations. Global events will almost certainly affect the goals that managers set, the decisions they make, and how they must coordinate and lead the work of other people.

The opening of many world markets (e.g., in China), the development of free trade agreements (such as the General Agreement on Tariffs and Trade—GATT, and the North American Free Trade Agreement—NAFTA), growing economies around the world, and increases in technology that facilitate global partnerships and competition have all contributed greatly to increasing globalization.[4] Opening of markets to foreign firms coupled with economic development increases market opportunities but simultaneously leads to greater global competition. In order to compete effectively in global markets, firms have sought increasingly to outsource activities to people and firms in lower-cost countries like India and China.[5]

Globalization promotes greater involvement in international markets. Thus, firms moving into international markets increasingly need to learn about different cultures and the institutional environments in these markets.[6] Some firms have facilitated this learning process by developing multicultural management teams. These teams have managers who speak different languages and have knowledge about the markets and environments in different regions of the world in which the firms operate.[7] Because of the complexities of operating in multiple countries and regions, some firms focus their international operations in one or a few specific regions of the world. In this way, they can develop the knowledge of the culture, markets, and institutions to operate there effectively.[8] (In Chapter 3, we discuss in further detail globalization and how firms manage in a global environment.)

Although Andrea Jung had done an excellent job turning around Avon's performance (see A Manager's Challenge on page 8), for which she received much positive acclaim, she faced a new crisis. She had achieved much of Avon's growth through international expansion. Yet, it appears that she needed to make other changes to better manage the geographically diversified firm that she created. She also needed to increase Avon's efficiencies internally, as overhead costs soared along with a large number of low-selling products

Jung had to make significant changes in Avon in an attempt to recapture its success. The substantial reduction in management layers, elimination of 25 percent of the products sold, and the layoff of many managers whom she had recruited were among the changes she made. It appears that her changes are paying off with a return to growth in 2006. Andrea Jung appears to be a decisive manager who is likely to continue to be successful and warranting all the recognition bestowed on her for her managerial prowess.

A MANAGER'S CHALLENGE

Globalization

The Global Remaking of Avon—Again

When Andrea Jung became CEO of Avon in 1999, the company was reeling from poor performance. However, Jung implemented new strategies to turn the company around. She took risks by developing new products and expanded greatly Avon's presence in global markets. And, she displayed a passion for her work as a manager and compassion for those working for the company. Because of her efforts and success, she was highly acknowledged for her leadership and effective management. The contrast was great with other "notorious" managers of this time who were well-known for their poor performance and ethical lapses, such as the leaders of Enron and WorldCom. Jung was recognized as one of the "50 Most Powerful Women in America." In 2001, *Time*/CNN recognized her as one of the "25 Most Influential Global Executives." *Business Ethics* magazine has recognized Avon numerous times as one of the "100 Best Corporate Citizens" among U.S. publicly held companies.

The list of Jung's accomplishments as a manager and Avon's CEO is lengthy. However, problems occurred. After almost six years of growth exceeding 10 percent annually and tripling the earnings over the same time period, sales began to stall or decline in several markets. Avon had expanded its international operations to 143 countries under Jung's leadership, but the international diversity became a problem to manage. Industry analysts noted that not only had sales stalled but overhead was high because local managers handled most decisions in foreign markets (e.g., manufacturing, marketing) thereby disallowing the opportunity to gain economies of scale. After a tough six months in which Avon's stock price declined 45 percent (in December 2005), Jung decided that she had to make substantial changes. It was very difficult for her to do so because she was changing the organization that she built and that had been highly successful.

Perhaps the most significant change Jung made was reorganizing Avon's management structure, reducing much of the autonomy previously enjoyed by country managers. She eliminated 7 layers of management to reduce the layers from 15 to 8. This meant that she had to lay off 25 percent of her top 1,000 managers, many of whom she had hired. According to Jung, it was a very tough decision. She hired many new managers from top consumer products companies, such as Gillette, Kraft, PepsiCo, and Procter & Gamble, and began to manage Avon with an eye toward achieving the company's return-on-investment goals. Additionally, she eliminated about 25 percent of the least-profitable products sold by Avon and increased advertising by 83 percent. She also changed the company's product development processes, enabling the firm to introduce about 1,000 new products in 2006.

At least the changes appear to be having positive results. Total sales at Avon were up 8 percent in 2006, and analysts are recommending that investors buy Avon stock again. Many of them like the fact that 70 percent of Avon's sales come from outside the United States in markets with a lot of potential growth.

The job of a manager is never over. One minute your company's on top of the world. Then everything changes, and you're fighting back from the brink. That's what Andrea Jung, the CEO of Avon found after discovering that taking the company global was tougher than it seemed.

Sources: N. Byrnes, "Avon: More Than Cosmetic Changes," *Business Week*, March 12, 2007, 62–63; "Full-Year 2006 Total Revenue Up 8% to $8.8 Billion," www.avoncompany.com/investor/businessnews, February 6, 2007; M. A. Hitt, C. C. Miller, and A. Colella, *Organizational Behavior: A Strategic Approach* (Hoboken, NJ: John Wiley & Sons, 2006), 277–278.

Managing Resources

A major part of a manager's job is to manage the resources of the organization. The manager must ensure the efficient use of resources but also use the resources in ways that maximize the achievement of the organization's goals. Among the resources important to managers are financial capital, human capital, physical resources (buildings and equipment, for example), and technology. They build and manage a portfolio of resources.[9] To build the portfolio, they have to acquire and develop the resources needed to complete the organization's tasks. For example, managers need to recruit and select the best employees possible to join the organization. After becoming employees, managers need to continually develop the employees' knowledge and skills.[10] As they do so, the employees' value to the organization increases. This implies that managers need to be effective in evaluating people's skills in order to select the best and to know what skills they need to develop. Managers must also design and implement the means to promote learning in the organization.[11]

Once they have the portfolio of resources, managers have to then allocate and coordinate these resources to accomplish the required tasks of the organization.[12] Managers are also responsible for developing and implementing a strategy to use the organization's capabilities to accomplish its goals.[13] One of the major dimensions of coordination is the relationship with others, especially other managers in the organization and with the employees managed. So, managers' interpersonal and communication skills are paramount in this process. We conclude that managers largely get things done with and through people in the organization. As a result, how they manage human capital is critical to their success.

Xerox CEO Anne Mulcahy is largely credited with turning around that company's performance. But Mulcahy argues that it was Xerox's employees who were critical to the turnaround in the company's performance. She stated that ". . . attracting them, motivating them, keeping them—making Xerox an employer of choice—is critical to our drive back to greatness."[14] These comments suggest that staffing the organization with the best human capital possible and further developing the knowledge and skills of employees is critical for the success.[15] This conclusion emphasizes the importance of managing the organization's resources (especially the people) to its ability to compete and survive in an increasingly competitive environment.[16]

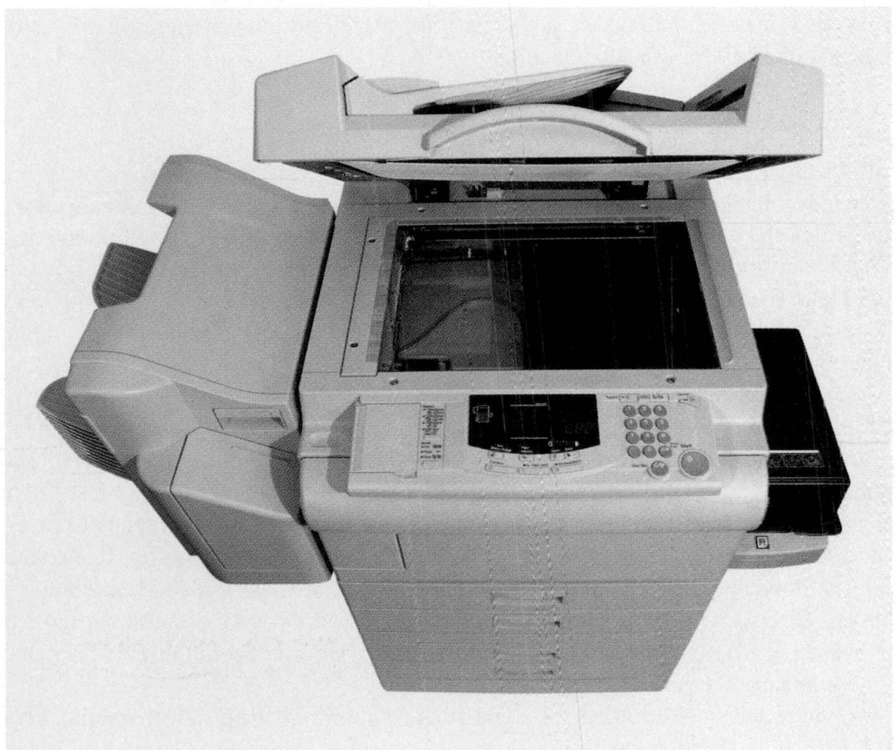

Executives at Xerox know that the company is more than just its machines. Xerox's CEO, Anne Mulcahy, has emphasized that the firm's human capital (people) are critical to the company's success in the highly competitive photocopier market.

Managing Strategically

Managerial challenges create an incredibly complex, dynamic, and competitive landscape in which most managers must operate. To survive and perform well in such an environment, managers throughout the organization need to manage strategically.[17] Managers at the top of the organization—CEOs such as Meg Whitman at eBay—establish goals and formulate a strategy for the firm to achieve those goals. To accomplish the goals, the company must effectively implement the strategy, which requires managers at all levels of the organization to set and accomplish goals that contribute to the organization's ultimate performance.

The increasing globalization and the enhanced use of technology have contributed to greater changes emphasizing the importance of knowledge to organizational success.[18] The importance placed on the intellectual capital of the organization requires managers to use their portfolio of resources effectively.[19] Of primary importance are intangible resources such as the employees and the firm's reputation. Managers are responsible for building an organization's capabilities and then leveraging them through a strategy designed to give it an advantage over its competitors. They usually do this by creating more value for their customers than competitors.[20]

BMW managers, for example, developed a strategy to use the firm's excellent research and development (R&D) capabilities to design and manufacture several new automobiles with the goal of increasing U.S. sales by 40 percent by 2008. The top managers at BMW made this decision at a time when other automobile manufacturers were reducing R&D expenditures to control costs. Capitalizing on its strengths and using them strategically to offer consumers more and better auto designs so far has given BMW an advantage over its competitors and contributed to its superior performance.[21]

Managers are responsible for forming the strategies of the major units within the organization as well. Because people in the organization have to implement the strategy, managers must focus heavily on the human factor. As they implement their strategies, they will encounter conflicting conditions. Often this means managing multiple situations simultaneously and remaining flexible to adapt to changing conditions. Additionally, achieving an organization's goals requires that managers commit themselves to always being alert to how they can improve and strengthen strategies in advancing the organization's vision. Finally, the dynamic competitive landscape entails substantial change. To adapt to this change, managers should be innovative and entrepreneurial; they should search continuously for new opportunities.

Managing Entrepreneurially

Managers should regularly search for new opportunities in the current marketplace or identify ideas that could create new markets.[22] Entrepreneurship involves identifying new opportunities and exploiting them. Thus, managers must be entrepreneurial. Entrepreneurial activity is not limited to new, small firms, however. Managers in large firms need to be entrepreneurial and create new businesses as well. Developing new businesses requires that the lead person, and perhaps others, take entrepreneurial actions. Given the amount of change and innovation encountered in most industries and countries, businesses cannot survive without being entrepreneurial.[23]

To be entrepreneurial, managers must develop an entrepreneurial mind-set. An entrepreneurial mind-set is a way of thinking about businesses that emphasizes actions to take advantage of uncertainty.[24] With an entrepreneurial mind-set, managers can sense opportunities and take actions to exploit them. Uncertainty in the environment tends to level the "playing field" for both large and smaller organizations and for resource-rich and resource-poor ones. Anyone can identify opportunities and exploit them to achieve a competitive advantage. This is how Microsoft beat its competitors, who were at one time larger and more powerful. To develop an entrepreneurial mind-set, managers must first be alert to new ideas and use them to create value for customers.[25]

Both large and small firms and new and established firms can be entrepreneurial. For reasons described earlier, they not only can be, they must be to survive. The original Polaroid, once an entrepreneurial company and a market leader in instant photography, no longer exists because it lost its entrepreneurial nature, and market share winnowed away with the development of digital photography technology (the firm that bought the rights to the Polaroid name is struggling). As a whole, small and new firms tend to be more entrepreneurial but often lack the ability to sustain this advantage. On the other hand, large, established firms are good at using their size to gain an advantage and sustaining their positions as long as new, rival products don't enter the market. However, larger firms have a more difficult time being entrepreneurial.[26]

Historical Approaches to Management

While many think that management is a very new concept, it is not. Even ancient civilizations encountered managerial challenges and found ways to cope with them. More than 1,000 years ago, Chinese leaders searched for an effective means of governing a large organization (government) and expressed the importance of open communications and consideration of people's needs. Additionally, Chinese leaders discussed the value of specialized labor, hiring and promotions based on merit, and the need to clearly describe jobs.[27] The modern field of strategic management owes its origins to an ancient Chinese warrior, Sun Tsu, and his book, *The Art of War*.

Management was practiced in many parts of the world many years ago. For example, consider how the pyramids were designed and built in Egypt so long ago. Completing these "wonders of the world" required a significant amount of planning, organization, and management of labor. Likewise, 2,000 years ago, the Roman Empire required effective management to build major monuments and an extensive network of roads and viaducts. Additionally, the development and spread of the Catholic Church throughout the world required a significant amount of planning, organization, and directing of people's efforts and activities.

The origins of what is often referred to as "modern management" are found in the Industrial Revolution, which began in England in the mid-eighteenth century and later spread to the United States and other geographic regions of the world. While many have contributed to the development of management thought and practices, Fredrick W. Taylor (1856–1915), an American engineer, is often credited as the "father of modern management." Taylor's work on linking workers' incentives to their performance provided an important base for motivation theory applied to the workplace. He argued that pay was only part of the reward and that employees should be provided regularly with feedback on their performance. His primary legacy is the principles of scientific management that form the base for many of the different functions, roles, and activities of managers that we explore in this book.[28] Recent research proclaims that scientific management was a sophisticated theoretical approach that contributed to other fields as well as institutional economics.[29]

Many other people have contributed to our notion of modern management theory and practice over the course of the last two centuries as well. Among them are Frank and Lillian Gilbreth, who developed the beginnings of time and motion studies to determine the most efficient manner in which to complete tasks. Alfred P. Sloan (former CEO of General Motors) and Chester Barnard (an executive of AT&T) both contributed to our knowledge of how to build an efficient and effective organization. While Sloan focused on the formal aspects of organizing such as the functions and divisions, Barnard emphasized the social characteristics of organizing such as cooperation, building common purpose, and the importance of communication. Mary Parker Follett and Douglas McGregor focused on the importance and value of leadership in organizations. Follett espoused principles related to the importance of integration and treating employees as partners. Similarly, McGregor is best known for promoting "Theory Y" leadership practices with positive assumptions about human nature in which positive leadership can bring forth greater efforts and levels of achievement from employees. And, Abraham Maslow and Frederick Herzberg made major contributions to our knowledge of motivation that are present in managerial practices today. Maslow is best known for his "hierarchy of needs" theory and Herzberg for proposing the independence of motivators and hygiene factors. Both of these individuals' ideas led to the concept of job enrichment used to design tasks that more effectively motivate employees and use more of their skills.[30]

We present a more detailed discussion of the history of management thought and practice in the appendix to this book. The ideas of these management pioneers are evident in the discussion of what managers do in the following sections.

What Do Managers Do?

In the opening profile about Blaine Halvorson, we learn that management has many dimensions. Halvorson's first attempt to design and sell clothes was successful because he created a product the market desired. Yet, he was unable to satisfy that demand. He did not know how to develop and manage an organization. His description of what he did in developing and managing Junk Food to be a successful company shows a number of managerial tasks that he had to complete, which include many of the functions described in this section.

There are several ways to examine managers' jobs aside from observing what managers do. Over the years, several systems have been developed to classify (a) managerial functions, (b) the roles in which managers operate, and (c) the characteristics and dimensions of managerial jobs. These typologies can provide useful ways to examine the varied nature of managerial jobs and responsibilities. In effect, they provide a road map for understanding what management is.

One way to think about the question "What do managers do?" is to analyze the work of managers according to the different functions that they perform. The first such classification system dates back at least 80 years, and, after more than eight decades, this system remains widely used by management scholars and writers.[31] A variation of this traditional typology forms the basis for the general sequencing of the chapters in this book (as well as most other textbooks on the subject of management). The four principal managerial functions most applicable to modern organizations are planning, organizing, directing, and controlling.

Planning

planning
estimating future conditions and circumstances and making decisions about appropriate courses of action

Planning involves estimating future conditions and circumstances and, based on these estimations, making decisions about what work the manager does and all of those for whom she or he is responsible. This function involves at least three distinct levels or types: strategic planning, which addresses strategic actions designed to achieve the organization's long-range goals:[32] tactical planning, which translates strategic plans into actions designed to achieve specific and shorter-term goals and objectives;[33] and operational planning, which identifies the actions needed to accomplish the goals of particular units of the organization or particular product lines in their respective markets.[34]

Planning is important in large and small organizations and in new and established companies. It may be even more important in new and small businesses because they rarely have the slack resources necessary to overcome major mistakes.[35] Firms that do not plan are frequently unprepared for unexpected events. When unexpected events occur, the firms' performance suffers, and they may have to take extraordinary actions.[36] Thus, planning is a highly important managerial function.

Organizing

organizing
systematically integrating resources to accomplish tasks

To conduct managerial work, resources must be integrated systematically, and this function is labeled **organizing**. It involves identifying the appropriate structure of relationships among positions, and the people occupying them, and linking that structure to the overall strategic direction of the organization. Because today's world is basically full of uncertainties and ambiguities, organizing is a critical function of managers. At its most basic level, the purpose of this managerial function is the attempt to bring order to the organization. Without it, chaos would ensue.

Most people think of the organization structure as represented by the organization chart. And, an organization chart informs others about some portions of the formal structure. Yet, organizing involves much more. For example, decisions about what units should be represented on the firm's project teams are a part of organizing.[37] The degree of autonomy granted to these units is a managerial organizing decision. Often firms producing

A MANAGER'S CHALLENGE

Change

Nestlé's Sweet Organizational Structure

In the 1860s, Henri Nestlé, who was a pharmacist at that time, began his company by developing a food for babies who were unable to breastfeed. Since this time, Nestlé has expanded its markets and acquired various companies including Alcon Laboratories Inc., Carnation, San Pellegrino, Spillers Petfoods, Ralston Purina, Dreyer's, and Chef America, Inc. Switzerland is the home of Nestlé's international headquarters and the location of the registered office of Nestlé's holding company, but the company still believes in decentralized operations. The company's policy is to adapt as much as possible to regional circumstances by decentralizing operations; in so doing, managers strengthen decisions made by providing their employees flexibility to make decisions locally. In turn, they will be better attuned to the specific issues in that given region and make more effective choices.

Nestlé is one of the world's *most* decentralized companies. With few levels of management, local employees, project teams, and task forces make personnel, marketing, and product policies and decisions. Via such decentralized decision making, the company strives to be an "insider" in every country in which it operates so it can respond more quickly to local market needs. Respecting the culture and customs of the individual countries in which it operates is also part of Nestlé's business code. Managers also encourage a structure that assures operational speed and personal responsibility, with a strong focus on results, reducing bureaucracy as much as possible. Members of Nestlé's management, at all levels, are strongly committed to the company, its development, and the culture that the Nestlé management and leadership principles express.

Although Nestlé is trying to remain decentralized, the need for operational efficiencies, company-wide needs for alignment and development of people, are placing limits on the decentralized organization. For example, Nestlé's margins are well below the industry average because it has duplicated separate IT and marketing support functions in most of the countries in which it operates. To help Nestlé has embarked upon the "Globe" project. The Globe project, which is short for "Global Business Excellence," is the biggest reorganization in the company's history. Its goal is to centralize the company's information technology centers around the world into five data centers and establish a common IT platform allowing the firm to consolidate and standardize its global business processes without losing the benefits of its decentralized management structure. To meet this goal, Nestlé needs to coordinate all of its suppliers, customers, and product data for its operations worldwide. In addition, Nestlé's managers want to optimize their industrial infrastructure while maintaining decentralization in all areas where its proximity to consumers and clients is critical for its success. In his letter to the shareholders in the *2006 Management Report*, Chairman and CEO Peter Brabeck-Letmathe discussed Globe and other projects designed to increase corporate efficiencies while maintaining the flexibility to maintain the firm's competitive advantage.

Nestlé is also restructuring some parts of the business and focusing on health and nutrition. Along with centralizing its IT operations while maintaining its decentralized managerial structure, Nestlé remains the world's largest food and drink company, reporting a 14 percent increase in profits for 2006. With additional acquisitions that include Jenny Craig and pharmaceutical company Novartis SE, Nestlé managers hope to transform Nestlé into a nutrition, health, and wellness company, with stronger innovation and branding along with improved efficiency. Some question Nestlé's ability to maintain the decentralized style of management as it continues to strengthen its product portfolio through acquisitions. They feel that Nestlé must consolidate to be competitive, thus, creating a more centralized managerial model.

Sources: "The Nestlé Management and Leadership Principles," Nestlé's Web site, April 2003, www.Nestlé.com; "Creating the Right Mix: Content and Technology," Factiva, 2002, www.factiva.com; "Nestlé Full-Year Profit Rises 14 Percent," *Business Week*, February 22, 2007, www.businessweek.com; W. Hall, "Nestlé to Centralize IT Centres," *Financial Times*, March 6, 2002, www.ft.com; P. Gumbel, "Nestlé's Quick," *Time Magazine*, January 27, 2003, www.time.com; "Letter to Shareholders," *Management Report 2006*, March 16, 2007, www.Nestlé.com.

modular products also have autonomous modular organization units.[38] Such units are becoming more common when integrating units from acquired businesses[39] and when establishing international subsidiaries.[40] As a result, the organizing function of management is complex and challenging.

Nestlé S.A. has had a "flat," or decentralized, organizational structure since its founding a century ago. This structure gives Nestlé's local country managers around the world a great deal of autonomy to satisfy customers in different markets. As a result, the company has achieved a significant amount of success using this structure. However, in recent times, Nestlé management has recognized that the decentralized structure has caused it to develop costly duplicate units and capabilities. The CEO of Nestlé, Peter Brabeck-Letmathe, spoke about the need for efficiencies and identified recent projects designed to reduce costs while maintaining excellence and the flexibility needed to deal with the uncertainties of operating in global markets. A Manager's Challenge on page 13 explains in more detail how he intends to do this.

Directing

directing
the process of attempting to influence other people to attain an organization's objectives

This function has typically had a number of different labels over the years. **Directing** is the process of attempting to influence other people to attain the organization's objectives. It heavily involves leading and motivating those for whom the manager is responsible, interacting with them effectively in group and team situations, and communicating in ways that are highly supportive of their efforts to accomplish their tasks and achieve organizational goals. Directing has several dimensions including leadership, motivation, communication, and the management of groups or teams among others.

Leaders must develop effective relationships with their followers, and their actions should result in fair outcomes for them, often referred to as justice.[41] Leaders can have a significant impact on an organization's outcomes—for example, on its innovation and performance.[42] Thus, the leadership exhibited by managers is highly important. Managers use leadership actions to manage change (to transform organizations and units).[43] A critical function for managers as leaders is to motivate their employees to be highly productive. To do so requires that the managers understand the individuals whom they manage and use the tools at their disposal to individualize the rewards for the employees tied to their performance.[44] Many managers focus their activities on directing teams in the current organizational environment. Thus, as leaders, they must find ways to direct the team while simultaneously motivating individuals, empowering both the teams and each individual member of the team.[45] For these reasons, directing is a challenging responsibility for managers.

Controlling

controlling
regulating the work of those for whom a manager is responsible

The word *controlling* sometimes has a negative connotation. Yet, **control** is a necessary and important managerial function. The essence of this function is to regulate the work of those for whom a manager is responsible.[46] Managers can accomplish control in several different ways, including setting standards of performance for employees in advance, monitoring ongoing (real-time) performance, and, especially, assessing the performance of employees on completed tasks. The results of these evaluations are then fed back into the manager's planning process. However, controlling employee behavior is a difficult task. If managers do not take great care in this process, they can elicit some unexpected and undesirable behaviors. Therefore, they must apply controls carefully and effectively.[47] Although they might want to avoid controls that are too tight for their employees, managers must also be careful to avoid overly loose controls. The lack of effective controls can lead to negative outcomes such as the Enron affair. Thus, managers must achieve a *balanced* set of controls.

Therefore, it is important to consider these four managerial functions as parts of a reciprocal and recurring process, as illustrated in Exhibit 1.1.

Managerial Roles

Some years ago, the Canadian scholar Henry Mintzberg proposed another approach to understanding managerial work.[48] Mintzberg based his classification system on research regarding how managers spend their time at work, primarily with regard to the roles they play. This way of viewing managers' work activities complements the functional approach; it provides additional understanding and insights on what managers do.

Mintzberg's typology of managerial roles entails three major categories—interpersonal, informational, and decisional—each of which contains specific roles. Together, there are 10 such roles in this typology, as shown in Exhibit 1.2 and described in the following sections.

Deb M. explains several interpersonal roles that she fulfilled in her managerial job (see A Week in the Managerial Life of Deb M. on page 16). Among those are the leader role and the liaison role explored next.

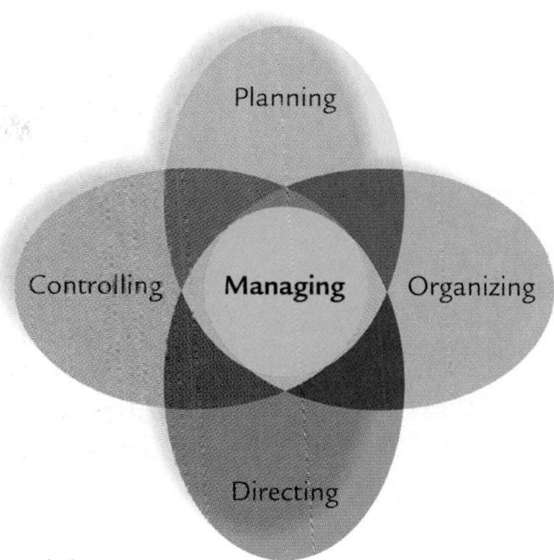

EXHIBIT 1.1

Managerial Functions

INTERPERSONAL ROLES Interpersonal roles are composed of three types of behavior and are derived directly from the manager's formal authority granted by the organization. They are:

1. ***The Figurehead Role*** This set of behaviors involves an emphasis on ceremonial activities, such as attending a social function, welcoming a visiting dignitary, or presiding at a farewell reception for a departing employee. A familiar term for this role of representing the organization, borrowed from the military, is "showing the flag." Over time, this behavior is important and is a necessary component of a manager's job. For example, the dean of a business school often finds it necessary to participate in figurehead activities such as commencement ceremonies, which are important for the long-term benefit of the school.
2. ***The Leader Role*** This role involves influencing or directing others. It is the set of responsibilities people typically associate with a manager's job, as the organization gives the manager formal authority over the work of other people. To the extent that managers are able to translate this authority into actual influence, they are exercising leadership behavior. A manager demonstrates leadership behavior when, for example, a newly appointed project team leader gathers her handpicked team members together and discusses the vision and goals for the team and how to accomplish them.
3. ***The Liaison Role*** This role emphasizes the contacts that a manager has with those outside the formal authority chain of command. These contacts include not only other managers within the organization but also many external individuals such as customers, suppliers, government officials, and managers from other organizations. It also emphasizes lateral interactions, as contrasted with vertical interpersonal interactions of a manager, and it highlights the fact that an important part of a manager's job is to serve as an integrator for his or her own unit and other units or groups. The liaison role applies to the situation where a marketing manager interacts with key customers to learn about their reactions to new product ideas.

EXHIBIT 1.2

Types of Managerial Roles

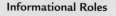

A week in the managerial life of DEB M.

Deb M. is the director of organizational effectiveness for a Canadian oil and gas company.

Question: Describe the type and range of managerial activities in which you were involved this past week.

Last week 70 percent of my time was spent in meetings with others. That's a bit high but not totally unusual.

One of the meetings I organized and led. Actually, it was a two-day work meeting with HR peers in other parts of the company. We were working on coordinating our HR activities such as recruiting and performance management across the company. We have four separate operating units, and each has its own HR department to some extent.

One of the other meetings involved making a presentation to our corporate senior management team regarding our compensation strategy. I was explaining how changes we proposed to make would help us better attract and retain employees with key skills.

I also had a meeting with my boss to review resource needs for my team in order to manage increasing workloads. I spent several hours interviewing job candidates for a new hire to join my team.

I also conducted an orientation session with a number of our managers to explain our new job evaluation system. The rest of the time was spent working on several efforts to better integrate and harmonize certain HR practices, such as pay, across the company. This involved both working with my subordinates as well as working on my own.

Question: What do you like best about your job as a manager?

One of the things I like best about my job is that I have the opportunity to influence the decisions and actions that will have a significant impact on the success of the company. Much of our success depends on the people we attract and select into the company and the performance current employees contribute. My job in HR and the work of my subordinates contribute directly to the quality of people we have and how well they perform.

Question: In the past year or so, what is the biggest change to which you have had to respond?

We are going through a lot of changes right now. We have changed our strategy and our structure, but most of these changes were planned. The unexpected changes have involved individuals who have either deviated from the agreed-to plan and/or have not shared key pieces of information that would have caused us to plan differently. In the first case, I've had to rely on my interpersonal skills to try and get the person back on track. In the second case, I've had to incorporate the new information and adjust our plans.

INFORMATIONAL ROLES This set of roles builds on the interpersonal relationships that a manager establishes, and it underlines the importance of the network of contacts built up and maintained by the manager.[49] The three specific informational roles are the following:

1. ***The Monitor Role*** This type of behavior involves extensive information-seeking in which managers engage to remain aware of crucial developments that may affect their units and their own work. Such monitoring typically deals with spoken and written information and "soft" as well as "hard" facts. A manager attending an industry conference who spends considerable time in informal lobby and cocktail lounge conversations in order to gather data on current developments in the industry provides an example of this role.
2. ***The Disseminator Role*** A manager not only receives information but also sends it. This often includes information that the receiver wants but otherwise has no easy access to without the help of the manager. A supervisor who learns about the firm's reorganization plans affecting his or her department and conveys that information to his subordinates is acting in a disseminator role. For example, Deb played a disseminator role when she made a presentation on her company's new compensation program to the firm's senior managers.
3. ***The Spokesperson Role*** A manager is frequently called upon to represent the views of the unit for which he or she is responsible. At lower management levels, this

typically involves representing the unit to other individuals or groups within the organization; at higher management levels, this typically involves an external component, presenting the organization's activities and concerns to external constituents, such as customers and suppliers.[50] When the manager of the western region meets with other regional managers and presents the views of his region's sales personnel about how well a proposed new sales incentive plan is working, he is functioning in a spokesperson role.

DECISIONAL ROLES The final category in the typology of roles relates to the decision-making requirements of a manager's job. There are four such decisional roles:

1. ***The Entrepreneurial Role*** Managers not only make routine decisions in their jobs but also frequently engage in activities that explore new opportunities or start new projects. Such entrepreneurial behavior within an organization often involves a series of small decisions that permit ongoing assessment about whether to continue or abandon new ventures. Playing this role often involves some risk, but the sequence of decisions usually limits this risk. Suppose, for example, that a lower-level production manager comes up with an idea for a new organizational sales unit. She then discusses the idea with her colleagues and, based on their reactions, modifies it and presents it to upper-level management. Such a manager is playing an entrepreneurial role that goes beyond her regular responsibilities.
2. ***The Disturbance Handler Role*** Managers initiate actions of their own, but they must also respond to problems or "disturbances." In this role, a manager often acts as a judge, problem solver, or conflict manager. The goal of such actions is to stop small problems from developing into larger ones. If a manager faces a situation in which employees cannot agree about who will do a particularly unpleasant but necessary task, the manager must settle the matter. In doing so, he or she is functioning as a disturbance handler. Deb M.'s actions to correct an employee's deviation from the plan represent the disturbance handler role.
3. ***The Resource Allocator Role*** Because resources must be managed efficiently in organizations and slack rarely exists, an important responsibility of managers is deciding how to distribute the resources. Such allocation decisions have a direct effect on the performance of a unit and indirectly communicate information to employees about the relative importance of the firm's activities. The manager of front desk services for a large resort hotel who decides how many and which clerks to assign to each shift is operating in a resource allocator role. Deb M.'s decisions related to the resources needed for her team and allocation of them represents the resource allocator role
4. ***The Negotiator Role*** Managers are often called upon to make accommodations with other units or other organizations (depending on the level of the management position). In this decisional situation, managers are responsible for knowing what resources they can or cannot commit to particular negotiated solutions. A manager who serves on a negotiating team to establish a new joint venture with another company functions in the negotiator role.

Decisional roles are particularly important in managerial responsibilities. Managers are expected to make decisions, and many of them have important performance implications. For example, managers have to decide when to develop and take new products to the market, when to develop new ventures, when to hire and lay off employees, and so forth. They are expected to make these decisions efficiently, with due speed but also comprehensively.[51] Frequently, there are no clearly correct paths to follow. Rather, decisions often require that managers exercise reasonable judgment and use their education, training, and experience.[52]

This typology of managerial work roles emphasizes the considerable variety of behaviors required by managers. Certainly, the extent to which any particular role is important varies considerably from one managerial job to another. The front-line supervisor of a group of bank tellers is likely to have a different mix of roles than the bank's executive vice president. Nevertheless, the 10 roles help to understand the total set of activities that managers usually have to perform over time.

A week in the managerial life of GREG K.

Greg K. is director of finance and accounting for a large division of a financial services firm.

Question: Describe the type and range of activities you were involved in, as a manager, this past week.

In my managerial job, I have a variety of activities in which I am involved, ranging from division project meetings to staff meetings to time to work on my own projects. Below is a brief overview of my activities this past week:

Monday: In the morning, I participated in a conference call with various management-level employees to discuss activity at one of our broker-dealers. The remainder of the day largely involved interacting with staff, completing my assignments, and reacting to various inquiries from other departments, divisions, and auditors.

Tuesday: On this morning I participated in a biweekly status call with our third-party administrator for one of our products. Following the conference call, I met with one of my direct reports (accounting manager) for our weekly staff meeting. We discussed the status of various department projects, staffing issues, upcoming projects, and current events affecting the division. Later that day I met with our accounting coordinator to discuss the status of a pricing project on which she was working.

Wednesday: This was a light day for meetings; however, I attended a one-hour training class regarding upcoming new product features that we will be offering. I then worked on several job-related projects.

Thursday: Thursdays are typically busy in the mornings due to a biweekly technology meeting in which I participate, and a weekly product meeting that I attend. This typically takes two or three hours of my morning when both of the meetings occur. This Thursday the head of our department held a monthly staff meeting to discuss general events affecting the department, the division, and the company.

Friday: Today began with a weekly investment meeting in the morning. I represent our division in this meeting, which includes other representatives from all divisions of the company. The remainder of the day was spent working on various normal tasks.

Aside from the meetings that I attend throughout the week, the remainder of my workweek typically includes other interactions with staff and completion of my other assignments (responsibilities as a "working manager"). I typically interact at least daily with our department head (the VP of finance). We discuss new requests and projects, staffing, status of current projects, and so forth. I also interact regularly throughout the day with my five direct reports to discuss projects and questions, and provide feedback. I also am responsible for approving all of our sales force travel and expense reports and approving sales support requests that come from our sales force.

Question: What do you like best about your job as a manager?

I need to answer this from two vantage points, one from the perspective of my direct assignments and one from a managerial perspective.

Regarding my direct assignments, the most rewarding part of my job is contributing to a division project that directly affects the division with findings and recommendations that are communicated to senior management. Feeling part of the division team is very rewarding.

As a manager, I enjoy problem solving and coaching my direct reports regarding problems that they encounter and complex tasks that they have to complete. My company offers several management development programs, and one that I found especially useful concerned leadership. I try to apply knowledge that I learned from the class to situations that arise in my job.

Question: In the past year or so, what is the biggest change to which you have had to respond?

From a management perspective, the most challenging change over the past year was terminating two employees (not my direct reports, but I was highly involved in the process) and adjusting accordingly on all facets of the job. I had not previously been involved in a termination, so it was challenging. The process included performance concerns, HR concerns, reallocating resources within the department to ensure completion of all assignments, and communication to other employees (a delicate matter).

Managerial Job Dimensions

Analyzing the dimensions of managerial jobs provides additional insight about the work. A British researcher, Rosemary Stewart, developed one particular approach.[53] Stewart proposed that three dimensions characterize a managerial job, regardless of its level and type of unit in an organization:

- the demands made on it;
- the constraints placed on it; and
- the choices permitted in it.

Analyzing managerial jobs in this way not only provides further understanding of what managers do but also permits direct comparisons of different jobs; for example, how the position of "manager of information systems" compares with that of "marketing vice president" or "plant manager."

Greg K. engaged in a number of activities that reflect each of the three dimensions of managerial jobs.

DEMANDS This dimension of management refers to what the holder of a particular managerial position must do. "Demands" involve two types: activities or duties to carry out and the standards or levels of minimum performance to meet. Demands can come from several sources, such as the organization, the immediate boss, or the organization of work activities. Typical types of demands include such behavior as attending required meetings, adhering to scheduled deadlines, following certain procedures, and the like. No doubt, for example, Meg Whitman has sales and performance targets to meet in her CEO position at eBay. Greg K. participated in several regular meetings each week, with his boss, his employees, and other department managers, for example.

CONSTRAINTS "Constraints" are factors that limit a manager's response to various demands. One obvious constraint for any manager is the amount of time available for an activity. Other typical constraints include budgets, technology, the attitudes of subordinates, and legal regulations. All managerial jobs have constraints. Consequently, managers need to develop a good understanding of how to minimize or overcome these constraints.

EXHIBIT 1.3 Two Managerial Jobs with Different Demands, Constraints, and Choices

	Job A: Project Team Manager	Job B: Fast-Food Restaurant Manager
Demands	• Develop new product with strong market appeal • Hold formal weekly progress meeting with boss • Frequent travel to other company sites	• Maintain attractive appearance of restaurant • Keep employee costs as low as possible • Meet standards for speed of service
Constraints	• 12-month deadline for product development • Project budget limit of $1 million • No choice in selecting team members	• Most employees have limited formal education • Few monetary incentives to reward outstanding performance • Federal and state health and safety regulations
Choices	• The organizational structure of the project team • Sequencing of project tasks • Budget allocations	• Selection of employee to promote to supervisor • Scheduling of shifts and assignments • Local advertising promotions

EXHIBIT 1.4

Managers' Skills

Technical	Interpersonal	Conceptual
• Specialized knowledge (including when and how to use the skills)	• Sensitivity • Persuasiveness • Empathy	• Logical reasoning • Judgment • Analytical ability

CHOICES This dimension underscores the fact that despite demands and constraints, managers always have the opportunity to exercise discretion. Thus, a manager regularly makes choices about what to do or not do, how to complete tasks, and which employees will participate in projects, among others. Frankly, discretion is an important part of managerial jobs. How they exercise it and the quality of the judgments that they make largely determine their effectiveness as managers. In her present and past managerial positions, Meg Whitman has faced a multitude of choices about how to make staffing decisions, how to demonstrate leadership, how to respond to changing market conditions affecting Internet use, and the like.

Exhibit 1.3 illustrates these three job dimensions for two different managerial jobs, a project team manager in a manufacturing company and a manager of a medium-sized fast-food restaurant. Although both are managerial jobs, their demands and constraints are quite different. Some of the choices permitted, however, are similar. The combination of the three dimensions determines the requirements to be a manager.

What Skills Do Managers Need?

Similar to other human activity, managing involves the exercise of skills, that is, highly developed abilities and competencies. Managers develop these skills through a combination of aptitude, education, training, and experience. Three types are critical for managerial tasks, particularly for the leadership component of management: technical, interpersonal, and conceptual (see Exhibit 1.4).

Technical Skills

Technical skills involve having specialized knowledge about procedures, processes, equipment and include the related abilities of knowing how and when to use that knowledge. Research shows that these skills are especially important early in managerial careers (see Exhibit 1.5), when leading lower-level employees and gaining their respect is often part of a manager's job. In addition, technical skills seem to be particularly critical in many successful entrepreneurial start-up firms, such as those involving Steve Jobs and Steve Wozniak at Apple Computer or Bill Gates at Microsoft. Technical skills, whether in an entrepreneurial venture or in a larger organization, are frequently necessary but usually are not sufficient for managing effectively. An overreliance on technical skills may actually reduce a manager's overall effectiveness. The first Apple computer designed and built by Jobs and Wozniak required their technical skills to start the fledgling company. However, as Apple grew, their technical skills became relatively less important because they employed technical specialists. Jobs and Wozniak were not, however, always readily able to exchange those technical skills for other, equally impressive leadership skills. As a result, the company had to search for other managerial talent, and did so with mixed success. After gaining considerable managerial experience in other business endeavors, Jobs subsequently returned to lead Apple in the late 1990s with the assistance of other able managers.

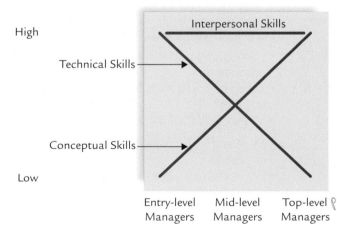

Interpersonal Skills
High
Technical Skills
Conceptual Skills
Low
Entry-level Managers
Mid-level Managers
Top-level Managers

EXHIBIT 1.5

Relative Importance of Managerial Skills at Different Organizational Levels

Interpersonal Skills

Interpersonal skills such as sensitivity, persuasiveness, and empathy are important at all levels of management, although particularly so at lower and middle levels. A longitudinal study of career advancement conducted at AT&T found evidence that such skills, measured early in careers, were important in predicting advancement in managerial ranks 20 years later. However, a lack of these skills may prematurely limit managerial advancement even when other skills exist, but these skills alone are unlikely to guarantee managerial success. Exhibit 1.6 summarizes the findings of one study that investigated reasons why some fast-rising executives eventually plateaued in their managerial careers, even when they appeared to start out with acceptable levels of interpersonal skills. As the management researchers suggested, "The charming but not brilliant find that the job gets too big and the problems too complex to get by on interpersonal skills [alone]."[54]

Conceptual Skills

Often called cognitive ability or cognitive complexity, conceptual skills such as logical reasoning, judgment, and analytical abilities are a relatively strong predictor of managerial effectiveness. These skills are often a major determinant of who reaches the highest management levels of the organization. A clear example of someone who was selected for a CEO job precisely because of his conceptual skills is Jack Welch, the former CEO at General Electric.

EXHIBIT 1.6 Who Succeeds? Who Doesn't?

Potential managerial leaders share traits early on:	Those who don't quite make it:	Those who succeed:
Bright, with outstanding track records	Have been successful, but generally only in one area or type of job.	Have diverse track records, demonstrated ability in many different situations, and a breadth of knowledge of the business or industry
Have survived stressful situations	Frequently described as moody or volatile. May be able to keep their temper with superiors during crises but are hostile toward peers and subordinates.	Maintain composure in stressful situations, are predictable during crises, are regarded as calm and confident.
Have a few flaws	Cover up problems while trying to fix them. If the problem can't be hidden, they tend to go on the defensive and even blame someone else for it.	Make a few mistakes, but when they do, they admit to them and handle them with poise and grace.
Ambitious and oriented toward problem solving	May attempt to micromanage a position, ignoring future prospects; may staff with the incorrect people or neglect the talents they have; may depend too much on a single mentor, calling their own decision-making ability into question.	While focusing on problem solutions, keep their minds focused on the next position, help develop competent successors, seek advice from many sources.
Good people skills	May be viewed as charming but political or direct and tactless, cold, and arrogant. People don't like to work with them.	Can get along well with different types of people, are outspoken without being offensive, are viewed as direct and diplomatic.

Source: Adapted from M. W. McCall, Jr. and M. M. Lombardo, "Off the Track: Why and How Successful Executives Get Derailed," *Technical Report #21* (Greensboro, NC: Center for Creative Leadership, 1983), pp. 9–11.

Welch was appointed to the top position at GE in 1981 and immediately set out to restructure the organization with the objective of making it more globally competitive. Over time and after several major changes in the organization, he reduced a significant amount of GE's bureaucracy and developed a more flexible organization. He also changed GE's corporate culture to one based on the greater empowerment of employees.

The Plan of This Book

After examining the nature of management in this chapter, we present the overall structure and plan of the remainder of the book. Following, we identify each part of the book and the chapters within it.

Part 1 provides an introduction to management and critical domains of managerial jobs. These chapters provide you with an introduction to the nature of management (Chapter 1) and its context. Two important contextual dimensions of managerial jobs are ethics and social responsibilities (Chapter 2) and international management and globalization (Chapter 3). Managers must act ethically and be sensitive to the social environment in which their organizations operate. The rest of the book follows the functions of management.

Part 2 examines the functions of planning and organizing. Chapter 4 examines the importance of and how managers make decisions in their jobs. An important decision made by managers is the strategy the organization must follow to achieve a competitive advantage. This aspect is explored in Chapter 5. Chapter 6 discusses the process of planning designed to implement the strategy throughout the organization. Finally, Chapter 7 explains how to organize the firm in order to effectively implement the strategy and operate an efficient organization.

Part 3 consists of five chapters dealing with the crucial managerial responsibility of leading. It begins with a discussion of managing human resource and diversity (Chapter 8). The next chapter discusses the topic of leadership, a critically important responsibility of managers (Chapter 9). Chapter 10 examines the topic of motivation, to provide an understanding of how managers can influence behavior in an organizational context. Chapter 11 turns to the role of groups and teams and how managers lead and govern teams' processes to guide their performance. Chapter 12 explores the topic of effective managerial communication.

Part 4 explores the nature of managerial control activities. Chapter 13 examines basic evaluation and control challenges in organizations. By contrast, Chapter 14 discusses operations controls that managers can use. Finally, Chapter 15 concludes the book by exploring organizational change. It discusses how managers can take a proactive role to facilitate organizational renewal and development within their firms.

Managerial Challenges from the Front Line

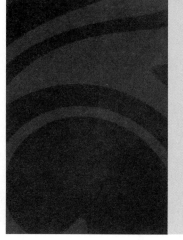

The Rest of the Story

We know from the opening profile that Blaine Halvorson's business, Junk Food, was successful. He and his partner Natalie Grof built the company alone until its annual sales reached $2 million. But then they had to develop and organization to expand it further. Today, Junk Food has 45 employees. He was creative and took entrepreneurial risks but also learned from his earlier mistakes to become an effective manager. In 2005, Delta Apparel acquired the company making Halvorson and Grof wealthy individuals. However, part of the agreement was that Halvorson would remain Junk Food's president and CEO and continue to build the business. Although he is compensated handsomely for reaching predetermined annual sales and profit targets, it is his responsibility to continue to find ways to take Junk Food to new heights.

Summary

- Management is the process of assembling and using sets of resources in a goal-directed manner to accomplish tasks in an organizational setting. It occurs in an organizational context.
- Managers face a number of significant challenges. Managerial challenges include managing change, managing resources, managing strategically, and managing entrepreneurially. Increasing technology and globalization has caused much organizational change, and companies must manage it effectively. Efficient management of resources is only part of the equation. Organizations must develop their resource portfolios and integrate resources to create capabilities that are then leveraged to achieve a competitive advantage. Managers select and implement a strategy designed to provide greater value to customers than do competitors. Finally, managers have to act entrepreneurially, even in large organizations, to identify and exploit opportunities.
- Management is an old concept dating back thousands of years; ancient Chinese rulers used management concepts of organization, specialization of labor, and strategy. The basis of modern management is traditionally thought to be scientific management proscribed by Frederick Taylor during the industrial revolution. However, a number of historical figures contributed to our knowledge of modern management. Other people have contributed to our knowledge of productivity (Frank and Lillian Gilbreth, for example), organization (Alfred Sloan and Chester Barnard), leadership (Mary Parker Follett and Douglas McGregor) and motivation (Abraham Maslow and Frederick Herzberg).
- What managers do can be understood through the functions that they perform. Among them are planning, organizing, directing, and controlling. Planning involves projecting the future conditions and tasks required to be successful in these conditions. Organizing involves identifying the appropriate structure of relationships among positions, and the people occupying them, and linking that structure to the overall strategic direction of the organization. Directing is the process of attempting to influence other people to attain organizational objectives with managerial activities such as leading, motivating, and communicating. Control is a necessary and important managerial function designed to regulate the work of those for whom a manager is responsible.
- A complementary way of viewing managerial work is through the roles that they fill. Managerial roles entail three major categories—interpersonal, informational, and decisional—each of which contains specific roles. Interpersonal roles include the figurehead, leader, and liaison. Informational roles include monitor, disseminator, and spokesperson. Finally, there are four decisional roles—entrepreneurial, disturbance handler, resource allocator, and negotiator.
- Managerial work can also be understood from the dimensions of managerial jobs. The dimensions include the demands and constraints placed on managers and the discretionary choices allowed by the job.
- To effectively perform the functions, fulfill the roles, and deal with the dimensions of the job, managers need several skills. Among these are technical, interpersonal and conceptual skills. All of the skills are important, but the mix and levels of the skills required to be effective vary by type of managerial job and level in the organization.

Key Terms

controlling 14
directing 14
management 5
organizations 6
organizing 12
planning 12

Review Questions

1. How is management defined, and what are its basic elements?
2. What are the four major challenges that managers face, and how do managers deal with them?
3. Who are the primary historical figures who have contributed to modern management, and what are their most important ideas?
4. What are the four primary functions of management and their contents?
5. What are the 10 managerial roles and their importance to managerial work?
6. How do each of the three dimensions of managerial jobs contribute to managerial tasks?
7. What are the three primary managerial skills, and how does their importance vary with the type and level of a manager's job?

Assessing Your Capabilities

Managerial Core Values

Rank the following statements as to how important they would be to you as a manager (with 1 being the most important and 16 being the least important).

______ Be professional
______ Cooperate with others in the organization
______ Make a profit in the short term
______ Solve problems
______ Achieve positive results
______ Deliver quality outcomes
______ Think in the long term
______ Satisfy your client
______ Communicate effectively with others
______ Offer superior value to constituents
______ Take risks in order to innovate
______ Lead to serve others
______ Motivate employees
______ Enjoy your work
______ Reach your goals
______ Build and maintain relationships with others

There are no right or wrong answers, but the ranking suggests the core values that will underlie your actions as a manager. For example, if you rank cooperating with others, leading to serve others, building relationships, communicating effectively, and motivating employees highly, you are likely to emphasize a service role. Alternatively, if you rank enjoying your work, making a short-term profit, and reaching your goals highly, your managerial activities are more likely to be opportunistic. Finally, if you rank solving problems, achieving positive results, delivering quality outcomes, and offering superior value highly, your managerial actions are likely to be results oriented. Compare your rankings with a few classmates and discuss why they are different for each of you.

Source: Adapted from: J. van Rekom, G. B. M. van Riel, and B. Wierenga, "A Methodology for Assessing Organizational Core Values," *Journal of Management Studies* 43 (2006): 176–201.

Team Exercise

Form teams of three to five people.

The H. J. Heinz Company has made a number of significant changes in its operations since 2002, when it spun off several noncore businesses. Some attribute recent changes to Nelson Pelz, a hedge fund manager and activist investor, who acquired over 5 percent of Heinz stock as an activist investor; others attribute the changes and performance improvement over time to the management of William Johnson, the CEO of Heinz. Obtain information about the company and the changes it has made over time. The following Web sites might be useful:

www.heinz.com/students.aprx
www.heinz.com/2006annualreport/2006heinzAR

You might also find helpful the following article in your library or online: A. Pressman, "Who's Really Shaking Up Heinz?" *Business Week*, March 12, 2007, p. 64.

Analyze the information you obtained and answer the following questions as a team.

1. What major challenges have Heinz managers faced over the last five years?
2. What managerial functions are evident in the actions taken by Johnson to improve his company's performance? Please link the actions and functions.
3. What managerial roles are displayed in Johnson's actions? Please relate the actions to specific roles.

Closing Case FedEx's Successful Internationalization

Federal Express always seems to be one package ahead of the game. As early as the 1980s, the company's founder. Fred Smith, knew Asia would become an economic powerhouse and began heavily expanding there. Today FedEx is Asia's premier carrier.

Companies desiring to compete in global markets need to be flexible in how, where, and what they provide customers. As early as 1979, Fred Smith, founder of FedEx, acknowledged that customer needs were constantly changing, and to be successful FedEx would need to implement strategies that would help it to be mobile and flexible and at the same time ensure strong customer satisfaction. FedEx has implemented successful strategies in Asia through a series of buyouts. Simultaneously, the firm has implemented innovative technologies creating a seamless experience for international customers using its services.

It was no accident that FedEx became the premier carrier servicing Asia. As early as the 1980s, Smith recognized the growing market in China and knew that Asia would become an economic powerhouse. So, in 1984, FedEx started operations in China and began the first direct express flight to the mainland in 1996. In 1989, FedEx paid $895 million to buy Tiger International Inc., a struggling hauler with rights to fly into most Asian airports and a management team familiar with the Pacific Rim. Wall Street did not like this decision because of the unpredictability of Asia, but FedEx saw the potential business opportunity in this region. It turned out to be a highly profitable decision. Its business in Asian countries has soared. In the past few years, the volume of goods shipped over FedEx's international network has drastically increased, with much of the growth coming from Asia. Currently FedEx operates 123 flights weekly to and from Asia, including 26 out of China alone. FedEx now controls 39 percent of the China-to-U.S. air express market compared to 27 percent for DHL International.

In January 2006, FedEx spent $400 million to buy out its partner in China, Tanjin Datian W Group. This gave FedEx full control over Datian's trucking fleet and its 89 distribution hubs. It also gave FedEx more control over services in secondary Chinese cities that are becoming more linked to the global economy as manufacturers shift factories further inland as they flee increasing labor costs in coastal regions. In addition, FedEx plans to close its Asian hub in the Philippines by 2008 and build a new $150 million super hub in the heart of one of China's fastest-growing manufacturing districts, Guangzhou. To provide customers with seamless services, FedEx recognized the need to provide all types of services that identify communication needs. In 2004, FedEx rebranded all the companies it owned in order to make customers aware of the breadth of its services.

Implementing the proper IT system to assist FedEx with the challenges of growing internationally was equally important. FedEx managers realized that when implementing an IT system, it should take into account the idiosyncrasies of different countries, custom authorities, and individual needs. FedEx knew it was important to provide detailed and accurate information to customs about customer shipments. Thus, it had to automate and electronically track all shipment documentation. So, FedEx installed the technology for customs authorities to review the documentation, in turn, simplifying the customs process and giving them the ability to identify and examine the inbound manifest of shipments quickly and accurately. The IT system also gives customers seamless clearance through customs, plus visibility of their shipments and customs procedures through to a receipt. A customer can go online from anywhere, conduct a transaction, or track a shipment. FedEx also runs all its own IT operations and develops much of its own technology. In order to achieve this, it has a large team of developers and IT personnel.

These initiatives have helped make FedEx successful, especially in the Asian market. FedEx's earnings increased 21 percent in 2005, and its stock price more than doubled between 2003 and 2006. The company's managers realized that in order to be successful, they needed to respond quickly to the changes and new challenges of the "flatter world." FedEx has been one package ahead of its competitors as a first mover in areas like Asia.

Questions

1. Why has FedEx been so successful in Asia?
2. Can competitors imitate FedEx's approach in international markets and take market share away from the company? Why or why not?

3. Is the FedEx move to close its hub in the Philippines and build a new one in China a good decision for its Asian operations? Please explain.
4. Can you identify the application of the managerial functions of planning, organizing, and controlling in FedEx activities? Please explain.

Sources: D. Goulden, "Managing IT for a Flat World," *Business Week*, October 2, 2006, www.businessweek.com; D. Foust, "FedEx," *Business Week*, April 3, 2006, www.businessweek.com; A. Counsell, "Doing More Faster and Better," *Financial Times*, February 14, 2006, www.ft.com; C. Shevlin, "Move out of Range to Think out of the Box," *Financial Times*, August 19, 2004, www.ft.com; S. Murray, "Putting the House in Order," *Financial Times*, November 8, 2006, www.ft.com; "FedEx Completes Acquisition of DTW Group," *Business Week*, February 28, 2007, www.businessweek.com; "FedEx Reports Solid Revenue and Earnings Growth," *Fedex.com*, December 20, 2006, www.fedex.com/us/investorrelations.com.

2

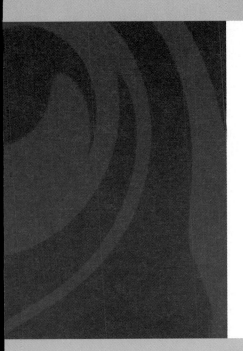

Social Responsibility and Managerial Ethics

Learning Objectives

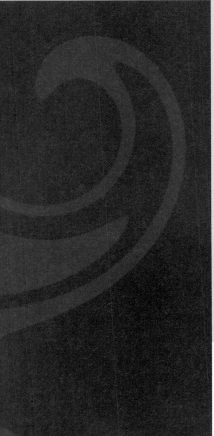

After studying this chapter, you should be able to:

- Describe why an understanding of basic approaches to ethical decision making and corporate social responsibility is important.
- Compare and contrast the efficiency and social responsibility perspectives.
- Explain the strategic corporate social responsibility approach.
- Explain the basic approaches to ethical decision making.
- Explain the aspects of moral intensity.
- Describe the actions that can foster a high degree of ethical behavior in an organization.

Managerial Challenges from the Front Line

Name: Sharon Anderson Wright

Position: CEO, Half Price Books

Outside work activities: Literacy and family literacy efforts; personally committed to Half Price Books mission of preserving the environment by reusing and recycling.

First Job out of school: Began working for Half Price Books at the age of 13, sorting and shelving paper backs.

Management style: Collaborative

Reportedly, Sharon Anderson Wright likes finding a good deal at a thrift store. This would probably not surprise you, unless you knew that Wright is the head of Half Price Books, the largest used book company in the country. Half Price Books was a company begun by Wright's mother, Pat Anderson, over a quarter century ago. Anderson, who, along with her boyfriend, diamond salesman Ken Gjemre, wanted to save trees by recycling unwanted books. "Nobody was recycling books then," says Wright. "They hated seeing all this great stuff thrown away." In 1972 Anderson and Gjemre opened their first store in a converted Dallas launderette.

Today, Half Price Books has some 85 stores in 14 states. (Most of the stores are in Texas.) It buys and sells books, magazines, and recorded material from individuals as well as leftover stock from publishers. The company sponsors literacy programs around the country and donates over 1 million books a year to schools, prisons, and hospitals all over the world. "These books are like manna from heaven to low-income families." Says Michael Hirschhorn, president of the National Alliance of Urban Literacy Coalitions. Besides donating books, the company is dedicated to recycling. Wright also encourages her 1,400 employees to pursue their own philanthropic activities. "It enriches their lives," she says, "and they enrich ours."

Half Price Book's success has created its own challenges, however. On the one hand, every new store it opens employs people in the community. On the other hand, expansion has meant that the company and its managers have had to invest money in information, finance, and other systems to properly run the business. These investments coupled with rising health care costs have squeezed margins to the point where the company had to decide recently whether or not to continue paying the health-care benefits for its part-time employees. The company had always provided both its full-time and part-time employees with the benefits.

You may be wondering, "Why should I care about corporate social responsibility or managerial ethics or whether or not my employees have health care benefits? Aren't these the types of issues philosophers worry about?" To answer this question, you only need to pick up a recent newspaper or business magazine. Everything from Wall Street trading scandals to accounting frauds at Enron, WorldCom, Tyco, and Global Crossing to environmental pollution problems with British Petroleum and corporate cover-ups seem to be in the press daily. For example, Citicorp lost billions in market value when it was revealed that a group of traders in the firm's London office had manipulated the bond market: A small set of traders disrupted the European bond market by placing 188 sell orders simultaneously (approximately $9 billion worth of bonds) on August 2, 2004. This drove the price of bonds in general down dramatically. The prices continued to drop even after the Citibank traders stopped selling. Just a few minutes later, the same traders then bought the bonds back at much cheaper prices than they had sold them for. This new buying triggered buying by other traders, and the prices rose. In the process, the Citibank traders made about $20 million in profits. Although the employees did not do anything illegal, their behavior was deemed unethical. In the end, Citicorp paid a $28 million fine to the Financial Service Authority for "failing to conduct its business with due skill, care and diligence, and failing to exercise proper controls over the London bond trading team."[1]

Clearly, poor managerial ethics and corporate social responsibility can generate negative publicity, hurt a company's stock price, destroy shareholder value, and, as a consequence, make it difficult for the firm to recruit high-quality employees. In contrast, good managerial ethics and corporate social responsibility can have a significant, positive consequence for employees, customers, shareholders, and communities.

Social Responsibility

Corporate social responsibility is concerned with the obligation corporations have to constituencies and the nature and extent of those obligations. Companies have a wide variety of constituencies including current shareholders, customers, employees, specific communities, society at large, governments, and so on. These constituencies typically have expectations of companies but do not always share the same expectations. In many instances, they have competing desires. For example, shareholders may want companies to maximize their returns, whereas local communities may want companies to give something back to them. Do companies have a higher obligation to shareholders or the specific communities in which they operate? Suppose a company's trucking activities created noise pollution that bothers citizens but falls well within the legal limits. Should the company take money from shareholders by paying them lower dividends and investing the money saved in exhaust and muffler systems in order to cut down engine noise? Suppose the safety standards for brakes on the trucks were different in two neighboring countries. Should the firm pay the extra cost and insist on the higher of the two standards for all its trucks? Do all their truck drivers, regardless of their nationality or employment location, have the same rights when it comes to equipment standards, such as those for brakes?

Questions such as these form the substance of social responsibility debates. Both corporate social responsibility and managerial ethics focus on the "oughts" of conducting business. Although several approaches to corporate social responsibility exist, an examination of two fundamental perspectives will help you reflect on how you personally view the issue and how you might effectively interact with others holding differing perspectives.

The Efficiency Perspective

efficiency perspective
the concept that a manager's responsibility is to maximize profits for the owners of the business

Perhaps no contemporary person presents the **efficiency perspective** of social responsibility more clearly than the Nobel Prize winning economist Milton Friedman.[2] Quite simply, according to Friedman, the business of business is business. In other words, a manager's responsibility is to maximize profits for the owners of the business. Adam Smith is perhaps the earliest advocate of this approach. Smith concluded nearly 200 years ago that the best way to advance the well-being of society is to place resources in the hands of individuals and allow market forces to allocate scarce resources to satisfy society's demands.[3]

MANAGERS AS OWNERS When a manager of a business is also its owner, the self-interests of the owner are best achieved by serving the needs of society. If society demands that a product be made within certain environmental and safety standards, then it is in the best interests of the owner to produce the product to meet those standards. Otherwise, customers will likely purchase the product from competitors. Customers are more likely to purchase from firms that comply with widely shared and deeply held social values, so it makes sense for businesses to incorporate those values into their operations and products. To the extent that the cost of incorporating society's values is less than the price customers are willing to pay, the owner makes a profit.

Critics of the efficiency perspective, however, argue that quite often customers and society in general demand safety, environmental protection, and so on only after firms have caused significant visible damage. For example, society might hold strong values about not polluting the water and causing heath problems. However, if the consequences of polluting a river are not visible and people are not immediately hurt, social pressure might not emerge in a manner to cause the owner to align his actions with societal values until years after the fact.

MANAGERS AS AGENTS In most large organizations today, the manager is not the owner. The corporate form of organization is characterized by the separation of ownership (shareholders) and control (managers). Managers serve as the agents of the organization's owners. Within this context, Friedman argues that managers should "conduct business in accordance with [owners'] desires, which will generally be to make as much money as possible while conforming to the basic rules of society, both those embodied in law and those embodied in ethical custom."[4] From Friedman's perspective, managers have no obligation to act on behalf of society if it does not maximize value for the shareholders. For example, a company should package products in recycled paper only if doing so maximizes shareholder wealth. Whether such an action satisfies or benefits a small group of activists is irrelevant. Managers have no responsibility to carry out such a program; in fact, they have a responsibility *not* to undertake such an action if it is more costly (and therefore does not maximize shareholder wealth). Similarly, charitable donations are not the responsibility of corporations. Instead, managers should maximize the return to shareholders, and then shareholders can decide if and to which charities they want to make their contributions. Simply put, the profits are not the managers' money, and, therefore, managers have no right to decide how or if they should distribute the profits to charitable causes.

From the efficiency perspective, it is impossible for managers to maximize shareholders' wealth and simultaneously attempt to fulfill all of society's needs. From the efficiency perspective, it is the responsibility of government to impose taxes and determine expenditures to meet society's needs. If managers pursue actions that benefit society but do not benefit shareholders, then they are exercising political power, not managerial authority.

CONCERNS WITH THE EFFICIENCY PERSPECTIVE The efficiency perspective assumes that markets are competitive and that competitive forces move firms toward fulfilling societal needs as expressed by consumer demand. Firms that do not respond to consumers' demands in terms of products, price, delivery, safety, environmental impact, or any other dimension will, through competition, be forced to change or be put out of business. Societal values not expressed through market forces should be reflected in governmental laws and regulations. As with competitive forces, companies that do not abide by these laws and regulations will also find themselves out of business. Unfortunately, however, corrective action often occurs only after people are injured.

In November 2006, 71 people became sick with symptoms of vomiting, nausea, and stomach pains after eating at various Taco Bells in a four-state region. Tests confirmed that these customers suffered from an *E. coli* infection. New Jersey had 33 confirmed cases, New York had 22, Pennsylvania had 13, and Delaware had two according to the Centers for Disease Control (CDC). Of the confirmed cases on the CDC list, 82 percent of the victims required hospitalization and 13 percent developed a form of kidney failure. Sales declined by an estimated 90 percent in the states affected, and Taco Bell closed 90 restaurants in the area. Sales fell across all of Taco Bell's restaurants by an estimated 20 percent.

After a month of investigation, officials were unable to pinpoint the source or cause of the outbreak, but CDC officials said that the people likely became ill from eating contaminated shredded lettuce. The assessment was based on a statistical analysis that examined the meals the people had eaten rather than tested food samples—virtually all the food sample tests came back negative. Lettuce is included in 70 percent of the menu items at the Mexican-style chain, which is based in Irvine, California.

Taco Bell decided not to take any chances. Greg Creed, president of Taco Bell Corp., stated, "Out of an abundance of caution, we switched our produce supplier for all of our produce, including white onions, for New York, New Jersey, Pennsylvania, and Delaware. Since the independent scientific laboratory tests on all of our ingredients have concluded negative for *E. coli*, we have no information regarding any Taco Bell ingredient linked to this outbreak." Taco Bell also threw out all lettuce provided by its former supplier.[5]

The other major concern with the efficiency perspective is that corporations can impose indirect consequences that may not be completely understood or anticipated. In economic terms, these unintended consequences are called **externalities**.[6] For example, the government of the United Kingdom enticed Nissan with tax and other incentives to build a new automobile plant there. However, the trucks going in and out of the plant created traffic congestion and wear on public roads that were not completely accounted for in the government's proposal. As a result, the government had to use tax revenue collected from U.K. citizens to repair the roads damaged by Nissan.

externalities
indirect or unintended consequences imposed on society that may not be understood or anticipated

However, even when externalities can be anticipated, consumers often cannot correctly factor in or may not be willing to pay for the costs. For example, the consequences of poor safety controls at a fertilizer plant (explosion, fire, toxic fumes, injury, and death) can be devastating. The question is, can fertilizer consumers correctly assess the costs of a chemical disaster and how much extra they should have to pay to cover the needed safety expenditures? If the answer is "no," a plant manager will be more likely to skip the necessary safety practices in order to keep costs low and make a profit. Only after a chemical disaster occurs will the impact of the externality (the disaster) be fully appreciated by consumers and, therefore, appropriately priced in the market.

The Social Responsibility Perspective

The social responsibility perspective argues that society grants existence to firms. Shareholders simply supply risk capital. Therefore, firms have responsibilities and obligations to society as a whole, not just to shareholders. Thus, while the efficiency perspective states that it is *socially responsible* to maximize the return to the shareholder, the social responsibility perspective states that it is *socially irresponsible* to maximize only shareholder wealth because shareholders are not the only ones responsible for the firm's existence. The most common form of corporate existence is one of *limited liability*—a privilege granted to corporations by society, not by shareholders.[7] In this form of existence, the financial liability corporations have to others is limited to the company and doesn't extend to its shareholders. In other words, creditors and people seeking redress (for example, if a chemical disaster occurs) cannot go beyond the assets of the corporation and seek repayment or restitution from the assets of the owners. Thus, the existence of the firm in general and the limited liability existence in particular are not solely a function of shareholders, and, therefore, the responsibilities of the firm cannot be restricted just to shareholders.

stakeholders
individuals or groups who have an interest in and are affected by the actions of an organization

STAKEHOLDERS From the social responsibility perspective, managers must consider the legitimate concerns of other stakeholders beyond just the firm's shareholders. **Stakeholders** are individuals or groups that have an interest in and are affected by the actions of an organization. They include customers, employees, financiers, suppliers, communities, and society at large as well as shareholders. Customers have a special place within this set of constituencies because they pay the bills with the revenue they provide.[8] Shareholders are also given special status, but in the stakeholder approach, shareholders are viewed as the providers of "risk capital" rather than as sole owners. Consequently, shareholders are entitled to a *reasonable* return on the capital they put at risk, but they are not entitled to a *maximum* return because they are not solely responsible for the existence of the firm. To maximize the return to shareholders would take away returns owed to the other stakeholders. Thus, managers must balance the returns shareholders earn against the legitimate concerns of customers, employees, financiers, communities, and society. The research evidence regarding the relationship between corporate social responsibility and financial performance is mixed,[9] meaning that there is no definitive evidence that being more socially responsible leads to higher financial performance.

CONCERNS WITH THE SOCIAL RESPONSIBILITY PERSPECTIVE One of the key concerns with the social responsibility perspective is that important terms such as *reasonable returns* and *legitimate concerns* cannot be defined adequately. Given that reasonable returns to shareholders and legitimate concerns of other stakeholders could come into conflict, not knowing exactly what is reasonable or legitimate makes it hard for managers to find the appropriate balance and act in socially responsible ways. This is why from a practical standpoint, even if you believe in the stakeholder framework of corporate social responsibility, making decisions that balance the interests of the different stakeholders is a significant challenge for which there is no magic solution. It is not only possible but quite likely that customers, employees, financiers, communities, and society at large will have conflicting and competing concerns. Moreover, it isn't clear from research whether or not greater corporate social responsibility leads to greater profits for firms.[10]

Consider the case of a manager in a corrugated box making factory. His customers want sturdy boxes that can be stacked several levels high. Society increasingly seems to want a higher use of recycled paper. However, boxes made of recycled paper either have higher costs for the same strength or lower strength at the same cost compared to boxes made of nonrecycled paper. Shareholders want competitive returns. In such a case, how would you determine the most socially responsible action? If customers tell you that boxes must meet a certain strength requirement regardless of whether they use recycled paper or not, does this outweigh the desires of the other stakeholders? Should you devote more money to researching and developing stronger recycled boxes even though it takes money away from shareholders today?

Even when you try to balance the concerns of competing stakeholders, it isn't easy, as Starbucks found out (and as illustrated in A Manager's Challenge, "The Eco-Cup at Starbucks"). Starbucks's quest to create a coffee cup made of recycled paper took 10 years, and in the end yielded a cup made with just 10 percent recycled paper. After reading the challenge, do you think Starbucks achieved the right balance among different stakeholders? If you were a shareholder, what would be your perspective? As a customer, how

A MANAGER'S CHALLENGE

Ethics

The Eco-Cup at Starbucks

The general success of Starbucks likely needs no summary. The company sells nearly $7 billion worth of coffee and other beverages across nearly 6,000 company-operated stores and 3,168 licensed operations in 37 countries around the world. In the process, Starbucks goes through nearly 2 billion cups annually. Although the company was started in 1971, it wasn't until 1996 that executives determined that they wanted to stop "double cupping"—giving customers a second cup to insulate the hot coffee in the first cup. That year Starbucks, along with Environmental Defense, held a competition for designs for a recycled cup.

This might seem like an easy target to achieve, but the design would need to meet several criteria. First, it would have to result in a product that would stand up well when filled with a hot beverage and held in a customer's hand. Second, it would need to not put off any odor that would compete with or detract from that of the beverage served. (Taste is highly influenced by smell.) Third, the product would need Food and Drug Administration (FDA) approval ensuring the recycled material was safe for direct contact with cold or hot beverages.

The contest in 1996 resulted in no winners. Most designs were rejected because they crumpled easily, smelled bad, or both. As a consequence, in 1997 Starbucks moved to a 60 percent recycled sleeve in place of the second cup. This "saved some trees" but was not what the company executives ultimately wanted. In 1999, the company tested a cup made of 50 percent post-consumer fiber but it was too flimsy and sometimes leaked.

In 2001, company executives made the decision to start over and work directly with a group of partners. They selected the pulp maker, Mississippi River Corp., the paper mill, MeadWestvaco, and the cup manufacturer, Solo Cup, to help them create an ecofriendly cup. The team finally came up with a design and product that received FDA approval in 2004. In January 2006, the cup was launched at select locations.

As early as 1996, Starbucks wanted to stop using a second container as insulation for its coffee servings. Hence began the company's quest to develop an "eco-cup" made out of recycled material. After much trial and error, in 2006, the company began successfully rolling out such a cup to its stores around the world, saving five million pounds of paper, or approximately 78,000 trees, a year.

Although the eco-cup is made up of just 10 percent postconsumer fiber, it will conserve 5 million pounds of paper per year and save approximately 78,000 trees. According to Starbucks's director of environmental affairs, Ben Packard, "We had our eyes on the prize of an earth-friendly cup. Ten percent is just the first step. Increasing the recycled fiber in any paper product for environmental reasons must be balanced with product durability and safety considerations. In the future, we will look for ways to increase the percentage of post-consumer recycled fiber contained in our cups, but first we want to be assured of the quality, safety and durability of these new cups. In the meantime, we are actively exploring additional innovations to reduce the environmental impacts of our paper cups and other packaging."

Sources: Starbucks's *Corporate Social Responsibility 2005 Annual Report*; "Creating the Eco-Cup," *Fortune*, October 2006, 42.

EXHIBIT 2.1

Comparing Efficiency and Social Responsibility Perspectives

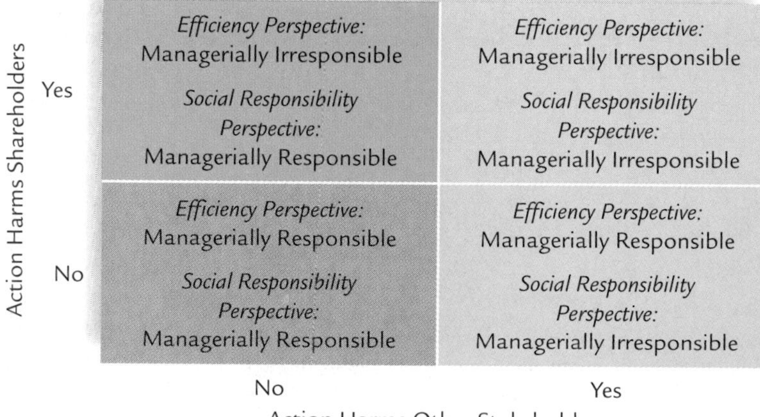

would you view the effort and results? If you were an employee, how would you view these efforts? Would they make any difference to you?

Comparing the Efficiency and Stakeholder Perspectives

The efficiency and social responsibility perspectives differ mainly in terms of the constituencies to which organizations have responsibilities. However, the two perspectives differ little in terms of how they evaluate actions that either harm or benefit both shareholders and society (see Exhibit 2.1). Their evaluations differ most markedly when actions help one group and harm the other. Actions that benefit shareholders but harm the other stakeholders would be viewed as managerially responsible from the efficiency perspective, but socially irresponsible from the social responsibility perspective. Actions that harm shareholders but benefit the other legitimate stakeholders would be viewed as managerially irresponsible from the efficiency perspective, but socially responsible from the social responsibility perspective.

How Corporations Respond to the Efficiency and Stakeholder Perspectives

How corporations react to the various pressures and constituencies connected to the topic of social responsibility varies widely. These reactions can be simplified and laid out on a continuum that ranges from defensive to proactive, as illustrated in Exhibit 2.2.

EXHIBIT 2.2 Corporate Responses

	Defenders	Accommodaters	Reactors	Anticipators
Belief:	We must fight against efforts to restrict or regulate our activities and profit-making potential.	We will change when legally compelled to do so.	We should respond to significant pressure even if we are not legally required to.	We owe it to society to anticipate and avoid actions with potentially harmful consequences, even if we are not pressured or legally required to do so.
Focus:	Maximize profits. Find legal loopholes. Fight new restrictions and regulations.	Maximize profits. Abide by the letter of the law. Change when legally compelled to do so.	Protect profits. Abide by the law. React to pressure that could affect business results.	Obtain profits. Abide by the law. Anticipate harmful consequences independent of pressures and laws.

DEFENDERS Companies that might be classified as defenders tend to fight efforts that they see as resulting in greater restriction and regulation of their ability to maximize profits. These firms often operate at the edge of the law and actively seek legal loopholes in conducting their business. Typically they change only when legally compelled to do so.

ACCOMMODATERS These companies are less aggressive in fighting restrictions and regulations, but they change only when legally compelled to do so. This type of firm tends to obey the letter of the law but does not make changes that might restrict profits if they are not required to.

REACTORS Reactor firms make changes when they feel that pressure from constituencies is sufficient such that nonresponsiveness could have a negative economic impact on the firm. For example, the firm might change to recycled paper for boxes only when the pressure from customers becomes strong enough that nonresponsiveness would lead customers to boycott their products or to simply choose a competitor's products that use recycled paper.

ANTICIPATORS Firms in this category tend to believe that they are obligated to a variety of stakeholders—customers, employees, shareholders, general citizens, and so on—not to harm them independent of laws or pressures that restrict or regulate their actions. Firms in this category not only abide by the law, but they might take action to avoid harming constituencies, even when the constituencies might not be aware of the potential danger. For example, a firm might take steps to protect employees from harmful chemicals within the workplace even before employees suffered negative side effects sufficient for them to demand work environment changes or before safety laws are passed.

Though we might imagine that firms adopting the efficiency perspective are more likely to be defenders, accommodaters, and reactors, while firms adopting the stakeholder perspective are more likely to be anticipators, we know of no research that has examined this specific association. The accompanying "Manager's Challenge" helps illustrate some of these corporate responses in the face of advancing technology. A Manager's Challenge, "Cleaning Up Dirty Little Engines" focuses on how firms making two-stroke engines for handheld power tools are responding to the emissions and pollution these engines create. As you read the feature, you might ask yourself what the motivation seems to be for each of the various firms mentioned to explore new combustion technology. For even the anticipators, are they motivated primarily to try and help the environment and reduce air pollution or are they motivated because they believe meeting or beating the proposed regulations with new technology could enhance their competitive position? What would you do if meeting or exceeding environmental or other societal goods potentially hurt your business? For example, what would you do if the technology for exceeding environmental standards for two-stroke engines resulted in engines that were 30 percent more expensive and at the same time weighed 20 percent more? What would you do if your market research suggested that commercial users of handheld tools (for example, trimmers or leaf blowers) were unlikely to pay the premium price or want the extra weight? After all, it is one thing for a consumer to deal with the extra weight for an hour or so once a week, but it is quite another thing for a small landscaping and yard work company to ask its employees to pack around 20 percent more weight six to eight hours a day, five days a week. What would you do if commercial sales accounted for half of your company's total sales?

The Strategic Corporate Social Responsibility Perspective

A more recent approach to corporate social responsibility tries to address the balancing act managers have to engage in when it comes to responding to the concerns of all the firm's stakeholders.[11] Called the **strategic corporate social responsibility perspective**, it argues that three fundamental criteria can guide managers.

strategic corporate social responsibility perspective a three-criteria model that can help managers focus on social areas where there is the highest possibility of creating shared value for the business and society

The first criterion takes an "inside out" approach. In other words, managers can look inside the company at issues that are more rather than less important as a function of the company's strategy and business activities. For example, if you are a manager at Wal-Mart, the labor-intensive nature of your business places a heavy emphasis on workers. In contrast, the capital-intensive nature of Boeing places a heavy emphasis on technology.

A MANAGER'S CHALLENGE

Technology

Cleaning Up Dirty Little Engines: Dealing with Technology

The whine of a two-stroke engine powering a leaf blower, chainsaw, or trimmer; the puff of blue smoke it emits; and the pungent smell of its oil and gas mixture are as common as a warm day in summer. Whether you are walking through a residential neighborhood or driving by the tidy landscape of an office building, you see, hear, and smell this multibillion-dollar-a-year industry. There are at least 30 million of these handheld products in use in the United States. Two million blowers, 2.5 million chainsaws, and 6 million trimmers are sold each year. About two-thirds of the sales are to consumers. The rest involve more heavy-duty products for commercial users. The Environmental Protection Agency (EPA) estimates that these blowers, trimmers, and the like contribute 5 percent of the total nonfactory hydrocarbon and oxides of nitrogen (NOx) emissions. (Manufacturers contend the number is closer to 2 percent to 3 percent.)

Two-stroke engines are so popular because they are extremely reliable, lightweight yet powerful, and fairly inexpensive. However, they are so dirty because unlike four-stroke engines, there is no separate intake and exhaust stroke, and, as a consequence, 30 percent of the gas-oil mix escapes unburned.

In 2006, the EPA allowed California to enforce new emission regulations—the third phase of emission regulations enacted in California in the last 10 years. In 1990, the California Air Resources Board (CARB) required emissions from handheld engines to be reduced by 30 percent by 1995. This was phase I. Phase II required a reduction of 80 percent from Phase I levels by 1999. Phase III required a further 40 percent reduction by 2007.

Fred Whyte, president of Stihl, one of the largest manufacturers of two-stroke handheld engines, echoed the sentiments of many manufacturers, "Is this the greatest challenge ever faced by handheld engine manufacturers? No question." Larry Will, vice president of engineering at Echo stated even more bluntly: "Meeting the regulations is one thing; meeting them and surviving is another."

Companies like Echo, McCulloch, Stihl, and other members of the Outdoor Power Equipment Institute enlisted powerful lobbyists to lower and delay the emission reductions. Representatives argued that the regulations would "virtually eliminate" all two-stroke engines and impose unreasonable cost burdens on consumers. Even if the standards could technically be met, the engines would cost 15 percent to 30 percent more. Given how price sensitive consumers are and given that "big-box" retailers like Home Depot, Wal-Mart, and Lowes control about two-thirds of consumer sales, no one wanted to be the first company to invest in the new technology and introduce the higher-priced products.

While virtually all the manufacturers were able to meet CARB's standards by 1995 simply by capturing more hydrocarbons in the exhaust, a further 80 percent reduction looked technically impossible. So in the mid-1990s, the manufacturers' association again took up the fight against the regulations.

However, three firms broke ranks: RedMax (a subsidiary of Japan's Komatsu), Tanaka, and Deere & Co. (the $13 billion-a-year farm machinery giant) tried to be anticipators. Although Deere had originally opposed the California standards, it subsequently lobbied both CARB and the EPA to *not* lower standards or delay their implementation. RedMax and Tanaka both created new technology for injecting a shot of pure air between exhaust gases and fuel intake that significantly reduced emissions in two-stroke engines beyond the Phase II CARB standards. Deere had perfected a new technological design they called "compression wave" for its Homelite brand that was similar to RedMax's solution. However, after big-box retailers pressured Deere to lower its prices on the higher-cost, lower-emission engines, Homelite lost $100 million over the next 21 months. Subsequently, Deere sold its Homelite division to TechTronics Industries of Hong Kong.

To meet the CARB standards and deadlines, virtually all the other manufacturers trying to sell the engines in California had to buy engines from RedMax and Tanaka. For example, Stihl had to buy 60,000 engines from RedMax. To meet the EPA standards set to take effect nationally in 2007, manufacturers such as Stihl, Echo, and Briggs and Stratton finally launched their own attempts at technological breakthroughs. For example, Stihl has moved from being a defender to an accommodater, and then to a reactor. At the cost of $12 million, Stihl developed an engine that acts like a four-stroke engine but is lubricated like a two-stroke engine and weighs only 10 percent more.

The result is that these once dirty little engines have gotten a lot cleaner. Over the last 10 years, improvements in outdoor power equipment design have resulted in the reduction of exhaust emissions by over 70 percent according to the Outdoor Power Equipment Institute.

Source: www.opei.org accessed January 8, 2007. C. Ratcliff, "Handheld Power Equipment Forecast 2006," *Grounds Maintenance*, December 1, 2005; E. Chapman, "Handheld Lawn and Garden Products," *Grounds Maintenance,* July 2003, 12; M. Boyle, "Dirty Little Engines Get Cleaner," *Fortune*, May 13, 2002, I146[B–L].

The second criterion takes an "outside in" approach. In other words, managers can look outside the company at issues that the company has an impact on. For example, suppose you are a Wal-Mart manager in charge of the energy costs consumed by all the company's stores. As such, you would have not only a big impact on the stores' energy consumption and greenhouse gas emissions, you would also be able to influence the power companies that produce electricity for your stores. For example, you might be able to get these companies to produce energy with fewer greenhouse gas emissions.

The third criterion takes an "outside out" approach. In other words, managers should look at social issues in general in terms of the extent to which they are problematic. Clearly, there are nearly an unlimited number of social issues to consider—everything from poverty to literacy to sanitation and beyond. However, the strategic social responsibility approach does not advocate looking at all social issues but rather assessing those that come into focus as a function of the first two criteria.

Taken together, the three criteria form a three-dimensional matrix that can help managers focus on those social areas where there is the highest possibility of creating shared value for society *and* the business. Exhibit 2.3 illustrates this matrix. Marriott provides an illustration of the framework in action. As a labor-intensive business, the quality and supply of people to do rather low-tech jobs is critical for the company. Most of Marriott's larger, upscale hotels are in large cities, such as New York. In these cities, chronic unemployment is a problem, and it tends to plague poorly educated individuals with fewer skills. Chronic unemployment leads to a number of socially undesirable consequences including homelessness and drug abuse. Marriott is a large employer of low-skilled labor. When all three criteria are used, social outreach efforts by Marriott help to chronically unemployed workers in large cities such as New York create the opportunity for shared value creation.

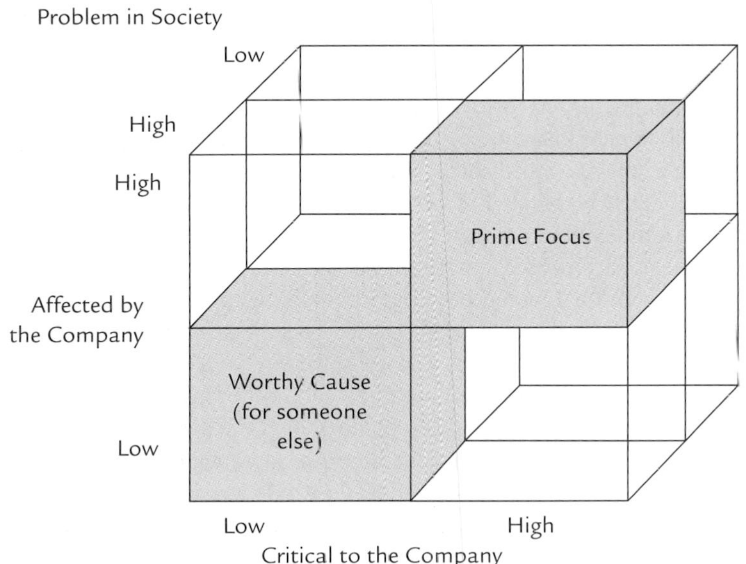

EXHIBIT 2.3

Strategic Corporate Social Responsibility: A Criteria Matrix

To address the issue, Marriott provides 180 hours of paid classroom and on-the-job training for chronically unemployed individuals. More than 90 percent complete the program and end up taking a job with Marriott. After one year, more than 65 percent are still in their jobs. This is both a high retention rate for the industry in general and a much, much higher rate of continued employment than is the norm for the chronically unemployed. In the end, individual workers benefit, Marriott benefits, and the communities in which the program runs benefit.

Suppose you were a manager in the human resource department at Marriott and someone suggested that the company should also get involved in another inner-city problem: HIV/AIDS. Should you recommend that the company invest its time and resources in this issue? Although it's an important issue, the problem is that HIV/AIDS does not seem to affect the key activities of the company, such as recruiting staff. Furthermore, because Marriott is a small employer in the scheme of this set of individuals, it does not seem that the company's actions could have a significant impact on the issue. The company lacks the potential to create shared value for society and the business. However, if you are a Marriott human resource manager in Bangkok, Thailand, or Johannesburg, South Africa, the same analysis might yield different conclusions. In Bangkok and Johannesburg, HIV/AIDS seriously affects the labor supply of low-skilled workers. This is a critical group for the company's operations. Furthermore, the company is a large employer in the two cities, and, therefore, its approach to preventative health care could have a significant impact on the incidence of HIV/AIDS in each city. As a consequence, what potentially is for Marriott in New York a "worthy cause for someone else" may be a "strategic corporate social responsibility issue" for Marriott's hotels in Bangkok and Johannesburg.

How the Ethics of Individual People Develop

managerial ethics
the study of morality and standards of business conduct

At its heart, **managerial ethics** is concerned with morality and standards of business conduct, especially among individuals. Managerial ethics begin at the top of the organization.[12] For ethical decisions and practices to permeate the firm, top executives must build a culture based on those values. This includes establishing codes of ethics, implementing ethics training for employees, and rewarding ethical behaviors (as we discuss later in this chapter). Moreover, it includes top executives behaving in an ethical manner *themselves.*

Although top managers can have an impact on the ethical (or unethical) behavior that occurs in a firm, much of what influences someone's perspective on what is or is not ethical happens long before they begin working. For example in your own case, you might consider what role your family, friends, peers, teachers, religion, job experiences, and life experiences have played in terms of your ethical beliefs. To explore this issue, think about a situation in which someone made a different ethical judgment from your own. What if you had been born in a different country, raised by a different family, attended a different school system, experienced different religious influences, had different friends, and held different jobs? Would you hold the same ethical values you do now? Would you reach identical ethical judgments to those you reach now?

There is little debate that family, friends, peers, teachers, religion, job experiences, and life experiences play a significant role in the development of individual ethical values and judgments.[13] What is debated is which factors play the strongest role because their influence varies from person to person.[14] This debate is unlikely to be resolved soon. Nor is its resolution necessary for our purposes. The primary reason for raising the issue is to realize that in order to understand how others make decisions, you need to understand something about their backgrounds.[15]

Simply labeling ethical judgments that are different from your own as wrong is likely to foster feelings of mistrust (in both directions) and hurt your working relationships. The greater the diversity there is in the workforce, the greater the need there is for tolerance and understanding. However, as a manager, tolerance does not mean simply allowing your subordinates to come to whatever ethical decisions they individually deem right. Because individual decisions can have consequences for the organization, managers often need to shape and influence the ethical thinking, judgment, and decision making of their subordinates.

Consider the following real case that was conveyed to us in a recent conversation. (We have disguised the names at the manager's request.) Imagine you are a manager in a publishing company. Your assistant manager has just recruited a new employee, Martha, from a key competitor. Martha worked for your competitor, Dresden, Inc., for 11 months after graduating from college. Dresden pays new employees a bonus based on how well they perform during their first year of employment. Prior to leaving the company, Martha had performed well enough to earn the $10,000 bonus from Dresden. When she interviewed with your assistant manager, Martha asked for a $10,000 bonus upon being hired by *your* company. Part of the reason your assistant manager agreed to do this is because Martha had been exposed to a number of strategic operations and marketing plans in her first year of employment at Dresden. Given her somewhat junior position in the company, she had not been asked to sign, nor had she signed, a "noncompete" clause that would have prevented her from taking a job with a competitor for a specific time period or disclosing the strategic knowledge she had gained while working for Dresden. Legally, she was free to take the job with you and bring and share all her knowledge with you.

Your assistant manager comes to you and asks if it is okay to try and get Martha to disclose as much as she knows about Dresden's marketing plans. What is your response? If you were Martha, would you have any ethical misgivings about taking the new job and then relating all you knew about your previous employer's strategic plans? Suppose on the off-chance, Dresden had paid you the end-of-year bonus prior to your leaving the company. Would that have any bearing on what you would or would not reveal to your new employer?

So how should you make decisions like these? Are there ethical approaches you can look to for guidance? The answer is that there are some basic approaches. The basic approaches have been around for a long time. This is in part because the challenge of ethical decision making is not a modern one. **Ethical dilemmas**, or the choice between two competing but arguably valid options, have confronted people throughout history.

ethical dilemmas
having to make a choice between two competing but arguably valid options

In the next section, we will describe these basic approaches for two reasons. The approaches can help you understand how other people approach ethical dilemmas and help you avoid **ethical lapses** or decisions that are contrary to an individual's stated beliefs and policies of the company.

ethical lapses
decisions that are contrary to an individual's stated beliefs and policies of the company

Again, it is important to keep in mind that the workforce is becoming increasingly diverse. As a result, now more than ever before, you are likely to encounter people who respond to ethical dilemmas differently. Research finds significant differences among managers from different nationalities.[16] A recent study examined the extent to which salespeople from the United States, Japan, and Korea viewed a set of actions as posing an ethical issue or not.[17] For example, unlike American and Japanese salespeople, Korean salespeople in one study did not think it was unethical to ask customers what price a competitor had quoted them. For example, in most places in the United States, a real estate broker cannot legally tell you how much someone else offered on a house you also want to buy. What do you think? Do you think asking a customer for information on the price submitted by your competitors is ethical or not?

From this same international study, researchers found that Korean salespeople did not think that giving free gifts was much of an ethical issue, while American salespeople did. General Motors shares this general "American" view and has a policy that restricts the giving of gifts. For example, in a conversation with the president of GM's Asia Pacific region, he mentioned that he could not pay for the golf game of the president of the Philippines when they were discussing a potential new factory in the country. Do you think GM's policy is appropriate, or has it gone too far?

Without understanding how or why others come to different conclusions, it is easy to label people holding the "wrong" beliefs as inferior. For example, in a recent study, Chinese and Australian auditors working for the same multinational accounting firms reached different decisions about proper ethical conduct because of different cultural assumptions. Chinese auditors looked to their peers whereas Australian auditors looked to themselves for guidance in making ethical decisions. This reference point reflects the cultural group orientation of Chinese and the individual orientation of Australians.[18] If either set of auditors simply judged the other wrong without a sensitivity to how culture might influence ethical decisions, imagine how difficult it might be for them to work together on a global audit team. Research has shown that ethnocentricity, or the view that your perspective is correct and that the views people in other cultures hold are inferior, tends to hurt managerial effectiveness. This is especially true in culturally diverse or international contexts.[19] So, it is important for new managers to examine the basic approaches to ethical decision making and recognize that individuals' backgrounds, including cultural values, influence their decisions and behavior.

As we stated, the second reason for examining basic approaches to ethical decision making is to avoid ethical lapses. Ethical lapses are more common than you might think. The pressures emanating from both the external environment and internal company environment often can be overwhelming. This is especially true if managers lack a systematized way of thinking through dilemmas. For example, suppose you were a sales manager about to report your current quarterly sales. You are short of your target. The policy is that you can only report sales for which a contract has been signed. You have a signed letter of intent but not a contract from a customer—a customer that has purchased from you before. The value of the deal will take you over your target and will trigger a bonus for you and the salesperson in charge of this account. The salesperson has told you that if the sale goes through, the customer will sign a contract dated prior to the close of the quarter. You barely missed your sales target last quarter. The company has a strong performance culture. In other words, if you don't perform, you don't have a career. Under pressures like these, can you imagine how it might be possible to make a decision contrary to your stated beliefs?[20]

Basic Approaches to Ethical Decision Making

Several frameworks, or approaches, to making ethical decisions exist. We examine four of the most common: the utilitarian, moral rights, universalism, and justice approaches. An understanding of the basic approaches to ethical decision making will help you as a manager to examine your own personal ethics and work more effectively with employees whose ethical perspectives are different.

The Utilitarian Approach

utilitarian approach
focuses on the consequences of an action

The utilitarian approach focuses on consequences of an action. Simplified, using a **utilitarian approach**, you try to make decisions that result "in the greatest good." For example, assume you are trying to sell grain to a developing nation, and a customs agent demands an extra fee before he will clear your shipment. From a utilitarian perspective, you would try to determine the consequences of the options available to you. For example, you could (1) pay the money, (2) not pay the money and let the grain sit there, or (3) seek intervention from a third party. Which action would result in the greatest good? If there are starving people waiting for the grain, would you argue that the "good" of saving lives outweighs the "bad" of paying an illegal bribe?

Keep in mind when talking about whether an outcome is good or bad that people may see the same outcome differently. In other words, the "goodness" or "badness" of an outcome is often subjective. Factors such as culture, economic circumstances, and religion can all affect those subjective judgments. For example, what if keeping the shipments of grain moving was needed to keep 2,000 people employed. Would you argue that the good of saving 2,000 jobs justified paying off government officials? What if unemployment were high in the region?

The Moral Rights Approach

moral rights approach
focuses on examination of the moral standing of actions independent of their consequences

The **moral rights approach** to ethical decisions focuses on an examination of the moral standing of actions independent of their consequences. According to this approach, some things are just "right" or "wrong," independent of consequences. When two courses of action both have moral standing, then the positive and negative consequences of each should determine which course is more ethical. Using this approach, you should choose the action that is in conformance with moral principles and provides positive consequences.

To illustrate this, suppose you have an ongoing supplier relationship but no written contract. Is cutting off the supplier with no warning in order to switch to a different supplier with lower prices ethical or not? From a moral rights approach, if not honoring unwritten commitments to suppliers is simply wrong, then it could be argued that it would be unethical to cut the supplier off with no warning. Conversely, if operating without a contract is simply a business convenience, then you might easily make the case that changing suppliers is just a matter of business, not ethics.

The managerial challenge here is that the moral standing of most issues is debatable. For example, you might want to say that it is wrong to lie. But is it wrong to make your competitors think you are about to enter one market when you are really about to enter another so as to gain a competitive advantage over them? Is it just wrong to say you are not working on a particular new technology when you actually are in order to influence your competitors not to invest in the new technology and thereby have an advantage when you finally perfect the technology? In many companies, both explicit policies as well as corporate values often serve a vital role in defining what is right or wrong when there is no universally accepted determination.

The Universal Approach

Immanuel Kant, perhaps one of the most famous moral philosophers, articulated the best-known ethical imperative, or **universal approach**. Simplified, Kant's moral imperative was "do unto others as you would have them do unto everyone, including yourself." If you follow this approach, you should choose a course of action that you believe can apply to all people under all situations and that you would also want applied to yourself. At the heart of universalism is the issue of rights. For Kant, the basis of all rights stem from freedom and autonomy. Kant believed that actions that limit the freedom and autonomy of people generally lack moral justification. Now let's return to the customs agent and bribe scenario we just discussed. Based on the universal approach, it might be difficult to justify paying bribes to government officials. To meet the "do unto others as you would have them do unto everyone" criterion, you would have to be willing to let everyone use bribes as a means of getting the ends they desired.

universal approach
choosing a course of action that you believe can apply to all people under all situations

The Justice Approach

The **justice approach** focuses on how equitable the process and outcomes are.[21] In general, costs and benefits should be equitably distributed, rules should be impartially applied, and those damaged because of inequity or discrimination should be compensated.

justice approach
focuses on how equitably the costs and benefits of actions are distributed

DISTRIBUTIVE JUSTICE Managers ascribing to **distributive justice** distribute rewards and punishments equitably based on performance. This does not mean that everyone gets the same or equal rewards or punishments; rather, they receive equitable rewards and punishments as a function of how much they contribute to or detract from the organization's goals. From this perspective, it would be wrong for a manager to distribute bonuses, promotions, or benefits based on arbitrary characteristics, such as age, gender, religion, or race. This is the basic rationale behind the U.S. Civil Rights Act of 1964. Under this law, even if a manager has no intention of discriminating against a particular minority group, if a minority group can demonstrate inequitable results (called *disparate impact*), legal action can be brought against the firm. For example, if 50 percent of a firm's applicants for promotion were women, but 75 percent of those receiving promotions were men the data could be used to file a claim of discrimination based on the underlying notion of distributive justice.

distributive justice
the equitable distribution of rewards and punishment, based on performance

PROCEDURAL JUSTICE Managers ascribing to **procedural justice** make sure that people affected by managerial decisions consent to the decision-making process and that the process is administered impartially.[22] Consent means that people are informed about the process and have the freedom to exit the system if they choose. As with distributive justice, the decision-making process cannot systematically discriminate against people because of

procedural justice
ensuring that those affected by managerial decisions consent to the decision-making process and that the process is administered impartially

arbitrary characteristics, such as age, gender, religion, or race. Recent research involving employees across multiple countries consistently suggests that perceived justice relates positively to desired outcomes such as job performance, trust, job satisfaction, and organizational commitment and negatively relates to outcomes such as turnover and other counterproductive work behavior.[23] Procedural justice is generally studied and interpreted within the context of the organization. However, the findings of a recent study show that factors external to the firm can also have strong effects: In one study, violent crime rates in the community where a plant resided led researchers to correctly predict that workplace aggression in that plant would occur, whereas the plant's procedural justice climate did not.[24]

compensatory justice
if distributive and procedural justice fail, those hurt by the inequitable distribution of rewards are compensated

COMPENSATORY JUSTICE The main thesis of **compensatory justice** is that if distributive justice and procedural justice fail or are not followed as they should be, then those hurt by the inequitable distribution of rewards should be compensated. This compensation often takes the form of money, but it can take other forms. For example, compensatory justice lies at the heart of affirmative action plans. Typically, affirmative action plans ensure that groups that have been systematically disadvantaged in the past, such as women or minorities, are given every opportunity in the future. For example, special training programs could be instituted for women who were passed over for promotions in the past because they were denied access to certain experiences required for promotion.

The Moral Intensity Factor

moral intensity
the degree to which people see an issue as an ethical one

As we have pointed out so far in the chapter, one of the challenges of ethical decision making for a manager is that for many issues and consequences, people do not have identical perspectives. They differ in whether they see a situation as involving ethics and in how they would determine their course of action. So the practical question is whether managers can help people come to more common views on the "moral intensity" of issues.[25] **Moral intensity** is the degree to which people see an issue as an ethical one. Moral intensity has six components, as illustrated in Exhibit 2.4: (1) magnitude of the consequences, (2) social consensus, (3) probability of effect, (4) temporal immediacy, (5) proximity, and (6) concentration of effect.[26] In other words, the overall moral intensity of a situation is the result of adding each of these components together. As a manager, you can use this framework

EXHIBIT 2.4

Factors of Moral Intensity

both to anticipate the moral intensity of an issue and to diagnose the reasons for differing views people have about that intensity.[27]

The **magnitude of the consequences** associated with the outcome of a given action is the level of impact anticipated. This impact is independent of whether the consequences are positive or negative. For example, laying off 100 employees because of a downturn in the economy has a lower impact than if 1,000 employees join the ranks of the unemployed. Likewise, many people would judge a 20 percent increase in the price of lawn fertilizer to be of a lower magnitude than 500 people killed or seriously injured because of an explosion in the fertilizer plant caused by poor safety procedures.

magnitude of the consequences
the anticipated level of impact of the outcome of a given action

Social consensus involves the extent to which members of a society agree that an act is either good or bad. For example, in the United States, there is greater social consensus concerning the wrongness of driving drunk than speeding on the highway.

social consensus
the extent to which members of a society agree that an act is either good or bad

Probability of effect concerns the likelihood that a given consequence will happen. For example, even if people agree that 500 people dying from a chemical explosion is a very bad consequence, the intensity of the issue rises and falls depending on how likely people think a chemical explosion is. For example, one of the reasons so many countries have restricted cigarette advertising is because smoking can cause health problems, including serious ones such as lung cancer. However, cigarette ads and smoking itself have not been completely outlawed in part because the probability of the effect is not 100 percent. The higher the probability of the consequence, the more intense the sense of ethical obligation. Because people are highly likely to be injured if they are in a car accident, the intensity regarding the moral obligation of auto manufacturers to make safer cars with options such as side-impact air bags is increasing. However, because there is no certainty that you will be in an automobile accident, the law does not require many of the available safety features.

probability of effect
the moral intensity of an issue rises and falls depending on how likely people think the consequences are

Temporal immediacy is the fourth component of moral intensity. It is a function of the interval between the time an action occurs and the onset of its consequences. The greater the time interval between the action and its consequences, the less intensity people typically feel toward the issue. For example, even if industrial pollution were certain to lead to global warming and result in catastrophic changes to weather patterns, because the consequences are likely to happen 50 years from now, the moral intensity of industrial pollution is much less than if the effects were to happen next year.

temporal immediacy
a function of the interval between the time the action occurs and the onset of its consequences

Proximity is concerned with the individual's physical and psychological closeness to the outcome. All other factors being equal, the closer the decision maker is or feels to those affected by the decision, the more the decision maker will consider the consequences of the action and feel it has ethical implications. Proximity can involve physical closeness as well as psychological and emotional closeness and identification. Consequently, an affinity between the decision maker and those affected could be a function of many factors including people's nationality, cultural background, ethnic similarity, organizational identification, or socioeconomic similarity. For example, if you feel a psychological and emotional affinity for young people, then making a decision to lay off workers based on their seniority (meaning younger workers will get laid off first) will have greater moral intensity for you. Likewise, a decision to close down a poor performing but slightly profitable factory that could put your parents and neighbors out of work will also likely have greater moral intensity for you than the closing of a different factory would.

proximity
the physical, psychological, and emotional closeness the decision maker feels to those affected by the decision

The **concentration of effect** is the extent to which consequences are focused on a few individuals or dispersed across many. For example, even though laying off 100 people has a lower magnitude of effect than laying off 1,000 people, laying off 100 people in a town of 5,000 has a greater concentration of effect than laying off 1,000 people in city of 10 million.

concentration of effect
the extent to which consequences are focused on a few individuals or dispersed across many

The importance of these six facets of moral intensity is twofold. First, as a manager, you can use these facets to anticipate issues that are likely to be seen as significant ethical dilemmas in the workplace.[28] If you can better anticipate issues that are likely to become ethical debates, you have more time to prepare for and may be more effective at handling ethical dilemmas. Second, if you are working with a group that is using the same basic ethical approach and still can't agree on the ethical course of action, you can use these facets to determine the source of the disagreement.[29] The disagreement may stem from different perceptions of the situation on one or more of the moral intensity components.

A MANAGER'S CHALLENGE

Globalization

Laboring for Nike Around the World

Even with celebrities like Tiger Woods sporting its apparel, Nike has had trouble shifting the spotlight off of the workers who toil to make its products. Nike has contracts with over 800 factories in more than 50 countries. About 450,000 workers, mostly in Asian countries, produce Nike shoes and clothing at these factories. However, none of these people are directly employed by Nike.

According to critics, the people employed at these factories are subjected to substandard working conditions, such as exposure to dangerous toxins and carcinogens, poor ventilation and/or air quality, forced overtime, sexual harassment, and corporal punishment and abuse. In addition, critics have argued that the workers do not receive a fair wage and that many are so young their employment violates child labor laws.

According to the chairman and founder of Nike, Phil Knight, the company has been through four key "chapters" in its efforts to improve conditions:

> In the first chapter, we upgraded processes and conditions behind closed doors. The second chapter began with critics bringing working conditions in underdeveloped countries to the attention of the world. After a bumpy original response, an error for which yours truly was responsible, we focused on making working conditions better and showing that to the world. These codes led to a third long chapter on the development of corporate and independent monitoring programs. The fourth chapter charts the beginning of collaborative efforts to address compliance issues. Creating change has proved more challenging than anyone imagined when corporate codes were first developed.

As Knight indicated, Nike's third chapter took shape in 2003 when it and a handful of other apparel companies allowed factory condition audits to be posted on the Internet by the Fair Labor Association (FLA), a sweatshop monitoring group (www.fairlabor.org). According to the FLA's 2006 annual report, Nike had 856 factories that were subject to the FLA audits to which the FLA made 22 independent visits. For its own internal audits, Nike employs its own staff of 1,000 labor-practices managers to run a program called Safety, Health, Attitude of Management, People, Environment (SHAPE). According to the FLA's 2006 annual report, Nike conducted 509 SHAPE assessments and gathered base-level environmental, safety, and health data on 650 factories in 52 countries. It also conducted 99 presourcing evaluations. Of these, 80 factories were approved and 19 were rejected.

Nike contracts with other companies to manufacture its sporting goods. Frequently these companies outsource the work to factories with low-cost labor in countries abroad, similar to this factory in Ho Chi Minh City, Vietnam. In recent years, numerous human rights organizations have called attention to the terrible conditions workers at these factories endure, casting Nike in a negative light. If Nike executives had used the moral intensity framework outlined in the text, could the company have averted the bad publicity?

Nike has also agreed to apply U.S. safety standards for air quality to its foreign suppliers and converted its use of toxic chemical solvents to water-based products in the assembly of its footwear. The firm has also increased the age requirements for all the factories it subcontracts with. Footwear manufacturers must employ workers who are at least 18 years old; apparel workers must be 16 years old. These standards exceed those established by the International Labor Organization. However, the company stresses that critics fail to appreciate that many workers in places such as Indonesia and China would be without work or working in much worse conditions if Nike did not contract for shoes and clothes to be manufactured there. Nike argues that its efforts allow workers to gain skills and knowledge that can help them build a better life.

Nike still faces several practical challenges when it comes to improving contractors' factories, despite its sizeable investment in money and manpower to do so. For example, Nike ultimately can withdraw its contracts from noncompliant factories. However, even this is a challenge as it found in Indonesia when it terminated a contract with a substandard supplier. The company employed 7,000 workers, all of whom lost their jobs because 100 percent of the factory's work was done for Nike.

If Nike executives were to use the moral intensity framework, how would they assess the positive and negative consequences for workers in these factories? What is the level of social consensus regarding the rightness or wrongness of certain working conditions? How strong do people feel about employing children, even indirectly through contractors? How likely are the negative consequences of poor working conditions, and how quickly might they occur? How close or distant will the public feel to workers thousands of miles away? When there are 450,000 workers around the world involved, how concentrated will the effects of Nike's efforts really be, and how will the public perceive its changes?

Sources: Fair Labor Association, *2006 Annual Public Report*; Nike, *Fiscal Year 2004 Corporate Responsibility Report*; A. Maitland, "Big Brands Come Clean on Sweatshop Labor," *Financial Times*, June 10, 2003; D. Akst, "Nike in Indonesia, Through a Different Lens," *New York Times*, March 4, 2001.

Nike had to deal with a lot of negative media coverage regarding the alleged use of child labor in factories it did not own but that manufactured its shoes (see A Manager's Challenge, "Laboring for Nike Around the World"). Nike executives were both caught off guard by the intensity of the global and domestic public scrutiny and somewhat unprepared to respond at first. If Nike executives had used the moral intensity framework, could they have better anticipated and predicted public reaction? Would the framework have helped them make some anticipatory changes in how they manage the manufacturers around the world that make Nike's shoes?

How People and Firms Can Make Better Ethical Decisions

While the media helps put in front of us the ethical misconduct of high-profile people, such as CEOs of major companies, there is some evidence that ethical misconduct at all levels is rising.[30] If this is the case, a significant challenge remains to you as a manager: How can you foster and encourage ethical decisions?

The Manager

As we mentioned at the outset of the chapter, part of the reason for exploring various approaches to ethical decision making is to help you refine your own approach so that when pressures arise, you can make decisions consistent with your ethical framework and avoid ethical lapses. To this end, there is perhaps no substitute for taking personal responsibility for your decisions.

Even after you have become more comfortable and explicit about how you would resolve ethical dilemmas, the question still remains: How much should you change your approach to fit in with others or try to change their approaches? If you were at Nike, how hard should you work to change the public's perception, persuading them to see the positive benefits workers enjoy? Although it is probably impossible to argue that one of the approaches presented in this chapter is best, applied consistently, each approach will result in a consistent pattern of ethical decision making. Even if people don't always agree with your decisions, they will appreciate the fact that you are consistent.[31]

The Organization

Just as managers try to foster ethical decisions, organizations have a significant impact on ethical decision making. The overall culture of the company can play a significant role. For example, the emphasis on keeping customers happy and income flowing in seemed to contribute to a number of rather lax audits by the accounting firm Arthur

Andersen (which subsequently went out of business) of companies like Enron and WorldCom. In contrast, firms can also have a positive impact on ethical decision making and behavior. In many firms, senior managers go out of their way to encourage their managers to behave ethically. Codes of ethics and whistle-blowing systems are perhaps two of the more visible efforts.

code of ethical conduct
a formal settlement that outlines types of behavior that are and are not acceptable

CODES OF ETHICS Many firms have adopted codes of ethics to guide their managers' decision making. A **code of ethical conduct** is typically a formal one-page to three-page statement outlining the types of behavior that are and are not acceptable. Exhibit 2.5 reprints the Johnson & Johnson credo, one of the oldest among U.S. corporations. The credo was first adopted in 1945 and has been revised four times to its current version.

An examination of 84 codes of ethics in U.S. firms found three specific clusters of issues addressed in these statements.[32] The first main cluster included items that focused on being a good "organizational citizen." The second cluster included items that guided employees to restrain from unlawful or improper acts that would harm the organization. The third cluster included items that addressed directives to be good to customers. Each of these three clusters was then further divided into subcategories. Exhibit 2.6 provides a list and description of the clusters and specific categories of issues addressed in these

EXHIBIT 2.5

Johnson & Johnson Credo

We believe our first responsibility is to the doctors, nurses, and patients, to mothers and all others who use our products and services. In meeting their needs everything we do must be of high quality. We must constantly strive to reduce our costs in order to maintain reasonable prices. Customers' orders must be serviced promptly and accurately. Our suppliers and distributors must have an opportunity to make a fair profit.

We are responsible to our employees: the men and women who work with us throughout the world. Everyone must be considered as an individual. We must respect their dignity and recognize their merit. They must have a sense of security in their jobs. Compensation must be fair and adequate, and working conditions clean, orderly, and safe. Employees must feel free to make suggestions and complaints. There must be equal opportunity for employment, development, and advancement for those qualified. We must provide competent management, and their actions must be just and ethical.

We are responsible to the communities in which we live and work and to the world community as well.

We must be good citizens—support good works and charities and bear our fair share of taxes. We must encourage civic improvements and better health and education.

We must maintain in good order the property we are privileged to use, protecting the environment and natural resources.

Our final responsibility is to our stockholders. Business must make a sound profit. We must experiment with new ideas. Research must be carried on, innovative programs developed, and mistakes paid for. New equipment must be purchased, new facilities provided, and new products launched. Reserves must be created to provide for adverse times.

When we operate according to these principles, the stockholders should realize a fair return.

Cluster 1

"Be a dependable organization citizen."

1. Demonstrate courtesy, respect, honesty, and fairness in relationships with customers, suppliers, competitors, and other employees.
2. Comply with safety, health, and security regulations.
3. Do not use abusive language or actions.
4. Dress in businesslike attire.
5. Possession of firearms on company premises is prohibited.
6. Follow directives from supervisors.
7. Be reliable in attendance and punctuality.
8. Manage personal finances in a manner consistent with employment by a fiduciary institution.

Unclustered Items

1. Exhibit standards of personal integrity and professional conduct.
2. Racial, ethnic, religious, or sexual harassment is prohibited.
3. Report questionable, unethical, or illegal activities to your manager.
4. Seek opportunities to participate in community services and political activities.
5. Conserve resources and protect the quality of the environment in areas where the company operates.
6. Members of the corporation are not to recommend attorneys, accountants, insurance agents, stockbrokers, real estate agents, or similar individuals to customers.

Cluster 2

"Don't do anything unlawful or improper that will harm the organization."

1. Maintain confidentiality of customer, employee, and corporate records and information.
2. Avoid outside activities that conflict with or impair the performance of duties.
3. Make decisions objectively without regard to friendship or personal gain.
4. The acceptance of any form of bribe is prohibited.
5. Payment to any person, business, political organization, or public official for unlawful or unauthorized purposes is prohibited.
6. Conduct personal and business dealings in compliance with all relevant laws, regulations, and policies.
7. Comply fully with antitrust laws and trade regulations.
8. Comply fully with accepted accounting rules and controls.
9. Do not provide false or misleading information to the corporation, its auditors, or a government agency.
10. Do not use company property or resources for personal benefit or any other improper purpose.
11. Each employee is personally accountable for company funds over which he or she has control.
12. Staff members should not have any interest in any competitor or supplier of the company unless such interest has been fully disclosed to the company.

Cluster 3

"Be good to our customers."

1. Strive to provide products and services of the highest quality.
2. Perform assigned duties to the best of your ability and in the best interest of the corporation, its shareholders, and its customers.
3. Convey true claims for products.

EXHIBIT 2.6

Categories Found in Corporate Codes of Ethics

Source: Donald Robin, Michael Giallourakis, Fred R. David, and Thomas E. Moritz, "A Different Look at Codes of Ethics." Reprinted from *Business Horizons* (January–February 1989), Table 1, p. 68. Copyright 1989 by Indiana University Kelley School of Business. Used with permission.

written codes. Most firms did have items in each of the three clusters, though not in all 30 subcategories.

A study of codes of ethics for firms in the United Kingdom, France, and Germany found that a higher percentage of German firms had codes of ethics than British or French firms (see Exhibit 2.7).[33] Although only about one-third of the European firms in this study had codes of ethics, approximately 85 percent of U.S. firms have formal codes.

In a separate study, researchers found that important differences in codes of conduct exist among U.S., Canadian, and Australian firms.[34] For example, the codes of ethics differed substantially in terms of whether they explicitly stated what was acceptable ethical conduct on issues such as gifts, meals, entertainment, etc. toward domestic government officials (87 percent of U.S. firms, 59 percent of Canadian, and 24 percent of Australian firms).

Exhibit 2.8 provides information about the content of the codes of ethics for the firms that had formal codes. While 100 percent of the European firms covered issues of acceptable and unacceptable employee behavior in their codes, only 55 percent of U.S. firms covered these issues. By contrast, only 15 percent of the European firms covered issues of political interests (i.e., business-government relations) and 96 percent of U.S. firms covered these issues in their codes.

EXHIBIT 2.7

Adoption of Codes of Ethics

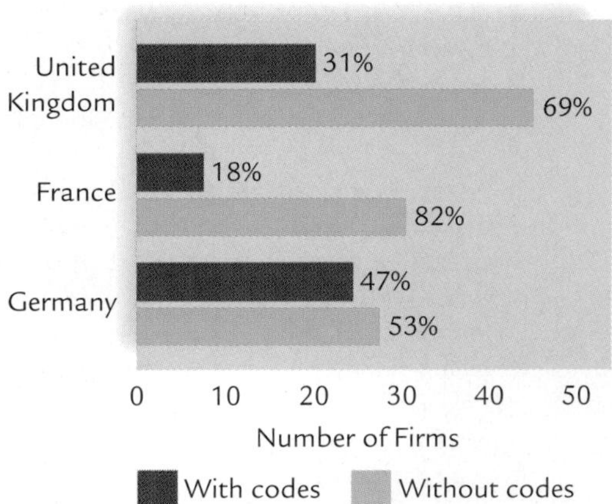

Research indicates that executives believe codes of conduct are the most effective way of encouraging ethical behavior on the part of their employees.[35] If a given firm had a code that covered all 30 categories listed in Exhibit 2.6, employees would have a comprehensive guide for their behavior. Unfortunately, the research does not support a strong link between having codes of ethics and actual employee behavior. Firms without formal codes seem to have no higher or lower incidents of unethical behavior than those with formal codes.[36] This may be because simply having a formal statement written down is not sufficient. For example, although nearly all *Fortune* 500 firms in the United States have codes of ethics, only about one-third have training programs and ethics officers, and only half have distributed formal codes to all their employees.[37]

SUCCESSFULLY IMPLEMENTING CODES OF ETHICS Actions speak much louder than words; employees are unlikely to conform to the formal code unless other actions taken by the organization reinforce the code and communicate that the company is serious about compliance.[38] In some companies "ethics officer" or ombudsman are being instituted. These individuals are responsible for getting ethics information and policies out to employees and also ensuring that their concerns and observations of misconduct are reported to senior managers so corrective actions can be taken.

	UNITED KINGDOM N = 33		FRANCE N = 15		GERMANY N = 30		TOTAL EUROPEAN COUNTRIES		UNITED STATES N = 118		SIGNIFICANCE
Subjects	**Number of Firms**	**%**	**Number of Firms**	**%**	**Number of Firms**	**%**	**Number of Firms**	**%**	**Number of Firms**	**%**	**Europe vs. U.S.**
Employee conduct	33	100	15	100	30	100	78	100	47	55	SIG
Community and environment	21	64	11	73	19	63	51	85	50	42	NS
Customers	18	39	14	93	20	67	52	87	96	81	SIG
Shareholders	13	39	11	73	18	60	42	64	NA	NA	NA
Suppliers and contractors	7	21	2	13	6	20	15	19	101	86	SIG
Political interests	4	12	3	20	5	17	12	15	113	96	SIG
Innovation and technology	2	6	3	20	18	60	26	33	18	15	SIG

NS = Not significant NA = No comparable data available SIG = Significantly different

EXHIBIT 2.8 Subjects Addressed in Corporate Codes of Ethics

Communication. For maximum impact, communicating a company's ethical standards needs to take a variety of forms and be repeated. It is not enough to simply send out a one-time memo. Rather, the company will need to communicate the code in memos, company newsletters, videos, and speeches by senior executives repeatedly over a period of time if people are to take the content of the message seriously.

Training. For the code of ethical conduct to be effective, people will likely need training.[39] For maximum impact, the training needs to be engaging. For example, Motorola developed approximately 80 different short cases. Each case presents a situation requiring a manager to make a decision. Participants in the training program are asked to individually and collectively decide what they would do in similar situations. They then compared their decisions to those of senior executives, including Motorola's CEO, and what these executives believe is in keeping with the firm's code of ethics.

Lockheed Martin also has taken an engaging approach to ethics training—with an interesting and innovative twist. In the late 1990s, the company developed a board game based on Scott Adam's "Dilbert" character. The game consisted of 50 ethical dilemmas players (employees) had to make decisions about. Participants found this approach to be more satisfying than traditional ethics training they had received. They also seemed to recall the learning points more effectively. Later when the Dilbert craze wore off, Lockheed Martin used real business ethics problems as a basis for discussion. The company also has an ethics hotline employees can call for advice if they are experiencing a business dilemma.[40]

Although officials at organizations often think that ethics training programs are effective, current research is less conclusive. What we can say based on research is that the greater the psychological and emotional involvement of participants in the training, the greater their retention of the learning points. This may explain why Lockheed Martin's experience with ethics training has been positive.

Reward and Recognition. In addition to communicating the code to employees and training them, it is critical to make sure that those who comply with the code are recognized and rewarded. Otherwise, employees will simply view the code as the "formal rhetoric but not the real deal." ExxonMobil is a company that does this. It regularly celebrates the story of an individual who has honored the company's code of conduct, even when doing so might have cost the company money. For example, when a government official in a developing company solicited a bribe from one of ExxonMobil's drilling teams in exchange for permission to drill there, the team manager refused to pay. The drilling team and their expensive equipment sat idle for more than a week at a cost of over $1 million. Finally, the government official admitted that all the paperwork and permits were in order and the team was allowed to proceed. ExxonMobil celebrated this incident in its newsletter to reinforce to its employees that the company takes its code of ethical conduct seriously and rewards people who honor it, even if it costs the company money.

Whistle-Blowing. A **whistle-blower** is an employee who discloses illegal or unethical conduct on the part of others in the organization. Although some firms have implemented programs to encourage whistle-blowing, most have not.[41] As a group, whistle-blowers tend *not* to be disgruntled employees but instead are conscientious, high-performing employees who report illegal or unethical incidents. In general, they report these incidents not for notoriety but because they believe the wrongdoings are so grave that they must be exposed.[42] For example, Randy Robarge, a nuclear power plant supervisor, never intended to be a whistle-blower. To Robarge, raising concerns about the improper storage of radioactive material at ComEd's Zion power plant on Lake Michigan was just part of doing a good job.[43]

whistle-blower
an employee who discloses illegal or unethical conduct on the part of others in the organization

Research suggests that the more employees know about the internal channels through which they can blow the whistle and the stronger the protection of past whistle-blowers, the more likely they are to initially use internal rather than external channels, such as the media, to call attention to problems.[44] IBM receives up to 18,000 letters a year from employees making confidential complaints through IBM's "Speak Up" program. Firms such as Hughes Tool Co., General Motors, and Bloomingdale's offer financial rewards to employees who report valid claims.[45] In general, research suggests the following steps can be effective in encouraging valid whistle-blowing:[46]

- Clearly communicate whistle-blowing procedures to all employees.
- Allow for reporting channels in addition to the chain of command or reporting incidents to one's boss.
- Thoroughly investigate all claims based on a consistent procedure.
- Protect whistle-blowers who make valid claims.
- Provide moderate financial incentives or rewards for valid claims.
- Publicly celebrate employees who make valid claims.

Examples Set by Top Managers. The examples top managers set—both in terms of how they behave personally and how they reward, punish, or ignore the actions of others—probably has the biggest impact on ethical conduct.[47] The examples these people set can severely damage the best intentions and implementation of any corporate ethics program. Middle managers are rarely persuaded by top executives to "do as I say not as I do."

Leaders at Enron, such as Ken Lay and Jeff Skilling, set an example of reporting growth at any price. Standard accounting rules were ignored so that higher revenues and profits could be recorded immediately. Once one rule, law, or policy is ignored by senior officers, who is to say that others shouldn't be? This pattern of illegal and unethical conduct was not confined to Enron but was complemented by the behavior of senior partners in the accounting firm that was supposed to monitor and certify Enron's accounting practices—Arthur Andersen. In an effort to retain Enron's auditing business and its more lucrative consulting engagements, leaders at Arthur Andersen ignored Enron's accounting irregularities despite their legal and ethical obligation to report them. In the end, leaders even instructed subordinates to destroy and shred documents (against company policy and legal statutes) in an effort to hide wrongdoing on both sides.

But by following the steps outlined earlier, managers can catch problems before they become national media events and seriously damage the firm's reputation. In addition, new laws in the United States both protect and reward whistle-blowers. Employers cannot

"The fish rots from the top of the head." The saying relates to the fact that people in an organization take their cues from the person leading it. Convicted of lying to federal officials about a stock trade, in 2004, homemaking maven Martha Stewart was sentenced to prison. The price of stock in her own company, Martha Stewart Living Omnimedia, plummeted as a result of the scandal: Having once traded for as much as $40 a share, it dropped to under $10 per share, taking a considerable toll on the company and Stewart's net worth.

discharge, threaten, or otherwise discriminate against employees because they report a suspected violation of the law. Employees who blow the whistle on companies with federal government contracts can actually receive a small portion of the judgment if the company is found guilty. For example, Jane Akre was one of the first to receive such a reward. Akre was given $425,000 when she blew the whistle on her employer, a TV station, which was deliberately distorting the news.[48] However, an award of $52 million to three men who blew the whistle on SmithKline Beecham, a large drug company, really grabbed people's attention.[49] And an even bigger eye-opener occurred when two men, Jim Alderson and John Schilling, shared a $100 million whistle-blower award granted on a $1.7 billion fine paid out by HCA, the largest hospital chain in the United States, for helping to disclose Medicare fraud.

How Governments Can Foster Ethical Behavior

The governments of the United States and many other countries have also tried to foster ethical behavior. For example, the U.S. government has enacted a number of laws and regulations designed to achieve this objective. Perhaps the most discussed, given today's global environment, is the Foreign Corrupt Practices Act.

Few issues of ethical behavior have received more attention than questionable payments or bribes. For American managers this is the heart of the **Foreign Corrupt Practices Act (FCPA)**. The act was passed in 1977 primarily because U.S. firms were making payments to foreign government officials to win government contracts and receive preferential treatment.

Foreign Corrupt Practices Act (FCPA)
a law prohibiting employees of U.S. firms from corrupting the actions of foreign officials, politicians, or candidates for office

One of the key incidents that sparked the FCPA was the revelation that Lockheed Corporation had made over $12 million in payments to Japanese business executives and government officials in order to sell commercial aircraft in that country. Subsequent discoveries showed that nearly 500 U.S. companies had made similar payments around the world, totaling over $300 million.

Lockheed's chairman at the time, Carl Kotchian, argued that the payments represented less than 3 percent of the revenue gained from the sale of aircraft to Japan. Kotchian also claimed the sales had a positive effect on the salaries and job security of Lockheed workers, with beneficial spillover effects for their dependents, communities, and shareholders. He said he was "between a rock and a hard spot": If he made the payments, people would say they were unethical; if he did not make the payments, a competitor would, and some Lockheed workers would lose their jobs. Do you agree with Kotchian? Whether you do or not, can you figure out which ethical approach he seems to be following? Is it a moral right approach, justice approach, or utilitarian approach?

Until the passage of the FCPA, these dilemmas were purely ethical ones. Upon its passage, they became legal ones: The FCPA made it illegal for employees of U.S. firms to corrupt the actions of foreign officials, politicians, or candidates for office. The act also outlaws an employee from making payments to *any* person when the employee has "reason to know" that the payments might be used to corrupt the behavior of officials. The act also requires that firms take steps to provide "reasonable assurance" that their transactions are in compliance with the law and to keep detailed records of them.

The FCPA does not cover payments made to business executives, though. For American managers, payments made to executives are ethical decisions, not legal ones. The FCPA also does not prohibit payments to low-level government employees to perform their duties in a more timely manner—duties they normally would have performed anyway. These types of payments are typically called *facilitating payments.* For example, a payment of $100 to a customs inspector not to delay the inspection of an imported product would not violate the FCPA because the payment simply facilitates something that the customs inspector would do anyway. However, the payment of $100 to pass a product *without* inspecting it would be a violation of the FCPA because the payment would entice the customs agent to do something he or she is not supposed to do.

Companies can be fined up to $1 million for violating the FCPA. Individuals face a $10,000 fine and up to *five years in prison.* Clearly, a $1 million fine is not a deterrent when deals can be worth $100 million. Rather, the prison terms for individuals are the real teeth in the law.

Managerial Challenges from the Front Line:

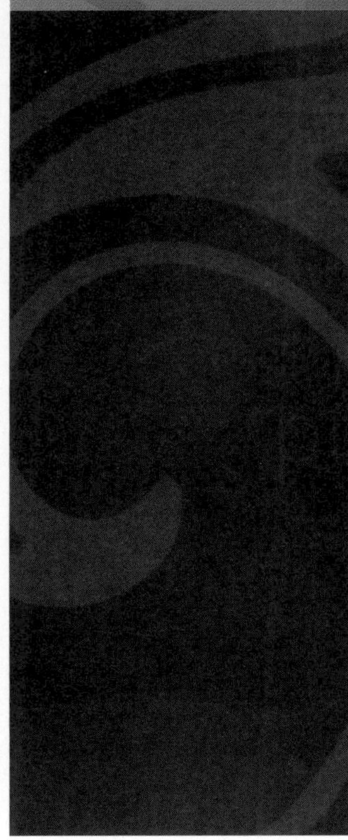

The Rest of the Story

After her mother died of lung disease in 1995, Sharon Anderson Wright became the CEO of Half Price Books. "I think we've grown more than she could have imagined," said Wright about her mom, In fact, even though the company now has about double the number of stores it did in 1995, it has never taken a lot of debt. Nonetheless, the growth of the business, forced the firm to become more organized, which has involved investing additional finances in things like computer and inventory systems. The expansion also made it too costly to maintain full healthcare benefits for part-time workers, a decision that Wright said she made "not lightly."

Wright still lives in her childhood Dallas home with her children and husband, Ken (who also works for the company). She pays herself a relatively small, five-figure salary. Employees are also paid modestly but are given shares in the company. Wright says that she and her sister, Ellen O'Neal, the executive vice president of Half Price Books, have turned down many buyout offers from competitors and venture-capital firms. "We could have been rich many times over," she says. "But my mom made a commitment to do the right thing, and it's my job to uphold it."

Sources: H. Landy, "Founder's Daughters Write Their Own Chapter," *Fort Worth Star-Telegram,* May 12, 2007, 1C, 6C; "Strong Results Fuel Chain's Decision to Add Stores," *Fort Worth Star-Telegram,* January 9, 2007; J. Lynch and G. Cosgriff, "Shelf Help," *People,* May 20, 2003, 127, 2p, 3c.

The general debates concerning ethics and social responsibility have raged for generations. The purpose of this chapter has not been to resolve the debate but rather to examine the assumptions and rationales of fundamental perspectives. If there were a magic formula for meeting these challenges, there would likely be little need for bright, capable people as managers wrestling with these issues (we could just turn the problem over to computer algorithms). Nor would there be much excitement in being a manager. We hope this examination enables you to evaluate your own views so that you will be prepared when situations arise concerning ethics or social responsibility. Perhaps then the pressure of the moment will be less likely to cause you to take actions that you might later regret. Understanding the general frameworks also helps you to better appreciate others who have differing perspectives and, thereby, interact more effectively with them.

Summary

- Poor judgments regarding social responsibility and lapses in ethical decision making can inflict irreparable damage on the value of a firm. As a consequence, as a manager, you need to be able to make sound, ethical decisions and encourage your subordinates to do likewise.
- The efficiency perspective argues that "the business of business is business." Therefore, a manager's obligation is to maximize shareholders' returns. The values of society should only be reflected in a manager's decisions insofar as those values are codified by law.

- The social responsibility perspective argues that corporations owe their existence not just to shareholders, who provide risk capital, but to society at large. As a consequence, managers should provide a reasonable return to shareholders while also meeting the legitimate concerns of society.
- The strategic corporate social responsibility approach argues that the best social responsibility is that which creates shared value for society and the business. Determining which issues have the highest probability of fulfilling this objective comes from assessing the activities that are key to the business, issues that the company affects, and issues that are of concern to society.
- The four basic approaches to ethical decision making include utilitarian, moral rights, universal, and justice approaches. The utilitarian approach is based on the premise that the right thing to do is that which brings about the greatest good. The moral rights approach assumes that there are principles with moral standing and that actions should be consistent with those principles. The universal approach is based on the notion that actions should be guided by principles that you believe should be universally applied, including to yourself. The justice approach is predicated on the notion that costs and benefits should be equitably distributed, rules should be impartially applied, and those damaged because of inequity or discrimination should be compensated.
- Moral intensity is the degree to which people see an issue as an ethical one. It is influenced by six factors: (1) the magnitude of the consequences, (2) social consensus, (3) the probability of effect, (4) temporal immediacy, (5) proximity, and (6) the concentration of effect.
- When it comes to fostering ethical decisions and behavior throughout an organization, few things are more important than the example set by senior executives. Codes of conduct, communication, training, and rewards (and punishments) are all additional steps that can have an effect on the decisions and behavior of employees.

Key Terms

code of ethical conduct 46
compensatory justice 42
concentration of effect 43
distributive justice 41
efficiency perspective 30
ethical dilemmas 39
ethical lapses 39
externalities 31
Foreign Corrupt Practices Act 51
justice approach 41
magnitude of the consequences 43
managerial ethics 38
moral intensity 42
moral rights approach 40
probability of effect 43
procedural justice 41
proximity 43
social consensus 43
stakeholders 32
strategic corporate social responsibility perspective 35
temporal immediacy 43
universal approach 41
utilitarian approach 40
whistle-blower 49

Review Questions

1. What is the major premise of the efficiency perspective regarding corporate social responsibility?
2. What are the key concerns with the efficiency perspective of social responsibility?
3. What is the fundamental objective of the strategic social responsibility approach?
4. What are the key differences between managerial ethics and corporate social responsibility?
5. Contrast and compare the utilitarian approach, moral rights approach, universal approach, and justice approach.
6. What are the six factors that influence moral intensity?
7. What are five powerful means of enhancing the influence of formal codes of conduct on actual employee behavior?
8. What is a whistle-blower?
9. What is the Foreign Corrupt Practices Act?

3. He could pay a large sum of money ($1 million deposited to a Swiss bank account) to a "consultant" who had "debottlenecked" problems like this before and who promised Pignatelli that he could fix the situation quickly.
4. He could pay money "under the table" directly to government officials to obtain the permissions needed to run the refinery economically.

Pignatelli considered each option. Playing it straight would likely take several months and possibly years before government authorization could be obtained. In the meantime, the refinery would not operate or would operate at such a low capacity that it would lose millions of dollars. Pignatelli was not certain that pressure from his partners would influence government officials. He wondered about the effect of going to the media. Given the current cost of the project, the thousands of jobs that depended on an operating refinery, and time pressures, $1 million seemed like a small price to pay to a consultant to get things debottlenecked. He might be able to gain approval for even less money if he went directly to government officials.

Questions

1. What should Pignatelli do? What would you do and why?
2. Pignatelli seems to be leaning in the direction of hiring a consultant who might use part of the money for bribes. If Pignatelli does not pay the bribes directly, does this absolve him of responsibility?
3. Bribes are illegal in Italy. Even if bribes are common practice there, does this justify paying them?
4. Does Pignatelli have a responsibility to Italian citizens to build an environmentally friendly refinery above and beyond what the law requires? Is it appropriate for Gulf to spend this extra money and essentially take it away from shareholders?
5. How would you feel if you were a lower-level employee in the company and learned that Pignatelli intended to pay bribes to get things "debottlenecked"? What would your ethical obligations be? Should you ignore the situation or confront Pignatelli? Should you inform your direct boss or go to the media?

Source: Personal conversations with Nicolo Pignatelli.

3

International Management and Globalization

Learning Objectives

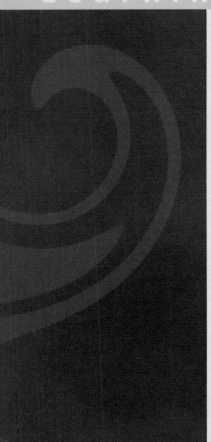

After studying this chapter, you should be able to:

- Explain what globalization is and how it affects firms and countries.
- Identify and differentiate the two major elements of the global environment.
- Name and explain the three major dimensions of an institutional environment.
- Define the term *culture* and identify four primary cultural dimensions.
- Describe the five international market entry strategies and explain when to use each strategy.
- Explain the three types of international organization focus.
- Discuss the benefits and challenges of managing across cultures.
- Describe how to effectively manage multicultural teams.
- Define the term *global mind-set* and explain its importance for managers.

Managerial Challenges from the Front Line

Name: Steve Radewych

Position: Vice President, Supply Chain Management, Americas Operations

Alma mater: Ryerson University (undergraduate degree); University of Waterloo (master's degree)

Outside work activities: Recreational cycling; would like to start playing golf again

First job out of school: Supply-chain planner

Business book reading now: *The Toyota Way*

Hero: The workers on the shop floor. They rarely get the credit they deserve.

Motto to live by: Treat others as you want to be treated

What drives me: A passion to learn

Management style: Collaborative

Pet peeve: People who cut in a line

Steve Radewych works for Celestica, Inc., a major provider of electronics manufacturing services and products. Celestica, which has its headquarters in Toronto, Canada, started out as a single, wholly owned subsidiary of IBM but was spun off in 1996. Today, Celestica's 40 electronics manufacturing and design centers around the world generate nearly $9 billion in revenues.

Radewych manages a team that provides manufacturing and supply chain services to firms that have outsourced these functions to Celestica. He says he has encountered several challenges as a manager, but two stand out in recent years. The first was moving Celestica's manufacturing from high-cost to low-cost geographic regions. The process required closing a number of high-cost manufacturing plants and starting others in regions of the world where the costs are considerably lower. A number of its manufacturing operations in North America and Western Europe were closed and new ones opened in Asia and Eastern Europe. Now, the company has large manufacturing operations in China, Thailand, the Czech Republic, and Mexico; only six electronics manufacturing services are in the Americas (Canada, United States, Brazil, and Mexico).

Radewych refers to the change that was made as "global growth management." In one particular role as part of a global customer unit team, it was his job to both design and manage Celestica's supply chain network across sites in three different global regions (Americas, Asia, and Europe). The goal was to increase the services and revenues in the customer accounts across these regions. But, it also required close and effective relationships with customers and suppliers, which was no easy task. Take, for example, one major account for a computer-networking company, which grew from about $40 million annually to almost $4 billion a year. In the case of that account, Celestica manufactured the goods in several locations and had to interface with key suppliers there, such as large-memory and high-end-processing device producers. Achieving coordination across the different organizations, different geographic regions, and operations was quite complex.

The challenges to which Radewych refers are international in orientation. In recent years, the amount of outsourcing of manufacturing from high-cost regions such as the United States and Western Europe to regions of the world where labor and other operating costs are lower, such as Asia and Eastern Europe, has increased substantially. As a company that serves as a supplier of outsourced manufacturing services, Celestica had to provide low-cost manufacturing while maintaining the required quality in order to compete. Closing manufacturing facilities and developing new ones in different countries with different cultures and institutional environments was a significant challenge for Radewych and his colleagues at Celestica. For example, the institutional environments are generally less well developed in a number of the Asian countries (e.g., China, Thailand, Malaysia), and their cultures often differ considerably from those in Western countries.

The second challenge mentioned to satisfy customers and to "grow their business," requires a careful coordination among the customer, the various manufacturing sites used within Celestica, and multiple suppliers. Take the case of the major networking firm: Multiple Celestica manufacturing sites were used, with predominantly the circuit-board assembly done in Asia, and the box and configuration done in high-cost geographic areas. Celestica also had to coordinate with suppliers in different geographic regions. Thus, understanding and being sensitive to the different cultures and means of operating as well as building relationships with parties across organizations and cultures were critical to Radewych's success.

In this chapter, we examine many of the issues Radewych faced as he worked to expand Celestica's operations. We begin discussing globalization and its effects on markets and businesses. We then examine the different institutional and cultural environments of countries and the strategies firms use to enter international markets, the reasons firms use each strategy, and the risks that they pose. We also discuss something Radewych had to learn to deal with firsthand: managing people and teams across cultures. We examine both as they have become highly important in our global economy and with multinational companies such as Celestica. Finally, we discuss what's called a "a global mind-set," what it is, and the importance for managers like Radewych to have one.

Globalization

Globalization refers to the flow of goods and services, capital (money), and knowledge across country borders. Globalization enhances the economic interdependence among countries and organizations across countries.[1] According to Thomas Friedman, the author

globalization
the flow of goods and services, capital (money), and knowledge across country borders

of the popular book, *The World Is Flat,* we are in the third stage of globalization, with the first involving internationalization of countries, the second involving companies moving into international markets, and the current and third stage involving individuals collaborating (and competing) on a global basis.[2] The increasing interdependence among countries, companies, and even individuals across country borders has reduced the influence that national governments can have on their economies.[3]

Increasing globalization has dramatically changed the competitive landscape in recent years for everyone. For example, when coupled with new technology, especially in information systems, small firms now have access to markets and resources in other countries. This has allowed them to compete effectively with larger and often more established firms.

A MANAGER'S CHALLENGE

Globalization

Made in China

As I tucked my seven-year-old boy into bed one evening, he said, "Wow, Mommy, I can't believe my bed says 'Made in Canada.' Finally I have something that doesn't say 'Made In China.'" A bit taken aback, I asked him why he was so surprised. He calmly began pointing to all of the items in his room that were exported from China. What I did not realize, but my son did, is that a majority of his toys and furniture were made in China. From 1998 to 1999, U.S. imports from China increased $71.2 billion. It is expected that China's trade surplus will exceed $140 billion this year, according to a Chinese government official. So far in 2006, China's exports exceeded imports by $110.0 billion. So what does this mean for the U.S.?

Financial markets are beginning to recognize that the emerging Chinese economy is boosting global growth. Some economists believe that the growing number of products imported from China is one reason inflation has remained low in the United States. This has encouraged banks to keep interest rates low, stimulating U.S. investment and growth. The purchase by China's central bank of billions of dollars of U.S. Treasury bills has also likely kept U.S. interest rates low.

Americans are exporting more goods to China as well. In 2006, these exports were up 20 percent. Some American corporations feel that without China, they would be less efficient, less profitable, and would have to pay lower wages to their workers in the United States. So whether Americans realize it or not, China has had a major impact on the United States' recovery following the country's 2001 recession.

However, China's growing trade surplus—the fact that it exports more than it imports—is becoming a sore point with some of its trading partners, including the United States. U.S. textile lobbyists, for example, are concerned that massive amounts of Chinese imports have cost thousands of Americans their jobs. Collectively these lobbyists have filed a petition to limit the importation of certain clothing products. China is also under some pressure from the United States to increase the value of its currency, the yuan. This would help make China's exports more expensive and U.S. imports into China more competitive.

Finally, U.S. retailers complain it often takes too long to receive Chinese imports, costing them sales. They feel that to compete with the European retailers, it's important to replenish merchandise faster to keep up with current trends. As a result, they are beginning to consider buying some of their merchandise locally.

Sources: D. Cohen, "The Global Reverbs of China and India," *Business Week*, February 9, 2006, www.businessweek.com; P. Bhatnagar, "Is 'Made in U.S.A.' Back in Vogue?" CNN Money, March 1, 2006, www.cnnmoney.com; A. Yeh, "US-China Trade Relations Take a Turn for the Worse," *Financial Times*, November 5, 2004, www.ft.com; C. Swann, "Strong Exports Help to Offset U.S. Trade Deficit," *Financial Times*, July 12, 2006, www.ft.com; R. Lenihan, "Value-Conscious Americans Are Long-time Fans of Chinese Goods," CNN Money, May 22, 2006, www.cnnmoney.com; Editorial, "Don't Blame Job Woes on China," *Business Week*, October 13, 2003, www.businessweek.com; The Associated Press/Beijing, "China's Trade Surplus to Extend $140B," *Business Week*, November 5, 2006, www.businessweek.com.

Additionally, even firms from economies that are less developed can better compete in international markets as well.[4]

According to Friedman, globalization has gone beyond the point where small and large companies have moved into international markets. Today, the world is at the point where even individual people are collaborating (and competing) with one another on a global basis.[5] Friedman suggests that the increased globalization has made all of us, regardless of our country of origin, "next-door neighbors"—and competitors.[6]

In the professional services area, many functions have shifted to countries like China and India because their workers have the ability to do a quality job at a much lower cost. Many U.S. firms are outsourcing services such as software development and tax-return preparation to India. Some U.S. companies are sending their U.S. employees to India for surgery because it is less expensive there, and the quality of the care is excellent.

India and China are expected to be major players in the global economy over the next 30 to 40 years. Some have argued that the combined economies of China, India, Brazil, and Russia are likely to be greater than the total economies of the G6 countries (Canada, France, Germany, Japan, United Kingdom, and United States) by the year 2040.[7]

Toyota is an example of a global company that has enjoyed a substantial amount of success internationally. It is poised to become the world's number one automaker. In 2006 alone, General Motors and Ford laid off 46,000 employees while Toyota moved forward opening new plants in the United States and other parts of the world. Over 50 percent of Toyota's sales revenues come from outside of Japan.[8] Toyota has emphasized high quality and reliability and thereby forced many of its competitors to do the same or lose market share. Toyota's employees and managers are strongly encouraged to continuously search for ways to improve the process that reduces the costs of manufacturing cars and increases the quality of the autos manufactured.[9]

Undoubtedly, globalization has both positive and negative effects on most countries as suggested in *The World Is Flat*, mentioned previously. It provides opportunities for companies to expand and grow by entering new foreign markets. It can also improve the economic development of countries. Yet, competition from foreign firms entering their home markets can harm some local companies. Some of the questions about China relate to their effect on U.S.-based firms and their employees in the United States. Competition in U.S. markets from Chinese firms has seriously harmed U.S. furniture and textile firms. Thus, government officials have to weigh the benefits of globalization against the costs. Often these officials are under significant pressure by different constituencies to institute trade barriers that make it more difficult for foreign firms to compete effectively in their home markets.

Understanding a Country's Environment

Wal-Mart, the biggest company in the world, employs over 500,000 employees across the globe. The company serves 49 million customers in international markets via 2,700 stores, and enjoys sales of over $67 billion in international markets.[10] To continue to grow and be profitable, it is important for Wal-Mart to know which markets to enter and how to compete in them. There are two major aspects of a country's environment that managers need to understand: institutions and culture. We discuss each next.

The Country's Institutional Environment

Each country has a distinct institutional environment composed of economic development, political-legal, and physical infrastructure dimensions. The **institutional environment** consists of the country's rules, policies, and enforcement processes. This, in turn, influences the behavior of the individuals and organizations that operate within the country.[11]

institutional environment the country's rules, policies, and enforcement processes that influence individuals' and organizations' behaviors that operate within the country boundaries

THE ECONOMIC DEVELOPMENT DIMENSION Countries vary in their level of economic development. Economic development and growth is vital to most countries because it contributes to better living standards and the health and welfare of citizens.[12] Economic

Workers ride tricycles past the first Wal-Mart store in Shanghai as preparations are made for the grand opening of China's 48th store. Wal-Mart is the biggest company on the planet, employing more than a half-million people in 2,700-plus stores worldwide.

development is important to local and foreign firms as well because it opens up greater market opportunities for them.

Country economies may be classified into developed, emerging, and developing economies. Some countries, such as the United States and Japan, have highly developed economies. Others such as Sudan and El Salvador have less-developed economies. Still others, like China and India, have economies that are not highly developed but are growing rapidly. These economies are classified as emerging.[13] For example, the countries in Western Europe have developed economies, whereas most of the countries in Eastern Europe have emerging economies.

Developed economies tend to be larger than less-developed or emerging economies. They also tend to have more-effective capital markets. In effective capital markets, people and businesses are readily able to borrow money from banks and other financial institutions or raise it by selling shares in stock markets. Developed economies tend to be larger than those in other countries. Emerging economy countries like China often have rapidly growing economies and their capital markets tend to be young and underdeveloped. Finally, the weakest economies exist in developing economies.

THE POLITICAL-LEGAL DIMENSION This dimension of the institutional environment refers to a country's political risks, regulations, laws, and the enforcement of them. Governments develop laws and policies to govern the behavior of their citizens and organizations operating within the country's boundaries.[14] Among the important regulations that affect businesses are those related to the way foreign firms operate. These regulations include laws that put tariffs and quotas on imported goods, laws that dictate the way employees are treated, and laws dictating how publicly traded firms listed on major exchanges in the country must behave.

For example, after China began to open its markets (partially at least), all foreign firms entering the country were required to form joint ventures with Chinese firms. Foreign firms' behaviors were regulated in order to protect local firms that often lacked the resources and capabilities needed to compete with firms from developed countries. In recent years, the Sarbanes-Oxley Act, often referred to as SOX, enacted by the United States in 2002, was designed to curtail scandals like the ones at Enron and WorldCom. Both domestic and foreign firms registered on U.S. stock exchanges must adhere to the provisions set forth in SOX. For example, all CEOs and CFOs must certify that the financial statements published by the firm are accurate and satisfy the rules set forth by standards in the industry and legal requirements. Almost 1,300 companies restated their earnings in 2005 because of SOX, which is more than any other previous year since records have been maintained.[15]

Primarily, the rules established by the law are intended to make the management of public firms more transparent. Yet, the rules can be excessive and discourage investment from abroad. Furthermore, an increasing amount of companies are going private (buying back their publicly traded stock) in order to avoid having to deal with the costly reporting rules required by the law. Thus, in late 2006, the U.S. Securities and Exchange Commission announced a number of "deregulation" orders designed to make compliance with the law less onerous on businesses.[16] Laws such as SOX play an important role in countries' institutional environments.

Among the important laws are those regarding intellectual property rights. When the laws related to and enforcement of intellectual property rights (e.g., patents) are weak, firms with valuable technologies are reluctant to bring them into the country. And, if they do enter the country's markets, they may not use the valuable technology in the market there or will guard it carefully to ensure their local partners don't access it. However, when barriers to such knowledge exist, they reduce the value of the joint venture, especially to the local partner. Local partners in developing and emerging markets often have goals of learning technological and managerial capabilities from their more-capable foreign partners.[17]

THE PHYSICAL INFRASTRUCTURE DIMENSION Institutional infrastructure is critical to the operation of businesses within a country because they facilitate business communications and the movement of goods from their source to the ultimate consumer. Physical infrastructure includes the amount and quality of roads and highways, number of telephone lines (per capita), and number of airports, etc. The availability of physical infrastructure often plays an important role in decisions to enter a new international market by a foreign firm because they tend to perform more poorly in countries where the infrastructure is not well developed.[18] Therefore, countries that wish to attract foreign investment must try to develop their physical infrastructure.[19]

Without the physical infrastructure, it is difficult for firms to distribute their products to potential customers. Thus, they either have to sell to smaller markets because they are unable to reach as many potential customers, or they have to distribute their products in much more costly ways. In either case, the firm earns lower profits than it would if the country's physical infrastructure was more well developed.

Table 3.1 depicts clusters of selected country institutional environments. As shown, the developing countries (e.g., Nigeria, Brazil) with relatively weak economies and central regulations (largely government control/low political rights) form the first cluster. Emerging market countries form the second cluster. These countries are generally experiencing rather strong economic growth and are beginning to develop the other institutions needed for further economic growth (e.g., enhanced transportation, new laws and regulations such as intellectual property rights). The third cluster of countries has relatively advanced institutional environments exemplified by Western European countries. Finally, the most advanced institutional environments are in Japan and the United States.[20]

IMPORTANCE OF THE INSTITUTIONAL ENVIRONMENT Economic growth is vital to most countries because it contributes to the standards of living, health, and welfare of their citizens.[21] Economic growth is important to local and foreign firms as well. Higher rates of economic growth suggest greater market opportunities for all firms and attract new business development and foreign investments in the country's economy.

Beyond the attractiveness of a country's economic development and health, laws, regulations, political stability, and physical infrastructure play important roles in firms' behaviors. In particular, multinational firms seeking to invest in new international markets

TABLE 3.1 Country Institutional Environment Clusters

Cluster 1: This cluster largely consists of developing and transition economies. These countries are high in regulatory control and low in political rights. Brazil, Russia, and Nigeria exemplify this group of countries.
Cluster 2: This cluster largely consists of emerging market countries that are more advanced than Cluster 1 countries but still need greater development of institutional dimensions. These countries score a little higher on political rights but the lowest on monetary policy and second highest on investment restrictions. China, India, The Netherlands, and Singapore exemplify this group of countries.
Cluster 3: These countries have the second highest regulatory controls but also score high on political rights. They also have strong physical infrastructures. Countries in Western Europe dominate this cluster (e.g., Finland, France, Germany, Portugal, and Sweden).
Cluster 4: This cluster of countries has the most developed institutional infrastructure overall with balanced regulatory controls and political rights and strong economic and physical infrastructure institutional dimensions. Only two countries are in this cluster, Japan and the United States.

Source: M. A. Hitt, R. M. Holmes, T. Miller, and M. P. Salmador, Modeling country institutional profiles: The dynamics of institutional environments. Paper presented at the Strategic Management Society Conference, Vienna, November 2006.

need to understand these elements of a country's institutional environment. These institutional dimensions can greatly affect a firm's willingness to make direct investments in a country's markets. Furthermore recent research shows that the strong presence of multinational firms in a country strongly influences the development of its institutional environment. For example, the greater number of multinational corporations in a country the greater the pressure on its government to develop and enforce legislation to reduce corruption.[22] The influences are partly because of these firms' effects on the country's economic development and growth. Alternatively, corruption also discourages foreign companies from making major investments in a country.[23] As we will learn later in the chapter, institutional environments have major effects on firms' international strategies and especially affect which countries firms enter.

While institutional forces play an important role in determining firms' behaviors within a country, societal culture plays at least as strong a role. Culture's effects may be more pervasive because of its influence on human behavior. Next, we examine the nature of culture and its effects on individual and firm behaviors.

Culture

culture
a learned set of assumptions, values, and beliefs that members of a group have accepted and that affect human behavior

Although institutional forces play an important role in terms of how and where businesses globalize, a society's culture is critical. **Culture** is a learned set of assumptions, values, and beliefs that have been accepted by members of a group and that affect human behavior.[24] Some have referred to culture as a collective programming of the mind that has a powerful effect on individual behavior.[25] Although a culture can exist among any group of people, our focus is on national cultures.

Understanding culture is critical because it can dramatically influence how people observe and interpret the business world around them—for example, whether they see situations as opportunities or threats. A person's culture likely affects his or her opinion about the "right" managerial behavior. For example, only 10 percent of Swedish managers believe they should have precise answers to most questions subordinates ask them, whereas 78 percent of Japanese managers think they should.[26] As this specific example illustrates, culture can contribute to preexisting ways of interpreting events, evaluating them, and determining a course of action.

CULTURAL DIMENSIONS The most prominent studies of culture were conducted by Geert Hofstede and by a large number of researchers led by Robert House referred to as

GLOBE.[27] Both these complex studies identified at least four prominent dimensions of national culture: power distance, uncertainty avoidance, individualism versus collectivism, and gender focus.

Power distance is the extent to which people accept power and authority differences among people. Power distance is not a measure of the extent to which there are power and status differences in a group. Most countries have richer and poorer citizens, and more and less powerful citizens. Power distance does not suggest whether or not status and power differentials exist in a country but rather the extent to which people in the country accept any differences. In Hofstede's study, people from the Philippines, Venezuela, and Mexico had the highest levels of acceptance of power differences. In contrast, Austria, Israel, and Denmark had the lowest levels of acceptance.

power distance
the extent to which people accept power and authority differences among people

Cultures differ in the extent to which they need things to be clear or ambiguous. This dimension of culture has been labeled **uncertainty avoidance**. Citizens in nations high in uncertainty avoidance prefer clear norms (rules that govern behavior). Groups high in uncertainty avoidance create structures and institutions to reduce uncertainty. By contrast, groups that are low in uncertainty avoidance prefer to have fewer rules and tend to be more comfortable in ambiguous situations. For example, managers from Sweden, the Netherlands, and the United States are most comfortable with uncertainty. Managers from Indonesia and Japan are least comfortable with high uncertainty.

uncertainty avoidance
when cultures differ in the extent to which they need things to be clear or ambiguous

Individualism is the extent to which people's identities are self-oriented and people are expected to take care of themselves and their immediate families. People from the United States and Great Britain often score high on individual orientations. Individuals from these countries exhibit high emotional independence from organizations and institutions and tend to emphasize and reward individual achievement and value individual decisions. Alternatively, **collectivism** is the extent to which a person's identity is a function of the group(s) to which the person belongs (his or her family, firm, community, and so forth) and the extent to which group members are expected to look after each other. People from China, Venezuela, and Pakistan have high collective orientations. People from these countries tend to exhibit emotional dependence on organizations and institutions to which they belong, emphasize group membership, and value collective decisions.

individualism
the extent to which people's identities are self-oriented and people are expected to take care of themselves and their immediate families

collectivism
the extent to which identity is a function of the group(s) to which an individual belongs (e.g., families, firm members, community members, etc.) and the extent to which group members are expected to look after each other

Gender focus represents the extent to which people in a country value masculine or feminine traits. Countries emphasizing masculine traits value activities that lead to success, money, and possessions. Alternatively those emphasizing feminine traits value activities that show a caring for others and enhance the quality of life.

Countries such as the United States tend to emphasize masculine traits. In the United States, people often work many hours a week (usually over 60 hours), and take shorter vacations. In other countries that do not emphasize masculine traits, work is often valued less. Table 3.2 presents the culture scores of selected countries.

gender focus
the extent to which people in a country value masculine or feminine traits

Understanding cultures can be valuable for a number of reasons. For example, cultural characteristics can predict how managers will respond to socially responsible actions. Research has shown that managers in cultures that emphasize collectivism and are low in power distance engage in greater amounts of socially responsible activities than cultures with high individualism and high power distance.[28]

Globalization has greatly enhanced the extent to which cultural diversity plays a role in business. As companies globalize and expand their operations around the world, they create an increased opportunity and demand for people from different cultures to effectively interact together. Managers must interact and deal with suppliers, customers, and partners from different cultures. We discuss the management of cultural diversity within companies and relationships across cultures later in this chapter.

Knowing and understanding different institutional environments and cultures is important if managers are to make good strategic decisions about which foreign markets to enter and how to manage operations established in these markets. We examine these strategies next and discuss how different institutional and cultural environments affect the strategies chosen and how to implement and manage them.

TABLE 3.2 Cultural Values and Scores (for Select Countries)

	Power Distance[a]	Uncertainty Avoidance[b]	Individualism/ Collectivism[c]	Gender Focus[d]
Brazil	5.33	3.60	3.83	3.31
Canada	4.82	4.58	4.38	3.70
China	5.04	4.94	4.77	3.05
England	5.15	4.65	4.27	3.67
France	5.28	4.43	3.93	3.64
India	5.47	4.15	4.38	2.90
Japan	5.11	4.07	5.19	3.19
Mexico	5.22	4.18	4.06	3.64
Netherlands	4.11	4.70	4.46	3.50
Poland	5.10	3.62	4.53	4.02
Russia	5.52	2.88	4.50	4.07
United States	4.88	4.15	4.20	3.34

[a]Higher scores indicate higher power distance.
[b]Higher scores suggest more uncertainty avoidance.
[c]Higher scores indicate greater collectivism.
[d]Higher scores suggest greater gender equality whereas lower scores indicate male domination.

Source: Based on data from R. J. House, et al, eds., *Culture, Leadership and Organizations: The GLOBE Study of 62 Countries* (Thousand Oaks, CA: Sage Publications, 2004).

International Market-Entry Strategies

Choosing which international markets to enter and how to enter them is critically important to many small-, medium-, and large-sized firms in recent times. With the increasing globalization discussed at the beginning of this chapter, a large number of firms are servicing international markets at their birth. International markets are attractive to firms for several reasons. International markets increase the size of firms' potential markets and their sales revenue. When they sell more products abroad, these firms gain greater economies of scale, which, in turn, increases their potential profit. Firms can also gain access to special resources (e.g., lower-cost labor, valuable raw materials) in some international locations that can help them become more competitive in global markets. These are referred to as location advantages.[29]

The previous information suggests that firms have considerable motivation to enter international markets. Yet, all international markets are not created equal. As stated earlier, countries vary in their institutional environments and cultures. Thus, the attractiveness of countries' markets also varies. First, early in their internationalization efforts, firms prefer to enter markets that have similar institutional environments and similar cultures to their home country. This is because they better understand these environments and thereby take less risk entering these markets. This is important, especially for small firms with less capital, because entering international markets requires resources and learning about the new market and environment rapidly.[30] For these reasons and to reduce potential costs, firms also often cluster their international operations in one or a few geographic regions.[31] As firms gain more experience entering and operating in international markets, they are willing to enter markets where the differences in institutional environments and cultures are greater. Yet, the institutional environments and cultural differences also influence the means by which firms enter new international markets.

Firms can enter new foreign markets in a variety of ways. Each poses different risks and requires different levels and types of resources. Among the ways to enter a new market are by exporting products to the market, licensing products to firms there, either acquiring or creating strategic alliances with local firms, or establishing your own operations in the country. We explore each of these strategies next.

Exporting

The most common way of entering international markets is by exporting goods. This is especially true for smaller firms and for firms initially entering into foreign markets. **Exporting** involves manufacturing products in a firm's home country and shipping them to a foreign market. It is a popular entry strategy because of the lower capital requirements and risks. Exporting does not require establishing operations in the country, thereby avoiding a large capital investment. However, it does require the exporting firm to establish a means of marketing and distributing its goods within the country. Thus, it may have to combine exporting and strategic alliances with local firms in order to distribute their goods to customers. As a result, the costs of transportation and having to share profits with a local firm can reduce the profits a firm can earn from the international market. Therefore, although an export strategy is less risky, it is unlikely to provide big returns because of its associated costs. If the exporting firm's transportation costs are high, it might be limited to exporting only to countries in close proximity of their home base of operations. Exports are also particularly sensitive to fluctuations in exchange rates.[32]

exporting
manufacturing products in a firm's home country and shipping them to a foreign market

Licensing

Licensing arrangements allow a local firm in the new market to manufacture and distribute a firm's product. Usually, the licensing contract provides the specifications to maintain quality and the quantity to produce and sell along with the royalty percentages on the sales. In these cases, the licensor has low costs and takes little risk; the licensee takes the major risks. Yet, licensing is unlikely to produce major returns for the licensor unless the potential sales in the new market are large.

licensing
arrangements establishing how to allow a local firm in the new market to manufacture and distribute a firm's product

The Altria Group, owner of Philip Morris brand cigarettes, is losing sales in the United States due to declining cigarette use. Thus, it is searching for new markets for its products. Recently, it has signed a license agreement with two Chinese firms to manufacture and market cigarettes in China under the Marlboro brand. This arrangement might still be lucrative for the Altria Group because the market for cigarettes in China is large and growing.[33]

Although licensing has advantages, it also has disadvantages. The primary disadvantage is that the licensing firm has little control over its product and the use of its brand in the new market. This underscores how important it is for a firm's licensing contracts to be clear and enforceable. Unfortunately, contracts with Chinese firms often go unenforced. Remember, most of China's legal and regulatory institutions are relatively new. Thus, the Altria Group could experience problems if it doesn't like how China is using the Marlboro brand. Like exporting, licensing is also unlikely to produce big returns for a firm unless sales in the new market are large.

Creating Strategic Alliances

The most popular strategy for international expansion has become strategic alliances. **Strategic alliances** are cooperative arrangements between two firms in which they agree to share resources to accomplish a mutually desirable goal. Strategic alliances allow firms to share the costs and risks of entering new markets, and they provide the opportunity for firms to access resources they do not have. As such, it also allows them to sometimes learn new capabilities from their partners.[34] In this way, alliances can contribute to a firm's ability to maintain or increase its competitiveness in global markets.

strategic alliances
cooperative arrangements between two firms in which they agree to share resources to accomplish a mutually desirable goal

Moreover, strategic alliances allow firms to outsource functions they once did in-house to other companies abroad. A Manager's Challenge, "Outsourcing and Offshoring" explains the advantages and disadvantages of outsourcing. Although the strategy can give a firm access to better and cheaper service functions, it isn't always problem free.

Strategic alliances allow firms to outsource functions that they completed in-house previously. A Manager's Challenge explains the advantages and disadvantages of outsourcing. In general, outsourcing allows firms to gain access to better and often cheaper performance

A MANAGER'S CHALLENGE

Change

Outsourcing and Offshoring

It was late one evening and I was desperately trying to make a deadline for a class paper that was due the next morning. I still had research to complete, but while accessing articles on the Internet, my computer crashed. I tried everything possible to get my computer to properly run, but had no success. In desperation, I decided to call the computer tech support number that I had been given when I purchased my computer. When the tech support representative answered, I had a difficult time understanding him. After numerous attempts to understand his instructions, I realized that the language barrier was too much and asked to speak to a manager. With the help of the manager, I eventually was able to get my computer operating, but realized I had just experienced, firsthand, one of the criticisms of outsourcing services.

Even though many companies are using firms outside of the United States to perform functions such as IT support, research and design, accounting, and payroll, there are some who criticize the use of outsourcing. Cultural differences are one of the biggest reasons why critics say offshoring services fail. This is due to different communication styles and language barriers. Different approaches to completing tasks, along with different conflict resolution and decision-making styles are other explanations of how outsourcing services run into problems. Public concern over offshoring is beginning to increase according to a YouGov poll commissioned by Deloitte, the U.S. professional services firm. They found that more than 80 percent of 2,000 Americans surveyed wanted employers to call a halt to moving jobs to other countries. Another poll conducted in 2006 reported that compared to 2005, the percentage of people seeing the advantages of outsourcing fell from 29 percent to 13 percent. Others feel that outsourcing diminishes human interaction from our workplace and that by moving services overseas, we are taking away job opportunities from Americans. If this is true, what could firms gain from outsourcing?

Some proponents of outsourcing feel that moving jobs offshore means cutting labor costs, which, in turn, allows companies to sell their product(s) at a lower price. Outsourcing also converts fixed costs into variable costs, releasing capital that can be used elsewhere in the business. Consequently, investors often view outsourcing positively because a company can put more capital directly into revenue-producing activities. In addition, outsourcing allows companies to increase their efficiency by focusing human resources where they need them most. Companies have limited resources and outsourcing can help managers set their priorities more clearly.

One benefit for small businesses is that outsourcing can help give them access to the same economies of scale, efficiency, and expertise that large companies enjoy. Outsourcing providers also assume and manage a certain amount of risk for their companies. This can be beneficial because markets, competition, government regulations, and technology abroad often quickly change. Multinationals also are citing reasons for going offshore because of the ability to crunch product development times by working around the clock with tech centers around the world. Another opinion is that job loss, specifically in IT, is due to automation of tasks, not because of offshore outsourcing. It can be more costly to purchase the necessary tools and provide ongoing staff training than it is to turn certain services over to companies that are already experts in those fields.

Certainly the Internet has enabled a new marketplace for outsourcing, but companies should still weigh the advantages and disadvantages of outsourcing. An activity that directly touches the firm's customers is likely to be a core functional activity and, therefore, the company should handle it internally. But if the firm must make a large investment in technological systems or hire and train staff members whose skills the company cannot apply to its ongoing operations, outsourcing is likely to be beneficial.

Lastly, companies need to be sure that any outsourcing contracts include provisions for proprietary rights, security and confidentiality, legal compliance, fees and payment terms, and auditing. Intellectual property, in particular, is a major concern because different companies and cultures have different guidelines regarding its protection. As long as consumers continue to want more products and services for lower prices, outsourcing and competing with foreign workers will continue to be a business reality—regardless of whether or not the consumer sees the immediate benefits of offshore outsourcing.

Sources: A. Taylor, "Public Concern over Offshoring Rises," *Financial Times*, November 28, 2006, www.ft.com; E. Conant, "I Want My IT Guy," *Los Angeles Times*, May 20, 2006, www.latimes.com; A. McCue, "Culture Clashes Harm Offshoring," *Business Week*, July 17, 2006, www.businessweek.com; P. Engardio, "Outsourcing: Job Killer or Innovation Boost?" *Business Week*, November 8, 2006, www.businessweek.com; A. McCue, "IT Job Losses: Don't Blame Offshoring," *Business Week*, March 6, 2006, www.businessweek.com; "The Benefits of Outsourcings for Small Businesses," AllBusiness.com, February 17, 2006, www.businessweek.com; S. Ranger, ". . . And Most Deals Are Doomed from the Start," *Business Week*, April 13, 2006, www.businessweek.com; A. McCue, "Contracts Key in Outsourcing Success," *Business Week*, June 26, 2006, www.businessweek.com; G. Taillon, "Out of Options: Is Outsourcing The Answer?" Keep Media, November 1, 2004, www.keepmedia.com; L. Kletzer, "The Upside of Outsourcing," Keep Media, August 1, 2004, www.keepmedia.com; "Ask Before You Outsource," CNN Money, November 27, 2000, www.money.cnn com.

of functions. In this way, firms can compete better in international markets and even to enter and compete in some markets where they could not compete previously. The vignette also suggests one of the problems of outsourcing alliances. The differences in culture and language can lead to a less than satisfactory performance. For example, Dell experienced problems after it outsourced its customer support function to India. It received a substantial number of complaints and bad publicity that probably resulted in lost sales.

Not all strategic alliances are successful. A large number of them fail Yet equity-based alliances, such as joint ventures whereby companies share risks and rewards, tend to be more successful because the firm has more voice in and control of the activities completed by the alliance or venture. Trust also seems to be an important factor in the success of an alliance.[35] So is the way in which firms manage alliances. As such, many firms are establishing alliance management functions to increase the success because of the large number of strategic alliances firms are forming.[36]

A country's institutional environment affects the decision to enter its markets and the means chosen to enter. In addition to the particular institutions in place, the stability of the institutions is of interest to foreign firms. Uncertainty in the institutional environment can stunt economic growth, making markets less desirable.[37] At the very least, firms entering uncertain institutional environments need to do so in ways that lower their risk. Forming strategic alliances to share resources and risks is one way of doing so.[38] Uncertainty in the country's institutional environment also affects the type of alliance formed and the type of partner desired. For example, in uncertain environments, firms look for short-term partners. In more stable institutional environments, firms select alliance partners with whom they can work over the long term. In other words, they seek long-term returns from their alliance partnerships.[39]

Acquisitions

Acquisitions of local firms made by foreign firms to enter a new international market are referred to as **cross-border acquisitions**. The number of cross-border acquisitions has increased in recent years. Such acquisitions are more common among non-U.S. firms. For example, the number of cross-border acquisitions by European firms has grown dramatically in recent years. Even firms from emerging market countries have used this strategy as exemplified by the Chinese firm Lenova's acquisition of IBM's laptop computer business.

cross-border acquisitions acquisitions of local firms made by foreign firms to enter a new international market

In recent years, approximately 40 percent to 50 percent of acquisitions made worldwide are cross-border acquisitions.[40]Acquisitions of a local firm in order to enter a new foreign market have several advantages. For one, they provide a fast way to enter a market. Operations in the new market are immediate with the acquired firm's customers, facilities, and relationships (e.g., with suppliers, government units, etc.). It generally represents the largest new market entry of the different alternatives. Wal-Mart entered the United Kingdom and Germany using acquisitions of local firms in those countries.[41]

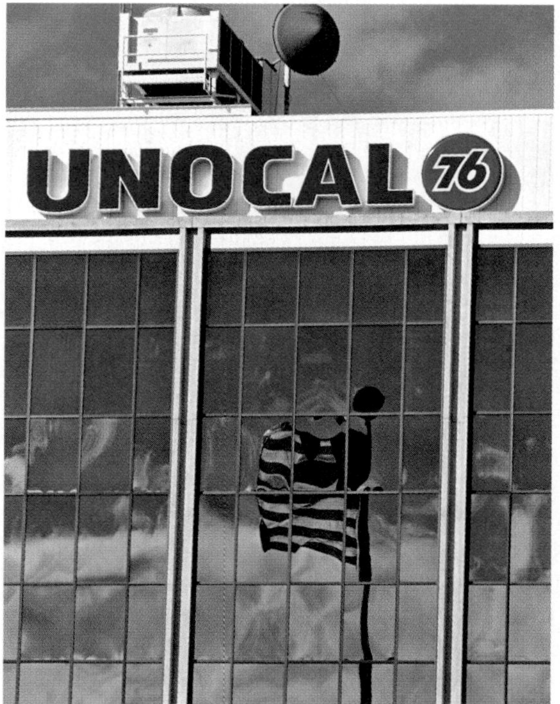

Globalization is fraught with difficulties. A Chinese firm found out as much when it tried to acquire Unocal, a large U.S.-based oil company. But U.S. citizens and Congress objected strenuously to the deal, effectively killing it.

Cross-border acquisitions are sometimes controversial with the local public or government. Such was true when CNOOC, the large Chinese petroleum company, attempted to acquire Unocal, a large U.S.-based oil company. CNOOC withdrew its bid because of objections from many in the U.S. Congress. Thus, there are disadvantages to cross-border acquisitions as well.

Cross-border acquisitions usually entail many of the potential advantages of acquisitions made within a firm's own home country. But if there are problems with a cross-border acquisition, they can be severe. For example, a common problem in acquisitions is the challenge of integrating two previously independent companies. Differences in the corporate cultures between the acquiring and acquired firms make integration difficult. Yet, cross-border acquisitions face a double-layered cultural integration problem.[42] Integration requires overcoming differences in corporate culture and national culture. Outside of selecting the right target, integration is the largest reason for the failure of acquisitions.[43]

Costs are another major disadvantage of cross-border acquisitions. It has become common for acquiring firms to pay a premium (more than market value) for target firms. Yet, premiums may be a larger problem in cross-border acquisitions because the acquiring firms frequently have less information on the target than in domestic acquisitions. And, research has shown that premiums are highest in host countries known for having a large amount of corruption.[44]

Therefore, if acquiring firms make the correct choice of target and do not overpay for the acquisition, it can be a positive opportunity to enter a new foreign market. Yet, the acquiring firm still must achieve integration, and that is likely to present a challenge.

Establishing New, Wholly Owned Subsidiaries

wholly owned subsidiaries
direct investments to establish a business in a foreign market in which the local firm owns and controls 100 percent of the business

Some firms prefer to establish a new, wholly owned subsidiary to enter a new international market. When a company creates a **wholly owned subsidiary** in a foreign country, it makes a direct investment to establish a business that it solely owns and controls there. Such a subsidiary is often called a "Greenfield venture."

Greenfield ventures afford the firm maximum control over the operations. Firms such as Starbucks—those with strong intangible resources including a good brand name, human capital, and so forth—may prefer Greenfield ventures to enter international markets because it allows them to buffer these assets from current and potential competitors in the new market.[45]

Greenfield ventures are often complex and expensive to launch. To maintain that control requires that the firm not only build its own facilities, it must establish relationships with suppliers, build distribution networks within the foreign country, and foster a positive relationship with potential consumers. Thus, they must attract customers from existing competitors or convince new customers to buy their product. Firms establishing Greenfield ventures must learn about the national culture and institutional environment—on their own. If the cultural distance or institutional distance between the home and host countries is high, a firm may experience difficulties establishing a new wholly owned subsidiary or making one that they establish to be successful. Therefore, the risks of establishing these subsidiaries can be quite high.[46]

With the development of the Chinese economy and the significant amount of cross-border trade between Western country firms and Chinese firms, UPS is establishing new wholly owned subsidiaries in Shanghai and FedEx is doing the same in Guangzhou. The firms entered the markets with Greenfield investments because they needed to ensure fast and reliable service and the desire to maintain control over their logistics operations.[47]

While wholly owned subsidiaries are valuable and allow firms to control their operations, they are risky and not always successful. EBay entered the China market with a partial acquisition of Eachnet.com in 2002 followed by a full buyout of the company in 2003, paying a total of $180 million for the company. In 2005, eBay invested over $100 million in marketing for its wholly owned Chinese subsidiary. Even with the acquisition, eBay was unable to manage the Chinese marketplace and fend off competition. Its primary competitor in China, Taobao, took market share from eBay's subsidiary. While Meg Whitman, CEO of eBay, has touted the Chinese market and eBay's Chinese subsidiary as a future growth engine for the company, in December 2006, eBay announced it was shutting down its main Web site in China and forming a joint venture with Tom Online, Inc., to operate in the Chinese market. Analysts said eBay lost market share because the company neither understood the Chinese market and culture nor quickly countered Taobao's challenge.[48] Now, eBay will use a Chinese partner to help it navigate the challenging Chinese market.

The decisions to enter foreign markets, what markets to enter, and how to enter them are very important. Yet, the management of international operations also affects their success. In the following sections, we explore the management of these international operations, first examining the corporate approach used. We then examine how to manage across cultures with emphasis on managing cross-cultural teams.

UPS China Express made its inaugural UPS flight to China in 2001. Some of operations UPS has established abroad, including its Chinese operation, have been accomplished via owned subsidiaries (which are sometimes called Greenfield investments). By owning their subsidiaries outright, firms like UPS have better control of their operations.

Managing International Operations

Companies must choose the manner in which they manage their international subsidiaries, and these choices carry important meaning for the management and flow of resources and information throughout the international operations in the company. Of critical importance is the degree of autonomy granted to the individual subsidiaries to develop and implement their own strategies. One of three different approaches—a global focus, region/country focus, or a transnational focus—reflects the focus of the home office.

Taking a Global Focus

globally focused organization
an organization that invests the primary authority for major strategic decisions in the home office

In a **globally focused organization**, the firm's home office makes major strategic decisions. Thus, the global organization has centralized authority, and the international subsidiaries usually follow the same or a similar strategy in each of their markets. These organizations normally attempt to market a relatively standardized product across geographic markets. Such an approach provides economies of scale and helps to manage the costs and thereby to enhance the profits. Thus, it helps firms to gain returns on innovative products developed in the home country market, especially firms that compete in markets where price is a critical competitive concern. In a globally focused organization, subsidiaries often share resources, allowing the most efficient allocation of resources throughout the company.

While a global focus has several advantages as noted previously, it also has some disadvantages. Because it does not allow the international subsidiary the flexibility to decide how to compete, it may be unable to take advantage of market opportunities when they occur. Furthermore an international subsidiary operating in a globally focused organization does not have the flexibility to react quickly to competitors' strategic moves. As such, they are vulnerable to competitors taking strategic actions with the intent of "stealing" market share in the local market. These international subsidiaries cannot respond easily to changes in customers' needs in the local market. Vodaphone used a global focus but then was unable to respond to local customers' needs in Japan and lost market share. Alternatively, Cemex, the third-largest cement company in the world, uses a global focus successfully. In this case, the type of product sold (e.g., ready mix cement) can largely be

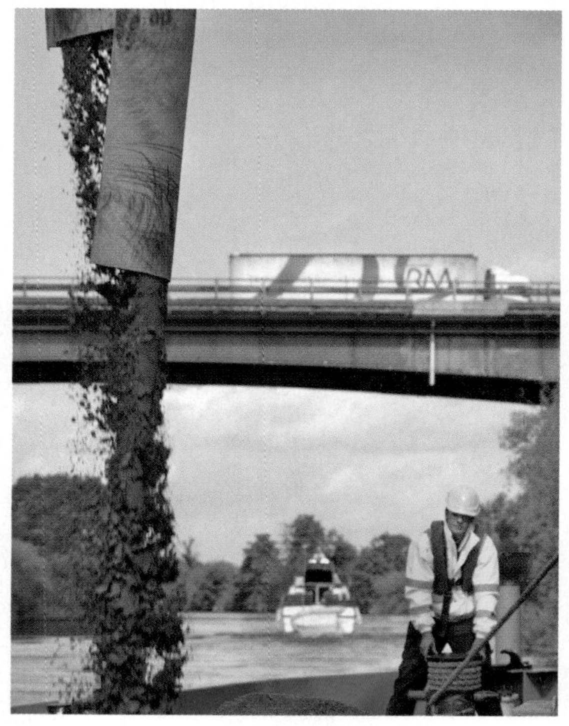

A worker helps load product at a Cemex dock in England. Cemex, a company headquartered in Mexico, has operations in Europe, North America, South America, and Asia. Because the company sells a largely standardized project—ready mix cement—it's been able to take a more centralized approach to globalization and achieve economies of scale as a result.

standardized. Cemex, headquartered in Mexico, has operations in North America, South America, Asia, and Europe. The centralized approach used by Cemex provides economies of scale and higher returns.[49]

Taking a Region–Country Focus

region–country focus
when the primary authority to determine competitive strategy rests with the management of the international subsidiary based in a region of the world or a specific country

In an organization using a **region–country focus**, the primary authority to determine competitive strategy rests with the managers of its international subsidiary based in a region of the world or a specific country. In this way, the region or country managers can tailor their strategies to local market conditions and demands. For example, subsidiaries can design, manufacture, and sell products that best satisfy local market customers. In this sense, subsidiaries can customize products for the local customers as opposed to the home office dictating product features. Thus, this type of organization is highly decentralized. The advantage of this approach is that it is flexible and allows a subsidiary to react quickly to changes in the marketplace. It can respond rapidly to competitors' strategic moves and can also respond quickly to take advantage of new market opportunities identified. It is most effective when the firm's subsidiaries operate in widely different markets indicated by countries with different cultures and different institutional environments. However, such an approach can be expensive for the company because it cannot achieve economies of scale. Furthermore, the diversity of strategies across markets may be difficult to oversee and govern from the home office. In particular, it may be difficult for home-office managers to evaluate the performance of subsidiary managers, especially if it requires assessing the value of the strategy chosen by that manager.

European multinational firms commonly use the region–country focused approach because they are operating in multiple countries with different institutional environments across Europe.[50] Unilever, a well-known European consumer products company, has traditionally used a decentralized approach to manage its international operations.[51]

Taking a Transnational Focus

transnational organization
an organization that strives to be simultaneously centralized and decentralized

Two well-known scholars and management consultants, Christopher Bartlett and Sumantra Ghoshal, developed the idea of a transnational organization. They suggest that a **transnational organization** is one that strives to be simultaneously centralized and decentralized. As such, its goal is to achieve global efficiency while maintaining local market responsiveness. In these organizations, strategic decisions are decentralized. Nonetheless, the organizations usually try to achieve global efficiency by having their subsidiaries share resources. Shared values, trusting relationships, and incentive systems that reward subsidiary managers for the firm's overall performance help facilitate this cooperation.

Effectively managed, this type of an organization often outperforms either of the other two types of organizations. Although it's easier to achieve either global efficiency or local responsiveness than it is to achieve both simultaneously, a company can do it. For example, Nissan CEO Carlos Ghosn used a transnational focus to turn around that automaker's performance. The different business units worked to achieve global efficiency while also maintaining responsiveness to regional markets. Thanks partly to the transnational focus, Nissan is now one of the top performers in the global automobile industry.[52]

While the overall focus, amount of authority delegated to subsidiary managers, and the degree of resource sharing across international subsidiaries are all important, managing diverse units across cultures and multicultural teams is critical to the firm's performance. Therefore, we examine these next.

Managing Across Cultures

In multinational firms with subsidiaries operating in multiple international markets, managers must often oversee, direct, and evaluate employees and other managers from different cultures and institutional environments. Managing people from a single country is a significant challenge; managing people operating in different cultures and institutional environments is often an extreme challenge—one that is very complex. It requires managers to understand cultural differences and how these differences affect employees' attitudes and behaviors.

cultural context
the degree to which a situation influences behavior or perception of the appropriateness of behaviors

high-context cultures
cultures where people pay close attention to the situation and its various elements

low-context cultures
cultures where contextual variables have much less impact on the determination of appropriate behaviors

Perhaps one of the most useful concepts for examining and understanding different countries' cultures is cultural context.[53] **Cultural context** is the degree to which a situation influences behavior or perception of the appropriateness of behaviors. In **high-context cultures**, people pay close attention to the situation and its various elements. Key contextual variables determine appropriate and inappropriate behavior. In **low-context cultures**, contextual variables have much less impact on the determination of appropriate behaviors. In other words, in low-context cultures, the situation may or may not affect what is considered appropriate behavior, but in high-context cultures, the context has a significant influence on this judgment.

For example, in Japan there are five different words for the pronoun *you*. The context determines what form of the pronoun *you* is appropriate for addressing different people. If you are talking to a customer holding a significantly higher title than yours, who works in a large company such as Matsushita, and is several years older, you would be expected to use the term *otaku* when addressing the customer. If you were talking to a subordinate several years younger, *kimi* is the appropriate pronoun. Table 3.3 provides a list of some low-context and high-context cultures.

With this in mind, consider some of the issues related to managing both people who come from low-context and high-context cultures. For example, imagine a team composed of one person each from the United States, Australia, Korea, and Japan. The team meets to discuss a global production problem and report to a senior executive from a client company. For the two people from low-context cultures (the United States and Australia), the phrase "say what you mean, and mean what you say" would not only be familiar to them but appropriate. Consequently, if the senior executive asked if the team could complete a specific task and the team had already discussed the impossibility of the task, the two team members from low-context cultures would most likely say "no." To say "yes" when you mean "no" would not be appropriate regardless of the fact that the senior executive from a client is in the room. These two people would likely view someone who said "yes" when he or she meant "no" with suspicion and at worst as untruthful.

But for the two team members from high-context cultures, the fact that the senior executive from a client is in the room asking the questions influences their perception of the appropriate response. For them, in this situation, saying "yes" when they meant "no" would be entirely appropriate. To say "no" without considering the context would be considered unsophisticated, self-centered, or simply immature.

Imagine then the manager's problem if the American replies that what the client is asking for is not possible while the Korean member of the team says it is. Not only will this confuse the client, but imagine the attributions that the American and Australian are likely to make about their Japanese and Korean team members, and, in turn, what the Korean and Japanese team members probably think of the other two. Without understanding the influence of culture context, the team trust and effectiveness could suffer.

TABLE 3.3 Low-Context and High-Context Cultures

Low-Context Cultures	High-Context Cultures
American	Vietnamese
Canadian	Chinese
German	Japanese
Swiss	Korean
Scandinavian	Arab
English	Greek

Source: Adapted from E. Hall, *Beyond Culture* (Garden City, NY: Doubleday, 1976); S. Rosen and O. Shenkar, "Clustering Countries on Attitudinal Dimensions: A Review and Synthesis," *Academy of Management Review* 10, no. 3 (1985): 449.

The key issue for managers leading multicultural teams is to recognize that neither high-context nor low-context cultures are correct or incorrect; rather, they are quite different. These differences influence the effectiveness of a manager's behaviors, including their communication, negotiation, decision making, and leadership skills. The previous case helps illustrate the concept and some of its implications. It points out that a lack of awareness of this fundamental dimension of cultural differences can lead to misinterpretations, mistaken attributions, mistrust, and ineffectiveness.

However, managing people working in different countries, cultures, and institutional environments is not the only complex managerial situation managers must confront in multinational enterprises. Even within countries, local workforces are becoming more culturally diverse. This is certainly true in the United States, which is considered a "melting pot" of many cultures. As globalization continues at a rapid pace, it is also becoming increasingly the case in many other countries. Many people of European descent, Asian ethnicities (e.g., Chinese, Korean, Japanese, Vietnamese), African ethnicity, Hispanic ethnicity, etc., coexist, living and working together in the same organizations and in similar jobs. Therefore, managers often have to manage multicultural teams within one organization in one location.

Managing Multicultural Teams

The first type of multicultural team is geographically dispersed across country borders. Although geographically dispersed, they often focus on regular business tasks such as developing new marketing programs and products. Yet, the team interacts somewhat differently than more traditional teams. Instead of face-to-face meetings, members frequently depend on technologically mediated communications, such as e-mail, Internet chat rooms, company intranets, teleconferencing, videoconferencing, and so forth.[54] Often the groups are called **virtual teams** because of their reliance on electronic communication.

virtual teams
teams that rely on electronically mediated communication

The forms of communication vary in their richness, leaving open the possibility that messages will be misperceived or misunderstood especially because the communications must cross cultures. When problems like this occur, it can disrupt the team's ability to complete its task(s). If misunderstandings occur early in the development team's formation, members may not trust, a characteristic important for the functioning of such teams. Trust is especially important for geographically dispersed multicultural teams because they often lack traditional direct supervision, must work more autonomously, and cannot coordinate with other team members as easily as more traditional teams.[55]

In these international teams, significant responsibility rests with the team manager to ensure effective function. Team managers need to build trust rapidly early in the development of these teams. Building trust rapidly is sometimes referred to as swift trust. **Swift trust** is the rapid development of trust in teams with positive and reciprocal communications about the team's task activities.[56] To build swift trust, the team manager must help members communicate with one another in a positive way, coordinate their efforts, and quickly eliminate any misunderstandings. To do this, the manager must have significant cultural knowledge and sensitivity in addition to effective managerial skills. The manager builds a unified vision and emphasizes collaborative outcomes with international teams for greatest success.[57]

swift trust
the rapid development of trust in teams with positive and reciprocal communications about the team's task activities

Developing a Global Mind-set

With the opening of world markets, firms from all over the world are formulating strategies to increase their presence in international markets. As such, these strategies and managers' abilities to manage diverse country operations and people from multiple cultures are critical to firm performance.[58] Because of this global evolution, the competitive terrain is changing in many international markets.[59] Competing in international markets, managing international operations, and managing multicultural teams requires managers to develop a global mind-set. A **global mind-set** is a set of cognitive attributes that allows an individual (e.g., manager) to influence individuals, groups, and organizations from diverse sociocultural

global mind-set
a set of cognitive attributes that allows an individual (e.g., manager) to influence individuals, groups, and organizations from diverse sociocultural and institutional environments

A MANAGER'S CHALLENGE
Globalization

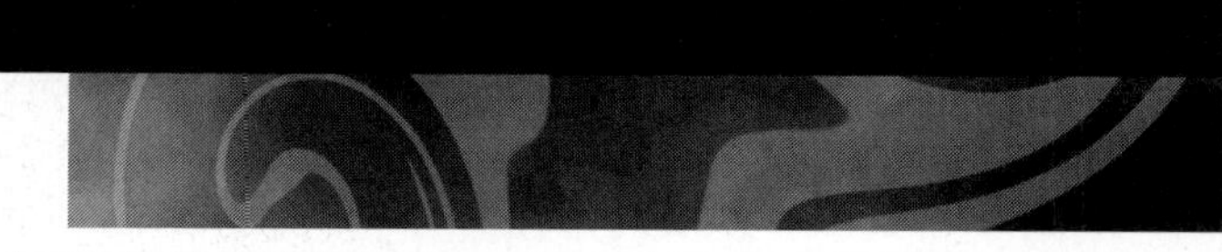

Cultural Integration or Cultural Disintegration?

How would you feel if you walked into a Buddhist temple and saw a middle-aged man dressed in a blue business suit burning incense in one hand while holding a cell phone in the other? How do people deal with the current multicultural world without losing their own cultural traditions and values? There's no doubt that globalization is changing not only economies but societies and their customs. Along with economic globalization comes cultural globalization. But how do people cope with and integrate these global changes into their culture?

Some people fear that because of globalization, societies are becoming homogenized. These people worry that we will one day have a worldwide "airport culture," that will homogenize the rich diversity of human civilizations. Critics of globalization feel that the process will lead to a bland uniformed identity. As a result, they feel threatened by cultural globalization and search for ways to resist foreign influences. For example, the Iranian government does not allow its citizens to own satellite dishes. France tried to protect the French language from being anglicized by inventing new French words for "fast food" and the "Internet" (*formue rapide* and *entre-reseau*). Similarly, the governments of some countries have aggressively sought to restrict the software and programming accessible to their citizens.

The control of media is a high priority for closed and highly controlled countries. Bangalore has gone through a tremendous transformation since 1991. Traditionally, Indian parents expected their children to live at home until marriage. Today, the situation has changed because young adults are offered new opportunities to earn a living, not available to their parents a generation ago. Young Bangaloreans are taking advantage of their newfound wealth and moving away from their families to live on their own. Bangalore women are also starting families later because of these increased opportunities, and there are more marriages based on choice rather than arranged by families. These cultural changes have resulted in a clash between the generations and a loss of some traditions.

There are others who feel that a global culture will help create a more peaceful society. While some are concerned that individual cultures will vanish, others have stated that there has been a surge of interest in local traditions. Thailand, a country once thought to be culturally homogeneous, has witnessed renewed interest in the history, language, literature, and culture of its local ethnic groups. Likewise, some Americans are beginning to recapture their traditional cultural values and consuming more ethnic products (foods and music). Some feel this is a reaction against mass consumerism. Further studies suggest that the return to one's ethnic roots has a soothing effect on Americans who have become lost in the superficiality of daily interactions. Other people feel that globalization and the revolution in communications technology will bring people together. After all, cultures have imported ideas and goods for thousands of years without losing their cultural identities. As a result of the increasing interconnection of cultures, old forms of diversity vanish, but they create cultural diversity. Globalization promotes integration and the fall of cultural barriers, which leads to a more peaceful society.

There are two definite opinions on the impact globalization is having on cultures. One is that cultural change can be a story of loss and destruction; the other is that cultural change can be a story of gain and creativity.

Sources: R. Frost, "As the World Flattens," *Business Week*, June 21, 2006, www.businessweek.com; D. Brooks, "All Cultures Are Not Equal," *New York Times*, August 10, 2005, www.nytimes.com; P. Loungani, "Globalization Without Tears," *Keep Media*, August 1, 2004, www.keepmedia.com; D. Rothkop, "In Praise of Cultural Imperialism? Effects of Globalization on Culture," *Global Policy Forum*, June 22, 1997, www.globalpolicy.org; P. L. Berger, "Four Faces of Global Culture," *Keep Media*, September 1, 1997, www.keepmedia.com; J. Breidenbach, "The Dynamics of Cultural Globalization. The Myths of Cultural Globalization," *Institute for International Cultural Studies*, 1999, www.inst.at; "Globalization Sparks Cultural Change in Bangalore," *Global Vision*, September 6, 2006, www.globalvision.org.

and institutional environments.[60] The composition of a team can influence such a mind-set. A. G. Lafley, the CEO of Procter & Gamble, reformulated his top management team so that at least 50 percent of its members came from outside the United States. Lafley's goal was to help his top managers adopt a global mind-set.[61]

While a global mind-set is important for operating multinational enterprises, some have expressed concerns about the globalization trend. As described in the box, globalization has created concerns on the part of some who believe that societies may lose their cultural identities over time. Others doubt this possibility and see the benefits of globalization. In addition to the economic benefits, it also facilitates the development of cultural sensitivity and understanding. There are countries that attempt to form barriers to globalization, refusing to participate in the economic globalization. Unfortunately, such actions will not stop the process. And, as the economic benefits accrue to other countries, the ones that create barriers are harmed the most because they lose out on economic development. Firms and managers that understand the value of unique cultures and institutions can adapt and use cultural differences to advantage. A global mind-set helps them do that.

Jagdish Sheth, a well-known scholar and consultant on international trends, argues that we can expect cultural integration over time—not cultural clashes. Sheth believes that Western cultures will not dominate the globe as some people fear. Rather, he believes Western societies such as the United States will adopt Asian cultural values because of the increase in economic power and influence of China and India and the greater acceptance and willingness by Westerners to assimilate diverse cultures. The United States and Canada, for example, are already multicultural with large minority populations, including ethnic Chinese and Indians. This cultural integration will lead to increased diversity within cultures and geographic regions.[62] As a result, the ability to manage multicultural workforces and serve multicultural consumer markets will continue to be more highly valued. These trends heighten why it's important for managers to develop a global mind-set.

Managerial Challenges from the Front Line

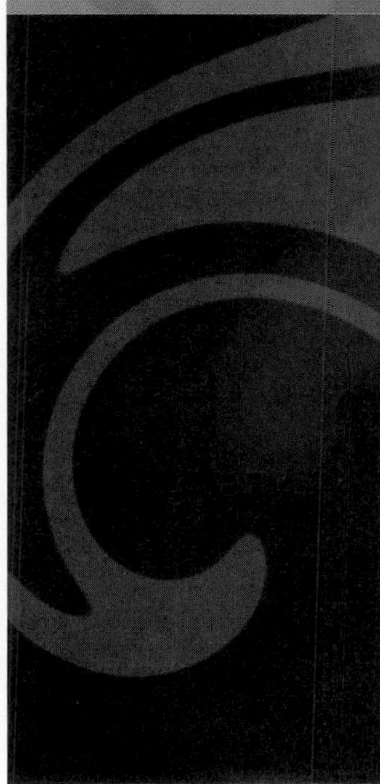

The Rest of the Story

As you learned, Celestica grew from one manufacturing site located in Toronto in 1994, to almost 40 manufacturing operations located in North America, Asia, Europe, and Latin America in 2007. During this time, Steve Radewych and his colleagues closed some higher-cost manufacturing plants in North America and Western Europe while simultaneously acquiring and building other plants in Asia and Eastern Europe where the costs are lower. But Celestica's goal wasn't just to cut costs but to better manage customer accounts and grow their business. Radewych was able to do this by creating global supply chain teams assigned to service particular accounts, like the one for the major computer networker, which grew from $40 million to $4 billion annually.

A supply chain manager, who managed all the relationships with Celestica's various manufacturing operations and suppliers, headed the global supply chain for the computer-networker account providing one person or team with which to interact for the service needed. "In a sense, we created an integrated global supply chain for our customers," says Radewych. To do this well, he and his colleagues had to put into practice many of the concepts explained in this chapter.

Summary

- Globalization refers to the flow of goods and services, capital, and knowledge across country borders. Globalization enhances the economic interdependence among countries and organizations across countries. In general, globalization has heightened the economic development and welfare of many countries but also created concerns about the homogenization of cultures.
- Two major elements of global environments are institutions and cultures. A nation's institutional environment consists of the country's rules, policies, and enforcement processes that influence individuals' and organizations' behaviors that operate there. By contrast, national culture is a learned set of assumptions, values, and beliefs that members of a group have accepted and that affect human behavior.
- Each country has a distinct institutional environment composed of economic development, political-legal, and physical infrastructure dimensions. Countries vary in their level of economic development. Country economies may be classified into developed, emerging, and developing economies. The political-legal dimension of the institutional environment includes the degree of regulation of economic actors, political behavior, laws and enforcement of them, and political risk. Institutional infrastructure is critical to the operation of businesses within a country because they facilitate business communications and the movement of goods from their source to the ultimate consumer. Physical infrastructure includes the amount and quality of roads and highways, number of telephone lines (per capita), number of airports, and so forth.
- Culture is a learned set of assumptions, values, and beliefs that members of a group have accepted and that affect human behavior. Some refer to culture as a collective programming of the mind with a profound effect on behavior. There are four prominent dimensions of national culture: power distance, uncertainty avoidance, individualism versus collectivism, and gender focus.
- Firms can enter new foreign markets via a variety of ways. Each has different risks and requires different levels and types of resources. Among the strategies are exports, licensing, strategic alliances, and acquiring or establishing subsidiaries abroad. Companies must choose how they manage their international subsidiaries, especially the degree of autonomy granted to the individual subsidiaries to develop and implement their own strategies.
- One of three different approaches reflects the focus of the home office: a global focus, a region–country focus, or a transnational focus. A globally focused organization has international subsidiaries that usually follow the same or a similar strategy, one which the firm develops centrally.
- In organizations with a region–country focus, authority is decentralized, and region or country managers can tailor their strategies to local market conditions and demands. A transnational organization is one that strives to be simultaneously centralized and decentralized in order to achieve both global efficiency and local market responsiveness.
- Managing people operating in different cultures and institutional environments is often a challenging task. It requires managers to understand the differences in these cultures and how those differences affect employees' attitudes and behaviors. For example, in geographically dispersed multicultural teams, rarely can managers schedule face-to-face meetings. They frequently depend on technologically mediated communications, such as e-mail, Internet chat rooms, company intranets, teleconferencing, videoconferencing, etc. Such teams are often called virtual teams because of their reliance on electronically mediated communication. In these international teams, significant responsibility rests with the team manager to ensure effective function. These managers need to build trust early in the formation of these teams.
- A global mind-set is a set of cognitive attributes that allows managers to influence individuals, groups, and organizations from diverse cultural and institutional environments. The globalization trend heightens the importance of managers building a global mind-set in order to effectively manage a multicultural workforce and serve multicultural consumer markets.

Key Terms

collectivism 65
cross-border acquisitions 69
cultural context 74
culture 64
exporting 67
gender focus 65
global mind-set 75
globalization 59
globally focused organization 72
high-context cultures 74
individualism 65
institutional environment 61
licensing 67
low-context cultures 74
power distance 65
region–country focus 73
strategic alliances 67
swift trust 75
transnational organization 73
uncertainty avoidance 65
virtual teams 75
wholly owned subsidiary 70

Review Questions

1. What is globalization, and how does it affect different countries?
2. What are the two major elements of the global environment, and why are they important?
3. What are the three major dimensions of an institutional environment and how do they differ?
4. What is culture and its four primary dimensions?
5. How are the five international strategies used to enter new foreign markets and when is each most useful?
6. What are the three types of international organization focus and how would you describe each?
7. Why do managers need to understand how to manage across cultures?
8. What are the primary factors with which managers must deal in managing multicultural teams?
9. What is a global mind-set and why is it important?

Assessing Your Capabilities

How Open Are You to International Work?

In our age of globalization, it is important for you to understand your feelings regarding international teams and assignments. Use the following exercise to assess your specific attitudes and behaviors associated with openness for international teamwork or an international assignment. Please carefully read each of the following statements and rate how it applies to you. Be honest!

	Never				Often
1. A year-long overseas assignment would be a fantastic opportunity for me and/or my family.	1	2	3	4	5
2. I have spent time overseas.	1	2	3	4	5
3. My friends' ethnic backgrounds are diverse.	1	2	3	4	5
4. Traveling the world is a priority in my life.	1	2	3	4	5
5. I visit art galleries and museums.	1	2	3	4	5
6. I was overseas before the age of 18.	1	2	3	4	5
7. My friends' religious affiliations are diverse.	1	2	3	4	5
8. I hope the company I work for will send me on an overseas assignment.	1	2	3	4	5
9. I attend the theater, concerts, ballet, etc.	1	2	3	4	5
10. Other cultures fascinate me.	1	2	3	4	5
11. I attend foreign films.	1	2	3	4	5
12. I am fluent in another language.	1	2	3	4	5
13. I travel within my own country.	1	2	3	4	5
14. I would host a foreign exchange student for one year.	1	2	3	4	5
15. I have moved or relocated substantial distances (i.e., state-to-state, overseas).	1	2	3	4	5
16. I eat at a variety of ethnic restaurants.	1	2	3	4	5
17. Foreign language skills should be taught in elementary school or earlier.	1	2	3	4	5
18. I attend ethnic festivals.	1	2	3	4	5
19. I have studied a foreign language.	1	2	3	4	5
20. I read magazines that address world events.	1	2	3	4	5
21. My friends' career goals, interests, and education are diverse.	1	2	3	4	5
22. If you took a vacation in Europe, locally owned hotel instead of a global chain.	1	2	3	4	5
23. My friends' first languages are diverse.	1	2	3	4	5
24. I watch the major networks' world news.	1	2	3	4	5

Scoring Key

Attitude

Add your total for questions 1, 4, 8, 10, 14, 17, 22. A score of 28 and above may be considered high, and a score of 14 or below may be considered low.

Past International Experiences

Add your total for questions 2, 6, 12, 15, 19. A score of 20 and above may be considered high, and a score of 10 and below may be considered low.

Comfort with Differences

Add your total for questions 3, 7, 21, 23. A score of 16 and above may be considered high, and a score of 8 and below may be considered low.

Participation in Cultural Activities

Add your total for questions 5, 9, 11, 13, 16, 18, 20, 24. A score of 32 and above may be considered high, and a score of 16 and below may be considered low.

If you scored high on two or more of the above and do not have any low scores, you may have a strong interest in and an aptitude for international work.

Source: P. M. Calguiri, R. R. Jacobs, and J. L. Fan, "The Attitudinal and Behavioral Openness Scale: Scale Development and Construct Validation," *International Journal of Intercultural Relations* 24 (2000): 27–46.

Team Exercise

1. Form teams of three to five people, and then examine the information presented in Tables 3.1 and 3.2 in this chapter.
2. As a team, develop written descriptions of the institutional environments and cultures of Brazil, China, France, and Japan. (Feel free to refer to the Internet or other sources to confirm the accuracy of your descriptions.)
3. Using these descriptions, develop a list of at least three important points regarding "ways of doing business" in each country that businesspeople from outside that country should understand.

Closing Case: Trying to Change the Corporate Culture of a Multinational Enterprise: General Semiconductor

When Ronald Ostertag took over the management of General Semiconductor, he realized quickly that he would have to change the $500 million company's culture for the firm to survive.

The first step Ostertag took toward changing General Semiconductor's corporate culture was to replace nearly every member of the company's senior management team. Job insecurity rapidly spread throughout the ranks. "I realized we needed to do something to develop a sense of teamwork," says Ostertag, suggesting that laying people off was not enough. "We needed to develop a culture of mutual respect that fostered cooperation and innovation."

However, changing General Semiconductor's culture was a significant challenge because the firm, an electronics parts manufacturer based in New York, had 60,000 workers around the world who spoke five different languages. Only 200 of those workers were employed in the United States. Its facilities outside the United States are in China, France, Germany, Ireland, and Taiwan.

After taking over as CEO, Ostertag decided to schedule a team-building meeting in which the new management team would decide on the company's guiding principles. "Our task," he says in retrospect, "was to put down on paper what our core values were and then make sure everyone was on the same page." A cohesive mission statement and a list of eight company values, which are called General Semiconductor's "culture points," came out of that meeting and were centered around goals like "quality," "integrity," "good customer service," and "on-time delivery."

Soon, everyone in the company knew the culture points and even carried them around on small cards. "They knew when they saw me coming, whether it was in the factory in Taiwan or Ireland or here, that I might come up to anyone and ask them to rattle off four or five of those values," says Ostertag. "I didn't mean it as a test, but more to show that that is what everyone here is striving for."

Unfortunately, Ostertag's changes did not occur quickly enough for General Semiconductor to fend off a hostile takeover. Believing that more improvements could be made and greater value extracted from General Semiconductor, Vishay Intertechnology purchased the company in 2001. Today, General Semiconductor is a subsidiary of the Pennsylvania-based firm.

Questions

1. In your opinion, what actions taken by Ostertag stood the most chance of changing General Semiconductor's culture?
2. Do you think requiring everyone in a multinational firm to carry around a card with the firm's core values on it can change a company's culture? Why or why not?
3. In your opinion, is Ostertag managing the cross-cultural operations effectively in the process of trying to change the firm's culture? Explain.
4. Did Ostertag appear to have a global mind-set? Why or why not?

Sources: S. Chin, "Vishay Finally Gets General Semi," *EBN*, August 6, 2001, 1c; C. L. Cole, "Optimas 2001—Global Outlook Eight Values Bring Unity to a Worldwide Company," *Workforce*, March 2001, 44–45; Vishay Intertechnology Web site, 2007, www.vishay.com.

Part Two

Planning and Organizing

4

Individual and Group Decision Making*

Learning Objectives

After studying this chapter, you should be able to:

- Explain the traditional model of decision making.
- Recognize and account for the limits of rationality in the decision process.
- Describe how risk and uncertainty affect decision making.
- List the conditions for when it is best to make decisions individually and when it is best to make them collectively.
- Name the steps to facilitate group participation in decision making.
- Describe the barriers to effective decision making and ways to overcome them.

*Portions of this chapter have been adopted from *Organizational Behavior*, Fifth Edition, by Richard M. Steers and J. Stewart Black with permission from the authors and the publisher.

Managerial Challenges from the Front Line

Name: Lurue Lord

Position: Co-owner, Lord Eye Center

Alma mater: Georgia Southern University

Outside work activities: Saltwater fishing, golf, and tennis

First job out of school: Paralegal with a Savannah, Georgia, law firm

Business book reading now: *How to Lead and Still Have a Life* and *The E Myth Revisited*

Hero: My parents because they were successful running their family business, and they taught me a strong work ethic and to act quickly.

Motto to live by: Enjoy life and enjoy your work.

What drives me: I am motivated by the challenge of success.

Management style: Total follow-through and mental toughness

Pet peeve: Dealing with low-energy people

In 1978, along with her husband, an optometrist, Lurue Lord established the Lord Eye Center in Statesboro, Georgia. Through the couple's hard work and dedication, the company grew and added offices statewide from Augusta in North Georgia to Brunswick in South Georgia. Today, Lord Eye Center is the largest privately owned optometric and optical business in the state.

Not unlike many small businesses, much of Lord Eye Center's early success was due to the fact that the Lords were heavily involved with its management. When they first established the business, Lurue had to make most of the decisions about almost every aspect of the company's operations—from how it tried to compete to who it bought supplies from. But as the business grew and spread geographically, Lurue faced an interesting challenge: Should she continue to make decisions in the same, hands-on way she always had? Or should she adopt a more employee-empowerment style of decision making?

Lurue faced this choice, in part, because as Lord Eye Center had grown there were simply more decisions Lurue had to make. Second, as the company prospered, the Lords were able to hire and train people who could potentially take on more decision-making responsibility. "I noticed our employees' ideas and ways of doing things were often very successful and that giving them more flexibility motivated them," explains Lurue. Third, making all the decisions herself took more time—time she wanted to spend enjoying some of the fruits of her labor.

Empowering your employees to make decisions is not without its risks, though. The optometric and optical business is a very competitive one.

Repeat business from existing customers is important, and "word of mouth" (positive or negative) can have a significant impact on a firm's ability to attract new customers. As a consequence, poor decisions today could affect the business far into the future.

So what should Lurue Lord do? Should she empower the firm's employees to make more decisions themselves, or stick with the tried-and-true approach that had driven the company to the point of success it enjoys today?

In the minds of many people, decision making is *the* most important managerial activity. **Decision making** is the process of specifying the nature of a particular problem or opportunity and selecting among the available alternatives to solve the problem or capitalize on the opportunity. In this sense, decision making has two aspects: the act and the process. The act of decision making involves choosing between alternatives. The process of decision making involves several steps that can be divided into two distinct categories. The first, **formulation**, involves identifying a problem or opportunity, acquiring information, and diagnosing the factors affecting the problem or opportunity. The **solution** phase involves generating alternatives, selecting the preferred solution, and implementing the decided course of action. Following the implementation of the solution, managers monitor the situation to determine the extent to which the decision was successful.

Like Lurue Lord, as a manager, you want to understand what factors affect the quality of decisions and what you can do to improve them. The models discussed next can help you better understand managerial decision making—both decisions made individually and those made in groups. Each is based on different assumptions about the nature of people at work.

decision making
a process of specifying the nature of a particular problem or opportunity and selecting among available alternatives to solve a problem or capture an opportunity

formulation
a process involving identifying a problem or opportunity, acquiring information, developing desired performance expectations, and diagnosing the causes and relationships among factors affecting the problem or opportunity

Individual Decision Making

It is no easy task to outline the details of the decision-making process. Research has been mixed about how individuals and groups make decisions.[1] Even so, at least three attempts to describe the decision-making process are worth noting. These three models are (1) the rational/classic model; (2) the administrative, or bounded rationality, model; and (3) the retrospective decision-making model. As you read about these models, pay special attention to the assumptions each makes about the nature of decision makers; also note the differences in focus.

solution
a process involving generating alternatives, selecting the preferred solution, and implementing the decided course of action

The Classical, or Rational, Model

The classical model, also known as the **rational model**, represents the earliest attempt to model decision-making processes.[2] This approach involves seven basic steps (see Exhibit 4.1).

rational model (classical model)
a seven-step model of decision making that represents the earliest attempt to model decision processes

Step 1 **Identifying Decision Situations** In the classic model, the decision maker begins by recognizing that a decision-making situation exists; that is, that problems or opportunities exist. A **problem** exists when a manager detects a gap between the firm's existing and desired performance. This is the situation we commonly associate with decision making and why decision making and problem solving often

problem
a gap between existing and desired performance

get talked about interchangeably. For example, you might discover that your subordinates just have more work than they can get done. As a consequence, you may decide to hire an additional worker.

opportunity
a chance to achieve a more desirable state than the current one

perception
a way one sees a situation based on experiences, personality, and current needs

An **opportunity** exists when a manager sees a way for the firm to achieve a more desirable state than the one it's currently in. For example, you might see an opportunity to capture greater market share because one of your key competitors is having some production problems relative to the installation and ramp up of new equipment. In response, you might decide to increase your firm's output to fill the gap left by your competitor's lower production levels.

THE ROLE OF PERCEPTION Managers often interpret situations differently. Some managers will see a situation as an opportunity; others will see it as a threat.[3] Your **perception**—the way you look at a situation—in large part is based on your own experiences, personality, and needs. As a result, when you first begin to examine a situation, it can be worthwhile to ask others what "their take" on it is.

The following "Manager's Challenge" illustrates how UPS tries to help its managers to make better decisions by broadening their perspective through giving them experiences that they normally would not have.

EXHIBIT 4.1

Classical Decision-Making Model

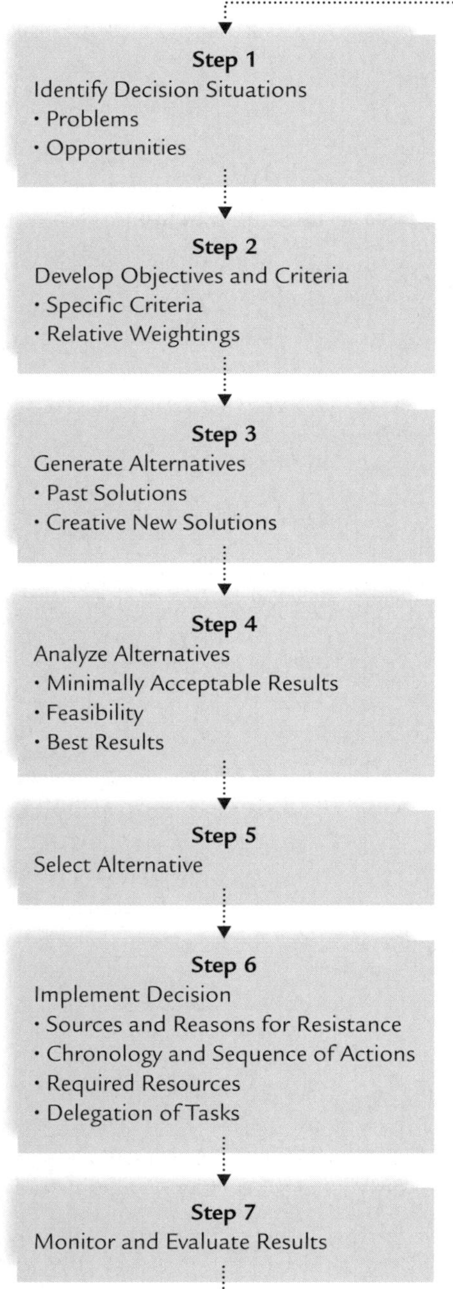

Step 2 Developing Objectives and Criteria Once you have identified a problem or an opportunity, the next step is to determine the criteria for selecting among the alternatives to deal with it. For example, before you can decide which job applicant to hire, you need to determine the outcome you're trying to achieve. If you need the new hire to be effective at sales, then good interpersonal skills might be a criterion. However, it is rare that a single criterion will be sufficient to guide the decision-making process, in part because one factor rarely produces all the desired results. For example, good interpersonal skills *alone* will not likely lead to great sales results; a person also needs to be motivated and understand the selling process.

When several criteria are involved, it is often necessary to "weight" the various criteria. For example, you might decide that a new hire's sales depend on four things: interpersonal skills, motivation, product knowledge, and understanding of the selling process. However, the impact of these factors might not be equal. As a manager, then, you might assign a weight to each criterion: for example, motivation, 30 percent; interpersonal skills, 25 percent; understanding of the selling process, 25 percent; and product knowledge, 20 percent.

Step 3 Generating Alternatives Once you've established your objectives and criteria, the next step is to generate alternatives that achieve the results you want. How exactly can you solve a particular problem or capture an opportunity? Most of us first consider alternatives we have successfully resorted to in the past. If the current situation is similar, past solutions can be effective. But if the situation isn't similar, we must generate new alternatives.

Even when a situation *is* similar, it's often worthwhile to pursue new, creative alternatives. Why? Because no two situations are exactly identical, and subtle differences may make a past solution less effective today. For example, suppose a sales manager needs to hire a new salesperson. In years past, a salesperson's product knowledge and industry experience seemed to be the keys to his or her success. The problem is that the products the firm currently sells have changed, as has the industry in which it operates. Increasingly customers are asking the firm's salespeople to develop "turnkey" solutions to their problems using new and different products. As a consequence, the sales manager might not only have to use different criteria for selecting salespeople but also generate different ways of finding them. For example, the manager might need to look for candidates previously employed in different but similar industries—people with different types of experience who can provide new and innovative solutions.

A MANAGER'S CHALLENGE

Diversity

Gaining a New Perspective on Decisions at UPS

Managing diverse perspectives in order to make better decisions is a tough balancing act for managers at United Parcel Service (UPS). On the one hand, UPS advertises that it runs the "tightest ship in the shipping business." The company has built a successful global delivery business by developing standard procedures for nearly all routine decisions, including how drivers should carry their keys when making deliveries. At the same time, UPS is increasingly a company of diverse and different employees. Half of all UPS's new employees are not white. As one senior manager noted, "We've got 330,000 U.S. employees. There are all kinds of personalities and all kinds of diversity. We need managers who can manage those individuals."

As a consequence, every year since 1968, approximately 50 senior managers participate in UPS's Community Internship Program (CIP): The managers leave their jobs and families for a full month to work at one of four CIP sites where they encounter a host of social and economic problems, including poverty. Whether they spend the month cleaning up dilapidated apartments or working with migrant workers, participants say the experience drives home new lessons about diversity. For example, during a month of working in New York, Tristan Christensen noted, "This internship has given me a better understanding of some of the hardships and challenges people face and why they make some of the choices they do. As a UPS manager, this understanding is the foundation for being able to connect to a diverse work group."

Patti Hobbs also did her internship in New York, working with teens who were addicted to drugs. She noted how impressed she was by the thoughtful suggestions these teens offered for keeping other teenagers off drugs. Back on the job, she broadened her use of group decision making to involve more staff members in problem-solving discussions, rather than only the highest-level managers. "You start to think there's no one person, regardless of position, who has all the answers," she explains. "The answers come from us all."

From her experience in San Francisco, Kim Campbell noted, "My experience at CIP was incredible. It has made me think about the people that directly and indirectly work for me and with me. Prior to this experience I was quick to judge. Now, I do not do that. I get to know the people and the situations they are in at home and work."

Since 1968, UPS has invested more than $15 million to send 1,300 of its middle managers to communities that suffer from poverty and other problems. Initiated by UPS founder James Casey, the program is designed to add diversity to the company's "brown" perspective.

Allen Sawbenbauer worked on a CIP in Tennessee and commented, "The experience gave me a better understanding of how I could have a better working relationship with my employees. Since returning, I have a better understanding of some of the challenges that my team—both management and nonmanagement—may face on a day-to-day basis. As a manager, CIP gave me the tools to work out problems with my employees, rather than making things more difficult for them."

Michael Lockard, a finance and accounting manager, helped inmates in a Chicago prison prepare for release by sharpening their interviewing and job-search skills. The experience shattered Lockard's preconceived notions about inmates and changed the way he approaches decisions at UPS. "I'm much more sensitive to the fact that we must make decisions on a case-by-case basis," he says. "Things are no longer black and white for me."

UPS has invested more than $15 million to send 1,300 of its middle managers through the program, at a cost of $10,000 per participant. Although executives cannot point to a financial return on this investment, feedback from participants indicates that they not only bring a new perspective to their work decisions, but they also come home inspired to volunteer in their own communities. "We will never really know how many lives we have touched," sums up a recent participant.

Sources: www.community.ups.com accessed January 9, 2007; B. Leak, "UPS Delivers an Eye-Opener," *Business Week,* October 10, 2005; K. Pelkey, "Resident Participates in Company's Community Internship Program," *Farmington Valley Post,* July 24, 2003; J. J. Salopek, "Just Like Me: UPS's Unique Intern Program Transforms the Perspectives of Leaders," *T&D,* October 2002, 52+; L. Lavelle, "For UPS Managers, a School of Hard Knocks," *Business Week,* July 22, 2002, 58–59.

Step 4 Analyzing Alternatives The fourth step in the process involves analyzing the alternatives generated. To begin, you need to determine which alternatives would produce minimally acceptable results. You can eliminate alternatives that are unlikely to at least achieve the minimally acceptable outcome. Next, you need to examine the feasibility of the remaining alternatives. Returning to our hiring example, you may have found three candidates for your sales position who would likely produce the minimally acceptable sales results. But one candidate's salary needs exceed your budget; therefore, that person is not feasible. Once you eliminate infeasible alternatives, the next step is to determine which of the remaining alternatives will produce the most satisfactory outcome. Typically, you apply the criteria and weights produced in Step 2 at this point. For example, of the two remaining candidates for the sales position, Jane and Martha, you might rate both people on each of the four criteria (see Exhibit 4.2).

Even though Jane scored lower than Martha on both sales and product knowledge, Jane is the better candidate. Her higher overall score is a function of scoring higher on the most important criteria (motivation and interpersonal skills).

subjectively expected utility (SEU) model
a model of decision making that asserts that managers choose the alternative that they subjectively believe maximizes the desired outcome

Step 5 Selecting Alternatives Selecting an alternative flows naturally out of your analysis. The classical model argues that managers will choose the alternative that maximizes the desired outcome. The **subjectively expected utility (SEU) model** exemplifies this idea. This model asserts that managers choose the

EXHIBIT 4.2

Applying Criteria in Analyzing Alternatives

Candidate	Criteria	Rating*	× Weight	= Score
Martha	Motivation	8	× .30	= 2.40
	Interpersonal	6	× .25	= 1.50
	Sales knowledge	7	× .25	= 1.75
	Product knowledge	6	× .20	= 1.20
			Total Score	= 6.85

Candidate	Criteria	Rating	× Weight	= Score
Jane	Motivation	9	× .30	= 2.70
	Interpersonal	8	× .25	= 2.00
	Sales knowledge	6	× .25	= 1.50
	Product knowledge	5	× .20	= 1.00
			Total Score	= 7.20

*1=Low; 10=high

alternative that they subjectively believe maximizes the desired outcome. The two key components of this model are the expected outcome produced by a given alternative and the probability that the alternative can be implemented. In our hiring example, Jane would seem to be the candidate who will produce the greater sales because she received the higher total score on the criteria believed to lead to sales success. The SEU model suggests that before you select Jane, you should assess the probability that if you offer Jane the job, she will come work for you. If Jane is the better candidate but won't work for you, then she really isn't the better candidate; Martha is.

Step 6 Implementing the Decision In the classical model of decision making, effective decision implementation has four components. First, you assess sources and reasons for potential resistance to the decision. For example, Joe, a district sales manager in your company, might resist the decision to hire Jane because Martha is his personal friend, and Joe told Martha he could help get her the sales job. Second, you determine the chronology and sequence of actions designed to overcome resistance to the decision and ensure the effective implementation of the decision. For example, you know that Joe believes that sales process and product knowledge are the most important things in hiring a new salesperson. You also know that Martha was rated higher on these criteria than Jane. Consequently, you might decide to first explain to Joe that in making your decision, you weighted motivation and interpersonal skills much higher than sales process or product knowledge and explain that company and independent studies support this weighting. Furthermore, you might assign Jane to a district sales manager other than Joe to ensure that she gets a good start with the company. You might also decide to place her in a month-long training program to better familiarize her with your products and send her to a one-week course on "The Selling Process" when it is next offered. Setting the chronology and sequence of actions leads naturally to the third step: an assessment of the resources required to implement the decision effectively. For example, you know it will cost you $4,500 for the sales training course for Jane. Moreover, you need to determine whether you could delegate implementation steps (such as scheduling Jane for "The Selling Process" course) to others and ensure these people understand and are held accountable for those steps and outcomes.

Step 7 Monitoring and Evaluating Results The final step in the classical model involves monitoring and evaluating the results of your decision. To do this, you must gather information and compare it to the objectives and standards you established. This is trickier than it seems. First, you must gather the *right* information, or you will distort the evaluation, or worse, make it meaningless. For example, in the case of hiring Jane, gathering information only on the number of sick days she has taken is unlikely to help you evaluate her early job performance. You might think it is silly that anyone would gather information on sick days taken when sales are what is important, but it is not uncommon for information that is easy to collect to obscure what is important. And often, the most important information is the hardest to gather. For example, gathering information on the number of sales calls Jane makes is much easier than gathering information on the attitude she presented to customers during those sales calls. Yet the latter may be more important than the former in terms of closing the sale. If you do not gather the appropriate information, you defeat the purpose of this last step. The key point here is that it is important to monitor and evaluate results in order to detect problems with the original decision and its implementation. This will allow you to take corrective actions promptly, if need be, before it's too late.

To many, the classical model makes considerable sense. However, it is important to understand the assumptions upon which it is built:

- The problem or opportunity is clear.
- The firm's objectives are clear.
- People agree on the criteria and weights used to make the decision.
- All alternatives are known.

- All consequences can be anticipated.
- Decision makers are rational:
  - They are not biased.
  - They process all relevant information.
  - They examine the immediate and future consequences of the decision.
  - They search for the alternatives that maximize the results they desire.

The potential weaknesses of the classical model are easily exposed if you just recall your own decision about what university to attend. How clear was the problem and your objectives? Did everyone (you, your parents, and your friends) agree on the criteria and weights for evaluating different schools? Did you know about and consider all universities you could possibly attend? Was your evaluation of the problems and opportunities related to attending each school completely unbiased, and did you review all relevant information? Did you look at the short-term and long-term consequences of your decision? Could you fully anticipate both the short-term and long-term consequences associated with attending each school? If you answered no to some of these questions, you're not alone. Research has shown that people are not as rational as the classical model assumes.[4] We can identify a series of factors that inhibit people's ability to accurately identify and analyze problems, as shown in Exhibit 4.3.

Thus, while the rational, or classical, model shows how decisions *should* be made, it falls somewhat short of describing how decisions are *actually* made.[5]

bounded rationality model (administrative model)
a model that assumes that people usually settle for acceptable rather than maximum options because the decisions they confront typically demand greater information-processing capabilities than they possess

The Bounded Rationality Model

Nobel Prize winner Herbert Simon developed an alternative decision-making model[6] called the **bounded rationality model**. It does not assume people are completely rational when they make decisions. Instead, it assumes that although people seek the best solutions, they usually settle for much less. Why? Because the decisions they face typically demand greater information and time to process than they possess. As a result, people seek a kind of "bounded" or "limited" rationality.

EXHIBIT 4.3

Factors That Hamper Accurate Problem Identification and Analysis

Factor	Description	Illustration
Information Bias	A reluctance to give or receive negative information	You are favoring Jane as the candidate and dismiss information about a performance problem she had at her last job.
Uncertainty Absorption	A tendency for information to lose its certainty as it is passed along	It is not clear how well Martha did in her previous job, but by the time the feedback gets to you, she is described as a poor performer.
Selective Perception	A tendency to ignore or avoid certain information, especially ambiguous information	Jane may have several employment alternatives and even be considering going back to school, but you ignore this and make her the offer.
Stereotyping	Deciding about an alternative on the basis of characteristics ascribed by others	Jane graduated from a private high school and went to a highly rated college on a partial scholarship so you figure she must be a great hire.
Cognitive Complexity	Limits on the amount of information people can process at one time	You initially have 200 applicants for the position but decide to eliminate anyone with less than three years' of sales experience.
Stress	Reduction of people's ability to cope with informational demands	Your company's market share is slipping because you don't have enough salespeople in the field, so you feel you just can't look at every bit of information on every candidate.

The concept of bounded rationality attempts to describe decision making in terms of three mechanisms. First, in the rational model, it is argued that people identify all possible solutions and then select the best alternative. Simon and other scholars have argued that this is not what people actually do. Instead, people examine possible solutions to a problem one at a time. If the first solution fails to work or they believe it is unworkable, they discard it and consider another solution. When they find an acceptable (though not necessarily the best) solution, people stop searching for new alternatives. Thus, if the first alternative is workable, the search-and-analysis effort is likely to stop.

Second, rather than using explicit criteria and weights to evaluate alternatives, the bounded rationality model argues that people use heuristics. A **heuristic** is a rule that limits the search to areas that have a high probability for yielding success. Thus, instead of looking everywhere for possible candidates for the new sales position, you might use a heuristic that says the best people for the job you have open are those already doing the job. Consequently, you might just try to hire someone away from your competitor. This could also help you make the decision more rapidly. This is why we often see companies recruiting yearly from the same universities—because in the past, graduates from those schools have performed well for the companies.

heuristic
a rule that guides the search for alternatives into areas that have a high probability for yielding success

The third mechanism is the concept of satisficing (not to be confused with *satisfying*). **Satisficing** involves choosing a minimally acceptable solution rather than searching exhaustively for the alternative that produces the best results. Whereas the rational model focuses on the decision maker as an optimizer, this model sees him or her as a satisficer. March and Simon explain:

satisficing
the tendency for decision makers to accept the first alternative that meets their minimally acceptable requirements rather than pushing them further for an alternative that produces the best results

> An alternative is optimal if (1) there exists a set of criteria that permits all alternatives to be compared and (2) the alternative in question is preferred, by these criteria, to all other alternatives. An alternative is satisfactory if (1) there exists a set of criteria that describes minimally satisfactory alternatives, and (2) the alternative in question meets or exceeds all these criteria. . . . Finding that optimal alternative is a radically different problem from finding a satisfactory alternative. . . . To optimize requires processing several orders of magnitude more complex than those required to satisfice.[7]

According to the bounded rationality model, the decision-making process is as follows:

1. Set the goal you want to pursue, or define the problem you want to solve.
2. Establish a minimum performance or criterion level. (When is a solution acceptable even if it is not perfect?).
3. Employ heuristics to narrow the solution to a *single* promising alternative.
4. If you cannot identify a feasible alternative, lower your aspiration level and search for a different solution (repeat steps 2 and 3).
5. After identifying a feasible alternative, evaluate it to determine its acceptability.
6. If the individual alternative is unacceptable, initiate a search for a different solution (repeat steps 3 to 5).
7. If the identified alternative is acceptable, implement the solution.
8. Following implementation, evaluate the ease with which the goal was (or was not) attained, and raise or lower the level of performance accordingly on future decisions.

This decision-making process is quite different from the rational model. We do not seek the best solution but instead look for a solution that is *acceptable*. Our search behavior is sequential—in other words, we evaluate one solution at a time. Finally, in contrast to the rational model, which prescribes how people *should* behave, the bounded rationality model is descriptive; that is, it describes how decision makers actually identify solutions to organizational problems.

The Retrospective Decision Model

A third model focuses on how decision makers attempt to rationalize their choices after they are made. It has been variously referred to as the **retrospective decision model**,[8] or *implicit favorite model*.[9]

retrospective decision model (implicit favorite model)
a decision-making model that focuses on how decision makers attempt to rationalize their choices after they are made

One of the most noted contributors to this perspective was MIT professor Peer Soelberg. Soelberg observed the jobs graduating business students chose and noticed that, in many cases, that students identified "implicit favorites" (the alternative they wanted) very early on. Nonetheless, the graduates continued to explore other alternatives and also selected a second-best alternative Soelberg labeled as the "confirmation candidate." For example, a student might identify a manufacturer in Arizona as her implicit favorite and select a high-tech firm in California as her confirmation candidate. Next, the student would attempt to demonstrate after the fact that her implicit favorite was superior.

perceptual distortion
highlighting the positive features of the implicit favorite over the alternative

Soelberg theorized that students were engaging in **perceptual distortion**—that is, they highlighted the positive features of their implicit favorites more so than they did the positive features of their confirmation candidates. For example, a student might heavily weight the fact that housing costs are cheaper in the locale of her implicit favorite—even though the overall cost of living there is no different than it is in the locale of her confirmation candidate. Ironically, Soelberg noted, the implicit favorite was typically superior to the confirmation candidate only in terms of one or two dimensions. Even so, the decision makers believed they were considering all factors and, therefore, making a rational decision.

intuitive decision making
the primarily subconscious process of identifying a decision and selecting a preferred alternative

Consider how many times you've made decisions this way while shopping for clothes, cars, stereo systems, and the like. You start with an item that catches your eye and then spend a considerable amount of time convincing yourself and the people around that it's the "best" choice. If your implicit favorite is the cheapest among the competition, you emphasize its price; if it is not, you emphasize its quality or styling. Ultimately, you end up buying the item you intuitively favored, feeling comfortable that you made the right choice. **Intuitive decision making** such as this isn't necessarily wrong.[10] Some research shows that not only are intuitive decisions often made more quickly but that their outcomes are as good or better.[11]

Types of Decisions

So which decision-making process do you think best describes your style? Are you a rational decision maker, a bounded rational decision maker, or a retrospective decision maker? Perhaps you are all three at different times depending on the type of decision.[12]

programmed decision
a standard response to a simple or routine problem

Most decisions can be divided into two basic types: programmed or nonprogrammed. A **programmed decision** is a standard response to a simple or routine problem. The nature of the problem is well defined and clearly understood by the decision maker, as are the possible solutions. For example, administrators making admission decisions often make programmed decisions. Also, at many universities admission criteria, such as grade point average and test scores, are well defined and a minimum threshold is set above which students are automatically admitted. Unions often make programmed decisions in terms of how companies treat their members—for example, using seniority to determine how the companies pay and promote union members. In all these decisions, specific criteria can be identified (grade-point averages and test scores for college admissions, and seniority levels for union promotions). High levels of certainty for both the problem formulation and the problem solution phases characterize the programmed decision-making process, and rules and procedures typically spell out exactly how people should respond.

nonprogrammed decision
a decision about a problem that is either poorly defined or novel

By contrast, **nonprogrammed decisions** are made in response to problems that are either complex or novel. For example, should a university president with limited funds expand the size of the business school to meet growing student demand, or should she expand the university's science facilities to bring in more federal research contracts? No alternative is clearly correct, and past decisions are of little help; instead, you must weigh the alternatives and their consequences carefully. In most organizations, the firm's hierarchy determines who makes programmed and nonprogrammed decisions. As Exhibit 4.4 shows, top managers usually face nonprogrammed decisions, and lower level managers typically encounter mostly programmed, or routine, decisions. Middle managers fall somewhere in between.

We need to make one final point about programmed versus nonprogrammed decisions. Programmed decisions are usually made through structured, bureaucratic techniques. For example, **standard operating procedures (SOP)** are often used for programmed decisions. SOPs specify exactly what should be done—the sequence of steps and exactly how each step should be performed. By contrast, managers must make nonprogrammed decisions using available information and their own judgment, often quickly.

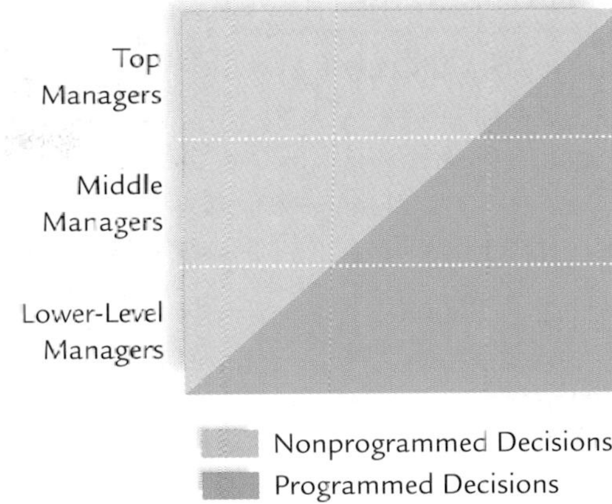

EXHIBIT 4.4

Decision-Maker Level and Type of Decision

Unfortunately, there appears to be a tendency for managers to let their programmed activities overshadow their nonprogrammed activities. Thus, if a manager has a series of decisions to make, he or she will tend to make those that are routine and repetitive before focusing on those that are unique and require considerable thought and have more ambiguity and uncertainty associated with their outcomes. This tendency is called **Gresham's law of planning**.[13] As a result, managers sometimes don't get to the more difficult and perhaps important decisions they must make. They either just run out of time or continue to occupy their time with programmed decisions.

The implications of Gresham's law are clear. As a manager, you must make decisions in a timely fashion. Check periodically to see whether you are spending your decision-making time wisely or if you are falling prey to Gresham's law. The matrix in Exhibit 4.5 can help you with this assessment.

standard operating procedure (SOP)
established procedure for action used for programmed decisions that specifies exactly what should be done

What Influences Effective Decision Making?

From a practical perspective, perhaps the most important question for managers is the following: "What influences *effective* decision making?" Exhibit 4.6 shows the general factors that influence a decision's quality.[14]

First are the characteristics of the decision maker. Earlier in the chapter, we discussed that we may not be as rational as we would like to believe. For example, we all have preferences and biases that we try to rationalize.[15] Moreover, we might lack familiarity with the problem or be too familiar with it and make a snap decision. There is also a limit to the amount of information we can process, which often leads us to satisfice.

Gresham's law of planning
the tendency for managers to let programmed activities overshadow nonprogrammed activities

Second is the nature of the problem or opportunity itself. The more ambiguous it is, the harder it is to be certain about the "right" decision.[16] Also, as we already discussed, people tend to put off making ambiguous decisions or make decisions without fully examining relevant information. The complexity of the problem can also affect the outcome. The more complex the problem is, the more challenging both the decision and its effective implementation are likely to be. The extent to which the problem is stable or volatile can also influence decision effectiveness. Clearly the more volatile the problem is, the greater the chance will be that the problem will change and the solution selected won't match the problem.

Third, the environment in which you make the decision will influence the decision. For example, time and resource constraints (people, money, equipment, and so forth) can influence a decision's effectiveness.[17] The more pressure you are under and the more constraints you have, the more likely it is that you will "miss" an important aspect of the decision.

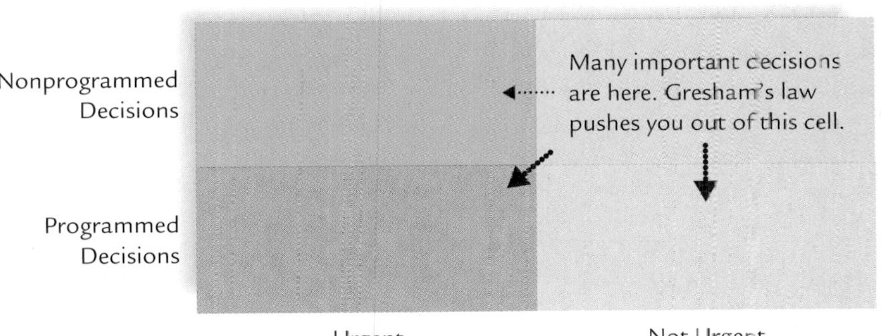

EXHIBIT 4.5

Gresham's Law of Planning

EXHIBIT 4.6

Influences on the Decision Process

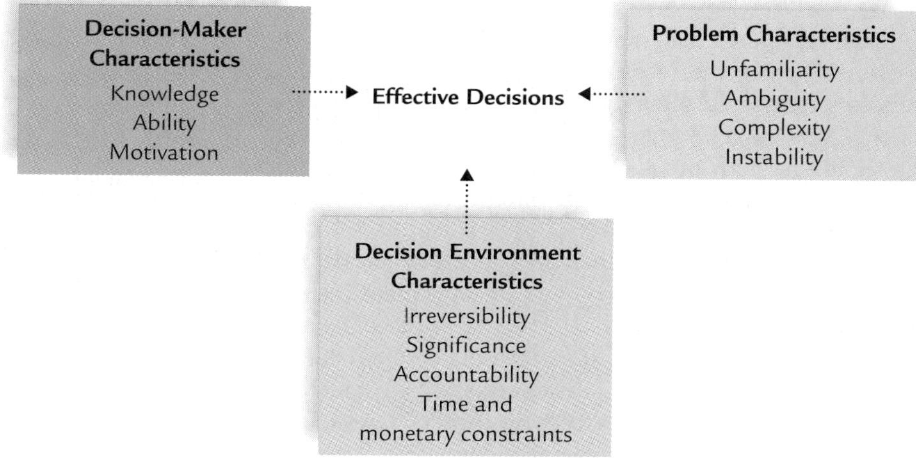

Finally, the importance of the decision can create its own pressures, which, in turn, can influence the effectiveness of the decision.

Group Decision Making

The three models described at the beginning of the chapter attempt to explain certain aspects of individual decision making. However, those models can also illuminate aspects of group decision making. Many of the basic processes remain the same. As with the classical (rational) model, both individuals and groups identify objectives. Both individuals and groups attempt to identify all possible outcomes before selecting one. Both individuals and groups satisfice and use heuristics when making decisions. Finally, both individuals and groups have implicit favorites and attempt to rationalize them.

What's different about group decision making is the social interaction, which complicates the dynamics. As shown in Exhibit 4.7, in some situations, group decision making can be an asset, but at other times it can be a liability. For example, groups are typically superior to individuals in that they bring greater cumulative knowledge to problems. But groups often arrive at decisions more slowly than individuals do.

- In *identifying alternatives,* individual efforts ensure that different and perhaps unique solutions are identified from various functional areas that the group can later consider.
- In *evaluating alternatives,* group judgment is often superior to individual judgment, because it involves a wider range of viewpoints.

EXHIBIT 4.7

Assets and Liabilities of Group Decision Making

Assets +	Liabilities −
• Groups can accumulate more knowledge and facts.	• Groups often work more slowly than individuals.
• Groups have a broader perspective and consider more alternatives.	• Group decisions involve considerable compromise that may lead to less than optimal decisions.
• Individuals who participate in group decisions are more satisfied with the decision and more likely to support it.	• Groups are often dominated by one individual or a small clique, thereby negating many of the virtues of group processes.
• Group decision processes serve an important communication function, as well as a useful political function.	• Overreliance on group decision making can inhibit management's ability to act quickly and decisively when necessary.

- In *choosing alternatives,* involving group members often leads to greater acceptance of the final outcome.
- In *implementing the choice,* individual responsibility is generally superior to group responsibility. Whether decisions are made individually or collectively, individuals perform better in carrying out the decision than groups do.

From the list in Exhibit 4.7, we cannot conclude that either individual or group decision making is superior in absolute. As a manager, you have to determine when it is best to make indvidual or group decisions. The "contingency model of participation" section later in the chapter will help you with this. First, though, let's look at a couple of common problems related to making group decisions.

Group Decision-Making Problems: Groupthink and the Escalation of Commitment

"Groupthink" can negatively affect a group's decision making. According to research done by psychologist Irving Janis, **groupthink** occurs when agreement among members becomes so dominant that it overrides a realistic appraisal of alternative courses of action.[18] The concept emerged from Janis's studies of high level policy decisions by government leaders. These included decisions by the U.S. government about Vietnam, the Bay of Pigs, and the Korean War. In analyzing the decision process leading up to each action, Janis found indications pointing to the development of group norms that improved morale at the expense of critical thinking. Exhibit 4.8 shows a model of how groupthink develops among groups.

groupthink
a mode of thinking in which pursuit of agreement among members becomes so dominant that it overrides a realistic appraisal of alternative courses of action

SYMPTOMS OF GROUPTHINK By studying both government and business leaders, Janis identified eight primary symptoms of groupthink. The first is the *illusion of invulnerability.* Group members often reassure themselves about obvious dangers, become overly optimistic, and are willing to take extraordinary risks. For instance, in the disastrous Bay of Pigs invasion in the 1960s, the United States operated on the false assumption that it could keep its invasion of Cuba a secret. Even after news of the plan had leaked out, government leaders remained convinced of their ability to keep it a secret.

Second, victims of groupthink tend to collectively *rationalize* and discount warning signs that should lead them to reconsider earlier decisions. Motorola fell prey to groupthink when it discounted Nokia's entry into the cell phone industry in the early 1990s. Collectively, Motorola executives convinced themselves that Nokia, a Finnish company that had traditionally made rubber boots and forest-industry products, didn't stand a chance. They also doubted that Europe would adopt a unified digital standard, which

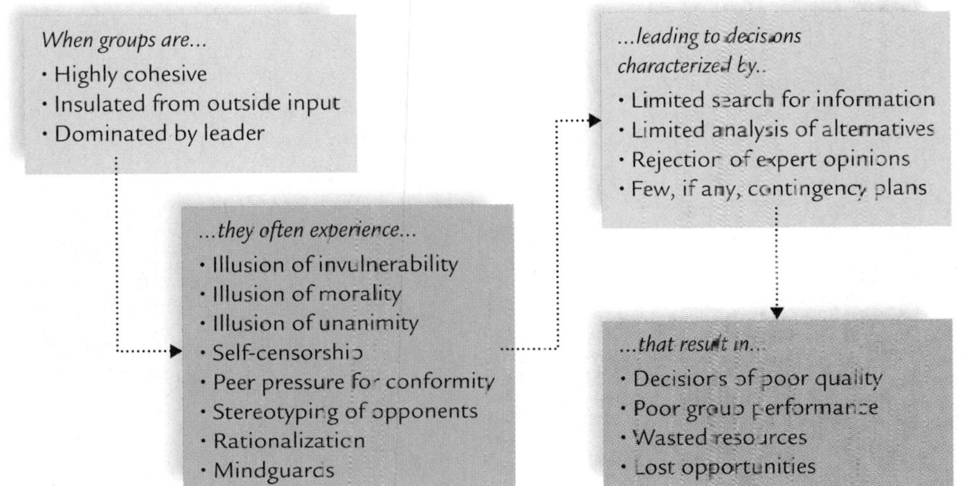
When groups are...
• Highly cohesive
• Insulated from outside input
• Dominated by leader
...they often experience...
• Illusion of invulnerability
• Illusion of morality
• Illusion of unanimity
• Self-censorship
• Peer pressure for conformity
• Stereotyping of opponents
• Rationalization
• Mindguards
...leading to decisions characterized by...
• Limited search for information
• Limited analysis of alternatives
• Rejection of expert opinions
• Few, if any, contingency plans
...that result in...
• Decisions of poor quality
• Poor group performance
• Wasted resources
• Lost opportunities

EXHIBIT 4.8

The Groupthink Process

Source: Adapted from Gregory Moorhead, "Groupthink: Hypothesis in Need of Testing," *Group and Organization Studies* 7, no. 4, December 1982, pp. 429–44. Copyright © 1982 by Sage Publications, Inc. Reprinted by permission of Sage Publications, Inc.

would allow Nokia to sell a large number of phones. And even if Europe did adopt the new standards, the size of the market there paled in comparison to the size of the U.S. mobile phone market. Over a 10-year period, Nokia captured market share, becoming the number one mobile phone company and the sixth most recognized brand in the world. Meanwhile, Motorola's global market share of mobile phones fell from 35 percent to half that.

You could argue that subsequently Nokia was subject to the same dynamics of rationalizing and discounting the warning signs relative to a new competitor that had affected Motorola. While Nokia was enjoying its overtaking of Motorola as the world's number one mobile phone company, it discounted the emergence of Samsung as a formidable competitor in part because it was not really in the mobile phone industry outside of Korea in any meaningful way until about 1999. However, from 1999 through 2007, Samsung went from not in the top ten manufacturers of mobile phones to number two in the world just ahead of Motorola in 2007. Much of Samsung's increase in global market share came from Nokia as its global share dropped from a peak of 40 percent to about 30 percent.

Third, groups that fall prey to groupthink often have an *illusion of morality.* That is, they ignore the obvious ethical or moral consequences of their decisions. For example, tobacco companies continue to run advertisements (especially in countries in which they are not legally restricted) about free choice about smoking, completely ignoring the medical evidence on the hazards involved.

Stereotyping the enemy is another symptom of groupthink. Members often stereotype leaders of opposition groups in harsh terms and refuse to listen to their opinions or negotiate with them. Groups suffering from groupthink also tend to engage in *self censorship*: They often minimize the seriousness of the doubts members raise and put tremendous pressure on them to agree to the group's consensus. Partly because of self-censorship, the *illusion of unanimity* forms. Members assume that individuals who remain silent agree with them. Finally, victims of groupthink often appoint themselves as *mindguards* to protect the leader and other members of the group from adverse information that could cause conflict over the correctness of a course of action. The mindguard may tell the dissident that he or she is being disruptive or nonsupportive or may simply isolate the dissident from other group members. For many years, FBI agents located in Washington, D.C., who expressed views contrary to the party line found themselves transferred to less desirable locations.

Organizational dynamics such as groupthink can lead companies to discount competitive threats. When the Finnish company Nokia—which had traditionally manufactured forest industry products, including rubber boots—entered the U.S. mobile phone market in the 1990s, competitors like Motorola didn't take it seriously.

CONSEQUENCES OF GROUPTHINK Groupthink can have several adverse consequences for the quality of decision making. First, groups plagued by groupthink often limit their search for possible solutions to one or two alternatives rather than all possible alternatives. Second, such groups frequently fail to reexamine their chosen action after new information or events suggest they need a change in course. Third, group members spend little time considering nonobvious advantages to alternative courses of action. Fourth, such groups often make little or no attempt to seek experts' advice either inside or outside their own organization. Fifth, members show interest in facts that support their preferred alternative and either ignore or disregard facts that fail to support it. Finally, groups often ignore possible roadblocks to their choice and, as a result, fail to develop contingency plans. This last consequence is similar to retrospective decision making—the decision is made and then data are selected that support the decision. Because peers reinforce the decision, unwillingness to reexamine and change directions is even more powerful than in individuals.

OVERCOMING GROUPTHINK Because a groupthink mentality poses such serious consequences for organizations, we must consider how to minimize its effects. Janis suggests several strategies. To begin, as a manager, you can reduce groupthink by encouraging each group member to evaluate proposals critically. Also, you can ensure members consider a range of alternatives by not initially stating their own positions outright but instead promoting open discussion. Other strategies for preventing groupthink involve getting more suggestions for viable solutions. This can be done by assigning the same problem to two independent groups. Or before the group reaches a decision, members can seek advice from other groups in the organization. Another technique is to invite experts outside the group to challenge members' views at group meetings.

Groupthink can also be prevented with strategies directed at the group members themselves. For example, for each group meeting, a member can be appointed to serve as a **devil's advocate**, a person whose role is to challenge the majority position.[19] Also, after reaching preliminary consensus, the group can schedule a second-chance meeting. This allows group members an opportunity to express doubts and rethink the issue.

devil's advocate
a group member whose role is to challenge the majority position

Groups can use the steps summarized in Exhibit 4.9 to minimize the likelihood of falling into groupthink.

EXHIBIT 4.9

Guidelines for Overcoming Groupthink

For the company
- Establish several independent groups to examine the same problem.
- Train managers in groupthink prevention techniques.

For the leader
- Assign everyone the role of critical evaluator.
- Use outside experts to challenge the group.
- Assign a devil's advocate role to one member of the group.
- Try to be impartial and refrain from stating your own views.

For group members
- Try to retain your objectivity and be a critical thinker.
- Discuss group deliberations with a trusted outsider and report back to the group.

For the deliberation process
- At times, break the group into subgroups to discuss the problem.
- Take time to study what other companies or groups have done in similar situations.
- Schedule second-chance meetings to provide an opportunity to rethink the issues before making a final decision.

Escalating Commitment to a Decision

escalating commitment
the tendency to exhibit greater levels of commitment to a decision as time passes and investments are made in the decision, even after significant evidence emerges indicating that the original decision was incorrect

Escalating commitment occurs when decision makers adhere to a course of action after they know it's a mistake. Have you ever continued to date someone even after it was clear you were not a good match? If so, perhaps you suffered from escalation of commitment. This same phenomenon occurs when managers "throw good money after bad."[20] For example, in the 1990s, banks around the world loaned billions of dollars to Asian countries. Even after it was clear in 1997 they would have great difficulty repaying their loans, the banks continued to loan the countries *more* money. Or consider the case of an individual who purchased a stock at $50 a share, but the price dropped to $20. Rather than sell, the investor bought more shares at the lower price. Soon the price declined further, and the individual was again faced with the decision to buy more, hold what he already had, or sell out entirely. The investor could not bring himself to sell and go back on the original decision. No doubt you can think of other situations in which people have stuck with decisions in spite of evidence that clearly indicate the original decision was wrong. The question is, why?[21]

At least three explanations are possible. First, we can point to individual limitations in information processing. People may be limited in both their desire and ability to handle all the information for complex decisions. As a result, errors in judgment may occur. For example, the company in which our stock investor purchased shares may have significant operations in countries in which negative changes in exchange rates are occurring or in which government regulations have changed. Our investor simply may not completely comprehend these issues and how they are hurting the company's performance and subsequent stock price. A second approach is to explain decision errors as a breakdown in rationality because of group dynamics. For example, our stock investor may have received the tip from a trusted friend or he could be the friend of the company's CEO and, therefore, have a strong emotional commitment. Although both explanations may help us understand the error, the work of Professor Barry Staw suggests that these explanations do not go far enough. "A salient feature . . . is that a series of decisions is associated with a course of action rather than an isolated choice."[22]

Staw suggested a model of escalating commitment (Exhibit 4.10). This abbreviated model shows that four basic elements determine commitment to an action. First, people are likely to remain committed to a course of action (even when it is clearly incorrect) because of a need to justify previous decisions to others. The social psychological literature on forced compliance supports this notion. In studies of forced compliance, when individuals are made to perform an unpleasant or dissatisfying act (e.g., eating grasshoppers) with no external rewards, after they comply, individuals generally bias their own attitudes to justify their previous behavior (e.g., eating grasshoppers is not a bad thing because they are high in protein). This biasing of attitudes is most likely to occur when the individuals feel personally responsible for the negative consequences and when the consequences are difficult to undo.

In addition, a norm for consistency influences commitment to a previous decision. That is, managers who are consistent in their actions are often considered better leaders than those who "flip-flop" from one course of action to another.

prospective rationality
a belief that future courses of action are rational and correct

Finally, two additional factors—the perceived probability and value of future outcomes—jointly influence what is called prospective rationality. **Prospective rationality** is simply a belief that future courses of action are rational and correct. When people think they can turn a situation around or that "prosperity is just around the corner," and when they highly prize the goal, they exhibit strong commitment to a continued course of action. They convince themselves that they can "pull victory out of the jaws of defeat."

OVERCOMING ESCALATION OF COMMITMENT Because escalation of commitment can lead to serious and negative consequences for organizations, we must consider how to minimize its effects.

1. First, as a manager, you should stress in your own mind and to others (superiors, peers, and subordinates) that investments made in the past are sunk costs—that is, you cannot recover them. All finance theory argues that managers should ignore sunk

costs in making future decisions, and they should consider only future costs and future anticipated benefits.
2. Second, you must create an atmosphere in which consistency does not dominate. This requires stressing the changing aspects of the competitive, social, cultural, and commercial environment surrounding a business and focusing on the importance of matching current decisions to current and expected fixture environments rather than to past decisions.
3. Third, you can encourage each member to evaluate the prospects of future outcomes and their expected positive value critically. You can invite experts from outside the group to challenge members' future expectations.
4. As with groupthink, a member can be appointed to serve as a devil's advocate to challenge the majority position.

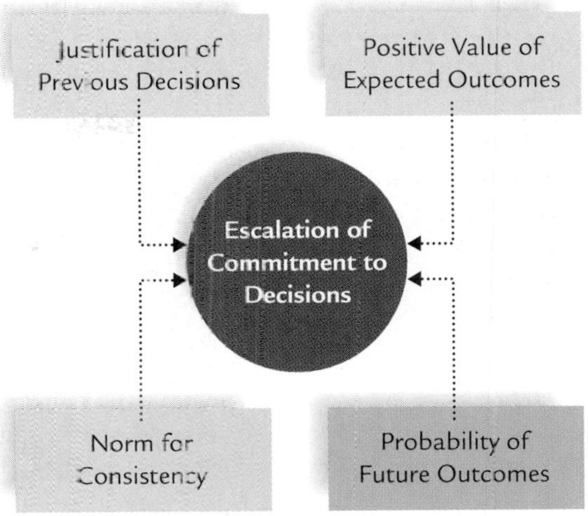

Justification of Previous Decisions

Positive Value of Expected Outcomes

Escalation of Commitment to Decisions

Norm for Consistency

Probability of Future Outcomes

EXHIBIT 4.10

Contributing Factors to Escalation of Commitment to Decisions

The Contingency Model of Participative Decision Making

Up to this point, we have noted that you cannot categorically state that individual decisions are better than group decisions or vice versa. However, most decisions aren't strictly made on an "individual" or "group" basis. The reality is that most managers face a continuum when it comes to involving others in decision making—from zero involvement (making an individual decision) to fully involving others (making a group decision). Research shows that the degree to which other people should be involved in a decision depends on the situation.[23] The key question, then, is how can you as a manager determine when to make a decision on your own and when to involve others?

Who Should Participate?

To determine some of the variables that make up good participative decisions, researchers have explored the question, "When participative decision making is effective, who should be involved?" First and foremost, research suggests that those participating in the decision-making process must have sufficient knowledge about the content of the decision. Companies such as Ford, FedEx, Procter & Gamble, and Boeing frequently put together **cross-functional teams** (teams consisting of members from different departments) to launch new products. Why? Because each member has unique knowledge that adds value to the decisions that need to be made to successfully launch these products.

cross-functional teams employees from different departments, such as finance, marketing, operations, and human resources, who work together in problem solving

However, in addition to having content knowledge, members also need to *want* to participate in group decision making. Not everyone does. However most people will want to participate if they believe (1) they have relevant content knowledge, (2) their participation will help bring about change, (3) the resulting change will produce outcomes they value or prefer, and (4) the organization values their participation, and it fits with the organization's goals and objectives. When General Motors first started encouraging more employee involvement in decision making, workers resisted the effort because they did not believe it was "for real." Historically, managers made decisions, and employees implemented them. As a consequence, GM's managers had to make a sustained effort to get workers to believe that they would take worker participation seriously.

Should the Involvements of Participants Be High or Low?

Like individual decision making, participative decision making involves related, yet separate, processes. Using the classical model of decision making, a participative group moves through the same seven steps, but the involvement of members can vary at each stage. Low involvement allows members to communicate their opinions about the problem and potential solutions but not make the final determination. High involvement allows members not only to communicate their opinions but to make final determinations. Thus, degree of involvement could range from high to low on each of the seven elements of the classical decision model.

EXHIBIT 4.11

Sample Configuration of Degree of Involvement and Decision Process

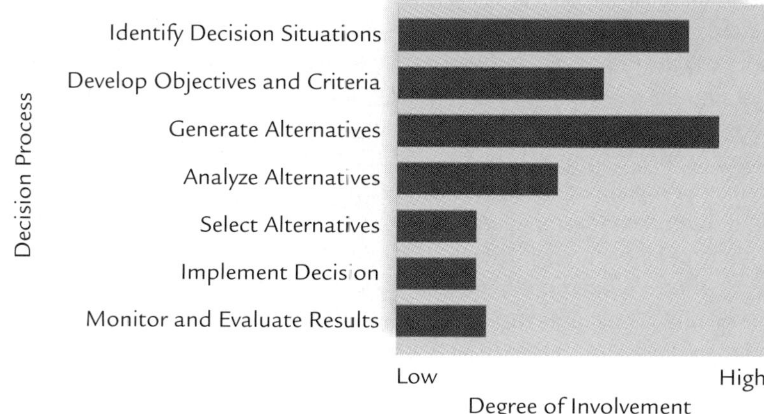

Exhibit 4.11 provides a sample in which a particular group has a high degree of involvement on the front end of classical decision making but low involvement on the back end.

So for which element of the decision-making process is high involvement more powerful? One study found that high involvement in three of the processes had strong impacts. Specifically, high involvement in generating alternatives, planning implementation, and evaluating results were significantly related to higher levels of satisfaction and work group performance.[24] The authors argued that involvement in generating alternatives was important because solutions almost always came from alternatives generated. They found that involvement in planning the implementation was important because the way a solution was implemented affected the outcome more than the solution itself. Finally, they noted that involvement in evaluating results was important because feedback is critical to beginning the decision cycle again.

One of the interesting findings from studies such as these is that members also need to understand group dynamics for participative decision making to be effective. For example, the ability of members to communicate and handle conflicts can be as important as their knowledge and the desire to participate. Being able to scan one's environment to identify problems is critical. After all, it is hard to begin participative decision making without members in your group who can recognize problems and opportunities. For generating alternatives, a critical capability is creativity. It is unlikely that a group can agree on a preferred solution without some conflict. As a consequence, managing disagreement effectively is a critical process skill. In this sense, much of the information in Chapter 11 on groups and teams and their effectiveness applies to effective group decisions.

Exhibit 4.12 provides a summary of the questions managers should ask themselves to determine whether participative decision making is likely to be effective.

On the basis of a long term research project, Victor Vroom and his colleagues Phillip Yetton and Arthur Jago also developed a theory of participation in decision making that has clear managerial implications.[25] It is possible to categorize this model as either a model of leadership or a model of decision making. The model considers how managers should behave in decision-making situations but also prescribes correct leader behavior regarding the degree of participation.

Although participative decision making is not always the best way to go, it does seem to work in many instances. Researchers have found four key reasons for this.[26] First, participation better clarifies for employees what they can expect relative to the issue being decided. Second, participation increases the likelihood that employees will work for rewards and outcomes they value. Third, it heightens the effects of social influence on behavior. That is, peers will monitor and exert pressure on one another to conform to expected performance levels. Finally, it enlarges the amount of control employees have over their work activities. This can help not only the organization achieve its goals but its employees achieve their goals, too, which should increase their job satisfaction.[27] That said, A Manager's Challenge, "Moving from Partners to Professional Managers" might surprise you. It illustrates one instance in which the move from *more* involvement in group decision making to *less* seems to have been effective.

1. Do potential group members have sufficient content knowledge?
2. Do potential members have sufficient process knowledge?
3. Do members have a desire to participate?
4. Do members believe that their participation will result in changes?
5. Do members positively value the expected outcomes?
6. Do members see participation as legitimate and congruent with other aspects of the organization?
7. If the answer to any of the above questions is no, is it possible to change the conditions?

EXHIBIT 4.12

Contingency Factors for Effective Participative Decision Making

Source: N. Margulies and J. Stewart Black, "Perspectives on the Implementation of Participative Approaches," *Human Resource Management 26*, no. 3 (1987), pp. 385–412.

A MANAGER'S CHALLENGE

Change

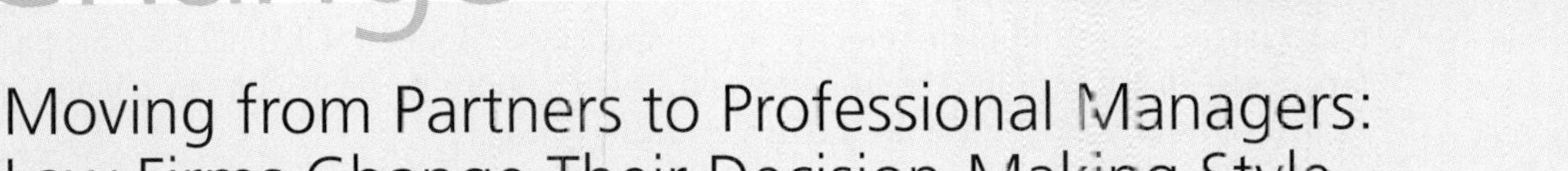

Moving from Partners to Professional Managers: Law Firms Change Their Decision-Making Style

Traditionally in most law firms, the firm's partners have jointly participated in all decision making. But what happens when a law firm grows dramatically both in terms of the numbers of lawyers it employs and also in terms of its office locations around the world? In this situation, you will have dozens and dozens of partners, and as a consequence, participative decision making can lead to bottlenecks.

With 2,700 lawyers working in 49 offices across 18 countries, DLA Piper is such a firm. As DLA Piper grew, it realized it needed a more centralized method of decision making. Instead of bringing all the firm's partners together to vote on initiatives and then manage their implementation, the chairman of DLA Piper now relies on professional managers who specialize in particular areas of expertise, including marketing, information technology, human resources, and finance—areas the partners aren't overly familiar with. "We realized that because of our size, we had to adopt a corporate model," states the joint CEO, Lee I. Miller. "It streamlines our decision making. We are able to react quickly, decisively."

Sometimes, however, partners accustomed to participative decision making have a hard time delegating decisions to professional managers. "At times it's a bitter pill," says a partner at the law firm Stellato & Schwartz. "When you ascend to the position of partner, it's based upon your ability to show loyalty, longevity, and business acumen. Inherent in those qualities is a desire to lead. But sometimes that desire has to be set aside for the good of the team." For their part, the managers who make decisions on behalf of law firms must constantly and carefully evaluate how the outcome of each major decision is likely to affect the firm and its partners.

Consider the situation at Wildman Harrold Allen & Dixon, an Illinois law firm where John Holthaus is executive director. Holthaus has no law degree but rather is an accountant who holds an MBA degree. His experience and education provide the technical and managerial background to make the myriad day-to-day decisions that keep the law firm operating smoothly. "I view my job as that of a hospital administrator who takes care of all the details so the doctors can take care of their patients," he explains. "I'm trying to make it easier for the attorneys to focus on serving their clients." Knowing that Holthaus understands the law firm's objectives and takes care of the business details, the partners have come to rely on him rather than getting bogged down in endless group meetings to make decisions themselves.

Source: Adapted from A. Palmer, "DLA Piper Makes Measured Progress Since Merger," *Legal Times*, June 2, 2006; J. T. Slania, "More Firms Mind Their Business: Corporate Model Helps Streamline Decision-Making," *Crain's Chicago Business*, January 28, 2002, SR10.

Decision Speed and Quality

Have you ever heard of Gavilan Computer? If you own a laptop computer, by all rights you should have, but odds are you haven't. In the early 1980s, Gavilan Computer had a virtual monopoly on the developing and soon-to-be-lucrative laptop market. But by 1984, the company had filed for bankruptcy. Despite a $31 million investment by venture capitalists, indecisiveness and long delays cost the company its early technological and market advantage. Competitors entered the market, and Gavilan failed to exploit its advantage. As one executive observed, "We missed the window."[28]

What happened to Gavilan happens frequently today—especially to companies in high-technology industries. In a series of studies of decision making in industries characterized by frequent change and turbulence—so called high-velocity environments—researchers Kathleen Eisenhardt and L. J. Bourgeois attempted to determine what separates successful decision makers and managers from unsuccessful ones.[29] In high-velocity industries (microelectronics, medical technology, genetic engineering, and so forth), high-quality, rapid decision making by executives and their companies is closely related to good corporate performance. In these industries, mistakes are costly; information is often ambiguous, obsolete, or simply incorrect; and recovering from missed opportunities is extremely difficult. What must decision makers in industries such as these do for their firms to prosper and survive?

Eisenhardt and Bourgeois found that five factors influenced a manager's ability to make fast decisions in high-velocity environments (see Exhibit 4.13). Three "mediating processes" that determine the manager and group's ability to deal with the quantity and quality of information moderate the five characteristics:

1. ***Accelerated cognitive processing.*** The decision maker must be able to process and analyze great amounts of information quickly and efficiently. Some people and groups can simply process information faster and better than others. The faster a manager can process information presented to him or her, the quicker the manager can make a decision.
2. ***Smooth group processes.*** To be effective, the manager must work with a group that has smooth, harmonious relations. This is not to say that everyone always agrees. Quite the contrary—members of effective groups often disagree. However, it is the way they disagree and resolve their disagreements that counts. Group members who share a common vision and who are mutually supportive and cohesive aid fast decisions.

In the early 1980s, Gavilan Computer was at the forefront of battery-operated laptop technology, having introduced the Gavilan SC laptop, shown in the photo. But by 1984, the company had filed for bankruptcy.

EXHIBIT 4.13

Factors of Fast Decision Making

1. *Real-time information.* Fast decision makers must have access to and be able to process real-time information—that is, information that describes what is happening right now, not yesterday.
2. *Multiple simultaneous alternatives.* Decision makers examine several possible alternative courses of action simultaneously, not sequentially (e.g., "Let's look at alternatives X, Y, and Z altogether and see how each looks."). This adds complexity and richness to the analysis and reduces the time involved in information processing.
3. *Two-tiered advice process.* Fast decision makers make use of a two-tiered advisory system, whereby all team members are allowed input but greater weight is given to the more experienced coworkers.
4. *Consensus with qualification.* Fast decision makers attempt to gain widespread consensus on the decision as it is being made, not after it is made.
5. *Decision integration.* Fast decision makers integrate tactical planning and issues of implementation within the decision process itself (e.g., "If we are going to do X, how might we do it?")

3. ***Confidence to act.*** Finally, fast decision-making groups must not be afraid to act. As we noted, some people are reluctant to make decisions in the face of uncertainty and fall victim to "analysis paralysis." Unfortunately, in high-velocity environments, uncertainty is constant. Fast decision makers must be willing to make choices even in the face of uncertainty.

Remember that this research focuses on high-velocity environments, not all organizational environments. In businesses characterized by relative stability (the funeral home industry, for example), rapid decisions might prove disastrous. Because stability allows time for more complete data collection and processing, managers in stable environments have less of a need to act quickly. Thus, as a manager of a team, you need to assess the time factors that characterize your industry. This will allow you to make better decisions.

Strategies for Improving Decision Making

As a manager, how can you improve the decision-making process in your organization?[30] At the beginning of the chapter, we mentioned that decisions can be divided into two phases: problem formulation and problem solution. Strategies to improve decision making can also be divided into the same two categories.

Improving Problem Formulation

Framing a problem involves deliberately and carefully examining the problem's nature in order to better solve it. The trouble is that groups often fail to look beyond what's familiar to them and "misdefine" problems. The following steps can help groups and managers improve their problem formulation.

One of the first steps to better decision making is better decision situation assessment. Exhibit 4.14 provides a simple set of questions related to the three categories of factors diagramed in Exhibit 4.6. You can ask yourself these questions in order to have a clearer picture of the situation and the potential pitfalls. In a **structured debate**, participants make use of techniques like a devil's advocate, multiple advocacy, and dialectical inquiry to better frame a problem. We discuss these techniques next.

structured debate a process to improve problem formulation that includes the processes of devil's advocate, multiple advocacy, and dialectical inquiry

DEVIL'S ADVOCATE As we explained earlier, a devil's advocate is a group member whose role is to disagree with the group. For example, if you asked a group of American

EXHIBIT 4.14

Questions Related to the Factors That Influence Decision Quality

Decision-Maker Characteristics

1. Do you have an implicit favorite solution?
2. Do you have a tendency to satisfice and go with the first workable solution?
3. Do you feel overwhelmed by the amount of information you have to process?
4. Do you feel a lack of knowledge about the problem?
5. Are you particularly unfamiliar or familiar with the problem?

Problem Characteristics

1. Does the problem seem quite ambiguous?
2. Is the problem substantially complex?
3. Does the problem seem stable or volatile?

Decision Environment Characteristics

1. Are you under significant time pressures to make the decision?
2. Do you face substantial resource limitations (people, money, equipment, etc.) relative to the problem and its solution?
3. Is the decision irreversible?
4. Are the problem and your decision of substantial importance?

automobile company executives why their sales are down, they might blame Japanese imports. In this case, a devil's advocate would argue that the problem lies not with the Japanese but with the Americans themselves and their poor product quality. This type of debate forces the group to justify its position and, as a consequence, develop a more precise and accurate picture of the problem and its underlying causes.

multiple advocacy
a process to improve decision making by assigning several group members to represent the opinions of various constituencies that might have an interest in the decision

MULTIPLE ADVOCACY **Multiple advocacy** is like the devil's advocate approach except that more than one opposing view is presented. Each group involved in making a decision is assigned the responsibility of representing the opinions of its constituents. Thus, if a university wants to enhance the campus's racial and cultural diversity, it might establish a commission including African Americans, Hispanics, Asians, women's groups, and so forth. The resulting dialogue should lead to the identification of a useful agenda for discussion.

dialectical inquiry
a process to improve decision making by assigning a group member (or members) the role of questioning the underlying assumptions associated with the formulation of the problem

DIALECTICAL INQUIRY **Dialectical inquiry** occurs when a group or individual is assigned the role of questioning the underlying assumptions of problem formulation. The group begins by identifying the prevailing view of the problem and its associated assumptions. Next, an individual is asked to develop an alternative problem that is credible but has different assumptions. By doing so, the accuracy of the original assumptions is reexamined. As a result, it forces group members to "think outside the box" and look at new ways to analyze the problem. Conducting a dialectical inquiry can be a particularly good way to overcome groupthink and escalation-of-commitment pitfalls.

Improving the Problem-Solution Process

To improve the problem-solution process, group members must be as thorough and creative as possible. Stimulating creativity expands the search for and analysis of possible alternatives. You can use the three techniques discussed next to do this.

brainstorming
a process of generating many creative solutions without evaluating their merit

BRAINSTORMING **Brainstorming** is a process of generating many creative solutions but not immediately evaluating their merit. It is a frequently used mechanism to provide a maximum number of ideas in a short period of time. During a brainstorming session, a group is given a problem and told to propose any ideas that come to mind to solve the problem. Once everyone's ideas are on the table, the group considers the positive and negative aspects of each proposal. Through a process of continual refinement, the best possible solution under the circumstances should emerge.

NOMINAL GROUP TECHNIQUE The **nominal group technique**, typically referred to as NGT, consists of four group decision-making phases.[31] First, individual members meet as a group, but they begin by sitting silently and independently generating ideas to solve a problem. Then, a round-robin procedure in which each group member presents his or her idea to the group follows. No discussion is initially allowed. The ideas are summarized and recorded (perhaps on a blackboard). After everyone has presented their ideas, the group discusses each idea. Finally, members conclude the meeting by silently and independently ranking the various ideas or solutions to the problem. The pooled outcome of the members' votes on the issue determines the final decision.

nominal group technique
a process of having group members record their proposed solutions, summarize all proposed solutions, and independently rank solutions until a clearly favored solution emerges

The NGT allows the group to meet formally, but it does not allow members as much free discussion; hence, the term *nominal* group technique. A chief advantage of the NGT is that everyone independently considers the problem without other members of the group influencing them. This technique, too, can be a particularly good way to overcome groupthink.

DELPHI TECHNIQUE The **delphi technique** never allows decision-making participants to meet face-to-face. Instead, a problem is identified, and members are asked through a series of carefully designed questionnaires to provide potential solutions. These questionnaires are completed independently. The results of the first questionnaire are then circulated to all the group's members (who are still physically separated). After reviewing the feedback, members are again asked their opinions. This process may continue through several iterations until group members' opinions begin to show consensus.

delphi technique
a decision-making technique that never allows decision participants to meet face-to-face but identifies a problem and offers solutions using a questionnaire

The Role of Technology

Much has been made in recent years about how technology affects individual and group decision making.[32] For routine but complex decisions, such as scheduling the flow of materials and products through a factory, technology can be a godsend. Computers and software can rapidly process amounts of information that would overwhelm a human being. For example, JetBlue became a successful and profitable start-up while other airlines lost billions of dollars. Part of JetBlue's success was due to its use of new technology.[33] By putting laptops and software in the hands of its pilots, the company didn't need scores of employees to make decisions about flight paths, schedules, fuel intake, and so on.[34] A Manager's Challenge, "Streamlining Decision Making at JetBlue" looks at how JetBlue accomplished this.

A MANAGER'S CHALLENGE

Technology

Streamlining Decision Making at JetBlue

David Neeleman, the founder and CEO of JetBlue, believes the airline industry underutilizes technology that could lower its costs. This is critical if you consider the fact that between 2000 and 2007, airline companies cumulatively lost $50 billion or more. During that time period, most commercial airlines cut or at least froze their IT budgets. By contrast, JetBlue nearly doubled its IT budget.

The company uses technology to make many of its daily managerial decisions. It is, in part, why JetBlue has succeeded whereas others have failed. For example, JetBlue uses workforce optimization technology called "Blue Pumpkin." Blue Pumpkin helps managers ensure the company has enough reservation agents on staff at peak call times. The first year the technology was used, the company achieved a 38 percent increase in service levels, a 30 percent improvement in agent productivity, and a 50 percent boost in management workload per agent.[35] The turnover among reservation agents in the airline industry overall that year was 30 percent, but JetBlue's was much lower. Today, the company has about 6 percent turnover among its reservation agents, which both increases the company's effectiveness and lowers its recruiting and training costs.

JetBlue also created the first "paperless cockpit." JetBlue equips all pilots with laptops so that they, instead of a separate set of employees at the company's operations center, can access flight manuals and make preflight load and balance calculations. This saves JetBlue an estimated 4,800 man-hours a year.[36] It also allows the pilots to make their own decisions about load and balance adjustments when temperatures, wind strengths, and departure directions change. Each plane saves about 15 minutes prior to takeoff, translating into approximately 1,500 additional flights annually for JetBlue.

In addition, JetBlue equips both pilots and crewmembers with wireless devices that allow them to report and respond to problems such as weather delays and safety-related injuries, including those that involve passengers. The devices immediately convey the problems to JetBlue's managers via their BlackBerries, and employees can easily access the information via the company's intranet, JetBlue Event Management System (JEMS). Reportedly, even Neeleman wears such a wireless device to bed!

Sources: J. Wynbrandt, *Flying High* (John Wiley & Sons, 2004); B. Peterson, *Blue Streak* (New York, Penguin Group, 2004).

A wide variety of technologies allow members of groups to communicate with one another and make decisions without having to meet face-to-face. For example, via technology, members can simultaneously review a document and make real-time changes to it. Design teams like those in the automotive industry increasingly use this type of technology, and it can significantly reduce a company's travel costs. The practice isn't without its drawbacks though. A recent study found that computer-mediated communication decreases the effectiveness of groups: Compared to face-to-face groups, these groups take longer to complete their tasks and members experience less satisfaction.[37] To be

Managerial Challenges from the Front Line

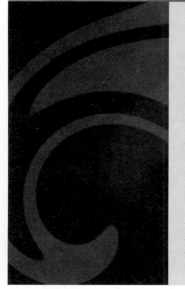

The Rest of the Story

Lurue Lord, in consultation with her husband, determined that she did need to delegate some decisions as well as stop doing lower-level tasks she had done for many years at Lord Eye Center. Today, the company has more policies and preset procedures that help employees make routine decisions. Lurue has also hired a new "area" manager to help her implement and manage some of the more difficult decisions and track employee and store sales. Nonetheless, Lurue continues to visit the company's various offices to gather firsthand information about the competitive and operational situation each faces, and she remains involved in key decisions such as those involving pricing, technology, and new store locations.

So far, Lord Eye Center, its employees, and a more relaxed owner are adjusting well to the change. In addition to finally taking some personal time to fish, play tennis, and golf, Lurue says she has more time to explore innovative ways to expand the business.

sure, organizations need to consider the pitfalls as well as the benefits associated with computer-mediated communication as a medium for group decision making.

Summary

- The classical model of decision making describes how people should rationally make decisions but does not describe how people actually make decisions.
- In real life, people do not have an unlimited amount of time to gather and evaluate alternatives. Instead, they evaluate their options sequentially and stop once they find one that satisfies their minimum objectives. This is called satisficing. Satisficing is an aspect of the bounded rationality model of decision making.
- The retrospective decision model, or the implicit favorite model, of decision making explains how decision makers intuitively make choices and then rationalize their decisions after the fact. Some research shows that decisions made this way can be quite effective.
- Managers tend to let their programmed activities overshadow their nonprogrammed activities. Thus, they tend to make routine and repetitive decisions before focusing on those that are unique and require considerable thought. This tendency is called Gresham's law of planning.[38]
- Although we cannot per se conclude that individuals make better decisions than groups or vice versa, there are conditions under which each can lead to better decision making. It's up to managers to figure out to what extent they should involve their employees in decision making based on the situation.
- Most people will want to participate in group decision making if they believe (1) they have relevant content knowledge, (2) their participation will help bring about change, (3) the resulting change will produce outcomes they value or prefer, and (4) the organization values their participation, and it fits with the company's goals and objectives.
- Techniques such as brainstorming, NGT, and delphi help ensure groups consider a broad range of options as well as their implications and outcomes. These techniques can help minimize group decision-making pitfalls such as groupthink and the escalation of commitment.

Key Terms

bounded rationality (administrative) model 90
brainstorming 104
cross-functional teams 99
decision making 85
delphi technique 105
devil's advocate 97
dialectical inquiry 104
escalating commitment 98
formulation 85
Gresham's law of planning 93
groupthink 95
intuitive decision making 92
heuristic 91
multiple advocacy 104
nominal group technique 105
nonprogrammed decision 92
opportunity 86
perception 86
perceptual distortion 92
problem 85
programmed decision 92
prospective rationality 98
rational (classical) model 85
retrospective decision (implicit favorite) model 91
satisficing 91
solution 85
standard operating procedure (SOP) 93
structured debate 103
subjectively expected utility (SEU) model 88

Review Questions

1. What is the basic premise of the rational (classical) model of decision making and how does it differ from the bounded rationality model?
2. How can selective perception influence decision formulation?
3. What is satisficing? How does it differ from satisfying?
4. How does the retrospective decision-making model work?
5. When are SOPs (standard operating procedures) most often used?
6. Describe Gresham's law of planning.

7. Why is analyzing the decision situation a key step in making better decisions?
8. What are the advantages and disadvantages of group decision making?
9. Describe what groupthink and the escalation of commitment are.
10. When should a manager engage in participatory decision making?
11. What techniques can managers use to improve group decision making and avoid pitfalls like groupthink and the escalation commitment?

Assessing Your Capabilities

What's Your Decision-Making Style?

Read each of the following statements. Indicate the extent to which you disagree or agree that this statement is descriptive of you. Be as candid as you can.

Statement						
1. I double-check my information sources to be sure I have the right facts before making a decision.	1 Strongly Disagree	2 Disagree	3 Somewhat Disagree	4 Somewhat Agree	5 Agree	6 Strongly Agree
2. I generally make snap decisions.	1 Strongly Disagree	2 Disagree	3 Somewhat Disagree	4 Somewhat Agree	5 Agree	6 Strongly Agree
3. When making decisions, I do what seems natural at the moment.	1 Strongly Disagree	2 Disagree	3 Somewhat Disagree	4 Somewhat Agree	5 Agree	6 Strongly Agree
4. I tend to put off making many decisions because thinking about them makes me uneasy.	1 Strongly Disagree	2 Disagree	3 Somewhat Disagree	4 Somewhat Agree	5 Agree	6 Strongly Agree
5. I use the advice of other people in making my important decisions.	1 Strongly Disagree	2 Disagree	3 Somewhat Disagree	4 Somewhat Agree	5 Agree	6 Strongly Agree
6. When making decisions, I rely on my instincts.	1 Strongly Disagree	2 Disagree	3 Somewhat Disagree	4 Somewhat Agree	5 Agree	6 Strongly Agree
7. I often need the assistance of other people when making important decisions.	1 Strongly Disagree	2 Disagree	3 Somewhat Disagree	4 Somewhat Agree	5 Agree	6 Strongly Agree
8. I avoid making important decisions until the pressure is on.	1 Strongly Disagree	2 Disagree	3 Somewhat Disagree	4 Somewhat Agree	5 Agree	6 Strongly Agree
9. I generally make decisions that feel right to me.	1 Strongly Disagree	2 Disagree	3 Somewhat Disagree	4 Somewhat Agree	5 Agree	6 Strongly Agree
10. I make quick decisions.	1 Strongly Disagree	2 Disagree	3 Somewhat Disagree	4 Somewhat Agree	5 Agree	6 Strongly Agree
11. I rarely make important decisions without consulting other people.	1 Strongly Disagree	2 Disagree	3 Somewhat Disagree	4 Somewhat Agree	5 Agree	6 Strongly Agree
12. I make decisions in a logical and systematic way.	1 Strongly Disagree	2 Disagree	3 Somewhat Disagree	4 Somewhat Agree	5 Agree	6 Strongly Agree
13. I postpone decision making whenever possible.	1 Strongly Disagree	2 Disagree	3 Somewhat Disagree	4 Somewhat Agree	5 Agree	6 Strongly Agree

14. When I make a decision, I trust my inner feelings and reactions.	1 Strongly Disagree	2 Disagree	3 Somewhat Disagree	4 Somewhat Agree	5 Agree	6 Strongly Agree
15. My decision making requires careful thought.	1 Strongly Disagree	2 Disagree	3 Somewhat Disagree	4 Somewhat Agree	5 Agree	6 Strongly Agree
16. I like to have someone to steer me in the right direction when I am faced with important decisions.	1 Strongly Disagree	2 Disagree	3 Somewhat Disagree	4 Somewhat Agree	5 Agree	6 Strongly Agree
17. When making a decision, I consider various options in terms of specific goals.	1 Strongly Disagree	2 Disagree	3 Somewhat Disagree	4 Somewhat Agree	5 Agree	6 Strongly Agree
18. I often make impulsive decisions.	1 Strongly Disagree	2 Disagree	3 Somewhat Disagree	4 Somewhat Agree	5 Agree	6 Strongly Agree
19. I generally make important decisions at the last minute.	1 Strongly Disagree	2 Disagree	3 Somewhat Disagree	4 Somewhat Agree	5 Agree	6 Strongly Agree
20. When I make a decision, it is more important for me to feel the decision is right than to have a rationale for it.	1 Strongly Disagree	2 Disagree	3 Somewhat Disagree	4 Somewhat Agree	5 Agree	6 Strongly Agree

In scoring your responses, simply write in the number you circled beside each item. Then, add up the total numbers you wrote in within each column. What emerges is a general profile of the decision-making styles that you tend to exhibit. Most people use more than one style but at the same time often have one or two styles they use more often, just as most people can use both hands but tend to favor using one over the other.

1. _______	6. _______	4. _______	5. _______	2. _______
12. _______	9. _______	8. _______	7. _______	3. _______
15. _______	14. _______	13. _______	11. _______	10. _______
17. _______	20. _______	19. _______	16. _______	18. _______
A Total	B Total	C Total	D Total	E Total

Column A: Logical Style

If your highest score is in Column A, this suggests that you make decisions in a logical fashion and rely on facts and information as they relate to your objectives or goals in guiding your final decision.

Column B: Intuitive Style

If your highest score is in Column B, this suggests that you trust your intuition and feelings and use them to make decisions.

Column C: Procrastinating Style

If your highest score is in Column C, this suggests that you are often uncomfortable making decisions. You tend to put them off until you are forced to make them.

Column D: Consulting Style

If your highest score is in Column D, this suggests that you value the input and perspectives of others and tend to consult with them before making important decisions.

Column E: Impulsive Style

If your highest score is in Column E, this suggests that you make decisions very quickly and do not feel the need to consult with others. Nor do you feel the need to consciously examine your own logic or feelings. Instead, you are comfortable going with what "pops" into your head.

Source: S. G. Scott and R. A. Bruce, "Decision-Making Style: The Development and Assessment of a New Measure," *Educational and Psychological Measurement* 55 (1995): 818–831.

Closing Case To Close or Not?

Dov Frohman, the general manager of Intel Israel, faced a tough decision in 1991: Should he keep his plant open with Operation Desert Storm looming—especially given the fact that Iraqi Scud missiles stood ready to strike Israel in just minutes? There was also reason to believe that missiles might be equipped with chemical warheads. Moreover, Israel's civil defense authority had suggested that the country's nonessential businesses temporarily close.

Frohman said one of the top factors influencing his decision was the uncertainty of the situation: "The radical uncertainty of the situation—not knowing how many missiles would fall, where they would fall, what kind of destruction they would inflict—threatened to bring our business to a halt, even before a single missile had been launched." He also took into account the general business implications shutting down would have. On the one hand, he was confident senior executives at Intel's headquarters in California would understand if he decided to shut down until the crisis passed. On the other hand, he knew Intel would need to get the microprocessors his plant normally produced somewhere else in the world. From Frohman's perspective, "Managing a major unit in a global corporation is a continual fight for resources." Therefore, a production interrupt, even a temporary one, might cause the company's senior executives to think twice about making any future investments in Intel Israel.

Frohman said he was concerned not only about the survival of Intel Israel but Israel's entire high-tech sector. Intel Israel was a key anchor of the country's still small but high-tech economy. "If we couldn't operate in an emergency situation, the trust of multinationals and venture capitalists in the stability of the Israeli business environment might crumble," he noted. Ultimately, though, Frohman's big concern was the safety of Intel Israel's employees: "People had a sealed room at home, and we had created them in all our main facilities, including the Jerusalem fab [fabrication plant]. But what about the daily commute?" He believed it was while commuting that employees would be at the greatest risk.

If Frohman decided to keep the operations running, how would he present the decision to employees? Should he order, request, strongly encourage, or simply offer them the option of showing up for work? After discussing the issues at length with his team, Frohman decided to keep the operations open. However, he would ask, not order, employees to come to work. "No one would be punished if they decided to stay home. I made it extremely clear to my direct reports that there would be no coercion: No manager was to pressure employees to come to work who did not want to."

Frohman said he communicated the decision to Intel Irael's workforce on Wednesday, January 18. The following day, with still no sign of missile attacks, most employees came to work. However, two days later, eight Iraqi Scud missiles hit Tel Aviv and Haifa around 2 AM. Fortunately, the missiles weren't laden with chemical warheads. However, at that point, Frohman had another decision to make: Should he stick with his original decision or close the plant and tell employees to stay home?

Frohman quickly met with members of his management team. The team had roughly 30 minutes to make a choice. The decision? To remain open. That morning, 75 percent of the employees scheduled to work the 7:00 AM shift at Intel's fab plant just outside Jerusalem arrived. Scud attacks continued on Saturday, but employee turnout at both the company's Jerusalem plant and its design center in Haifa remained at 80 percent.

Frohman talked to executives at Intel's headquarters about the situation. "I explained that we had decided to remain open, but we weren't forcing any employees to come to work who didn't feel comfortable doing so, and that so far turnout was quite good. They asked a lot of questions; we discussed the potential risks. But in the end, they were 7,500 miles away. Under the circumstances, they had to trust us." All totaled, the Scud attacks continued for six weeks, during which time, 39 Scuds fell in 18 separate attacks. Intel Israel operations remained opened and up and running the entire time.

A few years later, Intel decided to invest in and build a second semiconductor plant in Israel. Thereafter, the Haifa design center won the assignment to develop the Centrino portable-computing microprocessor. Then in 2005, Intel announced that it would spend an additional $3.5 billion to build a new fab plant in Israel. The investment was the single largest ever made by any company in Israel. Following the investment, Intel Israel's exports soared to $1.2 billion, accounting for 14 percent of all of Israel's electronics- and information-industry exports. Today, the company is the largest foreign-owned employer in Israel.

Questions

1. Do you agree with Dov Frohman's decision in advance of the actual missile attacks to keep Intel up and running? What about after the actual missile attacks began?
2. Do you agree that Frohman should have made the decision to remain open or close or should executives at Intel's corporate headquarters have made it?
3. What criteria would you have considered if you were in Frohman's position? How would you have weighted these factors?

Sources: Adapted from D. Frohman, "Leadership Under Fire," *Harvard Business Review* (December 2006).

Team Exercise

Form teams of four to six members. Read the following scenario. As a group, decide how you would answer each of the four questions at the end of the scenario.

While sitting in your office, you get a call from your company's plant supervisor. He tells you that a big customer wants you to a djust your assembly line to rush out a custom order. The plant supervisor says the decision is up to you. He needs to know what it is by tomorrow morning. The assembly line is currently in the middle of an extended, standard run, producing a product for five of your mid-sized customers. Your company competes in part by offering both low-cost products and good service. The vast majority of your mid-sized customers choose to do business with you because your prices are lower. You maintain your profitability with these customers by keeping your own costs low. Your principal means of achieving this is by assembling high volumes of standardized products. Many of your large customers appreciate your low price but are willing to pay a premium for customized service and alterations to the products that come off your line.

If you stop the line to make the changes in equipment needed to run the custom order, you will incur both costs and delays to your current standard run. You are about two-thirds of the way through your standard run but need one week more to finish it. The changeover will take approximately three hours to complete, and the custom run two days to complete.

You have made this particular changeover before but not in the last six months. You know the basics of the changeover, but the person most knowledgeable about the details is out sick but expects to return to work tomorrow. With the exception of two new employees, the company's nine assembly-line operators are fairly experienced and do not require close supervision, They are generally willing to be involved in decisions but are also happy just to "do their jobs."

1. Should you make this decision on your own or should you involve the group?
2. Are you inclined to stop the current run and make the changeover for the custom run? Why or why not?
3. If you insist that it's impossible to decide, what information must you have in order to make the decision?

5

Strategic Management

Learning Objectives

After studying this chapter, you should be able to:

Managerial Challenges from the Front Line

Name: Aaron Green

Position: Senior Marketing Manager, Wal-Mart Corporation

Alma mater: The Citadel (BA); Wake Forest University (MBA)

Outside work activities: Spending time with

For example, he spent time in the firm's merchandising department, in international operations, and in distribution centers, among other areas. He found his time in the program to be quite valuable because it gave him a more holistic view of the company. Green's first position after the rotation program was in merchandising as a buyer for landline telephones. It was during this job that he faced one of his toughest managerial challenges ever. The landline telephone market was highly competitive; Wal-Mart's competitors were aggressively advertising and pricing their products. As a result, the company's sales of landline telephones were declining. But to gain market share, the company couldn't increase its prices by very much because managers like Green knew consumers would simply buy their phones from other retailers, such as Target. As a result, profits were declining. Thus, there was a need to reverse the sales and increase the profits as well. Green faced a signifi-

Thus, Green faced a significant challenge. He needed to reverse the decline in sales and improve profits on the landline telephones. The challenge was substantial because Wal-Mart faced substantial competition; the aggressive marketing and pricing by competitors and the problems of suppliers made Green's challenge even more significant. He needed to determine how Wal-Mart could regain a competitive advantage in this product market. How would he handle his first big managerial challenge?

As described in the opening profile, Wal-Mart is the largest corporation in the world. It is not only an American icon, it has worked its way into U.S. culture. Businesspeople talk about the "Wal-Mart effect": Wal-Mart has affected the prices of goods, wage rates, and even economies in the countries where it does business. It has changed the way people do business not only in rural communities but also in large cities. It is described as perhaps the world's most important economic organization that is privately controlled.[1]

It is well-known that Wal-Mart employs a cost leadership strategy (explained later in this chapter). Thus, it is interesting that Wal-Mart was experiencing declining landline telephone sales because of aggressive marketing and pricing by its competitors and rivalry between its suppliers. This suggests that a firm's strategy is difficult to develop, implement, and sustain even by Wal-Mart.

The domestic automobile market provides another illustration of increasing competition. As recently as 25 years ago, only three major manufacturers—General Motors, Ford, and Chrysler—dominated the largest automobile market in the world, the United States. Chrysler was acquired by DaimlerBenz of Germany and is now DaimlerChrysler. Additionally, the market shares of both GM and Ford have fallen by nearly half in the last several years as foreign competitors, including BMW, Daewoo, Fiat, Honda, Hyundai, Isuzu, Kia, Nissan, Renault, Subaru, Suzuki, Toyota, and others have captured market share. In 2003, Toyota passed Ford in car sales in the United States and overtook GM in 2007 as the largest auto manufacturer in the world. This provides an example of how globalization has become a powerful force behind increasing competition. Communication and transportation technology only add to this competitive intensity.

Never has the need been greater to understand how to develop and implement effective strategies. Andrew Grove, the former CEO of Intel, observed that only the "paranoid" firms survive, primarily because they continuously analyze their external environments and competition, but also because they continuously innovate. Managers who help their firms gain a competitive advantage recognize that it is only temporary; they must be ready to change their strategy at any time based on their analysis of the competition and changes in their environments.[2]

Although the principles of strategic management are critical for top managers of a company, the principles also are applicable for managers at various levels of the organization. For example, a lower-level manager like Aaron Green might be responsible for a single product line in a company with many products. You can apply the principles presented in this chapter to create a strategy for a product line as well as for an entire company. In addition, even though top executives largely develop a company's strategy, the other managers and employees of the organization must then implement the strategy throughout the organization. Managers at all levels can do a better job of helping implement a strategy if they understand the strategic management process, how the strategy was developed, and its intended targets.[3] These topics are the focus of this chapter.

What Is a Competitive Advantage?

competitive advantage
the ability of a firm to win consistently over the long term in a competitive situation

Fundamentally, the objective of strategic management is to determine, create, and maintain competitive advantage. At its essence, the concept of **competitive advantage** is the ability of a firm to provide value to customers that exceeds what competitors can provide.[4] In the case of for-profit organizations, having a competitive advantage contributes to consistently higher profits than competitors.

A competitive advantage is created by having and managing resources to provide goods and services that meet the following criteria: (1) they provide superior value, (2) they are rare—competitors do not provide similar products and services in quality and quantity, (3) they are difficult to imitate, and (4) they are nonsubstitutable.[5] Hewlett-Packard (HP) is the market leader in printers. Clearly, this indicates that HP has a competitive advantage in this market. Thus, its products and services provided in this market meet the four criteria. Next, we explore each of the four criteria that lead to competitive advantage.

Superior Value

superior value
products and services that produce value for customers that is superior to the value provided by competitors

The essence of **superior value** as an aspect of competitive advantage is straightforward. Does the firm provide products and services that produce value for the customers that is superior to any provided by competitors? For example, FedEx was one of the first companies to introduce package tracking capability. It created a system for tracking a package all along its route. Thus, it was able to locate a customer's package at any point along the delivery route more effectively than its primary competitor, UPS. As a student, you chose the particular school that you attend because of the special value it provides you. For example, it may provide a superior education in the major of your choice. It also may provide a superior location or special place where you prefer to live. In recent years, Apple provides a superior product in the form of the iPod. Thus, Apple has a competitive advantage because it sells audio and video products that provide superior value to customers. This is sometimes referred to as a *comparative advantage* because compared to others, the firm provides superior value. It is also sometimes referred to as a *distinctive competence* because the superior product or service is the result of a competence that is distinctive.

Rarity

To hold a competitive advantage, no other firms can have the capabilities needed to provide the quality and quantity of products and services you produce. If even one other firm has similar capabilities, it can then provide the customers products and services of equal value. You may ask the question, "How many other firms hold similar capabilities?" If the answer is none and the capabilities held by the firm produce superior value for the customers, the firm clearly will hold a competitive advantage. Yet most competitive advantages are temporary because competitors are constantly trying to wrest an advantage from the market leader.[6] In particular, competitors often try to imitate market leaders.

Difficult to Imitate

Having capabilities that provide superior value for customers and that are rare will produce only a temporary advantage. Firms must try to avoid competitor imitation of these capabilities and must create barriers that make it difficult for others to imitate these capabilities to produce a competitive advantage.[7] These barriers can involve a variety of obstacles from tangible ones, such as size, to more intangible ones, such as a company's culture and corporate reputation.[8]

Disney's theme parks have been praised for having a comparative advantage in friendly employees. While Disney may provide superior value to customers with friendly employees, you may ask the question, "Is it easy for other firms to replicate this attribute?" If friendly employees represent a major contributor to offering superior value, Disney's advantage would likely disappear. But how easy is it to recruit, select, train, and keep employees who

Disney's characters—Mickey Mouse, Goofy, Pluto, and so forth—are well known and renowned the world over. As such, they give Disney a competitive advantage. So do the companies well-trained, friendly employees.

can and are willing to be very friendly to all customers over a long period of time? The harder it is for other firms with theme parks to hire, develop, and keep friendly employees, the longer Disney's comparative advantage may persist. Friendly employees clearly contribute to Disney's advantage, but other attributes also contribute to it. For example, the well-known and loved Disney characters (such as, Mickey Mouse, Goofy, Pluto) also contribute to Disney's advantage. Therefore, a competitive advantage may result from the combination of several factors, making it more difficult for competitors to imitate. Additionally, some advantages are more durable than others. Legal protection, such as patents, can prolong their existence. Many scientific patents are awarded for 17 to 20 years in length. Advantages like brand recognition can last a long time and may take years to deteriorate. The Disney "brand" has endured in the minds of children and their parents for over half a decade.[9]

Nonsubstitutability

In addition to the qualities identified previously, for a competitive advantage to be sustainable over time requires a low possibility of substitution. **Substitution** refers to fulfilling the customer's need by alternative means. Let's differentiate substitution and imitation with an example: Godiva chocolates are famous for their quality and unique flavor. They have an advantage with regard to taste and smoothness other companies' chocolates don't have. Godiva's specialized knowledge, which helped it to create this unique and highly valued flavor, makes it difficult for other firms to replicate, or imitate, the taste and texture of its chocolate. However, if Godiva is to sustain its competitive advantage, customers must find it difficult to find a substitute that equally satisfies their desire for the sweet taste and smooth texture obtained from the Godiva chocolates.

substitution
whether or not the customer's need that you fulfill can be met by alternative means

Turning a Competitive Advantage into Profits

Firms must manage their resources in such a way as to capture profits from their competitive advantage.[10] **Above-average returns** are the profits that are greater than the average for a comparable set of firms (usually compared by industry and size). These above-average profits are primarily a function of larger-than-average cost-price margins. For example, if, on average, a 250 megabyte USB drive costs $10 for firms in the hardware industry to produce, and, on average, the sales price within the industry is $15, the average profit margin

above-average returns
profits that are above the average for a comparable set of firms

is $5. More than $5 in profit on all such USB drives sold would represent an above-average return. Importantly, customers must perceive that they receive value. If they do so and the firm can earn above-average returns, the firm is creating value for its shareholders and usually for all of its stakeholders.

In the following sections, we examine specific aspects of the strategic management process, including the formulation and implementation of strategy. Strategy is developed and implemented with one basic objective—achieving a competitive advantage.

The Strategic Management Process: Setting Direction

Strategic management is a type of planning process in which managers (1) establish the organization's general direction and objectives, (2) formulate a specific strategy, (3) plan and carry out the strategy's implementation, and (4) monitor results and make necessary adjustments. To understand what this means, we need to examine each step in this overall process (see Exhibit 5.1).

Determining the Firm's Strategic Vision

strategic vision
provides a view of the firm over the long term and what it should achieve in the future

The first step in the strategic management process is the determination of the firm's strategic vision. The **strategic vision** provides a view of the firm over the long term and what it should achieve in the future.[11] Some use the term *strategic intent* to describe the strategic vision.[12] For example, the strategic vision for Xerox Corporation is to be "the World's Document Company." Kellogg's strategic vision is to have "Kellogg's Products on Every Table in the World." As these examples illustrate, a vision for a firm captures its general identity, direction, and level of aspirations. The strategic vision is the heart of the strategy and strategic plan.[13] In practice, an effective statement of strategic vision is short, compelling, and provides a general understanding of the organization's aspirations while engendering passion among the managers and other organization members. The vision and mission are closely integrated.

Formulating the Firm's Mission Statement

mission statement
a statement that articulates the fundamental purpose of the organization; the statement often contains several components

Although statements of strategic intent are typically only a sentence in length, mission statements are usually much longer. A **mission statement** articulates the fundamental purpose of the organization and often contains several components, among them:

- Company philosophy
- Company identity or self-concept

EXHIBIT 5.1

Strategic Management Process

- Principal products or services
- Customers and markets
- Geographic focus
- Obligations to shareholders
- Commitment to employees[14]

An example of a mission statement is provided in Exhibit 5.2. As the example illustrates, mission statements describe the purpose of the organization, and should support and be consistent with its strategic vision. One of the major differences between statements of strategic vision and mission statements is that mission statements tend to be much more specific in terms of the values and the primary focus of the organization.

To determine what strategy to pursue requires an analysis of both the firm's external environment and internal resources and capabilities. Kenneth Andrews probably first advanced this view in the early 1970s.[15] The results of an assessment of both need to be integrated to determine the appropriate objectives and to formulate the strategy necessary to achieve them.

Conducting an External Environmental Analysis

You must thoroughly analyze the external general environment and the industry and competitor environment because each can significantly affect the strategy a firm might develop, as well as whether the firm is likely to succeed or fail.[16] Although the general environment's effects are often indirect, they can be critical in formulating an effective strategy. Certainly, the forces in an industry and those associated with competitors are of particular importance when thinking about a company's strategy.[17]

The General Environment

A variety of forces in the **general environment** can influence the effectiveness of an organization's strategy to include sociocultural, technological, economic, political-legal, and global forces.

general environment sociocultural, technological, economic, political-legal, and global forces that can influence the effectiveness of an organization's strategy

SOCIOCULTURAL FORCES The **sociocultural forces** consist primarily of the demographics and the cultural characteristics of the societies in which an organization operates. Demographics are essentially the descriptive characteristics of people in the society, such as average age, birth rate, level of education, literacy rate, and so on. For example, in 1920 the average life expectancy was 53.6 years, and by 2010 it is estimated to be 77 years.[18]

sociocultural forces forces consisting primarily of the demographics and the cultural characteristics of the societies in which an organization operates

Demographics can significantly affect both organizational inputs and outcomes. For example, the average level of education and the birth rate in the United States combined can have a significant impact on the supply of workers with a given level of education and training. Specifically, a low birth rate and a modestly increasing level of education could result in a slow-growing or even declining number of technical workers. For example, in the 1990s, demand for workers with strong technical capabilities, such as software programmers, far outstripped supply in the United States.

Japan's population declined for the first time in 2005. By 2007, the number of people over 65 years of age will have more than doubled from 10 percent of the population to 21 percent in less than a generation. With one of the world's longest life expectancies (85.5

EXHIBIT 5.2

Mission Statement for the Internal Revenue Service

IRS Mission Statement

The IRS mission is to "provide America's taxpayers top quality service by helping them understand and meet their tax responsibilities and by applying the tax law with integrity and fairness to all."

Parents in SUVs line the parking lot at a Dallas Christian school while they wait to pick up their children. But "Would Jesus drive an SUV?" That's what some people began asking after concerns about the environment heightened people's awareness about the vehicles' CO_2 emissions. Changing societal values such as this are constantly changing the products people demand—changes astute managers need to be aware of.

for women and 78.5 for men), fewer workers will be supporting Japan's retirees than at any time in the country's history, and many of Japan's retirees will live so long that they are likely to use up their retirement savings before they die if they retire at age 65.[19] This may mean that younger workers will face higher government taxes to support social security systems for senior citizens.

Although demographics provide important data about the population, societal values help to translate those data into business implications.[20] Societal values are commonly shared desired "end states." In practical terms, societal values determine the extent to which an organization's products or services have a market. For example, consider the controversy surrounding sport utility vehicles (SUVs) in North America. Throughout the 1990s, SUVs, such as the Ford Explorer, Dodge Durango, and Chevy Suburban, were the fastest-selling automobiles. However, as concerns about the impact of pollution on global warming increased and the prices of gasoline rose, people began to develop a negative sentiment toward SUVs and pressured car companies to make "hybrid" cars. Instead of 12 miles to the gallon, hybrids get 50 or 60 miles to the gallon.

Astute managers need the ability to combine demographics and societal values in order to determine important implications for their organizations.[21]

TECHNOLOGICAL FORCES Technology is another external environment force that can critically affect organizations. A specific technological innovation can spell the birth and growth of one firm and the decline and death of another. Although the technological environment can be quite complicated, managers especially need to focus on two basic dimensions of the technology environment—product and process changes.

Product technological changes are those that lead to new product features and capabilities of existing products or to completely new products. Managers need to know what product technology changes are occurring, especially in their industries. Because firms increasingly win or lose as a function of their technological advantages and disadvantages, an awareness of technological advances at home and abroad is critical.

Process technological changes typically relate to alterations in how to make products or how to manage enterprises. For example, management information system (MIS) technology, such as that used by Wal-Mart (the largest retailer in the world with over $250 billion in annual sales), allows managers to track merchandise on a daily or hourly basis and thereby know which products are selling and which ones are not. This, in turn, allows them to effectively order merchandise so that they do not run out of hot-selling items (and miss out on the sales revenues) and avoid overstocking poor-selling items (and tie up valuable cash in inventory).[22]

Many North American steel manufacturers were driven into bankruptcy because virtually all of the largest firms were slow to adopt an important new process technology, the electric arch furnace. Most large (or what are called "integrated") steel companies made steel by starting with raw iron ore and melting and converting it to large steel slabs that were further rolled and refined. Electric arch furnaces allowed so-called "mini-mills" to start with scrap metal, melt it, and make it into steel products. Starting with scrap metal was significantly cheaper than starting with iron ore. Although the metal made in mini-mills cannot be made into such things as beams for skyscrapers, it can be made into sheet metal for making car exteriors, washing machines, toasters, and so on. Dofasco, Inc., of Hamilton, Canada, was the first, and at the time the only, integrated steel company to add this technology to its traditional steel-making processes. However, although the company now enjoys the benefits of the new electric arch furnace technology, it still took it nearly 10 years to adopt the technology after it was introduced.[23]

ECONOMIC FORCES A variety of economic forces in the external environment can also significantly influence organizations. Not all economic forces affect all organizations equally, however. The exact nature of the business and industry determines the specific factors that have the strongest influence on an organization.

Current economic conditions clearly can affect the demand for products and the costs of producing them. For example, the current level of inflation can directly affect how quickly costs increase, which in turn might reduce profits. The current level of unemployment can directly influence how easy or difficult it is to find the type of employees needed. Current interest rates can determine how expensive it is to borrow money or even how much money the firm can borrow to finance activities and expansions. When interest rates are low, home builders and mortgage loan providers generally experience higher demand for their services.

But economic activity is not static.[24] Economic activity tends to move in cycles. Although it is difficult to predict exactly when an upturn or downturn in economic conditions will occur, understanding that cycles exist and the key factors that move them is critical for managerial activities, such as planning. It is also important to understand that specific industry cycles can be more or less pronounced than the general economic cycle of the country. For example, the construction industry tends to have higher peaks and lower valleys than the overall national economy.

Perhaps the most difficult thing to determine about economic conditions is whether changes in the economy are temporary or whether they represent longer-term, structural changes. Structural changes significantly affect the current and future dynamics of economic activity. For example, the shift from an agrarian (agricultural) to an industrial economy and then from an industrial to a service economy were structural changes that took place in the United States. They affected where people worked, what work they did, the education level they needed to do the work. In many service companies, such as engineering, consulting, and law firms, the company's primary assets are its people. The knowledge held by these people represents intangible assets. This is in contrast to industrial companies, such as car manufacturers, which have millions of dollars in tangible assets like plants and equipment. As a consequence, while a car manufacturer may be able to replace a worker who leaves the assembly line with relative ease and feel only small effects of employee turnover, the same is not true for service companies. For example, when a star consultant leaves her firm, she takes with her most of her value to the company. Her understanding of clients' problems and solutions leaves with her. In some cases, the value is so closely tied to the individual that clients leave the company with a person's departure and redirect their business to wherever the star consultant works.

POLITICAL AND LEGAL FORCES Political and legal forces can have important effects on organizations. Laws frame what organizations can and cannot do. As a consequence, they can create both challenges and opportunities. For example, new pollution laws significantly increased the operating costs of coal-burning power plants. At the same time, these laws created new business opportunities for firms such as Corning, which developed and sold new filter systems to coal-burning power plants.[25] Tax laws can also have a profound effect on businesses. Controversial tax breaks for oil and gas exploration helped oil firms earn record profits when the price of oil increased substantially from 2005 to 2006.

Perhaps one of the most important political aspects of the external general environment is federal government spending. On the one hand, increases or decreases in government spending can have a significant impact on the overall economy. Total government spending at the local, state, and national levels accounts for about 20 percent of gross domestic product (the total dollar value of final goods and services produced by businesses within a nation's borders). More complicated, but perhaps even more important, is whether government spending increases or reduces the deficit. When federal spending pushes the federal deficit up, interest rates sometimes increase. As interest rates increase, money becomes more expensive for firms to borrow, and as a consequence, they typically borrow less. As firms borrow less, they expand their business activities at a slower rate or even contract their overall activity. This can push unemployment up, which in turn pushes consumer spending down. In combination this can create an economic downturn.

GLOBAL FORCES Although all managers should pay attention to the global environment, its importance depends on the organization's size and scope of business. When the percentage of international sales increases as part of total sales, the global environment becomes more important. For example, 70 percent of Coca-Cola's income comes from international sales in over 200 countries; consequently, the global environment is critical to the company's performance. Managers of multinational firms that operate in multiple countries must try to integrate those operations into an almost borderless enterprise. As Wal-Mart has grown internationally, it has had to become sensitive to the global forces in the general environment. Global forces affect each of the other four general environmental forces.

When analyzing a foreign country, there are two additional dimensions of the external environment that are typically examined in the context of a foreign country—institutional and physical environmental forces. They are often included in analyses of foreign countries primarily because of the vast differences among them in terms of institutions and physical characteristics.[26]

institutional forces
the country's rules, policies, and enforcement processes that influence individuals' and organizations' behaviors that operate within the country boundaries

physical forces
involve infrastructure that can affect existing and potential business operations in a country such as roads, telecommunications, air links, deepwater harbors, etc.

As explained in Chapter 3, **institutional forces** include the country's rules, policies, and enforcement processes that influence individuals' and organizations' behaviors that operate within the country boundaries.[27] The institutions that should be assessed include a country's government, labor unions, religious institutions, and business institutions because they can be (and often are) dramatically different from those "at home." These institutions also include the laws and regulations and economic factors as described in Chapter 3. **Physical forces** include infrastructure, such as roads, telecommunications, air links, arable land, deepwater harbors, mineral resources, forests, and climate, which can affect existing and potential business operations in a country. For example, China has vast coal resources deep in its interior, but they are not an attractive business opportunity because of the poor rail and road infrastructure in those regions.

Exhibit 5.3 summarizes the analyses of the general environment for Coca-Cola. The sociocultural information suggests that managers at Coca-Cola may desire to increase their marketing efforts to reach out to ethnic groups from countries and cultures in which drinking soft drinks, especially with carbonation, is not common. The information captured in the global dimension of the general external environment that managers at Coca-Cola should increase their efforts in emerging foreign markets with large populations, such as China.

A Manager's Challenge, "eBay Rethinks Its China Strategies," suggests that managers for the company did a poor job of analyzing China's general environment. In particular, eBay did not seem to understand well China's institutional environment. And, it underestimated its primary competitor in the Chinese markets, Taobao. Thus, the managers evidently

EXHIBIT 5.3

Description of the General Environment of Coca-Cola

Sociocultural

- Demographics
  Baby boomers drinking less soft drinks as they age.
  U.S. population growth is slowing and much of the growth comes from immigrants who generally drink less soft drinks.
- Values
  Society is increasingly concerned about pollution and recycling.
  Increasing focus on health and the negative aspects of caffeine, carbonation, and sugar.

Technological

- New "canning" technology makes using recycled aluminum easier and cheaper.
- Internet opens up a new means of running promotion contests and activities.

Economic

- Slow economy reduces per-person consumption primarily due to fewer social occasions (parties) at which soft drinks might be served.
- Nearing end of economic downturn and prospects of economic recovery.
- Stricter liability for illness caused by beverage contamination.

Global

- Gradual increase in acceptance of carbonated soft drinks in other countries, such as India and China.
- Widely available electricity and increased ability to afford refrigerators in emerging countries and economies.

did a poor job of analyzing the competitor environment in China as well. These failures cost eBay hundreds of millions of dollars in investments made to enter and stay in the Chinese markets. In this case, eBay managers did not earn above-average returns.

The Firm's Industry and Competitor Environment

Michael Porter developed perhaps the most well-known model for analyzing a firm's industry and competitor environment.[28] This framework focuses on five **industry and competitor forces** (Porter's Five Forces) that can significantly influence the performance of organizations within an industry (see Exhibit 5.4). Porter's original research was designed to explain why some industries were more profitable as a whole than others and why some companies within industries were more profitable than other firms in the same industry. In general, research has supported the validity of this model.[29] Three of the five forces (the nature of rivalry, new entrants, and substitutes) involve competitors and the other two forces are customers and suppliers.

industry and competitor forces
five environmental forces (Porter's Five Forces) that can significantly influence the performance of organizations in an industry

The first dimension of this environment is the nature of rivalry among competitors. For example, it is important to understand the strength of competitors relative to your firm. If competitors are stronger, they are likely to take actions to gain market share from your firm. Thus, it might be important to focus on market segments that competitors avoid to build up the strengths of your firm. In the analysis, it is important to learn competitors' weaknesses. Their weaknesses may represent opportunities that you can exploit. The number of direct competitors also provides information on the nature of potential rivalry.

In large industries, such as automobile manufacturing, there are quite often different segments. And, the nature of rivalry can differ by segment. For example, in the subcompact segment of the auto industry, competition is largely based on price. However, in the luxury automobile segment, competition is primarily based on quality. Issues of safety, engineering, and comfort, dominate the ads for Mercedes, Lexus, BMW, and Infiniti.

A MANAGER'S CHALLENGE

Globalization

eBay Rethinks Its China Strategies

EBay invested over $100 million into the China market in 2005, seeking to dominate a market with an online population that is likely to exceed that of the United States in 2008 or 2009. However, eBay's decision in 2006 to close its Chinese auction business and give the control to Hong Kong billionaire Li Ka-shing's Tom Line indicates eBay failed to understand the Chinese market. EBay's attempt to use the same business model it used in the United States was unlikely to succeed. Thus, eBay, a global powerhouse in the Internet auction area, was a strategic failure, whereas its competitors, such as Gmarket, succeeded.

Gmarket, a Korean-based Web site that Yahoo! owns 10 percent of, is edging past eBay in the Internet auction business. In May 2006, Gmarket logged 17.2 million unique customers compared to 17.1 million for eBay. This is an amazing outcome because Gmarket only entered the Internet auction business in 2003. In 2005, Gmarket's revenues from transaction fees, advertising, and other earnings totaled $59.3 million—five times more than 2004. In addition, Gmarket gained even more access to capital with its NASDAQ public offering in July 2007.

First, Gmarket places less emphasis on an open auction format than eBay. Unlike eBay, it offers goods that can be sold at fixed prices, with an option to negotiate prices with a seller on an exclusive basis. Second, Gmarket makes certain those who sell their products on its site have the necessary marketing tools to properly promote their goods. An example of this is a marketing program called "lucky auction." Lucky auction gives buyers a chance to buy any product at a fraction of the market value. A seller invites consumers to bid within a certain price range (usually less than 10 percent of the retail value). Then, Gmarket's computer generates a random winner, though still giving the option to visitors to buy the product at a special offer price. Finally, Gmarket created incentive programs for retailers so they can offer online links to their own mini-home pages within the site. In addition, retailers can also issue discount coupons, run joint mileage point programs, and use an internal messaging service called G-messenger to chat instantly with sellers. Some shops on Gmarket also attract business by agreeing to donate $0.10 to a favorite charity every time a product is sold. Kim Chang Kwon, an Internet analyst at Daewoo Securities in Seoul, forecasted that Gmarkets' net profit for 2007 will jump 80 percent ($50 million), which is impressive growth.

Because the Asian market is becoming increasingly sophisticated and more choices are readily available, it is important for companies like eBay to be more connected to local markets and understand how cultural differences can play a vital role in dominating various markets. But eBay has not given up strategically repositioning itself in China. For example, eBay has decided to partner with a local company, Tom Online. By partnering with a local company, eBay managers hope to gain a better understanding of the local market and how to serve it better. In addition, the Chinese auction site of eBay has expanded a partnership with PayPal Beibao, the online payment services of eBay in China, and it will become the exclusive provider of text-based research advertising on Eachnet (eBay's Chinese auction site). With this alliance, eBay hopes to challenge other Chinese auction companies. Whether the help of this alliance or Tom Online will be able to turn around eBay's auction business in China is still unknown; hopefully these strategic changes will better position eBay in the Chinese market to be successful.

Sources: C. Nuttall and M. Dickie, "EBay's Strategy in China Shattered," *Financial Times*, December 19, 2006, www.ft.com; M. Ihlwan, "Gmarket Eclipses eBay in Asia," *Business Week*, June 28, 2006, www.businessweek.com; R. Hof, "EBay's China Challenge," *Business Week*, December 19, 2006, www.businessweek.com; C. Chandler, "An Upstart Takes on Mighty eBay," *Money*, November 15, 2004, www.cnnmoney.com; "EBay Expands Partnership Venture," *New York Times*, November 6, 2006, www.nytimes.com.

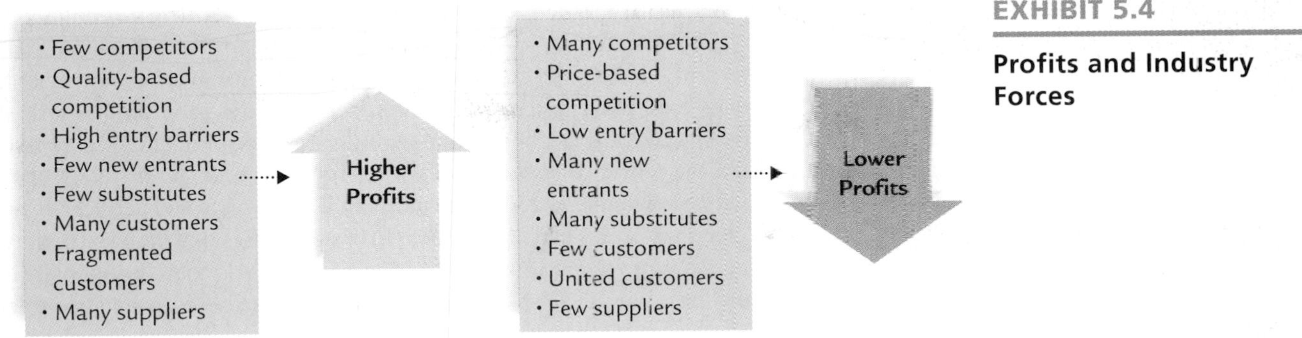

EXHIBIT 5.4

Profits and Industry Forces

The second dimension of the industry and competitor environment is the amount of difficulty firms encounter upon entering the industry. In general, new entrants will increase competition. Increased competition usually leads to lower profit margins because customers have more choices. Unless it is difficult and expensive for customers to switch from one company to another (this is typically called a *switching cost*), companies are forced to provide greater value to customers. American Airlines invented the frequent-flier program, to increase the switching costs. If customers decided to fly on a different airline, they lost the advantage of the upgrades or free flights offered by American Airlines. Where switching costs are low, competitors must offer greater value to attract and retain customers. This greater value usually comes from lowering profits.

entry barriers
the obstacles that make it difficult for firms to enter a particular type of business (industry).

Entry barriers are the obstacles that make it difficult for firms to enter a particular type of business. The larger the barriers, the more difficult it is to enter the business. So, larger barriers lead to fewer new entrants. For example, the barriers to enter the restaurant business are quite low. As a result, there are often many new restaurants opening each year (and many that fail as well). However, the barriers to enter the semiconductor business are high because a fabrication plant costs $6 billion to build.

A third environmental dimension is the potential for substitutes. This dimension focuses on the extent to which alternative products or services can substitute for existing products or services. Substitution is different from competition. It involves an alternative means of satisfying a customer's need. Generally, fewer available substitutes lead to greater profits. Different forms of transportation are substitutes (for example, bus, train, plane). People usually decide on which means of transportation based on the time required and cost.

CUSTOMERS Customers represent a critical component of an external environment. Organizations exist largely to serve customers, and, thus, managers focus their efforts on satisfying customer needs. As explained earlier in this chapter, when they provide customers value that is superior to the value provided by competitors, they achieve a competitive advantage. To the extent that there are relatively few customers and these customers are united, they have more power to demand lower prices, customized products or services, attractive financing terms from producers, and so on. The greater the power of customers, the more value they can extract. When customers are powerful, the firm is in a poor bargaining position, and its profits may suffer. When one customer buys a large amount of a firm's output, that customer also usually has power even if the firm has many other customers.

For example, Wal-Mart usually is in a powerful position with its suppliers because it purchases very large orders. It has power even with very large companies, such as Procter & Gamble, because of the amount it orders. This power was helpful to Aaron Green in making the adjustments to the purchase of landline telephones for sale in Wal-Mart stores.

Managers want to serve the firm's customers with superior value without allowing them to gain too much power.[30] The balance of power between the firm and its customers affects its ability to compete effectively and to earn above-average returns.

SUPPLIERS Managers must try to achieve a power balance with the firm's suppliers as well. If one or a few suppliers control a valuable good necessary for the products or services provided by the firm, the supplier will have considerable power. A supplier such as this likely can command a premium price or even limit access to the good. In this case, it may be difficult for the firm to earn an above-average return because of the high cost of the supplies. Regardless of the power of suppliers, it is important to build and maintain good relationships with them. Suppliers can contribute value to the products and services firms offer by customizing their processes and providing help in other ways that increase quality, improve the firm's marketing to its customers, lower its costs, and provide the supplies in a timely manner. Many firms have developed in-house units responsible for managing their strategic alliances with their partners, such as suppliers.[31]

Exhibit 5.5 presents a description of the industry and competitive environment for JetBlue. This exhibit provides examples of the different segments of this environment that you can analyze.

Internal Analysis

An analysis of the organization's internal capabilities is equally important to an analysis of its external environment. Of the various tools or frameworks for this purpose, the "value chain" approach proposed by Michael Porter is one of the most widely used.[32] The **value chain** consists of a set of key activities that directly produce or support the production of a firm's products and services offered to customers. Porter separates the internal components of a firm into five primary activities and four support activities (see Exhibit 5.5). The **primary activities** are those that are directly involved in the creation of a product or service and distributing it to the customer. As the label suggests, **support activities** facilitate the creation of the product or service and its transfer to the customer. Managers should assess the value these activities add to the product or service to gain an understanding of the firm's ability to compete. The absolute value of a product or service is a function of how many customers are willing to purchase the product or service and how much they are willing to pay for it. A firm makes a profit if it can provide a product or service whose value exceeds its costs. To determine where value is added in the firm's internal value chains, managers need to understand each of the nine activities in the chain, which we discuss next.

value chain
the set of key activities that directly produce or support the production of a firm's products and service offered to customers.

primary activities
activities that are directly involved in the creation of a product or service and getting it into the hands of the customer, and keeping it there

support activities
activities that facilitate the creation of a product or service and its transfer to the customer

INBOUND LOGISTICS This component of the value chain consists of activities that are designed to receive, store, and then disseminate various inputs related to the firm's products or services. Inbound logistics commonly includes raw materials, receiving, transportation,

EXHIBIT 5.5

A Description of the Industry and Competitive Environment of JetBlue

Competitors
- Rivalry
  Primarily based on price, which generally hurts performance.
  Many established and big players including profitable ones such as Southwest.
- New Entrants
  With $35 million anyone can start an airline; however, the frequency of past failure makes it less likely for new entrants.
- Substitutes
  As video conferencing gets better with faster connections, it may substitute for some face-to-face business meetings. It is less likely to substitute for leisure, tourist, or personal visit travel.

Customers
- Business travelers who want convenience.
- Leisure travelers who want low price.

Suppliers
- Airbus supplies all of JetBlue's planes (all are Airbus 320s).
- Many jet fuel suppliers, such as ExxonMobil.

All companies face a competitive environment characterized by their competitors, customers, and suppliers. Southwest became a celebrated airline by cutting costs and its ticket prices. Now other companies, including JetBlue, are using the same strategy.

inventory, and information. In the beer industry, inbound logistics involve getting hops, barley, and malt to the various brewing sites.

OPERATIONS The operations component of the value chain includes a variety of activities that transform inputs into the products and services of the firm. In addition, the operations segment of the value chain also includes activities (such as maintenance) that keep machines in working order. In the beer example, the firm's operational activities might involve producing the beer for different markets as well as the process of bottling and labeling the products.

OUTBOUND LOGISTICS Outbound logistics include activities that move the product or service from the firm to the customers. The beer producer needs to warehouse the finished product, process the orders, schedule delivery trucks, and distribute its products (either directly or through distributors) to stores, bars, ballparks, restaurants, and other places where it can be sold.

MARKETING AND SALES Marketing and sales activities are designed to inform potential customers about the products and services the firm has available and entice them to purchase them. The beer manufacturer, thus, advertises, promotes its products, and sells them.

SERVICE Service activities are designed to do what is necessary to ensure that the product satisfies the customer after the purchase and to increase the probability of a repeat purchase. Service activities may involve repair, supply of parts, installation, or product adjustments. They can also help the customer learn how to best use the product.

Each of these primary activities has associated costs. When done well, they enhance the firm's industry position and profitability if a customer is willing to pay more for them than they cost. The importance of the various activities changes depending on customer preferences. For example, in the fashion industry, customers often want the latest styles, colors, and fabrics soon after they are introduced. This places a premium on both inbound and outbound logistics to ensure that products can be delivered quickly to customers.

In addition to the five primary activities, there are four support activities. As illustrated in Exhibit 5.5, these activities cut across all five of the primary activities; that is, elements of a given support activity facilitate each of the five primary activities.

PROCUREMENT The activity of procuring usable and consumable assets is found in each of the primary activities. For example, not only must raw materials used in products be purchased in the inbound logistics activities, but also delivery trucks and scheduling software for the fleet must be purchased so that those materials can arrive for processing. The purchases of machinery and replacement parts are examples of specific procurement activities within operations. Firms often have purchasing departments, but various people, ranging from purchasing agents to secretaries, may handle procurement.

TECHNOLOGY DEVELOPMENT Technology development revolves around expertise and the tools or equipment related to the exercise of that expertise. The technology may be as simple or complicated as a supercomputer and related software. Although technology development concentrates on product development or process innovation, technology and the means by which a company applies it to tasks also has an effect on all five primary activities. Thus, technological capabilities play a key role in the value chain.[33]

HUMAN RESOURCE MANAGEMENT Given that no activity is completely removed from humans (humans even design and implement automatic processes and equipment), the process of acquiring, training, evaluating, compensating, and developing human resources is present in all five primary activities. Capable and motivated people can have a profound impact on all the activities of a firm so human resource management is a critical support activity. In service firms such as law, consulting, or accounting firms, the quality of the people is especially critical. Their expertise is the basis of the service provided. Therefore, this component of the value chain is critical to a service firm's fortune or failure.

FIRM INFRASTRUCTURE Although infrastructure usually brings plant, utilities, and equipment to mind, a firm's infrastructure has less to do with brick and mortar than with the administrative functions that support its primary activities. A firm's infrastructure consists of its planning, finance, accounting, legal, government relations, and other activities supplied by its various primary activities. For example, a firm is likely to need legal information on worker-safety standards for its operations department and legal information about "truth in advertising" for its marketing and sales departments.

All support activities have associated costs. Support activities enhance the firm's market position and profitability to the extent that they assist primary activities and contribute to final products or services that customers value. The importance of the support activities also changes depending on customer preferences. For example, in the fashion industry, customers' preferences for the latest styles, colors, and fabrics may increase the importance of planning information in the value chain. Planning information related to forecasting trends, buying seasons, purchasing cycles, and customer preferences would be valuable, in this case. Customers' preferences might also increase the importance of the firm's technology-development support activity. For example, technology that allows yarn to be dyed after it has been knit into sweaters rather than before could add value. This is exactly what Benetton of Italy did so that it could incorporate the latest color trends demanded by consumers as late in the manufacturing process as possible.

The value chain framework facilitates evaluation of the resources held and their ability to deliver value to the customer. The value chain framework enables a systematic and comprehensive analysis of the firm's activities.

LEVERAGING THE VALUE CHAIN The first step in managing the value chain for greater profits and performance is to determine where in the value chain there is potential to add the *greatest* value. Returning to the beer example, let's say that German customers value a rich-tasting beer and are less sensitive to price. If the quality of the beer's ingredients determines the flavor of the beer, procuring the highest-quality ingredients is a critical activity for the firm. Further, let's suppose that identifying high-quality ingredients is primarily a function of experienced buyers. Thus, the firm's human resource management systems of recruiting, selecting, and training these ingredient buyers must be superior. The power of the value chain model is that by segmenting the firm's business activities, managers can better understand the important linkages among them. However, managers must perform an analysis to identify which activities add the most value, and which linkages are the most important.

Recent research has suggested that to fully understand a firm's competitive position and advantage, not only do you need to analyze the firm's value chain but how suppliers, distributors, and other business partners fit into a "value net."[34] Because of today's increasingly tight connections among firms and suppliers, distributors, and other business partners, the strengths and weaknesses of one's partners throughout the entire value network affect the competitive position and advantage of a firm.[35]

EVALUATING THE MANAGEMENT OF RESOURCES Analyzing the firm's resources and capabilities places emphasis on building and exploiting the internal strengths of the company.[36] So, managers should develop valuable capabilities and use them to provide products and services to customers that are superior in value. These capabilities might be in technology, marketing, or another area of importance in the industry. Critical issues regard how managers obtain and bundle resources to develop capabilities, and how they then leverage those capabilities.[37] This suggests that managers should invest in strategic resources that have special value.[38] For example, in professional service firms, such as law and accounting firms, managers should acquire the very best lawyers and accountants available in the labor market.[39] Managers have to deploy the resources in the firm's resource portfolio.[40] Usually managers have to combine different resources to create a capability. For example, a capability to manufacture a product combines physical resources, such as plant and equipment, technology, and human capital.

Resources must be in a continual state of development. Some refer to this as dynamic capabilities.[41] As a final step, managers need to leverage the capabilities that they build in order to use the strategy formulated to earn above-average returns.[42] Some of the capabilities developed may become core competencies for the company.

core competence
focuses on an interrelated set of activities that can deliver competitive advantage in the short term and into the future

A **core competence** is an interrelated set of activities that can deliver competitive advantage in the short term and long term. Competencies are "core" when they (1) provide access to a wide variety of markets, (2) significantly contribute to perceived customer benefits of the end products or services, and (3) are difficult for competitors to imitate.[43] As an example, Honda believes that one of its core competencies is the technology behind its manufacturing of combustion engines. First, combustion engines have the potential to apply to a wide variety of markets and products. Honda uses its technology in the manufacture of motorcycles, cars, scooters, lawn mowers, snowblowers, and small electricity generators, among others. Second, customers value the performance of the combustion engines in these products. For example, better combustion can result in significantly better acceleration in cars and motorcycles. Third, combustion technology is hard to imitate. This is partly why Honda moved its engines into various car racing leagues such as Indy and even Formula One.

Integrating Internal and External Analyses

Although a variety of tools and techniques can help integrate the internal and external analyses, we focus on one of the most well-known and enduring approaches, SWOT analyses.

SWOT analysis
an analysis of the firm's strengths, weaknesses, opportunities, and threats (SWOT) to its continued operation

A **SWOT analysis** approach to integrate the separate analyses requires managers to consider their firm's strengths (S) and weaknesses (W), along with opportunities (O) and threats (T) for its continued operation. SWOT analysis is a basic framework for integrating the results of the analyses that guide the formulation of an appropriate strategy. In conducting a SWOT analysis, the firm should identify and evaluate its strengths and weaknesses. In doing so, understanding how to manage resources and core competencies can be of great help. Alternatively, managers can use the value chain framework previously discussed to analyze the firm's strengths and weaknesses. For example, what parts of the value chain does the firm do well, such as sourcing and marketing? What does it perform poorly, such as customer service or public relations?

The next step in the SWOT analysis focuses on the external environment. First, identifying the opportunities for the firm is important. For example, what products or businesses are about to enter the growth stage? What countries have conditions conducive to the growth of particular products or businesses? Are there new products that could become substitutes for the firm's products or new entrants into the market that could constitute serious threats?

The important insights of a SWOT analysis come after comparing and matching the organization's strengths and weaknesses and the environment's opportunities and threats. For example, Wal-Mart currently has many international opportunities. Wal-Mart's strengths include the ability to acquire, distribute, and sell large volumes of products to customers at low prices. However, as a result of its strong focus on the U.S. market, very few Wal-Mart managers have experience or knowledge of foreign markets. Fortunately for Wal-Mart, few competitors can capture immediately the new international opportunities that exist; however Wal-Mart must pursue international expansion opportunities because Carrefour, a French discount retailer, is also expanding internationally. Wal-Mart has responded to international opportunities. In 2007, Wal-Mart had more than 6,700 stores in 14 countries serving approximately 175 million customers per week. Wal-Mart knows that if an opportunity to make money exists in these foreign markets, a competitor will seek it out. To effectively respond, Wal-Mart has used partners with knowledge of specific international markets, developed managers internally, hired people who can help it expand internationally, and sometimes acquired existing operations in various countries.

Setting Strategic Objectives

Unless an organization translates its strategic intent and mission into specific performance goals, they will remain statements of good intentions and unrealized achievements. Furthermore, an analysis of the environment is an academic exercise unless the implications find their way into strategic objectives. **Strategic objectives** translate the strategic intent and mission of the firm into concrete and measurable goals. Setting strategic objectives is a critical step in the strategic management process because it facilitates a firm's ability to (1) allocate resources appropriately, (2) reach a shared understanding of priorities, (3) delegate responsibilities, and (4) hold people accountable for results.[44] Specifically, strategic objectives might address any of the following issues:

strategic objectives
objectives that turn the strategic intent and mission of a firm into concrete and measurable goals

- Revenue growth
- Profitability
- Customer satisfaction
- Market share
- Financial returns (for example, return on equity, return on assets)
- Technological leadership
- Cash flow
- Operating efficiency (for example, costs per unit, expense per employee)

It is important to note that strategic objectives differ from other performance objectives in one fundamental way: Strategic objectives are longer term in nature. They are not yearly objectives or goals. They represent targets the company aims for over the long term (typically five years or so). Although setting strategic objectives is critical, much of the time managers actually spend on strategic management is taken up in the subsequent steps of the process. These involve analyzing the organization's internal environment, formulating a strategy, developing an implementation plan, and monitoring the results.

The Strategic Management Process: Formulating a Strategy

There are at least three levels of strategy—corporate, business-level or competitive strategy, and functional or unit strategy.[45] The corporate-level strategy determines what business or businesses the firm wishes to operate. In other words, this level of strategy determines the markets in which the firm will compete.[46] The business-level strategy determines how a firm will compete in each of these markets.[47] Unit-level strategies focus on the operations of each function or unit and their contribution to help the firm achieve a competitive advantage.

While all levels of strategy are important, the most important for achieving a competitive advantage is the business-level strategy.[48] This is the focus of our analysis.

In many ways, the essence of formulating a competitive strategy is determining how the company is going to compete and achieve its strategic objectives, its mission, and ultimately its strategic vision. Next, we explain a set of generic strategies for achieving a competitive advantage.

Generic Strategies for Obtaining a Competitive Advantage

The two most-discussed generic strategies are cost leadership and differentiation.[49]

COST LEADERSHIP STRATEGY The **cost leadership strategy** involves competing by striving to be the lowest-cost producer of a product or provider of a service. Usually firms using this strategy charge slightly less than industry-average prices. To the extent a firm has lower costs than its competitors (for example, cost leadership) and can command prices similar to its competitors, it can achieve above-average profits. For a USB drive manufacturer to obtain above-average returns using a cost leadership strategy requires that it have lower costs than the industry average (for example, $7.50 with the industry average of $10) and provide the quality product that allows the firm to charge near the industry average price (for example, $15). In this case, the firm would make a profit of $7.50 instead of the industry average of $5. It is important to understand that the cost leadership strategy does not necessarily imply price leadership, meaning offering the lowest price. For example, if the cost leader had costs of $7.50 per disk but also charged the lowest price ($12.50), it would earn average returns (that is, the industry average of $5) per product sold. However, if its product quality was equal to competitors' products, it would likely sell many more products at that price and gain a large market share. Thus, the profit margin on each product does not fully project the value of a particular strategy.

cost leadership strategy
a strategy that involves being the lowest-cost producer of a product or provider of a service while charging only slightly less than industry average prices

There are a variety of means to achieve cost leadership. The use of special technology has become a common means. For example, managers might invest in the latest technology to reduce defects and increase the production "yield" (percentage of good chips manufactured) thereby reducing the average cost per chip. Managers can also gain cost leadership through economies of scale. For example, increasing overall output across the firm's factories can reduce cost per unit manufactured. Amazon.com has tried to achieve economies of scale (with better financial results more recently than at first) by selling more products through its existing sales channel (its Web site).

The Mexican company Cemex has used technology in a traditionally low-tech business to help it achieve a cost leadership position at home, and in international markets as well. Executives at Cemex have used information technology to improve efficiency and performance. To both reduce costs and use their assets more efficiently and effectively, executives use computers and global positioning system receivers in every cement truck to achieve more efficient routing and more precise delivery times. Previously, any number of problems could delay deliveries, including bad weather and traffic. Combining precise information about the trucks' whereabouts with plant output and customer orders, managers can calculate more precisely which truck it should use and how to reroute trucks if necessary. The system allows Cemex's managers to accurately direct trucks to be within 20 minutes of their delivery time instead of three hours.

The advanced state of the firm's internal information systems has allowed Cemex executives to expand beyond the borders of Mexico. Cemex executives have implemented a strategy of expansion into emerging markets in 14 countries, including Spain, Venezuela, Thailand, Egypt, and Puerto Rico. The company is now the third-largest cement producer in the world.[50]

DIFFERENTIATION STRATEGY Managers pursuing a **differentiation strategy** seek to make their product or service different from those of competitors on dimensions valued by customers. Achieving differentiation allows them to command a premium price. If managers can also keep costs at approximately the industry average, the premium price will allow the firm to earn above-average profits. For example, assume that a USB drive manufacturer was able to offer greater memory without substantially increasing the costs of

differentiation strategy
a strategy to gain a competitive advantage by making a product or service different from those of your competitors

manufacturing the disks and, as a consequence, could command a premium price (say $17.50 instead of $15) but keep its costs near the industry average of $10. In this case, the firm would make a profit of $7.50 per disk instead of the industry average of $5. Any number of characteristics might provide the basis for differentiation.

There are a variety of ways to differentiate products and services—style, quality, reliability, speed, fashion, durability, and so on. The key is to add differentiation that customers (or at least an important segment of customers) value at a cost that produces a superior margin. In other words, the cost increase to add the differentiation has to be less than the price premium customers will pay for the differentiation. If it costs you 20 percent more to make your product more reliable, but customers will only pay 20 percent more for this differentiation, then it will not generate above-average profits.

Starbucks is known for charging a premium price for its coffee. To do so, it has special means of differentiating the product it provides customers. In particular, it differentiates the flavor of its coffee by buying premium coffee beans and using a specially formulated roasting process. In this way, it differentiates the product through specific characteristics of the product. Yet, Starbucks also differentiates what it provides to the customer in other ways. Starbucks's executives refer to it as the "experience." The intent is to provide excellent service to customers. So, it trains service providers well and rewards them for providing high-quality service. Finally, because of the quality coffee, excellent service, and pleasant atmosphere in Starbucks's stores, Starbucks's brand has value as well. So, Starbucks differentiates through its product, service, experience, and brand reputation.[51] Some of the differentiation comes from product characteristics (the flavor of the coffee), and other dimensions of the differentiation come from related but less direct factors (the Starbucks experience and its brand reputation).

Firms seeking to differentiate their products often invest in research and develop and emphasize the importance of learning new capabilities in order to stay ahead of their competition. However, the firms must also have the capability to exploit the knowledge they gained and the innovative products they developed. Thus, they have to distribute their

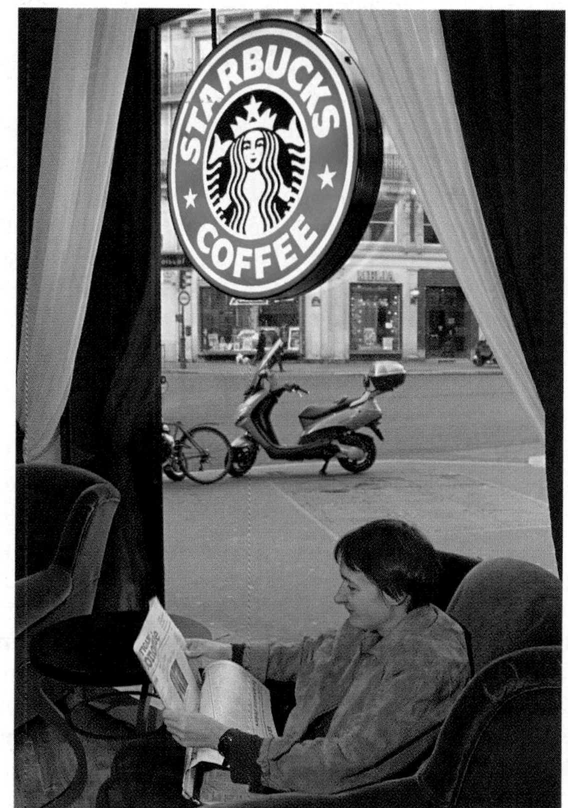

Starbucks differentiates itself from its competitors on a number of fronts: via its quality products and service, its brand reputation, and the special Starbucks "experience" it creates for customers.

products effectively and convince customers of the valuable characteristics of new products introduced to the market.[52] Yet, firms known for differentiating their products tend to attract competitors trying to imitate, or differentiate, their own products in similar locations.[53] Because of this fact, firms must not only "run harder and differently than their competitors, they must also run smarter."[54]

Using a differentiation strategy is risky, though. Hyundai found this out the hard way after it decided to change from a cost leadership strategy to a differentiation strategy. At one time, Hyundai produced smaller, low-cost (and often low-quality) automobiles. It later invested a substantial amount of its resources to change its products in order to compete with Toyota, Nissan, and Honda. As a result, Hyundai was able to successfully develop, manufacture, and market a high-quality automobile. However, despite receiving quality ratings in excess of its major competitors, it was unable to achieve the sales increases needed to achieve desired profits. As a result, Hyundai's profit declined by 34 percent in 2006. Unfortunately, despite high-quality and significant advertising, it has not been able to change its brand reputation in the minds of consumers.[55]

To be successful with a differentiation strategy, firms must continuously search for market opportunities and develop new products to exploit those opportunities.[56] To do so often requires firms to be bold and innovative in all areas of their business.[57] That is, they must simultaneously search for new opportunities and take actions (innovate) to gain and sustain competitive advantages.[58] This is the approach A. G. Lafley, the CEO of Procter & Gamble, and Jeffrey Immelt, the CEO of GE, advocate and use.[59]

STRATEGIC SCOPE A firm can limit the scope of its strategy (its **strategic scope**) by focusing on a specific segment of customers. Although the restriction reduces the total volume and revenue the firm can obtain from a product, it does not necessarily affect its ability to earn above-average returns. For example, Ferrari differentiates its product based on style and performance and focuses on a very narrow segment of customers (not many people can afford a $250,000 car). A narrow scope strategy can also be applied to cost leadership. To the extent that the cost leader can provide products or services sufficiently valuable to command prices near the industry average for some targeted segment of customers, it can achieve above-average profits. Thus, firms can follow a **focused differentiation strategy** or a **focused cost leadership strategy**.

strategic scope
the scope of a firm's strategy or breadth of focus

To succeed when pursuing a **focus strategy**, there must be significant differences among the firm's targeted customers or among geographical segments of its customers. A **customer segment** is essentially a group of customers who share similar preferences or place a similar value on product features. For example, in selling cars, clear segments exist. Some people value gas mileage while others value performance. Thus, manufacturers of a high-performance sports car focus on a different segment of customers from those who prefer small economy cars. Geographical segments may also be a factor. For example, customers in different locations may prefer different product features: In southern locales, people demand more cars with air conditioning. In northern locales, they demand more four-wheel drive vehicles to cope with snow. Customers in hot and humid climates prefer clothes made with cotton while those in drier and cooler climates prefer clothes made with wool.

focus strategy
a strategy that targets a particular market segment. The strategy may be a focused cost leadership strategy or a focused differentiation strategy

customer segment
a group of customers who have similar preferences or place similar value on product features

Commonly, firms that follow a focus strategy are more likely to make only incremental improvements in their products over time.[60] But, managers pursuing any one of the four generic strategies (see Exhibit 5.6) must understand, a current competitive advantage may be obsolete in the near future. Firms that offer more products in a particular market segment have higher survival rates. In other words, they reduce their risks by offering more product variations.[61] Regardless, to have a sustainable competitive advantage, managers must continually build a series of temporary competitive advantages, replacing old ones with new ones.

The pharmaceutical industry requires differentiation to be a major competitor (unless firms want to produce generic drugs, in which case, imitation and cost leadership are more appropriate strategic actions. As explained in A Manager's Challenge, "Major Changes Ahead for Merck," to develop new drugs that differentiated the firm from its competitors.

EXHIBIT 5.6

The Value Chain

Source: Adapted from Michael Porter, *Competitive Advantage* (New York: Free Press, 1985).

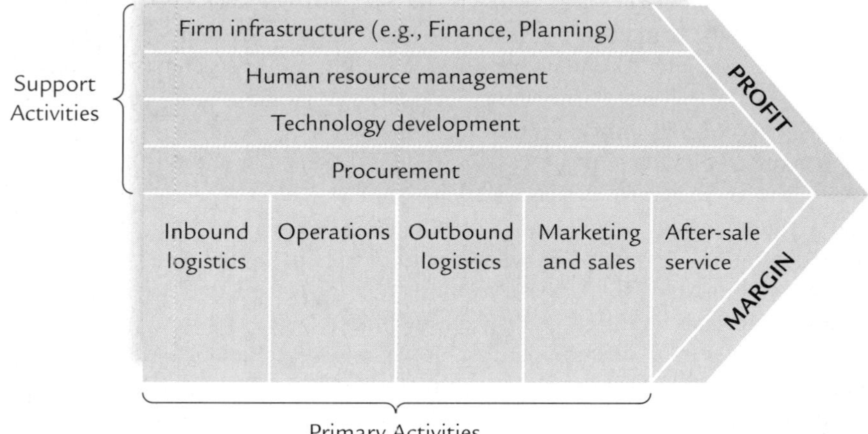

As such, it lost market share and experienced many problems. The company's new CEO, Dick Clark, is making major changes to enhance Merck's capability to differentiate its product lines from competitors, providing superior value to customers and regaining its competitive advantage. To create this value for customers while simultaneously managing resources efficiently to earn above-average returns is a major challenge. Clark must increase Merck's investments in R&D while simultaneously reducing costs. His initial efforts appear to be successful, though. However, we will need to observe Merck over the long term to see if his strategies are sustainable.

Other Generic Strategies

There are at least two other important "generic" strategies that managers can use to gain a competitive advantage—an integrated differentiation-cost leadership strategy and a multipoint competition strategy. We examine each in turn.

integrated differentiation-cost leadership strategy
a set of actions designed to differentiate the firm's product in the marketplace while simultaneously maintaining a low-cost position relative to its competitors.

INTEGRATED DIFFERENTIATION-COST LEADERSHIP STRATEGY An **integrated differentiation-cost leadership strategy** involves a set of actions designed to differentiate the product in the marketplace while simultaneously maintaining a low-cost position relative to competitors. This strategy is difficult to develop and implement effectively because some of the objectives of both strategies often conflict with one another. For example, achieving differentiation may require substantial investments in R&D to develop innovative products and in advertising to inform the market of the benefits of new products. It is difficult to achieve economies of scale when continuously introducing new products to the market. Additionally, a cost leadership strategy often emphasizes efficient manufacturing, making retooling to produce new products a challenge.

Michael Porter once recommended against such a strategy referring to it as "stuck in the middle"—firms trying to achieve both are likely to do neither and become stuck in the middle. Yet the globally competitive landscape increasingly requires that firms build high-quality and unique products of value and do so with an efficient cost structure. In some industries, firms are unable to survive without doing so. Having access to global markets and using sophisticated information technology can help firms achieve economies of scale and recoup major R&D investments, making this strategy feasible. Target Stores use this strategy by building a strong, distinctive brand for quality goods while competing with other department stores, such as Wal-Mart, that focus on low costs.[62]

multipoint competition strategy
a strategy that involves competing with firms across markets by using strengths in one market to overcome weaknesses in another market.

MULTIPOINT COMPETITION STRATEGY A **multipoint competition strategy** involves competing with firms across markets by using strengths in one market to overcome weaknesses in another market.[63] The competition can occur across product markets, geographic markets, or both. For example, at one time UPS was the market leader in ground shipping and delivery whereas FedEx was the market leader in overnight delivery. However, UPS entered the overnight delivery market, and FedEx bought trucks and other ground shipping

A MANAGER'S CHALLENGE

Change

Major Changes Ahead for Merck

With Merck facing about 265 potential Vioxx class-action lawsuits alleging personal injury and economic losses, with a number of their blockbuster products' patents expiring in the next two years, and with investors pressing for more cost-cutting strategies, Merck is redefining how it does business. In May 2006, the drugmaker hired Richard (Dick) Clark as the new chief executive officer. Clark's charge was to revive the company from a series of missed targets, reduce operations to cover the costs of litigation over Vioxx, and develop new blockbuster products to counteract the anticipated losses from high-earning drugs with expiring patents, such as Zocor and Fosamax.

The first step identified by Clark was to radically shift the company culture and change how employees work together to instill greater accountability in the various departments. Clark wants to create aggressive, disciplined, and efficient operations. He feels that a good strategy can be positive, but without the appropriate culture and systems needed to successfully implement those strategies, the strategy will fail. Central to this change is a commitment to talk directly with employees, and investors, about how he wants to change Merck's culture and how he plans to reach the firm's ambitious earning goals through 2010.

Essentially, Clark is trying to create "One Merck," where "silos" are eliminated and the company is more collaborative. In September 2006, the company asked employees to provide input on a potential new generic drug business. The review concluded that the company should remain a pure drug company. Clark felt that this process was essential because it showed that Merck would operate in an atmosphere where anyone could question openly the company's assumptions and goals. Clark continues to launch several initiatives to boost communication, including briefing employees around the world through Webcasts. He feels the only way to improve management's credibility is to share the company's goals with all employees.

A second step is the targeted acquisition of a "critical priority." A critical priority is a company with revenues that could immediately help Merck, plus provide a complimentary pipeline of products. Merck is searching for more established businesses, particularly in the biotech industry. For example, Merck paid $1.1 billion in December to buy Sirna, a small biotech company based in San Francisco. This acquisition was due to Sirna's gene-silencing technology that holds promise for developing cancer and other drugs. Merck is targeting only 9 areas of research at Sirna, as opposed to 32. Merck feels it would be better to focus on specific areas, like cancer and heart disease, rather than try to cover all the bases.

Merck is also examining ways to drastically cut costs, particularly in the marketing area. In addition, Clark plans to globally restructure the company, cutting 7,000 jobs, which equates to 10 percent of its workforce. Merck expects that this workforce reduction will save the company $500 million in 2007 and another $100 million in 2008.

Lastly, Merck's focus is on developing new products because the patents on two of its best-selling drugs will expire in the next few years, making them vulnerable to generic competing drugs. Merck's "niacin project," in essence, is designed to tweak niacin, a well-known vitamin that raises "good" cholesterol. The hope is that this will be a new blockbuster drug for the company. In addition, Merck will restructure manufacturing operations, and it will rely more heavily on technology as opposed to sales representation to market drugs. It will apply Six Sigma, a quality control system, in research to speed drug development, and elsewhere in the company. Clark expects that with the help of two other new products, Gardasil (a vaccine for cervical cancer) and Januvia (a diabetes drug), and the cost savings, Merck should enjoy a 10 percent growth in annual earnings.

Clark admits that Merck failed to heed signs that it needed to quickly change how it did business and that it failed to focus on key business metrics. But with these new strategies, Merck strives to change with the industry and plans on using different business models to be more successful. With these initial changes, it appears that Wall Street is becoming modestly optimistic about Merck. A growing sense that Merck can weather the legal problems caused by Vioxx and that Clark's new strategies will work in the pharmaceutical industry, helped in early 2007.

Sources: C. Bowe, "Clark Sets Out Strategy to Change Merck," *Financial Times*, March 26, 2006, www.ft.com; A. Barrett, "Merck's Plan for Relief," *Business Week*, December 13, 2005, www.businessweek.com; L. A. Johnson, "Merck Net Drops 58 Percent," *Business Week*, January 30, 2007, www.businessweek.com; C. Bowe, "Man out to Shake Up Merck," *Financial Times*, March 26, 2006, www.ft.com; A. Barrett, "Merck: Out of the Ivory Tower," *Business Week*, March 6, 2006, www.businessweek.com; L. A. Johnson, "Merck, Wyeth Shares Fall After Reports," ABC News, January 30, 2007, www.abcnews.com.

assets to compete in that market. Thus, they compete with each other in both markets and also compete in many geographic markets, domestic and international. Recently, they have engaged in fierce competition in China in both service markets.[64] UPS has also been gaining market share by becoming a logistics company and making value chain activities, particularly for small- and medium-sized businesses operating in foreign markets.[65]

The Strategic Management Process: Strategy Implementation

After formulating a strategy, a manager must effectively implement it for the desired results to materialize. Some evidence indicates that an average strategy superbly implemented is better than a great strategy poorly implemented.[66] Consequently, strategy implementation is at least as important as strategy formulation.

Perhaps the most widely used strategy implementation framework is that developed by one of the largest and best-known strategy consulting firms, McKinsey Consulting. The framework is called the Seven S approach. About 20 years ago, McKinsey discovered that when many of its clients implemented the strategic plans that it recommended, clients' performance often declined. Essentially, McKinsey discovered that the reason clients were doing worse when they implemented the new strategies was because their clients implemented the strategies within old structures, cultures, skills, styles, and staff. These old activities and context of the organization were inconsistent with the new strategy. So, the new strategy often was ineffective. The key to successful strategy implementation is having an internal organization that is consistent with and supportive of the strategy.

If the strategy calls for entering new product or geographic markets, firms can choose to do so organically, through acquisitions, or by using strategic alliances. Organic entries involve developing the new products internally (this requires a strong R&D unit) or establishing operations in new locations, often referred to as Greenfield ventures. But, in some markets, acquisitions may be more attractive as a means of entry.[67] For example, even Wal-Mart has used acquisitions to enter or expand in some foreign markets such as the United Kingdom and Germany. Acquisitions not only provide immediate access to new markets, they also provide instant knowledge about these markets.[68] Perhaps one of the most popular and common approaches to entering new markets (and obtaining reliable sources of supplies) is strategic alliances. Although popular, alliances are not easy to manage and are not always successful.[69] However, they can be successful when balanced with the firm's own internal development and an alliance partner from which the firm can learn or gain access to valuable resources.[70]

In A Manager's Challenge, "Not All Strategies Work: The Home Depot Experiment," seems that Bob Nardelli attempted to change the firm's strategy from differentiation to an integrated differentiation-cost leadership strategy. However, neither was accomplished effectively so Home Depot appears to be "stuck in the middle." He emphasized managing costs through centralization decision making and replacing full-time staff in the stores with part-time employees. But, these actions reduced the entrepreneurial actions and, thus, decreased the differentiation. In turn, these actions allowed competitors such as Lowe's to increase their share of the market at Home Depot's expense. There was need for closer monitoring and evaluation of the outcomes of these changes. It also appears that Nardelli ignored the feedback from the market. As a result, Home Depot suffered, and Nardelli eventually lost his job.

Monitoring and Evaluating the Strategy's Implementation

The final step in the strategic management process is evaluation. Evaluation and feedback can improve the performance of individuals and also enhance the organization's performance. When a small number of managers are responsible for the organization's strategic, tactical, or operational objectives, their individual performance evaluations can often provide a rough indication of how the organization is doing. If the individual's personal objectives are tied directly to the firm's operational objectives, and they are all meeting or exceeding their goals, the organization as a whole is likely meeting its operational objectives.

A MANAGER'S CHALLENGE

Change

Not All Strategies Work: The Home Depot Experiment

In recent years, Home Depot has made several strategic changes. In 2007, it also changed its executive leadership. The company and CEO Bob Nardelli "mutually" agreed that he would resign. Institutional shareholders called for Home Depot's top executives and board members to be held accountable for manipulating stock options and for the sluggish stock price in an otherwise positive stock market. Nardelli's resignation from Home Depot highlighted the company's failure to properly manage the dissatisfaction of shareholders. For most of 2006, investors publicly stated their opposition to the sizable pay increase given to Nardelli despite a slump in the company's performance. Shareholders also were skeptical of Home Depot's strategy to expand internationally and in markets outside of retailing.

Under Nardelli's leadership, Home Depot had developed a strategic plan to improve the firm's financial performance following a slowdown in sales and a slump in the company's stock price. Some of the initiatives of the plan included reorganizing management so that Nardelli had more direct involvement in the company's retail business. A layer of management was removed that previously had distanced him from the day-to-day operations. He felt that more direct and focused management was necessary. Under this structure, Home Depot's five regional presidents in the United States, Canada, and Mexico reported directly to the CEO. Nardelli also eliminated a sizable number of full-time positions and replaced them with part-time staff to help reduce costs.

Another strategic initiative involved expanding beyond consumer retailing into the wholesale market by supplying building and maintenance materials to professional customers. Home Depot also initiated plans to enter the fast growing Chinese retail market. The company's top executives thought that if Home Depot could conquer international markets such as China, it would help "jump-start" the company's stock price.

Nardelli also invested $1 billion to centralize the control of Home Depot's information technology. To help generate the desired data, it implemented self-checkout aisles and inventory management systems. Nardelli wanted to be able to measure all actions taken in the company and hold managers accountable for meeting "their numbers." One of his favorite sayings was "facts are friendly." He implemented a military management model, which was a key part of the move to reshape Home Depot into a more centralized organization. For example, all employees were ranked on the basis of four performance metrics: financial, operational, customer, and people skills.

Unfortunately, the organization never fully embraced Nardelli's leadership style. Many Home Depot employees could not embrace his military-style leadership and resented the replacement of many thousands of full-time store workers with legions of part-time employees. Some of their managers describe a demoralized staff and say a "culture of fear" caused customer services to wane.

The CEO's reputation also suffered because of Wall Street's affection for the firm's smaller archrival, Lowe's, whose stock price has increased more than 200 percent since 2000, while Home Depot's shares declined 6 percent in the same time period. Many felt that Nardelli's plan lacked a customer focus. Nardelli alienated customers by cutting experienced staff, which led to persistent complaints that there weren't enough workers in Home Depot stores to help the do-it-yourself customers.

In addition, Nardelli's relationship with Wall Street analysts was often poor. Wall Street analysts were unhappy with his strategy moving away from its core focus. Wall Street wanted results, but the lack of positive outcomes led to a low stock price. And the low stock price angered shareholders. Although the company spent $20.3 billion to buy back shares and issue dividends under Nardelli, investors experienced no gains in their share value. Nardelli's high pay package—more than $200 million in salary, bonuses, stock options, restricted stock, and other perks over the course of six years—exacerbated investors' frustration.

Even though Nardelli brought operational efficiencies that were needed, he failed to keep the entrepreneurial spirit alive in the stores. Despite his departure, Home Depot still faces the major strategic, financial, and management issues that remain.

Sources: H. R. Weber, "Home Depot General Counsel Resigns," *Business Week*, February 1, 2007, www.businessweek.com; A. Wardin, "Home Depot Unveils Shake-up," *Financial Times*, October 13, 2006, www.ft.com; "Home Depot Pay," *Financial Times*, January 24, 2007, www.ft.com; J. Politi, "Company Failed to Quell Shareholder Anger," *Financial Times*, January 3, 2007, www.ft.com; B. Grow, "Renovating Home Depot," *Business Week*, March 6, 2006, www.businessweek.com; B. Grow, "Out at Home Depot," *Business Week*, January 15, 2007, www.businessweek.com; J. Creswell and M. Barbaro, "Home Depot Ousts Chief," *International Herald Tribune*, January 4, 2007 www.iht.com.

Managerial Challenges from the Front Line

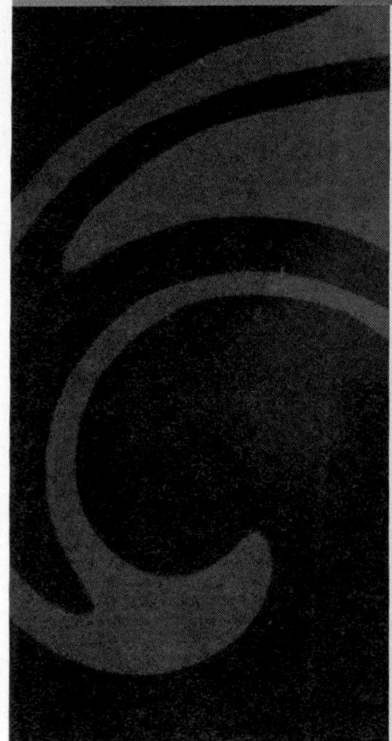

The Rest of the Story

Aaron Green's analysis showed that there was little differentiation across the different brands of landline telephones provided by Wal-Mart's suppliers. Thus, he decided that Wal-Mart could consolidate and use fewer suppliers. In so doing, select suppliers could sell a greater number of telephones and thereby maintain prices that were better for Wal-Mart overall in terms of its profits.

Green accomplished this by separating Wal-Mart's telephone business into segments: entry-level, mid-level, and high-level products. He then assigned one supplier to each level. This gave Wal-Mart's customers the variety they sought, and also ended suppliers' efforts to undercut each others' prices. As a result, Green was able to project the sales levels for each level thereby helping each supplier to manage its inventory and costs more effectively. The consolidation also allowed Wal-Mart to be more aggressive in its marketing and pricing, which helped it sell more telephones and earn a greater profit on each. The changes reduced costs by 30 percent, profits went up by 20 percent, and Wal-Mart's return on its investment in its landline telephone business increased by 50 percent. Thus, the changes were a rousing success.

Most organizations carry out annual or even quarterly organizational performance evaluations. Typically, the strategic results of these evaluations are given to the more senior executives, and the operational results are disseminated principally to lower-level managers. Similar to individual feedback, a company performs an organizational performance evaluation to reinforce efforts that have contributed to the desired results and to correct those that have not.

Summary

- Fundamentally, the objective of strategic management is to determine, create, and maintain competitive advantage. A competitive advantage is the ability of a firm to provide value to customers that exceeds what competitors can provide. It is created by having and managing resources to provide goods and services that provide superior value, rare, difficult to imitate, and nonsubstitutable.
- The strategic management process begins with the development of the strategic vision and mission for the organization. After establishing these, the organization should analyze its external environment and its internal resources. The results of these analyses help to identify the organization's strengths and weaknesses and the opportunities and threats in the external environment. The strategic objectives are developed and the strategy is formulated to achieve the objectives. Finally, the strategy is implemented.
- Analyzing the firm's external environment includes examining the general environment and the company's industry and competitor environment. The general environment consists of sociocultural, technological, economic, political-legal, and global forces. Analyzing the industry and competitor environment focuses on the five forces identified by Michael Porter. Three of the five forces (the nature of rivalry, new entrants, and substitutes) involve competitors; the other two forces are customers and suppliers.
- A comprehensive internal analysis of the firm's resources can be accomplished using the value chain. The value chain consists of a set of key activities that directly

produce or support the production of a firm's products and service offered to customers. Porter separates the internal components of a firm into five primary activities and four support activities. The primary activities are those directly involved in the creation of a product or service and distributing it to the customer. By contrast, support activities facilitate the creation of the product or service and its transfer to the customer.

- A SWOT (strengths, weaknesses, opportunities and threats) analysis can be used to integrate and interpret the results of the internal and external analyses. The SWOT analysis leads to the establishment of the firm's strategic objectives and the formulation of its strategy.
- Setting strategic objectives is a critical step in the strategic management process because it facilitates a firm's ability to (1) allocate resources appropriately, (2) reach a shared understanding of priorities, (3) delegate responsibilities, and (4) hold people accountable for results.
- The business-level strategies from which the firm can select include cost leadership, differentiation, focused cost leadership, focused differentiation, integrated differentiation-cost leadership, and a multipoint competitive strategy. The choice of strategy depends on market opportunities, competitors' actions, and the firm's resources and capabilities. The integrated strategy has been facilitated by globalization and technology and simultaneously sometimes necessitated by global competition. The multipoint strategy allows firms to compete with others across product and geographic markets.
- After formulating a strategy, managers must effectively implement it for the desired results to materialize. Oftentimes, in addition to organic growth, firms use strategic alliances and acquisitions to enter new markets. After implementation, managers need to monitor the outcomes to see if adjustments are necessary in the strategy or its implementation.

Key Terms

above-average returns 117
competitive advantage 116
core competence 129
cost leadership strategy 131
customer segment 133
entry barriers 125
focus strategy 133
focused cost leadership strategy 133
differentiation strategy 131
general environment 119
industry and competitor forces 123
institutional forces 122
integrated differentiation-cost leadership strategy 134
mission statement 118
multipoint competition strategy 134
physical forces 122
primary activities 126
sociocultural forces 119
strategic objectives 130
strategic scope 133
strategic vision 118
substitution 117
superior value 116
support activities 126
SWOT analysis 129
value chain 126

Review Questions

1. What is a competitive advantage, and what are the characteristics of a sustainable advantage?
2. What is the strategic management process? What are its major components?
3. How is an environmental analysis used to formulate a strategy?
4. What are the five dimensions of the general environment? Please explain each.
5. How do each of Porter's "five forces" affect the industry and competitor environment?
6. How can you use a value chain analysis to analyze the firm's internal resources? What are primary and secondary activities?
7. What is a SWOT analysis and how does it facilitate selecting the best strategy?
8. When is each generic business-level strategy most appropriate for use?
9. What are the strategic actions useful for implementing a strategy? Please explain each.

As a result, of these missteps, Blockbuster experienced net losses in the years of 2003 to 2006. Clearly, Blockbuster badly needs a new strategy.

Questions

1. How aggressively should Blockbuster move into selling video game players, games, and accessories versus its past focus on rentals? Why do you think it was slow to enter the DVD sales market?
2. Has the Blockbuster concept lost its novelty in the U.S. market? Can the subscription and online services help revive it?
3. Should Blockbuster increase its entry into international markets where digital-on-demand technology is not yet available?
4. In what other ways can Blockbuster try to redefine its core business and pursue other options in entertainment or home electronics? What strategy would you recommend to save the business?

Sources: P. Sweeting, "Fewer Rentals Leave Big Hole in Hollywood," *Video Business*, January 12, 2004, 7; E. Rivero, "Blockbuster Is the Latest Victim of Wall Street Alarmists," *Video Store*, December 21, 2003, 9; R. Sandomir, "Wayne Huizenga's Growth Complex," *New York Times Magazine*, June 9, 1991, S22–S26; S. G. Beatty, "Viacom's Blockbuster Rethinks Strategy," *Wall Street Journal*, November 20, 1995, Ai; C. Taylor, "The Movie Is in the Mail," *Time Canada*, March 18, 2002, 40; S. Diaz, "Digital Video Recorders Challenge Television-Advertisement Makers," *San Jose Mercrey News*, June 13, 2002; E. J. Epstein, "Hollywood's New Zombie," *Slate*, January 9, 2006, www.slate.com; R. A. Munarriz, "Date Netflix, Marry Amazon, Kill Blockbuster," *The Motley Fool,* February 14, 2007, www.fool.com; R. Duprey, "Coinstar Counting on Future Growth," *The Motley Fool,* February 12, 2007, www.fool.com; www.blockbuster.com, accessed, February 14, 2007.

6

Planning

Learning Objectives

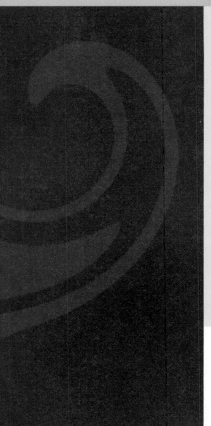

After studying this chapter, you should be able to:

- Define *planning* and explain its purpose.
- Differentiate between strategic, tactical, and operational plans.
- Describe the interrelationship between an organization's types of plans and the levels at which they are developed.
- Explain the planning process.
- Discuss budgeting as a planning tool.
- List and explain the five characteristics of effective goals.

Managerial Challenges from the Front Line

Name: Matt Kincaid

Position: Restaurant Owner and Manager

Alma mater: Gonzaga University (BBA, MBA)

Outside work activities: Basketball, guitar, and spending time with my fiancé

First job out of school: Sold CUTCO knives for Vector Marketing Corporation

Business book reading now: *Crucial Conversations*

Motto to live by: I try to live by the saying: "Along the way of life, someone must have sense enough and morality enough to cut off the chain of hate. This can only be done by projecting the ethic of love to the center of our lives." —Martin Luther King, Jr.

What drives me: The idea that I can make a positive difference in the world and improve a person's life, or perhaps and hopefully, many peoples' lives.

Management style: I truly desire to be a servant leader.

Pet peeve: When people use both lowercase letters and capital letters integrated into the same words and sentences.

Matt Kincaid grew up understanding the value of hard work—his mother had a saying painted on a rock in their home stating that "he who rolls up his sleeves seldom loses his shirt." The saying became important to Kincaid's success as a franchise owner of a West Lafayette, Indiana, restaurant. The company that sold Kincaid the franchise charges a franchise fee and provides market projections, marketing plans, and training to owners as to how to operate their restaurants. Kincaid depended heavily on the information the corporation gave him.

Kincaid soon encountered problems, however. Fewer customers visited the restaurant than he had anticipated based on the data the company gave him. He knew he needed to take action. However, given that he had not prepared for this and the fact that he had gone deeply into debt to finance his purchase of the franchise and its operation, his degrees of freedom seemed to be small. People in his market area did not respond well to the corporation's slogan encouraging them to eat healthy. And the corporation had no other franchises in Indiana, so there was no brand recognition.

Kincaid decided that building brand recognition for his restaurant would fall upon his shoulders alone. He developed flyers and hired college students to distribute approximately 200 per day each week. He also had them pass out $1 coupons at large college events, such as football games. He had shirts printed with his logo and wore a different one each day. He also tried to get newspaper stories that somehow related to his restaurant published.

All totaled, Kincaid estimated that he worked about 100 hours per week trying to make the business a success. He says a key problem was that he had depended on the market data, marketing planning, and operations manuals provided by the corporation that sold him his franchise. It seemed that the information on effective operations was useful. However, the other market projections and marketing plans were not helpful. Kincaid needed to do his own analyses of the market and develop plans for serving it to get more customers into his restaurant. Not doing so had caused him considerable problems in the first year or so of its operation.

The challenge with which Matt Kincaid had to deal clearly illustrates the importance of fully analyzing your firm's market and formulating a plan to compete effectively in it. Thankfully, Kincaid had gained a significant amount of business-operation knowledge through his education, which he applied, along with hard work, to overcome his initial lack of research, analysis, and planning. Kincaid's example shows the importance of following the planning process. Planning is especially critical in highly competitive markets. It helps firms to achieve and maintain an advantage over their competitors.[1]

On the one hand, strong competition means that if an organization, business unit, or individual manager fails to plan and, as a consequence, drifts off course or loses momentum, competitors are likely to overtake it. On the other hand, the speed of change and rapid flow of information increasingly require business plans that are flexible and dynamic. In today's world, a rigid plan can be as fatal as no plan at all. Increasingly, as a manager, you must not only be aware of local competitors but also competitors based in other parts of the world.

Effective planning at all organizational levels can have a significant impact on the firm's performance. Without effective planning, Procter & Gamble (P&G) might have failed in its efforts to enter and compete successfully in the Eastern European and Chinese markets. But, the company's activities in these markets turned out to be successful, in part, because the company's managers had a plan and regularly reevaluated and changed it. Managers need to continuously analyze and understand their external markets, and adjust their plans accordingly. Today, the instantaneous availability of information, rapid changes in economies, markets, and the political environments of countries in which firms do business affect planning efforts. Managers need to be prepared to adapt to changes that occur rapidly, no matter what their plans are.

This requires managers to accurately analyze their internal resources. For example, current research suggests that an organization's human capital is absolutely critical to the successful implementation of a firm's strategic plans.[2] So, managers must have the necessary human resources available in order for the firm to be successful. Certainly, the link between human capital and a firm's performance is evident at both P&G and General Electric (GE). These two companies are known for having excellent leadership development programs, and both companies have been high performers in recent years.[3]

An analysis of the organization's internal resources and external environment helps a manager determine the company's strengths, especially the organization's core competencies, along with its weaknesses and how they might affect its future plans.[4] This analysis can also identify the other resources managers will need to implement their plans and

General Electric (GE) has one of the best leadership development programs of any company in the world. People from different companies around the globe go through GE's prestigious programs to learn the fine art of corporate planning and improve their managerial skills. Former GE managers are also highly sought-after in the marketplace.

ultimately achieve their goals. Research has shown that effective analyses and planning are important to success in large firms[5] and in small- and medium-sized firms as well.[6] Says Jeff Immelt, the CEO of GE: "Most people just assume that big companies are slow and lethargic. But if you get good processes, you can make size an advantage."[7] GE has developed an effective strategy and an excellent planning process to help implement the strategy. This chapter examines types and levels of planning along with the planning process that firms should use.

An Overview of Planning

objectives
the end states or targets that a company's managers aim for

plans
the means by which managers hope to hit the desired targets

planning
a decision-making process that focuses on the future of an organization and how it will achieve its goals

strategic plans
plans that focus on the broad future of the organization and incorporate both external environmental demands and internal resources into managers' actions

Few activities are more basic to management than deciding where the company is going and how it is going to get there. An organization's **objectives** are the future "end states" targeted by its managers, whereas **plans** are the means by which managers achieve the objectives. **Planning**, then, is essentially a process to determine and implement actions to achieve organizational objectives. From this perspective, setting organizational objectives has to precede the development of organizational plans. Without objectives or targets, plans are of little value. Objectives help set direction, focus effort, guide behaviors, and evaluate progress.[8] We now explore the types of plans that exist, the basic planning process, and the methods for implementing plans effectively.

Types of Plans

Most organizations of any size offer more than one product or service. As a consequence, they cannot develop a single plan to cover all organizational activities; they must develop plans for multiple levels.[9] For example, GE sells a variety of products and services ranging from jet engines to financial services. To understand the planning process for complex organizations, we need to differentiate among three types of plans[10] (see Exhibit 6.1).

STRATEGIC PLANS **Strategic plans** focus on the broad future of the organization. Incorporating both external information gathered by analyzing the company's competitive

	Strategic Plans	Tactical Plans	Operational Plans
Time Horizon	Typically 3–5 years	Often focused on 1–2 years in the future	Usually focused on the next 12 months or less
Scope	Broadest; the original plans with a view of the entire organization	Normally focused on a strategic business unit	Most narrow; usually centered on departments or smaller units of the organization
Complexity	The most complex and general because of the different industries and business potentially covered	Complex but more specific, with a more limited domain of application	The least complex, because they usually focus on small, homogenous units
Impact	Have the potential to have a dramatic impact, both positively and negatively, on the survival and success of the organization	Affect specific business units, but the effect on the entire organization is measured	Impact is usually restricted to a specific department or organization unit
Interdependence	High interdependence; must take into account the resources and capabilities of the entire organization and its external environments	Moderate interdependence; must take into account the resources and capabilities of several units within a business	Low interdependence; the plans may be linked to higher-level tactical and strategic plans but are less interdependent on these plans

EXHIBIT 6.1 Types of Plans: Key Differences

environment and the firm's internal resources, managers determine the scope of the business (products and services the firm provides) to achieve the organization's long-term objectives.[11] Research shows that the rigorous use of strategic plans is associated with superior financial performance.[12] As we explained in the previous chapter, strategic plans cover the major aspects of the organization, including its products, services, finances, technology, and human resources. Most strategic plans focus on how to achieve goals three to five years into the future. For example, a few years ago, Sonora, Mexico, which borders Arizona, developed a strategic plan to revitalize its economy. In evaluating Sonora's strengths and weaknesses, government officials decided that the most effective way to revitalize its economy was to take advantage of its beautiful beaches and to encourage tourism. It took several years to implement the advertising and follow-up efforts that attracted more tourists to the area.

TACTICAL PLANS **Tactical plans** translate strategic plans into specific goals for specific parts of the organization. Consequently, they often have shorter time frames and are narrower in scope. Instead of focusing on the entire corporation, tactical plans typically affect a single business within an organization and its product lines (one or more related product lines).[13] Although tactical plans should complement the organization's overall strategic plan, they are often somewhat independent of other tactical plans. For example, the tactical plans of the transportation department for Sonora called for improving the roads leading from the border with Arizona to the beach resorts. The tactical plans of the commerce department called for making special low-interest loans available to companies to build more luxurious hotels in the targeted region. While the tactical plans of the transportation and commerce departments were different, both served to support the overall strategic plan of Sonora.

tactical plans
plans that translate strategic plans into specific goals for specific parts of the organization

operational plans
plans that translate tactical plans into specific goals and actions for small units of the organization and focus on the near term

OPERATIONAL PLANS **Operational plans** translate tactical plans into specific goals and actions for small units of the organization. They typically focus on the short term, usually 12 months or less. These plans are the least complex of the three and rarely have a direct effect on other plans outside of the department or unit for which the plan was developed. For example, in the case of Sonora, the purchasing group within the department of transportation created an operational plan that called for the purchase of several new road graders and a new steamroller to facilitate the expansion of the main highway from two lanes to four. Research has shown that the formal plans for units or teams have effects on the long-range success of these groups. Therefore, while short term and less complex, they remain highly important.[14]

As summarized in Exhibit 6.1, strategic, tactical, and operational plans differ from each other on five important dimensions: time horizon, scope, complexity, impact, and interdependence.[15] Although these differences matter, the three types of plans should align and integrate with one another. Each type of plan generally aligns with a different level in the organization.

The Organizational Levels at Which Plans Are Developed

In addition to plans that address strategic, tactical, and operational issues of the organization, managers at different levels of the company face different planning challenges. Exhibit 6.2 provides a graphical representation of the three primary levels of a corporation. Managers at each level attempt to address somewhat different questions.

CORPORATE LEVEL Most corporations of even moderate size have a corporate headquarters. However, complex and large organizations often divide the various businesses of the company into large groups. The heads of these groups are typically part of the group of senior executives at the corporate headquarters. Executives at the corporate level in large firms include both those in the headquarters and those heading up the large corporate groups such as finance, human resources, legal, and so on. These corporate-level executives primarily focus on questions such as the following:

- What industries should we get into or out of?
- What markets should the firm be in? For example, is it time to move aggressively into China? If so, what businesses should move first?
- In which businesses should the corporation invest money?
- What resources should be allocated to each of the businesses?

Best Buy, a *Fortune* 100 company, has over 940 retail operations selling electronic and technical products and services. Best Buy retail stores often contain products and services from several of its different business units, including Five-Star Appliance, Future Shop, The Geek Squad, Magnolia Audio Video, and Pacific Sales Kitchens and Bath Centers. The corporate office decides where and in what stores to emphasize the various products and services and allocates the resources accordingly. For example, Best Buy has The Geek Squad operations within about 300 of its stores. It is currently implementing two major recent corporate decisions leading to major changes, as explained in A Manager's Challenge, "Corporate Plans Are Reshaping Best Buy." They are the "customer-centricity" program and ROWE. The customer-centricity program is designed to provide more tailored products and services to key types of customers in each location. According to Best Buy's 2006 annual report, this program is more labor intensive and, thus, more expensive (requires allocating more corporate resources to specific stores), but it also is producing higher sales revenues. Alternatively, ROWE allows employees to work where they can best be productive (they do not always spend a specified number of hours in the office). The company then measures employees on their results. ROWE has enhanced employee satisfaction (*employee engagement* in Best Buy terms) and reduced turnover since its implementation. So far, though, Best Buy has only implemented it at the firm's corporate headquarters, awaiting diffusion to the company's retail operations.[16]

BUSINESS LEVEL The next level is sometimes referred to as the strategic business unit (SBU) level. At this level, managers focus on determining how they are going to compete effectively in the market. For example, within Best Buy, The Geek Squad, and Magnolia

Best Buy's corporate office decides where and in what stores to sell and market the various products and services it sells. For example, Best Buy's Geek Squad—a division that provides customers with at-home computer support—operates out of only about 300 of the company's stores, rather than all of them.

Audio Video (home theater installment) operate as business units. In such business units, managers attempt to address questions such as the following:

- Who are our direct competitors?
- What are their strengths and weaknesses?
- What are our strengths and weaknesses?
- What do customers value in the products or services we offer?
- What advantages do we have over competitors?

In Chapter 5, we examined some of the tools business-level managers can use to answer these questions. However, these planning questions, which business-level managers must answer, focus more on how to compete effectively in the specific market. If coordination across different departments (finance, marketing, product development, and so on) or units within the business is required, managers are responsible for recognizing and ensuring that the coordination occurs.

FUNCTIONAL LEVEL At the functional level, managers focus on how they can facilitate the achievement of the competitive plan of the business. These managers are often heads of departments such as finance, marketing, human resources, or product development. Depending on the business's structure, this can include managers responsible for the business within a specific geographic region or managers responsible for specific retail stores. Generally, these functional managers attempt to address questions such as the following:

- What activities does my unit need to perform well in order to meet customer expectations?
- What information about competitors does my unit need in order to help the business compete effectively?
- What are our unit's strengths and weaknesses?

A MANAGER'S CHALLENGE

Change

Corporate Plans Are Reshaping Best Buy

Best Buy is leading the way in creating innovative ways to boost customer relations and employee retention. With a new strategic planning initiative, Best Buy is incorporating a "customer-centricity" program that tailors the products and services in its local stores to one or more of five customer-demographic groups. This is a leading new trend in the market. In addition, Best Buy is transforming its culture, once known for long hours and hard-driving bosses, to one that emphasizes a "results only work environment" (ROWE).

Best Buy is one of the largest U.S. consumer electronic retailers. Its marketing strategy is customized to local stores targeting one of five customer groups. The five customer groups include: the affluent professional who is able to spend large amounts of money on top-quality products, the younger male interested in new games and technology, the family man wanting practical technology, the busy suburban mom who is looking for technology for her child(ren), and the small business owner who is looking for profit-enhancing products and needs technical support from Best Buy's service teams. The introduction of the segmented stores with more focused staff was also necessary because of the increasing complexity of the electronic products sold by Best Buy.

Along with the new customer-centricity program, Best Buy implemented ROWE, which focuses on employee results only, removing the old dogma that equates physical presence with productivity. With ROWE, the goal is to judge employee performance on output instead of the number of hours worked. Work is no longer a place where you go, but something you do. The company soon hopes to have all 4,000 employees at corporate headquarters on ROWE, and the initiative has already become part of the entire company's recruitment and employee-orientation programs. Best Buy is also in the process of identifying ways to roll out ROWE to its retail stores. No other retailer has ever before tried such a plan.

Some Best Buy employees feel the customer-centricity program is too costly. Other employees regard ROWE as just a flextime program with a different name. They feel that working offsite will lead to people working longer hours and destroy the boundary between their work and personal time.

But so far, both programs seem to be working. The 67 stores remodeled using the customer-centricity format have outperformed Best Buy's other stores. And since the implementation of ROWE, the average voluntary turnover experienced at corporate headquarters has decreased. Employee "engagement" (which measures employee satisfaction) is up, too, according to an audit of the company's corporate culture by the Gallup Organization. So, now the question remains, is the productivity up only because many employees are working longer hours or because they are more satisfied with the new work environment? And, will the cost and time involved in restructuring the company's local stores using a more customer-centricity model be worth it in the long run?

Sources: J. Birchallin, "Best Buy Leads the Trend for 'Bespoke' Stores," *Financial Times*, September 14, 2005, www.ft.com; M. Conlin, "Smashing the Clock," *Business Week*, December 11, 2006, www.businessweek.com; S. Smith, "Best Buy Unveils 'Consumer Centricity,'" *Keep Media*, May 17, 2004, www.keepmedia.com; J. Birchall, "Best Buy to Speed Up Revamp After Trial Success," *Financial Times*, April 2, 2005, www.ft.com; J. Birchall, "Best Buy Looks to Wider Horizons," *Financial Times*, June 7, 2006, www.ft.com.

The main focus of functional managers' planning activities is on how they can support the business and corporate plans. Functional-level managers are responsible for recognizing and ensuring effective and efficient operations. For example, if coordination between individuals within a unit is needed, it is their responsibility for facilitating it to enhance unit productivity. Store managers will be responsible for implementing Best Buy's customer-centricity program in each store. Functional unit managers (those in charge of finance, human resources, and so forth) are responsible for implementing Best Buy's ROWE program for the 4,000 employees at the company's corporate office.

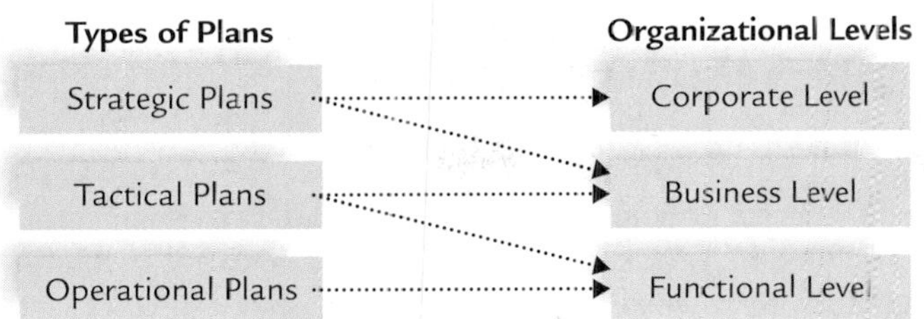

EXHIBIT 6.2

Interaction Between Plans and Levels

The Interrelationship Between Plan Types and Levels

Strategic plans are typically developed at the corporate level. Strategic planning is arguably the key planning responsibility of corporate managers. Corporate managers, however, tend not to be involved in developing tactical or operational plans. Business-level managers may be involved in developing strategic plans for their business units and are usually involved in developing tactical plans for their businesses. However, business-level managers typically are not involved in developing operational plans. In contrast, functional-level managers are not often involved in developing either strategic or tactical plans. Instead, their planning responsibilities largely focus on the development of operational plans. Exhibit 6.2 illustrates the general pattern of planning responsibility by organizational level. Keep in mind, however, that the specific pattern in any given organization could be different. For example, the size of the organization could affect the pattern. In small organizations, corporate managers often are involved in developing strategic, tactical, and operational plans. This is true in Matt Kincaid's case.

The Planning Process

The planning process has six key elements: environmental analysis, resources, objectives, actions, implementation, and outcomes (see Exhibit 6.3). In this section, we will examine each of these elements and the role they play in the overall planning process.

The first simultaneous stages of the planning process is an assessment of the external environments and internal resources. Managers who formulate or implement plans in the absence of any assessment of the environment and resources may very well fall short of producing the desired results. In contrast, managers who carefully scan the environment, understand their organizations' resources and capabilities, and incorporate the information gathered into the planning process can enjoy greater success from the plans they formulate and implement.[17] We discussed environmental analyses and analyzing internal resources

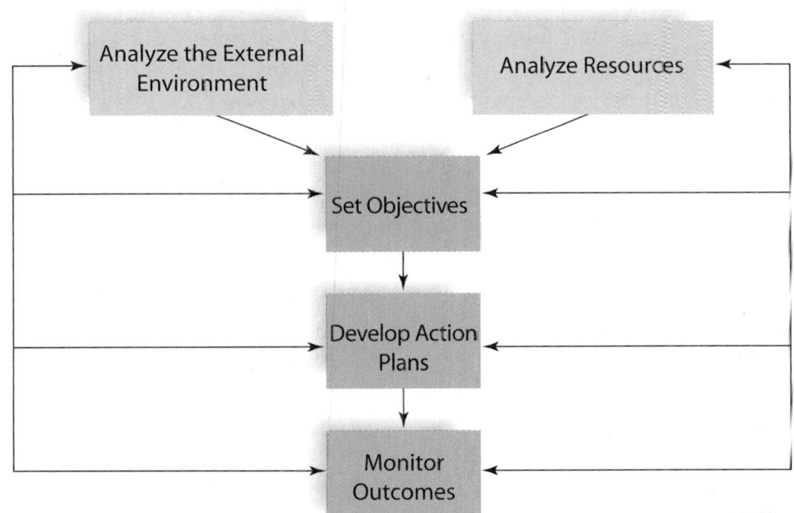

EXHIBIT 6.3

Planning Process

and capabilities in Chapter 5. Our focus here is more on the processes of analysis and how to incorporate them into the planning process

Analyzing the Firm's External Environment

Forecasts are challenging, critical tools for analyzing the environment and perhaps even more critical in highly uncertain environments. Benchmarking is another useful tool in assessing competitors. Next we discuss each.

FORECASTS One of the principal tools managers use to assess the business environment is a forecast. Forecasts are or can be made about virtually all critical elements in the environment that are likely to affect the organization or the manager's area of responsibility.[18] For example, if you were in the residential construction business, interest-rate forecasts would be important to you. Generally, as interest rates go up and borrowing money becomes more expensive, fewer people purchase new homes. Those who still purchase new homes would necessarily have to purchase less expensive homes than they would when interest rates were lower. The interest-rate forecast would influence the plan for the number of houses to build in the coming year, as a consequence.

Forecasts have a "cascading" effect. For example, if a manager forecasts that her firm will build only 1,000 homes instead of 1,500 homes over the next year because interest rates are expected to increase from 6 percent to 7 percent, then she would also likely forecast a decline in annual revenues. This may lead the purchasing manager to plan for smaller purchases of lumber and cause the human resource manager to plan for a smaller number of construction workers. The key point for managers is that it's vital to know your key forecasts and to keep track of any changes to them so you can develop appropriate objectives and action plans to compete within the projected environment.

ENVIRONMENTAL UNCERTAINTY Forecasting environmental uncertainty accurately is difficult. It is even more challenging in dynamic environments. Turbulent and uncertain environments are common in certain industries and in some countries. For example, in high-technology industries, such as the computer hardware and software industries, new technological developments are introduced regularly and can rapidly change the competitive landscape. Likewise, large economic changes can occur in developing and emerging economies sometimes because of unstable governments or major government policy changes (e.g., in some Latin American countries). Firms must incorporate this uncertainty into their planning process.[19] This information is important because it might affect a plan to enter a particular market or how much to invest in the subsidiary operations across several markets (e.g., subsidiaries in Brazil, China, and Poland).[20]

A key issue for managers and their planning activities is that the greater the environmental uncertainty, the more flexible their plans need to be. In some cases, managers may even develop contingency plans. **Contingency plans** typically identify key factors that could affect the desired results and specify what different actions will be taken if changes in key events occur.[21] For example, suppose you were a manager at KB Home, the fourth largest residential construction company in the United States.[22] Clearly, forecasts of future interest rates are important to the operation of the company. The forecast might call for interest rates to remain unchanged for the next year. But rather than solely rely on the forecast, it might be better to develop contingency plans. For instance, if interest rates go up one percentage point, people likely will buy fewer houses or less expensive houses. Your contingency plan might include offering reduced financing charges if customers choose certain upgrades in their homes, such as granite countertops. You could perhaps afford to offer buyers this incentive because the profits from the upgrades might be greater than the costs of the finance subsidies. By having this contingency plan in place before the change in interest rates, you are more prepared to respond, if it occurs.

contingency plans
plans that identify key factors that could affect the desired results and specify what actions will be taken if key events change

benchmarking
investigating the best results obtained by your competitors and noncompetitors and the practices that led to those results

BENCHMARKING Another popular tool for assessing the environment is benchmarking. **Benchmarking** can lead to strong positive results.[23] It involves investigating the best practices used by competitors and noncompetitors. In terms of results, managers might assess competitors with the highest revenue-to-employee ratio as a means of assessing productivity. Managers would then compare their own revenue-to-employee ratio to identify how they compared to competitors. An important part of this assessment, however, is identifying the practices that contribute to the high revenue-to-employee ratios. For example, they might find that the firms with the highest ratios have fewer levels of managers because they delegate decision-making authority to lower levels in the organization, thus, emphasizing participative management and employee involvement.

These same types of assessments might also be made of noncompetitors. The inclusion of noncompetitors has potential pitfalls and benefits that are different from benchmarking competitors. Clearly, noncompetitors face different business conditions that make appropriate comparisons difficult. For example, a telemarketing company that sells relatively inexpensive items over the phone will have a much lower revenue-to-employee ratio than a manufacturer of supercomputers. The telemarketing firm has a relatively labor-intensive business, whereas the supercomputer manufacturer has a technology-intensive business. Likewise, the inventory practices of a service firm will be difficult to apply directly to a manufacturing firm. However, by looking outside your set of competitors, sometimes you can find unique and significantly better ways of doing things.

Consider the case of Outback Steakhouse. Even though the steel industry is totally different from the chain-restaurant industry, Outback Steakhouse has incorporated, with great success, a motivational practice used by several steel "mini-mills." Outback's success depends on the performance of its restaurants. And the people most responsible for the performance of the restaurants are the firm's local managers. In particular, managers must hire the right people and motivate them effectively to ensure that they provide good food and service to customers. Thus, Outback needs highly motivated restaurant managers. The "best practice" that Outback adopted was giving the restaurant managers some ownership in the restaurants they managed. Therefore, if a restaurant made money, so did the manager. The manager felt more like an owner and less like an employee. The adoption of this best practice has helped Outback Steakhouse achieve significant success. Thus, even though benchmarking noncompetitors requires some judgment as to the relevant or appropriateness of practices, it can produce ways to gain a competitive advantage.

Assessing the Firm's Internal Resources

Another element in the planning process is an assessment of the required resources and the resources available to you. Managers should conduct this assessment simultaneously with the analysis of the external environment.

RESOURCES AVAILABLE You should identify the resources that are available to your firm because they affect what objectives you should establish and what plans you should formulate. Clearly, for a plan to be effective it must not only be well formulated but feasible to implement. If the resources required significantly exceed those available, you either must acquire new resources or design different actions. In assessing resources available, managers must ask themselves questions such as the following:

- What human capital do we have currently?
- Can people work on new and additional projects or will we need new people?
- Can we develop or acquire additional human capital if needed for new projects?
- What financial resources do we have available? Can we obtain additional funding from the debt or equity markets if needed?
- Do we have the cutting-edge technology or can we gain access to it at a cost-effective price?

Although these are certainly not the only questions managers would need to ask, they are typical of the questions managers need to ask to determine the portfolio of resource capabilities available in the organization.

Electronic Data Systems (EDS) illustrates the importance of this assessment. Rather than solely focusing on designing and selling computer-aided-design (CAD) products, EDS changed its strategy to selling "solutions" to its clients' product-development problems.

To make this change, the company needed new salespeople with different skills. When the focus was solely on selling CAD products, EDS sales representatives usually talked to middle-level executives in their clients' engineering and product-design departments. Trying to sell more integrated solutions required EDS salespeople to target more senior executives. In the end, EDS managers trained some of their best existing salespeople and recruited new salespeople as well.

Setting Objectives

After the external and internal analyses, the next element in the planning process is setting objectives. To design and implement specific actions requires knowing what you expect them to achieve.

PRIORITIES AND MULTIPLE OBJECTIVES One of the first challenges for managers as they set objectives is to determine priorities.[24] Not all objectives are of equal importance or value. Furthermore, some objectives might be important now and less important later. Without a clear understanding of which objectives are most important and temporal priorities, employees may be working at odds with each other or it might create unnecessary conflicts as well.[25]

Consider your own university. Most universities have multiple and sometimes conflicting objectives. For example, students feel they pay tuition in order to learn leading-edge content from the best professors the school has to offer. Universities cannot ignore the expectations of this important set of its constituents. At the same time, to generate leading-edge knowledge, universities must hire top researchers and fund their research. Without a clear idea of the university's priorities, department heads may find it difficult to determine how best to allocate their budgets to teaching and to research. How much of the budget should go toward activities that help develop the teaching skills of the faculty? How much should go toward funding research?

Temporal priorities among objectives can also exist. For example, suppose you are launching a new product in an established market with well-positioned competitors. You might decide that your current objective is to gain market share and thereby establish a presence in the market. You tell your salespeople to go after 10 percent market share and to offer discounts of up to 20 percent when needed to get the sale. However, after the product has a 10 percent market share, you might want the sales representatives to focus more on profitability objectives than gaining more market share. Without a clear understanding of this sequence in priorities, your salespeople would not be as able to help you achieve these objectives. If objectives are sequential, identifying that fact in advance helps subordinates better understand what you expect of them.

MEASURING OBJECTIVES Once the organization's objectives are clear to everyone, managers need to establish how to measure achievement of them. For example, a manager might determine that the organization's financial performance is the top objective. However, financial performance can be measured in a variety of ways.[26] It can be measured in terms of profits relative to sales or profits relative to the company's assets. For example, Nordstrom measures clerks' performance in terms of sales per hour. This is in contrast to many other retailers that only measure net sales. The difference in approach is important, if salespeople are measured on net sales, they will likely be motivated to work the greatest number of hours they can (to produce more sales). In contrast, Nordstrom's sales-per-hour objective causes clerks to focus on "sales efficiency," or selling the most in every hour they work. And, the best way to improve sales per hour is to sell to repeat customers because clerks know the types of things they like, how much they are likely to spend, and so on. Specific measures are important. Even slight differences, such as net sales versus sales per hour, can significantly influence employee behavior.[27]

The case of Dell is an interesting one as described in A Manager's Challenge, "Dell Rethinks Its Action Plans and Performance Measures." Essentially, Dell "took its eye off of the ball" after it became the industry leader and began emphasizing cost minimization to

A MANAGER'S CHALLENGE

Technology

Dell Rethinks Its Action Plans and Performance Measures

Michael Dell, the founder of Dell, Inc., started the company in part because of his dissatisfaction with the service he received from other personal computer companies. Dell launched his company with a broadly advertised commitment to quality. In addition, cost efficiency has been a longtime priority for Dell. As a result, the firm emerged as one of the fastest-growing companies in the 1990s and received accolades for good customer care. Yet in recent times, the company has experienced a number of performance-related problems, and its competitors have been gaining market share.

Service problems in particular have dogged Dell. Customers began complaining about long hold times and the fact that too many calls were being transferred from one technician to another. Like so many firms trying to minimize their costs, Dell had outsourced many of its service call centers overseas. It experienced problems because many overseas employees had poor English skills and could not understand customers' complaints or offer solutions. Thus, the outsourcing of the call centers contributed to the decline in the company's service quality.

Another reason Dell experienced trouble was because it was hard-pressed to keep up with the demand by individual consumers seeking help with the various personal computers and digital devices they owned. For example, Dell received a host of complaints from these customers about spyware, adware, and viruses and how to deal with them. Unfortunately Dell did not forecast the explosive sales growth of the home-computer market and lacked a good plan to develop the service capabilities to handle it.

According to Bobbi Dangerfield, who is Dell's director for U.S. consumer experience, the company's focus is now on ensuring that customer retention and satisfaction are considered in every transaction. According to Dangerfield, the most successful remedy is to make sure service representatives take ownership of a complaint. The representative is responsible for guiding the customer through the entire process. After resolving the service issue, the same representative e-mails or calls the customer with his or her name and supervisor's name. Other remedies include new policies limiting how many times a complaint can be transferred, thereby emphasizing that they should be resolved upon the customer's first phone call or e-mail. Following the implementation of this policy, the number of transferred calls fell 83 percent. To monitor the problems experienced by its customers, Dell is also beginning to utilize more customer and employee surveys to identify its own deficiencies and react aggressively to them.

Dell is also responding to the push for more home products by creating products like "DataSafe." DataSafe is actually a product that is a derivative of services already offered to corporations. However, it could potentially be beneficial for home-computer consumers. When consumers buy a new computer, they can update the data from their old computers using Dell's DataSafe Web site. Dell then loads the data onto their new computers for them, if they so desire. The market opportunity for this product is expected to be strong because many corporations and individual consumers hire computer technicians to transfer such data. In addition to DataSafe, the company is also discussing a new product that would automatically and remotely tune up consumers' personal computers.

Lastly, Dell has provided its phone support staff with more intensive training and has consolidated its product lines to make it easier for these people to address technical problems. The firm has also consolidated its support units and is building bigger call centers, which should provide more advancement and career-track opportunities for its call-center employees. This should help improve their retention and expertise. Well-trained employees who are motivated to provide quality service should lead to fewer complaints, and this, in turn, should lead to lower costs and free up Dell's workforce to increase the company's sales. Moreover, more satisfied customers will be willing to spend more money on Dell's products and tell other customers about their positive experiences with the company.

Sources: M. Kanellos, "Dell's Latest Push: Help at Home," *CNET News*, January 10, 2007, www.news.com; B. Hindo, "Satisfaction Not Guaranteed," *Business Week*, June 19, 2006, www.businessweek.com; P. Galuszka, "Service Is as Service Does: CEOs Talk the Talk, but Many Companies Don't Deliver," *Keep Media*, August 1, 2005, www.keepmedia.com.

You can't manage what you can't measure. That's why Nordstrom records the sales of its clerks on an hour-by-hour basis. The company found out that even slight differences in hourly sales can have a big impact on the motivation of clerks—assuming they know what those sales are. That's why Nordstrom makes the sales numbers available to everyone.

the detriment of customer service. All companies must manage their costs. However, overemphasizing costs can cause the firm to overlook other important market criteria. In this case, reducing costs became the primary measure of Dell's success. As a result, service quality suffered, which had a negative effect on the firm's overall performance. As we noted, Dell lost market share to its competitors, especially Hewlett-Packard. As a result, in 2007, Kevin Rollins, the CEO of Dell, resigned, and Michael Dell once again retook the reins of his company.[28] His goal is to restore Dell's position as the industry's market leader. To do so will require successful changes in the firm's strategy and especially its means of implementation.

Developing Action Plans

The next element in the planning process is the development of specific action plans. The action plans describe what the organization will do to accomplish the objectives it has established.

SEQUENCE AND TIMING A characteristic of an effective action plan is the sequence and timing of the specific steps or actions that must be taken.[29] One of the common tools used to graphically display the sequence and timing of the specific actions is a Gantt chart (see Exhibit 6.4). Time typically appears on the horizontal axis of the chart, and the tasks to be done appear on the vertical axis. The chart shows when actions are to start and how long they require for completion. It shows the sequence in which to complete the actions, whether a preceding action must be completed before a subsequent one can start, and the expected overlap in the timing of specific actions if any exists.

In addition to the planned sequence and timing of events, managers can plot the firm's actual progress on the Gantt chart as well. This allows managers to assess their progress against the plan and potentially make adjustments if needed. Today, sophisticated computer programs can assist managers in formulating and implementing plans involving literally hundreds of raw materials and components that must be brought together in the right amounts and sequences for the cost-effective production of finished goods.[30]

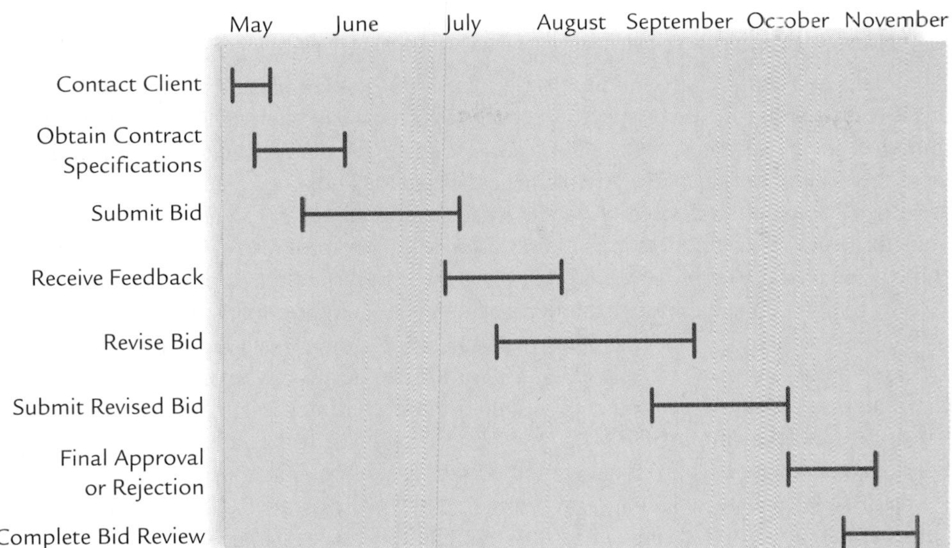

EXHIBIT 6.4

Gantt Chart

ACCOUNTABILITY The second key aspect of effective action plans is establishing who is accountable for the specific actions identified. Knowing who is responsible for specific actions facilitates coordination, especially if multiple people are involved in the execution of the plan. Accountability also increases the likelihood that the actions will be taken as planned in both quality and timing. Assigning accountability is especially important if managers need to change action plans during the course of their implementation (discussed next).[31]

Dell developed a team approach whereby every member of the team felt a shared accountability for implementing action plans and achieving the firm's objectives. Such an approach can be positive if the approach is complemented with the appropriate objectives and measures of success.[32] Unfortunately, Dell became almost obsessed with minimizing costs. In so doing, it invested only minimal amounts in R&D and eventually competitors were able to duplicate Dell's quality and excellent supply chain strategy. As a result, Dell lost its competitive advantage and with it, market share.

Implementing Plans

Action plans must be implemented. Like the quality of the plan itself the quality of the plan's implementation can affect the results achieved. Plans often fail in the implementation stage because of the inadequate assessment of resources required or the lack of accountability assigned to individuals for implementation. Yet, critically, the means of implementation must be carefully matched with the objectives to be achieved and the action plans designed.[33]

In the opening profile, we described actions taken by Matt Kincaid to increase the customer base of his restaurant. He had T-shirts printed with the restaurant's logo on it. He had college students distribute flyers, and he distributed discount coupons to attract more customers. Kincaid knew he would have to assume responsibility for these marketing activities, even though he was heavily focused on managing the restaurant's operations. This included ensuring that his employees were well trained and motivated to prepare quality food and deliver high-quality service. They also had to be committed to doing a good job and working as a team to achieve the restaurant's objectives.[34] Managing all of these diverse efforts required a significant amount of time on Kincaid's part. As he explained, he worked sometimes as many as 100 hours per week.

No matter how carefully the implementation is designed, managers still need to monitor and adjust implementation efforts when unanticipated events occur.

MONITORING THE IMPLEMENTATION Even if the previous steps in the planning process are done well, there is no guarantee that the plan will be successfully implemented.

This is why it is essential for you to monitor the implementation of the plan. In particular, you need to monitor three critical factors.

First, it is important to monitor the progress of the plan and its implementation. Are those responsible for taking specific actions well aware of their responsibilities and the timing of their expected actions? Are they adequately motivated and prepared to implement their portion of the plan? Are the necessary actions being taken at the right time? Are they being done at the desired or necessary level of quality? These are the types of questions that a manager needs to ask in order to monitor the progress of the implementation. Quite often plans have "milestones" that mark the progress of the implementation.

Second, the manager needs to monitor the level of support that the plan receives as it is being implemented.[35] This support might take the form of encouragement, money, or coaching. Few plans of any complexity or duration can be effectively implemented without continuous support. Are the other key supporters providing the encouragement needed? Kincaid found the support from his corporate franchisor to be lacking. As a result, he developed his own plan and implemented it without the franchisor's support.

Third, the manager needs to monitor the level of resistance. Many plans and their implementation involve change. To the extent that they do, resistance to the plan's implementation can occur. One of the general causes of resistance is people anticipate performing poorly when first doing new tasks. Even if they see that the change is good, they resist it because they fear failure at first. In these cases, managers may need to provide extra encouragement or provide training to ensure that employees succeed.

MAKING REAL-TIME ADJUSTMENTS As discussed in previous chapters, organizations exist in a dynamic environment; thus, most plans likely will need to be adjusted. As the environment changes, what was originally a perfectly acceptable objective can become unrealistic or too easily achieved, and therefore, may need to be changed. Likewise, what were perfectly reasonable time frames at one point may become unreasonable because of sociocultural, technological, economic, or political-legal changes. Events occur that cannot always be anticipated, requiring a change in the plans or their implementation.

In a phone company, one of the key principles is redundancy. If a catastrophic event occurs that knocks out a phone company's equipment, having a backup to the original equipment is necessary because obtaining replacement equipment quickly is difficult. AT&T learned this lesson after the September 11 attacks in New York City. Now, the company has 200 semitrailers of backup equipment ready for operation at a moment's notice.

Second, managers need to help employees recognize and accept the need to adapt plans in real time. To do so, managers likely should build capabilities that enable them to adapt effectively. These capabilities might include skills such as good environmental scanning and quick requirement and resource assessment. Thus, in today's dynamic environment, a fixed and rigid plan can be as dangerous as having no plan at all.

Monitoring Outcomes

The final element in the planning process involves monitoring outcomes. If the organization's objectives have been well defined from the outset of the planning process, there should be little question as to what outcomes to monitor or how to measure them. If the plan was expected to improve the firm's financial performance and to measure them in terms of increased sales, the outcome should be easy to gauge.

However, most plans also produce negative or positive unanticipated consequences.[36] Both can be valuable sources of learning. To monitor outcomes may require the use of specially designed information systems to capture and report these consequences on a real-time basis. Such systems can be particularly important for large, complex organizations. For example, most large firms carefully monitor the financial performance of their major business units. However, other types of information may be needed, too. For example, the success of all products provided to the market by the firm may be necessary.[37] If one product is not selling well, a company needs to identify the reasons for it. Therefore, managers should capture as much knowledge as possible when monitoring outcomes. There

A MANAGER'S CHALLENGE

Ethics

Wal-Mart's Green Initiatives

Wal-Mart had a rough year in 2006. A combination of legal troubles, public relations fiascoes, and labor issues made the retail giant more vulnerable to competitors. In November of that year, the company's same-store sales growth drifted into negative territory before rebounding to 1.6 percent in December. By contrast Costco and Target's sales were up 9 percent and 4.1 percent, respectively, in December 2006. And Wal-Mart's stock price was flat throughout 2006—an otherwise strong year for stocks.

But Wal-Mart is planning to implement a number of new initiatives to help improve its "low prices at the expense of everything else" image. For example, near the end of 2006, Wal-Mart began aggressively focusing on reducing greenhouse gas emissions and cutting waste. New initiatives such as these represent a fundamental shift in Wal-Mart's stance on a wide range of environmental and social issues. "For Wal-Mart to be successful and continue to grow, we must operate in a world that is healthy and successful," Wal-Mart CEO Lee Scott has told employees. Wal-Mart is revamping its overall environmental strategy with the assistance of Conservation International, a nonprofit environmental group that works closely with companies in creating environmental policies and initiatives. Wal-Mart has agreed to invest $500 million annually on environmental technologies at its stores. The new green initiatives include working towards a goal of producing no waste, providing fuel from renewable resources, and working closely with suppliers to promote good environmental practices.

One of Wal-Mart's goals is to increase the fuel efficiency of its U.S. trucking fleet by 25 percent over the next 3 years, and then doubling that increase in 10 years. Because Wal-Mart operates the largest privately owned truck fleet in the United States, increasing the fuel mileage of its trucks by one mile per gallon will result in savings of more than $52 million a year. So, the long-term savings will likely outweigh the short-term costs needed to increase the fleet's fuel efficiency. Furthermore, these actions are expected to please consumers, who are becoming more environmentally conscious.

Wal-Mart has also vowed to use 100 percent renewable energy, drastically reduce waste through recycling, and sell "sustainable" products that are more environmentally friendly. The company has said it will sell only fish that are certified to be from sustainable fisheries. Wal-Mart is also attempting to reduce by 25 percent the solid waste produced by its stores over the next three years, and it plans to work with suppliers to reduce product-packaging amounts and increase recycling. As well as being more environmentally friendly, less packaging on Wal-Mart's house-brand toys alone could save the company $2.4 million annually in shipping costs.

In addition, Wal-Mart is designing a prototype store that is 25 percent to 30 percent more energy efficient than existing stores. The firm is changing the lighting in stores to use more efficient bulbs and adding skylights for natural light, which has trimmed its electricity bill by 17 percent. Wal-Mart's efforts to sell more compact fluorescent bulbs illustrates its initiative to reduce the use of electricity, thus, decreasing the amount of its greenhouse gas emissions. Finally, Wal-Mart has implemented an initiative to sell a line of organic cotton baby clothes in Europe and Japan.

Whatever Wal-Mart's motivations are, many environmentalists are thrilled with these new initiatives. Because it is the world's largest company, Wal-Mart's efforts could have a broader impact. For example, it could have considerable effect on suppliers' standards and, thus, serve as an example to encourage the development and use of new energy-saving technologies. Environmentalists feel a key indicator of Wal-Mart's commitment will be its plan to release an initial environmental sustainability report, together with Internet data that external parties can use to evaluate its environmental progress.

Sources: J. Birchall, "Wal-Mart Picks a Shade of Green," *Financial Times*, February 6, 2006, www.ft.com; J. Carey, "Wal-Mart: Big Strides to Become the Jolly Green Giant," *Business Week*, January 29, 2007, www.businessweek.com; J. Birchall, "Wal-Mart Sets Out Stall for a Greener Future," *Financial Times*, October 25, 2005, www.ft.com; J. Birger, *CNN Money*, January 9, 2005, www.money.cnn.com; F. Harvey and E. Rigby, "Supermarkets' Green Credentials Attacked," *Financial Times*, September 14, 2006, www.ft.com.

also needs to be a feedback loop so that the company can use what they've learned to modify and improve the planning process.

Wal-Mart has developed some aggressive plans to become highly environmentally conscious in its operations. Yet, it has developed some very specific, measurable, and time-bound goals. For example, Wal-Mart has a goal to increase the fuel efficiency of its trucking fleet by 25 percent over a three-year period. In addition, Wal-Mart plans to include information on its Web site about its performance on these environmentally conscious initiatives. This will allow external parties to evaluate its progress toward reaching its stated goals. Wal-Mart is such a large company with strong market power, its efforts will encourage many more companies to develop and implement environmental initiatives as well. Given its well-articulated plans and precise statements of its goals, Wal-Mart has a high probability of being successful with its environmentally conscious initiatives.

Planning Tools

Managers use a variety of planning tools. In this section, we discuss two tools that managers widely use: budgets and goal setting.

Budgets

Managers use **budgets** to quantify and allocate resources to specific activities. Most organizations propose and set budgets on an annual basis, and they address a variety of issues. For example a **capital expenditure budget** specifies the amount of money a company plans to spend on specific items that have long-term use and require significant financial investments. These items might include things such as manufacturing equipment, land, and buildings.

Another common budget is an expense budget. An **expense budget** typically includes all primary activities on which the unit or organization plans to spend money and the amount allocated for each item during the year. Most profit and nonprofit organizations of a moderate or larger size use expense budgets, both for planning and for control purposes.

And most organizations have a two-phased process relative to budgets. The first consists of managers looking ahead and planning their needs. Thereafter, the organization develops a budget that specifies expected major expenditures or expenses. This **proposed budget** provides a plan of how much money the organization needs, and it is submitted to a superior or budget review committee. After the proposed budget is reviewed, often in the context of other proposed budgets, it receives approval (or requests for revisions and resubmission). An **approved budget** specifies the amount of money the manager is authorized to spend and what items can be purchased or expenses are allowed.

Two main approaches to the budgeting process are common. The first approach is typically called the **incremental budgeting approach**.[38] With this approach, managers use their approved budgets from the previous year as a starting point for developing the current year's budget. They then present arguments for why the upcoming budget should be more or less than the previous year's budget. Incremental budgeting is efficient because managers do not need to spend a significant amount of time justifying allocating money toward the same types of purchases or recurring expenses each year. The principal negative consequence of incremental budgeting is that it can result in "budget momentum." This means that money may be allocated to a unit in the future merely because the unit had been allocated money in the past. Consider the true case of a small town in North Carolina. Every year around Christmas, all the parking meters on the main street are turned off; people park free. Most of the city residents think that this is the city's way of giving folks a nice Christmas gift. Actually, it is the city council's way of maintaining its budget level given the incremental approach the mayor takes to budgeting. The council calculates the town's budget surplus toward the end of the year and computes how many days of free parking the city will need to use up the surplus. It then allocates that many days of free parking to maintain the same level of funding for the next year. As in this case, incremental budgeting can lead to the inefficient use of valuable resources.

budget
a tool used to quantify and allocate resources to specific activities

capital expenditure budget
a tool that specifies the amount of money to spend on specific items that have long-term use and require significant amounts of money

expense budget
a budget that includes all primary activities on which a unit or organization plans to spend money and the amount allocated for the upcoming year

proposed budget
a budget that outlines how much money an organization needs; it is submitted to a superior or budget review committee

approved budget
the budget specifies what the manager is actually authorized to spend money on and how much

incremental budgeting approach
a budgeting approach whereby managers use the approved budget of the previous year and then present arguments for why the upcoming year's budget should be more or less

The **zero-based budgeting approach** assumes that all funding allocations must be justified starting at zero each year.[39] The benefit of this approach is that items that cannot be justified on their current merits (regardless of their past merits and budgets) will not be allocated money. In general, this approach can lead to an overall more effective allocation of the organization's financial resources. However, zero-based budgeting requires an investment of time because each item must be justified each year.

zero-based budgeting approach
a budgeting approach that assumes that all funding allocations must be justified from zero each year

With either approach, managers typically use budgets as planning tools to determine priorities, required resources, and keys to implementation. In particular, because financial resources are usually scarce in most organizations, there is almost never as much money available as there are requests for its use. Allocating money among various activities forces managers to discuss the relative priority of the firm's activities. This is true at all three organization levels. For example, department managers are likely to find they have more demand for money than they have the resources to allocate. Similarly, corporate officers are likely to find departments and business units requesting more money than the organization has available to allocate. This leads to a determination of which units and their related activities are of highest priority and should receive budget approval.

In this sense, budgets can be an effective means of integrating and quantifying many aspects of the firm's corporate-, business-, and functional-level plans. Although the budgeting process does not guarantee that managers will make good decisions about the integration and coordination process nor that they will make good decisions about priorities, it does increase the likelihood of these key items being discussed and decisions made.

Goal Setting Criteria

Goal setting is a specific planning process for managing performance. Normally, goal setting is used at the individual level, although the principles are applicable to setting goals for teams, units, and organizations. The research suggests that effective goals can have a significant and positive effect on performance. The research also suggests that effective goals have five characteristics.[40]

SPECIFIC To be most effective, the goals for the firm, its units, and subordinates, should be specific. For example, a goal "to achieve the highest performance possible" is too vague. Rather, state the goal in specific terms, such as "to achieve a 10 percent return on assets during the next year" or "to gain a 15 percent increase in market share in the next six months." These statements are specific and detail which actual performance can be measured and compared.

MEASURABLE One way to determine that a goal is specific enough is by whether its achievement can be measured. For example, it would be highly difficult to measure the achievement of a goal "to reach the highest performance possible." What is the highest performance possible? How could a firm know when it is achieved? Yet, a goal to achieve a 10 percent return on assets or an increase of 15 percent in market share can be measured. These are specific and measurable goals. In addition, you need to actually measure progress toward the goal.

Goal setting is most effective when progress toward the goal is measured on a regular basis. The frequency of the measurement should depend upon the nature of the activities associated with the goal and its timing. For example, if the goal is to achieve a 10 percent return on assets over the next year, the goal can easily be assessed on a quarterly basis. Most companies develop and report their earnings each quarter. Whereas, if the goal is to increase market share by 15 percent in the next six months, the goal might be best evaluated on a monthly basis. The interim measures allow managers to know how the achievement of the goal is progressing and if any corrective actions are needed to ensure the achievement of the goal.

COMMITMENT Even if a goal is specific and measurable, those involved in its achievement must agree and be committed to it for the goal to be achieved. Thus, for organizational goals, this means that a substantial portion of employees must agree to them and be committed to their achievement. To achieve a 10 percent return on the firm's assets, many employees will have to do their jobs exceptionally well and take actions to minimize costs or to enhance revenues (or both). For unit goals, those in the unit must accept and be committed to the achievement of the goal.

Managers should be careful when gaining the commitment of their employees. Because managers are in a position of power, their subordinates often say what they believe their managers want to hear—even when it is not what the subordinates really think. For example, sales representatives may "agree" to the goal of increasing market share by 15 percent, but they may not believe they can do it. If so, they are unlikely to commit to the goal, and they will probably not achieve it. Thus, managers do not want superficial agreement to the goal but instead want a deep commitment to it. The research shows that one way to gain commitment to a goal is to allow employees to discuss and participate in the development of the goal. In doing so, the employees have a feeling of ownership.[41]

REALISTIC For people to be committed to the achievement of goals, they must be realistic. Research has shown that unrealistic goals (goals that are perceived to be unachievable) can produce several reactions from those charged with the achievement of them, none of which are good. First, some employees will ignore an unrealistic goal and set their own goals, which the organization may or may not desire. Other employees may become discouraged and their motivation to perform well will suffer. So, if sales representatives perceive that a goal of increasing market share by 15 percent in the next six months is not achievable, they are unlikely to work toward the goal.

Alternatively, goals that are too easy are not effective; they are not effective for at least two reasons: On the one hand, they do not inspire motivation. As such, people are likely to perform below their capabilities. On the other hand, easy goals are not effective because they do not deliver substantial results. Even if they are achieved, easy goals will not have a large effect on the results achieved at the organizational, unit, subordinate, or personal level.

TIME BOUND Even specific, measured, and realistic goals to which people are committed need to be time bound in order to be effective. Thus, goals need a specific time span within which they are to be achieved. Some goals will take a substantial time to achieve (for example, a year or more), whereas others will require shorter time intervals. For example, the goal of achieving a 10 percent return on assets was stated earlier in terms of a one-year time frame. Consequently, milestones should be set, and the goal measured on shorter time frames, such as every three months. By contrast, measuring progress toward the goal of increasing market share by 15 percent in a six-month time frame should probably be done

Managerial Challenges from the Front Line

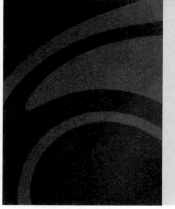

The Rest of the Story

With a lot of hard work and using his knowledge gained from his business education, Matt Kincaid achieved a successful outcome. His efforts helped build positive brand recognition for his restaurant in Indiana, and he was subsequently able to sell the business for a profit. Kincaid has since purchased a restaurant and a bar in Spokane, Washington. Despite the successful outcome of his West Lafayette, Indiana, venture, he says that he has learned some valuable lessons—the most important of which is to do your own research and develop your own plans before embarking upon a major business project.

every month. Having a time frame for goals is necessary in order to evaluate their success, and it also affects the realism of the goals. Perhaps it is unrealistic to expect large increases in market share in only six months, but such increases might be achievable in 12 to 18 months. Therefore, the time frame plays an important role in the goal-setting process.[42]

Summary

- Few activities are more basic to management than deciding where the company is going and how it is going to get there. Organizational objectives are the future end states targeted by managers, while plans are the means by which managers achieve the objectives. Planning, then, is essentially a process to determine and implement actions to achieve organizational objectives. This process includes an assessment of the organization's external environment and internal resources.
- Most companies of any size develop three different types of interrelated plans, strategic, tactical, and operational. Strategic plans focus on the broad future of the organization. Incorporating external information gathered by analyzing the company's competitive environment and the firm's internal resources, managers determine the scope of the business (products and services the firm will provide) to achieve the organization's long-term objectives. Tactical plans translate strategic plans into specific goals for specific parts of the organization. Consequently, they often have shorter time frames and are narrower in scope. Instead of focusing on the entire corporation, tactical plans typically affect a single business within an organization and its product lines (one or more related product lines). Operational plans translate tactical plans into specific goals and actions for small units of the organization. They typically focus on the short term, usually 12 months or less. These plans are the least complex of the three and rarely have a direct effect on other plans outside of the department or unit for which the plan was developed.
- In addition to plans that address strategic, tactical, and operational issues of the organization, managers at different levels of the company face different planning challenges. Managers at each level attempt to address somewhat different questions. Strategic plans are typically developed at the corporate level. Strategic planning is arguably the key planning responsibility of corporate managers. Business-level managers may be involved in developing strategic plans for their business units and are usually involved in developing tactical plans for their business. Functional-level managers largely focus on the development of operational plans.
- The planning process has six key elements: environmental analysis, resources, objectives, actions, implementation, and outcomes. Forecasts and benchmarking can be helpful in analyzing the organization's external environment. However, the uncertainty in this environment often makes analyzing it a significant challenge. Firms must currently have the resources or the ability to acquire them to implement the plans developed. Thus, analysis of the internal resources is necessary to establish realistic objectives. Next, the organization designs and implements the plan's action steps.
- Budgets are used to quantify and allocate resources to specific activities. Most organizations propose and set budgets on an annual basis. A capital expenditure budget specifies the amount of money an organization plans to spend on specific items that have long-term use and require significant financial investments. Another common budget is an expense budget. An expense budget typically includes all primary activities on which the unit or organization plans to spend money and the amount allocated to each during the year.
- Goal setting is a specific planning process for managing performance. The principles are applicable to setting goals not only for individual employees but for teams, units, and organizations. The research suggests that effective goals can have a significant and positive effect on performance, and five characteristics distinguish them: They are specific, measurable, realistic, time-bound, and have the commitment of those charged with the responsibility of achieving them.

that with a few modifications was ready for mailing. Tammy obtained several mailing lists that had the names of senior executives in medium-to-large companies. The mailing was sent out about five days early.

Inquiries regarding the program were 100 percent higher than other new programs that LDC had launched in the past. However, as the program's start date drew nearer, the ratio of inquiries to registrations was not good. Typically, 1 of every 10 people who contacted LDC for further information regarding a particular program ended up registering for it. However, eight weeks before the program's start, the inquiry to registration ratio was 100 to 1 (not 10 to 1). Only four weeks before the start of the program, only 10 participants had signed up. Pam was stressed about what she should do.

Questions

1. What adjustments would you make at this point? Would you cancel the program or run it at a loss?
2. Draw a Gantt chart of the sequence and timing of key activities. What insights does this give you regarding the plan and its implementation?
3. What do you think went wrong? What do you see as the strengths and weaknesses of the planning process used in this case?
4. LDC seemed to follow a planning process that had worked well for its mid-level managerial programs. Are there differences between senior executives and mid-level managers that might explain why the plan did not seem as successful as anticipated? Could these differences have been anticipated? Should they have been?

7

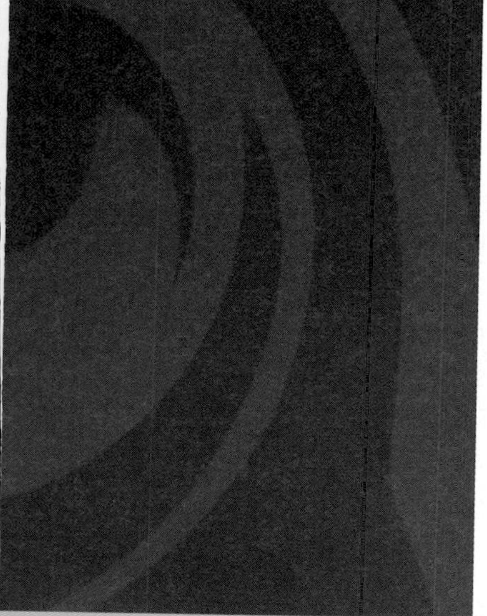

Organizational Structure and Design

Learning Objectives

After studying this chapter, you should be able to:

Explain the concepts of organizational structure and design.

Explain the concepts of differentiation and integration and their role in organizational structure and design.

Describe the concepts of formalization, informalization, centralization, and decentralization and discuss their interrelationships.

Identify the common structures used by organizations and describe the strengths and weaknesses of each of these structures.

Understand how network structures help firms manage their value chain activities and contribute to achieving a competitive advantage.

Describe how environmental factors and the organization's strategy influence organizational structure.

Explain the types of organizational structure important for firms to use when operating in international markets.

output. For example, two independent product divisions in the same company might each sell products to the same hospital to meet the customer's overall needs. **Sequential interdependence** exists when the outputs of one group become the inputs of another group. For example, at Boeing the raw materials of aluminum provided by the firm's purchasing department become the inputs of the firm's pressing department. That department then shapes the aluminum sheets for doors and its outputs become the inputs of the door assembly department.

common output

sequential interdependence
when the outputs of one group become the inputs of another group

Because organizations often have many alliances, a network structure becomes important for implementing this type of cooperative strategy.[4]

It is important for current and future managers to understand the fundamentals of organizational design and structure so that they can better prepare for implementing structures to make them effective. There are usually multiple structural options. Consequently, it is

reciprocal interdependence
when two or more groups depend on one another for inputs

Reciprocal interdependence exists when two or more groups depend on one another for inputs. For example, at Boeing the new-product development department relies on the marketing research department for product ideas to investigate, and marketing research relies on new-product development for new products to test on customers. In principle, the greater the interdependence, the greater the need for cooperation, and, thus, the more important it is to achieve integration.

uncertainty
the extent to which organizations cannot accurately forecast future input, throughput, and output factors

Another factor that can influence the need for integration is uncertainty. **Uncertainty** for a firm refers to the extent to which the firm cannot forecast accurately future input, process, and output factors. The more difficult it is to accurately forecast these factors, the greater uncertainty the firm faces. When there is greater uncertainty, there is greater need for integration and coordination because as events unfold, individuals and organizational units have to coordinate in real time their responses to the events.

Integration and coordination can be achieved through a variety of mechanisms.[15] The appropriateness of each mechanism relates to the level and type of interdependence and the extent of uncertainty in the environment. Among these mechanisms are rules, goals, and values.

RULES Rules establish guidelines for behavior and consequences under specific conditions. Basically, rules are the standard operating procedures (SOP) for the organization. In general, the more task independence that exists within the organization, the more useful rules are as an integration mechanism. In contrast, the more task interdependence and uncertainty that exist, the less useful rules are as an integration mechanism. For example, a manager in the promotion department of a record company would find it difficult to use rules for coordination and integration to implement concert cancellations due to weather, travel problems for the band, or any number of other unpredictable factors. Rules might work well in the accounting department of the record company where the environment is stable and the requirements are largely standard but would likely be less effective in the dynamic environment and requirements of the advertising and promotion department.

GOALS As task uncertainty and interdependence increase, the use of preset rules become less effective to coordinate tasks. Consequently under these conditions, goals are a more effective coordination mechanism than rules. Instead of specifying what individuals should do, goals specify what outcomes individuals should achieve. Effective goals define measurable outcomes and often require high levels of effort to achieve. Specifying the outcomes, but not the process, gives employees greater flexibility to determine how they will accomplish their tasks. It also facilitates integration by ensuring that people are working toward the same outcomes. For example, university professors encounter students with a wide variety of needs and situations. Rather than provide professors with set rules, the university typically sets goals in terms of student proficiency. These goals ensure that professors are working toward the same outcome but have the flexibility to respond to different needs and situations faced by individual students.

values
fundamentally important behaviors, activities, and outcomes

VALUES In conditions of high task uncertainty and interdependence, values become an important coordinating mechanism. The **values** in an organization identify fundamentally important behaviors, activities, and outcomes, such as customer satisfaction. But unlike goals, values do not necessarily represent measurable outcomes. Thus, values are a better integrating mechanism than goals when there is high uncertainty and high interdependence. Shared values facilitate coordination under these conditions because those holding the same values all work toward the same outcomes while maintaining flexibility in the process of how they are accomplished.

Exhibit 7.2 helps illustrate the level of appropriateness of rules, goals, and values in conditions of low to high levels of uncertainty. The exhibit also helps illustrate the partial overlap among them. As a matter of practice, it is impossible to specify the line where rules are no longer effective and goals should be used. Likewise, an exact boundary between the use of goals and values cannot be specified. Managers need to understand the relationship of rules, goals, and values with different levels of uncertainty and to use judgment in applying them.

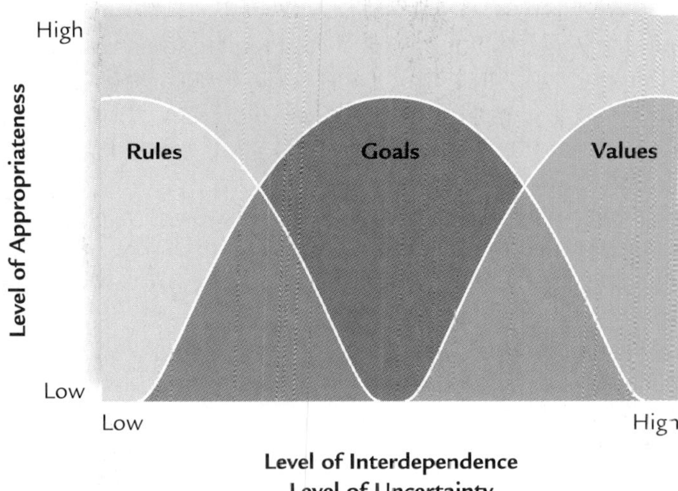

EXHIBIT 7.2

Appropriateness of Rules, Goals, Values

Formalization

One way to balance both differentiating (separating) and integrating people and activities is through formalization. **Formalization** is the defined structures and systems in decision making, communication, and control in the organization. These mechanisms usually explicitly define where and how people and activities are independent along with how they are integrated. While all organizations have to manage differentiation and integration, they vary substantially in how much formalization they use to accomplish this.

formalization
the official and defined structures and systems related to the decision making, communication, and control in an organization

Officially designating the line of authority within an organization is a common way of achieving formalization. A firm's **line of authority** specifies who reports to whom. It is often called line of authority because in organizational charts a line is typically drawn between subordinates and their bosses. Although it is important to follow the line of authority in many situations, there may be times that managers and employees go outside of the line of authority to seek special expertise needed to resolve a problem.

line of authority
specifies who reports to whom

More formal organizations also tend to stress unity of command. **Unity of command** suggests that an employee should have only one boss. Thus, people working in a highly formal organization with a strong orientation to unity of command are likely to have one boss who directs their work and evaluates their performance. The matrix structure used by Luiz Freire's company, Halliburton, violates the unity of command principle as we explain later. Yet such a structure has advantages that frequently offset the problems caused by people having two or more bosses.

unity of command
the notion that an employee should have one and only one boss

More formal systems also often limit a supervisor's span of control. **Span of control** refers to the number of employees reporting to a given supervisor. More formal organizations tend to have narrow rather than wide spans of control. The logic for this is that normally the fewer people a manager has to supervise, the more closely the manager can oversee and control them. However, several factors can influence the effectiveness of span of control. First, the nature of the task is an important factor. Usually, the more routine subordinates' tasks, the wider the effective span of control can be; managers can effectively supervise more subordinates if they have predictable and routine tasks. Another factor influencing effective span of control is subordinates' capabilities. Generally, the greater the subordinates' capabilities are, the less close supervision they require—thus, a larger span of control can be effective. Also, managerial capabilities influence effective span of control. The greater the manager's capabilities are, the wider the span of control that a manager can handle effectively. Integrating these three factors, we can see that if a manager is highly capable and his or her subordinates highly skilled, a wider span of control is possible. Exhibit 7.3 provides a brief summary of key factors that influence the effective span of control.[16]

span of control
the number of employees reporting to a given supervisor

Consistent patterns of span of control can affect the overall "shape" of the organization. Narrow spans of control throughout the entire organization tend to result in a **tall organization structure**, or one that has multiple layers with significant vertical differentiation. Wide

tall organization structure
a structure that has multiple layers or is high in terms of vertical differentiation

EXHIBIT 7.3

Factors That Influence the Span of Control

- *Job complexity*—Jobs that are complicated require more managerial input and involvement and, thus, the span of control tends to be narrower.
- *Job similarity*—If one manages a group of employees performing similar jobs, the span of control can be considerably wider than if the jobs of subordinates are substantially different.
- *Geographic proximity of supervised employees*—Because employees who work in one location are more easily supervised than employees in dispersed locations, physical proximity to employees tends to allow a wider span of control.
- *Amount of coordination*—A narrower span of control is advisable in firms where management expends much time coordinating tasks performed by subordinates.
- *Abilities of employees*—Supervisors who manage employees who are more knowledgeable and capable can have a wider span of control than supervisors managing less knowledgeable and capable employees. The greater the abilities of employees, the less managerial inputs are required and, thus, a wider span of control is possible.
- *Degree of employee empowerment*—Because employees who are trusted and empowered to make decisions need less supervision than employees with less autonomy and decision-making discretion, supervisors who empower their employees can have a wider span of control.
- *Ability of management*—More capable managers can manage more employees than less competent managers. The abilities of managers to educate employees and effectively respond to their questions lessen the need for a narrow span of control.
- *Technology*—Communication technology, such as mobile phones, fax, e-mail, workshare software, can allow managers to effectively supervise employees who are not geographically proximate, have complex and different jobs, and require significant coordination.

flat organization structure a structure that has fewer layers in its hierarchy than a tall organization

span of control throughout the organization will generally lead to a more **flat organization structure**. Given similar number of employees, a flat organization will have fewer layers in its hierarchy than a tall organization. Exhibit 7.4 shows examples of tall and flat organizational structures, as well as span of control.

The external environment largely affects the appropriateness of a tall or flat organization. Tall and formal organizations tend to be slower at making decisions and responding to changes in the business environment. As a result, tall and formal organizations tend to be best suited to stable external environments.[17] Because many organizational environments have become more dynamic, managers often respond by trying to "flatten" their organizational structures—often removing whole levels of hierarchy and people in the process (often referred to as downsizing). They do this so that information does not have to travel as far (from the bottom to the top) for decisions to be made, and as a consequence they can make and implement them faster.[18]

Nonetheless, implementing and managing flat structures can be a challenge. As environmental uncertainty increases for many organizations, managers often design flatter structures so that information can flow faster and decisions can be made more quickly. However, the environmental uncertainty also tends to result in more nonroutine tasks, which often require more narrow spans of control, creating taller, rather than flatter, organizations. Thus, flatter organizations and wider spans of control with more nonroutine tasks are only possible if subordinates and managers have stronger capabilities. Technology can arguably help companies remain flat by influencing the effective span of control.

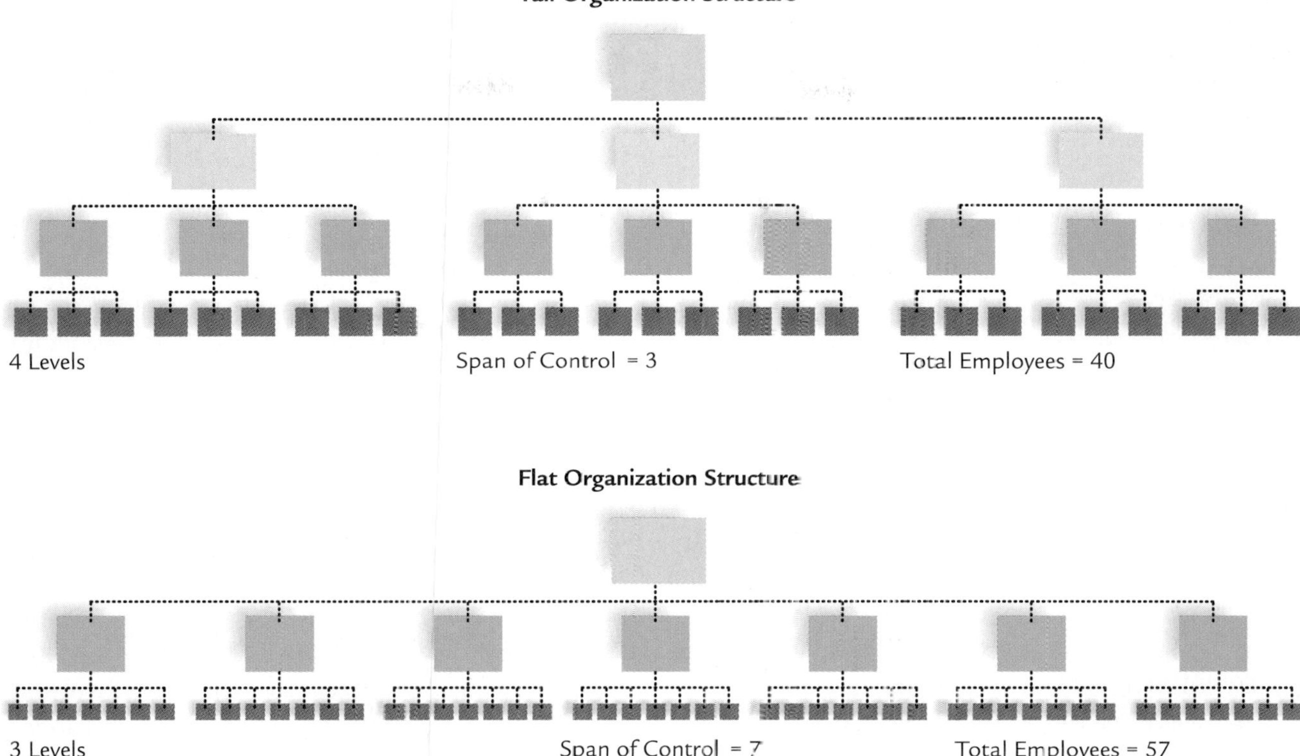

EXHIBIT 7.4 Tall and Flat Organization Structures

In summary, formalization mechanisms, such as span of control, line of authority, and chain of command, work to both differentiate and integrate people and their activities. They do so in an explicit and official way.

In A Manager's Challenge, "AES Gives Power to the People," structure by empowering lower-level employees to make major decisions. To ensure accountability and increase the probability of success, AES also provides its employees incentive compensation based on the company's performance. Thus, they will be motivated to help the company perform well. AES also operates a more informal organization with no human resources, operations, purchasing, or legal affairs departments. Furthermore, it encourages employees to seek advice from one another and managers in different parts of the company before making major decisions. This process fosters informal communication across the company's units and levels. AES's organizational structure and approach have been very successful. The company's return on invested capital grew 11.3 percent in 2005.[19]

Informalization

While virtually all organizations have some degree of formalization, even the most formal organizations also have some degree of informalization. The **informal organization** consists of the unofficial but influential means of communication, decision making, and control that are part of the habitual way things get done in the organization. Informal structures for decision making, communication, and control usually are not represented in organizational charts, yet they are common in the day-to-day operations of most organizations.

informal organization the unofficial but influential means of communication, decision making, and control that are part of the habitual way things get done in an organization

Both the degree of formalization and the degree of informalization can vary from company to company. It can also vary across countries. For example, one study compared U.S. and Japanese firms and found that the Japanese relied much more on informalization.[20] Japanese companies accomplish much of their decision making, communication, and control through informal, face-to-face meetings between people who do not have formal reporting relationships. This process is referred to as *nemawasi*. When nemawasi ensues, informal conversations occur in which incremental decisions are made. Consequently, by

A MANAGER'S CHALLENGE

Diversity

AES Gives Power to the People

AES, one of the world's largest electric-power producers, has been able to achieve a remarkable level of success through its informal organization and empowerment of its employees. In addition, employees in the field make many large acquisition decisions.

The company has been successful because its local units are empowered to make their own decisions yet are held accountable for their own profitability.

Many AES managers and employees see this empowerment as beneficial because it gives them a great deal of flexibility and freedom. It's as if they are running their own businesses versus working for other people. They also feel more creative and motivated. As a result, turnover is lower. AES even allows lower-level employees to make critical, multimillion-dollar decisions such as acquiring new subsidiaries. The system works because prior to making a decision, AES employees are expected to ask for advice (often by e-mail) from other people in the company, including senior managers.

Another reason for AES's success is due to the way the company is structured—its organization is very flat. For example, the company has never established separate corporate departments for its human resources, operations, purchasing, or legal affairs functions. Multiple teams work under a single level of management so bottom-up decision making is the norm. Fewer levels of management and shorter lines of communication accelerates decision making. Consequently, the company is nimble and can quickly respond strategically to changes in the marketplace.

Employee incentives programs have also contributed to AES's success. For example, the company gives an employee the option of earning a salary plus bonus (incentive) compensation in lieu of hourly and overtime pay. About 90 percent of AES's employees have chosen the salary-plus-bonus option. It is important to note that when standards and incentives are in place, employees are less likely to need intervention from "centralized" managers. AES feels that by giving the employees the power to make decisions, they will be more prone to support the company and will be more successful, which in turn will make the company more profitable. The culture thrives on individual empowerment, developing more capable employees, and holding them accountable for company performance with compensation through stock options. AES's people-oriented culture and empowered management has resulted in a low turnover rate and high employee satisfaction.

Sources: "A Worldwide Power Play," *Business Week*, November 27, 2000, www.businessweek.com; T. W. Malone, "Pioneers That Cultivate a New Model of Work," *Financial Times*, August 11, 2004, www.ft.com; G. Lee, "AES Corporation: Rewriting the Rules of Management," *Ray Shan's Journal*, December 6, 2005, www.rayshan.com; H. Wee, "A Nasty Short-Circuit at AES," *Business Week*, October 4, 2001, www.businessweek.com.

the time an official meeting is held to make the formal decision, the decision has already been made informally. In China, much is accomplished through relationships referred to as *guanxi*. Guanxi is developed over time. Basically, trust evolves between two people who take actions that benefit one another. In other words, reciprocity is expected. Guanxi is an important dimension of the informal organization in Chinese organizations.[21]

Centralization and Decentralization

centralized organizations
organizations that restrict decision making to fewer individuals, usually at the top of the organization

decentralized organizations
organizations that tend to push ...cision-making authority down ... lowest level possible

In addition to the organization structure's formalization and informalization, its extent of centralization or decentralization is also important. Centralization and decentralization refer to the level at which decisions are made, at the top of the organization or at lower levels. **Centralized organizations** tend to restrict decision making to fewer individuals, usually at the top of the organization. In contrast, **decentralized organizations** tend to push decision-making authority down to the lowest possible level. For instance, European multinational organizations tend to be decentralized and allow units in different countries to make decisions according to local conditions. Often this enables them to adapt to government demands and different consumer preferences.[22]

For many years, Philips, a large multinational electronics firm headquartered in the Netherlands, exemplified a decentralized international organization. Philips operated in over 60 countries around the world, and many of the larger-country units enjoyed considerable freedom and autonomy. For example, even though the V2000 videocassette recorder (the first VCR) was developed at the company's headquarters, the North American division of Philips refused to purchase and sell the product in the United States and Canada. Instead, North American Philips purchased a VCR made by a Japanese rival and resold it in the United States and Canada under the Philips brand name.

Japanese firms, on the other hand, exhibit a stronger degree of centralization and tend not to delegate decisions as frequently as either European or American firms.[23] Most Japanese multinational firms operate like centralized hubs into which information flows, and from which decisions are announced to foreign subsidiaries. Japanese firms have encountered increasing complaints from host nationals in local subsidiaries about a "bamboo ceiling"—the fact that host nationals are sometimes excluded from strategic decision making because Japanese expatriates sent by headquarters to ensure more centralized control occupy nearly all key positions in the subsidiary.[24] A major "bamboo ceiling" was broken when Sony named Howard Stringer, a citizen of Great Britain, as the CEO of Sony in 2005. At the time, Sony's performance was suffering, and Stringer was charged with the task of turning it around. However, Sony's performance has not rebounded since he was named CEO, thus clouding his future as the leader for the Japanese company.[25]

Sometimes it is perceived that formalization and centralization are essentially the same, and that informalization and decentralization are also synonymous. This is not the case (see Exhibit 7.5). A highly formal organization may be centralized, but a formal organization can also be fairly decentralized. For example, as we illustrated previously, Philips is a fairly decentralized company in that decisions are pushed down into the organization. At the same time, however, Philips is also relatively formalized. Lines of authority, chain of command, official policies, and so on are prevalent. In contrast, the U.S. military is both formal and centralized.

Similarly, a highly informal organization can be either decentralized or highly centralized. For example, on average, Japanese firms are relatively centralized but at the same time function through a high degree of informalization. Likewise, it is quite common for family-owned businesses to be both centralized and informal. That is, the owner makes most of the decisions, but informal connections, communication, and control, rather than the formal structures or rules, determine how tasks are accomplished. In contrast, Club Med is fairly decentralized and informal. Each general manager of a resort is fairly free to make decisions that meet the needs of his or her unique market. Club Med achieves coordination through an array of informal relationships among general managers and corporate managers.

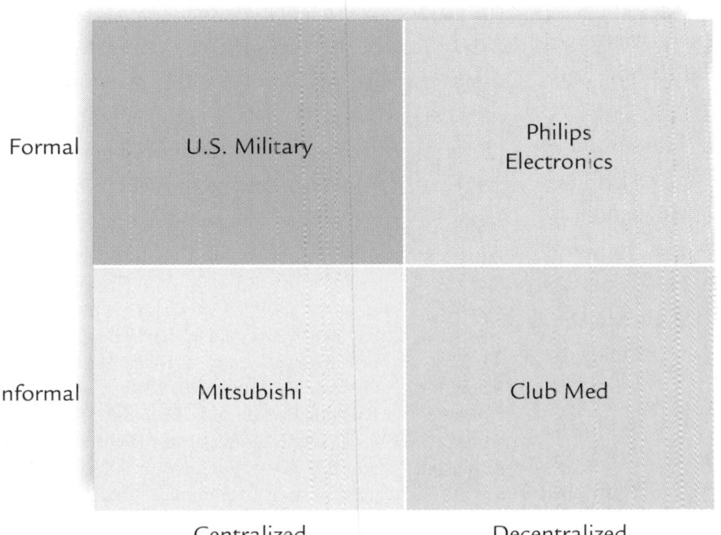

EXHIBIT 7.5

Combinations of Formal/Informal and Centralized/Decentralized

Some research suggests that the more intense the firm's information needs are, the more formal and centralized its IT (information technology) structure becomes.[26] Other research shows that the strategic use of decentralized structures allows units to adapt important new procedures to fit their needs and environment. In this way, they are more able to successfully get their subsidiaries and divisions to adopt new programs such as quality management standards and approaches.[27]

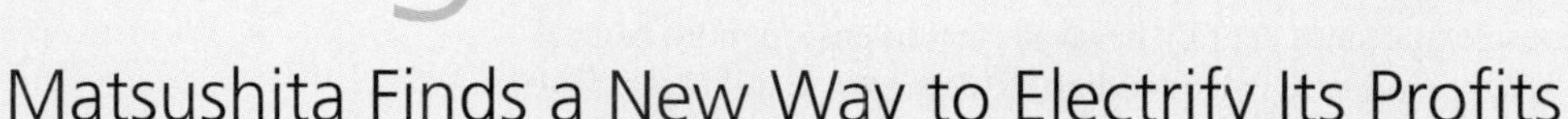

A MANAGER'S CHALLENGE

Change

Matsushita Finds a New Way to Electrify Its Profits

In 1994, Matsushita's then-CEO Teruo Tanni resigned abruptly from the firm saying his departure was due to the company's sagging fortunes, for which he took responsibility. Tanni's sudden departure shocked many in Japan's corporate world because CEO ousters are almost unheard of there. It seemed especially odd for Matsushita, which had commonly adhered to traditional Japanese-style management. Subsequent to Tanni's resignation, Chairman Matsushita asked the most junior of Matsushita's executive vice presidents to manage the company. His selection sent a strong message that the company wanted to change how it managed the business. This was reinforced when the company failed to keep ex-CEO Tanni on its board of directors.

Matsushita wasted no time reorganizing following Tanni's departure. The company also subsequently hired a new CEO, Kunio Nakamura, who played a pivotal role turning the company around. A three-year strategic plan was developed in which its approach was referred to as "Four-S Management" indicating "simple," "small," "speedy," and "strategic." The company's new management team wanted to simplify the company's managerial approach and make it less hierarchical.

Decentralizing decision authority to Matsushita's lower-level managers was essential to this plan. In so doing, the company removed an entire layer of management at headquarters, and the heads of the operating divisions were given full responsibility for product development as well as production and finance. Basically, each division had the autonomy to operate its own business, with Matsushita acting as the "shareholder" of each division.

Such decentralization and focus on individual responsibility is unusual in Japan, where group-oriented decision making is the norm and centralized authority is common. However, the change positively affected the heads of divisions, encouraging them to be more entrepreneurial. In addition, all managers from the lowest to the highest levels were required to provide Nakamura with a personal, three-year "revival" plan for each of their divisions or departments. By centralizing the company's research and development operations, each individual then had authority and responsibility directly provided by the CEO, which, in turn, created a flat organizational structure. Nakamura also ended the internal rivalries that led some divisions to develop identical products by centralizing the R&D operations.

Ultimately, the restructuring of Matsushita led to the recovery of the company. With the reduction in management levels and reorganization of 30 divisions into four groups with shared R&D facilities, the company cut costs and achieved a 50 percent operating profit for 2002. Eliminating product lines, merging operations, and centralizing R&D reduced costs; nothing was sacred, not even the corporate structure, which included the lifetime employment system established by the founder Konosuke Matsushita. Today, the $75 billion company is one of the biggest consumer electronics makers in the world and is receiving the benefits of the changes because Matsushita is achieving its best profit performance in a decade. Many are shocked at the changes made at Matsushita because they were antithetical to the Japanese culture. Yet, one would imagine that the company's stockholders are pleased with the outcomes.

Sources: I. Kunii, "Matsushita on the Mend," *Business Week*, December 30, 2002, www.businessweek.com; K. Hall, "Matsushita's Transformer Steps Down," *Business Week*, June 30, 2006, www.businessweek.com; "Management Tradition Be Damned," *Business Week*, October 31, 1994, www.businessweek.com; M. Nakamoto, "Reforms Drive Up Profits at Matsushita," *Financial Times*, February 5, 2005, www.ft.com; "News and Events," Panasonic, www.panasonic.net March 1, 2007.

Matsushita went against tradition and decentralized decision-making authority to its various divisions and departments. Today, it is largely decentralized, with centralized R&D operations to eliminate the duplicate products developed by divisions within the company trying to compete against each other. Thus, Matsushita was simultaneously decentralized and centralized (in different areas). The outcomes of the change in structure were dramatic and positive. The company's profits have increased greatly since the change.

Common Organizational Structures

A variety of organizational structures exist, but six structures represent the most common forms. We examine each of these basic structures although you can obtain variations by combining more than one structural form. In reality, most organizations do not have pure forms but rather have hybrids. After we review these basic organizational structures and briefly examine their general strengths and weaknesses, we then move to a more detailed discussion of the conditions that determine which type of structure a manager should adopt.

Functional Structure

Perhaps the simplest structure is the functional structure (Exhibit 7.6). The functional structure is used to organize the firm around traditional functional areas, such as accounting, finance, marketing, operations, and so on.[28] This structure is one of the most common types because it separates the specialized knowledge of each functional area through horizontal differentiation and can direct that knowledge toward the firm's key products or services.

Firms with operations outside their domestic borders might also adopt a functional structure. The key difference between a purely domestic organization and a multinational organization with a functional structure is the scope of the responsibilities functional heads in the multinational firm bear. In a multinational, each department has global responsibilities. Although each subsidiary might have a local human resource manager, the top human resource manager in the company (usually in the home office) is responsible for directing worldwide human resource activities, such as hiring, training, appraising, or rewarding employees. This structure is most commonly used when the technology and products of the firm are similar throughout the world.

The major advantages of this structure include the following:

- It is well suited to small to medium-sized firms with limited product diversification.
- It facilitates specialization of the firm's functional knowledge.
- It reduces the duplication of the firm's functional resources.
- It facilitates coordination within the firm's functional areas.

A global functional structure can also reduce headquarters–subsidiary conflicts because it integrates operations throughout the world into their functional areas and charges functional department executives with global responsibility. This, in turn, enhances the overall international orientation of managers. For example, the higher a

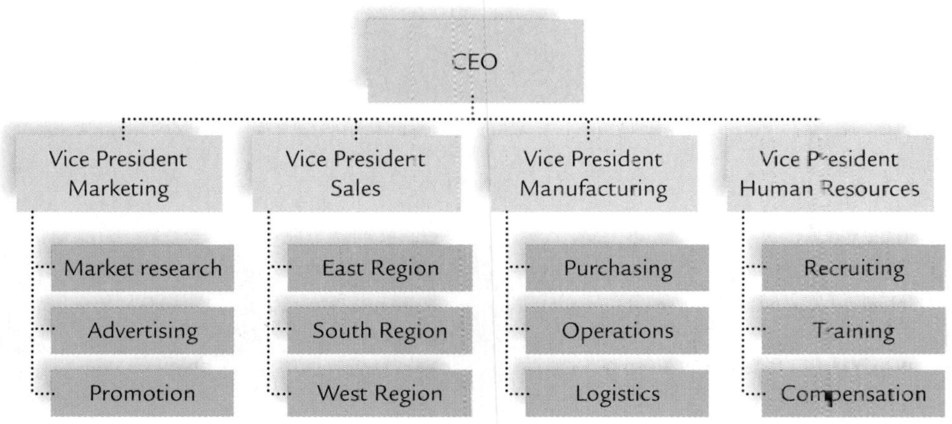

EXHIBIT 7.6

Functional Structure

marketing manager rises in the marketing department, the more that manager needs to think about and understand the firm's global marketing issues.

The primary weaknesses of this structure include the following:

1. It often creates problems of coordination across the firm's functional groups.
2. It leads to a narrow view of the organization's overall goals.
3. It can limit the attention paid to customers as functional groups focus on their specific areas.
4. It can result in the organization responding slower to market changes.
5. It often burdens chief executives with decisions that involve multiple functions.

In an international setting, a functional structure has disadvantages when the firm has a wide variety of products and these products have different environmental demands, such as different government restrictions or standards, customer preferences, or performance qualities. This weakness is exacerbated when different functional departments experience different demands across geographical areas. For example, if accounting practices are similar between the United Kingdom and France but advertising approaches differ, this will tend to exaggerate coordination difficulties between the accounting and marketing departments.

Product Structure

profit center
a unit or product line in which the related expenses are deducted from the revenue generated

In a product structure like that shown in Exhibit 7.7, the firm is organized around specific products (or services) or related sets of products (or services). Typically, each product group contains all the traditional departments a functional structure has, such as finance, marketing, operations, human resource management departments, and so on. Each product is generally treated as a **profit center**. That is, the expenses related to a product are subtracted from the revenues generated by the sales of that product. Most commonly, the heads of the product or services units are located in the headquarters of the company. However, this is not necessarily the case. For example, the headquarters for Honeywell's commercial and residential control product group is in Minnesota, whereas the headquarters for its commercial flight instruments product group is in Arizona.

The principal advantages of a product structure include the following:

1. Individuals in different functional areas within the product group focus more on the specific products and customers.
2. The performance of the firm's products (profits and losses) is typically easier to evaluate.
3. There is usually greater product responsiveness to market changes.
4. It often reduces the operating decision-making burden of the top executive.

The major disadvantages of the product structure include the following:

1. Duplication and lack of economies of scale for functional areas (for example, IT, finance, human resources, and so on).

EXHIBIT 7.7

Product Structure

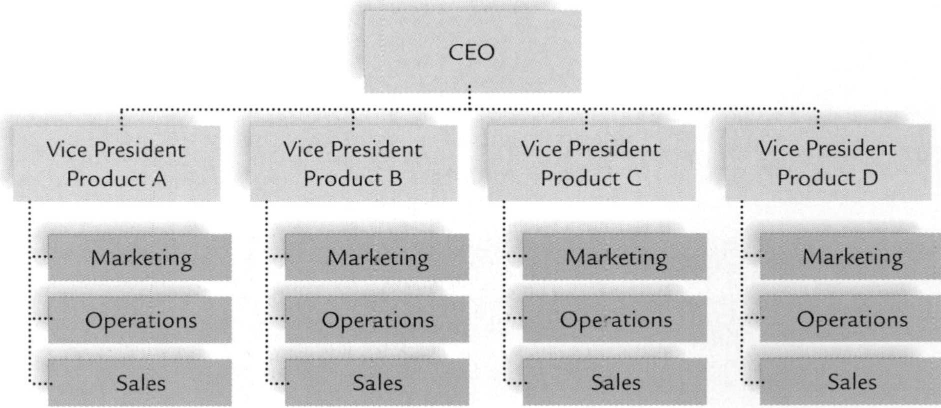

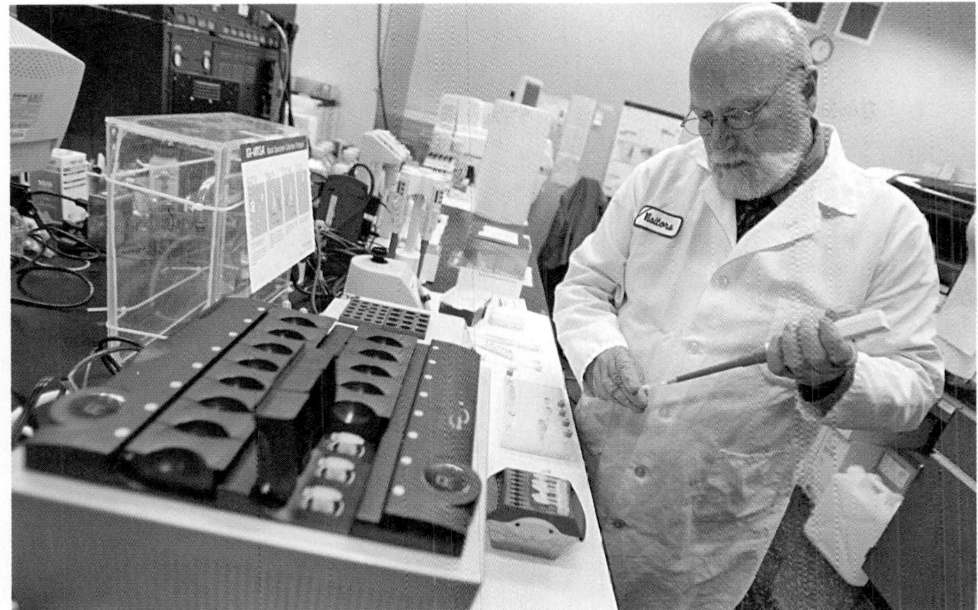

Multinational firms, such as Becton Dickinson, a medical products firm based in Franklin Lakes, New Jersey, frequently use global product structures. They typically do so when their customers' needs for a given product are similar throughout the international markets in which the firm participates.

2. It can create problems for customers who purchase products across multiple product groups.
3. Sometimes there are conflicts between the firm's corporate objectives and the objectives of its product groups.
4. There is an increased likelihood of conflict between different product groups and greater difficulty coordinating across product groups.

Multinational firms also use global product structures. This typically occurs when customer needs for a given product are similar throughout the international markets in which the firm participates. After Becton Dickinson adopted a global product structure, the head of the biosciences unit became responsible for global strategy formulation and implementation of those products.

Division Structure

The division structure can be viewed as an extension of a product structure. Exhibit 7.8 provides a partial organizational chart of the division structure of Becton Dickinson, a medical products company. Divisions typically consist of multiple products within a generally related area, though specific products may not necessarily be closely related. General Electric (GE) has over 11 different business units, organizing a diversified portfolio of

EXHIBIT 7.8

Division Structure

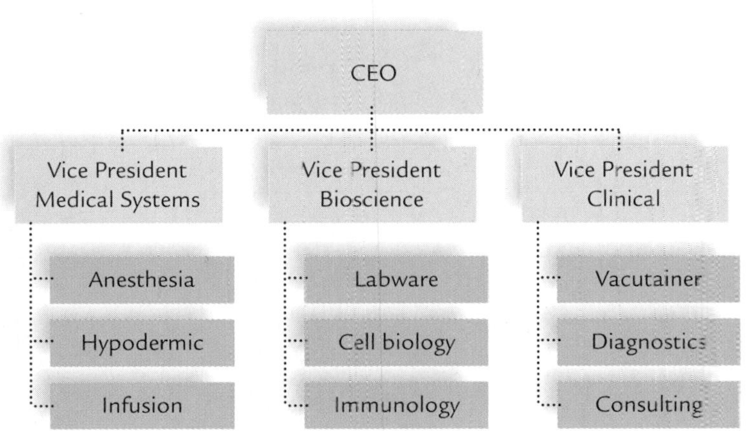

products including financial services, transportation, energy, insurance, medical systems, and entertainment products.

Within each unit, there are broad arrays of product groups and specific products. For example, the Medical Systems Division within GE consists of 12 different product groups, such as cardiology, radiology, emergency room equipment, and products related to orthopedics and sports medicine. Within each of these groups are many more specific products. Clearly, it takes a significant size and diversity of products to justify the creation of a division structure. A division structure also facilitates the use of modular products each of which is different but which contain some of the same parts. Thus, modular parts are produced and assembled in different ways to produce several different products.[29] Typically, in a division structure, all functional activities are located within each division.

The following are common strengths of a division structure:

1. Organizing various product families within a division can reduce functional duplication and enhance economies of scale for the firm's functional activities.
2. To the extent that product families within a division serve common customers, customer focus is often stronger.
3. Cross-product coordination within the division is easier.
4. Cross-regional coordination within product families and within the division is often easier.

The following are common disadvantages of a division structure:

1. Typically it is only appropriate for large, diversified companies with significant numbers of specific products and product families.
2. It can inhibit cross-division coordination.
3. It can create coordination difficulties between division objectives and corporate objectives.

Similar to domestic firms, multinational firms often use this structure. In this case, each division is charged with global responsibility. Because a division structure is generally an extension of a product structure, it has many of the same advantages and disadvantages. For large, diversified multinational firms, the division structure is one of the more common structures used.

Customer Structure

As the name implies, customer structures are organized around categories of customers (Exhibit 7.9). Typically, this structure is used when different categories of customers have independent needs that differ from each other. For example, industrial customers might purchase a different set of products than retail customers.

The primary strengths of this structure include the following:

1. It facilitates in-depth understanding of specific customers.
2. It increases the firm's responsiveness to changes in customer preferences and needs as well as the firm's responsiveness to actions taken by competitors to better serve customers.

EXHIBIT 7.9

Customer Structure

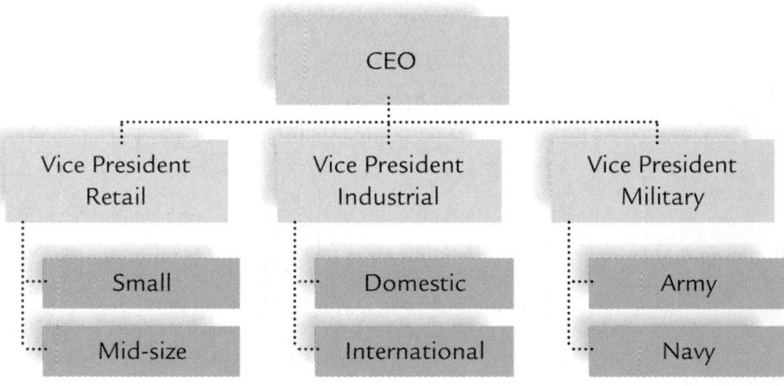

The primary weaknesses of this structure include the following:

1. It typically produces duplication of functional resources in each of the customer units.
2. It often makes it difficult to coordinate between customer units and corporate objectives.
3. It can fail to leverage technology or other strengths of one unit across other units.

Many multinational firms find this type of structure difficult to implement because customers differ across regions and countries. For example, even though IBM initially had a consulting unit focused on government customers, it found it difficult to organize the unit on a global basis because different governments had different needs and requirements for selecting computing-solution providers. Thus, while government customers in the United States were significantly different in their needs from other IBM customers, the advantage gained by focusing on this customer segment was not possible across the rest of the world.

Geographic or Regional Structure

As Exhibit 7.10 shows, firms can develop an organizational structure around various geographical areas or regions. Within this type of structure, regional executives are generally responsible for all functional activities and products in their regions. For example, a Western regional vice president might be responsible for all key business activities in the states of Washington, Oregon, California, Nevada, Montana, Utah, Idaho, Wyoming, Colorado, Arizona, and New Mexico. The individual regions are often treated as profit centers. Thus, each region's profitability is measured against the revenues it generates and the expenses it incurs.

The major advantages of a geographic or regional structure include the following:

1. It typically leads to in-depth understanding of the market, customers, governments, and competitors within a given geographical area.
2. It usually fosters a strong sense of accountability for performance among regional managers.
3. It increases the firm's responsiveness to unique changes in the market, government regulations, economic conditions, and so forth for the geographic region.

The major disadvantages of a geographic or regional structure include the following:

1. It often inhibits coordination and communication between regions.
2. It can increase conflict and coordination difficulties between regions and the firm's corporate office.
3. It normally leads to duplication of functional resources across regions.
4. Separating production facilities across multiple regions can inhibit economies of scale.
5. It can foster competitive behavior among regions, which is particularly frustrating for customers who have operations across multiple regions.

Multinational firms commonly employ geographic or regional structures.[30] This is primarily because customers' demands, government regulations, competitive conditions,

EXHIBIT 7.10

Geographical/Regional Structure

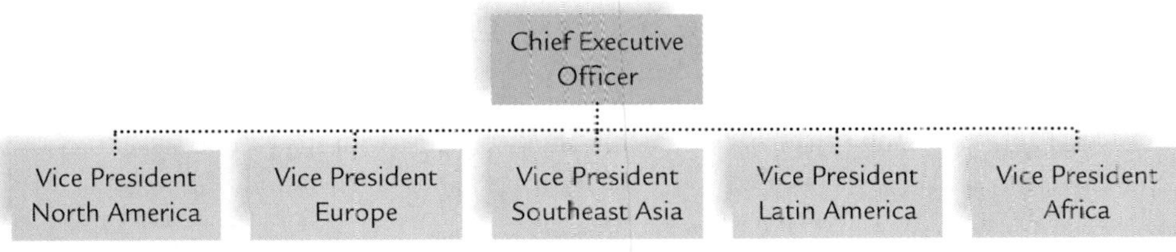

Strengths:
- Facilitates local responsiveness
- Develops in-depth knowledge of specific regions or countries
- Creates accountability by region
- Facilitates cross-functional coordination within regions

Weaknesses:
- Often creates cross-regional coordination difficulties
- Can inhibit ability to capture global scale economies
- Duplicates resources and functions across regions

the availability of suppliers, and other factors vary significantly from one region of the world to another. The size or scope of the region is typically a function of the volume of business. For example, in consumer products companies, the Middle East and Africa are often included in the European region because the volume of sales in these areas is too small to justify separate regions (EMEA—Europe, Middle East, and Africa). On the other hand, for most oil and gas companies with a geographic structure, the Middle East is a separate region because of its importance as a source of oil.

Matrix Structure

A matrix structure, such as the one shown in Exhibit 7.11, consists of two organizational structures superimposed on each other. As a consequence, there are dual reporting relationships. That is, one person essentially reports to two bosses. These two structures can be a combination of the general forms already discussed. For example, the matrix structure might consist of product divisions intersecting with functional departments or geographical regions intersecting with product divisions. This is the structure used by Halliburton as described in the opening profile. As we explained, Luiz Freire is a regional manager. He coordinates with country managers and product or project managers. The two overlapping structures used are often based on the two dominant aspects of an organization's environment.

The major strengths of a matrix structure include the following:

1. It typically facilitates information flow throughout the organization.
2. It can enhance decision-making quality because before key decisions are made, the organization considers both intersecting perspectives.
3. It is best suited to a changing and complicated business environment.
4. It can facilitate the flexible use of human resources.

The major disadvantages of a matrix structure include the following:

1. It often makes performance evaluations more complex because employees usually have two bosses.
2. It can inhibit the organization's ability to respond to changing conditions quickly.
3. It can diffuse accountability.
4. Conflicts can occur when the firm attempts to integrate the differing perspectives and objectives of intersecting units.

Multinational companies frequently use matrix organization structures, as exemplified by Halliburton. They are used often because although economies of scale for global product, division, or even customer structures are compelling, regional differences relative to governments, cultures, languages, and economies are also strong. However, matrix structures are especially difficult to manage in multinational companies. ABB, a large industrial company based in Switzerland, for many years had a regional division matrix structure. However, in the late 1990s, senior executives at ABB determined that the

EXHIBIT 7.11

Matrix Structure

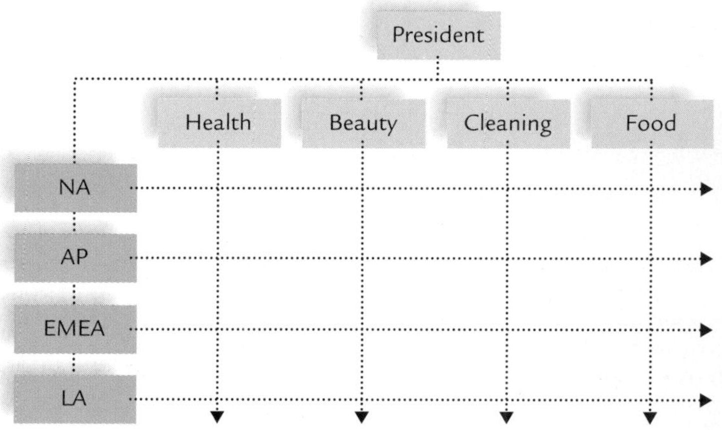

conflicts and difficulties of managing the matrix outweighed the benefits so they changed to a global division structure. Even though such changes are positive, they also are difficult to design and implement. Thus, it requires much planning for major changes in structure.[31]

Mixed Organizational Structures

As we mentioned earlier, although there are pure structural forms, any combination of the basic organizational structures is possible. The typical objective of a mixed, or a hybrid, organizational structure is to gain the advantages of one structure and reduce its disadvantages by incorporating the strengths of different structures. Because many of these hybrid structures are reflected in contemporary organizational forms, we explore this issue in more depth in the next section; however, Exhibit 7.12 provides an example of a hybrid functional-product-customer structure.

Network Organizational Structures

There are a variety of contemporary organizational structures. Many of them do not have common labels or names. This is, in part, because many of them have their essence in the configuration of organizational units and activities and organizational charts cannot easily depict them. One way of addressing these forms is by using the value chain concept introduced in Chapter 5. A major part of creating a contemporary structure involves reconfiguring the firm's value chain in an effort to gain cost savings and specialization benefits and improve integration and coordination.

Often these contemporary structures are referred to as network structures. There are several versions of network structures, ranging on a continuum from "low networked" to "high networked." In the low-networked structures, the quantity and magnitude of externally

EXHIBIT 7.12

Hybrid Structure

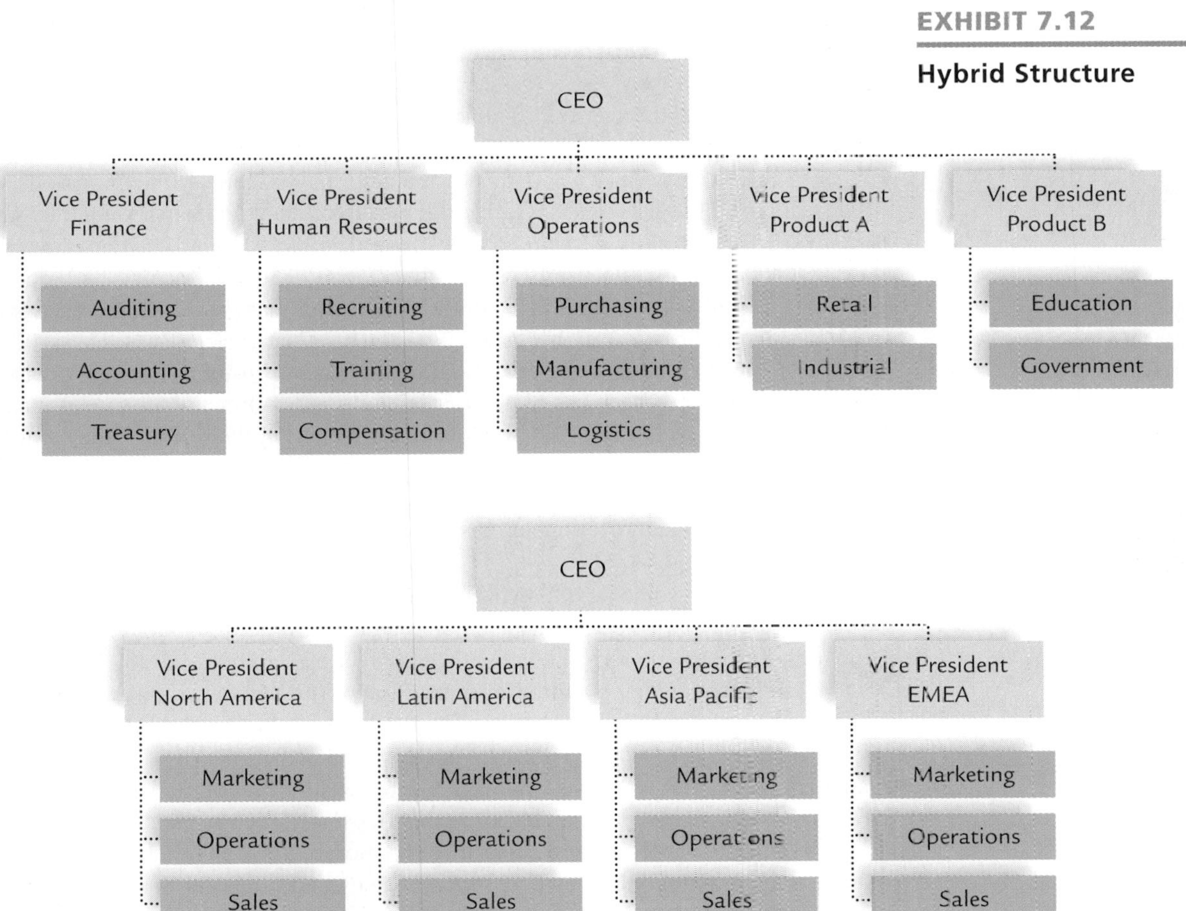

EXHIBIT 7.13

Outsourced Structure

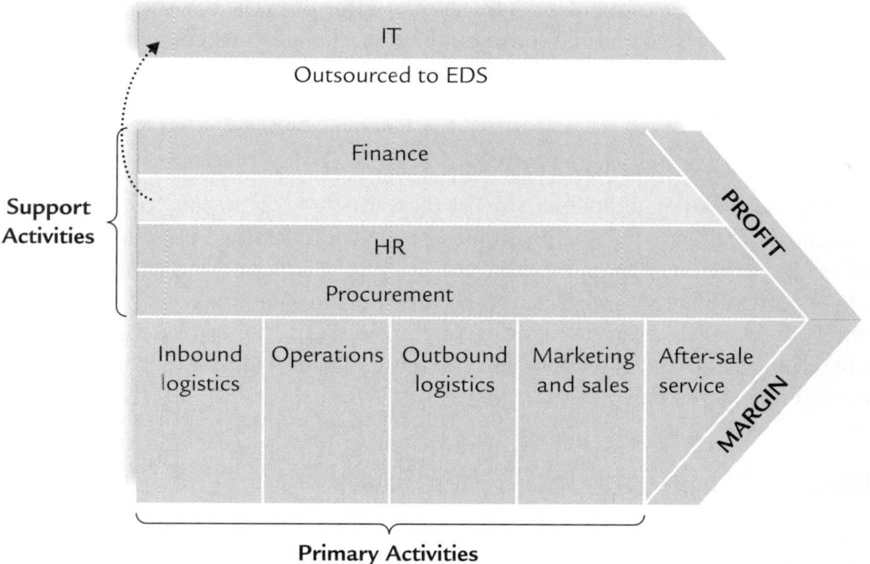

networked activities is limited. That is, a firm owns and executes most of its primary and support value chain activities and networks, and outside organizations are used for only a limited number of more minor value chain activities. In contrast, the high-networked structures include a larger quantity and magnitude of externally networked activities. In these structures, the number of externally networked value chain activities often exceeds those owned and executed internally by the firm.

One of the most common ways of networking with an external organization is to outsource a value chain activity. Outsourcing is the practice of taking a significant activity within the organization and contracting that activity out to an independent party. For example, in 2007 the European Space Agency signed a multibillion-dollar contract with EDS to perform virtually all the agency's IT functions.[32] A major portion of EDS's revenues comes from performing virtually all IT functions for a variety of customers (see Exhibit 7.13).

Nike outsources nearly all its shoe manufacturing, essentially the operations segment of the primary activities in its value chain. It is networked with its many contract manufacturers. Nike is so tightly networked that it can design a shoe at its Beaverton, Oregon, headquarters, send the blueprints via satellite to one of its contractors, and receive back by FedEx a prototype shoe from the contract factory all within a week. Increasingly, activities that executives once believed could only be done internally, such as IT, human resource administration, design, manufacturing, sales, and customer support, are being outsourced today. Technology has made it possible to network activities together and retain reliability as well as lower costs. Much of the outsourcing that occurs today is to companies in another country. All Nike's manufacturing contractors are located outside of the United States. Many outsourced activities are going to companies in India, particularly in IT.[33] Yet, the Indian government outsourced the processing of visas to a U.S. company in 2007.[34]

The available technology allowing communication and coordination to occur between distant locations and among multiple people on a real-time basis facilitates network-type structures. Some refer to this context as the digital era. Technology allows people to coordinate and to integrate their activities even though a formal organization does not bind them together.[35] Use of this new technology to "network" (coordinate and integrate) diverse people, activities, and organizations creates new and sometimes significant challenges for managers. As noted previously, managers must ensure that all activities are completed effectively—not an easy task if people are only loosely related to their organization.

In high-networked structures, firms have more value chain activities networked to external organizations than owned and executed internally. Assume a clothing design company formulated a strategy to compete by having superior design, world-class raw

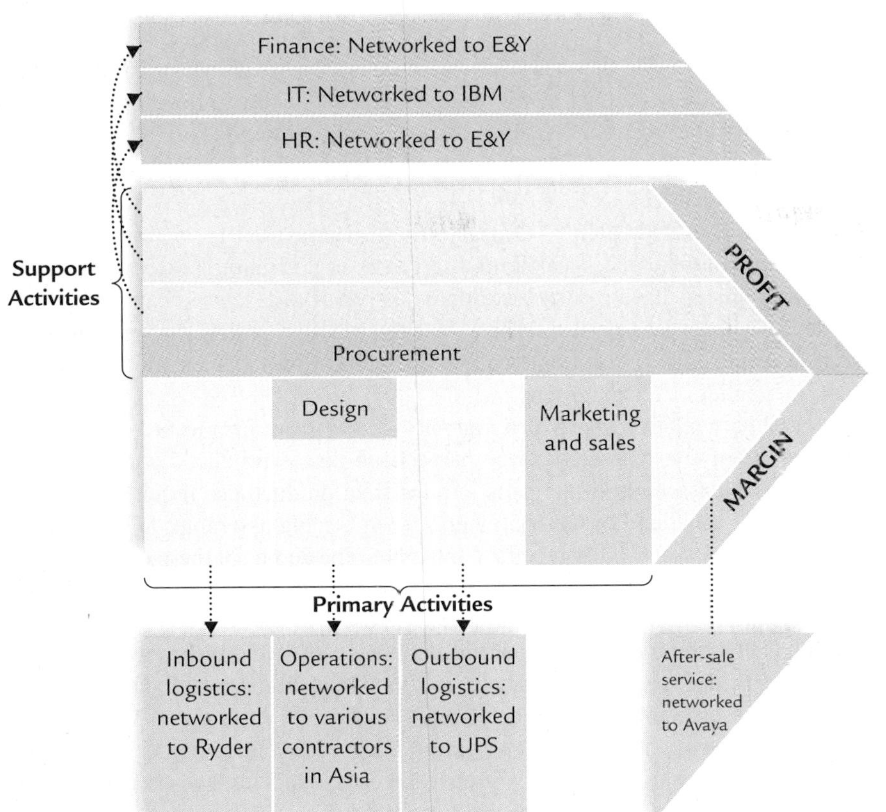

EXHIBIT 7.14

Network Structure

materials, and close relationships with retailers. Based on this strategy, the firm may own and control only a few elements of the entire value chain, such as design, procurement, and sales, but virtually nothing else. The firm could network with a company such as Ryder to perform its inbound logistics. It could network with various contractors in Asia to manufacture the clothes as designed. The firm could contract with UPS to perform all the outbound logistics. It could outsource customer service to Avaya to handle its customer services. IBM or EDS could run the IT functions. Ernst & Young could manage the HR, finance, and tax functions. In this way, managers of the company could focus their energies on the critical dimensions of the value chain, such as design, procurement, and sales, that are the most likely to provide a competitive advantage (see Exhibit 7.14).

Similar to the more traditional structures, **network structures** have both advantages and disadvantages. One of the most compelling potential advantages is that networking allows managers to focus on core competencies or the activities that are most likely to yield competitive advantage. By concentrating on core activities, managers can do them better. However, the "noncore" activities that are networked must also be performed effectively. It takes time, attention, energy, and skill to manage these relationships with external organizations. Simplified, network structure can provide greater focus and specialization on specific value chain activities, and it also requires oversight, coordination with the organizations that are performing the networked activities, and the integration of their outputs into the firm.

network structures formal or informal relationships among units or organizations (for example, along the firm's value chain)

Designing Organizations

Fundamentally, in designing organizations managers face the challenge of capturing both specialization and integration advantages while minimizing the often mirror-image disadvantages. So then, "How should the managers decide to actually structure an organization?" The two main determinants of this decision are the external environment and the strategy of the company.

The External Environment

A key factor in determining the match between the environment and organizational structure is environmental uncertainty.[36] We offered a relatively simple description of environmental uncertainty earlier in this chapter. Next, we expand this view with two related but separate constructs: the extent to which the environment is (a) complex and (b) dynamic.

environmental complexity the breadth and depth of differences and similarities in an organization's external environment

ENVIRONMENTAL COMPLEXITY **Environmental complexity** is fundamentally the breadth and depth of differences and similarities in an organization's external environment. Complex environments have greater breadth and depth of differences than simple environments. The differences and similarities can be assessed along many dimensions, but there are several core categories. These core categories include products, customers, technology, competitors, suppliers, and geography.

The complexity relative to products can vary widely from firm to firm. For example, a BIC pen consists of approximately seven parts. Each part is produced with relatively low technology, and the assembly of the parts into the final product also requires relatively low technology. At the other end of the continuum, when Boeing assembles a 787 jumbo jet, it has a huge breadth of over 1 million parts to integrate. The depths of these components range from a simple metal bolt to a panel composed of rare composite materials. Thus, Boeing has a highly complex product environment, especially relative to the BIC pen's environment.

Customers constitute another important dimension of environmental complexity. For example, McDonald's serves hamburgers to millions of customers each day, but the difference among these customers is relatively small compared to the group's overall size. In contrast, Toyota serves millions of customers each year, but their needs are different enough that key aspects of Toyota cars, such as the suspension and emissions systems, are very different from one region of the world to another.

Technology is another important dimension of environmental complexity. Technological complexity includes both the diversity of the technology required and the level of its sophistication. For example, Alcatel-Lucent Technologies utilizes analog, digital, and photonic technologies in its telephone and communication products. But the technology involved in both the manufacturing of its photonic switches for transmission of data along fiber optic lines and in the actual products Alcatel-Lucent makes is of a depth that many people with PhD's in physics have difficulty understanding it.

Competitors constitute an important dimension of environmental complexity. A larger number and greater diversity of competitors produce more complex environments. For example, in

A firm's environmental complexity relates not only to the competition that surrounds it but also its products, customers, technology, and geography. In terms of product complexity, consider Boeing: The company's planes, such as the 787 Dreamliner shown here, can consist of more than a million parts. The huge number of parts alone makes the operation more difficult to structure and coordinate.

the design and manufacture of commercial aircraft, Boeing has a fairly complex product environment, but it simultaneously has a much more simple competitor environment. Basically, its only direct competitor is Airbus. This does not mean that competing against Airbus is easy but only that its competitor environment is more simple than the environment of The GAP. The GAP competes with thousands of clothing manufacturers and labels for the same customers.

Suppliers are an additional dimension of environmental complexity. The greater number and diversity of suppliers lead to more complex environments. For example, despite having a more simple competitor environment, Boeing has a complex supplier environment. While Boeing designs most of the commercial aircraft it produces, it uses hundreds of suppliers, some making such large components as the entire tail sections of Boeing's planes.

The final dimension, geographic complexity, is included because it tends to have a significant impact on all the dimensions previously mentioned. This is principally because the more geographic regions covered the greater the probability of differences across the other categories. For example, the greater the number of countries in which a firm operates the greater the probability that dissimilarities will exist between the countries (their governments, laws, customer preferences, language, etc.). These differences are likely to increase the breadth and depth of differences relative to products, customers, technology, competitors, and suppliers. Consequently, greater geographic scope increases the complexity of the environment.

Environmental Dynamism

The second element contributing to the overall uncertainty of the environment is the extent to which the environment is static or dynamic.[37] Static environments may have few or many factors, but these factors tend to remain stable over time. For example, the manufacturing technology for pens and the component parts has changed little in the last 30 years. In contrast, factors in dynamic environments change rapidly. For example, advancements in composite materials and electronics have changed significantly for commercial aircraft manufacturers over the last 30 years. The fashion industry operates in an even more dynamic external environment. Benetton faces an environment in which colors, fabric, and styles change not just year to year but season to season. Firms facing dynamic environments often describe them as "white water" environments in reference to the challenges of navigating a raft down the changing rapids of a river. A rapidly changing external environment typically requires quick internal organizational changes.

While we note the effects of change in several chapters, we discuss at length, in Chapter 15, why organizational change is difficult, and systematic methods for enhancing its success.

By combining the dimensions of simple-complex and static-dynamic, we can create a four-cell matrix that provides a broad backdrop against which organizational design structures can be placed (see Exhibit 7.15). In general, the more complex and dynamic the environment

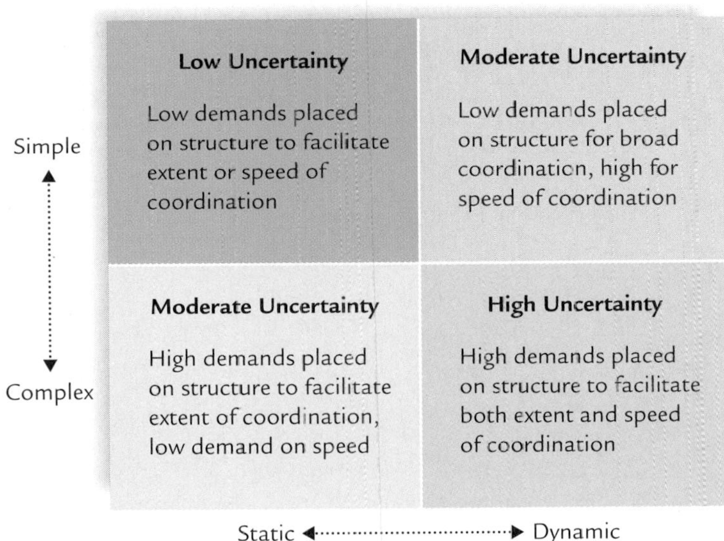

EXHIBIT 7.15

Matrix of Organizational Uncertainty

is, the more the organizational structure needs to coordinate different groups' efforts and the greater the speed with which this coordination needs to occur. This means that the more complex and dynamic the firm's environment, the more the structure will need to make use of mechanisms that facilitate coordination and integration, such as values, teams, and liaisons.

The Organization's Strategy

The second major element that managers must consider in designing their organization's structure is the company's strategy.[38] Unfortunately, there are no simple rules to use to match a particular structure to a company's strategy.

However, there are a few principles that can help to understand the relationship between strategy and structure.

A major principle is that the structure should complement and leverage the strategy. But, it is difficult to determine if a given structure complements or leverages the strategy.[39] However, we can gain important insights into this principle by examining one of the most common strategy formulation approaches. As we discussed in the previous chapter on strategy, one of the common means of formulating strategy is to determine the company's core competencies or resources that produce value, which is hard to imitate and is scarce, for customers. By focusing on these identified competencies or resources, we can more easily evaluate the fit or misfit of a proposed structure with the strategy.

Additionally, companies commonly use a division structure to complement a multiproduct strategy. Firms with such a strategy seek to operate in diverse product markets.[40] GE uses this strategy to manufacture and sell household electronic products and jet airplane engines and to provide financial and entertainment services. For each product or service market, it has a separate division.

Organizational Structures in an International Context

Our focus so far in this chapter has been on the basic organizational structures in both domestic and international contexts. Now, we examine organizational structure in an international context. Although more firms today are beginning as international organizations because of the technological reach, some are moving into international markets after they gain some level of maturity and managerial capabilities. Most start in one country and for a period of time focus on the customers within that country. Although international organizations would be easier to understand if they evolved steadily and systematically, they do not do so. However, there is a general relationship between the nature of the firm and its structure. This relationship was first proposed over 30 years ago[41] and has generally been supported[42] recently.[43] Exhibit 7.16 summarizes this theory and its findings.

EXHIBIT 7.16

International Strategy and Structure

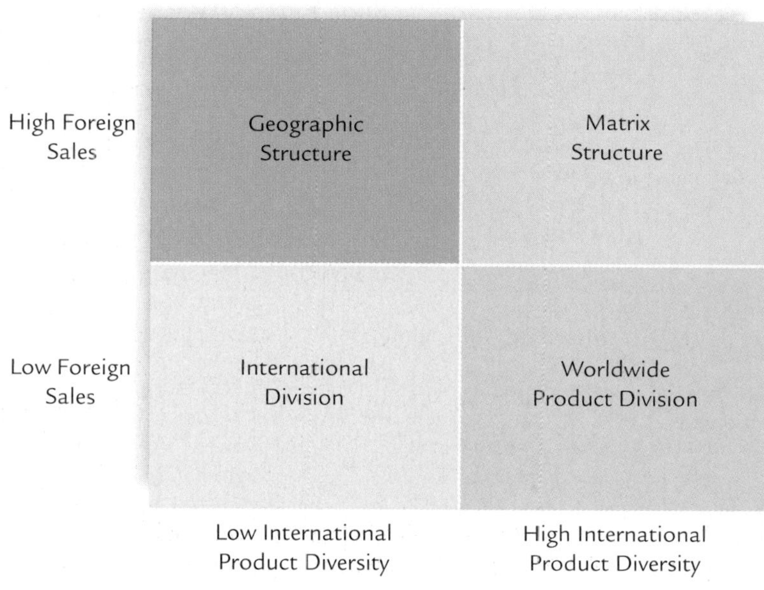

The first dimension of the matrix is the extent of foreign sales. For example, Nokia makes 97 percent of its sales outside of its home country in Finland. The second dimension of the matrix is the extent of product diversification. Product diversification is the extent to which the firm has many different products across many different segments and even industries.[44] For example, Nokia sells primarily mobile phones and network equipment for mobile phone systems. This represents fairly low product diversification. In contrast, GE has many different products across such diversified industries as jet engines, lighting, medical equipment, television and broadcasting, plastics, and power plants. Firms with low foreign sales and low product diversification generally form an international division to manage their international sales. Because there is not much in foreign sales to manage and because the products are relatively similar, it is more efficient to manage the international sales of all products in a single unit—the international division.

Firms having low product diversification with high foreign sales usually employ a geographic structure. This was the case with Nokia for a number of years. It was divided into four major geographic regions: Europe and the Middle East and Africa (EMEA), North America, Latin America, and Asia Pacific.

Firms with low foreign sales but high product diversification typically use global product divisions because the foreign sales are more effectively managed in units aligned with each product. Alternatively, firms with high foreign sales and high product diversification frequently use a matrix structure. This was the case for ABB. Similar to GE, ABB is a large industrial company with a highly diversified set of products ranging from train locomotives to power transmission. Because these products are significantly different, ABB needed to manage each independently. However, because international sales are a large percentage of overall sales, the company also needed a geographic structure. In combination, this formed a product-geography matrix structure.

Thus, while there are some associations between strategy and structure in international firms, the development of international organizations can be divided into two basic states: initial international structures and advanced international structures. Although most international organizations rarely use advanced international structures early, there is no consistent sequence that companies follow. Rather, the size of the organization's international sales, product diversity, size of foreign R&D, and foreign manufacturing determine the advanced global structures.[45]

A DOMESTIC ORGANIZATION WITH AN EXPORT DEPARTMENT As firms venture into foreign markets, they usually begin with a limited number of products. Typically, the products to be sold in foreign markets are designed and produced in the domestic market. Consequently, the primary international task is exporting the products to foreign markets. To manage these foreign sales, most firms simply add an export department to their existing structure to handle specialized tasks, such as international shipping and customs regulations.

A DOMESTIC ORGANIZATION WITH AN INTERNATIONAL DIVISION When the volume of exports exceeds the capabilities of a few specialists, firms commonly establish an international division. International divisions typically are responsible for all functional activities relative to international markets. The international division often has its own small departments for accounting, finance, marketing, and sales. However, production activities are not usually part of the international division. Products are produced within the normal domestic organizational structure and modified as needed for the international division. Consequently, the products often sold by the international division typically have broad appeal, and there are relatively few customer differences across countries.

Adding an international division has a number of advantages. First, it is an efficient means of dealing with the international market when a firm has limited experience. The focus on international activities and issues within the division can foster a strong professional identity and career path for its members. It also allows for specialization and training in international activities, which can be valuable when the firm moves more heavily into the international marketplace and needs employees with global market knowledge. The focus on international markets, competitors, and environments can also facilitate the development of a more effective global strategy. Furthermore, because the top officer of the international division often reports to the firm's CEO (or a similar senior executive), international concerns often receive a high level of corporate support with this structure.

However, international divisions are sometimes vulnerable because they depend so heavily on other divisions for products and support. Because domestic sales of a particular product are often the largest percentage of a product's overall sales, low priority may be given to international sales. Other parts of the firm that supply products and services to the international division may be unwilling to make modifications that cost them time and money, even if the changes could facilitate greater international sales.

ADVANCED GLOBAL STRUCTURES When international sales as a percentage of the firm's overall sales increase, and as the organization expands into a larger number of countries, it becomes increasingly difficult to maximize the benefits of an international division and minimize its weaknesses. When the organization outgrows its initial international structure, it can choose from among six advanced global structures. As mentioned, there is no particular sequence from one structure to another. The six advanced global structures correspond to the basic functional, geographic or regional, product, division, customer, and matrix structures already discussed, except that they have a global rather than a domestic scope.

Increasing globalization is contributing to a number of the changes in the organizational structures used by domestic and multinational firms. As we explain in the following "Manager's Challenge," globalization has contributed to increasing **outsourcing** (networked structures), flatter organization structures, more flexible structures and increasing integration (strategic alliances, for example). Thus, over time, many firms are using more advanced global structures, and these structures are common across country boundaries and cultures.

outsourcing
the practice of contracting out a significant activity within the organization to an independent party

Organizing to Think Globally and Act Locally

Given the increasingly international environment in which organizations compete, it is important to examine one other factor that managers must consider when designing organizational structures—whether the organization satisfies global or local demands.[46] A **global approach** involves the integration of activities on a coordinated, worldwide basis. Firms are likely to use a global approach when the benefits gained from worldwide volumes, efficiencies, or economies of scale are significant. These benefits include economies of scale for production, greater leverage of high-cost distribution networks, and higher leverage of expensive R&D activities. In a variety of industries, the minimally efficient production scale is beyond what a single market could support. For example, Boeing's break-even point for a new commercial aircraft is approximately 300 airplanes, with each airplane costing in excess of $100 million. This requires total sales of $30 billion. To achieve an acceptable return on its investment, Boeing must try to develop airplanes that will have global appeal because the U.S. market alone is not large enough to absorb the sales needed for a reasonable return. The high level of R&D and scale economies require that firms centralize activities such as product development and manufacturing.

global approach
integrating the firm's activities on a coordinated, worldwide basis

In contrast, differences among countries and customer preferences are two key factors that drive companies toward a local approach. A **local approach** involves differentiating activities in each country served. Firms often use a local approach when the benefits from location-specific differentiation and adaptation are significant and factors such as economies of scale are small. Procter & Gamble (P&G) was forced to use a local approach for a laundry detergent it developed. Initially, P&G wanted to develop one detergent, Visor, for all European countries served to capture the efficiencies of a single development, manufacturing, and marketing effort. However, it found significant differences between countries. For example, it found that Germans prefer front-loading washers, whereas the French prefer top-loading washers. This created a problem because detergent was not distributed as well among the clothes when poured into a front-loading washer. P&G solved the problem by developing a plastic ball into which detergent could be poured and that then could be thrown in with the clothes in a front-loading machine. The plastic ball was designed to dispense the detergent gradually though small holes as the ball bounced around in the clothes while they were being washed. Thus, P&G had adapted the product to fit customers' needs in the German market.

local approach
differentiating the firm's activities country by country

A MANAGER'S CHALLENGE

Change

Globalization and Organizational Structures

Because businesses are increasing their sales, manufacturing, research, and management internationally, they are also changing how they do business. Globalization has changed the labor market, created flexible work settings, flattened organizational structures, and increased the ability of firms to network across nations. In addition, globalization is linking markets and governments, creating more opportunities and exposures for people and firms.

Outsourcing

IT companies have led the way in terms of global sourcing. These firms discovered over 30 years ago that IT functions could be performed at lower costs abroad. (Today, U.S. software engineers earn, on average, $75,000 a year compared to similarly skilled workers in India, who earn less than $10,000 annually). As a result, electronics companies, such as Motorola, Texas Instruments, and Intel, began sending manufacturing operations abroad to reduce their operating costs and speed product development by taking advantage of time zone differences and lower wages. Many other firms have followed their lead by outsourcing work ranging from software development to HR administration and even accounting and finance functions.

Flexibility

Organizational systems, processes, and people are working with fewer detailed rules, procedures, and levels of management. Instead, they are being given greater autonomy and are being empowered to be creative and take initiative. Partly because of globalization, businesses are also beginning to customize their employment contracts with workers, who are increasingly engaging in telecommuting and job sharing. In addition, employees are being empowered to make decisions with fewer levels of management.

Flat Organizational Structures

Many companies expanding their business globally often decentralize the employee benefits function. Instead, they are using local managers to create employment plans and job designs, develop financial strategies, and select insurance carriers in each country. Companies are also using global approaches by benchmarking local country designs, incorporating strategic plans that meet local compliance measures, and ensuring that local insurance carriers meet minimum-security standards and evaluate catastrophic exposures. Employees are learning new skills and taking on more challenging assignments to earn pay increases because there are fewer vertical positions for domestic promotions. IT advances are allowing employees to communicate directly across the globe, thereby decreasing the need for middle managers to control communications. In other words, employees are less likely to be required to communicate through the "chain of command."

Integration

Many characterize the 1980s as an era of quality, the 1990s as an era of reengineering, and the twenty-first century as an era of integration. Integration has allowed companies to network with other companies, enhancing their competitiveness by giving them access to complementary resources.

Studies have shown that with globalization, the gross domestic product is growing for countries participating in the global economy. However, the wealth of countries with trade barriers and protectionism is declining. Thus, globalization has increased opportunities, but governments must open their markets to take advantage of these opportunities. Yet, there are disadvantages as well with some fears that local cultures and traditions may be lost over time.

Sources: R. Garnick, "Globalization's Gloomy Guses Must Adapt," *Business Week*, March 21, 2006, www.businessweek.com; R. Hof, "Web 2.0 Has Corporate America Spinning," *BusinessWeek*, June 5, 2006, www.businessweek.com; S. Borgatti, "21st Century Organizational Trends," Analytic Technologies, www.analytictech.com 2001; B. Fung, "Technology Advances and Globalization Are Changing the Face of Risk," *Aon Focus*, February 20, 2006, www.aon.com.

As the P&G example illustrates, the greater the differences between countries and the more significant these differences are for a product or service, the greater the need is for a local approach. However, forces can simultaneously push toward global and local emphases, requiring firms to be globally integrated and locally responsive. In the case of P&G, the manufacturing process was globally integrated because making detergent is basically continuous; that is, like many chemical products, the final product is delivered after a long process of mixing various chemicals in different states and temperatures until the desired chemical reactions create the final product. Thus, the process cannot be stopped at discrete points and finished elsewhere, nor is it economical to alter the process to create different detergents. Both of these factors necessitated a global approach concentrating the manufacturing activities without many modifications being made for local markets. On the other hand, the significant differences in washing machines between Germany and France required attention to local needs.

In general, firms heavily involved in international business face strong pressures for both integration and differentiation. They need specialists for certain functions, such as marketing to Germans, dealing with French government officials, and complying with U.S. accounting rules. However, they also face greater needs for integration. Using one or more of the following structural mechanisms—direct contact, liaisons, and teams—can meet these increased integration needs.

DIRECT CONTACT Often, direct contact is an important means of integration by sharing information. One of the largest firms in the world, Matsushita, has an interesting way of accomplishing this. Because R&D is vitally important in the consumer electronics industry, Matsushita has a large central research and development lab, as explained earlier in the chapter. To ensure that managers are informed about activities in the lab, and to ensure that lab scientists understand emerging market needs around the globe, Matsushita holds an annual, worldwide, internal trade show. Senior managers throughout Matsushita's worldwide operations gather and examine research results and potential new products. Managers also provide to R&D scientists information about market differences, customer preferences, and competitor positioning. The result is a massive sharing of information through direct contact that has helped Matsushita maintain its competitive advantage.

liaisons
individuals designated to act as a "bridge" or connection between different areas of a company

LIAISONS **Liaison** roles are designed to enhance the links, and, therefore, information flows, between two or more groups, including teams, departments, divisions, and subsidiaries. Part of Matsushita's success in the videocassette recorder (VCR) market was due to a purposeful liaison: The vice president in charge of Matsushita's U.S. subsidiary was also a member of the senior management committee of the Japanese parent company and spent about a third of his time in Japan. This facilitated the link between headquarters and the United States, which was the most important consumer market for VCRs. In addition, the general manager of the U.S. subsidiary's video department had previously worked for many years in the video product division of the production and domestic marketing organization in Japan. This created a strong link between the product division in Japan and the U.S. subsidiary. Also, the assistant product manager of the U.S. subsidiary had spent five years in Matsushita's central VCR manufacturing plant in Japan. Via these three individuals, Matsushita ensured there were vital links at the corporate, product, and factory levels between Japan and the United States.

TEAMS When integration needs arise across an array of functional areas, teams can serve as an effective integration mechanism. Philips uses teams as an integrative mechanism. For example, Philips has long had an office of the president, as opposed to a single CEO. The office of the president consists of technical, commercial, and financial executives. Furthermore, for each product, there is a team of junior managers from the firm's commercial and technical functions. These teams integrate various perspectives and information on a single product to ensure that they resolve interfunctional differences early and that they integrate necessary design, manufacturing, and marketing needs and concerns from the outset in an effort to increase the success of a product.

Managerial Challenges from the Front Line

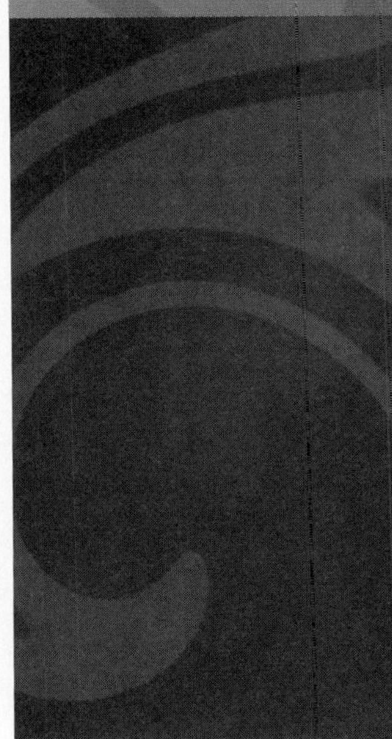

The Rest of the Story

While a matrix structure often slows some response activities because of the need to make joint decisions and coordinate actions prior to implementing them, in Halliburton's case, the structure worked very well. The challenge presented by the competitor required a coordinated response. The matrix structure facilitated this response because managers already had established working relationships and coordinated their efforts on a regular basis. Thus, they were able to jointly ensure that employees understood the overall benefits of working for Halliburton and assure them that the company valued them as employees.

Luiz Freire traveled extensively, visiting his project teams in the field to discuss the issues with them. This extensive effort on the part of Freire and his colleagues was effective. Halliburton lost very few employees to the competitor, and the turnover among professional employees was no greater during this period than other more normal time periods. Managers were pleased they were able to keep the high-quality human capital that Halliburton works hard to attract, develop, and retain.

Summary

- A firm's organization structure can be defined as the sum of the ways in which it divides its labor into distinct tasks and then coordinates them. The structure provides the blueprint for the reporting relationships, controls, authority and decision making in the organization. Organizational design is the process of assessing the firm's strategy and environmental demands and determining the appropriate organizational structure. Often, organizational structure is discussed in terms of organizational charts. Organizational charts illustrate relationships among units and lines of authority among supervisors and subordinates through the use of labeled boxes and connecting lines.
- Important dimensions of the organizing process include differentiation and integration. Differentiation is the extent to which tasks in the organization are divided into subtasks and performed by individuals with specialized skills. The main benefit of differentiation is greater specialization of knowledge and skills. Integration is the extent to which various parts of the organization interact, coordinate, and cooperate with each other. The primary benefit of integration is the coordinated actions of different people and activities to achieve a desired organizational objective.
- Formalization, informalization, centralization, and decentralization are structural dimensions that balance and help to manage differentiation and integration. Formalization is represented by the defined structures and systems in decision making, communication, and control in the organization. These mechanisms usually explicitly define where and how people and activities are independent along with how they are integrated. The informal organization consists of the unofficial but influential means of communication, decision making, and control that are part of the habitual way things get done in the organization. Centralization and decentralization refer to the level at which decisions are made—at the top of the organization or at lower levels. Centralized organizations tend to restrict decision making to fewer individuals, usually at the top of the organization. In contrast, decentralized organizations tend to push decision-making authority down to the lowest possible level.

- There are six common organization structures, functional, product, division, customer, geographic or region, and matrix. The functional structure is used to organize the firm around traditional functional areas, such as accounting, finance, marketing, operations, and so on. In a product structure, the firm is organized around specific products or related sets of products. Divisions typically consist of multiple products within a generally related area, though specific products may not necessarily be closely related. Customer structures are organized around categories of customers. Firms can develop a structure around various geographical areas or regions. A matrix structure consists of two organization structures superimposed on each other. As a consequence, there are dual reporting relationships.
- One of the most contemporary structures is the network structure. A common network structure results from outsourcing. Often, firms outsource noncore activities of their value chain so that they can focus on core activities that give them a competitive advantage.
- Designing organizations must be done within the context of the organization's external environment and its strategy. The environment's complexity and dynamism are important in designing organizations. Environmental complexity is fundamentally the breadth and depth of differences and similarities in an organization's external environment. Static environments may have few or many factors, but these factors tend to remain stable over time. Dynamic environments change constantly. The structure should complement and leverage the strategy. A division structure is commonly used to complement a multiproduct strategy.
- Firms usually begin with simple structures, such as an international department or international division, as they venture into international markets. However, their international structures grow more complex over time as they enter more countries. The structures chosen usually depend on the amount of the firm's foreign sales and degree of product diversification.

Key Terms

centralized organizations 176
cognitive differentiation 171
decentralized organizations 176
differentiation 170
environmental complexity 188
flat organization structure 174
formalization 173
global approach 192
informal organization 175
integration 171
interdependence 171
liaisons 194
line of authority 173
local approach 192
network structures 187
organizational charts 170
organizational design 170
organizational structure 170
outsourcing 192
pooled interdependence 171
profit center 180
reciprocal interdependence 172
sequential interdependence 171
span of control 173
tall organization structure 173
task differentiation 171
uncertainty 172
unity of command 173
values 172

Review Questions

1. What are the concepts of organization structure and organization design, and how do they differ?
2. What are differentiation and integration, and what is their role in organization structure?
3. How are formalization, informalization, centralization, and decentralization interrelated, and how can organizations use them to balance differentiation and integration?
4. What are six common organization structures and their strengths and weaknesses?
5. How does a network structure facilitate managing activities and help a company achieve a competitive advantage?
6. How do environmental factors and the organization's strategy affect the type of structure it should adopt?
7. What organization structures are most effective for organizations operating in international markets? Explain why.

Assessing Your Capabilities

Risk Taking Orientation

Answer the following questions using the scale below:

1. I prefer to think of opportunities in the future as opposed to focusing on past outcomes or even current tasks.	1 Strongly Disagree	2 Disagree	3 Neutral	4 Agree	5 Strongly Agree
2. If I had $100 to invest, I prefer to do so in a way that ensures a return (e.g., 5 percent CD) and no loss of the original amount invested, rather than one in which I could potentially earn as much as a 20 percent return on my investment but with a reasonably high risk of earning no return and potentially losing a portion of the original investment.	1 Strongly Disagree	2 Disagree	3 Neutral	4 Agree	5 Strongly Agree
3. I like to work with new ideas and undertake new tasks because they motivate me.	1 Strongly Disagree	2 Disagree	3 Neutral	4 Agree	5 Strongly Agree
4. I dislike regular change, preferring instead a steady work environment in which my tasks are predictable.	1 Strongly Disagree	2 Disagree	3 Neutral	4 Agree	5 Strongly Agree
5. When I am given a task to accomplish, I prefer autonomy to complete it in the way I desire.	1 Strongly Disagree	2 Disagree	3 Neutral	4 Agree	5 Strongly Agree
6. Rules and established procedures are very helpful in getting a job done.	1 Strongly Disagree	2 Disagree	3 Neutral	4 Agree	5 Strongly Agree
7. When given a new task to do, I find the careful directions and oversight of a supervisor to be helpful and comforting.	1 Strongly Disagree	2 Disagree	3 Neutral	4 Agree	5 Strongly Agree
8. I believe in being aggressive (as opposed to passive) in accomplishing tasks that I am assigned.	1 Strongly Disagree	2 Disagree	3 Neutral	4 Agree	5 Strongly Agree
9. In most situations, I feel most comfortable when people undertake traditional roles (e.g., traditional gender roles).	1 Strongly Disagree	2 Disagree	3 Neutral	4 Agree	5 Strongly Agree
10. When considering complex decisions with uncertain outcomes, I prefer to make the decision alone because I can do it faster than in working in a group.	1 Strongly Disagree	2 Disagree	3 Neutral	4 Agree	5 Strongly Agree

Scoring Your Answers:

Add the numbers you assigned as responses to questions 1, 3, 5, 8, and 10 (Set 1) and those assigned to questions 2, 4, 6, 7, and 9 (Set 2). Subtract the total score for Set 2 from the score for Set 1.

If the resulting score is positive, you prefer to take risks and feel comfortable operating in ambiguous and uncertain situations. The highest positive score you could obtain is +20.

If the resulting score is negative, you prefer a more certain and structured environment with less risk. The lowest negative score you could obtain is −20.

Kimberly-Clark eventually presented a new and different organizational structure in early 2004. Rather than organize products by the "grow, sustain, and fix" categories, management announced that it would organize around personal care, washroom products, and emerging markets. Specifically, management planned to combine the company's North American and European personal care groups under one organizational unit. The same would happen for products related to the washroom business. In addition, management planned to create an "emerging markets" business unit to maximize the growth of all Kimberly-Clark's products in Asia, Latin America, and Eastern Europe.

Questions

1. Why would Kimberly-Clark executives restructure the company based on "grow, sustain, and fix" categories? What disadvantages might result from such a structure?
2. Was the organizational structure presented by Kimberly-Clark executives in 2004 better than the first structure proposed? Why or why not?

Sources: "Company Profile," Kimberly-Clark, www.kimberly-clark.com, March 5, 2007; J. Neff, "K-C Huggies Plans Baby Wipe, Wash Line," *Advertising Age*, December 8, 2003, 49–50; S. Solley, "Kimberly-Clark Rejigs to 'Repair' Weak Brands," *Marketing* (UK), July 31, 2003, 3; "Kimberly-Clark Earnings Fall in 2Q," Associated Press, July 24, 2003; S. A. Forest and H. Dawly, "Pulp Fiction at Kimberly-Clark," *Business Week*, February 23, 1998.

Part Three

Leading

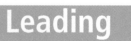

8

Managing Diverse Human Resources

Learning Objectives

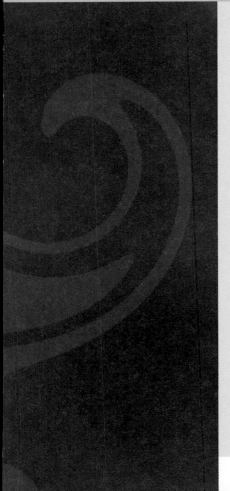

After studying this chapter, you should be able to:

Explain why maximizing the potential of the firm's human resources is important for both a company's human resource management department and all managers.

Explain how a firm's human resource capabilities affect its strategy.

Highlight the key aspects of getting the right people in the right jobs

Outline the effective methods for selecting job candidates.

Highlight the keys to effective socialization and training.

Describe various methods for providing employees feedback on their performance.

Discuss the various compensation and reward systems commonly used by firms.

Discuss why managing diversity is increasingly important in the light of globalization.

Managerial Challenges from the Front Line

Name: Jean-Jacques Beaussart

Position: Chief Procurement Officer, National City Corporation

Alma mater: Columbia University

Outside work activities: Travel, reading, hiking, and gardening

First job out of school: Engineer

Business book reading now: *Good to Great* and *Think Outside the Box*

Hero: Bill Gates

What drives me: Excellence

Management style: Tough but fair; I always strive for excellence and demand it of those around me.

Jean-Jacques Beaussart was born and raised in France but lived in both Morocco and Latin America before moving to the United States and attending Columbia University, where he graduated with a master's degree in engineering. Later, Beaussart received an Executive MBA from Fairleigh Dickinson University, in New Jersey. As the chief procurement officer for Cleveland-based National City Corporation, one of the nation's top financial holdings companies, he oversees more than $2 billion in annual purchases and a team that manages various aspects of this function.

Not long after Beaussart was hired into his National City Corporation position, he encountered a delicate human resource issue. One of his key subordinates, who had been with the company for several years, was near retirement age. The subordinate's past performance ratings had been good. However, Beaussart felt like the overall performance of his team could definitely be better. So, he subsequently raised the group's performance targets.

After several months, though, Beaussart felt that the subordinate nearing retirement age was not meeting the new standards that he had set. Beaussart spoke with the individual and communicated the gap he perceived between the individual's actual performance and the target. Six months later at the end of the year, the individual's performance still fell short of the target.

Beaussart faced a difficult challenge. On the one hand, he had data that demonstrated the subordinate had failed to meet his goals. As a manager, he could work with the company's human resource department to potentially fire the subordinate. This presented a problem in that the individual might claim he were discriminated against because of his age—especially if he were let go and replaced by a younger individual (which, given his age, would most likely be the case). Still, Beaussart felt like the hard facts supported his contention that if the individual were terminated, it would clearly be due to his poor performance, not discrimination.

On the other hand, the individual did have a great deal of knowledge he had obtained over the course of his 30 years of experience. Beaussart felt that it would be a shame to lose this knowledge. In addition, the individual had clearly had other strengths and skills. How, as a manager, could Beaussart resolve the situation?

As the opening case illustrates, as managers we have to think carefully about how we manage people—human resources. On the one hand, letting a poor performance persist will hurt a unit's overall performance, as Jean-Jacques Beaussart was acutely aware. On the other hand, losing the knowledge, experience, and other assets employees have to offer if they can be retained and managed effectively hurts a unit too.

Although people have always been integral to business, they are even more important these days. Why do we say this? The reason is that as we move deeper into a service and information economy, it is people rather than plant and equipment that constitute a higher portion of competitive advantage. For example, when fixed, tangible assets, such as plant and equipment, contribute a lion's share of a company's output, you could replace someone who left with someone new without significant negative impact on overall performance. However, when a business is largely service and information oriented, the more the critical assets of the company are not tangible but rather intangible. These assets include the company's culture, brand, leadership, customer service, knowledge and so on In most cases, people either are the essence of these intangible assets or directly affect them. As a consequence, the key assets of the company are essentially walking out the door each evening and back in the door (hopefully) the next morning.

For example, Nordstrom is a well-known clothing retailer. It clearly has good products—pants, shirts, dresses, shoes, etc—and its stores are nicely constructed and laid out. However, its success lies much more in its service reputation than these tangible aspects of the company. Its superior customer service is not embedded in some piece of equipment or display unit somewhere. It is inculcated in its people and embodied in its culture. If you take people out of a service culture, what do you have left? Clearly, the answer is, "Not much." This is why we say that human resources and the effective management of them is increasingly a critical factor in an organization's success.

This points to two key managerial implications: (1) managers' ability to attract, develop, leverage, and retain superior human resources will increasingly have a direct effect on the organization's success[1] and (2) as a manager, your career success or failure will increasingly depend on how well you manage the human resources for which you are responsible.[2] However, not only are human resources and their effective management in general more critical than ever before, but so is the diversity of employees and, therefore, a manager's ability to work with a wide variety of people.

As a result of these changes in the nature of our economy and competition, human resource management has evolved in recent years, particularly the strategic aspects of it.[3] In this chapter, we underscore the importance of this link. We also stress the need for individual managers to enhance their ability at identifying and selecting employees who have the knowledge, skills, and capabilities the organization needs to compete and fostering and retaining those employees with good development, compensation, and reward systems.

The traditional view of human resource management (HRM) activities focuses on planning for staffing needs, recruiting and selecting employees, orienting and training staff, appraising their performance, providing compensation and benefits, and managing their career movement and development. In most organizations, the human resource department has a special and specific role relative to these activities. However, the reality is that while human resource departments play an important role, managers implement and execute these activities. For example, although a firm's HR department likely sets the policies and practices for hiring people, managers typically interview and select the candidates. Similarly, although the HR department is likely to create employee performance appraisal forms and processes, managers are the ones who actually assess employee performance. Thus, although it is important for you to understand the role a company's human resource department plays, it is even more important for you as a future manager to understand how to manage human resources well. How can you manage your human resources effectively? In general, you need the following capabilities:

- You need the ability to *recruit* and *select* the right people.
- You need the ability to effectively *socialize* and *train* people in your unit.
- You need the ability to effectively *evaluate* their performance.
- You need the ability to determine *reward* systems that will motivate them to perform at a high level.
- You need to know what additional experience or education your subordinates need to *develop* to advance in their careers.

One of the most enlightening studies on the importance of effective HRM and career success looked at cases of career derailment. The study found that the number one reason for managerial career derailment, or, in other words, the number one reason why managers who got *on* but then at some point were *bumped off* upwardly mobile career tracks, was their inability to successfully carry out the activities associated with effective HRM.[4] Consequently, managers with better human resource skills place themselves squarely in a superior position for upward movement and greater opportunities and responsibilities.

The Strategic Role of Human Resource Management

As we discussed in the chapter on strategic management, a firm obtains a competitive advantage by creating and leveraging products and services that provide value to customers but are hard for competitors to copy. For example, Southwest Airlines has been one of the few airlines to consistently deliver profits since deregulation in 1978 in the United States. Why? Is it Southwest's unique planes? No. The company only operates Boeing 737s, but anyone can buy these planes from Boeing. Is Southwest's secret to a competitive advantage its reservation system? No. Until the Internet made it easy for many people to go online to make reservations, Southwest was not part of the major reservation systems that most travel agents used to book flights. This actually put Southwest at a competitive disadvantage because travel agents had to call the company rather than look on their computer screens—as they could do for United, American, Delta, and other airlines—in order to find out ticket prices, availability, and book a reservation. So what has accounted for Southwest's competitive success? By their own account, Southwest's executives believe it is their people and the way they manage their human resources that has been and continues to be the key to the company's success.[5]

Human Resources and Strategy Formulation

Traditionally people have looked at human resources as a department not involved in strategy formulation. However, this is a perspective that is changing.[6] Increasingly, executives are looking at their people and their present and future capabilities to determine what the company's competitive strategy ought to be.[7] As one executive put it, "In football, if you have a quarterback with a great throwing arm, does it make sense to design an offense built upon the run?" Recall from our discussion in the strategic management chapter that a competitive advantage comes largely from creating value for customers via resources that are hard for competitors to copy. The capabilities employees possess are often hard for competitors to

Having earned a profit for more than 30 years straight, Southwest Airlines is a success story in the beleaguered airlines industry. The company's executives say they believe it's Southwest's employees who give the firm a competitive advantage.

copy. To the extent that these capabilities also create value for customers, they become a source of competitive advantage and, therefore, can play a role in what the company's competitive strategy ought to be.

This is part of the Southwest Airlines success. Even though United and other airlines can go out and buy identical Boeing 737s, they have a hard time attracting, selecting, training, and retaining employees who can consistently serve you with a smile. Yet, many customers value the smiles and friendly service they get from Southwest Airlines employees compared to the condescending or rude service they often get from employees on other airlines. The fact that the Southwest Airlines' business model has existed for 30 years and very few if any other airlines have been able to copy it—especially the intangible aspects associated with its people—shows how hard copying the aspects of human resources can be and what powerful competitive advantages they can convey.

Human Resources and Strategy Implementation

Clearly, a firm's human resources should not drive every strategy. However, it is hard to think of any strategy that a firm can effectively implement without the proper management of its human resources. For example, earlier in this text we introduced Nordstrom's and how it competed in part through superior service. This superior service comes largely from Nordstrom's employees, not technology, the physical structure of the stores, or other resources in the company. If Nordstrom's managers do not select employees who have a natural orientation to customer service, if managers do not train them in specific techniques and practices of customer service, and compensate and reward them for superior customer service, then the superior customer service that is a core element of the company's strategy will fail to materialize. Consequently, both executives in charge of the HR function and managers throughout an organization need to manage the firm's human resources in a way that supports and helps implement the company's strategy.[8]

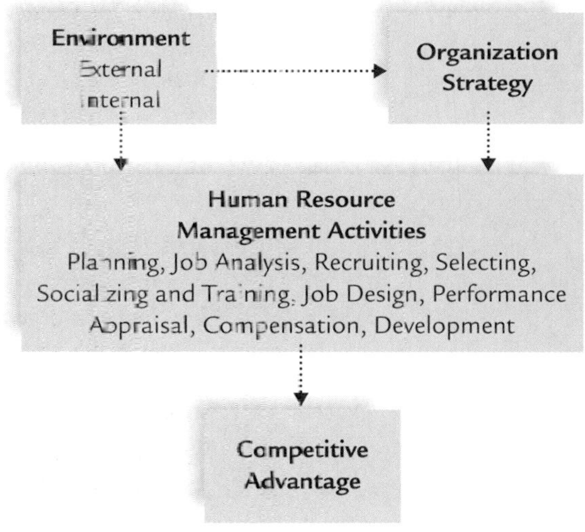

EXHIBIT 8.1

General Framework of HRM

Exhibit 8.1 incorporates these various perspectives into a strategic framework of HRM. As the figure illustrates, specific human resource activities (planning, job analysis, recruiting, selecting, socialization and training, job design, performance appraisal, compensation, and development) exist within the context of the firm's strategy and environment. The fit of these human resource activities with the firm's strategy and environment leads to competitive advantage for the organization and for the individual manager.[9]

Human Resource Management Activities That Get the Right People

To this point, we have explored the link between competitive advantage and HRM and have also briefly examined the importance of the fit between HRM practices and the firm's strategy. We now outline the key HRM activities listed in Exhibit 8.1.

Simplified, there are two main HRM goals: (1) getting the right people and (2) maximizing their performance and potential. Although there are a number of activities related to these two general categories, all managers need to get the right people into the right place at the right time and then help them maximize their performance and future potential. However, it is important to appreciate that someone who is right for one organization might not be right for another. For example, a brilliantly creative person might be right for a firm like 3M that competes by creating innovative products, but he or she would be the wrong employee for an organization that competes via cost leadership and low prices, such as America West Airlines (now a part of US Airways).

You cannot hire the right people without understanding and aligning the company's HRM activities with its corporate strategy.[10] Although it is necessary to discuss each of these activities separately, you should not forget that they are related and that success or failure in one activity can significantly influence the success or failure of another. For example, Disney's ability to select "cast members" (employees) with a happy disposition to work in its theme parks enhances the effectiveness of the "friendly service" training they receive. These two activities combined help keep millions of guests pouring through the gates into the parks each year.

Planning

Human resource planning involves assessing the firm's future human resource needs (demand), determining the availability of the type of people needed (supply), and creating plans for how to meet those needs (fulfillment). At the organizational level, human resources planning is sometimes a shared responsibility among human resources specialists and executives in other functional areas of the firm like accounting, finance, marketing, and operations.

FORECASTING DEMAND Forecasting demand involves determining how many and what type of employees the firm needs at some point in the future (for example, one or five years). This is done considering the firm's strategy and the general business and economic environment. For example, many Japanese electronics firms estimated in the mid-1990s that the sales of electronic music and games would increase at double-digit rates over the course of the next two decades, and that much of the assembly work needed to put together the various components of the music- and game-playing machines would require relatively low-skilled and low-cost labor.

ASSESSING SUPPLY At the time, much of what these firms produced for export to other countries was assembled in Japan. As they looked at the future labor supply in Japan, two key facts emerged. First, based on demographic trends, it was clear that the population of Japan in the 19 to 35 age range (the most common age of assembly workers) was going to shrink. Second, based on economic growth expectations, many of these companies forecast that labor costs were going to increase significantly. Thus, many of the managers in electronics firms in Japan determined that the demand for low-cost and low-skilled labor for product assembly would outstrip the supply of these types of workers in Japan.

FORMULATING FULFILLMENT PLANS The firms analyzed that demand would outstrip supply by approximately two to three million people by the turn of the century. To address this shortfall, many of these senior executives and government officials examined the possibility of allowing immigrants to Japan to fill the labor shortage and lower the labor costs. However, this approach generally lacked political and popular support. As a consequence, many executives of these electronic firms decided to automate some aspects of component manufacturing and also examined the automation of final assembly. However, while some components could be manufactured cost-effectively through automation, automating final assembly turned out to be too costly. On a quality and cost basis, human hands in this case were superior to a robot's. As a consequence, most of the executives in these firms decided to aggressively move final assembly operations offshore to countries with a good supply of semiskilled and low-cost labor, such as China, Vietnam, and Indonesia.

Even though the HRM department might be specially charged with looking at human resource planning, individual managers must also be skilled planners as well. As a manager you will want to be able to determine the number and types of employees you will need in your units, assess the supply in the marketplace, and develop a plan to get the right people. Just as with the organization, as a manager, you cannot distinguish between a "right" and "wrong" employee without considering your firm's strategy. For example, after his first departure from Apple, Steven Jobs started a company called NeXT to compete in the high-end computer and work station market. Within just a few years, Jobs decided to shift the firm's strategic orientation from hardware to software. For managers in product development, this meant that they needed more programmers and fewer engineers and that they initially needed fewer employees overall. Because the market for software programmers was tight, NeXT managers focused their efforts on attracting dissatisfied programmers at other companies by highlighting the exciting things that they were doing at NeXT.

To fulfill your employment needs, you may need to consider the use of part-time or temporary employees. This can give you the flexibility to meet temporary increases in demand for your product or service. It also allows you to reduce your workforce more easily if demand falls as well as to try out employees before hiring them permanently if demand remains strong.

Alternately, you might decide to outsource specific workforce demands[11] Many U.S. companies outsource their customer service and telemarketing jobs to companies operating abroad. In a sense, this offloads the fluctuations in demand for call center representatives to another company that specializes in these tasks and has concentrated capabilities in hiring and training people for these jobs.

Job Analysis

Doing a job analysis is a critical but often overlooked human resource activity. **Job analysis** is done to determine the scope and depth of a job and the required skills, abilities, and knowledge that people need to do the jobs. For example, when Motorola decided to shift its strategic orientation away from simply filling customer orders to creating world-class quality products, its managers analyzed the nature of the firm's factory jobs in light of the new strategy. Unfortunately, many of the company's employees were underqualified based on the new criteria. Managers had to decide whether to try to train the existing employees and get them to the level required or whether to let them go and replace them with more capable employees who could handle the new quality control systems and procedures.[12] In the end, Motorola did both but focused heavily on training existing employees.

job analysis
determination of the scope and depth of jobs and the requisite skills, abilities, and knowledge that people need to perform their jobs successfully

The data and insights that come from a job analysis are typically used to create a job description, or a list of duties and capabilities required for the job. Typically, this leads to a job specification, or a statement that describes the skills, experience, and education that a candidate should have to perform the job.

Recruiting

Recruiting is primarily concerned with determining who you want to attract and undertaking activities to entice those targeted candidates to apply for specific positions within the organization. As with the other activities we have already discussed, the desired pool of candidates depends on the firm's strategy. Whether you can get the type of person you want is a different story. It depends on what you have to offer them versus your competitor.

Let's assume you know who you want and now want to attract them to your company. The key here is knowing what your "target" recruits want. Consider the case of UPS in Germany.

When UPS expanded into Germany, managers had a difficult time selecting good drivers because they simply were not attracting high-quality applicants. Several factors contributed to this, most notably the fact that the brown UPS uniforms were the same color that Nazi youth groups wore during World War II. UPS was not offering what high-quality, prospective drivers wanted and was, in fact, offering something they did not want (brown uniforms).

Let's assume that you now have attracted the right people. Next, you need to ensure that what you offer is more attractive to your target candidates than what they already have or might get from a competing offer. People will always care about money, but if that is all you stress, that is the only element on which you can compete for talent. In the case of UPS in Germany, the company discovered that the freedom they gave employees to determine their own routes appealed to the professional nature of their targeted drivers. This in turn differentiated UPS's employment offering from those of other firms.

Once you have determined the nature of your target candidates, what they would find attractive in an employment offering, and feel that you have a compelling offering, then you need to generate actual job candidates. There are a variety of methods for this. Each one has its strengths and weaknesses and, as a consequence, you should use them as the situation dictates.

In today's high-tech world there are some interesting and new ways of finding the right recruits. For example, Guru.com, highlighted in A Manager's Challenge, "Guru's Gamble on Freelancers," functions a bit like a cyberspace matchmaker of freelance workers and the firms that employ them.

A MANAGER'S CHALLENGE

Technology

Guru's Gamble on Freelancers

The term *freelance* comes from the Middle Ages: Knights would put themselves up for hire because they were not beholden to a specific king. Therefore, they were free to fight and use their lances for any noble who would pay them. Now fast forward to the twenty-first century: With the explosion of broadband Internet connections and cheap telecommunication, the world of virtual employees who freelance for a while or for their entire careers has arrived. Freelancers like the arrangement because they can work for different companies without having to relocate, and they can move from one interesting project to another. For employers, freelancers offer flexibility in terms of "headcount" that simply isn't possible with permanent workers. Using freelancers, employers can more easily move the headcount up or down as demand dictates. They are also able to choose from an almost unlimited field of skill sets for each specific project they need help with.

There are scores of freelancer sites on the Web designed to bring "knight" and "noble" together. The largest is Guru.com. The privately held company has over 616,000 registered professional freelancers, who specialize in over 160 professional categories, including everything from Web site design, programming, graphic design, and business consulting to administrative

As a manager, would you be inclined to use skills tests psychological tests, and even artificial intelligence to ferret out the best job applicant? If so, how much would you be willing to pay to screen each candidate? What is the value of this approach for selecting the best employees?

support. Guru.com also has over 30,000 registered employers, including companies like Bristol-Myers Squibb, Cedars-Sinai Medical Center, Hewlett Packard, IBM, Johnson & Johnson, The National Geographic Society, University of Michigan, United States Navy, and Viacom International Incorporated.

Inder Guglani is the founder of Guru.com. Guglani had been a FedEx executive for seven years. Armed with this experience, an MBA from Carnegie Mellon University, and a bachelor of commerce degree with honors from Delhi University, he raised $400,000 to launch Guru.com in August 2000.

Fundamentally, the way it works is that employers seeking professional expertise post their projects or contract work on Guru.com for free. Professionals seeking work either register as a free (Basic) member or a subscribing (Guru) member (about $130 a quarter). Professionals place quotes on the posted projects in what is called a "closed auction" type of bidding, meaning no one competing for a project can see their competitors' bids. Freelancers base their bids for a project on either hourly rates or the total project cost. The employer then selects the best person for the job.

Once a project is finished, it is usually uploaded to the temporary "Workroom," which is only accessible to the contracted parties. Employers have the option of placing project funds in a neutral escrow account (Guru.com's SafePay Escrow) at the beginning of a project, where they are safely held until the employer approves project work and releases payment to the freelance professional. This way the freelancer knows that the funds are there to pay them once the project is completed and approved. Guru.com's Dispute Resolution Department, which works to resolve conflicts between employers and freelance professionals, supports the SafePay Escrow system. Both services are very important when the parties are in different cities or even halfway around the world. Finally, once the project is completed, employers and professionals leave feedback on each other. The escrow process seems to be working very effectively, with only a small percentage of cases (less than 5 percent) needing any form of mediation and even a smaller percentage (less than 1 percent) requiring the services of an arbitrator. Escrow payments increased fourfold between March 2005 and December 2005.

In February 14, 2006, Guru.com announced a 58 percent increase in the annual amount of total revenues earned by Guru.com professionals. "Continued adoption of the Guru.com Web site to find, manage, and pay contract professionals helped us complete another year of strong growth in transaction volume. Introduction of the escrow and dispute resolution services to enable employers and professionals to conduct transactions with complete security proved to be an important innovation for us, sending customer satisfaction to higher levels," said Guglani.

Sources: www.Guru.com, accessed January 24, 2007; A. Puranik, "Online Freelance Marketplaces," Entrepreneur.com, August 19, 2005.

JOB POSTING **Job posting** is a popular internal recruiting method whereby a job, its pay, level, description, and qualifications are posted or announced to all current employees. Increasingly, companies post their jobs electronically through e-mail or on the company's Web site. Job postings help ensure that all qualified employees have an opportunity to apply for a particular job. Job posting can also help current employees get a better idea of the types of jobs available to them and the qualifications needed to be successful in those jobs. This can allow them to plan their careers. On the negative side, job postings can generate unqualified applicants who need to receive explanations about why they were unqualified and did not get the job. Without adequate explanation, they are likely to wonder whether the job was really "open" when it was posted. If employees begin to doubt the process of posting jobs, it can generate skepticism and limit the candidates the company has to choose from.

job posting
an internal recruiting method whereby a job, its pay, level, description, and qualifications are posted or announced to all current employees

ADVERTISEMENTS Advertisements in general or in specialized publications can also be an effective means of generating job candidates. National business newspapers such as the *Wall Street Journal* cast a wide net. Professional magazines such as *HRMagazine* cast a very specialized net. Regional or local publications, such as your city newspaper, focus on the local labor pool. Increasingly, companies are using the Internet as a source of advertising job openings. As use of the Internet matures, it is likely to develop regional and industrial segments that will facilitate a more targeted advertising of jobs.[13]

EMPLOYMENT AGENCIES Employment agencies can also be effective in generating job candidates in some fields. The agency's effectiveness is largely a function of how well it understands your organization and the requirements of the specific job. Agencies tend to be expensive and usually not cost-effective for low-level and low-paying jobs. In contrast, most openings at the senior management level use executive search firms as part of their recruiting efforts. As their fee for finding an acceptable candidate, these firms typically charge at least one-third of the successful candidate's first-year compensation.

EMPLOYEE REFERRALS Managers may find current employees a great source for job candidates.[14] Current employees with tenure in the organization understand the organization, its culture, and often the particular job that needs to be filled. They usually know something about an applicant as well: work history, educational background, skills and abilities, personal characteristics, and so on. Given that their recommendation puts their own reputation on the line to some degree, current employees tend to recommend individuals whom they believe will do well. Their personal relationship with the recommended candidate allows employees not to just sell the company on the individual but to sell the individual on the company. In general, research suggests that current employee referrals are one of the most effective recruiting methods. Employee referrals are less effective when the firm is looking for a different type of employee than they currently have. Current employees tend to recommend people like themselves. As a result, a company pushing into international activities or new technology may find their employees don't know people in these new areas to refer.

SCHOOL PLACEMENT CENTERS School placement centers are also a popular source of job candidates. Placement center offices can range from those found in high schools, technical schools, and junior colleges to universities and advanced degree programs. Given an adequate amount of time and clear job specifications and requirements, school placement centers can do much of the prescreening for an employer, filtering out unqualified candidates. This can save the firm time and money in the recruiting process.

Schools are also increasingly using video conferencing capabilities to set up "virtual" interviews and online job fairs. Technology helps firms broaden their candidate search, reaching places to which they may not be able to travel physically. The weakness of school placement centers is that they often deal with so many companies and students that they might not know enough about either to conduct ideal screening.

THE INTERNET Companies are discovering that the Internet is a powerful recruiting tool. Most major companies use their corporate Web sites to list jobs and attract candidates. In addition to using their own sites to attract candidates, companies are increasingly using sites such as Monster.com. Monster.com now has over 41 million résumés in its database and is the number one online job search site. Careerbuilder.com and Yahoo!'s Hotjobs.com are two other sites where companies frequently post ads. These and other sites now have the ability to screen résumés for companies so that the human resources staff do not have to.

Selecting

Successful selection is a function of effective planning, analyzing, and recruiting, as well as applying appropriate selection techniques.[15] Even if you get a good set of candidates before you, you need to determine which one is best for the job. For example, international banks, such as Bank of America or Citibank, have no trouble attracting people to overseas positions because international experience is important in the increasingly global banking industry. However, managers selected for overseas assignments sometimes fail and have to return home early at a cost of about $150,000 per employee. This is costly for employers, but it can also hurt employees' careers. These failures are partly a function of poor identification of the characteristics that lead to success in an overseas assignment and also a function of limited use of effective selection techniques to make sure you get the right people.[16]

valid selection technique a screening process that differentiates those who would be successful in a job from those who would not

One of the key points to keep in mind about any selection technique is that if legally challenged, the organization must be able to demonstrate that the selection technique is valid. A **valid selection technique** is one that can differentiate between those who would be more successful in the job and those who would be less successful. For example, educational background is often used in selecting new hires because knowledge typically has a proven relationship with job performance. That is, it is hard to perform well in a job for which you do not have the requisite education and knowledge. There are a variety of selection techniques; each has its own strengths and weaknesses.

INTERVIEWS The most widely used selection technique is the interview. In most cases, the interview is unstructured. An unstructured interview is one in which interviewers have a general idea of the types of questions they might ask but do not have a standard set of questions. As a consequence, interviewers might ask different candidates different questions. With different questions and responses, comparing candidates can be like comparing apples and oranges. Not surprisingly, a major weakness of unstructured interviews is that they tend to have low levels of validity.[17] In contrast, **structured interviews**, in which interviewers ask a standard set of questions of all candidates about their qualifications and capabilities, can be quite valid. Carefully recording interviewees' responses on a standardized form and taking approximately the same time to interview each candidate can further enhance validity. Exhibit 8.2 provides tips for interviewers, and Exhibit 8.3 provides tips for interviewees.[18] However, legally there are some questions in the United States that you cannot ask. For example, you cannot ask if someone is married or if they plan to have children. You cannot ask about race, religion, birthplace, national origin, or age.

structured interview
one in which interviewers ask a standard set of questions of all candidates about qualifications and capabilities related to job performance

WORK SAMPLING A variety of techniques can be classified as work sampling. Essentially, these techniques attempt to simulate or exactly duplicate the job the person would be doing if hired. The underlying rationale is straightforward: If you perform poorly or well in the work sample, you will likely perform similarly in the real job. In general, the main strength of work sampling techniques is that they make a reasonably accurate prediction of how a candidate will do in a job. The main drawback is they tend to be time and cost intensive.

WORK SIMULATIONS Work simulations typically involve situations in which job candidates perform work that they would do if hired or work that closely simulates the tasks they would perform. For example, when Nissan set up its new assembly plant in Tennessee to

EXHIBIT 8.2

Tips for Interviewers

1. Plan the interview by reviewing the candidate and the job specifications.
2. Establish rapport with a friendly greeting and start the interview with a nonjob question.
3. Follow structured set of questions.
4. Avoid questions that require or solicit a simple *yes* or *no* response.
5. Try not to telegraph, or give cues for, the desired answer.
6. Make sure the candidate has plenty of time to answer—do not monopolize the conversation.
7. Listen carefully and paraphrase key candidate answers to be sure you understand what they meant to say.
8. Ask for specific, not general, examples of the candidate's experience and accomplishments.
9. Leave time at the end of the interview to answer questions from the candidate.
10. At the close make sure the candidate knows what the next steps are and approximate timing.
11. After the candidate leaves, review your notes and highlight important points while they are fresh in your mind.

EXHIBIT 8.3

Tips for Interviewees

1. Prepare for the interview by researching the company through articles and its own Web site.
2. Smile and provide a warm greeting and firm handshake if the interviewer extends his or her hand.
3. Make sure that your overall appearance (hair style, clothing, makeup, and so on) match the nature of the business and culture of the company.
4. Watch your nonverbal behavior to ensure that you maintain good eye contact and convey enthusiasm without being overly expressive with your hands or other body movements.
5. Try to solicit the interviewer's needs early in the interview.
6. Early in the interview be sure to get a complete picture of the job through questions such as, "Can you tell about what has led people to succeed in this job in the past?"
7. Explicitly relate yourself and capabilities to the interviewer's needs through statements such as, "You mentioned that one of the keys to this position is the ability to motivate others. In my experience at XYZ . . . ."
8. Take your time before answering; you do not need to begin talking the instant the interviewer asks a question.
9. Conclude the interview by thanking the person for the opportunity and expressing your interest in the company and the position.

assess applicants' manual dexterity skills, a key requirement for assembly line workers the company required them to assemble flashlights. At Motorola, technical writing job candidates are given a piece of equipment, shown how to use it, given time to practice using it, and then are required to write a technical description of the equipment and an operation manual. This gives Motorola a clear idea of those who can write technical material well.

ASSESSMENT CENTERS Assessment centers typically use any number of selection tools, including work sampling and simulation techniques, in order to get a broader and richer sense of the fit of the employee to the job. Typically, candidates are required to go through a number of exercises, and each exercise is designed to capture one or more key aspects of the job. For example, a supervisor's job might require good prioritization skills. To assess this skill, the assessment center might set up an "in-basket" exercise. The exercise consists of an in-basket filled with letters, memos, and reports that the candidate must read and then prioritize. This activity demonstrates the individual's ability to recognize and respond to high-priority items. In general, research shows that assessment centers are an effective selection method for new hires as well as for applicants moving up in a firm. However, using an assessment center to screen candidates is typically time and resource intensive.[19]

WRITTEN TESTS Written tests are also widely used. This is due to the fact that employers can administer the tests cost effectively to a large number of job candidates. Cognitive ability and intelligence tests measure an individual's general cognitive complexity and intellectual ability. Although the validity of these tests has been mixed, they do seem to be acceptable predictors for supervisory and management jobs. Personality tests are more controversial. Although they can be reasonably good predictors of people's ability to work well with other particular personalities, they have not been good overall predictors of job performance.[20] Integrity tests are a more recent development. These tests try to assess the general level of a person's honesty. In general, they seem to be of debatable validity.[21]

Written tests have the advantage of generally being inexpensive to administer, but the results are more valid regarding how applicants will perform in general rather than in a specific job.

BACKGROUND AND REFERENCE CHECKS Employers perform background checks to verify factual information provided by the applicants they have interest in hiring. Between 10 percent and 15 percent of applicants either lie about or exaggerate factual information. As a consequence, checking to make sure applicants graduated with the degrees they claim, from the schools they cite, and held the jobs with the responsibilities they describe can be quite valuable. The objective of reference checks is to get candid evaluations from those who have worked with the job candidate. However, recent legal judgments against past employers that made negative statements about their former employees have led employers to provide only factual information, such as title, years employed, and so on. On the other hand, court rulings have suggested that employers can be held liable for not conducting adequate checks. For example, financial service firms need to ensure that individuals involved in security transactions have not been convicted of a felony in the past.

PHYSICAL EXAMINATIONS Companies that require physical examinations as part of the selecting process typically do so because the job has high physical demands. In addition to helping them select physically qualified candidates, physical exams also protect firms. First, the physical exam information may help firms reduce insurance claims. Second, it may help protect the firm from lawsuits by identifying high-risk applicants, such as someone who might experience a heart attack from the physical strains of the job. However, given recent legislation in the United States, managers must be careful to ensure that the physical requirements being screened in the examination relate to job performance and are not sources for discrimination.[22] For example, BNSF Railway requires some of its employees to take a medical examination to prevent employee injuries. At one point, the company included testing a genetic factor only for employees claiming work-related carpal tunnel syndrome. Subsequently, a court ordered BNSF to stop testing employees because the test had nothing to do with an employee's current degree of carpal tunnel syndrome. Drug testing is another screening mechanism companies use to ensure that employees' judgment and capabilities are not impaired while on the job.

Up to this point we have covered a large number of specific techniques so it may be helpful to review the basics as illustrated in Exhibit 8.4. Planning for who you need is the first major task. You need to establish what the demand and supply balance for employees looks like in your industry in order to determine how you will fulfill your needs. The strategy of the organization and an analysis of the firm's jobs clearly affect these activities. Once the major planning is done, then it is a matter of recruiting and attracting the desired candidates. The last step is to select the best people to hire.

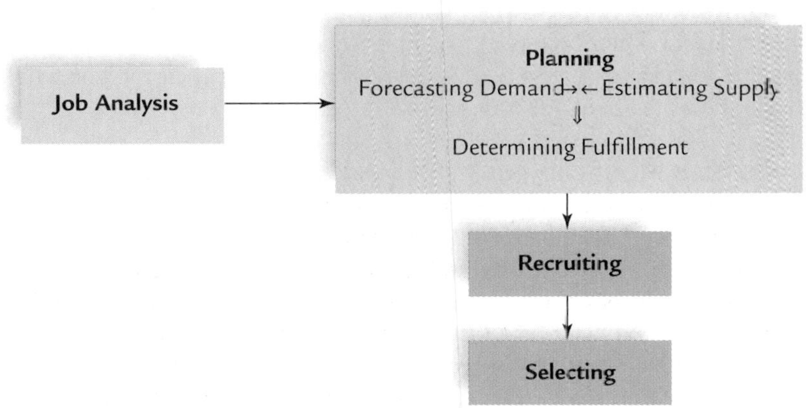

EXHIBIT 8.4

Key Aspects of Getting the Right People

Human Resource Management Activities That Maximize Performance

Once the right people are in the right positions, managers need to ensure they are performing well. What constitutes maximum performance and potential is largely a function of the organization's strategy. For example, 3M chooses to compete on new product innovation and strives to have the majority of its revenue come from products that are less than five years old. It, therefore, needs employees who can think of and test new ideas. For 3M, maximum performance and potential are largely defined in terms of employee innovations. Based on this, 3M undertakes a variety of activities to maximize employees' creativity. Five specific categories of activities can significantly influence employee performance and potential.

Socialization and Training

Just as early life experiences can shape the general character, personality, and behavior of people, so too can early training and socialization experiences shape important aspects of employees' performance.[23] For example, early training and socialization each affects (1) the probability that new hires will stay with the firm, (2) the extent to which they will perform well, and (3) the degree to which they will develop to their full potential.[24]

Managers can use a variety of training methods to enhance the performance and potential of employees. We cover several here. Although early career training is important, in today's changing environment, training and learning are likely to become career-long necessities

ORIENTATION One of the first opportunities for an organization to shape the expectations and behavior of new employees is during orientation programs.[25] Typically, these programs provide a broad overview of the industry, the company and its business activities, its key competitors, and general information about working for the company (such as key policies, pay procedures, and fringe benefits). Work-unit orientation sessions are typically more narrow and are generally designed to help the new employee get up to speed on the new job, coworkers, the work-unit's policies, procedures, and expectations. To maximize the effectiveness of orientation programs, managers should consider doing the following:[26]

- Keep paperwork to a minimum to avoid information overload. Do include paperwork that must be completed immediately.
- Include an informal meeting with the individual's immediate supervisor.
- Alternate heavy information, such as that related to benefits and insurance, with lighter live or video presentations from corporate officers.
- Provide a glossary of terms unique to the organization.
- Match each new employee with a "buddy" (that is, an experienced worker) based more on personality compatibility than similarity of jobs.

ON-THE-JOB TRAINING TECHNIQUES On-the-job training (OJT) is the most widely used training technique in organizations. As Exhibit 8.5 illustrates, there are a wide variety of techniques that a manager can use to train employees. Over your career, you will likely be exposed to most, if not all, of these approaches.

OFF-THE-JOB TRAINING TECHNIQUES The most common off-the-job training occurs in a classroom. The training program may be only an hour, or it may be several weeks in length. In-house experts (employees of the company) or outside experts from industry or education fields, such as a university professor, may conduct the training program. The program may involve lectures, case studies, discussions, videos, simulations, or computer-based training. Many computer-based training programs now adjust the program's content and difficulty level based on how well the individual is doing. Formal correspondence courses and online learning are sometimes used for off-the-job training.

EXHIBIT 8.5

On-the-Job Training Techniques

1. *Expanded Responsibilities.* This training technique expands the job duties, assignments, and responsibilities of an individual.
2. *Job Rotation.* Also called *cross-training*, this practice moves individuals to various types of jobs within the organization at the same level or next-immediate-higher level for periods of time from an hour or two to as long as a year.
3. *Staff Development Meetings.* Meetings are usually held offsite to discuss facts of each individual's job and to develop ideas for improving job performance.
4. *"Assistant to" Positions.* Promising employees serve as staff assistants to higher-skill-level jobs for a specified period of time (often one to three months) to become more familiar with the higher-skilled positions in the organization.
5. *Problem-Solving Conferences.* Conferences are held to solve a specific problem being experienced by a group or the organization as whole. It involves brainstorming and other creative means to come up with solutions to the basic problems.
6. *Mentoring.* A guide or knowledgeable person higher up in the organization helps a new employee "learn the ropes" of the organization and provides other advice.
7. *Special Assignments.* Special tasks or responsibilities are given to an individual for a specified period of time. The assignment may be writing up a report, investigating the feasibility for a new project, process, service, or product, preparing a newsletter, or evaluating a company policy or procedure.
8. *Company Trainers.* Special programs can cover such topics as safety, new personnel procedures, new product or services, affirmative action, and technical programs.
9. *Outside Consultants.* Recognized experts are brought to the company to conduct training on such topics as goal setting, communications, assessment techniques, safety, and other current topics of importance. They often supplement training done by company trainers.
10. *Consultant Advisory Reviews.* Experts in specialized fields meet with various managers and employee groups to investigate and help solve particular problems. The emphasis is on problem solving rather than training.
11. *Reading Matter.* A formal program is created to circulate books, journals, selected articles, new business material, and so on to selected employees. An effective program also includes periodic scheduled meetings to discuss the material.
12. *Apprenticeship.* Training is provided through working under a journeyman or master in a craft. The apprentice works alongside a person skilled in the craft and is taught by that person. Apprenticeship programs also often include some classroom work.

Source: Adapted from W. P. Anthony, D. L. Perrewé, and K. M. Kacmar, *Strategic Human Resource Management* (Fort Worth, TX: Harcourt Brace Jovanovich, 1993).

TECHNICAL, INTERPERSONAL, AND CONCEPTUAL TRAINING Orientation and training programs can have a variety of objectives. However, at a fundamental level, these programs are intended to address employees' technical, interpersonal, or conceptual abilities. An employee's technical skills can range from being able to read and perform simple math to being able to program a supercomputer. As mentioned earlier, when Motorola made a strategic commitment to quality, it discovered that over a third of its employees could not read, write, or do math at a level that the new quality control program required. This discovery led to a massive technical training effort.

Because very few employees work in isolation, improved interpersonal abilities are the target of a wide variety of training programs. Programs such as these might address skills such as effective listening, conflict resolution, negotiation, and coaching. In a recent study, executives cited poor interpersonal skills as one of the biggest problems associated with new college or MBA graduates.[27]

The final category is conceptual abilities. This category includes a variety of skills and abilities, such as problem solving, decision making, planning, and organizing. A given training program might be designed to address just one, two, or all three of these categories.

Regardless of the category the program is designed to target, most successful programs provide participants with several things:

- An understanding of what the correct employee behavior is and is not.
- A clear knowledge of why certain behaviors are correct or incorrect.
- Sufficient opportunities to practice the desired behaviors.
- Feedback on their performance with further opportunities to practice and improve.

An important part of training is evaluating its effectiveness.[28] The simplest way to do this is by using the "smile index"—that is, by gauging the satisfaction of the participants who received the training. This is often gathered just after the training is finished via a questionnaire. Participants who do not like the training they receive will be unlikely to retain it and use it in a beneficial way. However, just because participants enjoyed the training or thought it was useful does not guarantee that it will have the intended impact. A more rigorous assessment of training would involve a pretraining and post-training assessment. This would involve assessing the knowledge and skill levels of participants before the training and at some point afterward. If the training is intended to improve on-the-job performance, such as quality, you might assess the impact of the training by comparing important metrics. For example, in the case of a manufacturing company, you might measure the defects per 1,000 units assembled before and after the training. However, although a reduction in defects might tell you if the training had the intended effect, it will not tell you if the training was cost-effective. Determining this is much more complicated. In general, you have to assess both the direct costs of the training (such as the cost of trainers) and the indirect costs (such as the productivity lost due to workers being in the training instead of on the job). You then have to compare these costs to the benefits, such as the savings from having fewer defective products returned. However, one key challenge is determining the period over which to add up the benefits. For example, if higher quality is saving you $100 per day in returns, should you estimate the total value of these savings over the course of a week, a month, a year, or several years? Your answer will dramatically affect your calculations—and, therefore, whether the training was worth it.

Job Design

job design
the structuring or restructuring of key job components

Job design focuses on the structuring or restructuring of key components of a job. A job design typically includes the job's responsibilities. Thus, while job analysis focuses on what the components of a job actually are, job design is the process of determining which components ought to be put together and how they should be arranged to enhance performance.[29] For example, does an assembly line worker work in isolation and repetitively attach a given part to a product, or does he work in a team with others building an entire unit? Dell is one company that has assembly line workers work in teams that assemble entire computer units. In some texts, job design would be much earlier in the sequence than we have placed it. In general, for a brand new job that has never been filled before, job design does take place early in the sequence. Also, traditionally jobs were designed and then appropriate people were selected to fit into the jobs. The reality of today's dynamic environment has changed that approach. In some cases, it is possible and appropriate to

A General Mills employee in Minnesota visits her child at an onsite daycare center at the corporation's headquarters. General Mills is among the 100 best companies to work for, according to Working Mother magazine. Employees can flex or compress their work schedules, telecommute, or job-share, and maternity and paternity leaves are very generous.

design jobs and then try to match people to them, but in other cases, jobs might need to be designed or redesigned to fit the available people. There are also situations that require a combination of both fitting the person to the job and fitting the job to the person. For example, **job sharing** involves two people working part time in the same job. Effective job sharing requires two individuals who can coordinate well and have similar capabilities. It has become popular with working mothers who have to balance family and professional demands. Increasingly, technology is allowing managers to design and redesign jobs in ways that make them more flexible, productive, and satisfying to employees. For example, JetBlue, a relatively new airline and one of the most profitable, saved money by having its reservation agents work from home instead of putting money into large call centers. Improved communications technology has been one way to provide that flexibility.

job sharing
situation in which two people share the same job by each working part-time

During the early and mid-1990s, reengineering became a popular concept regarding the design or redesign of work. **Reengineering** involves rethinking and radically redesigning business processes to achieve dramatic improvements in performance, such as cost, quality, service, or speed.[30] Computer and information technology today have allowed organizations to design more enriched, satisfying, and productive jobs. Increasingly, organizations are looking at ways to give employees more flexibility in the way they accomplish their work. For example, at IBM before a major reengineering project, customer financing approvals involved four different people performing very specific, narrow, and repetitious jobs. One person reviewed the customer's financial strength by accessing a standardized database. Another reviewed the company's past payment history with IBM. A third examined whether the financing request was within or outside prescribed norms IBM had established. And one person then compared the contract to the standards IBM had established. Redesigning the job for one person to do all four steps and supporting that with needed technology produced important results. First, employee satisfaction with the job went up because it was much more interesting to employees, and productivity went up as well by nearly 1000 percent. Maximizing subordinates' performance and your unit's performance is your goal as a manager regarding effective job design.

reengineering
fundamental rethinking and radical redesign of business processes to achieve dramatic improvements in critical, contemporary measures of performance, such as cost, quality, service, or speed

Evaluating Employees' Performance

Before organizations or managers can encourage or correct the actions of employees, they must know how the employees are doing.[31] The performance appraisal process should (1) establish performance objectives and standards, (2) measure the performance of employees against those standards, and (3) give employees feedback about that measurement and evaluation.[32] As we stated before, the strategy of the firm must drive the objectives of a job and its associated performance standards. When Motorola decided that it would compete on quality, it set "six sigma" as its standard. A six-sigma quality standard allows for only 3.4 defects per 1 million opportunities. For Motorola, this had wide-ranging implications from the factory floor to the corporate kitchen. On the floor, this meant that only 3.4 products per million produced could have a defect. For the kitchen, it meant that only 3.4 muffins for every million baked could be burnt. Although six sigma was not immediately achievable for Motorola, it did have a significant impact on the performance of the company's employees.

For most managers, the performance appraisal is perhaps the most important, yet most difficult, human resource activity. Sometimes employees are not quite measuring up to the firm's standards and have to be told as much; however, few people like to give or receive negative feedback. Still, without this feedback, neither employees nor organizations can maximize their performance. As a consequence, all managers need to understand the key factors that drive effective performance appraisal systems and be skilled at implementing them.

GRAPHIC RATING SCALES Perhaps the most popular method of providing performance feedback is through graphic rating scales (see Exhibit 8.6). A graphic rating scale typically lists a set of qualities upon which to evaluate the employee. The employee's level of performance on each of these items is then rated in terms of a graduated scale. The scale typically ranges from 1 to 5. The degree of specificity concerning the definition of each point on the scale can range from one-word descriptors (e.g., 1 = poor) to complete sentences (e.g., 1 = Does not meet the minimum standards).

The popularity of graphic ratings is due to two main factors. First, they are relatively quick and easy for managers to complete. Given that most managers have many employees whom they must evaluate and are typically not rewarded for writing up high-quality evaluations, they have a natural incentive to complete the evaluations as quickly as possible. Second, it is easy to quantify the results and compare employees' performance ratings.

However, there are two key limitations that as a manager you should keep in mind relative to graphic rating scales. First, the characteristics being evaluated may not be clearly defined; thus, they are left to individual interpretation. Consequently, one manager might focus her interpretation of "interpersonal skills" on conflict resolution abilities, while another manager might focus his interpretation on listening skills. Given the two different interpretations, it is difficult to compare the employees evaluated by the two different managers. Furthermore, the two different managers might have different interpretations of

EXHIBIT 8.6

Graphic Rating Scale

Employee name: ____________________ **Dept.** ____________

	Excellent	Good	Average	Fair	Poor
1. Quality of work	☐	☐	☐	☐	☐
2. Quantity of work	☐	☐	☐	☐	☐
3. Cooperation	☐	☐	☐	☐	☐
4. Dependability	☐	☐	☐	☐	☐
5. Initiative	☐	☐	☐	☐	☐
6. Job knowledge	☐	☐	☐	☐	☐
7. Attitude	☐	☐	☐	☐	☐

the rating scale. One manager might only allow the top 5 percent of employees to receive a high rating of "5 = excellent." Another manager might interpret a "5" as applicable to the top 20 percent of employees. Once again, the different interpretations would make comparing employees rated by different managers difficult.[33] This incomparability is important because over 85 percent of firms use performance appraisals to determine merit increases, bonuses, and promotions.

behaviorally anchored rating scales (BARS)
a performance appraisal system in which the rater places detailed employee characteristics on a rating scale

BEHAVIORALLY ANCHORED RATING SCALES **Behaviorally anchored rating scales (BARS)** are designed to reduce the disadvantages associated with graphic rating scales. The two scales are similar in that managers rate employee characteristics using a quantitative scale. However, with behaviorally anchored rating scales, the characteristics are specified in greater detail and described in terms of behaviors rather than abstract qualities (see Exhibit 8.7). The greater specificity and link to behaviors reduces, but does not eliminate, the potential for different raters to evaluate employees differently.[34] Some potential for bias remains.[35]

EXHIBIT 8.7

Behaviorally Anchored Rating Scale

Source: Table from *Strategic Human Management* by William P. Anthony, Pamela L. Perrewé, and K. Michele Kacmar, p. 456. Copyright © 1993 by Harcourt Brace & Company, reproduced by permission of the publisher.

Position: ______________________

Job dimensions: ______________________

Plans work and organizes time carefully so as to maximize resources and meet commitments.	9	
	8	Even though this associate has a report due on another project, he or she would be well prepared for the assigned discussion on your project.
	7	This associate would keep a calendar or schedule on which deadlines and activities are carefully noted, and which would be consulted before making new commitments.
	6	As program chief, this associate would manage arrangements for enlisting resources for a special project reasonably well, but would probably omit one or two details that would have to be handled by improvisation.
Plans and organizes time and effort primarily for large segments of a task. Usually meets commitments, but may overlook what are considered secondary details.	5	This associate would meet a deadline in handing in a report, but the report might be below usual standard if other deadlines occur on the same day the report is due.
	4	This associate's evaluations are likely not to reflect abilities because of overcommitments in other activities
	3	This associate would plan more by enthusiasm than by timetable and frequently have to work late the night before an assignment is due, although it would be completed on time.
	2	This associate would often be late for meetings, although others in similar circumstances do not seem to find it difficult to be on time.
Appears to do little planning. May perform effectively, despite what seems to be a disorganized approach, by concerted effort, although deadlines may be missed.	1	This associate never makes a deadline, even with sufficient notice.

360-degree feedback
performance appraisal system in which information is gathered from supervisors, co-workers, subordinates, and sometimes suppliers and customers

360-DEGREE FEEDBACK The rationale behind 360-degree feedback appraisal systems is that a person's performance should be viewed from multiple perspectives.[36] Most **360-degree feedback** systems involve collecting appraisal evaluations from an employee's boss, peers, subordinates, and even the employee. In some companies, evaluations are also collected from suppliers and customers, depending on the nature of interaction the employee has with these constituencies, or groups of people. The positive aspect of 360-degree feedback is that because data are gathered from multiple sources, employees are encouraged to focus on all of the firm's key constituencies. This reduces the incentive, for example, for employees to simply cozy up to the boss but work poorly with their peers or subordinates. The major drawback is the time and energy it takes to collect, process, and effectively feed the data back to the individual. In addition, a recent study shows that 360-degree feedback might not have the validity attributed to it that it should. Between 1995 and 2005 the percentage of U.S. companies using some form of 360-degree evaluation more than doubled from 25 percent to 60 percent.[37]

critical incidents
recording of specific incidents in which the employee's behavior and performance were above or below expectations

EFFECTIVE PERFORMANCE FEEDBACK Regardless of the appraisal system used, the results of the evaluation need to be fed back effectively to employees to make a positive difference in their performance. First, if the employer's expectations concerning unacceptable, acceptable, or superior performance were not clear to the employee prior to the appraisal, a negative evaluation is not likely to motivate the employee or improve his or her performance. Consequently, the performance expectations must be clear and acceptable to the employee from the outset. Second, if the employee believes that, as the manager, you are biased in your observations, your assessment will not have the effect you desire. This is why recording both positive and negative **critical incidents** is important. This simply involves the recording of important, specific incidents in which the employee's behavior and performance were above or below expectations. This record then allows you to avoid remembering only the most recent events that occurred with regard to the employee. It also facilitates your ability to talk about specifics in the appraisal interview.[38] This brings us to a brief list of recommendations for an effective performance appraisal interview:

1. Review the key work objectives, goals, or standards against which the employee's performance is measured.
2. Summarize the employee's overall performance by reviewing specific positive and negative incidents.
3. Discuss causes of weak performance and listen carefully to the employee's explanation.
4. Discuss different ways to improve the employee's future performance and encourage the person's input.
5. Establish an agreed approach, timetable, and review process for future improvement.
6. Establish key objectives, timetables, and standards for the upcoming performance period.
7. Leave the meeting on an encouraging and positive note.

These may seem like simple steps. Nonetheless, they can go a long way toward improving how well you handle one of the most difficult yet important challenges you will face as a manager. A Manager's Challenge, "Nissan Imports Human Resource Management Techniques" reveals, new human resource practices with which you are unfamiliar can be a challenge for both senior managers to get implemented and for middle managers to adopt and use. What do you think of the changes Nissan introduced? Do they simply reflect a Western bias for how to manage people?

Compensation

Although rewards and compensation can be instrumental in getting the right people, their primary function is retaining and maximizing the performance of employees once they have entered the organization. Rewards by their nature are designed to encourage desired behaviors. As already discussed, desired behaviors must be linked to the firm's strategy. Thus, reward systems also must be linked to the firm's strategy.

MANAGER'S CHALLENGE

Globalization

Nissan Imports Human Resource Management Techniques

Carlos Ghosn and his management team brought Japan-based Nissan Motors back from the brink of near-bankruptcy in large part by importing non-Japanese HRM techniques. Born in Brazil, raised in Lebanon, and educated as an engineer in France, Ghosn speaks five languages and has worked all over the world. After French automaker Renault bought 44 percent of Nissan in 1999, top management brought him in as Nissan's CEO.

He and the 17 Renault managers who joined him at Nissan faced the difficult challenge of turning around a company hobbled by inefficient human resource traditions. These traditions included focusing mainly on hiring new college graduates to replenish the management ranks, promoting managers based on seniority, compensating managers based on their positions, and *not* requiring managers to provide performance appraisals or feedback to their subordinates.

Ghosn and his managers drew on French and U.S. management practices to help turn around Nissan. When he became CEO, he quickly established a series of cross-functional teams to examine the company's processes and recommend reforms. Instead of traditionally selecting team members based on their length of tenure, Ghosn and his managers chose members based on their enthusiasm for change. The teams' proposals became part of a multipronged plan to boost operating margins, reduce costs, and cut debt. Ghosn again violated Japanese human resources tradition by involving middle managers—managers who previously would have had no say in such matters—in the implementation of the plan.

Ghosn and Kuniyuki Watanabe, the senior vice president for human resources, also instituted a new system of merit-based reviews. Watanabe was familiar with these techniques from his days with Nissan's U.S. operations. "Giving your personal appraisal directly to the individual is not a job Japanese [managers] are used to doing, and I hated it [at first]," he remembers. "But it was great training for me. I'm fine with it now," says Watanabe. However, many other Japanese managers at Nissan weren't. For most managers, it involved a radical change from implicit and informal goal setting and performance feedback to a more explicit and formal approach.

On top of this, Nissan changed to a more Western model of rewarding, promoting, and developing managers based on performance rather than seniority. "We're moving to a system where it doesn't matter if you've been in the company 10 years or 40 years," Watanabe adds. "If you contribute, there will be opportunity and reward." This means middle managers have to make tough judgments about performance and potential and communicate their decisions and rationale.

The changes seemed to make a positive, if painful, difference. Nissan's operating profit improved, and its costs and debt dramatically fell. Another indicator of Ghosn's success: Leading Japanese corporations started following his lead and importing more non-Japanese and potentially more effective human resources practices to improve the performance of their firms.

Sources: A. Taylor, "The World According to Ghosn," *Fortune*, November 2006; M. Roman, "Carlos Ghosn: Move Over I'm Driving," *Business Week*, April 5, 2004; D. Welch, "How Nissan Laps Detroit," *Business Week*, December 23, 2003, 58–60; C. Dawson, "Ghosn's Way," *Business Week*, May 20, 2002, 27+.

PAY Most firms establish a pay structure based on the level in the company and type of position. A **pay structure** establishes a range of pay for a particular position or classification of positions. The most common element of any pay structure is the wage. Wages tend to be structured on a per hour basis or a fixed amount by calendar year. When structured by calendar year, the wage is typically referred to as salary, and the most common calendar division is annual although payment of the salary is typically divided and made monthly.

pay structure
a range of pay for a particular position or classification of positions

Traditionally, salary structures have been hierarchical and segmented. Most companies are now moving to **broad band systems** in which the range of pay is large and covers a wide variety of jobs.[39] Exhibit 8.8 provides a graphic illustration of a traditional pay structure and a more modern broad band system. The major advantage to a broad band

broad band systems
pay structures in which the range of pay is large and covers a wide variety of jobs

EXHIBIT 8.8

Traditional and Contemporary Pay Structures

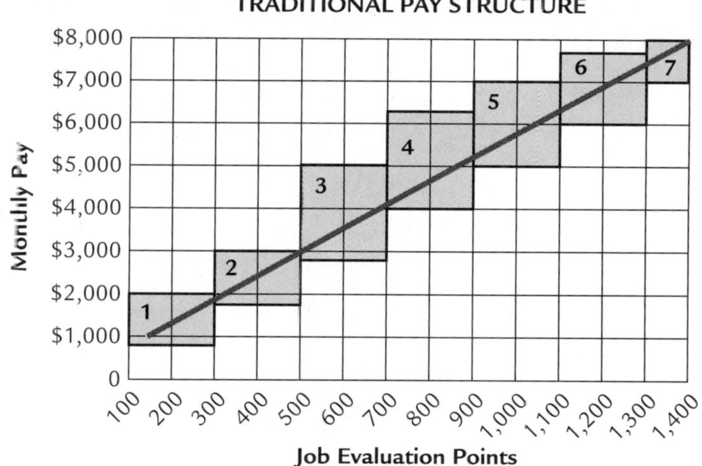

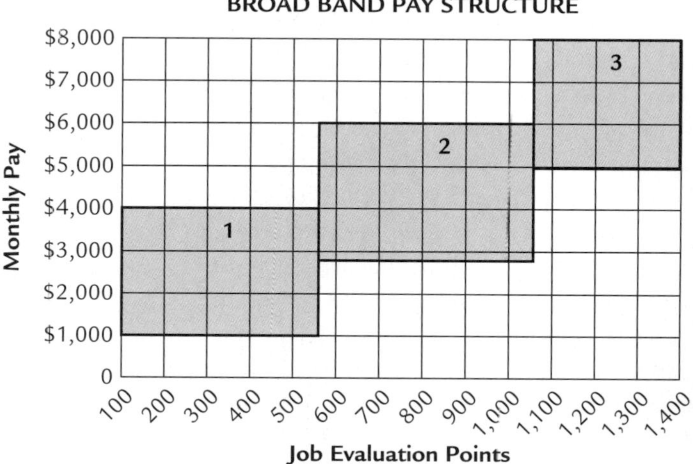

system is the greater flexibility it gives organizations to match an employee's pay to his or her individual value and changing labor market conditions.

at-risk compensation pay that varies depending on specified conditions, including the profitability of the company; hitting particular budget, revenue, or cost savings targets for a unit; or meeting specified individual performance targets

incentive plans systems that tie some compensation to performance

Another important pay trend is the movement away from an individual's total compensation package being primarily composed of salary and toward a greater portion of compensation being at risk.[40] **At-risk,** or **variable compensation**, is simply pay that varies depending on specified conditions. These conditions might include the general profitability of the company; hitting particular budget, revenue, or cost savings targets for a unit; or meeting specific individual performance targets. Increasingly, companies are placing a higher portion of employees' total compensation "at risk." This is primarily because if total compensation is made up of salary and if salaries are raised at a level comparable to inflation, inflation and subsequent salary increases can add significantly to company costs. On the other hand, if a higher percentage of compensation is tied to performance, higher compensation costs only occur with higher performance. Consequently, **incentive plans**, or approaches that tie some compensation to performance, are increasingly being spread throughout the organization, whereas traditionally they were reserved for only the most senior managers.

BENEFITS Traditional benefit plans include items such as medical, dental, and life insurance. In some cases, certain benefits are mandated by law at the state or national level. Companies operating internationally find that the laws regarding mandated benefits differ substantially from one country to another. In the past, companies used to compete for employees and retain them in part through offering attractive benefit plans. However, as companies added more features to the plans to make them attractive to a broader base of employees with differing needs, companies found themselves paying 20 percent to 40 percent of salary in benefits. To reduce the soaring benefit costs and still meet differing employee needs, companies began to offer **cafeteria-style plans** in which employees had a set number of "benefit dollars" that they could use to purchase the specific benefits that fit their particular needs.

cafeteria-style plans benefit plans in which employees have a set number of "benefit dollars" that they can use to purchase benefits that fit their particular needs

REWARDS AND MOTIVATION Although the human resource department has much of the responsibility for reward and compensation systems, effective rewards are more than the dollars paid out in salaries and bonuses or the dollars tied up in health care and other benefits. Although individual managers can influence pay increases and the like, they also have the greatest control over equally powerful rewards such as recognition and praise. Consequently, it is important for you to understand the broad range of rewards and how they influence the performance of your employees, which we discuss at greater length in Chapter 10. Still, it is important to point out here that employees are often rewarded for doing one thing and yet expected to do another. For example, as Motorola began to shift from simply shipping products to producing world-class quality products, employees continued to be rewarded for timely shipments (with quality levels well below six sigma). Furthermore, employees were punished if shipments were late, even if the quality levels of the late shipments approached six sigma. Because rewards were not aligned with the firm's new strategy, results of the six-sigma effort at Motorola were less than what senior executives expected. As another example, most stockbrokers at retail brokerage firms are rewarded with bonuses based on the volume of transactions they complete. This leads many brokers to "churn" individual investors' accounts. That is, brokers buy and sell shares in order to generate commissions even though the investment objectives of the investors did not justify such frequent transactions. As a consequence of this churning and the associated fees charged to customers, investors often take their accounts to competing brokerage firms. In the end, the reward structures encourage churning, but churning ultimately hurts firm revenue and broker commissions because customers defect.

Employee Development

One of the most powerful motivators for people to join organizations and to perform is the opportunity to grow and develop.[41] Career and employee development systems are designed to respond to that particular motivation and to ensure that the human capabilities needed in the organization are being developed. The **career paths** organizations want employees to embark upon to prepare for certain responsibilities is largely a function of the firm's strategy. For example, Sony is simultaneously trying to capture global efficiencies and respond to local market conditions. As such, Sony tries to capture economic efficiencies by manufacturing nearly all its small, handheld video cameras for markets throughout the world at a single factory in Japan. Yet, it also tries to sell these cameras in a way that appeals to different local tastes across the globe. Consequently, Sony places a high premium on career paths involving international experiences—especially for employees at the top of the organization. The company also utilizes integrated teams—that is, employees from various functional areas such as market research, engineering, sales, and finance—who work together to develop new products. Sony, therefore, places a premium on employees working in several functional areas over the course of their careers, or what is referred to as **cross-functional job rotation**.

career paths sets and sequences of positions and experiences

cross-functional job rotation opportunities for employees to work in different functional areas and gain additional expertise

As we have said, creating career and development systems often falls upon the shoulders of the firm's human resource function. Usually, though, it is individual managers who are the most knowledgeable about the development needs of specific employees and are often those to whom these people go in search of career guidance. In addition, managers develop reputations as being effective or ineffective at employee development. Their reputations often affect the quality of the subordinates they attract, which in turn affects the performance of their units. Consequently, career-path development is actually a critical activity for managers.

PROMOTION Employees can and should expand and improve their capabilities on the job. This need not always involve a promotion. However, for a large percentage of an organization's employees, part of the driver of development is promotion to positions of greater responsibility and pay.

In large companies, promotions often involve relocations as well. For example, many employees within IBM say that the company's initials stand for "I've Been Moved." With an increasing percentage of couples who both work, these relocations, especially international relocations, can be challenging.[42] For **dual-career couples**, finding a job for the employee's partner, especially in a foreign country, can be a serious obstacle to the person accepting a promotion and transfer. Even if a transfer or interim job can be located for the spouse, work visa restrictions can prevent the person from working in a foreign country. To cope with this challenge, companies are expanding their spouse relocation assistance programs and are also forming informal associations so employees interested in relocating, and employees who have already relocated, can exchange information about job opportunities and other aspects of accepting international assignments.[43]

dual-career couples
couples in which both partners work full-time in professional, managerial, or administrative jobs

TERMINATION. Despite your best efforts to recruit, hire, train, compensate, and manage the performance of your employees, you may find that you have to terminate, or fire, an employee. Firing for cause usually involves the termination of an employee for criminal behavior, such as theft of company property, or for violating the company's policies, such as sharing confidential information with its competitors. Most companies have detailed and written policies about the criteria for "cause terminations" and the steps that a manager must follow to fire an employee who meets these conditions. An employee can also be fired for failing to perform. Again, most companies have detailed policies about what must be done first before an employee can be fired for a poor performance. Often these policies involve the following:

1. Informing the employee of the performance standards
2. Formally and specifically documenting incidents of poor performance
3. Informing the employee of these performance failures, reiterating the job's standards, and outlining timeframes and actions for improvement
4. Formally informing the employee of the consequences of failing to meet the standards within the timeframe established

If the employee's performance does not improve sufficiently subsequently to taking these measures, many companies require his or her manager to work with a specialist in the human resources department to actually fire the employee.

Layoffs. Layoffs involve the termination of groups of employees because of economic or business reasons. Research has demonstrated that companies that do not conduct layoffs in a *reasonable* manner are less able to attract and retain good employees in the future.[44] In many cases by contract or law, companies have to provide a certain amount of advance notice before they can conduct a sizable layoff. Clearly, "reasonable" is open to interpretation, but practices that are reasonable include outplacement aids such as résumé-writing assistance, career counseling, office space access, secretarial help, and job-hunting assistance. Often companies outsource these activities to other companies that specialize in helping laid off workers find employment.

Labor Relations

Labor relations come into play when formal unions represent employees for the collective bargaining of their wages, benefits, and other terms of their employment. Unions represent a large proportion of employees in some industries, such as the automobile manufacturing and airline industries. For example, in the airline industry, not only are many lower-paid employees, such as baggage handlers, unionized, but so are highly paid employees, such as pilots.

Although the percentage of U.S. employees represented by unions has declined over the course of the last 50 years,[45] good labor relations remain critical for many companies. Managers walk a fine line between meeting the needs of unionized employees and meeting the needs of their employers.

Managing a Diverse Workforce

When we use the term *diversity*, we are talking about differences among people, including their age, gender, race, religion, cultural background, education, mental and physical disabilities, sexual orientation, and so on. Clearly, the U.S. workforce is in the midst of a sweeping demographic transformation. For example, from 1980 to 2020, the white working-age population is projected to decline from 82 percent to 63 percent (see Exhibit 8.9). During the same period, the minority portion of the workforce is projected to double (from 18 percent to 37 percent), and the Hispanic or Latino portion is projected to almost triple (from 6 percent to 17 percent).

This demographic shift is a function of two primary drivers. First, a larger number of younger Americans (ages 0 to 44) are ethnic minorities. Second, an increasing number of white workers are reaching retirement age and leaving the workforce. These are the "baby boomers"—people born from 1946 to 1964. Between 2000 to 2015, the largest increase in the younger U.S. population is projected to be among people of Hispanic or Latino descent (see Exhibit 8.10).

Gender and Diversity

Along with ethic dimensions of diversity, gender is another important aspect. Women constitute 46 percent of the U.S. labor force. More than 59 percent of U.S. women are employed outside the home, 75 percent of whom work full time. In 2005, the largest percentage of employed women (38 percent) worked in management, professional, and related occupations; 35 percent worked in sales and office occupations; 20 percent worked in service occupations; 6 percent worked in production, transportation, and material moving occupations; and 1 percent worked natural resources, construction, and maintenance occupations. Approximately 4 million women were self-employed in nonagricultural industries. These self-employed women represented 5 percent of all employed women.[46]

Despite their high participation rate in the workforce overall and in business in particular, women have been underrepresented in managerial positions. Some people refer to this phenomenon as hitting the "**glass ceiling**," meaning that women can "see" into the executive ranks, but an invisible barrier prevents them from being promoted in proportion to their representation in the workforce. Although the glass-ceiling phenomenon is changing, it is changing slowly. For example, in 1995, 8.7 percent of all *Fortune* 500 corporate officer positions were held by women, compared to 16.4 percent in 2005.[47]

glass ceiling
an invisible barrier that prevents women from promotion to the highest executive ranks

As business globalizes, the glass ceiling phenomenon gets even more complicated. One would naturally expect that as businesses globalize, a person's international work experience would become more important—at least for an executive's career. To ensure

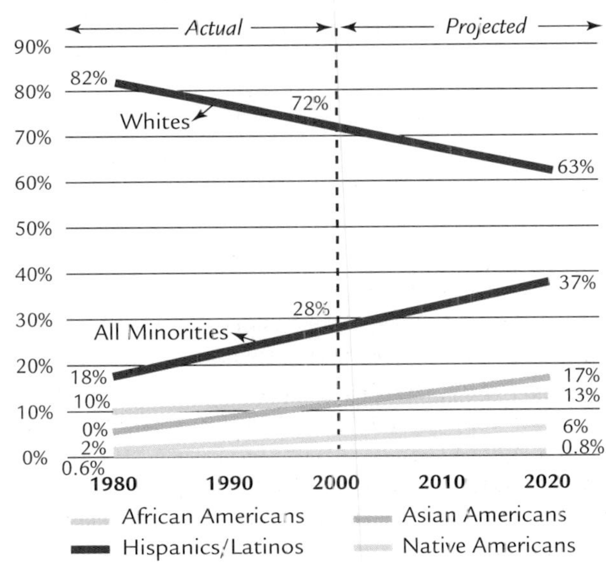

EXHIBIT 8.9

U.S. Workforce Demographic Changes, 1980–2020

Notes: Population projections are based on historical rates of change for immigration, birth, and death. Pacific Islanders are included with Asian Americans. Alaska Natives are included with Native Americans. Projections for Native Americans are based on the 1990 Census. The Census category "other races" is not included.

Sources: U.S. Census Bureau, 5% Public Use Microdata Samples (based on 1980, 1990, and 2000 Census) and U.S. Population Projections (based on the 2000 Census).

EXHIBIT 8.10

Projected Changes in the U.S. Population by Age and Ethnicity, 2000–2020

Notes: Population projections are based on historical rates of change for immigration, birth, and death. Pacific Islanders are included with Asian Americans. Projections based on the 2000 Census are not available for Native Americans.

Source: U.S. Census Bureau, 5% Public Use Microdata Samples (based on the 2000 Census).

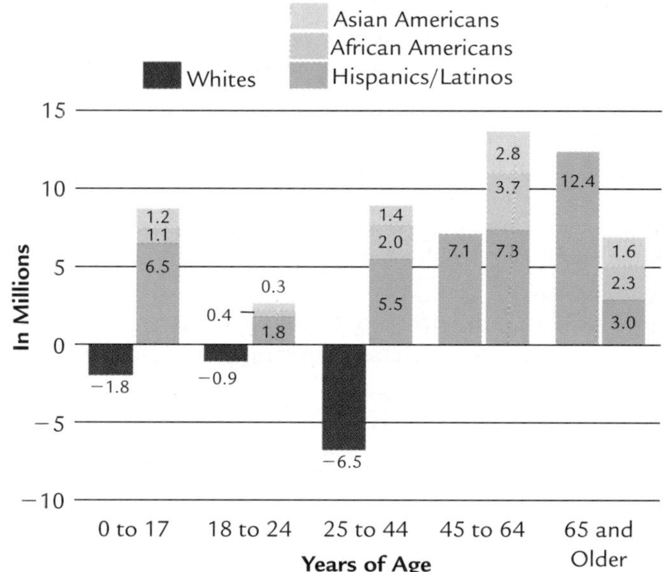

that equal opportunity was afforded all citizens regardless of gender, race, or other difference, the Civil Rights Act of 1991 requires U.S. firms to abide by the same nondiscrimination laws relative to their U.S. personnel overseas as their U.S. employees residing in the United States.[48] One of the specific implications of this law is that unless a particular host country prohibits women from occupying managerial positions, a U.S. firm cannot discriminate against a woman candidate being sent overseas on assignment even if the norms and values of the host country would make it difficult for a women to be effective.

When the Civil Rights Act of 1991 was passed, only 3 percent of U.S. expatriate employees—employees sent overseas on temporary assignments for three to five years—were women. This occurred despite the fact that 41 percent of all U.S. managers were female. This suggests that there may have been some gender bias in the selection of U.S. expatriate managers. If U.S. firms increasingly require an international assignment as part of a person's development for top management positions, given that only 3 percent of those receiving this opportunity were women, they may find the glass-ceiling problem even more challenging in the future.

The specific countries to which managers might be sent for development opportunities only complicate the situation. For example, because Japan is the United States' second largest trading partner, U.S. firms are likely to send employees to operations in Japan. However, in Japan, less than 1 percent of all managers are women. This may suggest that in the traditionally male-dominated society, female expatriate managers from the United States might have difficulty being successful. Yet, the Civil Rights Act of 1991 mandates that the gender of a U.S. candidate cannot be a factor in the selection decision. It is interesting to note that despite initial inclinations to think that women expatriates would have a more difficult time in Japan than male expatriates, research actually suggests that women expatriates do just as well as men in Japan.[49]

Sexual Harassment

Over the last 10 years, sexual harassment has become a major workforce issue, especially given the significant financial penalties that can be assessed to organizations that allow it to occur. Sexual harassment takes two basic forms. The first is sometimes termed *quid pro quo*. It involves requests or implied suggestions that sexual relations are required in exchange for continued employment or benefits, such as a promotion. The second form involves actions that create a "hostile environment." A hostile environment can be created through jokes, touching, comments, pictures, and other means of communicating unwanted sexual innuendos. Sexual harassment suits have increased dramatically over the last several years. As a consequence of the judgments (which are often several hundred thousand dollars), companies are increasingly offering training programs to try to help managers understand the law and avoid such incidents.

Laws and Regulations Affecting Human Resource Management

Because peoples' good intentions to treat everyone fairly regardless of gender, race, ethnicity, age and other differences do not always show up perfectly in their actions, an important set of established laws and regulations have been put in place. Many of these have a significant impact on the management of human resources. For example, a group of flight attendants for Delta Airlines filed suit because Delta had weight limits for flight attendants. The attendants claimed they experienced discrimination because although weight limits were applied to all flight attendants, both male and female, there were no similar standards applied to pilots. Delta first argued that the weight limits were legal because certain size limitations were necessary for flight attendants to perform their jobs in the limited space on planes. Despite this argument, Delta later dropped the weight requirements for all flight attendants.[50]

Exhibit 8.11 provides a summary of the laws enacted in the United States that have had a significant impact on human resource practices and policies. The basic intent of most of this legislation has been to ensure that equal opportunity is provided for both job applicants and current employees. Because the laws were intended to correct past inequalities, many organizations have either voluntarily implemented or been pressured by employees and other constituencies to implement **affirmative action programs** to ensure that organizational changes are made. These programs may involve such things as taking extra effort to inform minority candidates about job opportunities, providing special training programs for disadvantaged candidates, or paying special attention to the racial or gender mix of employees who are promoted.

affirmative action programs hiring and training programs intended to correct past inequalities for certain categories of people based on gender, race and ethnicity, age, or religion

Keep in mind that the intent of most of the legislation and regulation in the United States is designed to provide equal opportunity. This, however, does not prevent organizations from using certain criteria that you might think of as discriminatory, if it can be demonstrated that the criteria are **bona fide occupational qualifications (BFOQ)**, or qualifications that have a direct and material impact on job performance and outcomes.[51] For example, you might think that refusing to hire male employees who have a mustache or beard (or requiring them to shave them before being hired) would constitute discrimination. However, Disney has such a policy for its theme park workers and has prevailed when taken to court. Disney was able to retain the policy despite legal challenges because the company was able to demonstrate statistically that customers reacted better to and were more satisfied with clean-shaven park employees than those with beards and mustaches. In Disney's case, being clean shaven is a BFOQ.

bona fide occupational qualifications (BFOQ) qualifications that have a direct and material impact on job performance and outcomes

Diversity and the Firm's Performance

At this point, there has been more than 20 years of research on diversity and its relationship to the performance of small groups and larger organizations.[52] The results of these studies are mixed. Some studies have found a positive relationship between the level of a firm's diversity and performance, whereas other studies have found a negative relationship. More recent studies have found that there is not a simple, linear relationship.[53]

In general, as managers you can think of diverse groups having both assets and liabilities. All of the differences among group members can potentially constitute assets for the group. These include their different perspectives, knowledge, experiences, education, values, orientation, and so on. They allow the group as a whole to see and consider more angles than a more homogeneous set of individuals and perspectives likely would have. This can be particularly valuable in situations where an organization needs innovation and new ideas.

However, these differences can also become liabilities. This is because all the points of diversity that provide different perspectives can be potential sources of friction. Diverse work groups often encounter the following problems:

- Communication problems and misunderstandings
- Mistrust

EXHIBIT 8.11

Major U.S. Federal Laws and Regulations Related to Human Resource Management

Act	Requirements	Covers	Enforcement Agency
Thirteenth Amendment	Abolished slavery	All individuals	Court system
Fourteenth Amendment	Provides equal protection for all citizens and requires due process in state action	State actions (e.g., decisions of governmental organizations)	Court system
Civil Rights Acts of 1866 and 1871 (as amended)	Grant all citizens the right to make, perform, modify, and terminate contracts and enjoy all benefits, terms, and conditions of the contractual relationship	All individuals	Court system
Equal Pay Act of 1963	Requires that men and women performing equal jobs receive equal pay	Employers engaged in interstate commerce	EEOC
Title VII of CRA	Forbids discrimination based on race, color, religion, sex, or national origin	Employers with 15 or more employees working 20 or more weeks per year; labor unions; employment agencies	EEOC
Age Discrimination in Employment Act of 1967	Prohibits discrimination in employment against individuals 40 years of age or older	Employers with 15 or more employees working 20 or more weeks per year; labor unions; employment agencies; federal government	EEOC
Rehabilitation Act of 1973	Requires affirmative action in the employment of individuals with disabilities	Government agencies; federal contractors and subcontractors with contracts greater than $2,500	OFCCP
Americans with Disabilities Act of 1990	Prohibits discrimination against individuals with disabilities	Employers with more than 15 employees	EEOC
Executive Order 11246	Requires affirmative action in hiring women and minorities	Federal contractors and subcontractors with contracts greater than $10,000	OFCCP
Civil Rights Act of 1991	Prohibits discrimination (same as Title VII)	Same as Title VII, plus applies Section 1981 to employment discrimination cases	EEOC
Family and Medical Leave Act of 1993	Requires employers to provide 12 weeks of unpaid leave for family and medical emergencies	Employers with more than 50 employees	Department of Labor

Source: Raymond A. Noe, John R. Hollenbeck, Barry Gerhart, and Patrick M. Wright, *Human Resource Management: Gaining a Competitive Advantage* (Burr Ridge, Ill: Richard D. Irwin, 1997), p. 107. Copyright 1997. Reproduced with permission of The McGraw-Hill Companies.

- Conflict and incompatible approaches to resolving the conflict
- Lower group cohesiveness and greater subgroup formation based on elements of diversity such as language, race, or gender

In practice, diversity is a two-edge sword. Diversity can lead to new ideas, innovation, and higher performance but it does not happen automatically. To the extent that the differences lead to conflict and to the extent that the conflict is not managed well, the group's performance will suffer.

Leveraging the Diversity of Your Firm's Workforce

With this in mind, the practical question for a practicing manager is, "How can I limit the liabilities and leverage the assets of diversity?" One of the first things to consider is the complexity of the problems or opportunities you face. If on the one hand, the situation is rather simple and straightforward, a highly diverse team or workforce might not outperform a more homogeneous one with equal job capabilities. If, on the other hand, the situation is complex and multifaceted, then the multiple perspectives of members of a diverse group can add value. In this situation, assuming the potential liabilities, such as conflict, are well managed, diversity does seem to lead to a higher performance.

In addition to paying attention to the situations in which a diverse group of employees might excel, there are several other actions you as a manager can take to leverage the assets of diversity and limit the liabilities:

- ***Know yourself.*** How much exposure have you had to people with different ethnic, racial, religious, educational, or cultural backgrounds to your own? How tolerant and understanding of the differences have you been? How comfortable were you? How curious were you?
- ***Prepare yourself and your employees.*** How skilled are you and your employees at listening, communicating, negotiating, and resolving conflicts?
- ***Provide support.*** Are there support groups for minority employees to keep them from feeling unappreciated and wanting to leave the organization? To what extent do minority employees have mentors who can help them understand and become an effective part of the organization?
- ***Guide behavior.*** Do you monitor the behavior of your subordinates and peers? Do you consistently and positively reinforce behaviors that foster tolerance and the effective use of diversity? To what extent do you privately provide negative feedback to employees who display intolerance or other problem behaviors?

From both a domestic and international perspective, workforce diversity is only going to increase. One of the ways you can distinguish yourself from others and add value to your organization is by working effectively with your subordinates, peers, customers, and suppliers with diverse backgrounds. The Manager's Challenge box, "Marriott Embraces and Leverages Diversity," shows how one company successfully meets the diversity challenge.

How Globalization Is Affecting Diversity

Not only is the U.S. workforce becoming increasingly diverse, but globalization is increasingly causing multinational companies to hire a more diverse set of employees. Many people argue that the world is getting smaller. However, from a human resources perspective, the world is getting larger! If you look at the history of most multinational corporations (MNC), upon their founding they operated primarily in one or a very limited number of countries. However, as the firms grew, they expanded into more and more countries. Telecommunication and transportation technologies in particular have facilitated this expansion. Now, companies such as Marriott, Philips, and Citicorp operate in over 60 countries around the world. For them, that translates into employees speaking over 40 different languages, dealing with 60 different governments, interacting with 10 different major religions, and coping with hundreds of different customs, holidays, and traditions. As companies expand into new countries and cultures, the world for them gets larger and more complicated.

A MANAGER'S CHALLENGE

Diversity

Marriott Embraces and Leverages Diversity

Among Marriott's over 100,000 employees in the United States, 60 percent are minorities and 54 percent are women. Together, these employees speak over 50 languages. The majority of Marriott employees work in entry-level jobs from housecleaning to laundry and food services. Given the changing demographics of today's employees, Marriott's managers must find a way to seek out and leverage an increasingly diverse workforce. However, for Marriott it is not enough to simply get warm bodies in the door to work. Because Marriott competes on its service reputation, managers need workers who will not just do their jobs but will do them in a way that makes customers feel great. In addition, because the company promotes from within (more than a third of its managers start out in entry-level positions), Marriott's managers need to attract and retain the best of its entry-level employees.

Among Marriott's entry-level employees, many lack good work habits, have difficulty managing money, experience domestic abuse, or have inadequate child-care arrangements. In addition, many entry-level workers are immigrants who speak limited or no English or have limited education and skills. "It's critical that we become more skilled at managing this workforce," states Donna Klein, who directs Marriott's "work-life" programs.

To find out more about its unskilled workforce, Marriott managers conducted a study and learned that its workers faced various challenges. For example, it found that its existing child-care program barely scratched the surface of this group's needs. The study also found that about one-quarter of the workers had literacy problems. In response, Marriott initiated an on-site English as a second language (ESL) program during work hours.

Despite these efforts, managers were still busy offering advice about family conflicts and child-care solutions, and sometimes loaning money to employees for urgent bills. Instead of attending to the needs of its customers, notes Clifford J. Erlich, Marriott's senior vice president for human resources, "Many managers spent 15 percent of their time doing social work."

As a result, Marriott managers changed their HRM programs. They added programs such as social services referrals, parenting classes, and child-care facilities to attract and motivate hourly workers—and keep turnover lower than that of competitors.

To attract, motivate, and retain the entry-level, hourly workers upon which it relies, Marriott has developed landmark programs such as social-services referrals, parenting classes, and child-care facilities. Responding to the needs of its employees has helped the company keep its turnover rates low and sustained its reputation for exceptional service.

After a number of changes were made to U.S. welfare programs, Marriott's management instituted a program called "Pathways to Independence" to help welfare recipients become productive Marriott workers. As part of the program, participants learn business skills like work punctuality as well as life skills like money management. For a $5,500 per-person investment (half funded by government subsidies), more than 3,000 former welfare recipients now work for Marriott—a new labor pool that, importantly, has a below-average turnover rate.

Critics say Marriott's managers are too paternalistic. But the company's success stories show how these alternative approaches have added value. For example, Thong Lee has worked for Marriott for 16 years. A bartender in the Seattle Marriott, Lee learned English through the hotel's classes and used his Marriott stock and pay to buy rental properties. He also remembers when his boss shut down the hotel laundry for a day so the staff could attend his mother's funeral.

Responding to the changing composition of the U.S. workforce and needs of its entry-level employees has helped sustain Marriott's competitive position and its reputation for exceptional service. Moreover, the company's continued growth has created even more opportunities for the personal and professional development of its employees—a fact that managers highlight to attract and retain workers. It also doesn't hurt that Marriott is 1 of only 22 companies to consistently make *Fortune's* "100 Best Places to Work" list—an accomplishment that further enhances managers' ability to recruit and retain good employees.

Sources: "100 Best Companies to Work For," *Fortune*, January 22, 2007; "Marriott Makes Major Strides Toward Diversity Goals, Setting Industry Standards," Hospitalitynet.org, July 21, 2006; A. Wheat, "The Anatomy of a Great Workplace," *Fortune*, February 4, 2002, 75+; J. Hickman, "America's 50 Best Companies for Minorities," *Fortune*, July 8, 2002, 110.

Most firms cannot simply avoid expanding overseas. Consider where the world's workers will be in the future compared with where they are now: Exhibit 8.12 indicates that most of them will be in developing countries. Given that most of the large MNCs are headquartered in developed countries and most of the workers in the future will be in developing countries, continued expansion abroad seems inevitable.

As firms continue to expand outside their home countries, they will continue to confront a variety of diversity-management challenges. For example, do the selection techniques that work in one country also work in another? Can one performance appraisal form apply to all operations around the globe? Must a company adapt or change its reward systems from one country to the next? If it must adapt, how can a firm avoid the risk of employees perceiving these differences as inequitable? What must a firm do to ensure that it provides developmental opportunities for employees in all its operations? For example, recently a Korean multinational firm was seeking to fill its top global marketing position. Is the best person for the job Korean? How does a global firm ensure that it finds and develops the best possible talent wherever in its worldwide operations that talent might be located? When a firm needs to send employees abroad, how does it select these individuals? How should it train these employees prior to their international assignments? And how should they evaluate these employees when real changes in exchange rates, government price controls, and other external factors affect the bottom-line results of an overseas operation? These are just a few of the human resource questions managers will have to try to answer in today's increasingly global and diverse environment.

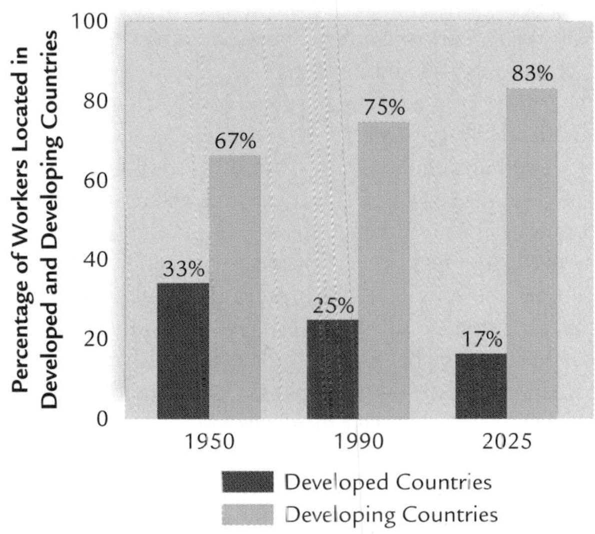

EXHIBIT 8.12

Where the Workers Are

Source: U.S. Department of Labor, 1997.

Managerial Challenges from the Front Line

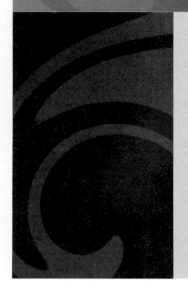

The Rest of the Story

After careful consideration, Jean-Jacques Beaussart decided that the best thing to do during his subordinate's end-of-year performance appraisal was to tell him that his performance that year had been unacceptable. However, Beaussart saw value and strengths in the individual and wanted to construct a set of responsibilities that put those strengths to their best use. Specifically, the individual was good at managing contracts, negotiations, and working with suppliers, many of which he had dealt with for years. After some discussions, the two men agreed to change the subordinate's job to one that focused on managing the company's outsourcing and offshoring activities—an important new task for National City Corporation. The new job design was a great fit with the subordinate's capabilities, and his resulting performance the following year was good. Thus, Beaussart was able to turn a bad situation into a win-win arrangement for both his procurement team and the longtime employee.

Summary

The capabilities of a firm's employees will influence both the company's strategy (its formulation) and how well it gets executed (its implementation). Because human resource capabilities are hard for competitors to copy, they can be a source of competitive advantage for firms.

- Getting the right people in the right jobs has four fundamental components. First, managers must plan for their human resource needs. This consists of three related activities: (a) forecasting their human resource demand, (b) estimating supply, and (c) determining fulfillment. Second, managers must do a job analysis to determine the nature of the firm's jobs and their requirements. Third, managers must interest the right people in the company and its job opportunities (recruit them). Fourth, managers must select the right people for the jobs.
- Unstructured interviews are most commonly used to select employees, but they are less valid than structured interviews. Methods such as work sampling, whereby candidates perform tasks identical or similar to the work they would be doing if hired, tend to be more valid indicators of who would be a better employee.
- Effective socialization and orientation should be done very early in the employee's tenure with the company. Paperwork and information should be kept to only what is required to avoid overload. Employees should meet their supervisors early in the process. Pairing a new hire with a "buddy" (more experienced employee) can also be helpful.
- Effective training can involve both formal (classroom or computer-based) training as well as on-the-job training. In both cases, effective training requires (a) a clear understanding of what is and is not correct or desired behavior and why that is the case, (b) sufficient opportunities to practice the behavior, and (c) feedback on the person's performance with further opportunity for them to practice and improve.
- Because it is simple and efficient, a graphic rating scale is a commonly used method of assessing the performance of employees. Behaviorally anchored rating scales are also common and provide richer descriptions of levels of performance. During a 360-degree feedback appraisal, multiple people assess the employee's performance.
- Most compensation systems consist of wages and salaries, at-risk pay, and benefits. At-risk compensation is typically tied to performance results and, therefore, moves up or down with performance. Benefits, such as health care, typically have a monetary value of 20 percent to 40 percent of an employee's wages or salary.

- A well-managed diverse workforce can exceed, in many cases, the performance of a nondiverse, or homogeneous, workforce. Managing a diverse workforce will become even more important in the future as firms continue to globalize and search for tomorrow's employees in developing countries.

Key Terms

360-degree feedback 222
affirmative action programs 229
at-risk, or variable compensation 224
behaviorally anchored rating scales (BARS) 221
bona fide occupational qualifications (BFOQ) 229
broad band systems 223
cafeteria-style plans 225
career paths 225
critical incidents 222
cross-functional job rotation 225
dual-career couples 226
glass ceiling 227
incentive plans 224
job analysis 209
job design 218
job posting 211
job sharing 219
pay structure 223
reengineering 219
structured interview 213
valid selection technique 212

Review Questions

1. Why is it important to keep the firm's strategy in mind when engaged in human resources activities such as selection?
2. What are the principal aspects of job analysis?
3. What does it mean for a selection technique to be valid?
4. How are structured interviews different than unstructured interviews?
5. Identify three written tests used in selection and describe their validity.
6. List the five things that organizations can do to make orientation programs more effective.
7. What are the key differences between graphic rating scales and behaviorally anchored rating scales?
8. List seven steps that an organization can take to make performance appraisal sessions more effective.
9. Why are organizations moving away from traditional pay structures to more broad band pay structures?
10. What is the purpose of affirmative action programs?
11. What is the difference between quid pro quo and a hostile environment in cases of sexual harassment?
12. Describe three things you can do to improve your capability to manage greater diversity in the workforce.

Assessing Your Capabilities

Indicate the extent to which you agree or disagree with the following statements. Be as candid as you can.

1. I sympathize with the homeless.	1 Strongly Disagree	2 Somewhat Disagree	3 Neutral	4 Somewhat Agree	5 Strongly Agree
2. I acknowledge others' accomplishments.	1 Strongly Disagree	2 Somewhat Disagree	3 Neutral	4 Somewhat Agree	5 Strongly Agree
3. I am wary of others.	1 Strongly Disagree	2 Somewhat Disagree	3 Neutral	4 Somewhat Agree	5 Strongly Agree
4. I distrust people.	1 Strongly Disagree	2 Somewhat Disagree	3 Neutral	4 Somewhat Agree	5 Strongly Agree

The steps that Alliant's managers have taken to promote diversity are innovative in two ways. First, rather than make the human resource department solely responsible for diversity, senior managers have demonstrated their active support and involvement. Second, the diverse composition of the steering team and diversity council helped these groups address diversity on a larger scale.

The expanded set of ongoing diversity initiatives include the following:

- Employee Resource Groups—These groups serve as a resource for employees and provide an opportunity to participate in diversity initiatives across the company. Existing affinity groups include the "Multicultural Business Council," the "Women's Network," and the "Alliant Pride Network."
- Diversity and inclusion awareness training for all employees.
- Diversity recruiting initiatives in key business units.
- Supplier diversity and development program.
- Community networking, support, and involvement.
- International days and "holidays around the world" celebrations.
- A printed diversity calendar distributed to all employees.
- Ongoing employee engagement surveys regarding the firm's organizational culture and diversity awareness.

Questions

1. Why is Alliant so committed to diversity of its human resources? How will this benefit the company?
2. Alliant Energy does not publicly report the results of its supplier-diversity initiatives. Do you think it should? What measures should be used to determine if its supplier-diversity initiatives are effective?
3. Do you believe the company is forcing the issue of diversity? Is it necessary to make diversity training mandatory for all employees? Explain your answer.
4. Independent surveys suggest that companies cannot easily quantify the effects of diversity. How would you suggest that Alliant measure the costs and benefits of having a diverse workforce?

Sources: "Alliant Energy 2006 Proxy Statement," *Alliant Energy 2005 Annual Report*; "Alliant Energy Corp.," Business Record (Des Moines), June 11, 2001, 18+; N. Mueller, "Wisconsin Power & Light's Model Diversity Program," *Training & Development* (March 1996): 57–61; and Alliant Web site, www.alliantenergy.com.

Team Exercise

Divide into teams of four and read the following short scenario. Assign one person to play the role of the female firefighter who finds the firehouse's sexually hostile environment disturbing. One person should play the role of the captain of the firehouse. One person should play the role of the other female firefighter. Finally, one person should play the role of a human resource manager for the fire department.

The female firefighter complaining about the sexually hostile environment has asked for another meeting to hear what the captain plans to do about the situation. The captain must make a decision and then explain it. The questions at the end of the exercise are designed to stimulate thinking and suggest potential courses of action.

You are the captain of a firefighting squad consisting of 12 firefighters, two of whom are women. Your squad is on duty for 24 hours and then off duty for 24 hours at a time. When on duty, you all live together in the firehouse where you eat, sleep, train, relax, and hang out together. Some days are so intense with emergency calls that you do not have time for anything else. Other days are quite slow.

Good firefighting skills are vital to your team. A significant amount of trust is also important. For example, if you were injured in a burning building, you would want to know that your team members would be able to get you out.

In most firehouses, including yours, the addition of women has happened only recently. All women firefighters have to pass the same physical and skill tests that men do. However, male-oriented conversation, humor, and activities, such as weightlifting, have traditionally helped squad members bond with one another.

One of your newest female recruits has complained to you that the firehouse is a sexually hostile work environment. She says that the jokes she overhears are full of offensive humor and that several of the guys have offensive pictures inside their lockers. She is physically as strong as a couple of the guys and has performed well. Because the firehouse is an older one, there are no separate locker rooms or showers. Although separate shower times have been scheduled, the recruit also complained that some of the guys had "accidentally" walked in when she was showering because they "forgot" the schedule.

You have talked about the complaints to the other female member of your squad, who has been in your unit for nearly a year. She disagrees that the firehouse's environment is sexually hostile but will not go into any details. Her performance has been okay but not high.

1. What actions would you take as the captain?
2. What would satisfy you as the individual lodging the complaint?
3. What should the human resources manager do about this situation? How much of the decision should be left to the discretion of the firehouse captain?
4. Suppose that other squad members tell you that a couple of the younger, single male firefighters might act a bit "macho" when they talk among themselves. If you confront these men about the problem, what will you do if they allege that the new female recruit is wrongly eavesdropping on their private conversations?

Managerial Challenges from the Front Line

Name: Taylor Ridout

Position: Owner and Operator, The Shoppes at Brownstone Village, Arlington, Texas

Alma mater: University of Texas at Austin (BA in Advertising)

Outside work activities: Taking my two-year-old daughter for a drive

First job out of school: Events coordinator for a trading-card company

Hero: My parents

Motto to live by: Several, including: "trust your instincts"; "think, execute, and balance"; and "do the right thing"

Management style: Firm, but friendly

When she was growing up in Arlington, Texas, a city in between Dallas and Fort Worth, Taylor Ridout used to go to a nearby skating rink. Over the years, though, Ridout stopped going there because it had become somewhat dilapidated and rundown. However, a few years later, after graduating from college, and with the help of her father, a developer, she bought the rink!

Now, at the age of 29, Ridout has totally remodeled the structure and turned it into a retail complex of boutique stores and restaurants called "The Shoppes at Brownstone Village." She not only owns the complex but also one of its restaurants and a winery in an adjacent building that was later added to the mall. Developing and marketing the site haven't been major hurdles for Taylor, given her educational and family background. That has been almost easy compared to the challenge of developing an appropriate leadership style to manage the complex's hundred or so employees and vendors.

In her first job out of college, Taylor obtained plenty of marketing savvy and experience by coordinating events at the Super Bowl and World Series for her employer, a trading-card company. She found the job really interesting, and even exciting, but after her daughter was born, she realized that she needed to reduce the extensive travel involved in her event-coordinating job and find something closer to home that did not require frequent out-of-town trips. That's when she decided to follow her father's footsteps and try her hand at developing a piece of property and then operating and managing the newly formed entity.

The Shoppes at Brownstone Village opened in November of 2004, and immediately became a popular local shopping destination. Customers flocked to the stores and even created a typical good-news-bad-news problem: Too many cars, too few parking places. But that problem was not as difficult for Taylor to solve as figuring out how to lead all the employees and vendors who worked for and with her. As she says, her natural tendency is to "want everybody to be friends."

Thus, that philosophy of congeniality guided her leadership approach in the early months following the Shoppes' opening. However, she soon found that this approach wasn't working very well and that many employees were performing in a rather indifferent and laid-back manner.

As Taylor Ridout had to learn at the beginning of her managerial career, leadership is an undeniably critical part of the overall management process. It lies at the very heart of that part of managing that deals with "Leading" (the title of this Part of the book). Without leadership, organizational performance would be minimal. Indeed, it would be difficult if not impossible to talk about the accomplishments of twenty-first-century organizations of all types—whether in business, government, education, or other settings—without referring to the role that leadership played in those successes. Clearly, leadership is important to organizations, and to society at large. What is not so clear is how to increase its presence in organizations and its effectiveness. That is the managerial challenge—the one faced by Taylor Ridout. But she is no exception.

Leadership is, above all, a process of influence. As such, it is not a set of behaviors limited to the chief executive officer, the executive vice president, the director of manufacturing, the regional marketing manager, or, for that matter, a sports team's coach or captain. It is a process that almost anyone can exhibit, and *potentially anywhere* in an organization.

However, although acts of leadership in an organization can be widespread and commonplace, often they are not. The central issue, then, both for organizations and for individual managers, is to turn leadership potential into reality. The very fact that so many articles and books have been, and continue to be, written on the topic of leadership is a good indication that this challenge is not being met well by either the typical organization or the practicing manager.

In this chapter, we will first confront three age-old questions: What is leadership? Are leading and managing the same? Does leadership differ across national cultures? We then explore the relationship between leadership and its close cousins, influence and power. Following this, we identify different sources and types of power and analyze issues in how to use power effectively. This provides a background for examining the basic elements of the leadership-influence process: the leader, the followers, and the situation. Throughout this discussion of the process of leadership, we explain different theoretical approaches at the place where they are most relevant to a particular part of the process. The chapter concludes by examining whether there are effective substitutes for leadership.

What Is Leadership?

Although *leadership* is a familiar everyday term, it's nevertheless far more complex than you might assume. That's what makes it such an interesting and intriguing subject. Let's look at how organizational scientists have defined the term *leadership*. Unfortunately, there is no clear consensus because, as one prominent scholar observed some years ago, "There are almost as many definitions of leadership as there are persons who have attempted to define the concept."[1] Consistent with most definitions, however, we define **organizational leadership** as an interpersonal process that involves attempts to influence other people to attain a goal.

organizational leadership an interpersonal process that involves attempts to influence other people in attaining organizational goals

While there is general agreement that leadership is an influence process, there is less agreement on (a) whether the definition must refer only to influence used by those occupying a designated leadership position (a "manager," "president," "chairperson," "coach," and so forth), (b) whether the influence must be exercised deliberately and for the specific attainment of the group's or organization's goals, and (c) whether the compliance of others must be voluntary. Our view on each of these issues follows.

As we explained out the outset of this chapter, *anyone can exhibit* acts of leadership behavior in an organization, and those acts are not limited only to persons holding designated leadership positions. In particular, this means that leadership should not be thought of as occurring only, or even mostly, at the top of the organization. Leadership can also be seen in the actions of the first-line supervisor who inspires her subordinates to increase their attention to safety procedures to avoid production downtime. The group member who champions his team's new product and convinces others of its potential demonstrates leadership. The human resources manager who makes sure—without being ordered to—that those in the human resources division treat all applicants for positions with the company respectfully and equitably shows leadership. Workers who set an example for their coworkers by continually seeking ways to improve processes and working conditions exhibit leadership.

Ordinarily, however, people in positions that are labeled managerial or supervisory have more opportunities to exert leadership. Also, leadership behavior is expected more frequently from supervisors and managers than from other types of employees. Such expectations often profoundly affect the behavior of both those who hold leadership positions and those around them. Expectations count! For instance, the pharmaceutical giant Johnson & Johnson (J&J) prides itself on its dedication to ethics in management. As such, J&J subordinates expect their managers to demonstrate such standards—to lead by example, in other words. A manager who does not abide by the ethical principles of the company, or who is even perceived as not adhering to them, is likely to lose first the trust of his subordinates, followed by his or her ability to lead them effectively.[2] The accompanying Manager's Challenge, "A Cautionary Tale," describes an example of where these kinds of issues were raised, rightly or wrongly.

People act as leaders for many reasons, and their efforts are not necessarily aimed solely at the attainment of a group's or organization's goals. In other words, leaders' motives can be directed at multiple objectives, including their own objectives, instead of the organization's. People's motives are seldom single-focused. However, for the sake of our discussion, in this chapter we will assume that leaders are seeking the attainment of the organization's goals, regardless of their personal objectives.

The use of coercion to gain compliance ("do this or you will be fired" threats) is not typically considered leadership. However, the dividing line between what is, and is not, coercion is often very difficult to determine. Probably the safest generalization is this: the greater the degree of purely voluntary actions by followers toward the leader's intended direction, the more effective the leadership.

effective leadership influence that assists a group or organization to perform successfully and meet its goals and objectives

The preceding discussion raises a further key issue: What is **effective leadership**? Put most simply, it is influence that assists a group or an organization to meet its goals and objectives and perform successfully. This implies that effective leadership is "enabling" behavior—that is, it is behavior that helps other people accomplish more than if there had been no such leadership.[3]

By their actions, those who exhibit effective leadership add an extra ingredient to the sum of the efforts of many people and thereby help them to achieve together more than they would have otherwise. Effective leadership unlocks the potential that resides in other people.

A MANAGER'S CHALLENGE

Ethics

A Cautionary Tale

When people in management positions become increasingly successful within organizations, they are typically rewarded by being promoted to higher-level positions that provide expanded leadership opportunities. That, for most people, is the good news. The cautionary, if not bad, news is that their actions are often much more closely scrutinized. Nowhere is this more true than with respect to their ethics. This was the situation Julie Roehm found herself in.

Roehm completed an undergraduate engineering degree at a major university in the United States, and then went on to an MBA program at one of the top-rated business schools in the country. When she graduated, she had the luxury of choosing among several attractive job offers in marketing. She joined the Ford Motor Company in its marketing leadership program. Subsequently, she was appointed as brand manager to lead the introduction of the then new Ford Focus, the car that at that time was replacing the Escort in Ford's lineup of vehicles. Reported Roehm: "We did crazy, out-of-the-box things that were intended to connect with a younger audience—live TV commercials, personalization packages like a 'road-trip package,' and little gems that fit in the O in the word Focus on the back of the car."

Because of her success on the Focus project, she was offered a higher-level marketing job with Chrysler. Again, she achieved great success—this time by marketing Dodge trucks. Soon, she was promoted to oversee the marketing of all three of Chrysler's brands.

Without a doubt, Roehm had become highly visible not only at Chrysler but also outside of the automobile industry. So much so that Wal-Mart hired her in early 2006, not only to oversee all the company's marketing communications but also to revamp totally its entire approach to advertising. Now she was in a position to exercise even more influential leadership. And, now she was even more in the spotlight than ever before.

Roehm proceeded to solicit advertising agencies to bid for Wal-Mart's advertising account. The review and competition among agencies for the contract was a seven-month process that ended in October 2006, with the award of the $580 million account to ad agency DraftFCB. But less than two months later, Wal-Mart fired Roehm, cancelled the agreement with DraftFCB, and announced it was reopening the review process. What had happened? Why the sudden turn of events?

Wal-Mart gave no official explanation. In the days immediately thereafter, Roehm stated, "The history books are littered with companies who sought change and then decided they didn't want it. . . . I still don't know specifically what happened here." However, the press reported that Wal-Mart was concerned about several apparent ethical lapses by Roehm, such as accepting an invitation to a reception and dinner at an upscale New York restaurant that was sponsored by one of the competing agencies—the agency that ended up being awarded the account—despite strict company rules against accepting gratuities and gifts. She also was reported seen riding in the Aston-Martin of DraftFCB's CEO before the completion of the review.

Whether Roehm's behaviors, if true, would add up to what most people would consider ethical lapses meriting her dismissal might be debatable. What is not is the fact that even the perceptions of possible violations of an organization's rules become intensely magnified as a manager assumes higher levels of responsibility. At the very least, therefore, leaders should assume that any behaviors they engage in that even give the appearance of an ethical infraction will be called into question.

Sources: R. Berner, "My Year at Wal-Mart," *Business Week,* February 12, 2007, 70–74; M. Creamer, "Unruly Julie and the Scandal That Rocked the Ad World," *Advertising Age,* December 11, 2006, 1+; "Scandal Puts Wal-Mart Ad Account Up for Grabs," http://money.cnn.com, December 7, 2006; D. Kiley, "An Open Letter to Wal-Mart, Julie Roehm and Draft/FCB," *Business Week* Online, www.businessweek.com, December 14, 2006; www.chicagogsb.edu/news/daa2006/04-roehm.aspx.

Leading and Managing: The Same or Different?

Leading and managing are two terms that often are used interchangeably. But are they really the same? In recent years some scholars have argued that the terms are different.[4] They argue that leadership involves creating a vision for organizations or units; setting, communicating, and promoting new directional goals and procedures, and inspiring subordinates. These

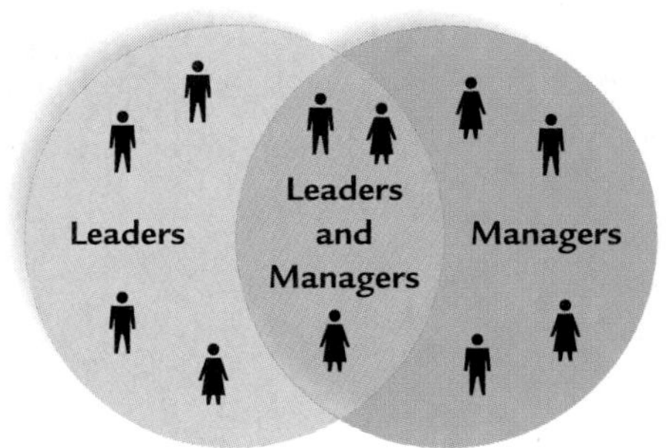

EXHIBIT 9.1

The Overlapping Roles of Leaders and Managers

activities can be contrasted with more mundane, task-oriented "managerial" functions, such as dealing with interpersonal conflicts, planning and organizing, and, in general, implementing the goals set by others (the organization's leaders).

When leading and managing are defined in these ways, then, of course, they are different. However, if we consider managing from a broader perspective, as it is throughout this book, then the two activities do not differ as much as might appear on the surface. That is, managing *ought* to involve most of the kinds of activities that are included in the leader's role. Removing such "leading" activities from managing makes an artificial distinction between the two and relegates managing to a routine, almost trivial activity—which it is not.

The relationship between leading and managing can be illustrated using a Venn diagram, similar to those encountered in mathematics classes. The diagrams consist of circles that are completely independent of each other, circles that overlap one another completely, or circles that partially overlap. Imagine all the leaders from one organization in one circle and all the managers from that same organization in another. The two circles are likely to be partially, but not totally, separate, as shown in Exhibit 9.1. Some people can be leaders, and some people can be managers; but many people can be *both* leaders *and* managers. Bluntly, leadership is a very important component of management, but management is more than just leadership. It includes other tasks that don't directly involve influencing people.

Thus, although not all leaders are managers, and not all managers are leaders, modern organizations need most of their managers to engage in leadership behaviors such as those that foster innovation and creativity, inspire other people, and improve their organization's performance. Consequently, in this chapter and in this book, we view organizational leadership as a process that should be included as a significant part of the managerial role, but it is definitely not the total role.

Does Leadership Differ Across National Cultures?

Does leadership differ fundamentally from country to country? Nobody knows for sure, although researchers are attempting to find out.[5] As some observers point out: *"Leadership* is a fairly modern concept. It did not appear in English-language usage until the first half of the 19th century and has been primarily the concern of Anglo-Saxon influenced countries. Prior to that, and in other countries, the notion of *headship* has been more prominent, as in the head of state, chief, or other *ruling* [italics added] position."[6] Or, as another scholar put it, "The universality of leadership [as a part of the managerial role] does not . . . imply a similarity of leadership style throughout the world."[7]

Experts on Southeast Asia, for example, point out two essential cultural features of leadership there: the requirement for order and compliance and the requirement for harmony.[8] The "order" requirement involves traditional values that support the acceptance of hierarchies, conformity, and deference to authority. The "harmony" requirement involves not only the obligations of the subordinate to the superior but also the obligations of the superior to respect the subordinate and care for his or her welfare. This style can be summarized by the word *paternalism,* whereby a leader is regarded as the provider, or "father," who will take care of the subordinate in return for responsible behavior and performance. In addition to Asia, it is a style often found in Central and South American countries where these is a strong emphasis on collective values as opposed to individual values.[9]

Despite such differences, some similarities in leadership practices—such as giving subordinates more participation in the decision-making process—are beginning to appear with increasing regularity around the world.[10] The results from the GLOBE project, the most recent and comprehensive international study of leadership, appear consistent with this conclusion as Exhibit 9.2 shows.[11] According to the data collected for this study, certain leader attributes, such as "trustworthy" and "decisive," are viewed as positive across all cultures. Likewise, other attributes, such as "dictatorial" and "asocial" are universally viewed as negative. However, how other attributes, such as "cautious" and "ambitious," are viewed depends heavily on a particular culture and its values. Some cultures view them positively, but other cultures view them negatively.

EXHIBIT 9.2

The Effect of Culture on Attitudes Toward Leaders' Attributes

Examples of Leader Attributes Universally Viewed as *Positive* +	Examples of Leader Attributes Universally Viewed as *Negative* −	Examples of Leader Attributes Viewed as *Positive* or *Negative* Depending on the Culture +/−
+ Trustworthy	− Noncooperative	+/− Ambitious
+ Encouraging	− Irritable	+/− Individualistic
+ Honest	− Dictatorial	+/− Cunning
+ Decisive	− Ruthless	+/− Cautious
+ Communicative	− Egocentric	+/− Class Conscious
+ Dependable	− Asocial	+/− Evasive

Source: P. Dorfman, P. J. Hanges, and F. C. Brodbeck, "Leadership and Cultural Variation: The Identification of Culturally Endorsed Leadership Profiles," In R. J. House, P. J. Hanges, M. Javidan, P. Dorfman, and V. Gupta (eds.), *Leadership, Culture, and Organizations: The GLOBE Study of 62 Societies* (Thousand Oaks, CA: Sage Publications, Inc., 2004) pp. 667–718.

Because of expanding industrialization, the need for effective leadership has become a worldwide phenomenon. Precisely *how* that need is being met in specific organizations and countries, however, still appears to be influenced by cultural circumstances and traditions. Nevertheless, the picture of particular leadership styles and practices around the world at the beginning of the twenty-first century could change dramatically during the next few decades. It already is in some places, as exemplified by Yifei Li, head of Viacom's China MTV.[12] Yifei Li is trying to lead a youth-oriented firm operating in the mostly older, male-entrenched regulatory bureaucracy of China. She is normally confident, brash and up-front, but when interacting with the authorities she modifies her style somewhat. A century ago, or even a decade ago, her natural leadership style would unlikely to have been tolerated let alone accepted in that kind of setting.

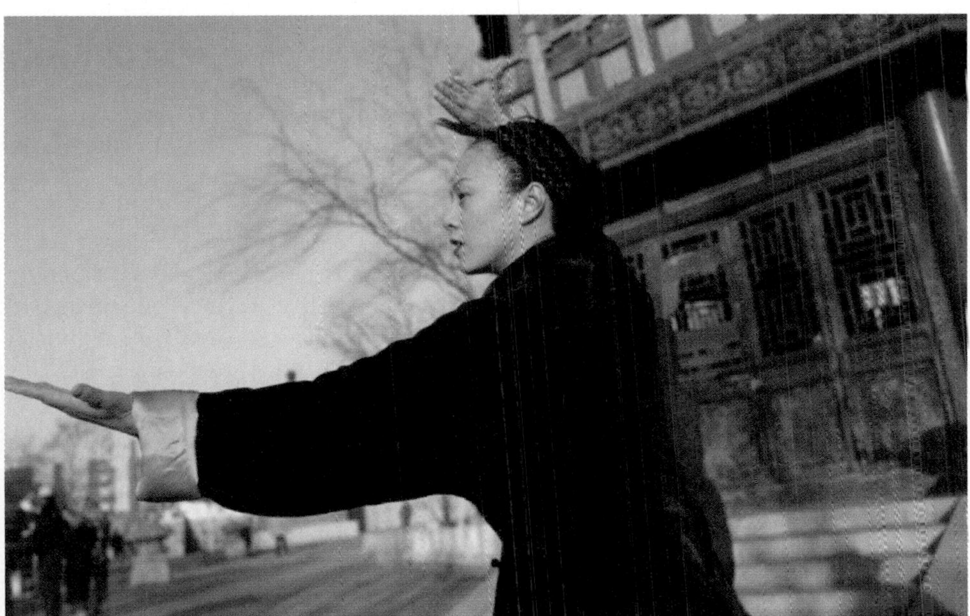

Yifei Li is the Managing Director of MTV Greater China, Executive Vice President of MTV Networks Asia, and the Chief Representative of Viacom China. Smart, confident, and female, Yifei Li has had to take a different approach to dealing with male business people in that country. "Particularly as a woman in China, you have to be a little bit softer, and humble," she has said. Yifei Li made The Asian Wall Street Journal's "Ten Women to Watch in Asia" list in 2005 and 2006.

Leadership and the Use of Power

power
the capacity or ability to influence

It is virtually impossible to study leadership as a type of social influence without also taking into account the idea of power. **Power** is typically thought of as the capacity or ability to influence. Thus, the greater a person's power, the greater the potential for influencing others. Power can be used "to change the course of events, to overcome resistance, and to get people to do things that they would not otherwise do."[13] However, the fact that a leader, or anyone else, has power does not guarantee that he or she will use it—or use it well. Possession and use are two different matters.

Whether a leader will use power depends on many factors. One principal reason leaders resist using their power, even when they can, is because they believe doing so will generate negative reactions. As has been said, "For many people, power is a 'four-letter' word."[14] The famous, but somewhat exaggerated, statement of this view of power was made more than a century ago in Britain, when Lord Acton wrote to Bishop Mandell Creighton that "power tends to corrupt [and], absolute power corrupts absolutely."[15]

It is not too difficult to think of an organization where a would-be leader used power inappropriately. This was illustrated several years ago when a chief executive officer of a consumer products manufacturer was removed from office, even though he had presided over a major turnaround that had brought the company out of bankruptcy. The reason he was dismissed was because of the way he used his power to intimidate subordinates. On occasion, he even threw objects at them when he was angry. His actions so severely damaged morale at the company that the board of directors had no other option but to find a new CEO.[16]

It would be misleading, however, to regard power only from the perspective of the damage it can do. In many circumstances, a leader's skillful use of power can produce positive outcomes. Frequently, though, the problem in organizations is not that leaders use too much power but rather that they fail to use the power available to them.[17] This was noted by two behavioral scientists who have studied leadership extensively when they said: "These days power is conspicuous by its absence. Powerlessness in the face of crisis. Powerlessness in the face of complexity . . . ."[18]

Types and Sources of Power

position power
power based on a person's position and rank in an organization

personal power
power based on a person's individual characteristics

Power, however used, does not arise spontaneously or mysteriously. Rather, it comes from specific and identifiable sources. The two major types of power, based on their sources, are position powers and personal powers.[19] **Position power** is based on a manager's rank in an organization. **Personal power** is based on a person's individual characteristics.

Clearly, someone who wants to be a leader could have large amounts of both types of power, which should facilitate the exercise of influence. For example, think about whether Taylor Ridout, featured in the opening profile, had access to both types of power and whether this helped her to exercise influence. There are also circumstances where a would-be leader might be low on both types of power, in which case the task of leading obviously would be more difficult. For instance, a lower-level manager who lacks the initiative to develop new products or programs and who is a poor communicator would find it difficult to inspire subordinates to put out extra effort to make changes and reach new goals. This manager lacks personal power and would be unlikely to be promoted—thus, also failing to increase his position power.

In many situations, though, a potential leader who is low on one type of power—for example, a person occupying a relatively junior-status position—can compensate for that by having very strong personal leadership characteristics that are recognized by other people, regardless of the person's formal status in the organization.

To help us better understand the nature of power in organizations, it is helpful to think about several subtypes of position power and personal power (see Exhibit 9.3).[20]

POSITION POWERS The powers associated with a position, include legitimate power, reward power, and coercive power.

legitimate power (or formal authority)
a type of position power granted to a person by the organization

Legitimate Power. **Legitimate power** is a type of position power granted to a person—for example, a manager—by the organization. It is sometimes called **formal authority.** In

EXHIBIT 9.3

Types of Power

Position Powers	Personal Powers
Legitimate—How much authority does the organization give to your position?	**Expert**—Do you have knowledge that others need?
Reward—Are you able to give others the rewards they want?	**Referent**—Do others respect you and want to be like you?
Coercive—Are you able to punish others or withhold rewards?	

the work setting, legitimate power is intended to give a manager the right to expect compliance by his or her employees. However, in today's organizations, with increasing levels of education of the workforce and changing societal norms about what is "legitimate" authority, the effectiveness of this type of power has distinct limits. Often, subordinates will disagree about the scope of a manager's authority; that is, they question the boundaries of what are "appropriate requests." For example, many managers used to expect their secretaries or assistants to make personal appointments for them and perform other nonwork-related services. Today, the relationship between a manager and his or her assistants has changed, and these types of requests are generally not considered legitimate.

The precise scope of legitimate authority in today's complex organizations is ambiguous, and the resulting agreement between manager and subordinate can typically be more implicit than explicit, leaving room for potential conflict. In addition, the extent of a manager's formal authority is bounded by subordinates' perceptions of that person's credentials. If the basis of a person's selection for a managerial position is questioned, the leverage of legitimate power is somewhat reduced. For example, take a medium-sized firm where the CEO decides to appoint a close relative who has little knowledge of the business to an executive-level position that in the past has been filled by employees who have worked their way up through the ranks. In this case, subordinates may not acknowledge that the relative has a right to the formal power that would normally be associated with the position, and thus they might not respond to requests rapidly and enthusiastically. This would probably be especially the case in many Western work situations, but perhaps not as much so in Asian cultures, where family connections are viewed as more appropriate for determining who should occupy high-level positions. In essence, though, in most organizational settings, formal authority represents power, but it definitely is not unlimited power.

reward power
a type of position power based on a person's authority to give out rewards

Reward Power. One of the strongest sources of position power for any manager is **reward power**, that is, the authority to give out rewards, especially differing amounts of highly valued rewards to different people. In any hierarchy, this power can have significant effects on others' behavior because it involves dispensing relatively scarce, but desired, resources. Only a few people, at most, can receive plum assignments; only one or two subordinates usually can be given the largest yearly performance bonus; only one person can be awarded the promotion. One positive aspect of rewards is that they have a "signaling" effect. They let subordinates know, for example, where they "stand" with the boss and give them an idea of what they must do to improve their standing. On the negative side, rewards can sometimes "demotivate" those who do not receive them or receive what they believe to be insufficient amounts of them. Because the use of reward power can have potentially important consequences, both good and bad, managers need to use rewards carefully and skillfully and be very alert to how subordinates perceive the administration of them.

coercive power
a type of position power based on a person's authority to administer punishments, either by withholding something that is desired or by giving out something that is not desired

Coercive Power. **Coercive power** is the power to administer punishments, either by withholding something that is desired, such as a raise, or by giving out something that is not desired, such as a letter of reprimand. In typical organizations, such power is used sparingly these days, at least directly and overtly. However, coercive power is sometimes used indirectly in the form of implied threats. A manager, for instance, can let her employees know that noncompliance with her requests will result in an assignment to the least desired projects or committees. A manager in charge of assigning shift work could subtly influence subordinates by assigning those who do not agree with his policies to a series of inconvenient split shifts.

A major problem with the use of coercive power is that it can cause recipients to avoid being detected by disguising their objectionable behavior, rather than motivating them to perform in the desired manner. Furthermore, the use of coercion can generate retaliation. Threatening employees with reduced hours or a pay cut if they don't take on more duties or accept a less than generous incentive plan might result in work slowdowns, an increased number of faulty parts, or complaints to government regulators. Any of these actions clearly would be counterproductive.

It should also be noted that although people with higher-level positions have greater ability to apply coercive power, its use is not confined to managers and supervisors. Potentially, anyone has coercive power. For example, a lower-level employee can harm someone higher by withholding valuable information or making a situation more difficult than it might otherwise be. This use of coercive power by subordinates may be subtle, but in some cases it may actually be quite effective for that reason.

PERSONAL POWERS Personal powers are attached to a person and stay with that individual regardless of the position or the organization. For those who want to be leaders, personal powers are especially valuable because they do not depend directly or only on the actions of others or of the organization. The two major types are expert power and referent power.

expert power
a type of personal power based on specialized knowledge not readily available to many people

Expert Power. **Expert power** is based on specialized knowledge not readily available to many people. It is a potential source of power because other people depend on, or need advice from, those who have that expertise. The best example of expert power in everyday life is the physician-patient relationship. Most people follow their doctors' directives not because of any formal position power but because of the potential negative consequences of ignoring their expertise. Given today's increased percentage of knowledge workers (those who have special expertise) and the increased use of highly sophisticated knowledge in many types of contemporary organizations, it is becoming imperative for most managers to have some type of expertise. Having expertise may not necessarily set a manager apart from his or her subordinates, but not having it may greatly diminish the effectiveness of various forms of position power.

Expert power is not confined to higher organizational levels. Lower-level employees can possess some of the most specialized, and yet most needed, knowledge in an organization.[21] One only needs to observe a boss trying to find a particular document in a file to appreciate the expert power that an administrative assistant often has in certain situations; or to watch the high-level executive waiting impatiently while the technician makes repairs on a computer or fax machine. These examples illustrate the fact that dependencies create an opportunity for expertise to become power, whatever the position a person holds.

About a decade ago, Jack Welch, then CEO of General Electric, used this principle deliberately by introducing the idea of "mentoring up" into the organization. He started by requesting that several hundred of his worldwide executives reach down in the ranks and pick younger, "Webified" subordinates to teach them the intricacies of the Net. Based on this experience, the upper-level executives indicated that they had become more receptive to receiving input from those in lower-power positions.[22]

referent power
a type of personal power gained when people are attracted to, or identify with, that person

Referent Power. When people are attracted to, or identify with, someone, that person acquires what is called **referent power**. This power is gained because other people "refer" to that person. They want to please that person or in some way receive acceptance. Referent power often can be recognized by its subtle occurrences. A subordinate, for example, may begin using gestures similar to those of his superior or even imitating certain aspects of his speech patterns. Or, the subordinate might find his opinions on important work issues becoming similar to those of his boss.

For anyone in a leadership position in a work setting, being able to generate referent power is clearly a great asset. It is a cost-free way to influence other people. Referent power makes it possible to lead by example rather than by giving orders. A manager can use her referent power to change work habits, for example. If she comes in early, stays late, takes shorter breaks, and finishes her work rather than putting it off until the next day, her subordinates may model themselves on her behavior and change their own work habits as well.

A problem with referent power, however, is that it is not obvious how such power can be deliberately and easily developed. There is no formula for how to increase your referent power, and attempting to get others to like or admire you can frequently cause the opposite reaction. Certain personal attributes, such as honesty and integrity, obviously help. Also, experience and a demonstrated record of success certainly help. The basic lesson seems to be that the referent power of a potential leader is built up over time by consistent actions and behavior that cause others to develop admiration for them.

The accompanying Manager's Challenge, "Lighting the Way at Amazon.com," describes someone who has both types of personal power, expert and referent, and is using them to make major organizational changes.

Using Power Effectively

There are at least four key issues for managers to think about in relation to the use of power (as shown in Exhibit 9.4):

- How much power should be used in a given situation?
- Which types of power should be used?
- How can power be put to use?
- Should power be shared?

HOW MUCH POWER TO USE? The answer to this question seems to be: Use enough to achieve objectives but avoid using excessive power. Using too little power in organizational settings can lead to inaction, and this is especially the case when change is needed but strong resistance exists or is anticipated. Often, managers seem reluctant to wield power because of anticipated opposition. Yet, the use of power is sometimes the only way to accomplish significant change. As management author Jeffrey Pfeffer said, "Managing with power means understanding that to get things done, you need power—more power than those whose opposition you must overcome."[23]

Using too much power, though, also can be a problem. When more power is used than is necessary, people's behavior may change, but resentments and reactions often are self-defeating to the power user in the long run. In many organizational situations, people have a sense of what is an appropriate amount of power. If that sense is violated, a manager may actually undermine his power for the future. Excessive use of power in work organizations, like excessive use of police force in civil disturbances, can result in potentially severe negative reactions.

WHICH TYPES OF POWER TO USE? Answers to this question depend on characteristics of the situation and circumstances: What has happened before, what type of change is needed, what amount of resistance is expected, where is opposition located, and the like. Each type of power, whether a position power or personal power, has a particular impact.

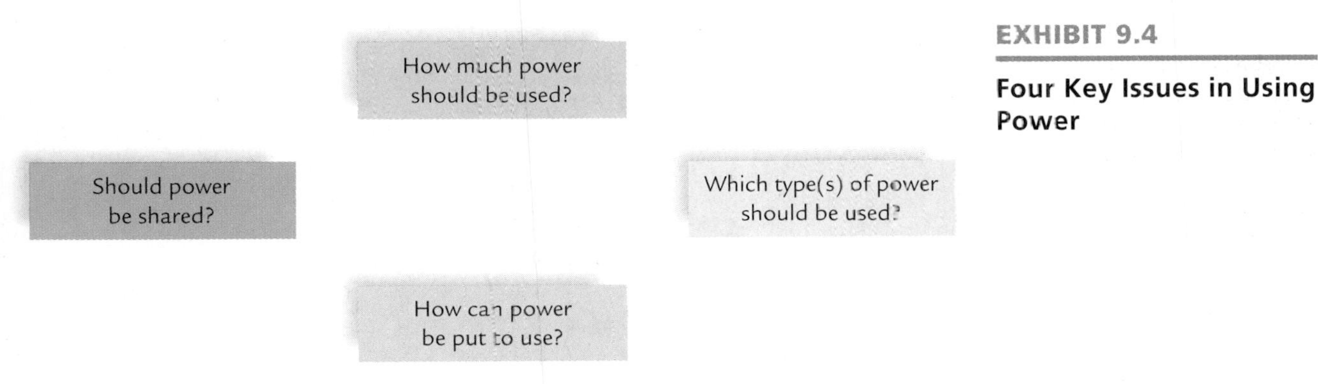

EXHIBIT 9.4

Four Key Issues in Using Power

A MANAGER'S CHALLENGE

Change

Lighting the Way at Amazon.com

Thomas J. Szkutak is using his background in lightbulbs and plastics to help the online retailer Amazon.com light the way to lower costs and brighter profits. Before joining Amazon.com as chief financial officer, Szkutak held the same position at GE Lighting, a Cleveland-based division of General Electric that makes a wide variety of lighting instruments for home and commercial use. Earlier in his career he was part of the management team for GE Plastics' business in Europe, Africa, India, and the Middle East. Jeff Bezos, Amazon.com's CEO, wanted Szkutak to help his company identify and implement changes that would "continue to drive down costs so that we can even further lower prices for customers."

How did Szkutak apply the personal powers and management skills he honed in lighting manufacturing and plastics production to his current role as CFO of a cutting-edge Internet-based retailer? It didn't hurt that his résumé included GE. GE is a recognized leader in corporate finance training. Every year, several hundred college recruits—the best and the brightest—go through its prized, two-year Financial Management Program in Ossining, New York, which was begun in 1919. These "star" graduates walk out of the course with the confidence that people will listen to them. Szkutak is no different.

Moreover, although GE Lighting employs 33,000 around the world and Amazon.com employs some 8,000 or so, the two companies face some similar challenges. Both are battling for global market share against formidable competitors and selling products to price-sensitive customers. Yet there are differences, as well—bottom-line differences. Whereas GE Lighting is a mature business that ekes out a relatively small profit margin of 10 percent year after year, Amazon.com is spending heavily to spur future growth and profits. Lower Wal-Mart-like prices are helping the e-retailer attract consumers interested in buying products other than just books, which has contributed steadily to continued growth and higher profitability for the company. "Lowering prices will go on for years and years, and that's just how we're going to do business," Bezos says.

So, why did Bezos choose Szkutak—whose management background is so concentrated in old-line manufacturing companies—for a key leadership position in a fast-paced online business like Amazon.com? It was precisely because of Szkutak's cost-cutting reputation at GE, where he and his managers constantly searched for creative ways to contain costs. Since cost cutting is one of Amazon.com's major priorities on the path to better profitability, Bezos believed the former GE executive would bring considerable expert power to his duties as CFO at Amazon.com. Szkutak also can wield referent power because GE's managers and finance executives are admired around the world, and he was a senior executive with the company for 20 years.

So has the bet paid off? Yes. 2003 marked Amazon.com's first full-year in the black. Since Szuktak's hiring, Amazon .com has dramatically streamlined its network of product distribution centers, one of its largest and most criticized expenses. Despite a rise in sales, the company has still managed to cut order fulfillment expenses significantly, thanks to better inventory software and smarter storage. It also honed its order "sorting" process, allowing it to ship roughly one-third more inventory with the same number of people. "They have made incredible progress in operations," said one industry research director.

Sources: M. E. Behr, "If at First You Don't Succeed," *CIO Insight,* November 2003, 51; R. Hoff, "Amazon & Co. Still Floating in Froth," *Business Week* Online, October 23, 2003; L. Chow, "All in the Grooming," *CFO Asia,* October 17, 2003; Adapted from Gene G. Marcial, "Amazon Turns a Page," *Business Week,* October 14, 2002, 172; "New CFO at Amazon.com," *Publishers Weekly,* September 9, 2002, 12; "Career Journal: Who's News," *Wall Street Journal*, September 3, 2002, B10; M. Soto, "Amazon.com Hires GE Executive as Chief Financial Officer," *Seattle Times,* August 31, 2002; S. Kaplan, "Amazon Riding High," *Video Business* 24, no. 17 (2004): 6; R. A. Manarriz, "In the Prime of Amazon's Life," *The Motley Fool,* March 9, 2007, www.fool.com.

Some types of power, especially referent and expertise, have relatively low costs. That is, their use generates little direct opposition. Thus, they would seem to be the powers to use whenever possible. The problem, however, is that they may not be strong enough to have an impact. If a manager has very little referent power, then trying to use that method is not likely to accomplish much. Similarly, if subordinates do not perceive the expertise of the manager as high, regardless of the actual degree of expertise, then the manager is unlikely to be able to motivate them to change. In such cases, the use of a form of position power, such as formal authority or reward power, might be necessary. However, the risks of creating a negative reaction are increased, thereby lessening the effects of such power.

HOW CAN POWER BE PUT TO USE? Power, in its various forms, provides the basis for influence. However, power must be converted into actual leader behaviors. The skillful use of different types of power is a type of expertise that anyone can develop. This means that the total amount of power available to you as a manager is not a fixed quantity but rather a resource that can expand or shrink over time.

To put power to use involves **influence tactics**, that is, specific behaviors that can affect the behavior and attitudes of other people. Exhibit 9.5 shows a representative sample of[24] tactics that can be employed. Different types of power match up with some tactics more than others. For example, a high degree of expertise would support the use of rational

influence tactics
specific behaviors used to affect the behavior and attitudes of other people

EXHIBIT 9.5

Types of Influence Tactics

Rational Persuasion: The agent uses logical arguments and factual evidence to show a proposal or request is feasible and relevant for attaining important task objectives.

Apprising: The agent explains how carrying out a request or supporting a proposal will benefit the target personally or help advance the target person's career.

Inspirational Appeals: The agent makes an appeal to values and ideals or seeks to arouse the target person's emotions to gain commitment for a request or proposal.

Consultation: The agent encourages the target to suggest improvements in a proposal or to help plan an activity or change for which the target person's support and assistance are desired.

Exchange: The agent offers an incentive, suggests an exchange of favors, or indicates willingness to reciprocate at a later time if the target will do what the agent requests.

Collaboration: The agent offers to provide relevant resources and assistance if the target will carry out a request or approve a proposed change.

Personal Appeals: The agent asks the target to carry out a request or support a proposal out of friendship, or asks for a personal favor before saying what it is.

Ingratiation: The agent uses praise and flattery before or during an influence attempt or expresses confidence in the target's ability to carry out a difficult request.

Legitimating Tactics: The agent seeks to establish the legitimacy of a request or to verify authority to make it by referring to rules, formal policies, or official documents.

Pressure: The agent uses demands, threats, frequent checking, or persistent reminders to influence the target person.

Coalition Tactics: The agent seeks the aid of others to persuade the target to do something or uses the support of others as a reason for the target to agree.

Source: G. Yukl, *Leadership in Organizations* (Upper Saddle River, NJ: Prentice Hall, 2002), p. 160.

persuasion. Someone possessing a great deal of referent power could more effectively use inspirational appeals than could someone with less referent power. A leader with little position power would have trouble using legitimating tactics.

The other major factor affecting the use of specific influence tactics is the circumstances of the situation, particularly with regard to the people targeted. Thus, if the target of influence is a person higher up in the organization, pressure would likely be an inappropriate and ineffective tactic. Likewise, exchange might work very well with a peer but perhaps be unnecessary in a typical situation involving subordinates. On the other hand, rational persuasion could be a potentially useful tactic in a wide variety of situations, whether with one's superiors, peers, or subordinates.

empowerment
sharing of power with others, especially by those with high amounts of position power

SHOULD POWER BE SHARED? In recent years, the concept of empowerment has become prominent in management literature.[25] In its broadest sense, **empowerment** simply means the sharing of power with others, where those with high amounts of power increase the power of those with less, especially with regard to decision making. This can be done on an organizationwide basis, but the individual manager or leader also can do it. A company that strongly embraces empowerment is Novo Nordisk, a Danish pharmaceutical company, with sales of almost $7 billion per year. The manager of one of its clinical units, for example, describes the organization as "a debating and arguing culture." However, he also points out that once a decision has been made, "externally, we show extreme loyalty to the company . . . grumbling after the fact isn't tolerated here."[26]

Those who advocate empowerment suggest that it is a key leadership practice for helping organizations perform at high levels and cope successfully with major changes.[27] Empowerment can also facilitate organizational commitment, learning, and innovation. However, for empowerment to take place, managers cannot simply declare that those below them have more power. They must provide the necessary means, such as, for example, delegating more formal authority to make specified decisions, offering increased training opportunities to develop expertise and self-confidence, providing more resources and access to information to implement effective decisions, and not rescinding the shared power at the first sign of trouble.

traits
relatively enduring characteristics of a person

The Leadership Process: Leaders

In this and the following two major sections, we turn to examining leadership as a process. As mentioned in the introduction to this chapter, this process—within organizational settings—has three fundamental components: leaders, followers, and situations. All three components need to be considered to gain a comprehensive understanding of how the process unfolds. As shown in Exhibit 9.6, what has been termed the "locus of leadership" is the intersection of these three variables: where and when the leader with a particular set of characteristics and behaviors interacts with a specific set of followers in a situation with certain identifiable characteristics.[28] Each component influences, and is influenced by, the other two, and a change in any one will alter how the other two interact.

We will discuss the impact of each of these three variables on the basic leadership process in this and the two sections that follow. In this first section on the leadership process, the focus will be on the leader: specifically, leaders' traits, skills and competencies, and behaviors.

EXHIBIT 9.6

Locus of Leadership: Intersection of the Basic Components of the Leadership Process

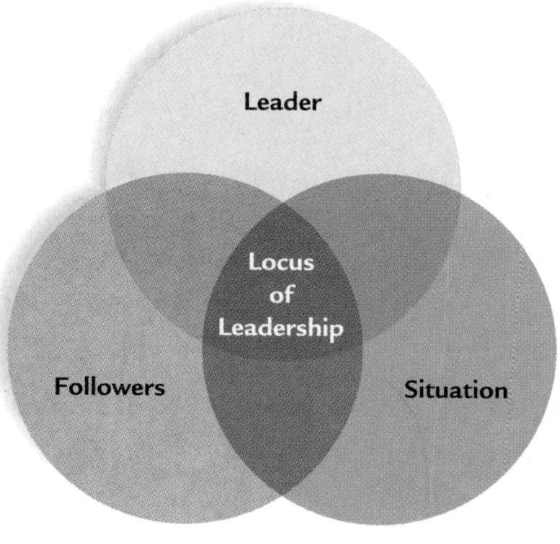

Leaders' Traits

One critical component of what leaders in managerial roles bring to the work setting is their **traits**, that is, the relatively enduring characteristics of a person. The scientific study of the role of leaders' traits has had a somewhat rollercoaster history: At the beginning of the twentieth century, the "great man"—note that it was not the "great person"—view of leadership was in vogue. That is, leaders, almost always thought of as only men in that era, were assumed to have inherited combinations of traits that distinguished them from followers. The notion, then, was that those destined to be leaders were "born' not made. As years passed, however, this theory faded away because of the difficulties of proving that traits were inherited. Instead, the focus shifted in the 1920s and 1930s to a search for specific traits or characteristics—such as verbal fluency, physical size, dominance, self-esteem—that would unambiguously separate leaders from nonleaders.

The current view is that although specific traits do not invariably determine a leader's effectiveness, they can increase its likelihood (at least in Western-oriented work environments).[29] As shown in Exhibit 9.7, among the traits that research has indicated are most apt to predict effective leadership are drive, the motivation to lead, honesty/integrity, self-confidence, and emotional maturity.[30]

- ***Drive:*** A high level of energy, effort, and persistence in the pursuit of objectives.
- ***Motivation to Lead:*** A strong desire to influence others, to "be in charge." Such a person is comfortable with the use of power in relating to other people.[31]
- ***Honesty/Integrity:*** Trustworthiness. Someone with this trait is a person whose word can be relied on consistently and who is highly likely to do what he or she says.[32]
- ***Self-confidence:*** A strong belief in one's own capabilities.[33] People with this trait set high expectations for themselves and others,[34] and they tend to be optimistic rather than pessimistic about overcoming obstacles and achieving objectives. In contrast to honesty/integrity, self-confidence is a trait that in the extreme can be a negative. It can result in a sense of infallibility and in an attitude of arrogance that can alienate potential followers. In other words, too much self-confidence can lead to what has been called "the shadow side of success."[35] That is, too much leadership success, paradoxically, can sow the seeds for later leadership problems. Moreover, no matter how much confidence managers have in themselves, their staffs, and their employees, nothing substitutes for preparation. The manager who relies on self-confidence at the expense of planning is setting the scene for potential disaster.
- ***Emotional Maturity:*** Remaining even-tempered and calm in the face of stress and pressure. People with maturity tend to accurately assess their own strengths and weaknesses; moreover, they are less likely to be self-centered and unduly defensive in the face of criticism.[36]

It is important to reemphasize that traits, such as those listed, do not guarantee that a person will become a leader or will necessarily lead effectively. Very few people possess exceptionally high levels of each and every trait. However, if a person has one or more of these relatively enduring characteristics, it increases their chances of being a successful

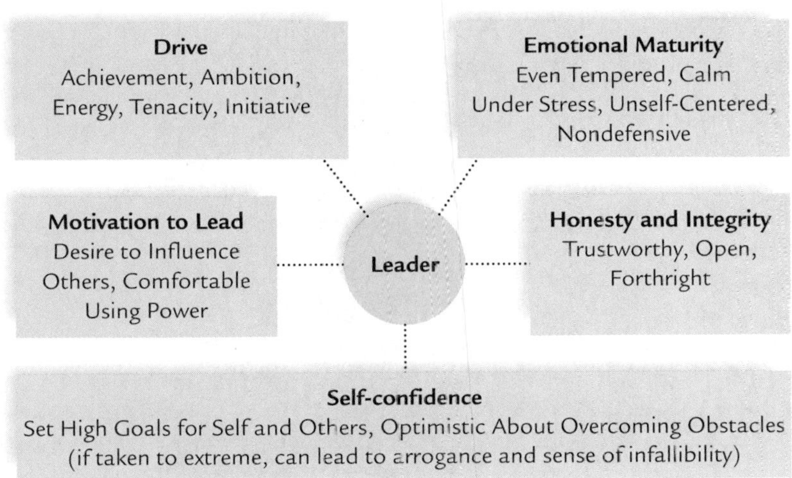

EXHIBIT 9.7

Leaders' Traits

Source: Adapted from S. A. Kirkpatrick and E. A. Locke, "Leadership: Do Traits Matter?" *Academy of Management Executive* 5, no. 2 (1991), pp. 48–60.

leader. Traits provide potential, but other factors such as skills, attitudes, experience, and opportunities determine whether that potential will be realized.

Finally, it must be stressed that most of the research on the relationship of personal traits to the effectiveness of leaders has not considered the impact of culture. It has focused primarily on Western, mostly American, work environments. Whether traits can universally predict successful leadership is still an open question (see the discussion of the GLOBE research project later in this chapter). It may be that in at least some other cultures, different traits would be equally or more influential. The very notion that specific personal qualities or leadership traits are critical to successful influence is itself open to question in many non-Western cultures. In countries such as Korea or Malaysia, for example, a person often is in a leadership position by virtue of ownership or family position; others show respect for that reason rather than because of certain personality features.[37]

THE SPECIAL CASE OF CHARISMA Charisma constitutes a set of traits that can produce an especially strong form of referent power. The term *charisma* has a theological origin and comes from the Greek word for "gift." It literally means "divinely conferred gift." Its relevance to organizational settings was first highlighted in the early decades of the twentieth century by the sociologist Max Weber.[38] Weber described the **charismatic leader** as someone who has influence over others based on the inspirational qualities of the individual rather than on that person's formal power or position. Thus, followers or subordinates are assumed to identify with that person because of those exceptional qualities. Many people would like to think they are endowed with charisma, but only relatively few people have these special powers. If they were common, they wouldn't be exceptional.

charismatic leader
leadership by someone who has influence over others based on individual inspirational qualities rather than formal power

The term *charisma* has been used particularly in the political sphere to describe those who are especially influential with large numbers of people. Examples include historical figures such as Mahatma Gandhi, Nelson Mandela, Winston Churchill, Mother Teresa, Martin Luther King Jr., and John F. Kennedy. In the business world, such people as Steve Jobs, Sam Walton, and Richard Branson come to mind.

Only in the last couple of decades has charisma been examined by scholars of organizational leadership. However, the topic has steadily received increased attention since then.[39] One of the first studies conducted found that charismatic leaders have traits such as:

- A strong need for power
- High levels of self-confidence
- A strong belief in their own ideas[40]

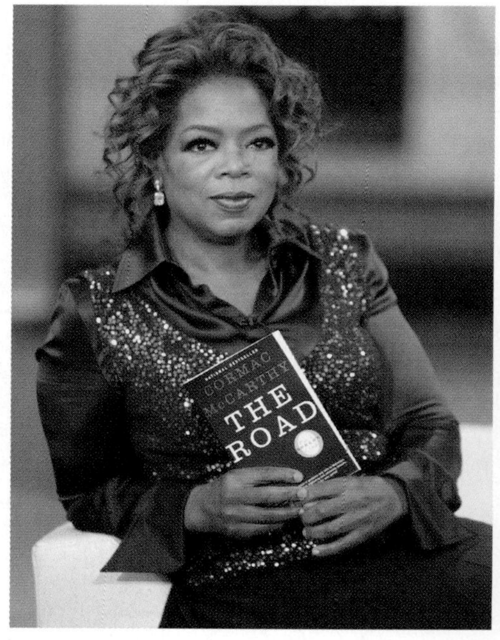

From her humble beginnings in rural Mississippi, Oprah Winfrey has become one of the most charismatic and influential leaders of our time. As the chairman of Harpo, Inc., Winfrey manages employees as she does audiences—with emotion and empathy.

With these kinds of traits, charismatic leaders, more than other types of leaders, are especially likely to:

- Model desired behavior[41]
- Communicate high expectations for followers' performance
- Be concerned with, and try to influence, the impressions of others
- Emphasize ideals, values, and lofty goals

The views of a business executive often described as charismatic, Herb Kelleher, the founder of Southwest Airlines, exemplify the last two points. Kelleher would always tell new employees: "I want you to be able to tell them [the employees' children] that being connected to Southwest Airlines ennobled and enriched your life—it made you bigger and stronger than you ever could have been alone."[42]

Based on several scholarly analyses, Exhibit 9.8 presents a summary set of attributes of charismatic leaders.

Since charisma is a type of "special power" possessed by relatively few people, can a typical manager or leader try to increase his or her charisma? It is clear that no one can create this type of power simply by assuming they have it, or by asking for or demanding it. It must be generated or conferred in some fashion. Although relatively few managers have the personality traits to produce easily or spontaneously the levels of charisma that certain renowned business and political leaders have achieved, most persons in leadership positions can increase the chances that their subordinates will be motivated to follow them and work with and for them.[43] The kinds of behavior, summarized in Exhibit 9.8, are ones that can be developed.

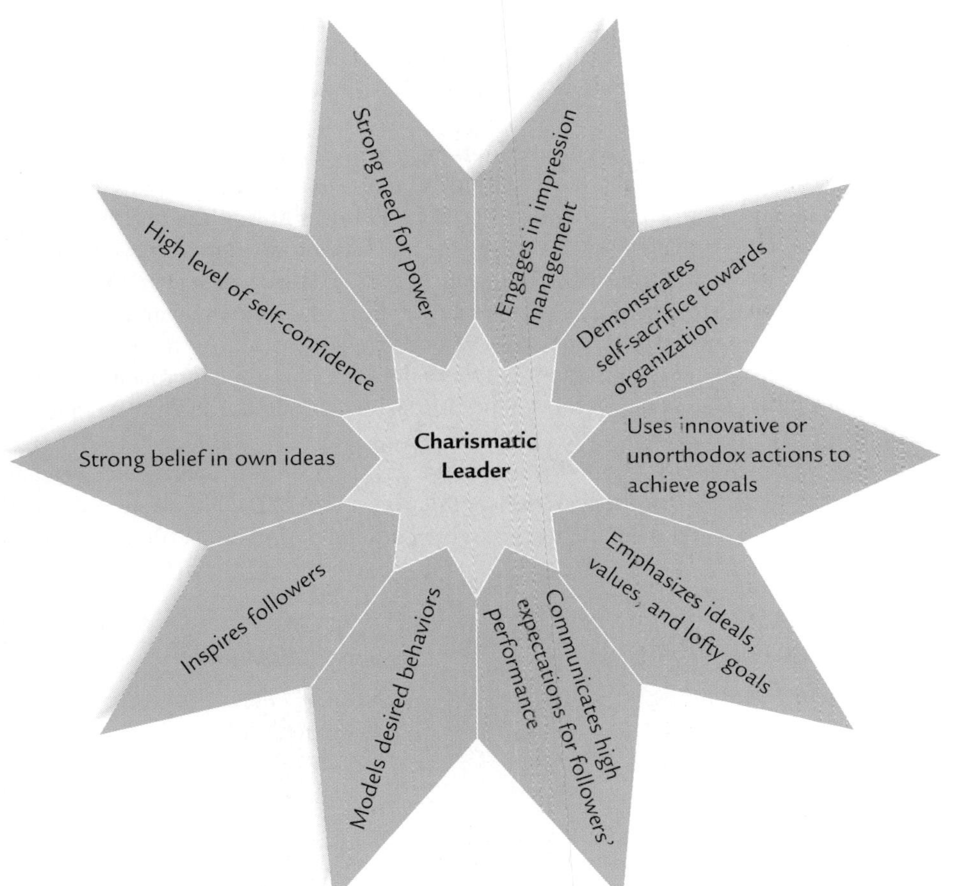

EXHIBIT 9.8

Attributes of the Charismatic Leader

One final point should be raised about charisma: its potential downside. A highly charismatic and overpowering leader does not always suit the requirements of the situation. Take, for example, the case of Christos Cotsakos, the former CEO of the online brokerage company E*Trade. Widely viewed as charismatic, Cotsakos, among his other traits, moved extremely fast. He modeled that behavior for his subordinates, even going so far as to sponsor a day of Formula One racing for his top aides. (He spent his "spare time" working on his PhD in economics at the University of London!) Cotsakos also was not shy about espousing company values and setting high goals: "At E*Trade, we're an attacker, we're predatory . . ."; "(Our culture) is all about getting people excited about how they can make a difference as a person and as a team . . ."; "(We have) a lust for being different . . .".[44] He was leader of E*Trade during the heights of the dot-com boom. When circumstances changed and the external environment became more competitively complex for dot-com firms, the company's directors released him as CEO and turned to someone with an apparently different style to guide the organization.

It should also be obvious that charisma can be used for harmful ends as well as good. Society and the world at large are all too familiar with how certain "leaders"—such as Adolf Hitler in Nazi Germany before and during World War II—used an apparently extreme level of charisma with disastrous consequences. Charisma represents a set of traits that confer special power, but that does not guarantee that it will always be used for worthy goals.

Leaders' Skills and Competencies

In Chapter 1 we discussed three types of skills that are important for anyone in a managerial position: technical skills, interpersonal skills, and conceptual skills. As we pointed out in that chapter, early in a managerial career the first two categories of skills—technical and interpersonal—loom especially large in determining whether someone will advance to higher organizational levels. As a person moves up in the organization, the relative importance of technical skills decreases, the importance of interpersonal skills continues to remain strong, and the importance of conceptual skills becomes increasingly critical.

In the last 15 years or so, two other sets of skills or competencies have become increasingly prominent in research relating to influence processes: "emotional intelligence" and "social intelligence." The first of these, **emotional intelligence**, has probably received the most attention to date;[45] one of its chief proponents has even gone so far as to say it "is the *sine qua non* [indispensable ingredient] of leadership."[46] The essence of emotional intelligence, as the name implies, involves an awareness of others' feelings and a sensitivity to one's own emotions and the ability to control them. These features are especially prominent in two major contemporary approaches to leadership that we will discuss later in this chapter: transformational leadership and authentic leadership.[47]

emotional intelligence involves an awareness of others' feelings; and a sensitivity to one's own emotions and the ability to control them

As shown in Exhibit 9.9,[48] emotional intelligence has been conceptualized as having five key components: self-awareness, self-regulation, motivation, empathy, and social skill. Three aspects of emotional intelligence seem particularly important for a manager to

EXHIBIT 9.9

Components of Emotional and Social Intelligence

Emotional Intelligence	Social Intelligence
• Self-Awareness	• Social Perceptiveness
• Self-Regulation	• Behavioral Flexibility
• Motivation	• "Savvy"
• Empathy	
• Social Skill	

consider: (1) it is distinct from IQ or cognitive intelligence; (2) although in part determined genetically, it probably can be learned or improved by training, coaching, practice, and—especially—effort; and (3) it seems obviously relevant to a leader's performance in an organizational setting.

An illustration of two managers who had contrasting levels of emotional intelligence occurred several years ago at a news division of BBC, the British media organization. A decision had been made to close a particular BBC unit, one that employed some 200 journalists. The executive who announced the decision to the employees exhibited self-centered behavior in addition to delivering the message in a brusque, uncaring manner. It created such a negative reaction that it appeared that the executive might have to call in company security. The next day, a different executive spoke with the same set of employees in a calm and understanding manner and with a high degree of empathy for their situation. He was actually cheered.[49]

Although social intelligence is somewhat similar to emotional intelligence, the two also differ. Whereas major components of emotional intelligence involve self-awareness and self-regulation, **social intelligence** focuses more on being able to "read" other people and their intentions. (See Exhibit 9.9.) Social perceptiveness is a principal ingredient. However, so is what has been called "behavioral flexibility," or the ability and motivation to modify your own behavior in response to what you perceive socially. Thus, like emotional intelligence, social intelligence puts a premium on being able to monitor your own behavior and adjust that behavior according to assessment of the social context and circumstances. A person who is socially intelligent is someone who has considerable tacit knowledge—knowledge that is not always directly made explicit—or, to use a more everyday term, is *savvy.* Again, as with emotional intelligence, social intelligence is both desirable and important for leadership and is something that a person can work on and presumably improve.[50]

social intelligence
the ability to "read" other people and their intentions and adjust one's own behavior in response

Leaders' Behaviors

For leadership to occur, a leader must transform traits and skills into behaviors. Thus, considerable research has focused on leaders' behaviors and their impact on subordinates and followers. As far back as the 1950s, researchers zeroed in on two fundamental types of leader behaviors: those involving assistance in the direct performance of the task, and those involving the interpersonal relationships necessary to support task performance. These two types of behavior have been called by various names over the years, but probably the easiest terms to remember are *task behaviors* and *people behaviors*. Exhibit 9.10 shows examples of these behaviors.

TASK BEHAVIORS The key aspects of task behaviors, also termed *initiating structure* behaviors, center on specifying and identifying the roles and tasks of the leaders and their subordinates. Such behaviors involve planning assignments, scheduling work, setting standards of performance, and devising the procedures to carry out the tasks.

EXHIBIT 9.10

Leaders' Behaviors

Task Behaviors (Initiating Structure)	People Behaviors (Consideration)
• Specifies roles and tasks	• Is friendly
• Plans assignments	• Is supportive
• Schedules work	• Shows trust and confidence in subordinates
• Sets performance standards	• Shows concern for subordinates' welfare
• Develops procedures	• Gives recognition to subordinates for their accomplishments

PEOPLE BEHAVIORS This dimension of leader behaviors has also been termed *consideration* or *relationship oriented.* Essentially, people behaviors include being friendly and supportive, showing trust and confidence in your subordinates, being concerned about their welfare, and recognizing them for their accomplishments.

These two dimensions of leadership behavior have been identified in a wide variety of research studies over the years. Thus, you might expect that the most effective leaders would rate high on both dimensions—that is, be both strongly task oriented and strongly people oriented.[51] This has not been conclusively demonstrated, however, although it has been fairly consistently found that leaders who score highest on people behaviors tend to have the most satisfied subordinates.

Do female leaders demonstrate different behaviors than male leaders? Some research shows that women are more likely than men to exhibit high levels of people skills. However, conflicting evidence and considerable controversy surrounds this issue.[52] What seems clear is that the *individual* differences among women and among men, and the specifics of a given organizational context, are probably more important than any relatively small overall average difference between the two gender groups as a whole.[53]

In terms of the behaviors of leaders, five decades of research seem to boil down to this: Effective leaders need to focus on *both* structuring the work (task behaviors) *and* supporting and developing good interpersonal relationships with and among subordinates (people behaviors). Looking at leadership in this way can help you assess your own leadership behaviors. Periodically ask yourself: "How am I doing on task behaviors, and how am I doing on people behaviors?"

APPROACHES TO LEADERSHIP THAT EMPHASIZE LEADERS' BEHAVIORS Among the major conceptual approaches, or theories, that have been proposed over the years to understand leadership in action, several have focused on leaders' behaviors.

Blake and Mouton's Managerial Grid. Several decades ago, an approach to improving leadership effectiveness was developed by psychologists Blake and Mouton that focused specifically on the two types of leader behavior discussed previously: orientation to tasks and orientation to people.[54] They coined the term *Managerial Grid* because it was proposed that each of these two dimensions could be thought of as going from a low score to a high score and the scores plotted on a graph. The central theme of this approach was that the best managers would be those highest on both dimensions—in effect, a high task-oriented and a high people-oriented leader. Those who were high on one dimension but low on the other were viewed as lacking in one or the other of the two critical skills needed for leadership success. Those who were in the middle on both dimensions were regarded as average or mediocre leaders.

This approach to leadership puts heavy emphasis on the leader, and gives relatively little attention to the attributes of the followers and, especially, the characteristics of the situation. A high-high leader was thought to be the best kind of leader, irrespective of who the followers were and what kinds of situations confronted the leader. The "managerial grid" approach could be thought of as a "universal" leadership theory—that is, one that says that there is one absolute best type of leader—one who is high on both types of behavior—under *all* conditions. Although this approach helped to highlight two dimensions of leader behavior that are clearly important, it ignores many important situational variables that affect both how leaders behave and how followers react. As noted previously, research has not confirmed that one type of leadership style, whether the so-called high-high style, or any other style, is universally appropriate and effective.

transformational leadership leadership that motivates followers to ignore self-interests and work for the larger good of the organization to achieve significant accomplishments; emphasis is on articulating a vision that will convince subordinates to make major changes

Transformational Leadership. Within the past couple of decades, many scholars who write about leadership have been advocating an approach that emphasizes a particular set of leader behaviors: those that inspire followers to make major changes or to achieve at very high levels. That approach is called **transformational leadership**. The original concept of transformational leadership, authored by a political scientist, James M. Burns, described it as a process in which "leaders and followers raise one another to higher levels of morality and motivation."[55] Later refinements of this approach—by social scientists specifically addressing organizational contexts—emphasized that leaders are transformational even if they don't necessarily appeal to "higher levels of morality and motivation," as long as they motivate followers to ignore their own self-interests and instead to work for the larger good of the organization.[56]

Transformational leaders, like charismatic leaders, inspire their followers. However, leaders do this not only because followers identify with them as is the case with charismatic leaders, but also by empowering and coaching them. In other words, followers are not required to be highly dependent on transformational leaders like they are on charismatic leaders. Also, whereas instances of charismatic leadership are rare, transformational leadership behavior is assumed to be potentially possible almost anywhere throughout the organization.[57]

Those who advocate greater transformational leadership in organizations typically contrast it with so-called **transactional leadership**,[58] as shown in Exhibit 9.11. The latter is regarded as leadership that is more passive. It emphasizes the exchange of rewards for followers' compliance. Whereas transformational leaders appeal to followers' organizational or "common good" interests, transactional leaders rely more on followers' pursuit of self interests to motivate their performance. In many respects, however, this distinction is artificial since individuals often act for both their own interests *and* organizational interests.

transactional leadership leadership that focuses on motivating followers' self-interests by exchanging rewards for their compliance; emphasis is on having subordinates implement procedures correctly and make needed, but relatively routine, changes

Another distinction drawn between transformational and transactional leadership by some experts is that the former involves motivating subordinates to make fundamental and creative changes, while the latter involves the implementation of routine changes and procedures. Again, this distinction is not always clear-cut in many organizational situations. In any event, a transformational perspective does focus on motivating people to make highly significant, or even unusual, achievements and accomplishments. Several studies have explored how transformational leaders influence their followers to achieve such exceptional results. One study of 12 CEOs, for example, found that transformational leaders (a) recognized the need for major changes, (b) helped subordinates prepare for and accept such changes, and, especially, (c) were particularly skillful in persuading subordinates to accept a new way of doing things. That is, they communicated a new vision within the organization. The study indicated that transformational leaders

- Viewed themselves as agents of change
- Were thoughtful risk takers
- Were sensitive to people's needs
- Stated a set of core values to rally around
- Were flexible and open to learning
- Had good analytical skills
- Had considerable confidence in their vision for the organization[59]

Another study of 90 leaders in both the corporate world and the public sector came to similar conclusions:

> [Transformational leaders] paid attention to what was going on, they determined what parts of events at hand would be important for the future of the organization,

EXHIBIT 9.11

Transformational Versus Transactional Leadership

	Transformational Leadership	**Transactional Leadership**
Leader gains subordinates' compliance by:	Inspiring, empowering, and coaching followers	Exchange of rewards and benefits
Appeals focus on:	Organizational and "common good" interests	Self-interest
Type of planned change:	Major organizational change	Routine changes

EXHIBIT 9.12

Guidelines for Transformational Leadership

Those Who Want to Be Transformational Leaders Should:

Develop a clear and appealing vision
Develop a strategy for attaining the vision
Articulate and promote the vision
Act confident and optimistic
Express confidence in followers
Use early success in small steps to build confidence
Celebrate successes
Use dramatic, symbolic actions to emphasize key values
Lead by example

Source: Adapted from G. Yukl, *Leadership in Organizations*, 3rd ed. (Upper Saddle River, NJ: Prentice Hall, 1994).

they set a new direction, and they concentrated the attention of everyone in the organization on (that new future). This was . . . as true for orchestra conductors, army generals, football coaches, and school superintendents as for corporate leaders.[60]

Exhibit 9.12 summarizes a set of guidelines for those who aspire to transform their organizations or their parts of organizations.[61]

Authentic Leadership. A recent and somewhat similar approach to leadership that focuses on leaders' behavior has been called "Authentic Leadership Development Theory."[62] Two contemporary factors have contributed to the interest in this approach: a spate of ethical lapses by some managers and companies in the past decade or so, and the development of an area of psychological theory and research called "positive psychology."[63] According to the proponents of this leadership approach, those who earn the designation from others as "authentic leaders" have high levels of (1) self-awareness, and (2) self-regulation. In other words, they know themselves well, and they behave in ways that are consistent with their own basic characteristics. Put another way, they do not try to come across as somebody they are not. Instead, they model self-awareness and regulation for their followers and, according to the theory, motivate them to act more authentically too. This approach is too new to know how influential it will become. Nevertheless, it is consistent with recent trends in organizations to place more emphasis on positive types of behavior by all members, leaders and followers alike.

The Leadership Process: Followers

We now turn our attention to the second key component of the leadership process: those who *receive* the leadership and influence, namely, followers or subordinates. The amount of research on followers has been considerably less than that on leaders. The fact is, however, that followers often impact a leader's success to a great degree.[64]

Followers have characteristics similar to leaders: personality traits, past experiences, beliefs and attitudes, and skills and abilities. What may be different, though, are the amounts and nature of these characteristics in relation to the leader's. Rarely would they be exactly the same. Also, in a work setting, followers typically have lower position power than the leader. However, in increasingly flatter and less hierarchical contemporary work organizations, that difference is not likely to be as great as in the past. The greater access to information by subordinates due to Internet technology, for example, is decreasing the difference in power. Such a decrease in the difference between followers' and leaders' formal authority is changing the very nature of the leadership process in today's organizations and thus presents new challenges to would-be leaders. In contemporary organizations, leaders cannot assume that they possess more expertise and knowledge than those in a subordinate position.

As the CEO of eBay, Meg Whitman (whom we previously mentioned in several earlier chapters) has had to adopt a different type of leadership style. Many of eBay's managers are young, creative, and very tech-savvy. They had resisted traditional corporate structures and control mechanisms that became increasingly necessary as eBay rapidly expanded. Whitman has managed to implement a more formal corporate structure that includes well-defined jobs, formal communication systems, and regular management meetings. Yet, under Whitman's leadership, eBay's culture remains creative and its structure more flexible than many similar organizations.

Not to be overlooked, moreover, is the fact that—in organizations—almost every leader is also a follower of someone else. Thus, most people in organizations have to learn how to become good followers as well as good leaders. The U.S. Military Academy at West Point recognizes this point by using cadets' first year to instruct them in the basics of followership. As a former West Point instructor stated: "[New] cadets don't know how to lead soldiers well. They don't know how to motivate or train or reward or discipline effectively." Consequently, the first year is used to teach them to be good followers and in so doing to demonstrate to them what makes an effective leader.[65] As a knowledgeable observer has pointed out: "Organizations stand or fall partly on the basis of how well their leaders lead, but partly also on the basis of how well their followers follow."[66] Learning how to be effective in a follower role can be a significant ingredient in becoming an effective leader, but this is not the same thing as saying that all followers can or will become good leaders.

How the Behaviors of Followers Affect the Leadership Process

Leaders influence followers, but the reverse is also true: Leaders act, followers respond, and leaders react to those responses. Especially important in these evolving interactions are the followers' perceptions of the leaders—that is, how followers view the leader's characteristics and behaviors versus what they think those should be.[67] In effect, followers tend to judge a leader's actions against particular standards or expectations they have in mind.[68] When expectations aren't met, followers may blame leaders for a group's or organization's failures; likewise, when expectations are met, leaders typically get the credit.

Some theorists argue that leaders in organizations, just like certain stars of athletic teams, frequently get excessive—and sometimes undeserved—credit or blame for outcomes.[69] For example, for many years it seemed that no story concerning Microsoft could be written without mentioning Bill Gates. Rightly or wrongly, he became the icon of the company. Articles commending or criticizing some new software product of the company seemed to place all the praise or blame squarely on the leader at the top: Bill Gates. It is likely, however, that others in his organization should have received a relatively greater share of the attention.

Hersey and Blanchard's "Situational Leadership Model"
a model that states that different types of appropriate leadership are "contingent" on some other variable, in this case "followers' readiness to learn new tasks"

APPROACH TO LEADERSHIP THAT EMPHASIZES FOLLOWERS' BEHAVIORS Although all theories or approaches to understanding leadership emphasize the importance of the role of the leader, there is one that puts particular attention on the followers: **Hersey and Blanchard's "Situational Leadership Model."** It is one of the earliest models of leadership and pays particular attention to followers. Although labeled a "situational" approach, it focuses primarily on a single aspect of the situation: followers' "readiness" to engage in learning new tasks.[70] Subordinates' readiness consists of two parts: their ability, and their willingness to undertake the task. The model advocates that certain types of leader behaviors are best, depending upon subordinates' readiness levels.

Despite some positive features of this model, there are some fairly obvious problems with its implementation. Subordinate readiness levels, for example, typically do not come in simple high and low combinations. More often, the combinations of ability and willingness cluster around the middle. Probably the most critical deficiency of the model, however, is that it considers only subordinate readiness as a feature of the task and organizational environment. It essentially ignores other possible major elements of the context, such as the amount and type of interaction subordinates have with other individuals or units in the organization, the culture of the group or organization, the history of past events, and the like.

The Leader-Follower Relationship

As we have stressed, in organizational work settings leaders and followers engage in reciprocal relationships: The behavior of each affects the behavior of the other. In cases where a leader has direct contact with a group of followers, such as in a work unit, two-person leader-follower relationships are built between a supervisor and each subordinate. Research shows that these relationships may vary considerably.[71] In other words, how a supervisor relates to his or her subordinates can be quite different from one subordinate to another.

leader-member exchange (LMX) theory
a theory suggesting that leaders develop different levels of relationships with different subordinates, and that the quality of these individual relationships affects subordinate behavior

APPROACH TO LEADERSHIP THAT EMPHASIZES THE LEADER-FOLLOWER RELATIONSHIP The importance of this relationship has led to the development of the **leader-member exchange (LMX) theory**.[72] Research based on this theory appears to suggest that the quality of such two-person relationships can strongly influence the effort and behavior of subordinates.[73] LMX theory focuses on the types of relationships that develop between a leader and a follower, rather than on only the behavior of the leader or the follower. According to the theory, the leader's central task is to build strong, mutually respectful, and satisfying relationships. However, the degree to which such relationships progress depends as much on the behavior and performance of the follower as on the actions of the leader.[74] Also, developing such deep relationships is not always easy so this approach can be time-consuming. In later versions of the LMX theory like the one shown in Exhibit 9.13, the leader-member relationship is viewed as taking time to develop across different stages—for example, from that of a "stranger" interaction, to an "acquaintance" relationship and, ultimately, to a "mature partnership."[75]

EXHIBIT 9.13

Development of Leader-Member Relationships over Time

Source: Adapted from G. B. Graen and M. Uhl-Bien, "Relationship-Based Approach to Leadership: Development of Leader-Member Exchange (LMX) Theory of Leadership over 25 Years: Applying a Multi-level Multi-domain Perspective," *Leadership Quarterly* 6, no. 2, Special Issue: "Leadership," (1995), pp. 219–47.

Relationship Characteristic	Relationship Stage: Stranger	Acquaintance	Maturity
Relationship-building phase	Role-finding	Role-making	Role implementation
Quality of leader-member exchange	Low	Medium	High
Amounts of reciprocal influence	None	Limited	Almost unlimited
Focus of interest	Self	..........▸	Team

Time ....▸

LMX theorists stress though that not all leader-follower relationships develop into the partnership phase, and some may not even get to the acquaintance stage. However, if the mature relationship phase can be reached, each party can exercise sizable influence over the other for the benefit of both themselves and the organization. What is significant about the LMX approach is that it places particular emphasis on how individualized leader-follower relationships develop and on the potentially important consequences that can flow from high-quality relationships.[76]

The Leadership Process: Situations

The third key element in the analysis of the leadership process is the situation surrounding the process. In addition to followers, the two most important categories of situational variables are the tasks to be performed and the organizational context.

Types of Situations Affecting the Leadership Process

TASKS The nature of the work to be performed provides a critical component of the situation facing leaders. Change the task, and the leadership process is highly likely to be changed. Research shows that two of the dimensions of tasks that affect the leadership process include whether the tasks are relatively structured or unstructured and whether they involve high or low levels of worker discretion.[77] For example, a manager of a group of newly trained but relatively inexperienced tax preparers at a firm such as H&R Block would probably need to use a fairly high degree of task-oriented leadership to be sure that precise guidelines were being followed in analyzing clients' returns. Alternatively, a project leader in charge of reviewing the work of a group of highly educated scientists doing advanced research in a pharmaceutical company such as Merck would probably be more concerned with ensuring a continuous flow of new scientific information and obtaining additional funding for the group even when it appears they are not producing immediately useful results. Therefore, this manager might use a more person-oriented, less directive form of leadership.

ORGANIZATIONAL CONTEXT The term *organizational context* in this instance means both the immediate work group (those who come in direct contact with a leader) and the larger organization (composed of all individuals and groups who do not usually have frequent, direct personal contact with a leader). A number of features of the organizational context can affect the leadership process.[78] Of particular importance is the fundamental culture of the organization—that is, its history, traditions, and norms. Someone formerly employed by a large and comparatively slow-moving company, for example, probably would find that the style of leadership he had used effectively there would not be equally effective in a fast-changing start-up entrepreneurial firm. The reverse also would be equally true: A leadership style consistent with the fun, informal culture at Ben & Jerry's Ice Cream would not necessarily work at a larger and more traditional firm, such as the Bank of America. These may be extreme cases, but they illustrate that an organization's culture is highly likely to determine what forms of leadership will succeed. In addition to culture, other important aspects of the organizational context affecting leadership include its structure (Chapter 7), its human resource policies (Chapter 8), and its pattern of controls (Chapter 13). Certainly, an example of a leader operating in a unique organizational context is Bill Green, the CEO of the global management consulting firm Accenture, as described in the accompanying A Manager's Challenge, "Leading Accenture When It Is Anywhere and Everywhere."

Leadership Approaches Emphasizing Situational Contingencies

FIEDLER'S LEADERSHIP CONTINGENCY THEORY This theory, developed several decades ago by psychologist Fred Fiedler, grew out of a program of research that centered on leaders' attitudes toward their coworkers. Like some other leadership models, this approach emphasized the degree to which a leader was especially task oriented or person

A MANAGER'S CHALLENGE

Globalization

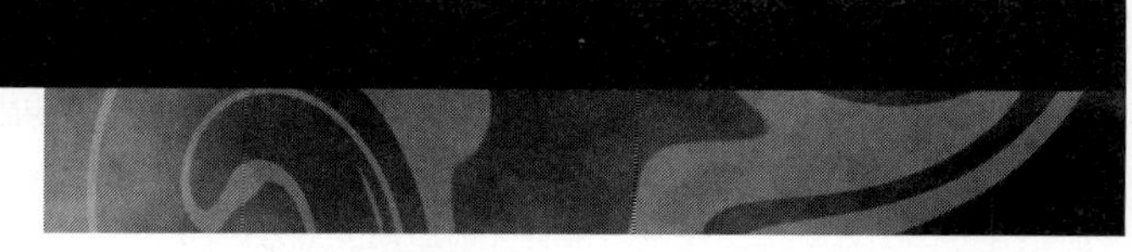

Leading Accenture When It Is Anywhere and Everywhere

Revenue of over $18 billion (in 2006). More than 140,000 employees. Offices in 150 cities—in nearly 50 countries. By almost any measure, the global management consulting and technology service company Accenture is big. It consists of a large percentage of highly educated professionals. But its size is not what distinguishes Accenture from other service-type companies. Rather, it is the fact that it has no operational headquarters. In that sense, it could be considered almost a "virtual" organization. Accenture's CEO, Bill Green, is based in Boston, but the firm's chief financial officer is located in Silicon Valley in California. The head technology officer lives in Germany. The executive in charge of human resources is based in Chicago. The leadership challenges for Green, who in a recent year flew more than 165,000 miles, are obvious.

Accenture was founded in 1989 when the partners in the management consulting part of the Arthur Andersen accounting firm split off to form their own independent company called Arthur Andersen Consulting. (The name was changed to Accenture in 2000.) At the time of its formation at the end of the 1980s, the partners could not agree on where to locate the firm's headquarters, primarily because many of them did not want to move from their present locations, and also because they knew they would be constantly traveling. Instead, they simply decided to incorporate in Bermuda and to meet on a periodic basis. Every six weeks Green and his 23-person, top executive team meet in some city almost anywhere in the world. "We land somewhere, meet clients in the area, meet employees, then get together as a team to make decisions—and head out again," he says.

Among the many potential difficulties faced by Accenture's top leader is trying to coordinate communication and interactions among his key subordinates when most of them, at any given time, are not only not in one location but may not even be in any location because they are in the midst of traveling. Even with advance planning, scheduling a conference call at a particular point in time can be a problem because the participants are in multiple time zones. According to one executive, the "magic hour" for a conference call is 1 PM London time, which is 9 PM in Beijing, midnight in Australia, and 5 AM in California. However, highly sensitive matters still require in-person meetings, likely causing extended travel for one or more of the participants.

Cell phones and the Internet make it easier to manage such a sprawling global enterprise. Each day, Accenture's employees log on to the company's internal Web site to indicate where they are working that day. This way, any employee no matter where they are at the moment, can eventually be reached. When employees are traveling and need to use an office, they simply find a spare desk in the closest local Accenture office. If Green is on the road, as he usually is, a phone call to his Boston office is automatically routed to the Accenture office where he is that day. When there is a need not only to hear other partners or clients but also to see them, videoconferencing provides the mechanism.

Leading any large company is difficult, and leading this kind of highly dispersed global company is especially so. Says one of Accenture's top executives: "Anyone who says managing this way is easy is lying."

Sources: C. Hymowitz, "Have Advice, Will Travel," *Wall Street Journal*, June 5, 2006, B1; S. Prasad, "IT Is Nothing More Than Servant to the Business," *Global Service*, March 12, 2007, www.globalservicesmedia.com/sections/ito/showArticle.jhtml?articleID=197801123; www.accenture.com.

oriented. Fiedler's theory was that leadership effectiveness would be contingent on a combination of the type of leader (relative task or person oriented) *and* the relative degree of favorability of the situation for the leader.[79] According to the theory, a favorable situation for the leader exists when three conditions are present:

- when relations with subordinates are good,
- when the task is highly structured, and
- when the leader has considerable position power.

An unfavorable situation would be when none of these conditions exist. For example, a vice president of finance who has been assigned the task of preparing the company's annual report, who will be able to work with the same team that produced the previous year's report, and who also is regarded as excellent by top management would be in a highly favorable situation. In contrast, the leadership situation would be less favorable for a senior manager asked to develop a new product in conjunction with a subordinate who had hoped to be promoted into the position now held by the new manager. The theory predicts that task-oriented leaders are most effective in highly favorable *or* highly unfavorable situations. On the other hand, high relationship-oriented leaders will do best in moderately favorable or moderately unfavorable situations. The reasoning, according to the theory, is that task-oriented leaders do not need to be especially sensitive to interpersonal relations in very favorable situations, but that in very unfavorable situations a strong task orientation by the leader is the only approach that will work. Conversely, when situations are neither especially favorable nor unfavorable, the theory presumes that leaders more attuned to other people's feelings will do best.

Probably the chief value of this leadership theory is that it highlights the importance of the nature of the situations leaders face, and it suggests how those situational conditions could make it harder or easier for leaders of particular types to be effective. From the perspective of this theory, it is more difficult for leaders to change their styles than to change the situation (or to match leaders with particular types of situations). It also clearly is a contingency theory and not a universal approach in which one type of leadership should work best in all situations.

HOUSE'S PATH-GOAL THEORY In the 1970s, House and his associates proposed what was termed a **path-goal theory of leadership**.[80] Essentially, this theory emphasized that the leader's job is to increase subordinates' satisfaction and effort by "increasing personal payoffs to subordinates for work-goal attainment and making the path to these payoffs easier to travel by clarifying it, reducing roadblocks and pitfalls, and increasing the opportunities for personal satisfaction en route."[81]

path-goal theory of leadership
a contingency theory of leadership that focuses on the leader's role in increasing subordinate satisfaction and effort by increasing personal payoffs for goal attainment and making the path to these payoffs easier.

Path-goal leadership theory draws heavily from expectancy theories of motivation (discussed in the next chapter). Thus, it assumes that the leader's role is to influence subordinates' estimated probabilities for being able to convert their efforts into performance that leads to desired rewards. Also, much like several of the other leadership approaches, path-goal theory emphasizes two basic types of leader behavior: supportive leadership (people oriented) and directive leadership (task oriented).

Like other contingency-type leadership theories, the path-goal theory of leadership assumes that a particular leadership approach will work better in certain situations than in others. The theory assumes that if the tasks your subordinates are doing are frustrating, boring, or highly stressful, a supportive-leadership style will help increase their enjoyment and reduce their anxiety, thereby raising their effort and satisfaction levels. By contrast, if their tasks are enjoyable and interesting, a supportive-leadership style won't make much difference. (See Exhibit 9.14.)

By contrast, a directive, task-oriented-leadership style, according to this theory, works well when your subordinates are inexperienced and their tasks are varied and unstructured. Such directive behavior is assumed to reduce the ambiguities of the situation and make it easier for subordinates to perform their tasks successfully. On the other hand, if your subordinates are highly experienced and their tasks are relatively structured, a directive-leadership style isn't necessary, and your subordinates might even resent it.

Unlike Fiedler's contingency theory, path-goal theory assumes leaders can modify their styles to suit the situation rather than having to have the situation changed to fit the leader. In essence, path-goal theory's primary value is in helping potential leaders to think systematically about what types of behavior on their part might work best in what types of situations.

EXHIBIT 9.14

Path-Goal Theory

Source: Adapted from R. J. House, "A Path-Goal Theory of Leader Effectiveness," *Administrative Science Quarterly* 16, no. 5 (1971), pp. 321–39.

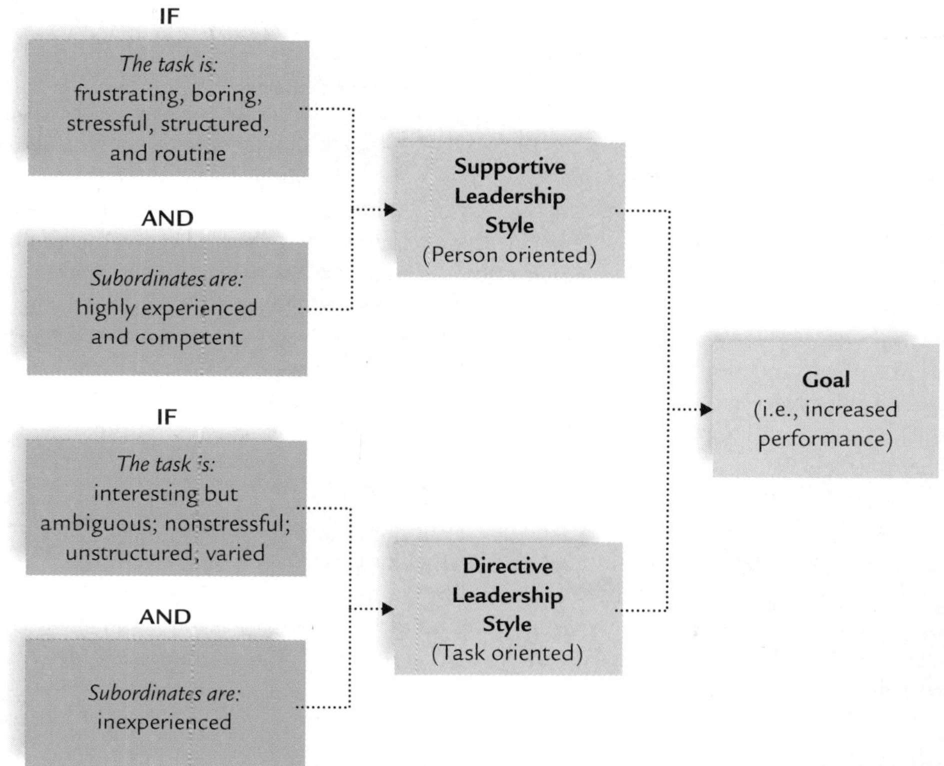

Are There Substitutes for Leadership?

In concluding this chapter, the question can be asked: Can there be substitutes for leadership?[82] The answer, at least in some circumstances, is yes. That is, a greater use of leadership behaviors is not always the only, or even the best, solution for some managerial problems. In certain work settings, other approaches can at least partially substitute for the need for leadership or can sometimes overcome poor leadership. Exhibit 9.15 shows some examples of this.

EXHIBIT 9.15

Examples of Possible Substitutes for Leadership

Source: Adapted from S. Kerr and J. M. Jermier, "Substitutes for Leadership: Their Meaning and Measurement," *Organizational Behavior and Human Performance* 22, no. 3 (1978), pp. 375–403.

Managerial Challenges from the Front Line

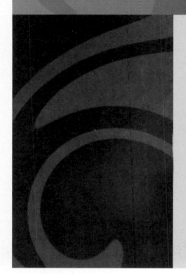

The Rest of the Story

Taylor Ridout, in her first months as a manager, quickly learned that "not everybody can be friends," and decided that she had to come up with a different style of management. After giving the issue considerable thought, she concluded that she needed to use a firmer leadership approach. "I realized that we had to have clear job descriptions and then empower employees to get the job done and to take responsibility for meeting their jobs' objectives. This was a big adjustment for me, but I realized it had to be done," says Ridout.

So far, her revised approach to leadership has been successful, and with the spaces in the complex fully leased out, she is looking for new sites in the north Texas area. She also has been designated one of the young leaders in her locale as part of a group honored as "40 [achievers] under 40."

Extensive training and experience, for example, can lessen the need for a leader's direction in fast-paced and complex jobs like those held by air traffic controllers or police and emergency workers. Decisions often have to be made so rapidly in these jobs that they don't allow time for intervention by a leader. Consequently, prior employee training may be able to substitute for such influence. Furthermore, in many technical and professional jobs, high levels of formal education reduce the need for close supervision. It is safe to assume that an attorney or scientist or computer programmer working for a company will probably not need the same amount of supervision, and certainly not the same type of supervision, as an employee with few skills working in a relatively new position. Similarly, workers with intrinsically satisfying jobs, like those involving the development of an exciting new product or service, would be unlikely to need leaders to increase their motivation. These examples point to the conclusion that the amount and type of leadership required can vary considerably from situation to situation. Too much attempted leadership, or too much of a particular leadership approach, sometimes can be as dangerous for the organization—and the would-be leader—as not enough leadership.

In addition to substitutes for leadership, there are also **neutralizers of leadership**, that is, aspects of the organization or work situation that can defeat the best efforts of leaders. Examples would be inflexible organization procedures that do not give leaders sufficient freedom of choice, or an organizational compensation policy that does not allow them to appropriately reward exceptional performance. Neutralizers, like substitutes, emphasize the importance of situational contingencies and how they can impact leadership. In the case of neutralizers, however, that impact is often dysfunctional.

neutralizers of leadership aspects of the organization or work situation that can hinder the exercise of leadership

Summary

- Leadership is a process of influence that can potentially occur anywhere in an organization—not just at the top. Although anyone can demonstrate leadership, those who occupy managerial positions generally have more opportunities to do so. The critical issue for both individual managers and for their organizations is how to convert leadership "potential" into actual, effective leadership.
- Leading and managing share many similarities, but they are not the same. Managing includes leading (influencing people), but it also involves various activities, such as

planning and organizing, which may not directly involve influencing other people. Not all leaders are competent at managing, nor are all managers effective leaders.

- Leaders potentially have available different kinds of power. Two major types are position power and personal power. Position power is based on a person's rank in the organization and can include legitimate (formal authority), reward, and coercive power. The two primary personal powers are expertise, which is based on a person's skills and knowledge, and referent power, which occurs when people are attracted to, or identify with, someone. The use of power raises several important leadership issues such as: how much power to use, what types of power to use, how best to put power to use, and whether and to what extent power should be shared.
- A useful way to look at leadership is as a process that includes three fundamental elements: leaders, followers, and situations. The intersection of these three components has been called the "locus of leadership." Especially important for leaders are their traits and competencies, their skills, and the kinds of behaviors they exhibit. Followers are a sometimes neglected part of the leadership process. However, they often determine its effectiveness. Particularly important is the leader-follower relationship. Situational circumstances provide both opportunities and constraints that impact how effective particular leadership behaviors will be.
- Leadership is not the only way to deal effectively with managerial problems. Greater levels of education and expertise on the part of employees can often reduce the need for direct leadership. Other variables such as rigid rules and procedures can neutralize the effects of leadership.
- Even though it may be difficult for a person to become a highly acclaimed leader, almost any person can improve their leadership capabilities.

Key Terms

charismatic leader 256
coercive power 249
effective leadership 244
emotional intelligence 258
empowerment 254
expert power 250
Hersey and Blanchard's "Situational Leadership Model" 264
influence tactics 253
leader-member exchange (LMX) theory 264
legitimate power (or formal authority) 248
neutralizers of leadership 269
organizational leadership 244
path-goal theory of leadership 267
personal power 248
position power 248
power 248
referent power 250
reward power 249
social intelligence 259
traits 254
transactional leadership 261
transformational leadership 260

Review Questions

1. What is leadership? Who can be expected to exhibit leadership in an organization?
2. Are leadership and management the same? Why or why not?
3. Differentiate between *position power* and *personal power*.
4. What kind of power are subordinates most likely to have? Why?
5. What is referent power, and how can it be developed? How is it related to charisma?
6. What is the role of emotional intelligence in leadership?
7. Why is it important to consider the characteristics of followers?
8. According to House's path-goal theory, what is the main responsibility of a leader?
9. What is the difference between a transformational and a transactional leader? Is one necessarily better than the other? How does each bring about change?
10. What is meant by a substitute for leadership?

Assessing Your Capabilities

How Power Oriented Am I?

Using the following scale, circle the number that best indicates the extent to which you agree or disagree with each statement.

Statement	1	2	3	4	5
1. The best way to handle people is to tell them what they want to hear.	1 Strongly Disagree	2 Somewhat Disagree	3 Neutral	4 Somewhat Agree	5 Strongly Agree
2. When you ask someone to do something for you, it is best to give the real reason for wanting it rather than giving reasons that might carry more weight.	1 Strongly Disagree	2 Somewhat Disagree	3 Neutral	4 Somewhat Agree	5 Strongly Agree
3. Anyone who completely trusts anyone else is asking for trouble.	1 Strongly Disagree	2 Somewhat Disagree	3 Neutral	4 Somewhat Agree	5 Strongly Agree
4. It is hard to get ahead without cutting corners here and there.	1 Strongly Disagree	2 Somewhat Disagree	3 Neutral	4 Somewhat Agree	5 Strongly Agree
5. It is safest to assume that all people have a vicious streak, and it will come out when they are given a chance.	1 Strongly Disagree	2 Somewhat Disagree	3 Neutral	4 Somewhat Agree	5 Strongly Agree
6. One should take action only when it is morally right.	1 Strongly Disagree	2 Somewhat Disagree	3 Neutral	4 Somewhat Agree	5 Strongly Agree
7. Most people are basically good and kind.	1 Strongly Disagree	2 Somewhat Disagree	3 Neutral	4 Somewhat Agree	5 Strongly Agree
8. There is no excuse for lying to someone else.	1 Strongly Disagree	2 Somewhat Disagree	3 Neutral	4 Somewhat Agree	5 Strongly Agree
9. Most people more easily forget the death of their father than the loss of their property.	1 Strongly Disagree	2 Somewhat Disagree	3 Neutral	4 Somewhat Agree	5 Strongly Agree
10. Generally speaking, people won't work hard unless they're forced to do so.	1 Strongly Disagree	2 Somewhat Disagree	3 Neutral	4 Somewhat Agree	5 Strongly Agree

Scoring

To obtain your score

1. Total your responses to questions 1, 3, 4, 5, and 9	Enter total here: ______________
2. Reverse score (5 becomes 1; 4 becomes 2, etc.) questions 2, 6, 7, 8, and 10.	Enter total here: ______________
Your MACH score is the total of both partial scores	TOTAL ________________

Analysis and Interpretation

This instrument was designed to compute your Machiavellianism (Mach) score. Machiavelli wrote in the sixteenth century on how to gain and manipulate power. An individual with a high-Mach score is pragmatic, maintains emotional distance, and believes that ends can justify means. The National Opinion Research Center, which used this instrument in a random sample of American adults, found that the national average was 25. The closer your score is to 50, the more Machiavellian you are in how you like to use power.

Source: Prentice Hall's Self-Assessment Library, ed. S. P. Robbins and T. A. Judge.

dock their pay, make them work overtime, or cut back on their hours. She couldn't shorten their lunch breaks or eliminate their coffee breaks. Only the overall company manager could impose sanctions of that sort. The problem was that if she tried to insist that a call handler use a new procedure or work certain hours and the call handler balked, she had no recourse. If she complained to the manager about her situation, she would be viewed as unable to do her job. She couldn't complain to her friends because they were part of the problem.

To combat her problems, Grace tried to act with a great deal of authority. For example, she insisted employees follow the new methods she had devised. As a result, she was met with hostility, and her friends stopped talking to her. One day she had had enough and berated a group of her friends about how they gave her no respect, were uncooperative, and were not doing their jobs. After all, she never asked them to do anything she wasn't willing or able to do herself. Still, morale was plummeting and productivity was falling. Grace felt like a failure at the job she had worked so hard to get, and, even beyond that, she felt she was losing her friends.

Grace knew that something was going to have to change. She needed to try something new, to somehow regain the respect of her subordinates and find a new way to inspire them to improve their performance and efficiency and to restore morale. And she had to accomplish all of this while still maintaining her friendships.

Questions

1. Which traits, skills, and behaviors associated with successful leaders does Grace possess? Are there characteristics she could enhance to improve her leadership ability?
2. Why did Grace have problems making changes and maintaining discipline when she first was promoted to a position that required leadership?
3. Analyze Grace's leadership situation in terms of her sources of power: Are there types of power she couldn't or shouldn't use? What types of power could she draw on, and how could she use those types to greatest effect?
4. Are there substitutes for leadership present in this situation? What neutralizers must Grace overcome to be an effective leader?

Source: Personal communication to the authors.

10

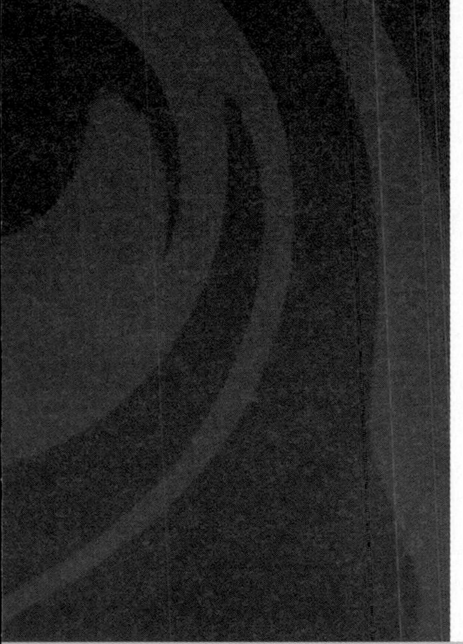

Motivation

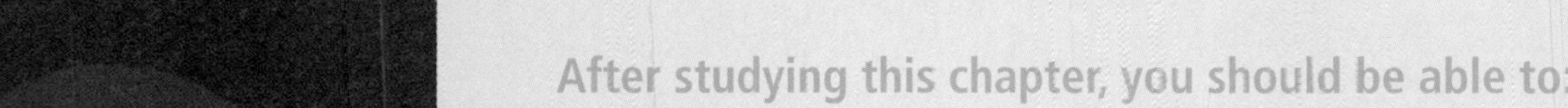

Learning Objectives

After studying this chapter, you should be able to:

Analyze the motivational forces present in a specific situation.

Identify the sources of an individual's motivation.

Differentiate between content and process theories of motivation and indicate how each can be helpful in analyzing a given motivational situation.

Explain how job enrichment can influence an employee's motivation.

Compare and contrast the various approaches to reinforcement and describe their relative advantages and disadvantages for use by managers.

Describe how values and attitudes toward work can influence motivation.

Managerial Challenges from the Front Line

Name: Elizabeth Hayes

Position: Programming Director, America Online, Inc.

Alma mater: University of Texas at Austin (B.A.)

Outside work activities: Reading, movies, museums, and yoga

First job out of school: High school teacher

Hero: Educators in general

Motto to live by: "Whether you think that you can, or that you can't, you are usually right." (Henry Ford)

What drives me: The desire to provide teachers with effective tools they can use to enhance learning

Management style: Delegator—enabling people with the tools and support they need to succeed

Elizabeth Hayes's career track since graduating from college has, primarily, combined the worlds of education and business. After spending her first several post-graduate years teaching high school English, she went to work for a major college textbook publishing company as a developmental editor and associate acquisitions editor. Although the "editor" title of her jobs indicated a close association with the world of words and writing, she simultaneously had to pay close attention to the bottom line in terms of signing authors to textbook projects that would eventually contribute positively to the company's income. Mistakes in judgment about which proposed books to sign and which ones to pass on could result in wasting valuable resources. Alternatively, making the right choices could generate significant profit streams over the years through future editions of successful books.

After several years, Hayes decided to leave the publishing industry and join Texas Instruments as a product manager in the company's education division. From that job she moved to her current position as a programming director of education service at America Online, Inc. (AOL). At AOL, Hayes is responsible for the editorial vision, integrity, and product direction of a no-cost Web portal that K–12 educators can use to find the right online resources and tools they need. She is also responsible for building the product and AOL's brand identity, identifying and working with strategic partners, and supervising programming staff. In this latter role, one of the biggest managerial challenges she faces is keeping her remotely located subordinates consistently motivated and challenged. As "virtual" employees, these subordinates often feel like they are left out and missing out on things happening in the office. Furthermore, with employees working at off-site locations, there is always the potential one of them will take advantage of being unobserved and avoid (for a while, at least) accountability.

Managers who can successfully motivate their employees are generally rewarded by their high performance. However, that is not so easy to accomplish. If it were, every employee would be an outstanding performer. One major obstacle is that conditions beyond a manager's or a company's control can affect employee motivation. Furthermore, these conditions keep changing. The state of the economy, for instance, constantly fluctuates, and this can influence the motivation level of many employees. Also, family and other personal circumstances can sometimes acutely affect their attitudes and level of effort.

Understanding these motivational forces has been a continuing challenge for managers ever since the beginning of the Industrial Age. However, what we want to demonstrate in this chapter is that regardless of factors not directly under one's control, it is still possible to influence the motivation of employees. Although Elizabeth Hayes faces some daunting challenges in trying to motivate her "remote" employees, she nevertheless can still exert influence. In other words, managers have many opportunities to affect the motivation of those who work with and for them—especially if they understand some of the basic principles involved in the motivational process. If you as a manager want to be able to demonstrate leadership, then you need to develop your capabilities to motivate those around you.

What Is Motivation?

When we use the term *motivation*, regardless of the setting, what does it mean? **Motivation** can be thought of as the set of forces that energize, direct, and sustain behavior. These forces can come from the person, the so-called "push" of internal forces, or they can come from the environment that surrounds the person, the so-called "pull" of external forces. It is, therefore, essential for managers to recognize the importance of both sets of factors when they are analyzing motivational causes of behavior.

motivation
set of forces that energize, direct, and sustain behavior

However, an overemphasis on one set of forces to the exclusion of the other can lead to faulty diagnosis and to actions that do not solve motivational problems. For example, a manager might assume that her subordinate's level of sales calls is low because he is lazy, when, in fact, appropriate incentives have not been provided that tap his needs or interests. The manager would be assuming the cause to be lack of an internal, push force, whereas a more accurate diagnosis in this case would focus on inadequate pull forces. This kind of misreading of motivation, which is easy to do, could lead to the loss of a potentially valuable employee. Likewise, a supervisor might assume that due to external, or pull, forces, a clerical worker is doing an especially good job in order to please his boss, when, in fact, the employee might be a person with strong push forces who is highly motivated no matter what kind of supervision he receives. In both of these examples, a broader view of motivational factors should lead to more valid and useful assessments.

Throughout this chapter, different types of motivational forces will be examined, with particular emphasis on what psychologists and other behavioral scientists have had to say about the content and process of motivation. First, though, we begin with a framework to analyze the sources of motivational forces in the work situation. Following that, several major behavioral theories of motivation are examined. In later sections of the chapter, attention is focused on how reinforcement systems and the situational context of work can affect the strength and direction of motivation.

Sources of Motivation

As shown in Exhibit 10.1, there are three basic categories of variables that determine motivation in the work setting:

1. The characteristics of the individual
2. The characteristics of the job
3. The characteristics of the work situation

The first category, the individual's characteristics, is the source of internal, or push, forces of motivation. This is what the employee *brings* to the work setting. Three variables contribute to an individual's push forces: The person's (a) needs—such as the need for security, self-esteem, achievement, or power; (b) attitudes—toward self, a job, a supervisor, or the organization; and (c) goals—such as task completion, accomplishment of a certain level of performance, and career advancement. Martin Franklin, the CEO of Jarden Corporation, a manufacturer of a diverse array of consumer goods, represents a perhaps extreme example of the push-type forces that an individual brings to the work environment. A marathon runner, Franklin's philosophy is: "For me, it's all about seeing how far you can go, be that in business, in helping people, or in athletics . . . . It would be a very sad day for me to say that I can't do more." [1]

The second category of motivational forces, which relates to the external, or pull, forces, focuses on the characteristics of a person's job—what the person *does* in the work setting. These characteristics include how much direct feedback the person receives, the person's work load, the variety and scope of the tasks that make up the job, and the degree of control the person has in terms of how he or she does the job.

The third category of motivational forces also consists of external pull forces. It relates to the characteristics of the work situation—what *happens to* the individual. This category has two sets of variables: the immediate social environment composed of the person's supervisor(s), work-group members, and subordinates; and various types of organizational actions, such as, for example, the firm's reward and compensation practices, the availability of training and development, and the amount of pressure applied to achieve high levels of output.

Taken together the three major categories of variables—individual, job, and work situation—can serve as a useful framework for analyzing the sources of motivation

EXHIBIT 10.1

Key Variables That Influence Motivation

INTERNAL (PUSH FORCES)	EXTERNAL (PULL FORCES)	
Characteristics of the Individual (examples)	**Characteristics of the Job (examples)**	**Characteristics of the Work Situation (examples)**
Needs • For security • For self-esteem • For achievement • For power Attitudes • About self • About job • About supervisor • About organization Goals • Task completion • Performance level • Career advancement	Feedback • Amount • Timing Work load Tasks • Variety • Scope Discretion • How job is performed	Immediate Social Environment • Supervisor(s) • Workgroup members • Subordinates Organizational Actions • Rewards & compensation • Availability of training • Pressure for high levels of output

whether the location is in Bangkok, Lima, or Chicago. The framework also forms a good basis for considering the major theories of motivation relevant to managing in organizational settings. We present these theories next.

Motivation Theories Applicable to Work Situations

Several theories of motivation are particularly relevant for work settings.[2] Each of these theories highlights one or more of the variables just discussed and displayed in Exhibit 10.1.

However, it is important to note that almost all these theories were developed by American behavioral scientists. Thus, an obvious question is: Do these theories apply only in the context of American culture and society, or can the theories be used to analyze motivation in other societies and cultures?[3] Unfortunately, the answer is not clear. Based on the available evidence, the best answer is that some of the theories can be applied widely across the world whereas others cannot. However, none of the theories should be automatically rejected because they originated in a particular cultural context, nor should they be routinely accepted as always applying equally well across different cultures. Instead, managers should view them as possible ways of looking at motivational problems and issues, whatever the context.

Psychologists typically categorize motivation theories into two types: *content theories* and *process theories,* as shown in Exhibit 10.2. The two types together provide us with a deeper understanding of motivation.

Content Theories

Content theories address the issue of what needs a person is trying to satisfy and what features of the work environment seem to satisfy those needs. Such theories try to explain motivation by identifying both (a) internal factors, that is, particular needs, and (b) external factors, particular job and work situation characteristics that are presumed to cause behavior. Two content theories, need hierarchy and acquired needs theories, focus on identifying internal factors. A third theory, the two-factor theory, focuses on identifying external factors.

content theories
motivation theories that focus on what needs a person is trying to satisfy and on what features of the work environment seem to satisfy those needs

NEED HIERARCHY THEORIES The most prominent need hierarchy theory was developed a half century ago by psychologist Abraham Maslow.[4] Maslow's theory appealed to managers because it was easy to remember. It contains five types of needs that are arranged in a hierarchy of strength and influence, starting with the most essential:

- ***Physiological needs:*** The need for the basic essentials of life, such as water, food, shelter, and so on.
- ***Security (safety) needs:*** The need to feel safe and secure.
- ***Social (belongingness) needs:*** The need to be loved and accepted by other people.
- ***Esteem needs:*** The need for self-respect and respect from other people.
- ***Self-actualization needs:*** The need to be personally fulfilled, to feel a sense of achievement and accomplishment, and especially, to develop one's own unique talents to their highest possible levels.

EXHIBIT 10.2

Motivation Theories

	Content Theories	Process Theories
Focus	• Personal needs that workers attempt to satisfy • Features in the work environment that satisfy a worker's needs	• How different variables can combine to influence the amount of effort put forth by employees
Theories	• Maslow's Need Hierarchy • McClelland's Acquired Needs Theory • Herzberg's Two-Factor Theory	• Equity Theory • Expectancy Theory

SAS Institute, one of the world's leading software developers, knows it's no better than the talent of the programmers who work for it. When the company's employees leave the building for the evening, CEP Jim Goodnight knows that it's his job to motivate them to come back the next day. Toward that end, SAS offers its employees a plethora of benefits unheard of at most companies—onsite daycare, extensive healthcare, an art museum, assistants to help employees with their day-to-day personal matters, and even live entertainment in the company's lunchroom.

Maslow's need hierarchy theory
states that people will first attempt to fulfill basic needs, such as physiological and safety needs, before making efforts to satisfy other needs, such as social and esteem needs

The essence of **Maslow's need hierarchy theory** is that an individual is motivated to satisfy the most basic needs first (such as physiological needs) and then, if those are satisfied, move to the next level. According to this theory, only when their most basic needs have been met will people be able to concentrate on satisfying higher-level needs. However, if these persons' basic physiological and security needs should become threatened, they would then be likely to revert to focusing on those lower-order needs. They would decrease their efforts to satisfy social, esteem, and achievement needs until or unless the threat has passed.

A good example of this theory occurred a few years ago at Ahlstrom Fakop, a Polish subdivision of the Finnish paper and power equipment manufacturer A. Ahlstrom. Plant managers were having trouble motivating employees in the formerly state-owned enterprise. Offering incentive pay had not worked. Only when managers let employees know that no one would be laid off if the firm's sales targets were met did employee morale pick up. The problem was that many of the employees were more concerned about keeping their jobs than increasing their pay levels as Poland moved from a state-controlled to a market economy.[5]

An even more extreme example of this principle occurred in the 1990s in the Los Angeles area. Young Thai nationals were working in garment workshops under conditions that approached slavery. For example, they were not allowed to leave the building in which they lived and worked (for up to 18 hours per day) for months and even, in some cases, years.[6] Need hierarchy theory clearly would have predicted that the workers would not have been concerned with satisfying higher-order needs like belonging, esteem, and self-actualization when their most basic needs—physiological and safety—were not being met.

The key to understanding a person's motivation, then, from a need hierarchy perspective, is to identify that person's most basic need that is not yet being met. For the Thai garment workers in Los Angeles, that level would be the most basic: physiological needs. Once a need has been satisfied, however, it ceases to be a motivator unless its fulfillment is threatened again. But, if it is threatened, that more basic need becomes the focus of attention, as in the Polish manufacturing plant example.

Many questions can be raised about need hierarchy theory. For example, do the needs occur in the same hierarchical order across all cultures and countries? Probably not. The theory was developed in an American context, and there is no convincing evidence that the hierarchy is universal, either from country to country or from one person to the next.

Not only does the hierarchy of needs probably not have the same order across different cultures, it almost assuredly is not ordered the same from one individual to another. Furthermore, different individuals have quite different satisfaction thresholds for each need. For example, someone who grew up in a poor family might go to extreme lengths as an adult to satisfy her need for financial security, even though she is quite well off. Individual differences in both the order of needs and the threshold for satisfying them clearly make it harder for managers to base their actions on the theory.

A somewhat more simplified variation of need hierarchy theory was published subsequent to Maslow by behavioral scientist Clay Alderfer. Alderfer's alternative version, labeled ERG theory for Existence-Relatedness-Growth, collapsed Maslow's five levels into three and provided a more straightforward way of thinking about need hierarchies. (Exhibit 10.3 provides a graphic comparison of the two classifications of needs.) ERG theory differs from Maslow's theory in some respects.[7] For example, it presumes that different levels of needs can be active at the same time. Thus, a lower level does not have to be completely or even mostly satisfied before higher-level needs can emerge. Also, Alderfer's version suggests that even though a lower-level need has already been satisfied, a person may revert back to focusing on such a need if he gets frustrated trying to satisfy a higher-level need. ERG theory presents an interesting alternative to Maslow's earlier, more complicated version, but the key point is that both theories focus on people's attempts to satisfy particular needs and on how that can affect the amount and direction of motivation.

From the standpoint of individual managers in an organization, there is probably relatively little they can do personally to affect employees' satisfaction of basic physiological needs. Managers, however, may have some opportunities to help ensure that employees' safety needs are not threatened and that security needs are met as much as possible.

By contrast, there are probably many ways managers can help employees obtain satisfaction of social, esteem, and even self-actualization needs. For example, at a company in Texas, managers encouraged their employees to "report" on fellow employees. As part of a program called "Caught in the Act," they asked employees to write a short note of praise when they saw another employee performing exceptionally well. The write-ups were then posted on the employee bulletin board and also reproduced in the company newsletter.[8] In this example, the satisfaction of the needs of both parties was probably increased: the self-actualization needs of the initiator for the "selfless" act of taking the time and trouble to write up the deeds of another employee, and the esteem needs of the recipient gaining public recognition.

In recent years, many organizations have provided their employees with innovative opportunities to satisfy a variety of different needs. For example, see the accompanying Manager's Challenge feature regarding work–life balance issues. Another example would be in those instances where employees can satisfy self-actualization needs by participating

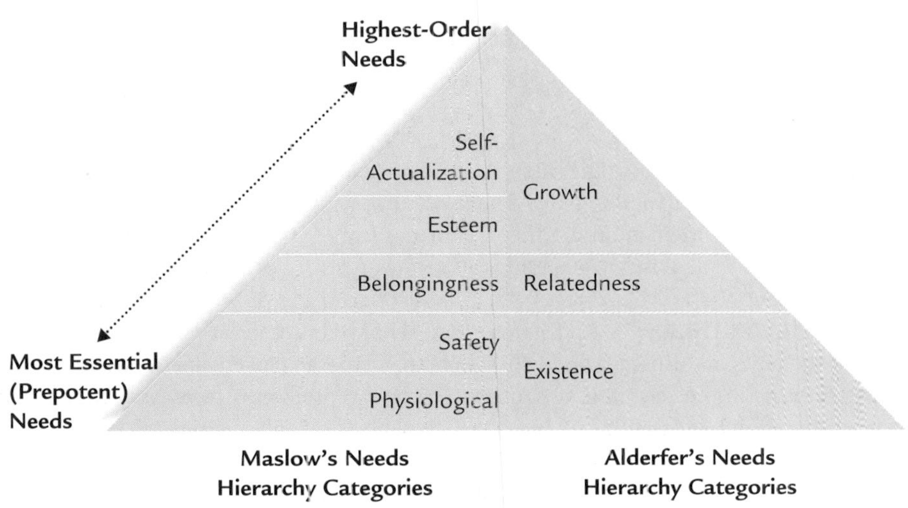

EXHIBIT 10.3

Maslow's and Alderfer's Needs Hierarchies Categories

A MANAGER'S CHALLENGE

Change

Helping Employees Achieve a Better Work–Life Balance

In 1998, Joyce Bordash, a manager at IBM, was expecting her second child and wanted to reduce her workload for a while. In decades past, personal needs like this received relatively little attention from managers. No matter what positions employees held, they were expected to put their work first. Usually they were told to either find a way to manage their personal lives on their own, or leave the company. In short, in terms of work–life balance, the equation was basically weighted toward 100 percent emphasis on company-related work needs and 0 percent concern by the employer about family and nonwork needs.

This one-sided balance has been changing considerably in recent years because of the greater prevalence of two wage-earner families changing societal norms, and stronger employee focus on the issue. For example, one survey showed that employees rated work–life balance as more important than job security, financial rewards, and career advancement. In another survey, 34 percent of 200,000 workers said that "the demands of their jobs seriously interfere with their private lives." More specifically, employees under the age of 35 indicated that work–life balance is *the* most important job-satisfaction factor. Still another survey found that almost 20 percent of managerial and professional personnel reported that a lack of work–life balance in their current jobs would cause them to look for other jobs in the following year.

As a result of these and similarly compelling findings, some organizations are realizing that by paying more attention to work–life balance issues, they can improve the motivation of their employees and encourage them to stay with their organizations. For example, major accounting firms, such as Ernst & Young (E&Y) and Deloitte and Touche (D&T), have instituted policies and practices that directly address the issue. E&Y has adopted a policy of having employees rate their managers on the extent to which they make work–life options available to their direct reports; those ratings are then made a part of the supervisors' performance reviews and bonuses. At D&T, a "mass career customization" program makes it standard policy to arrange flexible accommodation for the needs of employees in different phases of their careers and lives.

At IBM, Bordash worked out an arrangement with her manager that allowed her to work fewer hours per week, not only over the course of several months but several (actually, six) years! Soon after she returned to work full-time, Bordash was promoted to a vice president position. As she puts it, "the needs I have now are different than when [my children] were little, and will be different in the future…All the while with work and family, the balance point changes."

Sources: "Work–Life Issues Is Pushing One in Five to Quit," *Employee Benefit News* 20, no. 3 (2006): 3; "Getting a Life," *Electric Perspectives* 31, no. 3 (2006): 11–12; J. Lewison, "The Work/Life Balance Sheet so Far," *Journal of Accountancy* 202, no. 2 (2006): 5; M. Messmer, "Myth Busters: Breaking Through Workplace Misconceptions," *Strategic Finance* 88, no. 1 (2006): 12–13; D. Ortega, "Value-Added Employee Programs Can Help Recruitment Efforts," *Managed Healthcare Executive* 16, no. 5 (2006): 34–37; S. Shellenbarger, "Avoiding the Mommy Track," *Wall Street Journal* Online, February 23, 2007.

in company-sponsored events that allow them to volunteer with organizations like Habitat for Humanity and the Salvation Army. These programs give employees the opportunity to make a difference in their communities and at the same time to build camaraderie with their colleagues and increase their feelings of self-worth.

acquired needs theory
motivation theory that focuses on learned needs—such as those for achievement, power, and affiliation—that become enduring tendencies

ACQUIRED NEEDS THEORY Another content theory centered on needs was developed by an American psychologist, David McClelland.[9] This **acquired needs theory** focuses on learned, or acquired, needs that become "enduring predispositions" or tendencies of individuals, almost like personality traits, that can be activated by appropriate cues in the environment. McClelland considered three of these needs to be especially important (hence, his theory is sometimes referred to as the "three-need theory"): affiliation,

Since 1976, Habitat for Humanity has built more than 225,000 houses around the world, providing more than 1 million people with a safe, decent, and affordable place to live. Many managers encourage their employees to volunteer for Habitat for Humanity so as to give back to the community.

power, and achievement. However, most research has concentrated on the need for achievement.

According to McClelland's theory, a person who has a high need for achievement is someone who habitually strives for success or goal attainment in task situations (though not necessarily in other types of settings). The research data collected by McClelland and his associates indicate that high need-achievement individuals prefer to

- work on tasks of moderate difficulty
- take moderate risks
- take personal responsibility for their actions
- receive specific and concrete feedback on their performance

In other words, high need achievers want challenges, but realistic challenges, not impossible ones. Especially important from a managerial perspective, McClelland's theory suggests that "appropriate" training, that is, showing people how to recognize and respond to relevant achievement cues, can increase the need for achievement. However, this feature of the theory is controversial; many experts doubt the extent to which permanent changes in the need for achievement can be brought about by such training.

Is a need for achievement a universal motive? Is it, for example, as prevalent in Brazil as in the United States, or in India as much as in Germany? A study that was carried out across 20 countries appeared to show that achievement, along with power, is a universal motive.[10] Although the percentage of high-achieving people varied considerably from country to country, the critical point is that there are definitely people of this type in every culture that has been studied: "It seems that the primary goal of achievers everywhere is to attain recognition for themselves."[11]

Research findings show that there were fairly large changes in the level of achievement motivation in both Japan and the United States in the first several decades after World War II.[12] There was a definite overall decrease in achievement motivation in Japan between the 1970s and the beginning of the 1990s, especially in younger generations. This could be due, in part, to the increase in overall prosperity in Japan during that particular time span. On the other hand, younger people in the United States showed higher levels of achievement motivation at the beginning of the 1990s than their counterparts did in the late 1960s and early 1970s, perhaps reflecting the decreasing levels of economic security that occurred in the United States over that time span. Taken together, these findings seem to reinforce the conclusion that strong societal forces, such as changing cultural attitudes toward work and changing economic conditions, can influence achievement motivation. Research from the mid-1990s, incidentally, appeared to indicate that achievement motivation remained somewhat lower in Japan than in the United States, but that could change again with future societal changes in the two different countries.[13]

two-factor theory
motivation theory that focuses on the presumed different effects of intrinsic job factors (motivation) and extrinsic situational factors (hygiene factors)

TWO-FACTOR THEORY In the early 1960s, Frederick Herzberg, an American psychologist, proposed a motivation theory that came to be called the "two-factor theory."[14] This theory focused on the distinction between factors that can increase job satisfaction ("motivators") versus those that can prevent dissatisfaction but cannot increase satisfaction ("hygiene factors"). As shown in Exhibit 10.4, motivators are "intrinsic" factors directly related to the *doing* of a job, such as the nature of the work itself, responsibility level, personal growth opportunities, and the sense of achievement and recognition directly received by performing the work. The other factors, "hygiene" factors, are "extrinsic" to directly performing the job. They, instead, are associated with conditions *surrounding* the job. Hygiene factors include supervision, relations with coworkers, working conditions, and company policies and practices related to benefits and compensation.[15]

Within the past few years, General Electric has given some attention to the distinction between the two types of factors with respect to motivating its sales managers. The company's sales managers tended to complain more than other managers—about too much paperwork, too many lateral transfers, and too little time to talk directly with their customers. GE executives first started paying more attention to hygiene factors, such as cutting down on paperwork and bureaucratic "red tape" required of sales managers. Then they turned to motivator factors: They instituted new training programs and, in particular, gave sales managers total responsibility for individual clients, rather than having a different manager deal with each customer by product line.[16]

As shown in Exhibit 10.5, the two-factor theory predicts that "motivator" factors actively increase satisfaction, whereas hygiene factors only decrease dissatisfaction to the point where the employee is "neither satisfied nor dissatisfied."

The theory was an immediate hit with managers when it was first proposed some years ago because it contains a relatively simple message: If you want to motivate employees, focus on improving how the job is structured—what they *do*—so that they obtain positive job satisfaction. Simply taking care of the hygiene factors can prevent dissatisfaction but will have no effect on positive motivation.

EXHIBIT 10.4

Herzberg's Two-Factor Theory: Motivators and Hygiene Factors

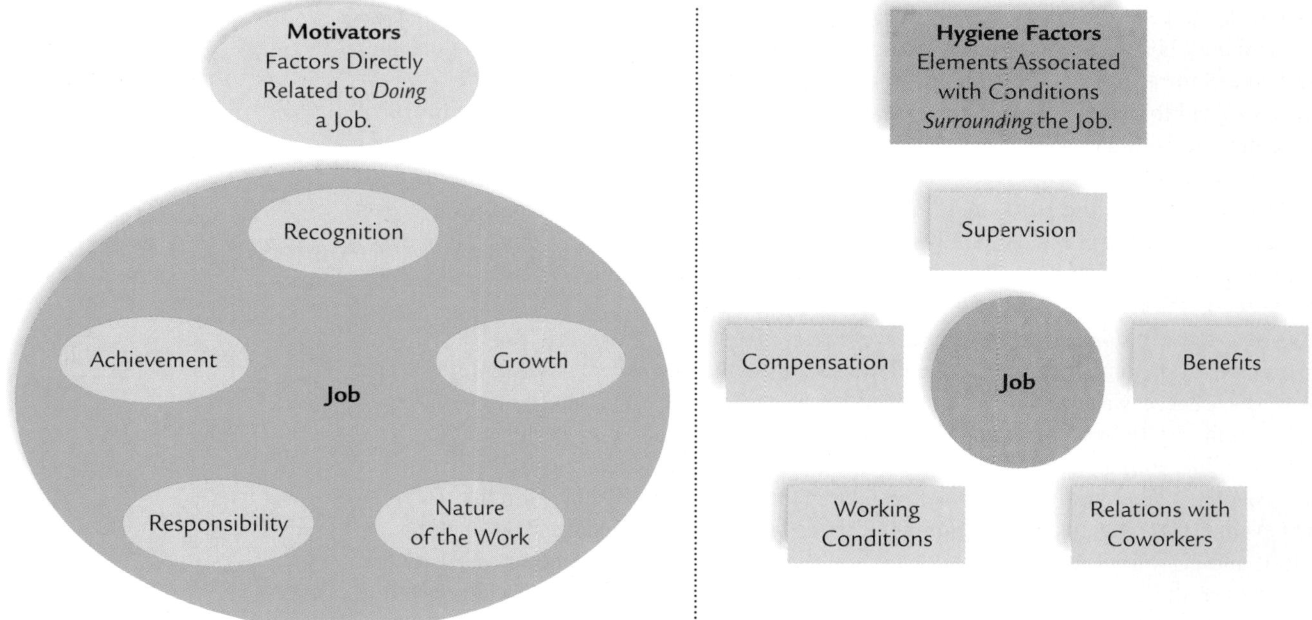

Although intuitively appealing, the two-factor theory has been criticized by many scholars as being overly simplistic. For one thing, research has shown that satisfaction and motivation are not the same thing. Reacting positively to something, such as being pleased with doing a more challenging set of tasks, does not necessarily mean that you will be more motivated to do your job better. Therefore, although changing the nature of the work can often lead to an increase in intrinsic satisfaction, it does not necessarily follow that employees will be more motivated to perform well. Critics contend that the theory blurs the distinction between satisfaction and motivation. Also, subsequent research has shown that it is impossible to distinguish clearly between variables that only increase satisfaction from those that only decrease dissatisfaction.

Motivators
Intrinsic Factors Related to the Doing of the Job Itself

Neither Satisfied nor Dissatisfied

Hygiene Factors
Extrinsic Factors Related to Conditions Surrounding the Job

EXHIBIT 10.5

Herzberg's Two-Factor Theory: Differential Effects of Hygiene Factors and Motivators

IMPLICATIONS FOR JOB DESIGN Despite these and other criticisms, the two-factor theory had one very important consequence in the years after it was proposed: an increased emphasis on how jobs are designed, that is on how different combinations of tasks are put together to form particular jobs.[17] If nothing else, the two-factor theory influenced both organizational scholars and employers to consider how the contents of jobs affect the motivation to perform them. Managers are realizing it is possible to revise jobs to give employees a greater feeling of responsibility, accomplishment, and achievement as GE did with its sales managers. The general approach to designing jobs that do this is called **job enrichment**.

job enrichment
increasing the complexity of a job to provide a greater sense of responsibility, accomplishment, and achievement

One of the most comprehensive approaches to designing enriched jobs with high potential for increased motivation is the "job characteristics model."[18] Developed by two organizational scientists, J. Richard Hackman and Greg Oldham, the **job characteristics model** emphasizes three components, as shown in Exhibit 10.6:

- Core job characteristics, such as skill variety and task significance
- Critical psychological states, such as experienced meaningfulness of work and experienced responsibility for outcomes of the work
- Expected outcomes, such as high internal work motivation and high work effectiveness.

job characteristics model
approach that focuses on the motivational attributes of jobs by emphasizing three sets of variables: core job characteristics, critical psychological states, and outcomes

Not every employee wants more responsibility, autonomy, and the like—but many do. In recent years, many companies have paid more attention to the motivational content of their employees' jobs. It seems to be paying off. For example, in a survey of U.S. workers conducted in 1977, only 17 percent of them said the work they do "is meaningful to me." By contrast, in 2002, the percentage was 66 percent. Likewise, the percentage of workers answering "my job lets me use my skills and abilities" jumped from 28 percent to 68 percent.[19]

The bottom-line message for managers is that if they can create or adjust jobs to include more of the "core characteristics" (see Exhibit 10.7), they may be able to increase the motivation and satisfaction of many of the employees who work in those jobs. A useful way for managers, who often have highly enriched jobs themselves, to think about enriching the jobs of their subordinates is to make those jobs more like their own!

EXHIBIT 10.6

Job Characteristics Model

Source: Adapted from J. R. Hackman and G. R. Oldham, *Work Redesign* (Reading, MA: Addison-Wesley, 1980).

Core Job Characteristics
- Skill Variety
- Task Identity
- Task Significance
- Feedback
- Autonomy

→

Critical Psychological States
- Experienced Meaningfulness of the Work
- Experienced Responsibility for Outcomes of the Work
- Knowledge of the Actual Results of the Work Activities

→

Outcomes
High
- Internal Work Motivation
- "Growth Satisfaction"
- Work Effectiveness
- General Job Satisfaction

Core Job Characteristics	Definition	Example
Skill variety	The degree to which a job requires a variety of different activities in carrying out the work, involving the use of a number of different skills and talents of the person.	The aerospace engineer must be able to create blueprints, calculate tolerances, provide leadership to the work group, and give presentations to upper management.
Task identity	The degree to which a job requires completion of a "whole" and identifiable piece of work, that is, doing a job from beginning to end with a visible outcome.	The event manager handles all the plans for the annual executive retreat, attends the retreat, and receives information on its success from the participants.
Task significance	The degree to which a job has a substantial impact on the lives of other people, whether those people are in the immediate organization or in the world at large.	The finance manager devises a new benefits plan to improve health coverage for all employees.
Autonomy	The degree to which a job provides substantial freedom, independence, and discretion to the individual in scheduling the work and in determining the procedures to be used in carrying it out.	R&D scientists are linked via the company intranet, allowing them to post their ideas, ask questions, and propose solutions at any hour of the day, whether at the office, at home, or on the road.
Feedback from job	The degree to which carrying out the work activities required by the job provides the individual with direct and clear information about the effectiveness of his or her performance.	The lathe operator knows he is cutting his pieces correctly, as very few are rejected by the workers in the next production area.

Source: Adapted from J. Richard Hackman and Greg R. Oldham, *Work Redesign* (Reading, MA: Addison-Wesley, 1980).

EXHIBIT 10.7

Core Job Characteristics in Job Characteristics Model

process theories
motivation theories dealing with the way different variables combine to influence the amount of effort people put forth

equity theory
a motivation theory proposing that individuals will compare their circumstances with those of others and that such comparisons may motivate certain kinds of behavior

Process Theories

Process theories of work motivation deal with the way different variables combine to influence the amount of effort people put forth. In other words, whereas content theories focus on *which* variables affect motivation, process theories focus on *how* the variables affect it. The four most prominent types of process theories are: equity theory, expectancy theory, social cognitive theory, and goal-setting theory. We discuss each next.

EQUITY THEORY Developed in the early 1960s by psychologist Stacy Adams, **equity theory** proposes that individuals will compare their circumstances with those of others, and that such comparisons may motivate certain kinds of behavior.[20] As one observer has pointed out, a particularly vivid example involves professional athletes:

> (Such) athletes often make the news by demanding that their contracts be torn up before their terms expire. The reason for this apparent lack of respect for contract law usually involves feelings by these athletes that the previously agreed on rates of pay are [now], by some standard [of comparison], not fair.[21]

Equity theory, as shown in Exhibit 10.8, assumes that people know what kind of effort and skills they put into their jobs and what kinds of outcomes (salary, promotions, etc.) they receive from their employer. The theory also assumes that individuals are likely to compare (a) the *ratios* of inputs to outcomes they receive to (b) the *ratios* of other people like their colleagues or acquaintances (within, or outside, their organization). Such comparisons determine whether the individual feels equitably treated. The most important

If	Is	Then	And I Am Motivated To
The ratio of my outcomes to my inputs	Equal to the ratio of the other's outcomes to inputs	I am satisfied	Do nothing
The ratio of my outcomes to my inputs	Less than (<) the ratio of the other's outcomes to inputs	I feel dissatisfied (Inequity)	Choose between • Increasing my own outcomes • Decreasing my own inputs • Reevaluating the other's inputs • Changing the referent • Leaving the situation

EXHIBIT 10.8 Basics of Equity Theory

assumption—as in the example of the professional athletes just cited—is that if the comparisons result in feelings of inequity in favor of the other persons, the individual making the observation will be motivated to take steps to reduce these feelings.

Equity theory states that people have a number of ways to reduce their feelings that others are "doing better" than they are. One way is to increase their outcomes, such as getting a salary increase or obtaining a promotion. Another response might be to decrease their inputs; for example, they might try to put less effort in the task and still receive the same level of outcomes, if possible. A third action might be to leave their jobs.

If people do not think they are being rewarded equitably, they have other ways of dealing with the situation. They might simply change the object of their comparison—that is, they might decide to compare themselves to different people, for example, neighbors instead of work colleagues. This involves no change of behavior but only a change in the way of looking at a situation. Likewise, people might reevaluate the inputs and outcomes of those with whom they are comparing themselves and rationalize that "she has more skills than I thought she did" or "his job isn't as good as I thought it was."

Unfortunately, equity theory has not been very successful in predicting *which* method people will use in a specific situation. However, the chief value of this theory is that it highlights the importance of how people's perceptions of equity in comparisons to others' circumstances can affect their motivation. In effect, equity theory emphasizes the "social" nature of motivation.

(It should also be pointed out that comparisons can result in feelings of inequity that favor the observer. In that case, the individual could take steps, such as increasing one's own inputs, to reduce the perceived inequity. However, the common sense assumption is that this kind of situation—where the other comparison person's ratio of outcome to inputs is perceived as being worse than one's own—will occur relatively infrequently.)

EXPECTANCY THEORY Psychologist Victor Vroom (mentioned in Chapter 9) formulated a motivation theory applicable to work settings that is based on people's expectations.[22] Although details of the **expectancy theory** can get complicated, the basics are easy to understand, and Exhibit 10.9 diagrams them.

expectancy theory
motivation theory that focuses on the thought processes people use when choosing among alternative courses of action with their anticipated consequences

Expectancy theory focuses on the thought processes people use when they face particular choices among alternatives, particularly alternative courses of action. Simplified, the theory proposes that two kinds of beliefs affect the amount of effort people will choose to put forth. One such belief (typically referred to as an "expectancy"), effort-to-performance, which is symbolized as ($E \rightarrow P$), is the probability that a certain amount of effort will lead to a certain level of performance: "If I try to do this, will I succeed?" The other belief (often called an "instrumentality" belief), performance-to-outcome, which is symbolized as ($P \rightarrow O$), is the probability that a particular level of performance will lead to (will be instrumental in obtaining) particular "outcomes" or consequences: "If I succeed,

EXHIBIT 10.9

Components of Expectancy Theory

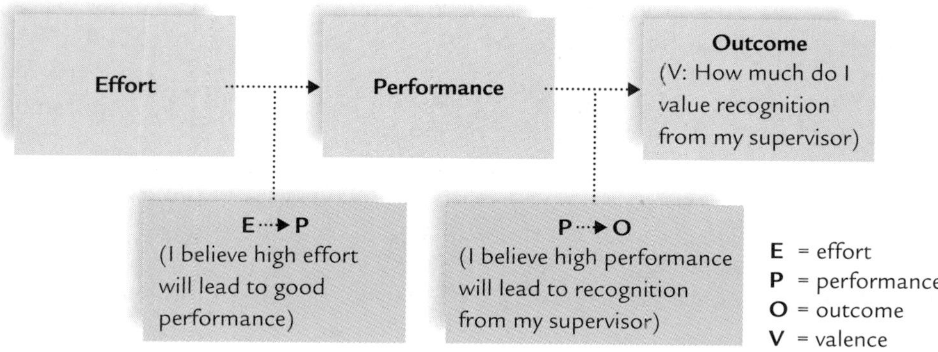

will I get praise from the boss?" The third key variable in the theory is the valence (*V*), or anticipated value, a person attaches to an outcome: "How much will I like praise from the boss if I get it?" If the valence of rewards offered is high, there is potential for increased motivation; likewise, if the anticipated value of those rewards is low, or the offered rewards are seen as irrelevant, motivation is likely to be weak.

Expectancy theory states that the three key variables interact in a multiplicative, not additive, manner to determine the amount of effort people will choose to expend on a particular task:

$$\text{Effort} = (E \rightarrow P) \times (P \rightarrow O) \times V$$

Since, according to the theory, these three variables are multiplied to determine the level of effort, a low value of any one of the three would result in very low motivation. For example, even if a sales representative strongly believes that a certain level of performance (like meeting a sales quota) will lead to a very desirable reward (like a bonus), her motivation will be low if she does not also have a strong expectation that her effort will lead to that level of performance. To restate: Both expectancies *and* the anticipated value of the outcome must be high for a person to be highly motivated.

A number of implications for managerial practice flow from this theory. For each of the theory's three key variables, managers can take steps to increase employee motivation. For example, the $E \rightarrow P$ expectancy can be modified in a variety of ways: If a person believes he doesn't have the skills needed to reach a certain level of performance, these perceptions can be changed. His manager might encourage him to get additional training and further practice, and by appropriately guiding and counseling him, build his confidence (thereby influencing his $E \rightarrow P$ expectancy). Employees who believe they are capable of performing well will be more motivated to achieve their goals.[23]

Additionally, by consistently recognizing employees' accomplishments, managers can increase those employees' perceptions of the probability of obtaining a desired outcome if they have performed well (thereby influencing the $P \rightarrow O$ expectancy). How many times, however, do employees perform at a level strongly desired by the organization only to find that, from their perspective, the organization ignores or does not sufficiently recognize their accomplishment? If this happens continually, their level of motivation is certain to decrease.

On the other hand, the reverse is true: If difficult but desired levels of performance are reached and the supervisor or organization recognizes it in an explicit way, future levels of motivation can be increased. Employees are more motivated to perform well when they have a very strong belief that they will be rewarded.

The following three organizational examples illustrate this: At the software firm Metiom, Inc., each year the 30 top sales representatives gain membership in an elite company group called "Inner Circle" and are rewarded with significant perquisites for themselves and their families. Every salesperson in the organization knows he or she has an opportunity to join the Inner Circle by performing exceptionally well.[24] At the Internet search firm Google, the company has, since 2004, distributed on a yearly basis a small number of awards, but ones that have amounted to a sizable amount of money. Thus, in 2005, two awards, called Founders' Awards, worth approximately $12 million in restricted stock, were given to two teams, each comprised of about 12 members. As Sergei Brin, one of Google's founders, said, "We have people who just do phenomenal things here. I wanted . . . to reward that." The company views it as a way not only to reward creative accomplishments but also to retain employees.[25] At Lloyds TSB Asset Finance Division, employees can nominate either individuals or groups who exemplify the company's values and perform at a high level. Ten winners are selected each month, quarterly winners are drawn from the monthly winners, and, in turn, an annual winner is selected from the quarterly awardees. As might be expected, each increasing level of award is more valuable. The bottom line: The program appears to have helped bring about higher levels of organizational commitment and performance.[26]

The following points sum up, from an expectancy theory perspective, the key ways that you as a manager—and not just the organization as a whole—can potentially influence employees' motivation:

- Identify rewards that are valued
- Strengthen subordinates' beliefs that their efforts will lead to valued rewards
- Clarify subordinates' understanding of exactly where they should direct their efforts
- Make sure that the desired rewards under your control are given directly following particular levels of performance
- Provide a level and amount of rewards that are consistent with a realistic level of expected rewards

One final issue relating to expectancy theory should be noted: Cultural circumstances can affect its application. For instance, in certain countries in the Middle East where there is a strong emphasis on fate, attempts to change effort → performance ($E - P$) expectancies might not succeed. Likewise, attempts to single out an individual for public praise in collectivistic cultures, such as those that exist in many Asian or Latin American countries, would not be as likely to motivate employees as it would in Germany or Australia, where individualism is a stronger cultural characteristic. (Recall from Chapter 3 our discussion of the "individualism-collectivism" dimension of culture.) A motivational approach that considers how people calculate the potential personal benefits of pursuing one course of action over another seems more relevant to most Western cultures than to cultures that place less emphasis on personal gain.

Although the psychological processes described in expectancy theory are not necessarily culturally bound, since they can occur anywhere, the frequency with which they occur probably is. For any culture, however, the key point is that expectancy theory is probably most useful in helping to understand and predict levels of motivation that involve deliberate choices in the amount of effort to be put forth, rather than forecasting routine behavior that is largely determined by habit.

SOCIAL COGNITIVE THEORY A process theory closely related to expectancy theory, and one that has received considerable recent attention among organizational scholars, is **social cognitive theory (SCT)**, developed by social psychologist Albert Bandura. For our purposes, we will concentrate on one key component of SCT: **Self-efficacy**. It can be defined as "an individual's... confidence about his or her abilities to mobilize motivation, cognitive resources, and courses of action needed to successfully execute a specific task within a given context."[27] In other words, self-efficacy is the extent to which a person believes he or she can accomplish a given task in a specific situation. Roughly, it is the equivalent of the $E \rightarrow P$ expectancy in expectancy theory. Such a belief has three dimensions: magnitude (how difficult the task to be accomplished is), strength (the certainty of its accomplishment), and generality (the extent to which similar but not identical tasks can be accomplished). Research to date appears to show conclusively that when individuals have high self-efficacy beliefs, their work-related performance is better.[28]

social cognitive theory
A process theory that, in part, describes how to increase an individual's sense of self-efficacy, thus increasing motivation

self-efficacy
an individual's confidence about his or her abilities to mobilize motivation, cognitive resources, and courses of action needed to successfully execute a specific task within a given context

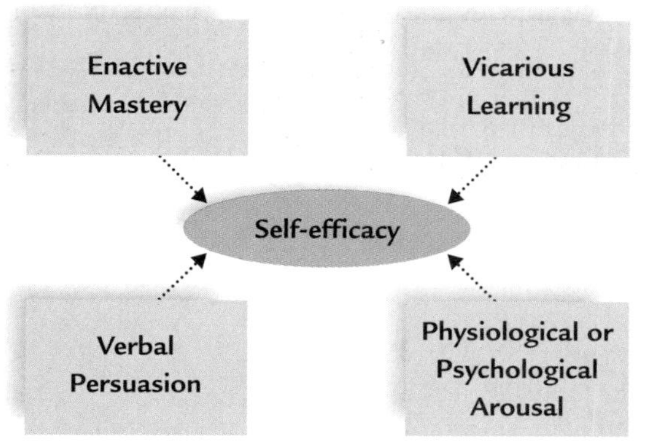

EXHIBIT 10.10

Social Cognitive Theory: Methods to Increase an Individual's Feelings of Self-efficacy

From a managerial perspective, you should be asking yourself this question: How can a person's self-efficacy beliefs be increased? As shown in Exhibit 10.10, SCT proposes four major determinants:

- ***Enactive Mastery Experience:*** Succeeding on a similar prior task *and* attributing that success to one's own capabilities rather than to luck or circumstances.
- ***Vicarious Learning/Modeling:*** Knowledge gained by observing or learning how others successfully perform a task and then modeling one's own behavior in a similar manner.
- ***Verbal Persuasion:*** Statements from others that convince a person that he or she can successfully perform the task.
- ***Physiological and Psychological Arousal:*** Potential energizing forces that can increase self-efficacy beliefs if the focus is directed to the task.

It should be clear from this discussion that if you are a manager there are several different ways to influence positively the self-efficacy of those who work with and for you. You can create opportunities for them to exhibit enactive mastery by taking on and succeeding in difficult tasks that they may have been initially reluctant to try to do. You can model successful behavior for them, or you can arrange working conditions so that they can learn from those employees most experienced and competent at the task. You can attempt to convince them that they should be able to do a task successfully, but this is not always easy to do. And, you can try to increase their energy levels by inspiring them or directing their emotions toward specific task accomplishments. An essential point to keep in mind is that these various approaches to increasing others' self-efficacy are not mutually exclusive. Several of them can be used together. And, as the accompanying Manager's Challenge, "Sales Potential All Bottled Up," illustrates, increasing a person's self-efficacy is something that can probably be done in many cultures.

goal-setting theory assumes that human action is directed by conscious goals and intentions

GOAL-SETTING A somewhat different type of process theory that has attracted considerable research attention in recent years is **goal-setting theory**.[29] "Goal-setting theory assumes that human action is directed by conscious goals and intentions."[30] Therefore, as Elizabeth Hayes learned in her supervisory position at AOL, if managers can influence goals and intentions, they can directly affect performance.[31] The level at which goals are set is a potentially powerful determinant of motivation, and obtaining a person's commitment to particular goals is crucial.[32]

The findings from goal-setting research point to two basic conclusions:

- More challenging (higher or harder) goals, if accepted, result in higher levels of effort than easier goals.
- Specific goals result in higher levels of effort than general or vague goals.[33]

These two principles in action were illustrated by a manager of a retail store when she used specific goals to motivate her employees to increase their sales during the holiday season. She decided to post the sales numbers from the previous season and the sales goal for the current season where everyone could see them. In this way, she thought the sales personnel would be motivated to improve. She was gratified when the first day's sales level showed a 40 percent increase over the same day a year before, which was even higher than the 36 percent increase she had set as a goal.[34]

Despite consistent findings supporting a goal-setting approach in a number of well-controlled experiments, one dimension of goal setting has produced inconsistent and often contradictory results: Whether goals that are set through a process of participation (by those who will be asked to meet them) result in higher performance levels than goals assigned by someone else such as a supervisor. Some research suggests that cultural factors may be particularly influential in determining whether or not participation is effective in the goal-setting process.[35] A study jointly conducted on American and Israeli university students showed that a lack of participation had a much more

A MANAGER'S CHALLENGE

Globalization

Sales Potential All Bottled Up

Mark Johnson (a real person whose name we have changed) was in a panic. He was meeting with his company's Asia Pacific Regional President in less than two weeks, and he would have to explain to him why sales were down 15 percent and profits were down 40 percent in the last six months since Johnson arrived.

Johnson was the managing director of a joint venture (JV) between Pepsi and a formerly state-owned enterprise that made and bottled carbonated cola and noncarbonated fruit beverages in Vietnam. The JV was established to bottle and distribute Pepsi beverages initially in southern Vietnam and eventually throughout the entire country. To everyone's delight, the JV did well during the first couple of years of operation. During that time, the JV's managers focused on the existing customers of the Vietnamese partner. These customers were other state-owned enterprises. Johnson was sent to the JV in its third year of operation in large part to add a consumer-focused marketing and distribution strategy to the initial institutional base of customers.

Soon after his arrival, sales and profits began to decline. When Johnson asked his sales manager, marketing manager, and individual salesmen why sales and profits were declining, they simply shrugged their shoulders or blamed the rainy season. Johnson was totally frustrated. The targets for consumer sales were clear. The commissions that salesmen would receive if they hit their sales targets were very lucrative by Vietnamese standards. With unemployment at 12 percent, Johnson could not understand how the Vietnamese salesmen would not be motivated by the reward system.

In a bit of desperation, Johnson went with one of the salesmen on some sales calls. What he discovered amazed him. First, even though his Vietnamese was not good, he could tell that the salesman was not comfortable with cold calls (calling on a new customer for the first time). Second, it was clear that Vietnam's distribution and retail industries were significantly more fragmented than in the United States. Therefore, to achieve a particular volume of sales, a salesman in Vietnam might have to make 10 times as many sales calls. Johnson also discovered that most of the roads outside the main cities of Vietnam were dirt; during the rainy season they became almost impassible for the motorcycles and bicycles that were the primary means of delivering products to retailers.

Although the salesmen acknowledged the performance expectations and lucrative rewards they would receive for meeting their targets, they were not motivated to try very hard. Why? Because they did not believe they had what it took to be successful. They knew how to deal with long-established institutional customers and take orders, but they had little experience making cold calls to small distributors and retailers.

Consequently, Mark decided to use the JV's existing salespeople to continue to sell to institutional customers but hire a different type of person for consumer sales and marketing. For these new salespeople, one of the solutions to the motivational issue was to provide them with the information, training, and skills they needed—for example, procedures for making cold calls and how to become more efficient in consumer distribution activities. In effect, Mark had to strengthen their effort to performance, $E \rightarrow P$, expectancies. This increased their beliefs that they could hit their sales targets with the new customers and, consequently, obtain the promised rewards.

As a result of these successful steps, sales increased substantially, and Mark has been promoted to a larger job in the region.

Source: Personal communications to author, J. S. Black, 1998–2007.

serious negative effect on the Israeli students than on the American students. The authors of this study interpreted the findings as consistent with cultural differences between the two countries.[36] This research suggests that participation in goal setting will be more effective in countries and cultures where collective decision making is the norm. Overall, however, the basic conclusion across accumulated research findings from many studies is that setting goals has a positive effect on performance, no matter how those goals are set.

Reinforcements and Consequences

Events that happen to people following their behavior—the consequence of their performance—can reinforce their tendencies to continue or discontinue that behavior.[37] The consequences can be positive, neutral, or negative and can vary from insignificant to overwhelming. The deliberate and appropriate application of them, however, provides a manager with a potentially powerful set of motivational tools.

Reinforcement Approaches

The two principal approaches that can be used to increase the probability of behavior desired by the manager or organization are positive and negative reinforcements, which are discussed next.

positive reinforcements desirable consequences that, by being given or supplied following a behavior, increase the likelihood of that behavior being repeated in the future

POSITIVE REINFORCEMENTS **Positive reinforcements**, often referred to as "rewards," are desirable consequences that increase the likelihood of behavior being repeated in the future. In many instances, the use of positive reinforcements, such as a manager praising an employee for good performance, strengthens the likelihood of that behavior in the future, especially if the subordinate does not see such praise as routine or insincere. However, positive consequences also can inadvertently reinforce behavior that is not wanted.[38] For example, an employee might take a risky shortcut to achieve an important performance goal. If the employee's manager does not realize that the shortcut behavior occurred and congratulates the person for reaching the goal, the risky behavior is also being reinforced.[39]

Another example of a manager's unintended reinforcement of the "wrong" behavior occurred in a public relations firm. The head of the firm gave his staff the task of producing a report on their company's history to celebrate the firm's tenth anniversary. The staff members, who often procrastinated when it came to routine tasks, underestimated the time the project would require and were in danger of falling behind. The deadline could not be put off, however, so the head of the firm allowed them to drop all their other work and even hired temps to help them. After a chaotic race to the finish line, the project was done and the head of the company gave the staff a bonus to reward them for their hard work. Given these facts, it is not hard to guess what the staff members learned about the effects of their procrastination. The example demonstrates how easy it is for managers to positively reinforce undesirable behavior with the best of intentions.

One of the foremost scholarly experts on the use of rewards, Steven Kerr, suggests that for positive reinforcements (rewards) to effectively motivate people in organizational settings, the rewards should be:

- ***Equitable:*** The size of rewards should be roughly related to the quality and/or quantity of past job-related performance.
- ***Efficient:*** The rewards must have some capacity to affect future performance; for example, by making clear that a particular level of future performance will lead to a desired reward.
- ***Available (capable of being given):*** Managers and organizations should not talk about or offer rewards that are not readily available, or are available in such small amounts that the recipients view them as not really rewarding at all. As Kerr states: "Organizations with minuscule salary increase pools spend hundreds of management hours rating, ranking, and grading employees, only to waste time, raise expectations, and ultimately produce such pitiful increases that everybody is disappointed and embarrassed."
- ***Not exclusive:*** The possibility of obtaining rewards should not be limited to only a small percentage of employees. The more people that are "ineligible," or excluded, from the possibility of obtaining the rewards, the less likely a given reward will have a widespread motivational effect.

- ***Visible:*** The rewards should be visible not only to recipients but also to others who possibly could obtain them in the future.
- ***Reversible:*** This does not refer to a reward that can be taken away once given. Rather, it refers to rewards that can be denied or not given in the future, if circumstances warrant. The classic example is a bonus. Unlike an annual pay raise, a bonus can clearly be a one-time-only reward. It also is a type of reward that can be given again in the future. That feature provides managers with a great deal of flexibility.[40]

NEGATIVE REINFORCEMENTS The *removal* of undesirable, or negative, consequences—that is, consequences a person performing an act does not want—can increase the likelihood of that behavior being repeated in the future. Removing undesirable consequences is referred to as **negative reinforcement**, just as the addition of desirable consequences is called a positive reinforcement. In both cases, they are reinforcing if they cause behavior to be maintained or increased. For example, a salesperson working in a sales territory with very difficult and demanding customers finds that, by putting in extra effort, the unpleasant experiences he has been encountering are reduced when he is transferred to a different territory. If he believes the transfer or promotion was a result of his hard work, the removal of the undesirable consequences (the difficult territory with difficult customers) has reinforced the likelihood that he will try hard to please his customers in his new territory. In this instance, both the company and the salesperson benefited from the negative reinforcement.

negative reinforcements
undesirable consequences that, by being removed or avoided following a behavior, increase the likelihood of that behavior being repeated in the future

Negative reinforcements, however, can also work against the best interests of the organization. For example, if a supervisor finds that giving a particular subordinate an "average" rating results in avoiding unpleasant confrontations with the person that have occurred in the past—when the subordinate was given well-deserved "below-average" ratings—the supervisor's current action is negatively reinforced. Thus, the supervisor will likely continue to give the subordinate "average" ratings, while the subordinate's performance will probably continue to be sub-par.

Both of these reinforcement mechanisms—positive reinforcements and negative reinforcements—*maintain or increase* particular types of behavior and performance. Thus, they provide managers with potentially potent ways to motivate desired behavior. However, if care is not taken, their use instead can lead to the continuation of behavior that isn't wanted. In contrast to these two reinforcement mechanisms for maintaining or enhancing particular behaviors, managers can use two other methods involving consequences, discussed next, to *decrease* the probability of behaviors occurring.

PUNISHMENTS **Punishments** are unwanted consequences given following undesirable behavior to decrease the likelihood it will be repeated. In some organizations, punishments are seen as an effective way to prevent behavior that is not wanted. However, many other organizations discourage punishments, often because their use is seen as either inappropriate or ineffective. Also, punishments can have the inadvertent effect of increasing behavior that isn't wanted. For example, punishing employees for absenteeism may result in more sophisticated excuses rather than better attendance. This example illustrates that it is typically quite difficult in organizations to make sure that punishments have only the intended effects managers want—and no reinforcement of undesirable behavior.

punishments
undesirable consequences given following behavior to decrease the likelihood it will be repeated

There are also many examples in organizations of punishment administered inadvertently, with possible undesirable consequences. These include giving increasing responsibility to someone who has shown that she can handle stress, or giving additional committee assignments to the person who has shown that he is exceptionally dependable in meeting commitments. Unless a manager is highly alert, unintended punishments happen more often than might be expected.

EXTINCTION Another way to decrease undesirable behaviors is to avoid providing any positive consequences as the result of that behavior. This process is referred to as **extinction**. It is a well-demonstrated research finding, and a fact of everyday work life,

extinction
the absence of positive consequences for behavior, lessening the likelihood of that behavior in the future

that behaviors that do not lead to positive reinforcements tend not to be repeated, or at least not repeated as much. Managers can use the principle of extinction to their advantage by deliberately not reinforcing employee behavior that they considerable undesirable. For example, a manager deliberately might refrain from reacting positively to a tasteless joke.

However, using extinction poses two challenges for managers. One is the inadvertent lack of attention to rewarding behavior that the manager should reinforce. A typical example of this in manufacturing organizations often occurs with respect to safety behavior. Frequently, supervisors take for granted safe work behavior and do not explicitly reinforce it. As a result, because safe behavior usually requires extra time and effort, employees gradually lose motivation to take these extra steps, and eventually an accident occurs. Another common example of the unintentional application of the principle of extinction occurs when an employee puts in extra effort on a key project but receives little or no recognition or acknowledgment from the boss. In this case, the employee is not likely to be motivated to behave similarly on the next key project—nor will other employees who observed the lack of response to the extra effort.

The second potential hazard of either the deliberate or unintended use of extinction is that it can leave the interpretation of important situations in the hands of employees rather than under the control of the manager. By contrast, explicit reinforcements and punishments provide employees with clear, or at least clearer, information regarding what their managers view as desirable or undesirable behavior and performance.

Exhibit 10.11 summarizes the effects of each of these approaches to the use of reinforcements.

Planned Programs of Positive Reinforcement

Organizations often institute programs to apply systematically the principles of reinforcement theory (often called "behavior modification" or "applied behavior analysis" programs). These programs involve four basic steps:

1. Specify desired performance precisely. (Example: "Lower and keep the accident rate below 1 percent.")
2. Measure desired behaviors. (Example: "Monitor safety actions A, B, C.)
3. Provide frequent positive consequences for specified behaviors. (Example: "Give semi-annual monetary rewards for performing a procedure safely 100 percent of the time.")

EXHIBIT 10.11 Reinforcement Approaches and Their Effects

Reinforcement Approach	Managerial Action	Effect	Example
Positive reinforcement	Provide desirable consequence	**Increase probability** of behavior being repeated	Highway construction supervisor receives bonus for each day a project is completed ahead of schedule.
Negative reinforcement	Remove undesirable consequence	**Increase probability** of behavior being repeated	Management stops raising output quotas each time workers exceed them.
Punishment	Provide undesirable consequence	**Decrease probability** of behavior being repeated	Habitually tardy crew member is fined the equivalent of one hour's pay each day he is late to work.
Extinction	Removable desirable consequence	**Decrease probability** of behavior being repeated	Group member stops making unsolicited suggestions when team leader no longer mentions them in group meetings.

4. Evaluate the effectiveness of the program. (Example: "Were accidents kept below 1 percent over the previous six-month period?") Then make progress public knowledge.[41]

Programs of this type have been effective in a wide variety of work settings and in parts of the world as diverse as the Middle East, Europe, and the United States.[42] It should be emphasized, though, that formal programs aren't needed for reinforcement methods to be effective. *Any* person in a managerial position can use these methods. They will be likely to have their greatest effect on the third of the three elements that make up the definition of motivation—the persistence of behavior.

How the Situation Influences Motivation

Although the point is sometimes overlooked, understanding motivation involves more than simply analyzing individual behavior. If we are concerned about behavior in work settings, then it is crucial to recognize—as emphasized in Exhibit 10.1 at the beginning of this chapter—the powerful influence the situational context has on motivated behavior,

Influence of the Immediate Work Group

The immediate work group affects many aspects of a person's behavior, particularly motivation. This is especially true for organizations operating in cultures and countries that have strong collectivist tendencies, such as those in Asia and Latin America.[43] In these cultures, the individual is likely to be heavily influenced by the **in-group**, that is, the group to which the person belongs, but less influenced by others who are not members of the in-group. Nonetheless, in almost any culture or organization, depending upon the circumstances, groups can strongly influence the motivation of individual members.

in-group
the group to which an individual belongs

What are those circumstances? Primarily, they involve (1) the existence of a group in which an individual is a member, the in-group, and especially (2) the strong desire of the person to be part of that group and to receive that group's approval. When this situation exists, the group's influence almost certainly will affect the level of effort or motivation a person exerts.

The direction of a group's influence on motivation will likely depend on its norms—the group's expected standards of behavior for its individual members. When those norms support the organization's goals, the group is likely to increase the motivation of its members to perform. When the norms oppose the organization's objectives, the group is likely to decrease the motivation of its members to perform. And, as originally demonstrated in a study many years ago, the more cohesive a group is, the more it can affect performance motivation in either direction—up or down.[44] (Group norms will be discussed in detail in the following chapter.)

A person's work group can affect motivational aspects of her work behavior other than just the level of performance. For example, a study of teenage workers in fast-food restaurants demonstrated that when an employee decided to leave the organization, it increased (not decreased) the desire of close friends to continue working at the restaurant. Although such a result might seem unexpected, the researchers explained the finding by hypothesizing that the friends who remained working at the restaurant had to reexamine ("justify") their reasons for staying, which resulted in a stronger determination to do so.[45] Thus, the social influence of the work-group friends in this study clearly affected the motivation of at least one type of behavior: staying with the organization.

Recently, Amway Company directly acknowledged that work groups influence motivation and completely changed the company's traditional door-to-door sales approach in China as a result. Amway stores with "work groups" have replaced individual door-to-door salespeople in China. The pay for each work-group member of a store is directly tied to the performance of every other member of the store, thereby motivating each person to contribute to the overall sales effort in the stores in which they work. In addition, Amway has provided leadership training that emphasizes the group impact on each person's motivation.[46]

Influence of Supervisors and Subordinates

Supervisors and subordinates, not just work-group peers, are also part of the immediate social environment that can influence employee motivation—either positively or negatively.[47] The impact of supervisors or leaders on the motivation of their employees is linked to their control of powerful rewards and potential punishments, as we discussed earlier. However, it is important to emphasize that the motivational impact of someone in a supervisory position is not the same for all subordinates; it is often uneven. The same supervisor can be a source of increased motivation for some employees and a source of dampened motivation for others.[48] Much depends on the one-on-one interpersonal relationships supervisors develop over time with each of their subordinates.

Subordinates can also influence the motivation of their superiors, especially through their ability to punish behavior by subtly withholding rewards. Although subordinates typically do not have the same amount of reward-punishment leverage as their superiors, they are not powerless.[49] For example, they could withhold some specialized expertise only they have (and their supervisor does not) if they are not pleased with an action of the supervisor. A systems analyst, unhappy with the assignment she has been given, could resist pointing out some key technical details to her boss. Although such behavior is unlikely to be overt, it can affect the supervisor's motivation to act in the future in ways that produce these kinds of reactions.

Influence of the Organization's Culture

Not to be overlooked is the impact that the culture of an organization as a whole can have on employees' motivation.[50] This influence on motivation is exercised primarily through norms—in this case, how the organization expects its employees to behave. Just as with a peer group, the more an individual wants to remain part of an organization, the more he or she will be influenced by that organization's culture. The organization can be considered simply a larger type of group, with its culture often having a less direct influence on employee motivation than the immediate work group, but an influence nonetheless. Organizations that have gone through mergers or acquisitions know only too well how the imposition of an unfamiliar corporate culture can have potentially devastating effects on the motivation of the members of the "new" entity.[51]

The Influence of Values and Attitudes Toward Work

No analysis of motivation in the work setting can be complete without considering how people's values and fundamental attitudes affect their work. These values and attitudes are especially sensitive to cultural differences within a country or across countries. Thus, to understand motivational issues in an international workforce or a diverse domestic workforce, managers need to pay attention to these differences.

Values

Chapter 3 already provided a general discussion of culture and cultural values. With that as a backdrop, we can look at the role of those values as they specifically affect motivation. Values can influence goals and intentions. They also affect what kinds of behaviors individuals will find rewarding and satisfying.[52]

Different cultures put different weights on particular values. Exhibit 10.12 shows how one set of scholars summarizes core value differences among three cultures from diverse parts of the world: American, Japanese, and Arabic.[53] The valence (desirability) of different rewards would be quite different across these three cultures. Thus, from an expectancy

	American	Japanese	Arabic
Core Values	Competition Risk-Taking Material Possessions Freedom	Group harmony Belonging	Reputation Family Security Religious Belief Social Recognition

Source: Reproduced by permission. Adapted from table 3.3 from *Multicultural Management 2000* by Farid Elashmawi and Philip R. Harris, Ph.D. Copyright © 1998, Gulf Publishing Company, Houston, Texas, 800-231-6275. All rights reserved.

EXHIBIT 10.12

Differences in Core Values Among Three Cultures

theory framework of motivation, for example, managers supervising employees from these three cultures would need to consider the types of rewards to offer in return for high levels of performance.

To illustrate how cultural values can motivate particular behaviors, recall from Chapter 3 that *individualism* is the subordination of a group's goals to a person's own goals, whereas *collectivism* is the subordination of personal goals to the goals of a group.[54] An interesting line of research dealing with this dimension of culture as it affects motivation was carried out with Asian and American college students. The research project compared the preferences of the two sets of subjects for allocating rewards to members of work groups: according to "equality" (every member gets an equal share of the rewards) or according to "equity" (members are rewarded in proportion to their individual contributions). The findings showed that although both Asian and American college students generally preferred equity as the basis for rewards, students from Hong Kong and Korean backgrounds tended to put relatively more emphasis on equality than did the Americans. This is in line with the basic hypothesis that those who are raised in a culture that values collectivism will be influenced by this value when put into a work situation. They will be more likely than those raised in an individualistic culture to consider the needs of everyone in the group, even if this means deviating somewhat from the generally preferred equity reward allocation. The research also showed that while Asian student subjects had a greater tendency to use equality as a basis for allocating rewards to in-group members, they did not necessarily extend this tendency to members of out-groups. Thus, Asian students were apparently distinguishing clearly between those two types of groups.[55]

work centrality
the degree of general importance that working has in the life of an individual at a point in time

Attitudes Toward Work

Understanding how different groups or cultures view the meaning of work, that is, how much the activity of working is valued, helps us to gain additional insight into motivational differences across cultures. The famous sociologist Max Weber was one of the first persons to point out these differences. Weber contended that in the "Christian" countries of his era (the late nineteenth and early twentieth centuries), Protestant religious values emphasized hard work and the accumulation of wealth. This idea led him to coin the well-known phrase "the Protestant work ethic."[56] According to Weber, many people in the United States and in northern European countries were assumed to be guided by such an ethic, whether or not they were literally "Protestants."

A body of scholarly research carried out in the last decades of the twentieth century on the meaning of work focused especially on ***work centrality,*** defined as "the degree of general importance that working has in the life of an individual at a point in time."[57] To measure work centrality, researchers asked working adult respondents to rate the importance of work to them and also to compare its importance to other major life roles such as leisure, family, and religion. Exhibit 10.13 shows the resulting overall score for four

EXHIBIT 10.13

Work Centrality: Country Differences

Source: Adapted from I. Harpaz and H. Fu, "Work Centrality in Germany, Israel, Japan, and the United States," *Cross-Cultural Research* 31, no. 3 (1997), pp. 171–200.

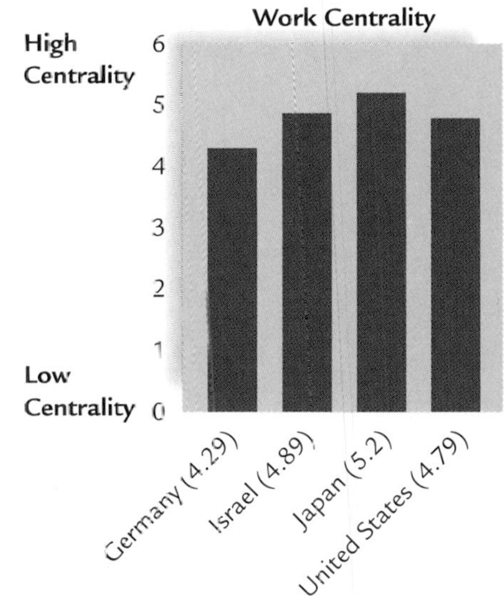

Managerial Challenges from the Front Line

The Rest of the Story

Elizabeth Hayes could have chosen to have only on-site employees. However, Hayes decided not to take this route because the basic nature of the work to be done is conducive to doing it remotely. Also, AOL is well set up to facilitate remote employment so she makes extensive use of the company's available technology. Moreover, being able to hire employees anywhere in the world gives her access to a wider range of talent.

Nonetheless, the challenge of motivating remote employees on a steady basis is ever-present. To deal with this, Hayes sets up clear performance goals and objectives for her subordinates and then gives them regular and very direct feedback on how their work is going. She does this by scheduling one-on-one meetings with each person at least once a quarter to review their performance. As a manager, Hayes also looks for opportunities to provide company-sponsored remote training classes and other growth experiences for those who report to her. She has also instituted virtual meetings to help foster a team feeling among her subordinates. The bottom line results are that customer use of AOL's educational Web portal has increased, and Hayes' employee retention rates are consistently high.

countries, on an index from low to high. The findings indicate that for these particular cultures work was relatively more important and more central to people's lives in Japan than it was in the other three countries, including the United States.[58]

Not all features of the work environment are valued equivalently by different groups of employees.[59] One research study,[60] for example, shed some light on this issue. The study was carried out on a sample of some 4,500 "knowledge workers and managers"—arguably a segment of employees that will be one of the most important to organizations in the future—from 10 large, technology-intensive companies (including those in aerospace, software, and pharmaceutical industries) that have major operations in North America, Europe, and Asia. Survey data were collected from this sample and analyzed by age, gender, and geographical region of the respondents. The respondents were asked what aspects of the work situation were most important to them. The findings demonstrated that there are differences by age, gender, and region. Factors such as "career advancement" and "professional career development" were rated more important by younger versus older employees. Women, at early stages of their careers, put more emphasis on job security and less on financial rewards, compared to men. At later stages, women put more importance on career advancement and professional development than did men in the sample. The major difference by region involved "international opportunities" (for career advancement). Asians and Europeans viewed these opportunities as more important than did Americans.

What are the motivational and managerial implications of these research findings? A major one is that they show that because work does not generate the same relative degree of importance among employees, managers face different challenges when it comes to motivating different employees or employees in different cultural contexts. As a result, specific incentives—such as pay raises, time off, or opportunities for career advancement—will not have the same motivational effect on all people in all situations. The message is that managers cannot assume that everyone else will value work, and different elements of work, in the same way that they do. A sensitivity to these differences, therefore, can be highly useful in addressing motivational issues and problems.

Summary

- Motivation results from a set of forces that energize, direct, and sustain behavior. These forces can either be internal, or "push," forces or external, or "pull," forces. Overemphasizing one of these two sets of forces to the exclusion of the other can result in misdiagnosing the motivational situation in an organizational setting. At any point in time, either or both types of forces may be active.
- The source of internal, or push, forces is the individual. A person's needs, attitudes, and goals are major push forces. The primary sources of external, or pull, forces are the characteristics of the job, and the characteristics of the work situation. Job characteristics include the degree of control allowed on the job, its degree of difficulty, and the feedback received from doing it. The characteristics of the work situation include a person's immediate supervisor, work-group members, and various organizational actions such as compensation and training.
- Those who have studied motivation in organizations generally classify work-motivation theories as either content or process theories. Content theories focus on the needs that the individual brings to the situation and the features of the work setting that can potentially satisfy those needs. Process theories focus on how different variables combine to determine the amount of effort that people expend on tasks.
- Research focused on content has helped managers understand how the design of jobs can affect the motivation of those who perform them. When a job is designed in such a way that it becomes more meaningful to the employee doing it, the result is called job enrichment.
- The consequences employees experience following their behavior can impact the likelihood of that behavior being exhibited in the future. The applications of desirable consequences, called positive reinforcements, increase the likelihood of behavior. Similarly, the removal of undesirable consequences, called negative reinforcements, can also have this effect. Applications of undesirable consequences, called punishment, can decrease future behavior but also have other unpredictable effects. Not applying any consequences, called extinction, can decrease the likelihood of a behavior occurring in the future.
- The values and attitudes employees bring to the work situation can strongly influence their motivation. Values vary across different categories of employees (e.g., younger versus older), and, especially, across different national cultures. Likewise, individuals' attitudes toward the importance of work in general—in other words, the "centrality of work"—can affect their reaction to various motivational attempts by their managers. The implication for anyone in a managerial role is that particular incentives that work quite well for some employees or some groups might not motivate others.

Key Terms

acquired needs theory 282
content theories 279
equity theory 286
expectancy theory 287
extinction 293
goal-setting theory 290
in-group 295
job characteristics model 285
job enrichment 285
Maslow's need hierarchy theory 280
motivation 277
negative reinforcements 293
positive reinforcements 292
process theories 286
punishments 293
self-efficacy 289
social cognitive theory 289
two-factor theory 284
work centrality 297

Review Questions

1. What are "push" and "pull" motivational forces? Give examples of each.
2. What are three major characteristics that determine motivation in organizations? What are some of the variables within each?
3. What are some of the characteristics of an individual with a high need for achievement?
4. How can managers affect motivation by changing a job's content?

5. According to equity theory, what might happen if a worker thought he or she was putting in more effort than a coworker, yet the coworker received a higher salary or larger bonus?
6. According to expectancy theory, what can a manager do to increase an employee's motivation? Does his or her culture make a difference?
7. How are content theories and process theories of motivation different?
8. What attributes do positive reinforcements need to have to motivate behavior?
9. What is the difference between a negative reinforcement and a punishment? Give an example of each.
10. What is work centrality? Why is it important for managers to understand this concept if they want to motivate their employees?

Assessing Your Capabilities

What Motivates Me?

Using the following scale, circle the number that best indicates how important each of the following items is in the job you would like to get.

Item					
1. Cooperative relations with my coworkers.	1 Not important	2 Slightly important	3 Moderately important	4 Very important	5 Extremely important
2. Developing new skills and knowledge at work.	1 Not important	2 Slightly important	3 Moderately important	4 Very important	5 Extremely important
3. Good pay for my work.	1 Not important	2 Slightly important	3 Moderately important	4 Very important	5 Extremely important
4. Being accepted by others.	1 Not important	2 Slightly important	3 Moderately important	4 Very important	5 Extremely important
5. Opportunity for independent thought and action.	1 Not important	2 Slightly important	3 Moderately important	4 Very important	5 Extremely important
6. Frequent raises in pay.	1 Not important	2 Slightly important	3 Moderately important	4 Very important	5 Extremely important
7. Opportunity to develop close friendships at work.	1 Not important	2 Slightly important	3 Moderately important	4 Very important	5 Extremely important
8. A sense of self-esteem.	1 Not important	2 Slightly important	3 Moderately important	4 Very important	5 Extremely important
9. A complete fringe-benefit program.	1 Not important	2 Slightly important	3 Moderately important	4 Very important	5 Extremely important
10. Openness and honesty with my coworkers.	1 Not important	2 Slightly important	3 Moderately important	4 Very important	5 Extremely important
11. Opportunities for personal growth and development.	1 Not important	2 Slightly important	3 Moderately important	4 Very important	5 Extremely important
12. A sense of security from bodily harm.	1 Not important	2 Slightly important	3 Moderately important	4 Very important	5 Extremely important

Scoring

To calculate your score, the items in each need set are added as follows:

Items: 2, 5, 8, 11 = Growth Needs Enter your score: ________________

Items: 1, 4, 7, 10 = Relatedness Needs Enter your score: ________________

Items: 3, 6, 9, 12 = Existence Needs Enter your score: ________________

Interpretation

If you considered all four items within a "need" category to be extremely important, you would obtain the maximum total of 20 points in each.

College students typically rate growth needs highest. However, you might currently have little income and consider existence needs to be most important. For instance, a student's scores of 20, 10, and 15 for growth, relatedness, and existence needs, respectively, would be interpreted to mean that her relatedness needs are already substantially satisfied. Her growth needs, on the other hand, are substantially unsatisfied.

Note that a low score may imply that a need is unimportant to you or that it is substantially satisfied. The implication, however, is that everyone has these needs. So a low score is usually taken to mean that this need is substantially satisfied.

Source: Prentice Hall's Self Assessment Library, ed. S. P. Robbins and T. A. Judge.

Team Exercise

1. Choose a job at least one of your group members knows a lot about. This will probably mean a job that one of you has held. Don't just pick a job at random because you really need to know all the responsibilities, drawbacks, challenges, plusses, and minuses of the job in order to do this exercise. This does not necessarily have to be the worst job you have ever held—many of those do not lend themselves well to redesign! Choose a job you feel has some potential to be redesigned.
2. Analyze the motivating potential of this job. Use the accompanying questionnaire to develop the numerical scores to plug in to the motivating potential score (MPS) formula. Come up with an initial MPS. **Insert the initial MPS score here.** ________________
3. Brainstorm ways to redesign the job so as to improve its motivating potential score. Try to think both rationally and creatively.
4. Once you have decided how you, as managers, could redesign this job so as to increase your employees' motivation to perform at a high level, compute the new MPS for the job. Use the same questionnaire items below. **Insert the revised MPS score here.**

   ____
5. Type a report to be handed in at the next class. The report should include
   a. The job—who held it and why you chose it.
   b. The job's initial MPS score with your reason for scoring it the way you did.
   c. A detailed look at your job redesign strategy
   d. The job's new MPS calculation

The motivating potential score (MPS) of a given job is defined as

$$MPS = \frac{TV + TI + TS}{3}(A)(F)$$

where:

TV = Task Variety
TI = Task Identity
TS = Task Significance
A = Autonomy
F = Feedback

Job Diagnostic Survey

How much autonomy is there in the job? That is, to what extent does the job permit a person to decide on his or her own how to go about doing the work?

1	2	3	4	5	6	7
Very little; the job gives a person almost no personal say about how and when the work is done.		________	Moderate autonomy; many things are standardized and not under the control of the person, but he or she can make some decisions about the work.	________		Very much; the job gives the person almost complete responsibility for deciding how and when the work is done.

and could be used for something more worthwhile. Henkelman could not help but feel let down and began to feel skeptical again. "Same old story," he thought. However, a few days later, Henkelman and his team were surprised to learn that the forklift expenditure was approved. Spirits boosted, Henkelman said, "It gave me the idea that we can make a difference. It made me feel that we weren't doing this work for nothing."

As Sandstrom transformed into a company managed by its employees, Henkelman saw the barriers to information begin to fade away. Although the lab had always ruled over the technical manuals, Henkelman and the other plant workers were now allowed to consult them if they wanted to resolve an issue. He eventually even received a password that gave him access to the formulas on the computer, an event unheard of in prior times. No longer paralyzed in a specific job role, he could update the formulas so the process flowed more smoothly. His attitude began to change in his work.

Henkelman's life began to turn around at the same time. He stopped drinking and got an apartment, where he lived alone. With so much spare time, he went into the office and explored the computer, teaching himself about the business. He filled his empty hours, but more importantly, he filled himself with knowledge, with confidence, and with hope. As a virtual new "owner" in the company, he thought it was his duty to understand every aspect of the business. In the old days, he had only learned what he needed to know to do his narrow job well. Now he wanted to understand the entire process, to help grow the business.

Henkelman and the members of the merit pay team also took on the challenge of redesigning an entirely new compensation system. Plant managers had previously used a mixture of seniority and favoritism to compensate their employees, who were unhappy about the situation. The workers believed that pay should more closely reflect employee performance: how useful a worker was on the job, how much a worker knew, and how well the person's tasks were done. These beliefs were not altogether contradictory to those of management; both groups wanted a highly skilled and effective workforce.

The first proposal drawn up by the team offered plant workers an incentive to cross-train in their jobs. However, when management and the team fully analyzed the numbers, they both concluded that the proposal was unrealistic. Rather than dismiss the issue, however, management asked for a proposal that made fiscal sense to almost everyone. Deep in the middle of the analysis, Henkelman came to the realization that he was beginning to think like an owner, not like an hourly employee. The new proposal found a way to pay for the added costs of training but at the expense of some paychecks. Some members of the team quit, but Henkelman was determined to stick it out. After months of hard work—meeting formally, debating with coworkers, striking a balance between paying incentives and maintaining equality among workers—the team came up with an innovative compensation system, which was eventually adopted by the company.

This was a critical turnaround in Henkelman's career. Despite the demands that management made on the team's process, Henkelman felt needed and alive for the first time in his working career. He noted, "Because of that I felt and still feel today that I have control of my destiny."

His attitude completely overhauled, Henkelman sought other responsibilities within the company to tap into his strengths. Taking a major promotion, Henkelman was put in charge of scheduling production and even became plant manager for a while. What he found is that neither job suited him. Always a doer, he found it difficult to delegate tasks to others. In a few months, a technician job opened in the lab. Generally, technicians had college degrees in chemistry, and Henkelman had not even taken chemistry in high school. But Bob Sireno, the lab's technical director, wanted Henkelman for the job. He eventually got it.

Henkelman put away his blue-collar shirt and moved to the lab. He would still do what he had always done—make paint—but instead of following orders, he would guide the process from the beginning to the end. His new job allowed him to work with customers, to develop new formulas, and to use his hands-on experience to solve problems where other less-experienced chemists had failed. Sireno admitted that in a year's time Henkelman had developed skills that had taken college graduates five years to develop. When a complex problem appeared, it was Henkelman who was chosen to solve the problem—shirt sleeves rolled up and mind determined to make it work.

With a new identity and a new attitude about work, Henkelman remains a valuable team member to Sandstrom Products. Instead of dreading the feuding and the tedium of mixing paint, he now looks forward to each new day, wondering what challenges he will overcome.

Questions

1. Using Maslow's hierarchy of needs, identify the basic needs that Leo Henkelman was attempting to fulfill. How did these needs manifest themselves? How were these needs eventually satisfied?
2. Assess the variables that affected Leo Henkelman's motivation—characteristics of the individual, of the job, and of the work situation.
3. Using the job characteristic model (see Exhibit 10.6), analyze Leo Henkelman's motivation: (a) as a worker on the plant floor prior to the introduction of "open book management"; and (b) as a technician in the laboratory.
4. The company's open book management approach was designed to get all employees to focus on helping the business make money. What do you think of open book management as a tool for motivating employees? In what kind of organizational circumstances would it work best? In what kind of circumstances might it be ineffective?

Source: Republished with permission of *Inc.* magazine, Goldhirsh Group, Inc., 38 Commercial Wharf, Boston, MA 02110. "Before and After," David Whitford, June 1995. Reproduced by permission of the publisher via Copyright Clearance Center, Inc.

11

Groups and Teams

Learning Objectives

After studying this chapter you should be able to:

Describe the similarities and differences between groups and teams.

Identify and compare different types of groups.

Name the factors that influence group formation and development.

Analyze the various structural and behavioral characteristics of groups.

Identify the advantages and disadvantages of self-managing, cross-functional, global and virtual work groups and teams.

Explain the differences in the various types of team competencies.

Distinguish between the two major types of group conflict, and discuss their causes and consequences.

Explain how managers can help their work groups develop into high-performing teams.

Managerial Challenges from the Front Line

Name: Stephen Ortiz

Position title (and company): Director of Marketing, Prairie Casino (Kansas), Harrah's, Inc.

Alma mater: Haskell Indian Nations University (AA); Washburn University (BBA, MBA)

Outside work activities: Bass fishing tournaments (in the Ozarks)

First job out of school: Staff Consultant, Enterprise Risk Services, Deloitte & Touche

Hero: Parents; both grandfathers; and my (late) friend Kelly D. Jones

Motto to live by: Live every day likes it's your last

Management style: Instill a vision and manage to that vision; collaborative

Steve Ortiz loves to spend time outside when he is not working, especially participating in bass fishing tournaments in the Ozarks. Ortiz's fishing accomplishments have been featured in over 20 articles in outdoor magazines in the past 10 years. He sees fishing as more an art than a sport, but he also feels that competing in bass tournaments helps to sharpen his competitive edge. As he says, "competitive fishing is much like running a business—good and bad decisions can make you a hero or a zero. The key is to learn from your decisions."

One of Ortiz's key decisions in life was to attend college. When he graduated from high school, that was not his top priority, but his father convinced him otherwise. After receiving his AA degree, he thought about getting an undergraduate degree in environmental science. However, the experience of working on an entrepreneurial venture to bring economic development to his reservation, coupled with the advice from a faculty member at a nearby university, influenced him to change his intended major and instead obtain a BBA in accounting, and subsequently an MBA degree as well.

After graduating, Ortiz joined the accounting firm of Deloitte & Touche and worked with a number of major clients on internal auditing and business process control issues. Following four years with D&T, he was hired by the gaming and entertainment company, Harrah's, to work in the marketing department of the company's casino near Topeka, Kansas. After several promotions, he is now the director of marketing for the casino.

One of Ortiz's biggest challenges occurred when he first joined Harrah's as a manager, prior to being promoted to the director of casino marketing. He was charged with growing the "VIP" customer segment of the casino's business. At the time, he was inheriting a unit that had subpar performance. The Kansas casino's customer service ratings (based on surveys) were some of the lowest of any of Harrah's facilities. Consequently, Ortiz had to study the internal workings of the department and analyze how the group's performance could be improved. He knew from extensive data the company had collected over the years that unless the employees who interacted with their individually assigned VIPs could become more satisfied with their jobs, then these important guests would not be satisfied and willing to spend more money. To change this situation was the challenge that Ortiz faced.

In the flatter and leaner organizations of the early twenty-first century—with their increased emphasis on speed and flexibility—being able to operate effectively in groups and teams, and to manage them, is even more important than it has been in the past. Organizations of all types and sizes, whether in business, government, health care, or other settings, are much more likely to use groups and teams than even a few years ago.[1] This represents a major change in the way organizations function. Consequently, it requires a change in the mind-set of both managers and their subordinates. People need to change their attitudes toward group work and emphasize teamwork instead of only individual work. This, in fact, was exactly the challenge that confronted Steve Ortiz in his former job as the director of casino marketing at a major Harrah's location.

Of course, there will always be a place for the brilliant employee working alone who produces a remarkable innovation or creative achievement.[2] Also, not all individuals or cultures adapt equally well to a group-oriented organizational environment; nor is creating groups always the most effective way to organize work.[3] Nevertheless, operating in global markets, organizations are now depending increasingly on highly networked and interconnected relationships involving groups and teams. Managing these networked relationships requires strong collaborative skills and the ability to work successfully with, and in, groups and teams. These skills are necessary to build social capital within an organization and with groups and organizations outside the organization as well. If they have these skills, managers are in a much better position to be able to lead and gain the acceptance and commitment of others in order to meet the important challenges faced by today's organizations.

Groups engage in a diverse set of activities, ranging, for example, from developing new products, to designing automobiles, to constructing budgets, to formulating strategic plans. Even those people who are inclined to be independent entrepreneurs eventually face this reality test: If an organization is not based on high-performance groups and teams, it likely will not be able to compete effectively in the current or future competitive landscape. Therefore, it is absolutely crucial that anyone aspiring to a career in management be able to meet two fundamental challenges: how to be an effective *member* of a group or team, and how to be an effective *leader* of a group or team. This was well summed up by eBay CEO Meg Whitman, who stated: "We hire people who aren't focused on me, me, me. One of the first questions I ask when I interview people is: 'What are the most effective teams you've been on, and how did those teams work?'"[4]

It is important to differentiate between groups and teams. They are the same under some circumstances and "not" the same under other circumstances. A **group** is typically defined as a set of people, limited in number (usually from 3 to 20 or so), who have some

group
a set of people, limited in number (usually from 3 to 20), who have some degree of mutual interaction and shared objectives

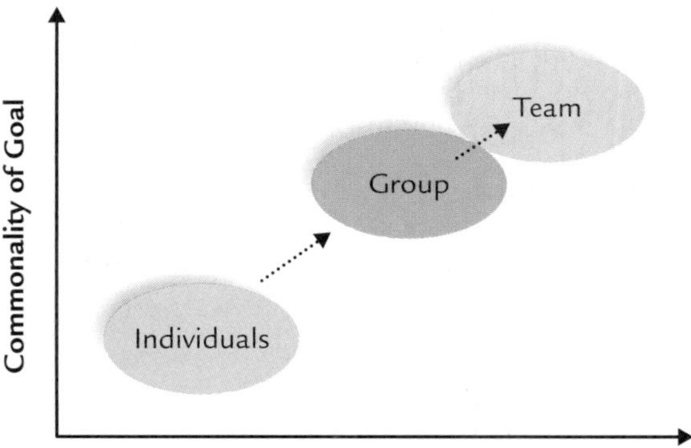

EXHIBIT 11.1

Individuals-to-Group-to-Team Continuum

Source: Adapted from M. E. Kossler and K. Kanaga, *Do You Really Need a Team* (Greensboro, NC: Center for Creative Leadership, 2001).

degree of interaction and shared objectives. A **team**, on the other hand, is a type, or form, of group. In effect, a team has additional characteristics beyond a "mere" group, including a higher degree of coordinated interaction and, especially, a stronger sense of members' personal responsibility for achieving specified group outcomes.[5] Also, groups that become teams typically have created a high level of identification with the group on the part of each member. In other words, it matters to members that they are a part of the unit.

A useful way to think about the relation between groups and teams is to view it as a continuum, as illustrated in Exhibit 11.1. Individuals are put into—or put themselves into—a group. The group may or may not go on to become a team.

Put simply, all teams are groups, but not all groups are, or become, teams.[6] A major objective in most of today's organizations is to have their work groups develop and evolve quickly so that they behave more like teams.

This chapter begins by briefly identifying the various types of groups that operate in organizational settings. Then we discuss how groups are formed and developed and what some of their most important characteristics are, such as their structure, norms, and degree of cohesiveness. This is followed by an analysis of a critical issue common to many groups, namely, conflict. The chapter concludes with a consideration of the challenges involved in improving group effectiveness.

Basic Types of Groups

Most people who work in organizations are part of at least one group, and often of several different groups. These groups can be of different types. One major distinction among them is simply whether they are "formal," that is, established by the organization, or "informal," established by particular individuals without direct involvement by the formal organization. The basic types of groups to which almost all organization members could belong are illustrated in Exhibit 11.2 and described here.

team
a type of group that has additional characteristics: a high degree of interdependent, coordinated interaction and a strong sense of members' personal responsibility for achieving specified group outcomes

Formal Groups

Within and across almost any kind of organization there are typically three fundamental types of formal groups: command (supervisory), project/task forces, and committees.

command (supervisory) group
a group whose members consist of a supervisor or manager and all those who report to that person

COMMAND (SUPERVISORY) GROUPS A **command (supervisory) group** consists of a supervisor or manager and all those who report to that person; for example, those who report to a particular production supervisor or to a sales manager in a department. These groups are usually considered to be the basic work units of an organization. Depending on the nature of the tasks assigned to each person, however, the amount of interaction among members may vary considerably from one command group to another. For example, in a clothing manufacturing plant, a group of workers may be assigned to work on a particular style of jeans. All of the workers construct the same garment, but because one is sewing the pocket to the leg while another is putting in zippers and yet another is topstitching the waistband, there is very little opportunity for interaction among them. Contrast this with a marketing team for a toy company, where the members meet frequently to discuss new products, schedule advertising campaigns, and decide on special promotional activities.

Command groups are usually considered relatively enduring, rather than temporary. Also, the membership in these groups changes relatively slowly. These factors together affect the nature and quality of the interpersonal associations among group members. The fact that you know that you will be interacting repeatedly with the same set of people for an indefinite length of time can have a powerful effect on your relationships with those other members.

project/task force
a temporary group put together by an organization for a particular purpose

PROJECT/TASK FORCES A **project/task force** is a group put together by an organization for a particular purpose, such as to design a new product or to work on a particular problem.

Type of Group	Features	Examples
Formal		
Command (Supervisory)	One supervisor with a number of subordinates Relatively enduring Membership changes relatively slowly	Clerical units Manufacturing assembly units Local sales managers reporting to a regional sales manager
Project/Task Force	Temporary Specific limited purpose Group members are aware of temporary nature of group	Product design teams Management information systems teams to develop upgraded computer systems Term project groups in university classes
Committee	Either permanent or ad hoc Meet only periodically Members have different permanent jobs and/or supervisors Membership typically does not represent an employee's highest commitment	Budget committees Safety committees Promotion review committees
InFormal		
Friendship	Group not originated by the organization Voluntary membership Obvious differences and boundaries between members and nonmembers	Group of employees who lunch together on Fridays Van pool group The "water cooler group"

EXHIBIT 11.2 Types of Groups

For example, Ball Aerospace put together a project team to develop the HiRise optical equipment for use aboard the Mars Reconnaissance Orbiter to obtain detailed photographs of the planet. The project team not only consisted of Ball Aerospace employees but also included specialists from several other organizations such as Jet Propulsion Laboratory (JPL), NASA, the Smithsonian, and several universities. The team pooled group members' expertise in such areas as climate change, glacial processes, polar geology, and landscape evolution. The result: a camera that produced what one publication called "stunning Mars images."[7]

Project teams and task forces differ from command groups in that they are intended to be temporary. They usually have a defined beginning and a specified ending goal. Their members know that once they complete the project or task, the group will likely cease to exist. This not only changes members' perceptions and their interactions with one another, but it also changes their relationship to the appointed leader of the project or task force group.

Because of the nature and importance of the goals and objectives set for them, though, task forces and project teams (really groups that may, or may not, become true teams) constitute some of the most critical group-like activities within, and frequently across, organizations, and they often involve virtual (non-face-to-face) group situations. The creation of project teams is not always a panacea for dealing with organizational issues; they can run into various kinds of problems such as lack of clear goals, insufficient resources to accomplish their objectives, and ineffective team leadership.[8] Nevertheless, most organizations of any size could not function for any extended period without using task forces and project teams.

committee
a group that is either permanent or temporary (ad hoc) whose members meet only occasionally and otherwise report to different permanent supervisors in an organization's structure

COMMITTEES **Committees** can be either permanent or temporary (ad hoc) in terms of the length of their existence. Typically, the most important feature of committees in organizations is that their members meet only occasionally and otherwise report to different permanent

EXHIBIT 11.3

Examples of Committees Present in Many Organizations

• Governance	• Compensation	• Oversight
• Executive	• Finance	• Audit
• Steering	• Safety	• Ethics
• Disaster planning	• Long-range planning	• Public relations

supervisors in the organization's structure (Exhibit 11.3). Thus, interaction is episodic, and for most members this is not the formal organizational group to which they have the highest degree of commitment. For instance, a budget committee might meet several times during a company's fiscal year, with the members likely coming from each of the firm's major departments or divisions. The primary jobs of the budget committee members, however, are in their own organizational work units, not serving together on the budget committee.

formal group
a group that is designated, created, and sanctioned by the organization to carry out its basic work and to fulfill its overall mission

The preceding types of groups are all examples of **formal groups**; that is, groups that are designated, created, and sanctioned by an organization to carry out its basic work and to fulfill its overall mission. However, in many respects, informal groups are just as, and sometimes more, important for a manager to pay attention to, and understand, than formal groups.

Informal Groups

informal group
a group whose members interact voluntarily

An **informal group** is one whose members choose to interact voluntarily with one another, not by organizational mandate. A typical example is friendship groups. Although there is no formal "joining" process, these groups often have fairly obvious boundaries between members and nonmembers. At any given time, people think they know (perhaps incorrectly from the point of view of others in the group) whether they are a member of a certain group or not. Just observing who eats lunch with whom, or who talks especially frequently to whom, for instance, is often a clear signal of a friendship group's boundaries. Informal groups can be fairly temporary, but more typically they last for considerable periods of time.

Most important for a manager is the fact that friendship groups and other informal groups can significantly affect the attitudes and performance of their members in relation to organizational tasks and objectives. A set of employees who were originally strangers, for example, might develop into an informal group after carpooling together over a period of time. If the conversations within this group focus on negative reactions to new organizational policies, then the group could become a source of opposition to those policies. However, informal groups often can provide considerable assistance to managers in dealing with organizational challenges. The key for the manager is whether the group can be influenced to support organizational and work group goals. To do this, managers need to be able to recognize important informal groups, gain an understanding of their norms, and identify where the leadership is within the group. If these steps are taken, then the potential exists for informal groups to become positive forces.

The Formation and Development of Groups and Teams

Groups in organizations form for many reasons and in many ways. Most often the company or organization deliberately puts groups together to serve stated organizational purposes. Informal groups, however, are another matter. They form more or less spontaneously on the basis of actions by their members and to serve those members' self-interests, which may or may not coincide with those of the organization.

What Influences the Formation of Groups and Teams?

The most important factors influencing the formation of groups in organizations are the goals of the organization, the opportunities for interaction and sharing mutual knowledge, and the psychological needs of potential group members.

ORGANIZATIONAL GOALS The goals and purposes of the larger organization directly affect the nature of its formal groups. The organization creates new groups, whether command, task forces, or committees, based on its judgment that needs are not being met adequately by either existing groups or the absence of any groups at all. (See A Manager's Challenge, "Are Teams Worth It?" regarding Bell Atlantic—now part of Verizon—for an example of groups being created where none existed before and how this turned out to be an effective change that has helped the organization meet its goals).

New groups may arise because of organizational growth, changes in the products or services the organization offers, or simply perceptions by key managers that greater efficiency and effectiveness can be gained by adding to, altering, or combining existing groups. It should also be noted, however, that occasionally companies will hire intact groups away from other companies—a practice called "lift-out"—instead of developing their own new group in order to jump start some new initiative.[9]

A key issue for organizations and managers when new groups are formed is whether they will be given adequate resources to accomplish their specific goals.[10] The leader of a

A MANAGER'S CHALLENGE

Change

Are Teams Worth It?

How do teams affect an organization's performance when a company is confronted with a major change? One of the best documented tests was conducted a few years ago by Bell Atlantic (which later merged with GTE to become part of Verizon). At the time, Bell Atlantic derived its corporate value from three areas: employee productivity, service quality, and employee satisfaction. All these contributed to the performance of the company's 45 consumer call centers, where about 6,000 sales consultants served the firm's residential customers.

The company decided to convert the call centers to a team structure over a two-year period to help support its corporate goals of shareholder value, customer satisfaction, and employee commitment. The sales consultants' jobs were unchanged by the conversion to a team structure. But in the centers where teaming had begun, a committee of employees and an assistant manager helped to identify and communicate team needs. Teams were seated together in work areas from which high dividing walls had been removed, and training related to team processes, cooperative communication, and problem-solving was provided. Teams also met weekly to discuss results and solve problems, and a special feedback system was developed to acknowledge members' efforts and share best practices with their colleagues.

According to 15 months of productivity data, the sales consultants who worked in teams outperformed the others in three of the company's four productivity measures. They generated an average of $21,000 more per year in sales revenue than their nonteamed peers—representing a potential total revenue gain of $127 million per year.

Teams also scored slightly higher on 13 service quality criteria, such as job knowledge, courtesy, and accuracy. Even larger gains were logged in employee satisfaction. The number of employee suggestions increased, participation in meetings went up, and employees became more active in identifying and solving problems. Given these positive results, Bell Atlantic chose to proceed with converting the remaining call centers.

Clearly, employees seemed to enthusiastically embrace the joint decision making, cooperative problem solving, and cross-training aspects of teaming. Other factors that helped the team concept succeed were the existence of team champions; thorough assessment of support systems such as communication, performance measurement and feedback, and continuous improvement; and, especially, a high-level plan of action that covered pre- and post-team implementation and plenty of training.

Source: A. Overholt, "Wireless in San Diego," *Fast Company*, January 2004, 84; P. S. Wisner and H. A. Feist, "Does Teaming Pay Off?" *Strategic Finance*, February 2001, 58–64.

team that developed the data storage system for a major product at Honeywell Defense Avionics stated, "My most important task . . . was to help this team feel as if they owned the project by getting them whatever information, financial or otherwise, they needed."[11]

If you are a member of a new group put together by the organization, you are likely to have a number of questions, such as

- Why am I, rather than someone else, in the group?
- What are the real reasons why the group was put together?
- What are my new responsibilities going to be?
- Are the stated objectives for the group realistic and are they the actual goals that will be measured?

Such questions naturally occur to anyone who becomes part of a new group, but they don't always get asked directly or openly. Managers who form groups, therefore, must anticipate questions such as these, whether or not they are raised directly, and must be prepared to provide necessary information and explanations. If you become responsible for putting together a new organizational group, you need to recognize that, as discussed earlier, the formation of a new group does not necessarily mean that a new team has been created. You may have the hope that your new group will develop into a team with a strong sense of shared responsibility for the group's performance and output, but cohesiveness and cooperation are not something that you can decree. Managers cannot simply declare new groups to be "teams" and expect that they will operate that way. Team development depends on managerial skills and follow-up actions to elicit true teamwork in more than name only.[12]

OPPORTUNITIES FOR INTERACTION AND SHARING MUTUAL KNOWLEDGE For groups to form and develop into teams, physical proximity clearly is a helpful factor. When people have the opportunity to work together closely, it can facilitate learning about similarities of interests and experiences. These similarities can provide a basis for the development of strong relationships that can assist the work of the group.

However, in this age of electronic communication, groups are often highly dispersed geographically. In such circumstances, it becomes even more critical to increase the opportunities for interaction of members, even if that is only via electronic messages. In other words, in dispersed "virtual" groups, it is essential to take steps to develop mutual knowledge—to find "common ground"—among members.[13] These steps could include such actions as conducting at least one initial face-to-face meeting, arranging possible visits by one or more team members to other members' local sites, encouraging each member to share information about their particular work context (time constraints, other task demands, local customs, and so forth), and, especially, taking extra efforts to make sure that each member has access to all relevant information.[14]

PSYCHOLOGICAL FACTORS There are many personal reasons that motivate organizational members to form closer relationships in groups, especially basic human needs for security, social support, self-esteem, and status. By belonging to groups, even virtual ones, employees are often able to fulfill needs that may not be well satisfied by the work itself. Thus, the feeling of belonging to a group at work can be highly rewarding for many individuals. It can be, in effect, a significant way for individuals to achieve a distinct social identity that is meaningful both for themselves and for others who interact with them.[15]

The Stages of Group Development

Whether groups are formed by the organization or by voluntary actions of individuals, they tend to move through distinct developmental stages as they mature.[16] One popular early statement on this issue utilizes an easy-to-remember set of terms for such stages: "forming" (getting acquainted), "storming" (expressing differences of opinion), "norming" (building consensus on basic issues), and "performing" (carrying out cooperative group

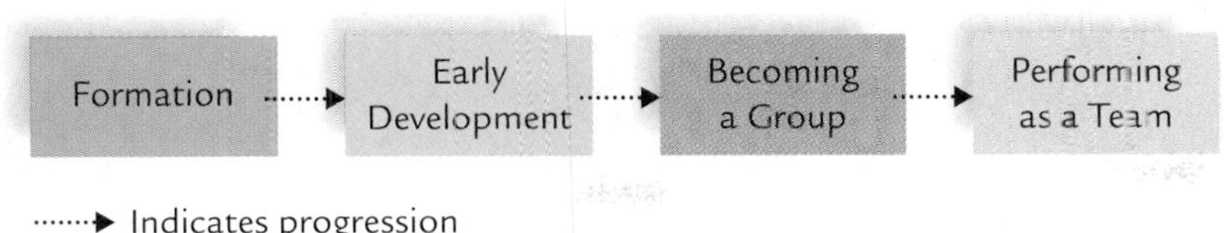

EXHIBIT 11.4

Stages of Group Development

actions).[17] Although this model has considerable appeal as a way to think about the phases of group development across time, it does not necessarily apply to all groups. As one set of management scholars has noted, "It seems unlikely that a single sequence can describe the development of all kinds of teams (groups)."[18]

Despite this fact, several identifiable stages do show up with some regularity in organizational contexts (Exhibit 11.4), and we will use the "forming," "storming, "norming," and "performing" labels to identify these stages.

FORMING If you are forming a new group, you will face some unique challenges. One kind of challenge is presented when potential team members are not used to a group-oriented approach to work. If they have been comfortable working alone, they are facing a significant change. Another kind of challenge in the formation stage is that the group's members will have lots of questions, whether they ask them openly or not. For example, they will want to know who is in the group and why they are there, who is leading the group, and where each person is "coming from" in terms of his or her existing attitudes and viewpoints. Nearly all new groups go through this "getting to know you" stage. ExxonMobil faced this situation when it formed two new teams—one in Finland and one in Texas—to design and build a new deep-draft caisson vehicle. Each team was made up of company engineers, outside contractors, and vendors. In order to succeed, each team had to forge strong bonds among its members immediately. The teams did many things to build camaraderie quickly, including having T-shirts made up with a logo each team designed and drafting their own mission statements, charters, and project plans.[19]

STORMING Following a group's formation and initial interactions, an early-development "storming" stage often settles in and may last for some time, depending on the nature of the group and its tasks. In this stage, members learn what is expected of them, what is acceptable behavior, and how well they relate to each other. Typically, members cautiously exchange, and sometimes jealously guard, information. If you are the group's leader, it is an important time for learning about how opinions within the group overlap or differ on key matters. Often, conflicts (hence the "storming" label for this stage) over group goals or the means to reach them may emerge in this stage. An analogy to adolescence in human development might be apt for helping to understand this stage.

NORMING In this stage, at least a minimum amount of consensus about the group's issues and norms (agreed upon standards of behavior) begins to appear, as well as a degree of individual identity with the group and its goals. How much cohesion and group identity will actually emerge will vary widely from group to group. A critical factor will be how well the group is meeting each member's needs and how well members think the group is being led. In this stage particularly, if you are in a leadership role you can have considerable impact on the group's development of its norms (see the next section) and thus help it to become a true team.

PERFORMING In this stage, a group is able to perform like a team and take actions as a coherent entity and not just as a set of loosely affiliated individuals. Internally, this means that the group is able to influence members' attitudes and behavior on matters of importance to the group, and externally it means that others within, or outside, the organization are being affected by its actions. Several years ago, for example, Sterling Winthrop, currently a part of the pharmaceutical firm Sanofi-Aventis, constructed a one-million-square-foot complex. Construction was finished early, on budget, and with an exceptional safety

Renowned chef Alain Ducasse owns top-rated restaurants in Monaco, New York City, and Paris. Over the course of nearly 20 years, Ducasse has employed more than 500 people. He takes a close interest in recruiting teams for his restaurants and selects, welcomes, and trains them before encouraging them to stand on their own two feet.

record. The company credits that feat to the development of an intense team identity. That team's identity was tied to members' shared beliefs about cooperation, commitment, and the individual value of each team member.[20]

Returning to the general issue of stages in the development of groups, whether a team's actions across these stages are continuously effective or not is another matter. Events internal or external to the group could still cause it to revert to an earlier stage of development, where it might need to re-form and attempt to become a "performing group" all over again. However, if a group has no specified ending point, that is, no "adjourning" phase, there is no reason why the performing stage cannot last indefinitely. To keep a group or team in this stage continually is a clear managerial and leadership challenge.

The Characteristics of Groups and Teams

All groups have certain characteristics or features that affect the degree and types of influence they have on their members and their level of collective performance. Some of these are structural, whereas others relate to the basic features of groups, such as their norms and the degree of cohesion among their members. For all these characteristics, it is important for leaders and managers to understand their likely effects. Particularly, managers need to be on the lookout for how changes, originating from both inside and outside the organization, can alter one or more of these characteristics, which in turn can have a profound impact on how well groups function and perform.

Structural Characteristics

Just like an organization has a structure (as discussed in Chapter 7), so do groups, except on a smaller scale. Four of the most essential structural features of groups are size, composition, differentiated roles, and differentiated status.

SIZE As one review of research on groups stated, "Current literature yields a consistent guideline [for determining the best size for a group]: [use] the smallest number of people who can do the task."[21] Similarly, another review of studies carried out in the United States found that member satisfaction decreased as groups got larger, and leaders' behaviors toward members became more task-oriented and less people-oriented.[22] Likewise, studies have tended to find that organizational productivity per employee decreased with increasing size.[23]

What is an optimal group size? There is no single answer to this question since it would vary based on the types of tasks facing the group. However, research shows that when a group's size increases, the sense of personal responsibility for its output or performance on the part of each individual member tends to decrease. The phenomenon of reduced effort per person in larger-size groups has been labeled **social loafing**.[24] Individuals in larger groups apparently are more likely than those in smaller groups to assume that other members will "carry the load." Also, in larger groups, individual members' specific contributions are less easily identified. This appears to be a major factor that encourages such "loafing."[25]

social loafing
the phenomenon of reduced effort per person in large groups

There are, however, some approaches that can be used to counter the social-loafing tendency. For example, it is possible to structure a group's tasks to encourage full participation by its members. The key lies in being able to readily identify the contributions of each member. One experiment using college swim team members found that the athletes swam faster in individual time trials than they did during relays. When the relay race was structured so that each individual's time was announced aloud at the end of his or her lap, the individuals actually swam faster during the relay than in the individual heats. Results such as these suggest that managers may be able to encourage higher individual levels of effort on group projects by building in some form of acknowledgment of each member's contributions to the final outcome of the project.[26]

Other research seems to indicate that social loafing in groups is less likely to occur in collectivistic cultures (see Chapter 4), such as those in Asian countries, than in more individualistic cultures, such as those in the United States or Australia, because of the much stronger group orientation in collectivistic cultures.[27]

Increasing **process costs**—costs related to coordinating people—are another reason why the performance of groups suffer when their sizes increase. As groups become larger, the number of person-to-person relationships increases significantly, and coordination becomes more cumbersome. Also, a larger size comes with additional opportunities for interpersonal conflicts among group members.

process costs
increasing costs of coordination as group size increases

The disadvantages of large group size must be weighed, naturally, against the potential advantages of having a more extensive pool of talent, skills, and expertise to boost the group's performance and take on additional problem-solving tasks.[28] Having too few people in a group, especially when tasks are many and complex, defeats the whole purpose of putting together people in the first place. Michelin Americas Small Tires unit learned this a few years ago when company management cut the size of sales teams in a cost-savings move, only to have to reverse course and double them just 18 months later because of increasing complaints from dealers.[29] In determining the best size for formal work groups, managers need to consider the probable losses due to process costs in relation to the likely gains due to larger integrated efforts.

Another managerial challenge related to a group's size is that it is not always constant; it can change, sometimes dramatically. These effects are illustrated by a relatively small company called Next Jump, Inc. It started out as a tiny venture organized by a group of friends. Those friends hired their friends. A "family tree" was even posted, showing the relationships among all the employees. In just three months, the company grew from 30 to 105 employees. As it grew, Charlie Kim, the company's CEO, tried to maintain the family feeling in the firm. Unfortunately, the idea of one large "team," with all members focused on the same goals, all working cohesively together, didn't work any more as the company got larger. Meetings fell apart and confusion and conflict increased. People started quitting. The "family tree" was taken down. Kim, in his managerial role, was experiencing the effects that a different size group can have on its members and on the management of it.[30]

COMPOSITION Groups may be composed of individuals who are very similar or very dissimilar. If the former is the case, we describe the group as *homogeneous*. If the latter is the case, the composition would be regarded as *heterogeneous*, or diverse. Most groups these days have some degree of diversity, and many have a great deal. As Exhibit 11.5

EXHIBIT 11.5

Examples of Diversity Within Groups and Potential Consequences

Types of Diversity	Potential Consequences
Observable Attributes	Affective Consequences
• Race	• Satisfaction
• Ethnicity	• Identification with the group
• Gender	• Conflict within the group
• Age	Cognitive Consequences
Underlying Attributes	• Innovation
• Values	• Amount and quality of new ideas
• Skills	Communication-Related Consequences
• Knowledge and Information	• Decreased frequency within group
• Tenure	• Increased frequency outside of group

Source: Adapted from Frances L. Milliken and Luis L. Martins, "Searching for Common Threads: Understanding the Multiple Effects of Diversity in Organizational Groups," *Academy of Management Review* 21, no. 2 (1996), pp. 402–23.

shows, there can be different types of diversity within groups, including obvious differences such as the race/ethnicity, gender, and age of members as well as less obvious differences such as members' values, skills, knowledge, information, and their length of time in the group and in the organization.[31] A Manager's Challenge, "Team Logica" shows how the diversity in the backgrounds and experiences of a team's members were harnessed as a strength.

Some managers deliberately take advantage of the diversity groups have to offer. For example, Jerry Hirshberg, the former president of Nissan Design who helped turn Southern California into a global center of automobile design, purposely combined employees with radically different professional and/or cultural backgrounds into teams. Hirschberg believes that the natural conflict in these diverse teams results in "moments of friction and collision [that lead to] opportunities for breakthroughs."[32]

The key managerial question is: Does a greater amount of diversity within groups more often help or hinder such outcomes as effective group functioning and performance? There is no simple answer to this question, especially given that there are different kinds of

Demographic differences, differences in interpersonal styles, and differences in values can lend a group strength. However, the same differences can also become the source of intragroup conflict. Managers should actively emphasize the common interests of members and discourage personal conflicts between them.

A MANAGER'S CHALLENGE

Diversity

Team Logica: Different Backgrounds Were No Obstacle

A round-the-world yacht race may not seem to have much in common with corporate management, but for Doug Webb, the CFO of a major information technology firm called Logica, the "exercise of human interaction against the sea" was a perfect metaphor for solid teamwork.

"I am sending this via email on the eve of Leg Five," he wrote of the 2000–2001 Global Challenge race, "a 6,020-mile crossing of the Southern Ocean from Sydney, Australia, to Cape Town, South Africa." Webb's crew had finished Leg Four in fourth place, up from ninth and only 4 minutes shy of first place. "That leg," Webb said, "showed a team working together more closely than it had at any time." The group had already weathered a collision with a fishing boat and a serious medical emergency that required evacuation of one of the crew. According to Webb, these obstacles actually helped to develop the team's cohesion.

How did these 13 amateur sailors, randomly assigned to one of 12 identical 72-foot yachts, manage to form close enough bonds to succeed through 10 months of being forced into close quarters, tense competition, and stormy seas?

In 2000–2001, Logica, an info-tech firm, put teamwork to the test. Sporting a crew of over a dozen diverse employees from all walks of life, "Team Logica" set sail on a multi-month race around the world. Called the BT Global Challenge, the contest is dubbed "the world's toughest yacht race." In terms of fostering teamwork, the trip was a success with Team Logica achieving a satisfying fourth-place finish.

The first success factor was preparation. After developing diverse teams including students, detectives, a ballet dancer, software engineers, marketing executives, and so forth, race organizers brought crews together nine months before the race to spend three days getting to know one another and learn how to communicate. Listening skills and the ability to give and receive feedback were stressed, as well as conflict management strategies. Other training sessions were conducted over the weeks to come.

Webb, who served as helmsman for Team Logica, recalls that one of his crew's earliest decisions was that all members would have different roles on board but an equal voice in decision making, though the skipper clearly had to make the most critical choices. Just as many different people in a successful firm can bring together their varied perspectives to work on a problem, so on board "a much broader base of expertise can be tapped, and ultimately better decisions are made."

The second factor was uncovering the key to converting a group of diverse team members into a cohesive team after the race was underway. Everyone on Team Logica brought different skills and had a different reason for being there. Some came to win; others came for the experience. By maintaining a relaxed atmosphere that included playing music on the deck loudspeakers, Webb's team managed to satisfy everyone's goals by making the rigors of going fast and trying to win into a unifying and enjoyable experience.

Some conflict could not be avoided. Skill differences among members caused some role shifting to occur during the race. With coaching, some members grew into their roles. Other members were given tasks they were better able to perform. Even Webb was replaced as watch leader, a transition he admits was for the best. There were occasional failures, but no one was ever blamed for them.

Communication was crucial to building trust, a key ingredient in a team whose members could literally be depending on one another for survival. Questions about responsibility surfaced after the accident with the fishing boat, for example, but uninhibited discussions among the crew soon restored confidence. Team Logica later successfully weathered 77-knot winds and 35-foot waves in an unexpected storm.

In the final leg of their 30,000-mile adventure, this group of former strangers became united around the task and worked effectively as a true team to achieve a satisfying fourth-place finish. As the leader of the winning boat, LG Flatron, put the challenge: "The single most significant thing is getting the crew to be responsible for the outcome."

Sources: D. Webb, "Rhyme of the Ancient Manager," *Forbes*, September 10, 2001, 76–77; H. Riley, "A Sea Change for the Better," *Supply Management*, November 15, 2001, 28–30; S. Tapsell, "Racy Business," *New Zealand Management*, February 2001, 14; D. van Knippenberg and M. L. C. Schippers, "Work Group Diversity," *Annual Review of Psychology* 58, no. 1 (2007): 515–541; F. Rink and N. Ellemers, "Diversity as a Basis for Shared Organizational Identity: The Norm Congruity Principle," *British Journal of Management* 18 (2007): 17–27; www.conradhumphreysracing.com.

diversity.[33] Research findings are only suggestive and not conclusive. However, they tend to show that increased diversity potentially:

- Has somewhat negative effects on members' reactions and interactions with each other;
- Has somewhat positive effects on increasing the quality of the outputs of members' thinking together as a group, presumably because a wider range of opinions and ideas are discussed; and
- Leads to decreased frequency of communication within a group but more communication with those outside the group.

In short, the challenge for a manager is to maximize the benefits that a group's diversity offers and minimize the potential disadvantages. This can be done by anticipating what some of those disadvantages might be and then directly addressing them. One way is for managers to give extra attention to developing strong group norms of cooperation. Also, since it is diversity in members' values and attitudes that is most likely to cause difficulties, managers need to help groups work through these initial differences and turn them into advantages rather than obstacles. The encouraging finding is that it appears that the longer a group works together, the more likely it is to find ways to do just that—to succeed in overcoming those initial differences in values and attitudes.[34] Whatever else can be said, though, one thing seems absolutely certain: The use of increasingly diverse work teams, especially—but not only—multinational groups, is becoming commonplace.[35] Therefore, the diversity challenges for managers are growing, not decreasing.

DIFFERENTIATED ROLES In groups of any size, different members perform different roles; that is, they occupy different positions with sets of expected behaviors attached to those positions. This is most vividly illustrated in certain athletic teams, where players have specialized roles when the team is on offense and different roles on defense. Roles in work groups are not always as clear-cut and can range from being fairly general, such as performing analytical duties, to being highly specialized with specific task assignments, such as monitoring particular pieces of equipment. More and more, however, organizations are attempting to loosen rigid role boundaries in groups in order to gain greater flexibility in meeting unexpected competitive and environmental challenges. The spirit of this change was illustrated by the following quote from a leader of the Electronic Media Team at the U.S. Information Agency: Referring to the new roles of team members, he said at the time, "in the old days, people had very specific job descriptions, and they rarely ventured outside of them." The challenge of teams is to get people and teams moving "outside the box" (that is, to think more creatively about how to fulfill their roles).[36]

One obvious type of role that is assigned or emerges in almost all groups is that of the leader. In the past, the leadership role in work groups has tended to be specialized and concentrated in one person, the supervisor. However, the clear trend in today's highly competitive organizations is to attempt to spread leadership functions as widely as possible among group members. This occurs especially in so-called self-managing teams, but it also is becoming more common even in typical command-type groups.[37] The principle involved is that if a group's leadership functions are more broadly shared and accepted, the group will be able to respond faster and more effectively to rapidly changing pressures and circumstances.

Two particular issues that groups face with respect to roles—and that you probably have faced in your own group experiences—are role ambiguity and role conflict. **Role ambiguity** refers to a situation in which the expected behaviors for a group member are not clearly defined. This can increase the stress level for that person. **Role conflict** emerges when a member has to fulfill two or more contrasting sets of expectations, such as taking time to be friendly with customers versus meeting a certain quota of customers served. Lina Echeverria, who at one time was the core technology director of glass ceramics at Corning, is one manager who faced a role conflict. Echeverria's effectiveness was evaluated on two primary criteria: (1) keeping Corning's research scientists happy, which involved adopting a relatively hands-off leadership style and letting them work when, how, and on what they wanted; and (2) keeping the company happy, which involved being a hands-on, directive leader, holding down costs, and making sure the research scientists were productive.[38] In such a situation, a manager has to make choices that are often very difficult.

role ambiguity
a situation in which the expected behaviors for a group member are not clearly defined

role conflict
a situation in which a member of a group faces two or more contrasting sets of expectations

DIFFERENTIATED STATUS LEVELS Not only do members have different roles in groups, they also often have different levels of status or rank. **Status** is the standing or prestige that a person has in a group, and it can be based on a number of factors, such as perceived leadership abilities, seniority, or special skills, among others.

status
the standing or prestige that a person has in a group, which can be based on a number of factors such as perceived leadership abilities, seniority, or special skills

Research has shown that status differences can strongly influence the interactions within a group.[39] For example, higher-status members tend to receive more communications than do lower-status members, and lower-status members tend to defer to higher-status members when groups are making decisions.[40] However, a group's communication and decision making are likely to be inhibited if the status differences within the group are too extreme. In this case, information relevant to the group's members would be less likely to be widely shared and, thus, not be given sufficient attention by the group.

Behavioral Characteristics

There are two chief features of groups and teams that involve behavioral-type characteristics: namely, the norms that develop in groups and the degree to which groups are cohesive.

Norms

Norms, as we indicated in our earlier discussion of informal groups and the stages of group development, are a group's shared standards that guide the behavior of its individual members. For example, when members of a group behave similarly toward supervisors or outsiders, such as stopping nontask conversations when they enter the room, they are demonstrating the effect of group norms. It would be very difficult, if not impossible, for groups to function if they did not have norms.[41] Each person's behavior would be too unpredictable for coordinated action to take place. Norms also help to reduce ambiguity; thus, they provide members with cues and useful guidelines about how to behave.

norms
a group's shared standards that guide the behavior of its individual members

Information provided by norms is particularly important for new members of a group who need to learn what is going on in the work situation as rapidly as possible. This was illustrated in the case of a manager who left her former employer to begin work at a technology company as a supervisor of a group of project managers. Within her first few days on the new job, the manager asked her assistant to set up individual meetings with several of her project managers. To her surprise, the assistant scheduled the meetings in the subordinates' offices rather than in the manager's office. When she inquired why, the assistant replied "that's how it's done [around here]." The manager realized that if she had insisted that the meetings be held in her own office, she would have violated a prevailing norm and potentially created unnecessary ill will.[42]

THE CHARACTERISTICS OF GROUP NORMS Group norms and their significance can be understood by reviewing several of their main features:

- Norms are usually established for the more important issues of concern to the group; for example, rates of minimally acceptable output or performance.

- Norms do not necessarily apply to all members of the group; some apply only to certain members (like the leader), usually based on the status or particular role of those members. For example, it may be acceptable for a senior member of a group, but not for a junior member, to arrive late for meetings.
- Norms vary in the degree of their acceptance by group members; some norms are accepted and endorsed by virtually all members, others by only a majority. For instance, norms regarding how to deal with work problems might be accepted by everyone, but norms regarding desirable attire might be endorsed by only certain members.
- Norms vary in how much deviation members are permitted in following them; in other words, some norms are very loose and permit a great deal of leeway in behavior, whereas other norms, especially those regarding key group issues, are much more restrictive.[43] For example, a member of a group who talks to outsiders about the group's internal problems might receive severe censure from fellow group members. By contrast, someone who merely talks louder than normal during meetings might be tolerated (up to a degree, at least).

THE DEVELOPMENT OF GROUP NORMS Norms do not suddenly and magically appear in groups. They seldom, if ever, develop in a purely spontaneous way. Rather, they arise out of interaction among group members. An example of a typical norm development process is shown in Exhibit 11.6. Key factors that often have a major influence on the process include the following:[44]

- ***Early behaviors:*** Typically, initial behaviors, especially in newly formed groups, establish standards for subsequent behavior. In committees, for example, the first few meetings help establish norms about how candid, or how indirect, the discussion of sensitive issues is likely to be. Such quickly established norms are often difficult to reshape or change later.
- ***Imported behaviors:*** Members of a group often bring with them standards of behavior that were prominent in their former groups. "When in doubt, stay with the familiar" seems to be the (sometimes incorrect) watchword of many people in organizations. When a high-status member imports a norm, as in the case of those with

EXHIBIT 11.6

Example of the Development of Group Norms

Source: Kenneth Bettenhausen and J. Keith Murnighan, "The Emergence of Norms in Competitive Decision Making Groups," *Administrative Science Quarterly*, 30 (1985), pp. 350–72.

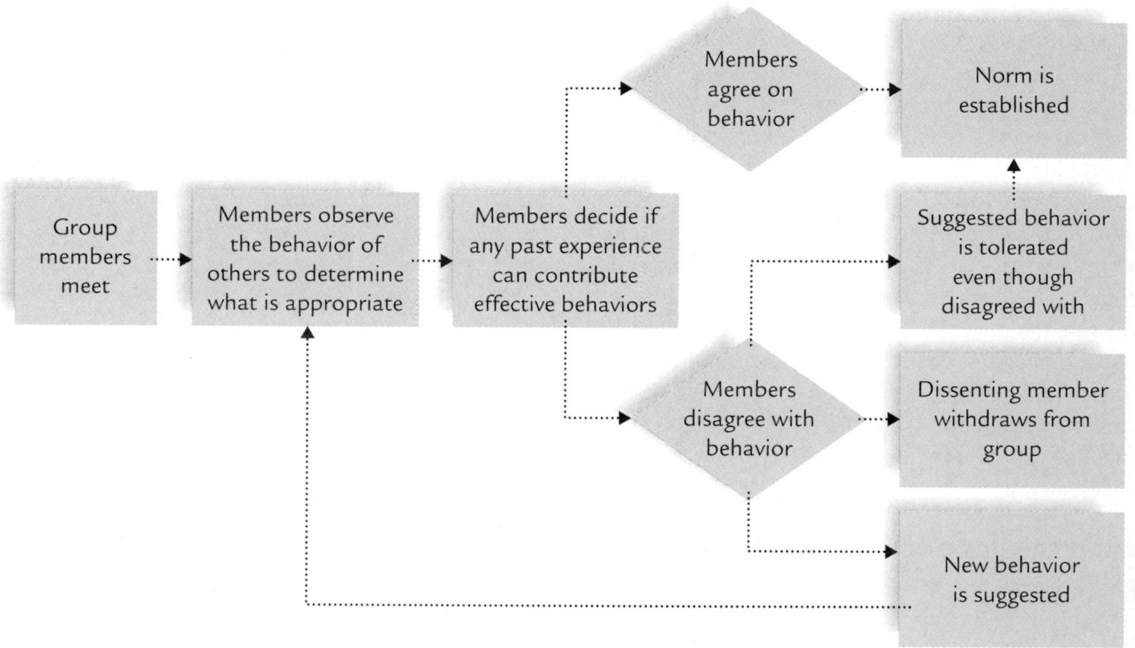

acknowledged expertise or high power, the prominence of that norm is likely to be strong. A new chief executive officer (CEO), for example, may believe in a norm of communication "only through channels" even though this may run counter to the organization's previous norm of "openness." However, because the new CEO's status is high, few are likely to challenge this imported norm.

- ***Critical events:*** A sudden challenge to the group, such as criticism from another group, can create specific and vivid responses that form the basis for how members should be expected to respond in the future. A time of crisis makes people particularly alert to cues in their environment and tends to reinforce norms that emerge from that period. In a corporation that has announced layoffs, for example, new norms regarding the overt display of diligent work habits may emerge.
- ***Explicitly stated standards:*** Not to be overlooked is the fact that leaders or high-status members of a group may simply assert that "this is how we will do it around here!" Newly appointed supervisors and athletic coaches, for example, frequently use this approach with their groups or teams.

THE EFFECTS OF GROUP NORMS The existence of strong norms tends to narrow individual differences in behavior and beliefs. This results in a certain degree of **conformity,** or close adherence to the group's norms, by the individual members. In the opening profile, Steve Ortiz at Harrah's was faced with changing existing norms that seemed to be inhibiting the performance of his group. Ortiz needed the group to adopt new and different norms supportive of his unit's revised objectives.

conformity
close adherence to the group's norms by the individual members

Whether such conformity is "good" or "bad" depends on the perspective of the viewer. If the norms support a manager's goals for a group—for example, that everyone should look for opportunities to make creative suggestions to improve the group's effectiveness—then the manager would regard conformity as very helpful. A few years ago, a large, national transit company reorganized around cross-functional groups following a decade of financial and labor problems; about half (42 percent) of the groups were successful and about half (48 percent) were unsuccessful. The successful groups had developed stronger norms of open communication and leadership, and they behaved more like teams.[45]

If norms conflict with the objectives a manager is trying to achieve, then greater conformity would be regarded as negative. The implication for you as a manager, therefore, is that you should be as concerned about the content or direction of group norms as about the amount of conformity to them.

From the point of view of an individual member of a group, norms can sometimes be too constraining. In that case, the individual may deviate from the group's expected attitudes and behavior. Such divergent actions or expressed views are potentially troubling to others in the group because they can threaten the group's solidarity and, perhaps, in extreme cases, even its existence. Therefore, the group sometimes imposes sanctions on the deviant in an attempt to bring about greater conformity. The classic case in certain Western work situations, particularly at the hourly worker level is the individual who works faster or slower than the group thinks he or she should. Sometimes labeled "rate busters" or "slackers," these people are often subjected to ridicule or ostracism to persuade or force them to work at a rate more in line with the group's norms.

Cohesion

Another major behavioral property of groups is their amount of **cohesion,** "the degree to which members are motivated to remain in a group."[46] Group cohesion is usually considered to have many advantages and to be highly desirable if it can be developed.[47] When managers and organizations attempt to turn groups into teams, they are, in effect, trying to generate stronger group cohesion. However, as we will discuss later, high levels of group cohesion don't always result in positive outcomes.[48]

cohesion
the degree to which members are motivated to remain in the group

THE DEVELOPMENT OF GROUP COHESION There are no sure-fire ways for you as a manager to build strong cohesion in groups that you lead or in which you are a member. However, the available research suggests three factors that can be potentially important in developing greater group cohesion:

- Strengthening the interpersonal attraction among group members;
- Generating a record of high performance and past success of the group;[49] and
- Fostering competition with other groups.[50]

The most consistently important of these factors appears to be the first, namely, whether members of the group think they have something in common with other members and tend to like being with them; that is, whether they feel like they belong to a true team. The evidence for the other two factors in bringing about cohesion is not as clear-cut. However, both past successes and current or anticipated conflicts with other groups also seem to unite members and increase their cohesion. This is especially true if a strong interpersonal attraction among members is already present. A group whose members don't especially like being with each other may disintegrate when faced with competition from external groups, rather than develop greater cohesion, which again places a premium on developing interpersonal bonds.

THE EFFECTS OF GROUP COHESION The increased cohesiveness of groups can have a number of potential advantages.[51] Chief among these is an increase in the quantity and quality of group interaction.[52] A second potential advantage of greater group cohesion is that the group has stronger influence on each member to conform to the group's standards or norms. Assuming—and this is a critical assumption—that those norms are positive from the manager's perspective, then this is a significant advantage. A third possible advantage is that cohesive groups appear to be more effective in achieving goals that group members accept, although research on this point is not totally consistent. A final possible advantage of higher group cohesion is that members tend to have greater satisfaction with the group.

As positive as these potential advantages might seem, high group cohesion sometimes can be a mixed blessing from a manager's point of view (see Exhibit 11.7). First, if the group has norms that do not support the organization's goals, then greater cohesion is definitely a minus. In this case, members may be more influenced in the "wrong" direction—as when, for example, a group of workers tolerates sexual harassment—than if there is little cohesion. Another possible disadvantage of strong group cohesion is that any deviance from the group's norms might not be handled well. Highly cohesive groups are more likely to reject any deviance, even if it represents creative ideas that could ultimately be useful to the group. Related to this is the danger that groupthink[53] (previously discussed in Chapter 4) may be accentuated in highly cohesive groups. Dissenting viewpoints expressed by a "devil's advocate" often can help a group critically examine its opinion or decisions.

Still another potential disadvantage of high group cohesion, but one that is frequently overlooked, is that the cooperation between groups may be adversely affected. For example,

EXHIBIT 11.7

Effects of High Levels of Group Cohesion

Positive Effects	Negative Effects
• Increased quality and quantity of group interactions	• Counterproductive norms may be emphasized
• Strengthened adherence to group norms	• Useful or creative ideas may be ignored if they deviate from established norms or values
• Increased effectiveness in achieving group goals	• Increased probability of developing groupthink
• Augmented individual satisfaction with group membership	• Potential decrease in intergroup cooperation

in developing and marketing a new product, problems may develop among a firm's production, marketing, and sales groups as they work together to develop and market a new product. If the production group is highly cohesive and has a norm of never allowing outsiders to know it has problems, it may be reluctant to notify other units that a key piece of equipment is not functioning correctly. Without this information, the marketing department might generate unrealistic expectations for the product's release date, and the sales teams then would promise higher numbers of the product to customers than would actually be available. Most organizations have many work groups; some have hundreds or more. The challenge, for higher-level managers, is to have these groups and teams work together and interact smoothly and reliably. So, it is a concern if high within-group cohesion hinders intergroup cooperation.

Emerging Types of Groups and Teams in Today's Organizations

Now that we have examined how groups form and develop and explored some of their basic characteristics, we are ready to look at some examples of particular kinds of groups and teams that are becoming increasingly prominent in today's organizations (see Exhibit 11.8). Not every organization will have each of these groups, but where they do exist they present some special managerial challenges.

Self-Managing Work Groups (Teams)

A relatively recent, but increasingly important, variant of a command work group is the **self-managed**, or so-called autonomous, group—a work group that has no formally appointed supervisor. These groups are similar to command groups in that the members coordinate their work as if they all reported to the same formally appointed supervisor. However, the group manages itself on behalf of the organization's objectives, and its members usually appoint their own informal team leaders.[54] The group is made up of a number of members with diverse skills that can be applied to the group's task. It generally is responsible for decisions concerning how to accomplish the work—which members will perform which tasks and in which order. Members also frequently do jobs traditionally associated with supervision, such as conducting team meetings and solving productivity problems. A major reason why some organizations—Xerox, Procter & Gamble, and General Motors, among many others—put together self-managing units is to develop more team-like group behavior than in more traditional command groups, and eventually to gain greater efficiency and effectiveness.[55]

self-managing (autonomous) workgroup a group that has no formally appointed supervisor but is similar to command groups in that the members coordinate their organizational work as if they all reported to the same formally appointed supervisor; members usually appoint their own informal team leader

EXHIBIT 11.8

Prominent Groups and Teams in Today's Organizations

Type	Potential Advantages	Potential Disadvantages
Self-managing	More team-like behavior	Not all employees want to manage themselves
Cross-functional/ New Product	Increased creativity Dispersed knowledge Speed to market	Increased group conflict
Global	Increased creativity from diversity of backgrounds	Paralysis Inaction Failure
Virtual	Increased speed of communication Decreased costs	Increased misinterpretation Lack of trust Difficult to manage

The idea of group self-management, however good it appears in principle, may not appeal to all employees whom it might affect. Furthermore, it cannot be assumed to fit into all types of cultures.[56] Therefore, managers and organizations who want to establish such groups need to consider the potential pitfalls and resistance to self-managed teams as well as the possible advantages.

Cross-Functional, New Product (or Service) Groups

Groups that draw their membership from distinctly different types of units within an organization, such as R&D and marketing, have been around for many years. However, their number and importance have increased markedly in recent years. A primary objective for such groups or teams is to bring to bear as much creativity and dispersed knowledge as possible on the task. A good example of a company's use of cross-functional teams is represented by dj Orthopedics. Given the highly competitive nature of the orthopedics products industry, the company needs to concentrate on new product development (NPD). To do this, it creates an NPD team for every project, consisting of members from the design engineering, manufacturing, quality, marketing, and regulatory units. Each team is given complete responsibility for the project from its start to finish and has oversight over all project tasks and elements. These cross-functional teams also are encouraged to try to solve any problems they face before having to involve higher managers to make final decisions.[57]

Other major objectives of cross-functional teams, especially in high-technology firms, are to speed the products to market while at the same time controlling or minimizing costs. This sounds good, but the reality is often that the outcomes are less favorable than expected because of the potential for increased conflicts in groups composed of members with widely varying initial perspectives.[58] To deal with this basic issue, research results suggest that managers should try to increase the following attributes of effective cross-functional groups:[59]

- members' feelings of "ownership" ("at-stakeness") of the group's decisions;
- transparency or openness regarding members' motivations, expectations, and personal agendas;
- "mindfulness" or, essentially, reaching high-quality decisions after examining all divergent points of view; and
- high levels of mutual cooperation ("synergy") and trust.

Global Teams

Another type of group that is becoming increasingly prominent, especially in larger organizations, is the multinational group (almost always referred to as a "multinational team"). It is usually a highly diverse group, whether or not it represents one or several functional areas, because members are often from very different cultural backgrounds. For reasons that we have already discussed, diverse teams potentially offer major advantages for organizations. However, reality is not always quite so rosy. All too frequently, the groups can end up in paralysis or even in failure.

One set of researchers divides up global teams into three general types: the destroyers, the equalizers, and the creators.[60] "Destroyers" are groups that turn out to be utter disasters; they channel their members' efforts and attention into unproductive conflicts and interpersonal attacks. For example, one member of a European destroyer team described the team environment candidly: "Those Brits on our team are too serious; the Germans are so stuck up about engineering that they don't think anyone else has a brain; and the French couldn't care less about production quotas." "Equalizer" types of teams are those that think they are doing well and have little apparent conflict, yet seem unable to produce any result other than one of mediocrity. Essentially, equalizers are underperforming teams that fail to take advantage of their cross-national diversity. "Creator" teams are those that directly accept and build on their differences and use them to enhance their creativity.

Virtual Teams

As mentioned earlier in this chapter, organizations are increasingly establishing virtual teams or groups composed of individuals who do not work together in close physical proximity. Members of virtual teams are often geographically dispersed, often with cross-organizational or cross-national membership.[61] As their names imply, such groups rarely, if ever, meet in person and instead conduct most or all of their business via electronic communication.

The increased speed of communication and decreased costs in meeting together are obvious advantages of these groups. Nevertheless, virtual teams have their own challenges and problems.[62] First, communication, though fast and sometimes nearly instantaneous, can be incomplete and easily subject to misinterpretation by the receiver.[63] Second, trust among group members may be very difficult to develop because of the absence of the typical getting-to-know-you socialization process that occurs with nonvirtual groups that meet face-to-face.[64] Third, managerial supervision may be more difficult than in a typical group. Issues that can crop up in any group, such as role ambiguity and social loafing, for example, may be intensified in virtual groups. See the A Manager's Challenge, "Stages in Virtual Teams," for an illustration of some of these issues in virtual teams that were used in FOODCO (not its real name), a large, nationwide and complex food distribution company composed of a number of different operating units.

Building and Managing Groups and Teams

Throughout this chapter in various places, we have mentioned some of the steps that you as a manager can take to increase the quality of group functioning and the satisfaction of group members. Here, in this section, we focus on three issues that are particularly critical in building and managing groups and turning them into true teams: developing team competencies, dealing with team conflicts, and improving group effectiveness.

Developing Team Competencies

As we have emphasized throughout this chapter, working with, and in, a group is different from simply doing your own individual job well. It is the interaction with other people, whether face-to-face or by electronic and other indirect means, that makes the difference. Therefore, to be able to perform effectively in a group, it is important that you develop competencies in teamwork. To be a competent team member is not necessarily the same thing as being a competent individual performer. A very useful way to think about what is required from you in a team situation is to consider three basic areas of teamwork competencies: **k**nowledge, **s**kills, and **a**ttitudes (KSAs).[65] Specific examples of team competencies in these three areas are shown in Exhibit 11.9.

EXHIBIT 11.9

Examples of Specific Team Competencies in Three Areas

Knowledge	Skills	Attitudes
• Knowledge of team mission, objectives, norms • Task sequencing • Team role interaction patterns • Understanding team work skills • Teammate characteristics	• Adaptability and flexibility • Mutual performance monitoring and feedback, self-correction • Coordination and task integration • Communication • Decision making and problem solving	• Team orientation • Shared vision • Team cohesion • Mutual trust • Importance of teamwork

Sources: Adapted from J. A. Cannon-Bowers and E. Salas, "A Framework for Developing Team Performance Measures in Training," in M. T. Brannick, E. Salas, and C. Prince (eds.), *Team Performance Assessment and Measurement: Theory, Methods, and Applications* (Mahwah, NJ: Lawrence Erlbaum Associates, 1997), p. 47.

A MANAGER'S CHALLENGE

Technology

Stages in Virtual Teams

Do virtual teams go through "life cycles" in the same way that many meet-in-person groups do? Do they face the same kinds of challenges at each stage of the cycle that those groups do? Those were the basic questions examined by researchers associated with the University of North Carolina (UNC).

It has been demonstrated that many teams, particularly project-like teams that have specific beginning and ending points, go through a set of stages in their development that could be called their life cycles. Although these cycles have been studied in various groups where members are located in relative proximity to each other and can have frequent in-person, face-to-face meetings, they seldom have been investigated in virtual teams composed of members who are geographically dispersed. This was the focus of the UNC-based study that was conducted in connection with an executive leadership institute.

Those attending the institute held mid- and upper-level managerial positions at "FOODCO," a real company given this fictitious name to protect its anonymity. FOODCO is a large, nationwide food products distribution company with some 20 operating subsidiaries. Its clients include fast-food chains, hospitals, universities, and free-standing restaurants. With the company's participation and encouragement, the 29 managers attending the leadership program were formed into four- or five-person virtual teams by the instructors. Each of the six teams were given a specific project objective (for example, to determine how to transfer the best practices from one division of the company to other divisions) and an eight-month timeline to complete their project and make concrete recommendations to top management (while continuing to do their regular jobs back at their own locations).

Virtual teams rarely, if ever, meet in person. Instead they work toward common goals by conducting most or all of their business via electronic communication. Because they allow organizations to hire and retain the best employees around the world regardless of where they are located, virtual teams are becoming more prevalent as businesses globalize.

The researchers found that the forming-storming-norming-performing description of a group's life cycle was well adapted to the development of these virtual teams. In the forming stage, the teams exhibited extremely high levels of optimism about doing the task and being able to work with their teammates. By the second or storming stage, reality had set in. Problems emerged, such as a lack of team leadership, the apparent lack of commitment from some members, and the difficulties related to coordinating the efforts among the far-flung group members. In the third stage, at least some of the teams, but not all, had proceeded to develop consensus norms about how to proceed, how to do a better job of sharing relevant knowledge, and how to obtain commitments to time schedules. By the fourth or performing stage, definite differences had emerged across the six groups with regard to how well they were meeting their project objectives in a timely fashion and without having to make "a mad dash to the finish."

What conclusions were learned from the study? Many of the problems faced by virtual teams—such as achieving agreements on responsibilities and on how to manage the project team's task at the same time as doing one's regular job—were very similar to those encountered by nonvirtual project teams, except more so! Almost all team participants agreed that the advice they would give future virtual teams was "start (getting organized) earlier!" They found—more than they had expected to—that the "virtual" aspects of their team greatly intensified the difficulties related to finding effective ways to communicate and coordinate with one another. Also, it was clear from this study that it was extremely important for higher-level executives to intervene in a timely way to help teams. In short, "to thrive, virtual project teams must be embedded in supportive corporate cultures." Although the teams in this study were virtual, the challenges they experienced were real.

Sources: Based on S. A. Furst, M. Reeves, B. Rosen, & R. S. Blackburn, "Managing the Life Cycle of Virtual Teams" *Academy of Management Executive*, 18, no. 2 (2004): 6–20; see also W. Combs and S. Peacocke, "Leading Virtual Teams," *T + D* 61, no. 2 (2007): 27–28; D. L. Paul, "Collaborative Activities in Virtual Settings: A Knowledge Management Perspective of Telemedicine," *Journal of Management Information Systems* 22, no. 4 (2006): 143–176.

Knowledge (K) in the group context refers to the necessary understanding of facts, concepts, relations, and underlying relevant information necessary to perform team tasks. As shown in Exhibit 11.9, examples of the kinds of specific knowledge that are especially useful in team situations include knowledge about the team's mission and goals, the sequencing of tasks faced by the team, fellow team members' roles and responsibilities, and teammate characteristics.

Skills (S) (as noted in Chapters 1 and 9) refer to highly developed behavioral and cognitive capabilities, such as emotional intelligence,[66] that are necessary to carry out team tasks and meet team goals. Among others, these skills include such competencies as adaptability and flexibility in relation to accomplishing team tasks, being able to monitor one's own performance and the performance of one's team members, being able to accept and give criticisms, and being able to assume leadership responsibilities within the group.

Attitudes (A) involve relatively stable feelings and beliefs about something. In other words, our attitudes, generally speaking, indicate how we view important parts of our environment. In group work situations, these attitudes would include those toward the concepts of teams and teamwork, the need for team cohesion, the assessment of a team's capabilities, and the level and importance of trust within a group.[67]

Dealing with Team Conflict

When people work together in groups, there is always the potential for conflict within the group. Conflicts can occur for a number of reasons and can have a variety of consequences. Although the effects of group conflict, such as a marked decrease in cohesion within the group, often can be negative, that is not always so. Some types of conflict, particularly task or substantive conflict (discussed next), potentially can have positive effects. For instance, a senior executive at Keane, an information technology firm based in Boston, views it this way: "We can agree our way into horrendous decisions. But when people are allowed to express their opinions, no matter how disagreeable, magic can occur. More ideas are put on the table, which can lead to more discovery, which can lead to quantum leaps in improvement and innovation . . . When marketing and engineering disagree violently about something, you've got a wonderful opportunity to figure out how to make improvements by meeting both [of their] objectives."[68]

The important point to remember is that conflict among members within groups is fairly common, and it is not always something to be avoided. In fact, the absence of any conflict at all can be a significant sign that the group is not openly generating a sufficient variety of viewpoints and potential approaches for solving problems and making good decisions.

TYPES OF GROUP CONFLICT Researchers have generally distinguished three basic types of group conflict: task, process, and relationship. **Task conflict** is conflict that focuses on differences in ideas about the nature of the issues facing a group and the group's objectives. It is also sometimes called cognitive (thinking)[69] or substantive conflict.[70] Research indicates that sometimes, but certainly not always, some amount of task conflict can be beneficial to the group,[71] especially for less routine and more complex tasks,[72] and when conflict is introduced deliberately as in the use of a "devil's advocate."[73] Similarly,

task conflict
conflict that focuses on differences in ideas and courses of action in addressing the issues facing a group

process conflict differences of opinion about the procedures a group should use to achieve its goals

relationship conflict interpersonal differences among group members

process conflict—differences of opinion about the procedures a group uses to achieve its goals—can be helpful but often may not be.

The other major type of conflict that can occur in groups, relationship conflict, is usually found to be almost always dysfunctional. **Relationship conflict** focuses on interpersonal differences and is sometimes called affective or emotional conflict.[74] It is usually a negative type of conflict for groups because it distracts focus from tasks and ideas.[75] It discourages rather than encourages members to consider multiple points of view and openly discuss ideas and solutions.

CAUSES OF GROUP CONFLICT There are many potential causes of group conflict, but they can usually be linked to one of the two types of conflict.

Potential causes of task and process conflicts include:

- Ambiguities regarding the task;
- Differences in goals, objectives, and perspectives (for example, stemming from differences in functional backgrounds)[76] among group members; and
- Scarcity (actual or perceived) of resources to accomplish the group's goals.

Potential causes of relationship conflicts include:

- Dissimilarities in the composition of the membership of the group, including demographic diversity (in age, ethnic/cultural background, gender, and so forth) and status/power differences;[77]
- Differences in the interpersonal styles of individual members; and
- Differences in values.[78]

Several of the potential causes of group conflict can occur together; for example, when a very diverse group that includes several people with distinctive interpersonal styles or quite different values encounters a highly ambiguous task. When there are multiple causes such as these, finding ways to deal with the conflict becomes even more difficult.

MANAGING GROUP CONFLICT If you are put in the position of leading a group, what can you do to help your group deal with conflict? Probably the most important managerial guideline for dealing with group conflict is to try to increase the ratio of substantive to relationship conflict.[79] This would mean, for example, strongly encouraging a culture of openness that allows members to express their different opinions about task methods and objectives, and also being especially receptive to novel or creative approaches to coping with the group's task requirements.[80] In this way, maximum amounts of relevant information can be brought to bear on the issues faced by the group,[81] and unintended groupthink tendencies can be minimized. In addition, you should help to clarify and reduce task ambiguities and try to get the group to focus on larger goals beyond the individual interests of members—goals, in other words, that emphasize the common interests of all the group members. Also, there is evidence to suggest that active attempts taken to avoid relationship conflicts can be an effective way to eliminate or at least reduce their harmful effects on members' satisfaction and performance.[82] The key overall point here is that it is difficult to avoid conflicts occurring within groups, but that conflicts of any type can be managed and potentially turned into productive group behavior.

intragroup conflict differences that occur within groups

intergroup conflict differences that occur between groups

Most of what we have been talking about so far applies to conflict *within* groups (**intragroup conflict**). In organizational settings, however, achieving coordination and reducing conflict *between* or among groups—**intergroup conflict**—is also important.[83] Strategies for managing intragroup conflict can apply equally well to intergroup conflict. Therefore, managers should look for opportunities to decrease unnecessary relational conflicts in those intergroup interaction situations and increase the focus on relevant substantive differences. Also, emphasizing larger, more organization-wide goals can help increase cooperation and, thus, performance.[84] So, for example, if sales and production can concentrate on the issue of improving customer satisfaction—to elevate it to the highest priority—then their differences on how many variations of a product to make and market can be minimized or resolved. As with intragroup conflict, the potential exists for positive effects from intergroup conflict, but again that conflict has to be faced and managed.

Improving the Effectiveness of Groups and Teams

Teams and groups are not static parts of organizations. They come into existence, go out of existence, and change over time. Additionally, and most important, their effectiveness and performance can be changed and improved. As a leader of a group, however, this is not necessarily easy to do. There is no magic formula to bring this about. Nevertheless, there are some useful approaches to consider that have the potential for helping to improve a group's performance in organizational settings.[85]

ASSESSING THE EFFECTIVENESS OF GROUPS What exactly do we mean by group effectiveness? What distinguishes highly effective groups from less effective groups? A survey of 61 U.S. companies revealed that about two-thirds used objective quantifiable criteria to measure group effectiveness; these included measures of production output, quality improvements, cost reductions, and turnaround times. A number of the companies also used more subjective criteria including member participation, cooperation, and involvement.[86]

How can we tell when a group is performing especially well? One of the foremost experts on group effectiveness, Richard Hackman, suggests there are three major indicators (Exhibit 11.10):[87]

1. Whether the group's outputs—products, services, or decisions—are valued by those that receive or use them. Are a committee's recommendations implemented? Does a product development group's creation ever get put into production? Is upper management satisfied with the performance of a customer service unit?
2. Whether the group's capacity for further cooperation among its members is maintained or increased.
3. Whether members gain satisfaction and a sense of growth and well-being from being part of the group. Outsiders are unlikely to regard a group or team as effective if the team's own members do not seem satisfied and are not experiencing feelings of accomplishment by being part of the group.

Most observers would probably say that the first of these criteria—acceptance of the group's outputs by others—is the most important one in organizational settings. However, if a group cannot achieve either of the other two objectives, it is highly unlikely that it will be able over time to produce valued output. Thus, all three are important components of group effectiveness.

EXHIBIT 11.10

Characteristics of Highly Effective Groups

- Any product or service they develop is highly desired and valued by customers.
- Increased cooperation among members is encouraged and achieved.
- Group membership increases individual members' feelings of satisfaction, personal growth, and overall well-being.

Source: J. R. Hackman (ed.), *Groups That Work (and Those That Don't): Creating Conditions for Effective Teamwork* (San Francisco: Jossey-Bass, 1990).

INGREDIENTS NECESSARY FOR GROUP EFFECTIVENESS For a group to perform effectively, it must be able to do at least three things especially well:

1. Exert enough effort to accomplish its tasks at acceptable levels of quantity and quality;
2. Obtain sufficient knowledge and skills to carry out its work; and
3. Use appropriate strategies to apply its effort, knowledge, and skills effectively.[88]

These three bases for achieving high levels of group effectiveness sound simple, but they are major challenges for leaders of groups. To ensure that these components are actually in place consistently, managers need to address several issues:

Develop Appropriate Group Structures To be effective, groups need clearly defined tasks and objectives that can motivate their members. Groups also need to be sized appropriately to their tasks, and they need a membership with a sufficient mix of skills and expertise. This means that if a leader has the option of choosing the group's members, those choices will often make a large difference in how well a group performs initially and what its capacity is to improve.

Develop Appropriate Support from the Organization[89] Groups operating within companies and organizations need support from their surrounding environment. For example, they need to be rewarded for effective collaboration.[90] They also need education and technical training for performing critical group tasks[91] as well as relief from their other duties, and access to necessary information. For instance, some years ago, managers in the U.S. Information Agency (USIA) found that after the agency was reorganized into self-managing teams, their major problems centered around a simple lack of administrative support.[92]

Obtain Appropriate Coaching and Consultation Assistance[93] In the day-to-day world of work, most groups need outside help (whether from inside or outside the larger organization) to reduce potential conflicts, to increase their coordination in terms of dealing with problems within the group, and to develop strategies for approaching the group's tasks. Increased collaboration is an important objective,[94] and the message here is that it is often the case that a group should not try to go it alone.

EXHIBIT 11.11 Enhancing Group Effectiveness

	POINTS OF LEVERAGE		
Necessary Processes	**Group Structure**	**Organizational Context**	**Coaching and Consultation**
Apply ample effort	Motivational structure of group task	Organizational reward system	Remedying coordination problems and building group commitment
Acquire sufficient knowledge and skill	Group composition	Organizational education/training system	Remedying inappropriate "weighting" of member inputs and fostering cross-training
Develop task-appropriate performance strategies	Group norms that regulate member behavior and foster scanning and planning	Organizational information system	Remedying implementation problems and fostering creativity in strategy development

Source: Adapted from J. R. Hackman (ed.), *Groups That Work (and Those That Don't): Creating Conditions for Effective Teamwork* (San Francisco: Jossey-Bass, 1990), p. 13.

EXHIBIT 11.12

A Checklist for Leaders of Groups

How well do you:

- ❑ Encourage members to learn from each other?
- ❑ Recognize and praise members for their contributions?
- ❑ Keep key people outside the [group] informed about its accomplishments?
- ❑ Promptly inform members about major developments that [may] affect them?
- ❑ Give [group] members authority to make [at least some] important decisions?
- ❑ Openly accept and respond to feedback from [group] members?
- ❑ Review the [group's] performance at the end of major tasks?
- ❑ Offer specific and concrete suggestions for how members can improve?
- ❑ Understand what motivates members to work hard?

Source: Adapted from G. L. Hallam, "Seven Common Beliefs about Teams: Are They True?" *Leadership in Action* 17, no. 3 (1997), pp. 1–4.

Exhibit 11.11 provides a summary of the preceding points and shows how the manager's attention to the group's structure, support from the organizational context, and relevant coaching and consultation can help increase each of the three ingredients necessary for group effectiveness: high levels of effort, sufficient knowledge and skills, and appropriate strategies for applying effort and skills. The points presented and summarized in the exhibit do not provide a "cookbook" for group or team success. Rather, they are useful guidelines for managers and organizations to consider as they attempt to help groups improve their performance. Likewise, Exhibit 11.12, based on extensive research,[95] provides a helpful checklist for those who assume leadership positions in groups and teams to measure how well they are fulfilling that role in their groups. If team members concur that their leader is doing a good job in these areas, then it is likely that the group (and not just the leader) will perform well.

Managerial Challenges from the Front Line

The Rest of the Story

Steve Ortiz was confronted with the overall challenge of generating more income from the VIP customer segment of the Harrah's casino for which he works. This meant that he had to increase his employees' motivation to serve these customers better. To accomplish this, Ortiz formed a "team-based" approach. He held the entire group of employees working with the VIPs accountable collectively for the results, and he gave the team a clear-cut target on a month-by-month basis. Specifically, he developed a system whereby a VIP could be assisted by any "host" (employee), as opposed to the former system of having each host monitor only his or her "own" players. This resulted in the entire "team" receiving recognition and, most importantly, it left VIP guests with the impression that it did not matter which particular host was assigned to them—they would get great service either way.

Within two quarters following the change, the Kansas facility's customer satisfaction scores had increased above the mean scores for the company, and VIP sales ended up 18 percent over the previous year and the highest in the seven-year history of the property.

Summary

- The terms *group* and *team* are often used interchangeably. However, it is sometimes useful to make a distinction between them. A group is typically considered to consist of a small number of people, usually between 3 and 20 members who interact around some kind of shared objectives. A team can be considered a type of group that has a higher level of coordinated interaction and, especially, a higher level of individual members' identification with the group. Some groups become teams and some remain "only" groups.
- Groups operating within organizations can be classified into different basic categories. One category is "formal" groups—for example, command, project, and committee groups—put together by the organization. The other category of groups are "informal," those formed by the voluntary actions of individuals rather than in response to an organizational directive. Informal groups often can greatly affect the success or failure of managers' actions.
- Three major factors influence the formation of groups: the organization's goals, opportunities for group members to interact and share knowledge, and people's psychological needs, such as those for security, social support, and self-esteem. Once groups are formed and their members begin to interact, they often, though not always, go through fairly predictable and sequential stages in their development. These stages have popularly been characterized as: forming, storming, norming, and performing.
- All groups, whether they are formal or informal, have structural and behavioral characteristics. Structural attributes include the group's size, its composition, and the different roles and levels of status of its members. A major behavioral feature of any group is its norms, or shared standards of behavior. Norms often influence the behavior of individual members in powerful ways. The level of cohesion, or the extent to which members want to remain a part of the group, is another significant behavioral characteristic.
- Several specific kinds of groups formed for particular purposes are becoming increasingly prominent in contemporary organizations, including: self-managing work groups, cross-functional groups, global teams, and virtual teams. Each of these types of groups has their own advantages but also some potential problems. For example, self-managing work groups can generate a strong sense of member involvement, but not everyone may want to work in this kind of group. The other three groups are well adapted to deal with particular kinds of problems and issues, but sometimes face major problems coordinating the efforts of their members.
- Almost any type of group will perform better if its team members have good teamwork competencies. Such competencies can be classified as knowledge (for example, about one's teammates), skills (for example, communication skills), and attitudes (for example, mutual trust). Some of these competencies are "transportable" and can be used in any situation; others are sometimes specific to a particular task, particular situation, or particular combination of a task and situation.
- All groups face the possibility of conflict developing among their members. These conflicts are generally of two types: task and/or relationship. There are many possible causes of group conflicts of either type. Regardless of the specific causes, research has tended to show that an effective way to deal with group conflict is to try to reduce the amount of relationship conflict among members and to use task conflict to bring out different, even novel, approaches to task methods and goals before decisions are reached.
- The effectiveness of almost any group potentially can be increased by focusing on the following issues: the appropriateness of group processes and group structure, the nature of the organizational context, and access to external coaching and consultation where necessary.

Key Terms

cohesion 323
command (supervisory) group 310
committee 311
conformity 323
formal group 312
group 309
informal group 312
intergroup conflict 330
intragroup conflict 330
norms 321
process conflict 330
process costs 317
project/task force 310
relationship conflict 330
role ambiguity 321
role conflict 321
self-managing (autonomous) work group 325
social loafing 317
status 321
task conflict 329
team 310

Review Questions

1. What are the similarities and differences between a group and a team?
2. What are the four stages of group formation? What are the important features of each?
3. Is there an optimum group size? Why or why not?
4. What is *social loafing*? Can managers do anything to minimize or eliminate it?
5. What effects can diversity have on group members and on group functioning?
6. Provide examples of role conflict and role ambiguity that illustrate the difference between the two terms.
7. Why are norms important to groups?
8. What is meant by group cohesion? Are high levels of group cohesion always desirable?
9. What are the advantages and disadvantages of virtual teams?
10. What are KSAs, and how do they relate to team competencies?
11. Can managers eliminate group conflict? Should they try?
12. What are three major indicators that can be used to identify high-performance groups?

Assessing Your Capabilities

How Good Am I at Building and Leading a Team?

Using the following scale, circle the number that best indicates the extent to which you agree or disagree with each statement.

1.	I am knowledgeable about the different stages of development that teams can go through in their life cycles.	1 Strongly Disagree	2 Disagree	3 Slightly Disagree	4 Slightly Agree	5 Agree	6 Strongly Agree
2.	When a team forms, I make certain that all team members are introduced to one another at the outset.	1 Strongly Disagree	2 Disagree	3 Slightly Disagree	4 Slightly Agree	5 Agree	6 Strongly Agree
3.	When the team first comes together, I provide directions, answer team members' questions, and clarify goals, expectations, and procedures.	1 Strongly Disagree	2 Disagree	3 Slightly Disagree	4 Slightly Agree	5 Agree	6 Strongly Agree
4.	I help team members establish a foundation of trust among one another and between themselves and me.	1 Strongly Disagree	2 Disagree	3 Slightly Disagree	4 Slightly Agree	5 Agree	6 Strongly Agree
5.	I ensure that standards of excellence—not mediocrity or mere acceptability—characterize the team's work.	1 Strongly Disagree	2 Disagree	3 Slightly Disagree	4 Slightly Agree	5 Agree	6 Strongly Agree

	1	2	3	4	5	6
6. I provide a great deal of feedback to team members regarding their performance.	1 Strongly Disagree	2 Disagree	3 Slightly Disagree	4 Slightly Agree	5 Agree	6 Strongly Agree
7. I encourage team members to balance individual autonomy with interdependence among other team members.	1 Strongly Disagree	2 Disagree	3 Slightly Disagree	4 Slightly Agree	5 Agree	6 Strongly Agree
8. I help team members become at least as committed to the success of the team as to their own personal success.	1 Strongly Disagree	2 Disagree	3 Slightly Disagree	4 Slightly Agree	5 Agree	6 Strongly Agree
9. I help members learn to play roles that assist the team in accomplishing its tasks as well as building strong interpersonal relationships.	1 Strongly Disagree	2 Disagree	3 Slightly Disagree	4 Slightly Agree	5 Agree	6 Strongly Agree
10. I articulate a clear, exciting, passionate vision of what the team can achieve.	1 Strongly Disagree	2 Disagree	3 Slightly Disagree	4 Slightly Agree	5 Agree	6 Strongly Agree
11. I help team members become committed to the team vision.	1 Strongly Disagree	2 Disagree	3 Slightly Disagree	4 Slightly Agree	5 Agree	6 Strongly Agree
12. I encourage a win-win philosophy in the team; that is, when one member wins, every member wins.	1 Strongly Disagree	2 Disagree	3 Slightly Disagree	4 Slightly Agree	5 Agree	6 Strongly Agree
13. I help the team avoid "groupthink" or making the group's survival more important than accomplishing its goal.	1 Strongly Disagree	2 Disagree	3 Slightly Disagree	4 Slightly Agree	5 Agree	6 Strongly Agree
14. I use formal process management procedures to help the group become faster, more efficient, and more productive, and to prevent errors.	1 Strongly Disagree	2 Disagree	3 Slightly Disagree	4 Slightly Agree	5 Agree	6 Strongly Agree
15. I encourage team members to represent the team's vision, goals, and accomplishments to outsiders.	1 Strongly Disagree	2 Disagree	3 Slightly Disagree	4 Slightly Agree	5 Agree	6 Strongly Agree
16. I diagnose and capitalize on the team's core competence.	1 Strongly Disagree	2 Disagree	3 Slightly Disagree	4 Slightly Agree	5 Agree	6 Strongly Agree
17. I encourage the team to achieve dramatic breakthrough innovations as well as small continuous improvements.	1 Strongly Disagree	2 Disagree	3 Slightly Disagree	4 Slightly Agree	5 Agree	6 Strongly Agree
18. I help the team work toward preventing mistakes, not just correcting them after the fact.	1 Strongly Disagree	2 Disagree	3 Slightly Disagree	4 Slightly Agree	5 Agree	6 Strongly Agree

Scoring

Add your scores for each question. Your score will range between 18 and 108.

Enter your total score here: ________________

Analysis and Interpretation

The authors of this instrument propose that it assesses team development behaviors in five areas: diagnosing team development (items 1, 16); managing the forming stage (2–4); managing the storming stage (10–12, 14, 15); and managing the performing stage (5, 17, 18).

Based on a norm group of 500 business students, the following can help estimate where you are relative to others:

Total score of 95 or above	=	You are in the top quartile
72 to 94	=	You are in the second quartile.
60 to 71	=	You are in the third quartile.
Below 60	=	You are in the bottom quartile.

If you need to work on your team-building skills, see S. A. Mohrman, S. G. Cohen, and A. M. Mohrman, Jr., *Designing Team-based Organizations* (San Francisco, CA: Jossey-Bass, 1995).

Source: Prentice Hall's Self Assessment Library. 12 ed. S. P. Robbins and T. A. Judge.

Team Exercise

Designing a Dream Team

The Situation

You have just met with the CEO of X-lent, a medium-sized clothing manufacturing company with factories in China and Mexico. X-lent sells to several large stores that carry moderately priced clothing in the United States. The CEO is concerned that her customers have expressed increasing dissatisfaction with X-lent's responsiveness to their complaints about product quality, the returned-order process, and the overall treatment by the company's employees when there is any kind of customer service problem. The CEO has asked your consulting group to make recommendations for a permanent customer service "dream team," which will develop and oversee plans and policies to address these issues.

Your team must now develop the recommendations that you will then present to the CEO and the top management of X-lent. (Remember, you are not designing or discussing your own team. You are making recommendations to the CEO as to the composition of the new X-lent team to be assigned this task.)

Assignment

Your group's assignment is to develop recommendations to present to the CEO. Your recommendations should, *at the least*, address the following issues. You are free to discuss other issues you feel may be important in the development of the new X-lent team.

Justify each of your answers. Do not just give one sentence responses. Explain *why* you believe your recommendations are appropriate and critical.

1. What type of group should this be? (Formal or informal? Command? Project? Committee?)
2. Discuss the best fit characteristics for this team (for example: size, composition, roles).
3. How should norms be established? This may relate to the type of team you recommend.
4. How much conformity and cohesion will be needed for this team to perform effectively? What could X-lent do to help the team develop an appropriate level of cohesion?
5. What team competencies will be most critical?
6. How can the organization assist the team in developing its effectiveness?

Source: Grace McLaughlin, Ph.D. (2006), used with permission.

Closing Case Uniting a Class-Project Team

It is 3 PM on the afternoon before the written part of your team project is due to be turned in for your management class. You are about to meet with the other members of your team to put the finishing touches on your paper. Each of them had originally agreed to provide two full pages of material, on disk and with a hard copy for editing. As your group members arrive for the meeting, you find out that most don't have even one page prepared and that several of those pages are handwritten. You realize there is a lot to do if this paper is going to be in shape to turn in by tomorrow's deadline. The parts must be integrated, typed, edited, polished, and proofread. Also some of the exhibits, especially a couple of the more detailed ones, still must be completed in final form.

There are six of you on the team. The varsity athlete, who made some especially good contributions in one of the team's meetings, has tried to get several of the other past meetings postponed or cancelled in order to accommodate her practice schedule. Unfortunately, again today her coach has told her she must attend a mandatory practice session from 4 PM to 9 PM. The international student, who has good oral but poor written English, always volunteers to help and has strong ideas. For some reason, though, this student always feels resented by you. The two of you just don't seem to get along. The fraternity president was aware that planning for this weekend's upcoming major social event would provide a conflict for this meeting, and so he is anxious to get the meeting over with and leave as quickly as possible. Surprisingly, however, he has apparently spent a lot of time polishing and editing his part of the paper and has provided a hard copy and disk copy of it. Another member, a drama department major, has just gotten the lead in the school play and has absolutely no interest anymore in this class project. Frustrated by past missed deadlines, willing to settle for a so-so paper, and unwilling to miss tonight's rehearsal, the actor has submitted a handwritten rough draft that you consider to be too short and skimpy on necessary details. The sixth member has travel reservations for early this evening. A marketing major, this member just finished scribbling down some self-described creative ideas, doesn't care who writes the paper, so long as it gets done, and is willing to lend the team a laptop computer.

As the team leader, you wonder how things could possibly have gone so wrong and what you are going to do now. In the back of your mind, however, you keep reminding yourself that this group is going to have to work together again next week to develop an oral presentation to give in front of the class and the instructor. You and the other members of the group have discussed in the past the fact that the syllabus makes clear that the grade for the project will be based on a combination of both the written paper and the in-class presentation.

Questions

1. Considering what you know about each member of the group, what type(s) of conflict would you expect to exist in this group? How would the group's productivity likely be affected?
2. What stage of development does this group seem to be in?
3. Keeping in mind issues discussed in this chapter, what would you, as team leader, do now?

Source: Case developed by Grace McLaughlin and Lyman Porter.

12

Communication and Negotiation

Learning Objectives

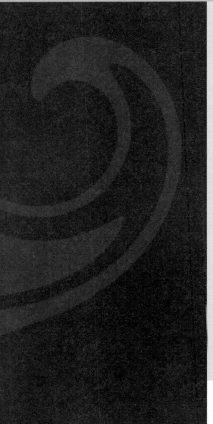

After studying this chapter, you should be able to:

- Explain why communication is vital for effective management.
- Describe the basic process of communication.
- Discuss how to choose the best mode and the appropriate media richness for effective communication.
- Analyze the impact of the organizational context on communication.
- Identify key barriers to effective communication.
- Explain various approaches to overcoming communication barriers, including intercultural barriers.
- Describe the basic process of negotiation.

Managerial Challenges from the Front Line

Name: Bridgette Chambers

Position title: Vice President of Enterprise Business Solutions, COMSYS

Alma mater: University of Houston (BS, Education); Texas A&M (MBA)

Outside work activities: Volunteering for not-for-profit organizations; family activities; golf

First job out of school: Started my own company

Business book reading now: *Competing on Analytics* by Thomas Davenport

Hero: My grandmother; former General Electric CEO Jack Welch; Alexander the Great

Motto to live by: Get it done...do it right . . . and be damn proud when you are finished with it.

What drives me: Relentless desire to always grow and accomplish the next objective

Management style: Management by objectives and accountability

Pet peeve: Second place

Bridgette Chambers, in her position as an upper-level manager at a technology services consulting firm, communicates almost constantly—in person, by telephone, and by e-mail. Hers is not a desk job. She is not sitting off by herself analyzing spreadsheets. Instead, Chambers is almost daily in the center of a whirlwind vortex of communications. As she puts it, "most of my day is spent communicating." If she were not a good communicator, she would not last very long in her type of job.

Following her graduation from college, Bridgette began her business career by becoming an entrepreneur. She started and built a small company called Trans Resolve Legal Services that she eventually sold after seven years. With that experience and background, she moved into consulting activities, such as setting up an outside sales component for a company. She subsequently managed consulting services activities for several organizations before joining her present firm, COMSYS, a $750 million publicly traded company that provides a variety of consulting and project services. Her current position is in the Enterprise Business Solutions division where she manages three different service lines: business analytics, business intelligence, and enterprise resource planning. In that role, she has eight direct reports and is responsible for more than 400 employees.

Earlier in her career, Bridgette did not always have successful communication experiences. With a low tolerance for poor performance and task failures, she was not always aware of her impact, as a leader, on others. Consequently, she sometimes created more ill will than the situation called for and certainly more than she had intended. "I failed to understand that not everyone wakes up in the morning with the same expectations of their day and objectives. I had to begin a journey of self-awareness and seek critical feedback."

Most of us, like Bridgette Chambers early in her career, take communication for granted because we do it every day. Communicating effectively, however, is not easy.[1] Accurate and persuasive communication within and between organizations, person to person, person to group, or group to group, is frequently, and sometimes unexpectedly, difficult, as the opening example demonstrates. Receivers often do not have a complete understanding of what senders mean. But the heart of **communication** is exactly that: the process of transferring information, meaning, and understanding from sender to receiver. And carrying out that process convincingly and proficiently is an absolute essential for a manager to exercise leadership. In fact, leadership is unlikely to be successful in the absence of excellent communication skills. The first step for a manager to become an outstanding leader, therefore, is to become an outstanding communicator.

communication
the process of transferring information, meaning, and understanding from sender to receiver

In this chapter, we start with an overview of the basic communication process, followed by an examination of the modes and media of communication. These topics provide a background for the next section on the organizational context of the communication process as it affects managers. Although the organization can facilitate managerial communication, it also can be one of the key sources of barriers to communication—interpersonal, organizational, and cultural—that are discussed in the following section. Then, the next section highlights some of the steps that managers can take to reduce or overcome these barriers.

The final parts of the chapter focus on one particular area of communication that is especially critical for managers—negotiation. In those sections, we discuss the impact of cultural influences on negotiation strategies and on the negotiation process itself. Throughout this chapter we need to keep in mind a basic perspective: Although communication is a universal human activity, successful communication is not habitual. It requires motivation, skill, and knowledge.

The Basic Model of Communication

How do people communicate? How do they send and receive messages? What factors can disrupt communication? Let's look first at the basic model of the communication process outlined in Exhibit 12.1.[2]

All communication involves four actions and five components. The four actions are encoding, sending, receiving, and decoding. The five components are sender, message, medium, noise, and receiver. The actions and components combine to transfer meaning from the sender to the receiver. The sender originates the message by **encoding** it, that is, by constructing the message. The message is the content of the communication. The sender then transmits the message through a **medium**. A medium is the method or means of transmission, not the message itself. Examples of media are spoken words, video, written memos, faxes, and e-mails. The receiver acquires, or receives, the message by hearing it, reading it, or having it appear on a fax or computer. The receiver then begins **decoding** the

encoding
the act of constructing a message

medium
the method or means of transmission of a message

decoding
the act of interpreting a message

EXHIBIT 12.1

Basic Communication Model

noise
interference with the transmission or decoding of a message

message, that is, interpreting it. Sometimes distractions interfere with the message; these interferences are called **noise**. Noise contributes to misinterpretations of the original message, and it is only through feedback, or verification of the original message, that communication problems can be uncovered and corrected.

The basic model of communication is fundamental and universal. That is, it occurs whenever communication takes place regardless of the culture or organization. However, although the basic acts and components of the communication process are the same everywhere, how the acts are carried out and the *nature* of the components are deeply influenced by cultural, organizational, and even personal contexts.[3] Who can send messages to whom, what kinds and what volumes of messages are sent, by what medium are messages transmitted, what sort of interference or noise is likely to occur, and what cues are available for decoding are just some of the many examples of the types of communication issues that can vary from manager to manager, from organization to organization, and from country to country.

Modes of Communication

Communication can occur in either a verbal mode or a nonverbal mode, as shown in Exhibit 12.2. Each mode has particular characteristics and related issues that managers must understand.

EXHIBIT 12.2 Modes of Communication

	VERBAL MODE (LANGUAGE USED TO CONVEY MEANING)		NONVERBAL MODE
	Oral	**Written**	
Examples	• Conversation • Speeches • Telephone calls • Videoconferences	• Letters • Memos • Reports • E-mail • Fax	• Dress • Speech intonation • Gestures • Facial expressions
Advantages	• Vivid • Stimulating • Commands attention • Difficult to ignore • Flexible • Adaptive	• Decreased misinterpretation • Precise	• Effectiveness of communication increases with congruence to oral presentation • Can emphasize meaning
Disadvantages	• Transitory • Subject to misinterpretation	• Precision loss in translation • Inflexible • Easier to ignore	• Meanings of nonverbal communication not universal

Verbal Communication

Most of us think of spoken words when we think of verbal communication. The key, however, is not that the words are spoken but that the words—language—are used to convey meaning. Consequently, when we talk about verbal communication, we mean *both* oral and written communication.

ORAL COMMUNICATION The spoken word has the potential advantages of being vivid, stimulating, and commanding. In most organizational situations, it is difficult for receivers—the listeners—to ignore either the speaker or the words spoken. Just think about the last time someone spoke to you directly. Even if you weren't interested in what the person had to say, wouldn't it have been difficult to simply ignore the person, turn, and walk away?

Also, oral communication is exceptionally flexible for both the sender and receiver. While you are speaking, you may try to make a point a certain way, but along the way change your words in order for the listener to understand you. Because oral communication is generally interactive, it can be quite responsive and adaptive to circumstances. However, this mode of communication has the major disadvantages of being transitory (unless recorded) and subject to considerable misinterpretation. Even when individuals use the same language, the subtle nuances of the spoken word may be missed or incorrect meaning attached to them. Oral communication between those whose first languages differ, as in many management situations today, simply multiplies the chances of intended meaning going awry.

WRITTEN COMMUNICATION When messages are put in writing, as in letters, memos, e-mail, and the like, the opportunities for misunderstanding the words of the sender are reduced. The receiver may still misinterpret the intended message, but there is no uncertainty about exactly what words the sender has used. In that sense, written communication has precision. However, not everyone writes well, and so greater precision does not necessarily lead to greater understanding. This is further complicated when the words need translation from one language to another. For example, Americans often write when requesting action "at your earliest convenience," meaning that the request is somewhat urgent, but Europeans frequently interpret it to mean they can respond whenever they want. Or consider how Northwest Airline's one-time slogan "Give Wings to Your Heart" was translated into Chinese: "Tie Feathers to Your Blood Pump." Because the writer (sender) does not know immediately how well or poorly the message is getting across, written communication has the disadvantage of not being very flexible. In addition, it is often not as vivid or compelling as oral communication. Although you might find it difficult to ignore someone speaking to you, it would probably be much easier to ignore a letter you received.

Nonverbal Communication

In direct interpersonal communication, nonverbal actions and behaviors often send significant messages. A whole range of actions, or lack of them, has the potential for communicating. The way you dress, speak words, use gestures, handle utensils, exhibit facial expressions, and set the physical distance to the receiver are just some of the many forms of nonverbal communication.

As a manager, keep in mind that when verbal and nonverbal messages are contradictory, receivers often give more weight to the nonverbal signals than to the words used. For example, you might say to your employees, "I have an open-door policy. Come and talk to me whenever you need to." However, if you never seem to be able to find the time to see them or rarely look up from your work when they enter your office, they will soon come to believe the nonverbal message, "I'm busy, don't bother me" rather than the verbal message, "I encourage you to talk with me at any time."

When nonverbal messages are consistent with the spoken message, the odds of effective communication taking place are increased. For example, suppose that in addition to saying you had an open-door policy, you looked up when employees entered your office, made eye contact with them, smiled, and turned away from your computer and the report on which you were working. In combination, what sort of message do you think you would be sending?

The problem for managers in many of today's organizations where they work with employees from different cultural backgrounds and often work across international borders is that there are no universal meanings to various nonverbal actions. For example, the traditional "OK" sign in the United States is a gesture for money in Japan and is a rather rude gesture in Brazil. You might think that just toning down your nonverbal gestures would be a good way to avoid inadvertent wrong messages. Such an effort would be fine in Finland, but someone in Italy or Greece might infer from your subdued, nonverbal cues that you are uninterested in the discussion. As a manager, you should learn about the nonverbal cues and gestures of countries and cultures with which you deal the most.

Media of Communication

The means of communication, or *how* information is transmitted from sender to receiver, are typically referred to as communication media (or, in the singular, medium). In organizations, there basically are a limited number of types of media that can be used. They range from the very personal and direct, face-to-face interaction to the very impersonal and indirect, bulletin-board notice. In between are telephone conversations, electronic messages, letters, memos, and reports.

Media have different sets of characteristics, such as the following:

- their personal-impersonal nature
- their speed in sending and receiving
- the availability of multiple cues to assist receivers in acquiring accurate meaning from the messages
- the opportunity to receive immediate and continuing feedback from the receiver

media richness
different media are classified as rich or lean based on their capacity to facilitate shared meaning

The term used to summarize these differences is called "**media richness**."[4] Different media are classified as rich, or lean, based on their "capacity to facilitate shared meaning."[5] (See Exhibit 12.3.) Thus, interpersonal face-to-face interactions, for example, would be regarded as rich because they provide several types of information and multiple ways to obtain mutual understanding between sender and receiver. By contrast, a general e-mail message sent to a number of receivers would be regarded as leaner because it lacks some of the features listed previously. The general principle here is that the more ambiguous and complex the issue is, the richer should be the medium of communication.[6]

Managers, consequently, should be sensitive to matching message with medium. Using face-to-face meetings to convey simple, straightforward information, such as the locations and times of future meetings, would be an unnecessary waste of a rich medium. That is, it would involve too much time and effort of both sender and receivers to obtain shared meaning of a relatively unambiguous message. On the other hand, using a memo, for example, rather than a face-to-face meeting, would probably be a poor choice for settling a serious disagreement with one's subordinates. The medium would be too lean to enable the manager to resolve a complicated, highly ambiguous matter, A Manager's Challenge, "E-mail," describes how one company dealt with the pros and cons of using the medium of e-mail. What is fastest may not be the best medium in all circumstances.

EXHIBIT 12.3

Factors Contributing to Media Richness

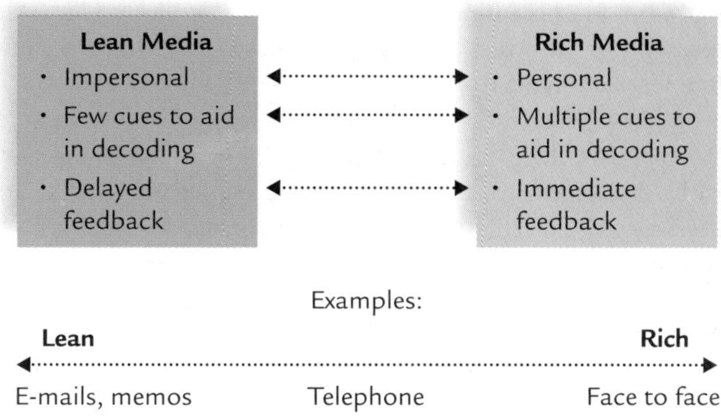

Hundreds of dispatchers at Burlington Northern Santa Fe Railway's Network Operations Center in Fort Worth, Texas, communicate constantly via the company's wireless network with locomotive crews across the country operating trains like this one. The dispatchers serve a function similar to that of air traffic controllers. Clear communication between the dispatchers and crews is imperative to prevent rail accidents.

Often, time pressures and distance make it relatively costly for a manager to use a richer rather than a leaner medium. The key point, however, if you are a manager, is to choose a medium that best suits the degree of potential ambiguity in the message, consistent with the constraints of circumstances and the resources of you and your organization. The choice of an appropriate medium should not be left to chance.

The Organizational Context of Communication

Managers do not deal with communication in the abstract. Rather, they deal with it within an organizational context. The structure and processes of organizations powerfully shape the nature and effectiveness of communication that takes place within and between them.[7] Organizations, whether businesses, hospitals, or government agencies, have a set of defining characteristics, all of which affect communication in one way or another.[8] Thus, organizations

- Are composed of individuals and groups
- Are oriented toward goals
- Have differentiated functions
- Have intended coordination
- Have continuity through time

Organizations of any size, regardless of country, are not simply a random set of individuals who by chance come together for a brief period with no purpose. The fact that they have goal orientations, structures, and coordination greatly influences the nature and amount of communication that takes place. This influence can be analyzed in terms of directions, channels, and patterns of communication.

Directions of Communication Within Organizations

Because organizations of any degree of complexity have both differentiated functions and a number of levels of positions with differing degrees of responsibility, the potential directions of communication within organizations can be classified according to the level for which a message is intended:

- **Downward communication** is sent from higher organizational levels to lower levels; for example, from the organization's top executives to its employees, or from supervisors to subordinates.

downward communication messages sent from higher organizational levels to lower levels

A MANAGER'S CHALLENGE

Technology

E-Mail: Blessing or Curse? Savior or Scourge?

The advent of e-mail in the early 1990s brought truly significant communication advantages to individuals and organizations. Almost overnight, those wishing to send written messages could do so far and wide to one person, or thousands, at virtually no cost and at almost instantaneous speed. It seemed a miracle to people who were used to communicating at a distance by postal mail or within companies by the distribution of office memoranda. Today, it's hard to imagine life without e-mail, instant messaging, or Web-conferencing. Consider: When was the last 24- or 48-hour period when you did not check your e-mail?

But, as with almost anything else in life, there are downsides as well as tremendous upsides to the use of e-mail. Who among us, for example, does not complain about being bombarded with unwanted e-mail spam? Another often-heard complaint about e-mail is that it is so easy to send e-mails, and to multiple recipients at one time, that recipients feel overwhelmed by the number of messages, many of which are seen as unnecessary. These are some of the obvious drawbacks of e-mail.

Are there also other important, intangible, and often hidden, costs to interacting by e-mail? Some companies are beginning to think so, particularly with regard to the issue of media richness. One of the major concerns is that the use of e-mail is a "lazy-person's" way to communicate when direct phone or in-person conversations would provide much richer communication. This is especially true when there are subtleties or nuances that need to be conveyed. As one manager put it, "you can't get to know someone through e-mail."

One company that recently took a step to reduce the use of casual e-mail and instead rely on relatively more person-to-person interaction was PBD Worldwide Fulfillment Services (a company providing call-center management and other services) in Alpharetta, Georgia. PBD's CEO instituted "no e-mail Fridays" and urged his employees to reduce the use of e-mail on the other days of the week. As a result, e-mail use in the company declined by over 80 percent, and, even more importantly, the company's clients have reacted positively and have increased their communications with PBD.

Easy-to-send electronic communication has both its ups and downs. Some people feel barraged by a constant onslaught of e-mails, for example. Others can't go without checking for their messages every few minutes.

"No e-mail Fridays" certainly would not work for many organizations. But one organization's need for such a policy highlights some of the unintended consequences e-mail can have. These have to be weighed against the medium's advantages. E-mail provides a great benefit—a classic case of "can't live without it"—but it is not cost-free.

Sources: D. Brady, "*!#?@ the E-mail. Can We Talk?" *Business Week*, December 4, 2006, 109; "Stoned on E-Mail," *Profit* (June 2005): 115; G. Browning, "Resolve to Develop your Email Intuition," *People Management* 11, no. 1 (2005): 102; G. Flood, "Tame the Mountain," *Information World Review 210* (2005): 18–19; S. Sweetham, "E-mail Tactics," *T&D* 60, no.1 (2006): 13.

upward communication messages sent from lower organizational levels to higher levels

lateral communication messages sent across essentially equivalent levels of an organization

- **Upward communication** is sent from lower organizational levels to higher levels; for example, from nonmanagement employees to their supervisors, or from a manager to her boss.
- **Lateral communication** is sent across equivalent levels of an organization; for example, from one clerical assistant to another, from the manager of product A to the manager of product B, or from the marketing department to the engineering design department.

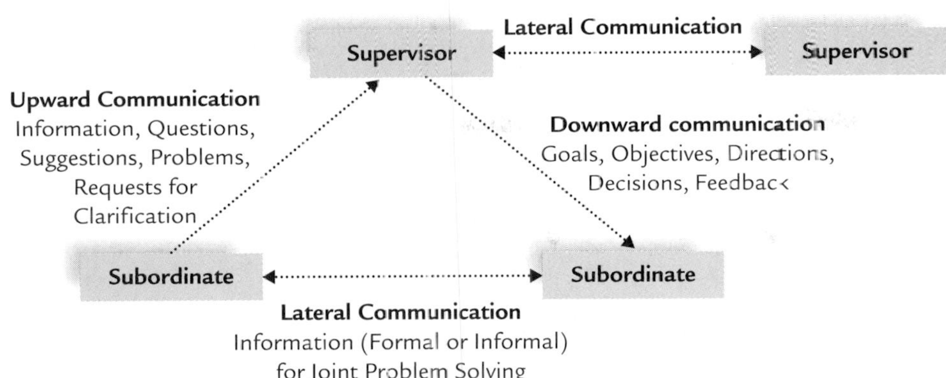

EXHIBIT 12.4

Directions of Communication within Organizations

The contents of communications within organizations usually vary according to the direction of the communication activity. As shown in Exhibit 12.4, downward communication typically involves such matters as goals, objectives, directions, decisions, and feedback. Upward communication commonly focuses on information, suggestions, questions, problems, and requests for clarification. Lateral communication is oriented toward exchanges of information—both formal and informal—that assist or affect coordination and joint problem solving.

The culture of an organization (or the culture of the country in which the organization resides) can affect the direction and nature of communication. For example, in an organization in which authority and hierarchy are stressed, upward communication might be more formal than in an organization with a more egalitarian culture. As a simple illustration, in a strongly hierarchical organization, a conversation might start with the subordinate addressing a superior several levels above as "Mr. or Ms. Jones." In many countries, such as Korea, the conversation might start by addressing the superior by his or her title, such as "Director Park." In organizations with less emphasis on hierarchy, the conversation might start by addressing the superior by his or her first name. Likewise, organizational or country culture can influence the frequency and flavor of upward communications. For example, in organizations with strong hierarchical values, upward communication tends to be less frequent.

Channels of Communication Within Organizations

Organizational channels, or routes of communication, consist of two fundamental types: formal and informal. Both types are essential for organizational functioning, and neither type can easily substitute for the other.

Formal communication channels are those that the organization authorizes, plans, and regulates and that are directly connected to its official structure. Thus, the organization's designated structure indicates the normal paths for downward, upward, and lateral formal communication. Formal communication channels (shown in Exhibit 12.5) are like highlighted roads on a map. They specify which organizational members are responsible for communicating information to levels above and below them and back and forth to adjacent units. Also, formal channels indicate the persons or positions to whom work-related messages should be sent. Formal channels can be modified, and, thus, they have some flexibility, but they can seldom be disregarded.

formal communication channels
routes that are authorized, planned, and regulated by the organization and that are directly connected to its official structure

Informal communication channels are communication routes that are not prespecified by the organization but that develop through the interpersonal activities of employees. These channels can appear, change, or disappear rapidly, depending on circumstances. However, they can also endure, especially where individuals have been working together over a period of time. If a specific pattern becomes well established, it would ordinarily be called a "network" (to be discussed later).

informal communication channels
routes that are not prespecified by the organization but that develop through typical and customary activities of people at work

Several important features of informal communication channels should be noted:

- They tend to operate more laterally than vertically compared to formal channels (see Exhibit 12.6) because they are not designated by the organization and its top officials.

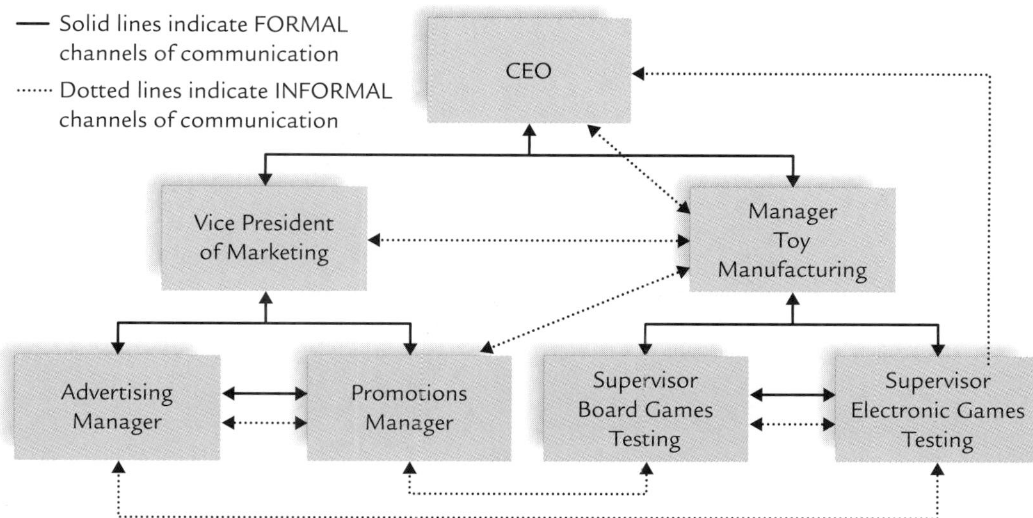

EXHIBIT 12.5

Formal and Informal Channels of Communication in Organizations

- Second, information flowing through informal channels often moves extremely fast, principally because senders are highly motivated to pass information on. The so-called "grapevine" is a classic example.[9] In recent years, the communication capabilities of the Internet have facilitated the emergence of large-scale, word-of-mouth networks. Some researchers propose that these mechanisms are poised to have a significant impact on the informal information flow in organizations.[10]
- A third feature is that informal channels carry work-related as well as nonwork information. Just because channels are informal does not mean that only gossip and other messages unrelated to jobs and tasks are carried by them. Crucial work-related information is frequently communicated this way as well. The downside is that some of the messages passed through informal channels are inaccurate or focus only on negative information. However—and this is important to emphasize—few organizations could exist for very long if they had to rely only on formal communication channels!

Patterns of Organizational Communication

communication networks identifiable patterns of communication within and between organizations, whether using formal or informal channels

Identifiable patterns of communication that occur with some regularity within and between organizations, whether using formal or informal channels, are typically called **communication networks**. Put another way, communication networks are stable systems of interconnections; networks involve consistent linkages between particular

EXHIBIT 12.6

Characteristics of Formal and Informal Communication Channels

Formal Communication Channels	Informal Communication Channels
• Authorized, planned, and regulated by the organization • Reflect the organization's formal structure • Define who has responsibility for information dissemination and indicate the proper recipients of work-related information • May be modified by the organization • Minor to severe consequences for ignoring them	• Develop through interpersonal activities of organization members • Not specified by the organization • May be short-lived or long-lasting • Are more often lateral than vertical • Information flow can be very fast • Used for both work-related and nonwork information

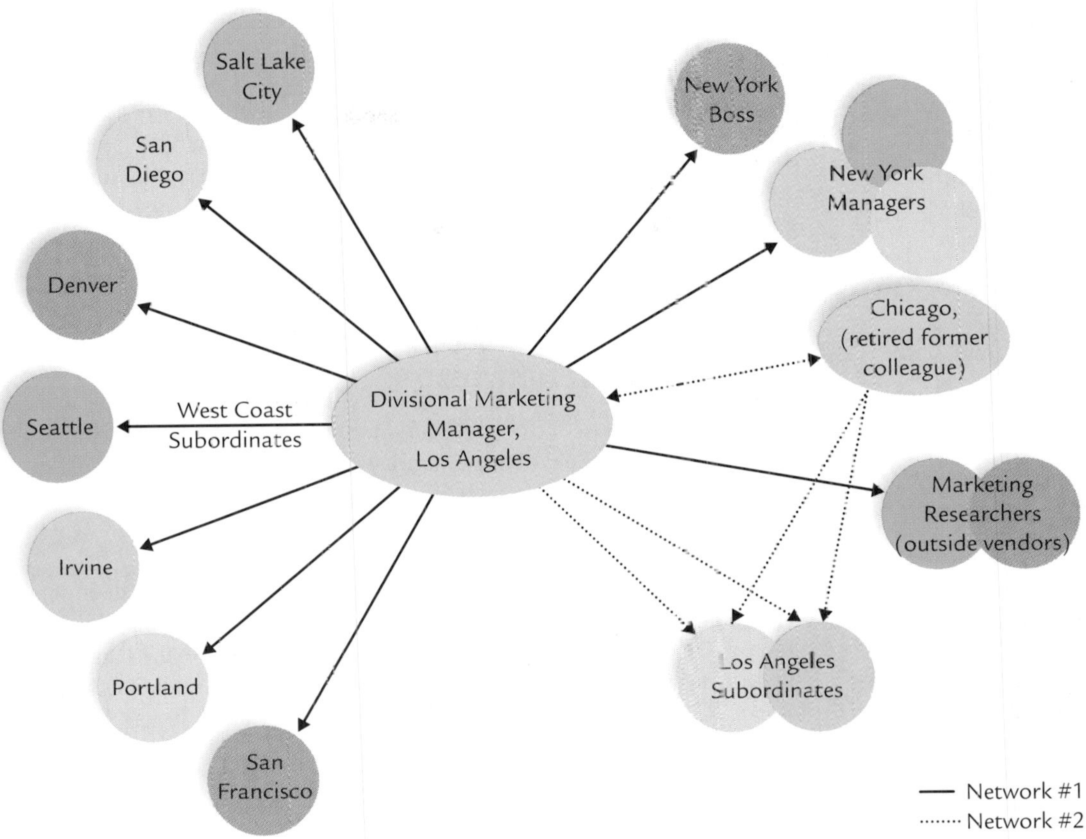

EXHIBIT 12.7

Examples of Two Organizational Communication Networks

sets of senders and receivers. For example, as shown in Exhibit 12.7, a middle-level divisional marketing manager in Los Angeles might have a particular network that involves her boss in New York, three key managers in other departments in the company's New York headquarters, her seven subordinates located in major Western cities, and two outside vendors of market research data. Another network for the same manager might involve two lower-level managers in other units in the firm's Los Angeles office and their former colleague and old friend who is now a sales supervisor in Chicago and who has access to inside information on how well new marketing approaches are working in that region.

An example of a larger, more organization-wide network would be the Coca-Cola Company's communication relationships between its headquarters in Atlanta and its bottlers and distributors around the world. Networks can also be formed across organizations as well as within. This is what often happens, for example, when sets of managers from two companies have to work together on issues that arise in an international joint venture.[11]

The importance of communication networks to managers is that they can provide significant and regular information (both of the formal and informal type) that might otherwise take a much longer time to obtain. This is especially so if various communication links had to be set up "from scratch" each time a new issue or problem came up. Also, when managers are members of established networks, it can make it easier for them to influence the other people or groups involved in the networks. Consequently, for both of these reasons, managers need to pay particular attention to what networks they can, and want to, be a part of, and to the composition of those networks. It is no accident that the term **networking** has come to signify a process that has the potential for gaining advantages for a manager (or anyone for that matter). It helps to have one or more sets of individuals with whom one can interact easily and regularly, thereby building a sense of confidence and trust.

networking
a process of developing regular patterns of communication with particular individuals or groups to send and receive information

In traditional Western organizations, it has always been relatively easy for men in management positions to establish various networks with other men (thus providing the basis for the phrase "old boys network"). However, at least until very recently, it's been much harder for women and members of underrepresented ethnic groups to establish similar helpful networks. Research suggests that organizational networks involving individuals from these latter groups are different in terms of both their composition and relationships from the traditional networks composed primarily of white males.[12] It does not make such networks any less important or useful to managers from these groups, but does serve to emphasize that network patterns of communication can vary based on a number of different situational circumstances, including the age, gender, and ethnicity of the individuals involved.

Barriers to Communication

Barriers that interfere with the communication process can arise from several different sources, including interpersonal, organizational, and cultural sources, as illustrated in Exhibit 12.8. Next, we discuss each of these sources.

Interpersonal Barriers

Obstacles to interpersonal communication can occur with either the sender or the receiver. The burden is simultaneously on both the sender and the receiver to ensure that accurate communication occurs. It is, however, the sender's obligation to choose the language and words—to encode the message—with the greatest possible precision. This is the lesson that Bridgette Chambers, discussed at the beginning of the chapter, had to learn. Precision is especially

EXHIBIT 12.8

Barriers of Communication

Level	Origin of Barrier	Affects Communication Between:
Interpersonal	• Selective perception • Frame of reference • Individual differences • Emotion • Language • Nonverbal cues	• Individuals or groups
Organizational	• Hierarchical (barriers resulting from formal structure) • Functional (barriers resulting from differences between functional departments)	• Individuals and/or groups within an organization • Individuals and/or groups in different organizations
Cultural	• Language • High- or low-context culture • Stereotyping • Ethnocentrism • Cultural distance	• Individuals or groups in different organizations with different national cultures • Individuals or groups from different organizational cultures • Individuals or groups from diverse cultural backgrounds within an organization

important if the sender is trying to persuade the receiver to do something in a language or communication style different from what the receiver prefers. For example, if you are trying to convince your boss to authorize a new project, and you use an informal style and choice of words, she may not be receptive to your request if she prefers a more formal approach. You will probably need to adjust your communication style to be effective in this case.

The receiver, of course, often can be the source of communication breakdowns. For example, the receiver might have a **selective perception** problem.[13] That is, the receiver might unintentionally screen out some parts of the intended message because it contradicts her beliefs or desires. For example, you might stress the increased productivity that would result from a proposed project, but your boss is focusing on the estimated cost of the project. Although selective perception is a natural human tendency, it hinders accurate communication, especially when sensitive or highly important topics are being discussed. Another way to state this point is that individuals tend to adopt **frames of reference**, or simplified ways of interpreting messages, that help them make sense of complex communications, but these shortcuts may prevent the intended message from being received.[14]

selective perception the process of screening out some parts of an intended message because they contradict our beliefs or desires

frames of reference existing sets of attitudes that provide quick ways of interpreting complex messages

Individual differences between senders and receivers in terms of such basic characteristics as their age, gender, ethnicity, or level of education sometimes can be the source of communication barriers. In general, it would be reasonable to assume that the fewer the differences the two parties have with regard to these kinds of attributes, the lower their communication barriers are. Research shows that even when these differences exist, they usually don't seriously impede good communication.[15] It is more a matter of a manager being very alert to the *possibility* that individual differences in sender and receiver characteristics could impose a significant obstacle to good communication, rather than assuming it will never be a barrier or, conversely, will always be a barrier.

Emotions can be another barrier.[16] How the receiver feels at the time can influence what gets heard or how it gets interpreted. You certainly have had the experience of feeling that someone was "touchy" or overly sensitive when responding to your message. As a consequence, comments that normally would be taken as mere statements get interpreted as criticisms.

Language can also be a barrier. Even for people who speak the same language, a given word or set of words can mean different things to different people.[17] For example, saying, "That's a bad haircut" to a 50-year-old means something completely different than if it were said to a 15-year-old. The 50-year-old will likely interpret the words to mean that the barber did a poor job. The 15-year-old will likely take the statement to mean he looks "cool."

Nonverbal cues can also be barriers to effective communication in two basic ways. First, people can send nonverbal signals without being aware of them, and, therefore, create unintentional consequences.[18] For example, you might make minimal eye contact with your boss while trying to convince her to approve your proposed project, and yet be unaware that you are doing so. Your boss might think the project has merit but interprets your low level of eye contact as an indication that you are hiding something. She might then reject a project that she would otherwise have authorized. Second, as we have already touched on, nonverbal cues can mean different things to different people.[19] A weak handshake might indicate politeness in Indonesia but communicate a lack of confidence in Texas.

See the accompanying "Manager's Challenge" for an example of how multiple communication barriers, including selective perception, differing frames of reference, and unintended nonverbal cues led to the sending of mixed messages.

Organizational Barriers

Just as interpersonal barriers can limit communication, so can organizational barriers. Organizational barriers can interfere with communication between individuals or groups within the same organization, between individuals or groups from two different organizations, or between entire organizations. The basis of these barriers lies within the hierarchical structure of organizations. All organizations of any complexity have specialized functions and more than one level of authority. This specialization creates a situation that is ripe for communication difficulties. For example, one person might come from marketing and the other from R&D. The person in marketing might think nothing of exaggerating whereas the person from R&D might always understate her points. Consequently, the marketer might

A MANAGER'S CHALLENGE

Communications

Communication Confusion

It was a car lover's dream. Two brothers, Jack and John Goudy, left their desk jobs to open their own auto repair shop. At first, just the two brothers did brake jobs and replaced exhaust systems. Then, as business grew, they hired a few workers and moved to a larger shop. Within a decade, Two J's Auto Repair was cranking in sales of half a million dollars per year, but then those sales reached a plateau and gradually began to decline. So John, who was in charge of sales and accounting, searched for a new way to improve business. He found it by using technology. John began integrating cutting-edge technology into the shop's office operations. But he had to convince his workers, including Jack, who spent more time in the shop than in the office, that his strategy for rebuilding Two J's would be successful.

John convened a staff meeting to communicate his new strategy to the employees. Armed with graphs and charts, he talked about profit sharing, employee involvement, and state-of-the-art technology. "From today on, we're a completely different business," he predicted. He did not know how prophetic that statement would prove to be. John's audience did not share his enthusiasm; in fact, they did not understand his message at all because they had received no previous training in the areas of finance, human resources, or the use of technology. They didn't understand the vocabulary he used or the ideas he was presenting. "It was a sea of blank faces with an occasional mutter here and there," John recalls. Thus, the flow of miscommunication at Two J's began.

John purchased a new computerized information system, which reduced the amount of paper communication generated by the office. But employees eventually discovered that the original estimates and the final invoices did not match each other, which caused them to believe that he was withholding work hours—and pay. Additionally, although John had provided his employees with an elaborate explanation of the profit-sharing plan (which they did not understand), they were skeptical of it because of mixed messages he sent: John often groaned about poor profits but would suddenly arrive at work driving a new sports car. Sensing declining morale, John started to hold daily "release meetings," designed to let employees voice their frustrations and concerns. But even these backfired. "John talked about working together like a football team," says one employee. But the meetings quickly dissolved into lectures. "John talked, we listened." Another employee observes, "It was clear John didn't care much about what we thought. He was too excited about his big ideas."

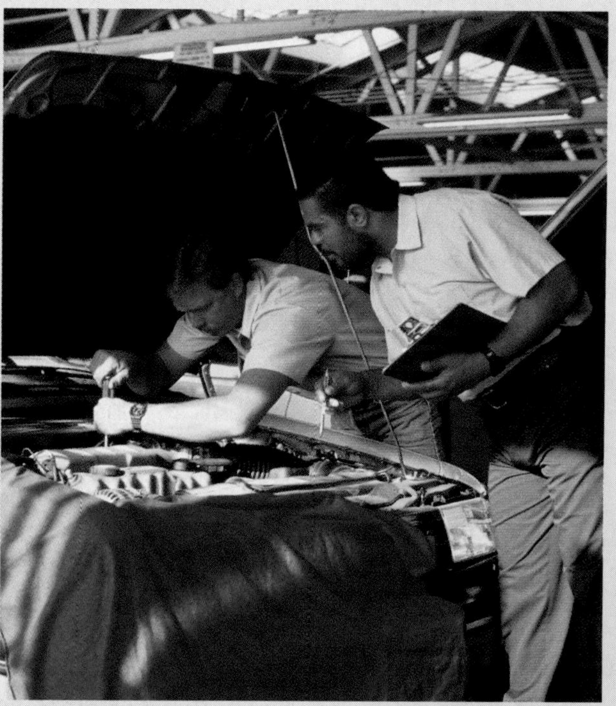

When Jack and John Goudy left their desk jobs to open their auto repair shop, it seemed like a car lover's dream. But poor communication between the two and their staff members turned their one-time dream into a nightmare. Fortunately, they realized their "failure to communicate" and were able to improve their situation.

Finally, despite John's efforts to attract new customers and provide better, faster repairs through technology, workers began to leave the shop for jobs with other companies. At first, he did not understand what had gone so wrong. He had not realized how grueling running his own business could be. He also knew that he was not a strong communicator. "Every day there were questions," he comments. "After a while, they just ground me down." When the company hit rock bottom, John started to get the message. He began to recognize the importance of communication—not only with customers, but with his own workers—and proceeded to make small changes. "Now [when I attend staff meetings], I bring a yellow pad, scribble, and listen."

Source : E. Conlin, "Company Profile: Collision Course," *Inc.*, December 1992, 132–142.

see the R&D employee as unimaginative and boring, whereas the R&D employee might view the marketer as superficial and careless. In addition, the two parties might come from different levels in the organization: A senior executive is likely to expect an explanation of how a proposed project broadly impacts the organization whereas a junior technical expert might be more likely to focus on the detailed schedule of the project.

Cultural Barriers

Communication and culture are tightly intertwined. Culture cannot exist without communication, and human communication only occurs within a cultural context. Since the act of communicating is so closely connected to the surrounding environment, culture can ease or hinder it. Thus, similarity in culture between senders and receivers facilitates successful communication—the intended meaning of a message has a higher probability of getting transferred if the sender and receiver share the same culture. The greater the cultural differences between sender and receiver, the greater the difficulty in communicating you should expect. Therefore, other things being equal, it should be easier, for example, for an American manager to communicate with an Australian subordinate than with a Greek subordinate. Or, for example, consider the differences of what "yes" means in two divergent cultures, India and the United States: An Indian manager working for Infosys in Bangalore noted that: "Indians have a difficult time saying no or that you're doing it the wrong way. Indians are more hierarchical and might not say anything unless asked." Thus, some American managers have observed that when Indians say "yes" to a request or a directive, they mean they will attempt to do it, not that it will necessarily get done or that they will take responsibility for it if it does not get done.[20]

Even small and relatively subtle differences between cultures, however, can impede communication, as Jeff Skoll, a Canadian, found out. Skoll, the CEO of a film company and formerly the first president of eBay, recalled that "the transition from the Canadian to the U.S. workplace was really an eye-opener. I found the Canadian way to be more subdued, polite, and . . . more indirect. In the U.S. . . . it turned out that such an approach was no longer effective. Not saying what you want to say out of regard for politeness or sensitivity doesn't seem to work as well here."[21]

Organizational cultures can also differ. The industry of an organization, for example, can influence its internal culture. Therefore, it is more likely that an executive at Warner Brothers could communicate successfully with an executive at Disney than with an executive at Exxon. It is not that extreme cultural differences prevent good communication; rather, the possibilities for breakdowns in communication increase in proportion to the degree of differences in the background and customs of the two parties.

The extent to which a sender and receiver differ in a high-context or low-context communication style also significantly influences the effectiveness of the communication. As we discussed in Chapter 3, individuals in high-context cultures tend to pay great attention to the situational factors surrounding the communication process and as a consequence substantially alter what they say and how they say it based on the context.[22] (See Exhibit 12.9.) Individuals in low-context cultures tend to pay less attention to the context and so make fewer and smaller adjustments from situation to situation.[23] Although the greatest differences in high and low context occur across countries, there are also such differences across organizations. For example, Japan is a high-context culture that has three distinct levels of language that a speaker uses depending on his or her status compared with that of the listener. Thus, there are actually five different words for "you" that are used depending on relative rank and status. However, even within Japan, communication is much more high context at Mitsubishi Heavy Industries than at Nintendo.

What is most problematic when individuals from high- and low-context cultures communicate with one another is that each often forms negative interpretations about the other's communication approach. Individuals from low-context cultures will tend to believe the wide swings in words and style indicative of people from high-context cultures is evidence of insincerity, hypocrisy, and even instability. These interpretations make trust difficult, and at the extreme, can make effective communication impossible. On the other hand, individuals from high-context cultures view the lack of change in communication style of individuals from low-context cultures as evidence of immaturity, selfishness, or lack of sophistication.

EXHIBIT 12.9

Communication Differences in High- and Low-Context Cultures

Source: www.crwflags.com/flow/flags.

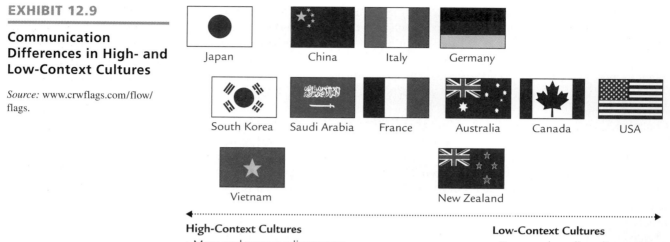

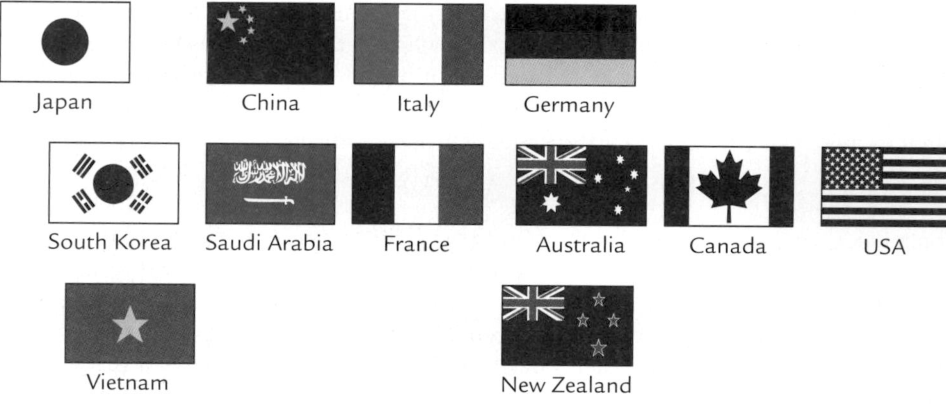

High-Context Cultures
- More and greater adjustments in messages
- Rank of receiver will probably affect message and medium
- Nonverbal communication cues may be very important
- Medium may be as important as message

Low-Context Cultures
- Fewer and smaller adjustments in messages
- Rank of receiver may or may not affect message or medium
- Nonverbal communication cues not as important
- Message is more important than medium

In Japan, managers are taught that to communicate effectively, you should "say what you mean, and mean what you say."[24] Vague directives and instructions are seen as a sign of poor communication skills. The assumption, therefore, is that the burden of proof for effective communication is on the speaker. In contrast, in cultures such as those in Arabic countries and in Latin America, the assumption is that both the speaker and the listener share the burden for communicating effectively. In cultures in which the speaker and listener both share communication responsibilities, the chances of unpleasant encounters, direct confrontations, and disagreements tend to decrease.

ethnocentrism
the belief in the superiority and importance of one's own group

Probably the greatest single cultural barrier that can affect communication across different departmental, organizational, regional, or national cultures is ethnocentrism.[25] **Ethnocentrism** is the belief in the superiority of one's own group and the related tendency to view others in terms of the values of one's own group. Ethnocentrism leads individuals to divide their interpersonal worlds into in-groups and out-groups. As we discussed in Chapter 11, in-groups are groups of people with whom you identify and about whom you care.[26] Members of the in-group tend to be trusted, listened to, and have information shared with them. Members of out-groups tend to be viewed with skepticism, if not suspicion, and are not given full information. This type of behavior exists in organizations as well as in interpersonal interactions. When British European Airways merged with British Overseas Airways Corporation some years ago to form British Airways, the ethnocentric orientation of each side almost led to the bankruptcy of the merged unit, which lost nearly $1 billion before the communication barriers were overcome.

stereotyping
the tendency to oversimplify and generalize about groups of people

Another cross-cultural barrier to communication closely related to ethnocentrism is **stereotyping**, the tendency to oversimplify and generalize about groups of people. The more firmly held the stereotype by a communicator, the harder it becomes for the person to overcome preconceived expectations and focus on the specifics of the message being sent or received. Stereotyping occurs both within and between cultures, and, thus, it affects communication in virtually all organizational settings. For example, suppose you are a technical service manager in a software company, and the president has a definite stereotype of people in your position. Generally, the president sees technical service managers as focused on details and unable to see the big picture. With a strong stereotype of this sort, the president might not recognize that you understand and are considering the competitive implications (not just the technical ones) of a new software tool.

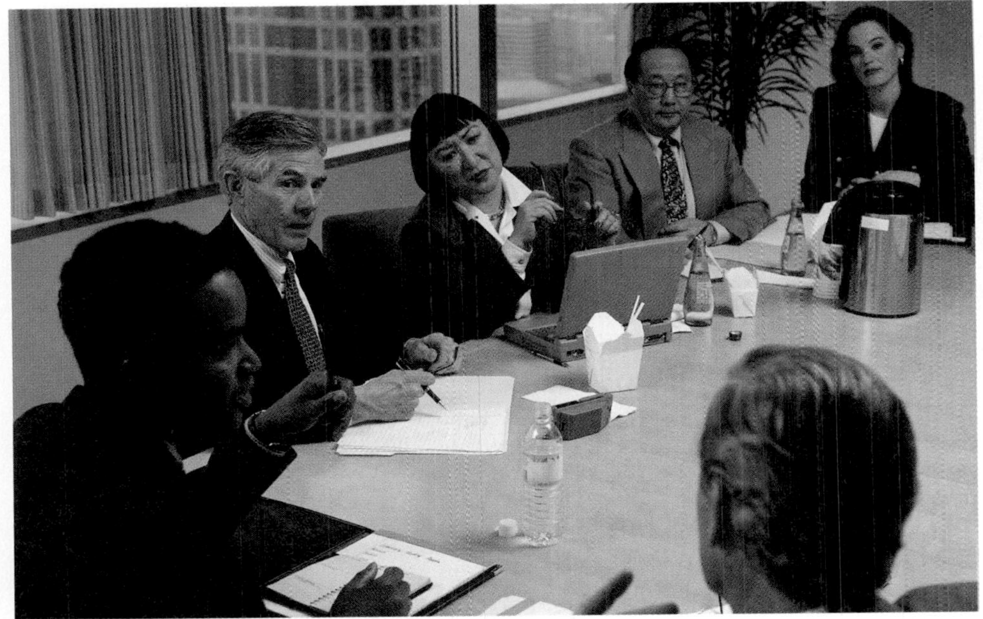

Cross-cultural communication problems can stem from language differences, but more subtle problems occur because of cultural differences and biases such as stereotyping *(the tendency to oversimplify and generalize about groups of people) and* ethnocentrism *(the belief that one's own culture, or group, is superior).*

A third major cultural barrier to communication can be labeled **cultural distance**.[27] This concept refers to the overall difference between two cultures' basic characteristics, such as their language, level of economic development, and entrenched traditions and customs. Cultural distance was illustrated by a study that gathered 21 senior executives from major corporations in Japan, the United States, Brazil, the United Kingdom, and India for a five-week period of cultural exploration. The executives attended lectures and seminars, built rafts and climbed cliffs together, and even traveled as part of fact-finding teams to one another's countries. Nevertheless, observers reported that communication remained a problem the entire five weeks.[28] Although much of the difficulty came from obvious language differences, a more subtle difficulty came from cultural differences. Many of the Japanese managers, attempting to fit in, adopted American nicknames, but they actually hated being called by them. The Americans couldn't understand why the Japanese were so quiet, not realizing that they felt that it was unwise to speak first at a meeting. The more senior the Japanese executive, the more he listens, and the executives on this trip were quite senior.

cultural distance
the overall difference between two cultures' basic characteristics such as language, level of economic development, and traditions and customs

Similarly, a development project undertaken by Alcan Aluminum Ltd. of Canada and the Chinese National Nonferrous Corporation brought together managers from both firms to learn more about each other's cultures. Even though a set of managers from China spent a whole year in Canada studying North American business methods, good communication remained an elusive goal throughout the period for both sides.[29] Examples such as these emphasize that the degree of cultural distance between people from different nationalities represents a potentially difficult communication barrier to overcome. The severity of the problem should not be underestimated.

Improving Your Communication Skills

The various barriers discussed in the preceding section can interfere with effective communication, but there are ways to deal with—or overcome—them, and improve your communication capabilities. How important is it for you to have a commitment to developing good communication skills? Consider this: According to a Graduate Management Admission Council (GMAC) Corporate Recruiters survey, recruiters said they were especially eager to find MBAs whose "soft" skills—intangible qualities such as leadership potential and communication expertise—are strong.[30] Similarly, the *Wall Street Journal*/Harris Interactive survey of recruiters found communication skills to be among those attributes of graduates most sought after.[31] As a *Wall Street Journal* article once put it: "Interpersonal communication . . . skills are what corporate recruiters crave most but find most elusive in MBA graduates."[32]

Given the obvious importance of this topic, in the remainder of this section we discuss some of the most essential approaches that are necessary for you to consider if you want to improve your communication abilities as a manager in organizations.

Improving Your Listening Skills

When it comes to improving one's communication skills, particularly verbal communication skills, most people first think of improving their speaking or writing skills. The fact, is, however, that it is also critical to do a better job of listening—an often neglected skill. It is typically overlooked as a communication skill because it is assumed to be so easy, whereas speaking and writing well are considered to be more difficult skills to master. Becoming a good listener, however, is not something to take for granted.[33]

LISTENING RATHER THAN TALKING YOURSELF The simple act of not always talking, but, instead, concentrating on listening to the other person is one way to improve your listening skills. Even those employed as recruitment interviewers sometimes lose sight of this basic principle. As David Ibarra, the director of talent acquisition for the health insurance company Well Point, has stated: "The most common mistake made by interviewers [is talking rather than listening]. You leave an interview not knowing who the candidate really is."[34]

BE MORE OPEN-MINDED Stereotyping, ethnocentricity, rigid frames of reference, and selective listening can all become barriers to comprehending the intended message of a sender. Consequently, one of the first things you should do to enhance your listening skills is to develop a greater awareness of your personal tendencies with regard to these barriers. Once you have a better awareness of these tendencies, you can monitor and control them during conversations. Part of the reason for direct and conscious attention to this area is that most people speak at about 120 words per minute and yet can listen at about a rate of 1,000 words per minute.[35] This creates the opportunity for our mind to wander or make judgments about what we are hearing. These tendencies then can take over and distort how we interpret what we hear.

empathy
the ability to put yourself in someone else's place and to understand his or her feelings, situations, and motives

DEVELOP EMPATHY Once you've examined your communication tendencies, the next step is developing empathy. **Empathy** is identifying with and understanding the other person's feelings, situation, and motives. To some extent, this requires thinking about the situation of other people, an activity that Bridgette Chambers had to learn to emphasize. What are their feelings relative to the topic at hand? What are their motivations? Why are they talking about what they are? These and other questions can help you enhance your understanding of the personal context of the message being sent.

LISTEN ACTIVELY The next step to improving communication is to take actions to ensure that you—the receiver—hear and understand what the sender is trying to communicate. In conversations, making eye contact is a good way to help speakers feel comfortable and convinced that you are sincerely interested in understanding what they have to say. It is important to focus on the content of the message being sent regardless of the style of its delivery. Even if people are not choosing the best words or are making grammatical errors, they may have something quite valuable to communicate. Focusing on style over substance can cause the value of the message to be missed. To make sure you understand what is being said, ask clarifying questions. Also, even when you think you have understood the message, it is a good idea to paraphrase, that is, restate what you think the message is. This can be put in the form of a question or statement. For example, you could ask, "So are you saying that . . .?" or you can put it more directly by saying something such as, "What I understand you to be saying is . . ."

OBSERVE NONVERBAL CUES As we discussed earlier in this chapter, observing nonverbal cues is vital to effective communication.[36] Listening more open-mindedly and actively to the words is only part of the task. You also need to concentrate on picking up on nonverbal signals. In cross-cultural settings, this means that you need to remember that a gesture or expression can have different meanings in different cultures. There is little substitute for learning about the nonverbal cues and gestures of the culture of those with whom you will be interacting.

Improving Your Sending Skills

There are many situations in which you will be the sender of a message. Effective communication can be enhanced by developing better sending skills.

SIMPLIFY YOUR LANGUAGE One of the first things a sender can do to enhance communication is to simplify the language in the message. Clearly, what is simple will vary depending on the audience. Simplifying may involve eliminating jargon that may not be familiar to all members of the audience. It may also involve choosing more succinct and active words and shorter sentences. Perhaps the best clue for spotting complicated and passive language is excessive use of prepositions. The more prepositions in a sentence, the higher the likelihood that the language could be simplified and the message could be stated more directly.

ORGANIZE YOUR WRITING Executives consistently complain about the poor writing skills of new managers.[37] Their complaints lie not in spelling or grammar mistakes, though clearly these should be eliminated, but in the lack of logical thought processes. As a manager, you are likely to write more reports and memos than you may want, and the effectiveness of those written communications will have an important impact on your career. Consequently, developing good writing skills is vital to being an effective manager. Nothing substitutes for practice.

UNDERSTAND YOUR AUDIENCE Perhaps the single best thing a sender can do to enhance the effectiveness of communications is to understand the audience.[38] For example, consider the following questions, which come from the material we have covered thus far in the chapter:

- What is the direction of the communication (up, lateral, or down), and does the receiver have any expectations concerning this type of communication?
- Is the communication formal or informal, and how should it be structured to have the intended impact on the receiver?
- Are there expectations from the receiver about the explicitness or implicitness of the message you want to send?
- Does the receiver have any biases for or against certain modes of communication (e.g., for or against e-mail, face-to-face conversations, and so on)?

If you do not understand the person or persons to whom you are sending a message, it is almost impossible to answer these questions. Knowing your audience is critical to improving your sending skills, particularly in cross-cultural settings. Exhibit 12.10 lists some tips to improve your cross-cultural communication.

Organization-Level Improvements in Communication

Organizations can take steps to change their policies and methods for how and when managers should communicate. Unfortunately, guidelines for this more structural approach are not as well developed as those for individual managers. A study of research and development laboratories within 14 large multinational firms, however, provides some suggestions.[39] The study produced strong evidence for the importance of **gatekeepers**, or so-called "boundary-spanning" individuals who are at the communication interface between separate organizations or between units within an organization. Large companies especially need to be able to structure the activities of gatekeepers to maximize their usefulness to the communication process and to make sure that the most critical information is both sent and received. Findings from the study indicated that communication could be improved by implementing rules and procedures that increased formal communication, replacing some face-to-face communication with electronic communication, developing particular communication networks, and even creating a centralized office to manage communication activities.

gatekeepers
individuals who are at the communication interface between separate organizations or between different units within an organization

EXHIBIT 12.10

Tips on Being a More Effective Cross-Cultural Communicator

1. Study general principles that apply to all types of intercultural communication.
2. Learn about the fundamental characteristics of the other cultures with which you will be working.
3. For high-context cultures, learn as many details in advance about the target organization(s) and their specific individual representatives.
4. For high-context cultures, use at least a few words or phrases in the listener's language.
5. For high-context cultures, be especially careful about body language and tone of voice.
6. For low-context cultures, organize written communications so that the major points are immediately and directly stated.
7. Study and respect communicators' preference for greater degrees of formality, especially compared with the typical American approach of casual informality.

Communication and Negotiation

negotiation
the process of conferring to arrive at an agreement between different parties, each with its own interests and preferences

In the last sections of this chapter, we focus on one particular type of communication that is becoming especially crucial for a manager to master—namely, negotiation. **Negotiation** can be thought of as the process of conferring to arrive at an agreement between two parties, each with its own interests and preferences. The purpose of negotiation is to see whether the two parties can arrive at an agreement that serves their mutual interests. Since reaching an agreement inherently involves communication, negotiation and communication are inseparably linked.

Why Managers Need Good Negotiation Skills

Today's managers often find themselves in the role of negotiator. This can occur in different types of situations. One type is during the ongoing day-to-day activities of the manager's organizational unit, where there is a need to negotiate a settlement or resolution of some kind of disagreement. This could be a disagreement between the manager and his own boss, between the manager and another manager from a different unit, or between the manager and one or more of his subordinates. Disagreements can also occur between subordinates or between entire departments. Typically, in these kinds of circumstances the manager would function as an individual negotiator.

The other basic type of negotiation situation in which managers could find themselves would be where they are part of a formally appointed negotiating team representing their unit or organization in discussions with representatives from another unit or organization. In either kind of negotiating situation, managers are taking on the role of facilitator—attempting to ensure that all parties can agree on a common course of action. Also, regardless of the specific features of the situation, the principles of effective approaches to negotiation can help settle any kind of disagreements that a manager might encounter—inside or outside an organization.

Achieving More Effective Negotiations

negotiation "interests"
a party's or parties' concerns and desires—in other words, what they want

negotiation "positions"
a party's or parties' stance regarding their interests

There are several ways managers can increase their chances of achieving successful negotiation outcomes. (See Exhibit 12.11.) One especially useful principle to keep in mind when serving as a negotiator is to focus on the two parties' *interests*, not their positions.[40] **Interests** are a party's concerns and desires—what they want, in other words. **Positions**, on the other hand, are a party's stance regarding those interests. Thus, an interest, for example, would be the desire by a subordinate to receive a specific challenging new assignment. A position, in this example, would be a statement by the subordinate that "I am the one who should receive this new sales territory because. . . ." It is easier to get agreement on interests instead of positions because: (a) for a given interest there are probably several possible positions that could satisfy it; and (b) behind two opposed

Less Effective	More Effective
• Positions	• Interests
• People Involved	• Problem/Issue
• Maintaining/Increasing Competition (Win/Lose Focus)	• Decreasing/Lessening Competition (Collaborative Focus)

EXHIBIT 12.11

Improving Effectiveness of Negotiations

positions, there are likely to be at least some interests of the two parties that are shared rather than in direct conflict with one another.[41] If these mutually compatible interests can be identified, the chances of reaching an acceptable conclusion to the negotiation are increased.

In the previous example, even though the boss is not able to give the desired new sales territory to this particular subordinate, a common interest may be identified—such as the desire of both parties to see that the subordinate's good performance in the past is rewarded with some other kind of challenging new assignment in the future—even though it can't be this particular assignment now.

A second, sound principle for negotiations (again, see Exhibit 12.11) is to focus on the problem or issue, rather than on the people involved, as we discussed in the section on conflict in Chapter 11. The key point here is that a negotiator should endeavor to concentrate on the substance of the disagreement rather than on who is doing the disagreeing or what they are like as people. This principle is well summarized in the advice to negotiators to "be hard on the problem, soft on the people."[42]

Another helpful principle for managers who are involved in negotiation (Exhibit 12.11) is to try to lessen the competition between the two parties (an "I win, you lose" situation) by establishing an atmosphere of collaboration (a "we all win" situation). **Collaboration** is an attempt to get both parties to attack a problem and solve it together, not have one party defeat the other, as in a win-lose athletic contest. Thus, both parties should be encouraged to develop creative solutions that increase the total amount of resources available to be shared or divided by the two parties.

collaboration
part of negotiation in which parties work together to attack and solve a problem

Finally, if managers find that negotiations are extremely complex, and the parties seem emotionally invested in the outcome, they can often request intervention by a neutral third party. Sometimes disinterested managers within the organization can be asked to serve in this role. The third-party negotiator can serve the role of judge, mediator, or devil's advocate. In the role of a judge, the manager handles negotiations and decides on the best possible course of action, which the parties then agree to follow. In mediation, the manager controls the negotiation process, but someone else makes the final decision based on the arguments presented—possibly a senior executive in the organization. As we have discussed in other chapters, a devil's advocate asks questions that may oppose the positions of both parties. The attempt here is for all parties to think about positions that they may not originally have considered.

Key Factors in Cross-National Negotiations

As noted earlier, as a manager you may find yourself a member of negotiating teams. With the greater frequency of international assignments, this may particularly be the case when working in situations that require negotiations across national borders. Because of the advances in transportation and communication technologies, along with expanding capital flows worldwide, organizations are engaging in ever-larger amounts of foreign trade and international business partnerships. Together, all this activity increases the importance of your being able to negotiate successfully in cross-national circumstances as well as in your own organization or country. There are three principal variables that determine the outcome of negotiations in general, and especially in these kinds of cross-national situations: the people involved, the situation, and the process itself.[43]

PEOPLE Despite some cultural differences in preferred negotiator characteristics, there seem to be preferred negotiator traits that are fairly universal. They include good listening skills, a strong orientation toward people, and high self-esteem, among others.[44] In

U.S. Managers	Japanese Managers	Chinese Managers (Taiwan)	Brazilian Managers
1. Preparation and planning skill[a]	1. Dedication to job	1. Persistence and determination	1. Preparation and planning skill
2. Thinking under pressure	2. Ability to perceive and exploit power	2. Ability to with respect and confidence	2. Thinking under pressure
3. Judgment and intelligence	3. Ability to win respect and confidence	3. Preparation and planning skill	3. Judgment and intelligence
4. Verbal expressiveness	4. Integrity	4. Product knowledge	4. Verbal expressiveness
5. Product knowledge	5. Listening skill	5. Interesting	5. Product knowledge
6. Ability to perceive and exploit power	6. Broad perspective	6. Judgment and intelligence	6. Ability to perceive and exploit power
7. Integrity	7. Verbal expressiveness		7. Competitiveness

[a] *Note:* Characteristics are listed in order of importance.

Source: L.L Graham and Y. Sano, *Smart Bargaining: Doing Business with the Japanese*, 2nd ed. (New York: Harper Business, 1988).

EXHIBIT 12.12 Important Characteristics Needed by Negotiators in Four Countries

addition, the ability to be influential in one's home organization appears to be a commonly favored personal attribute.

Opinions about the qualities of effective negotiators *do* vary in different countries, however. Exhibit 12.12 lists the qualities that managers from the United States and three other countries think are important for effective negotiators. As the exhibit indicates, the opinions about these qualities vary considerably by culture. For example, U.S., Japanese, Chinese (Taiwan), and Brazilian managers differ in the importance they attach to the "ability to win respect and confidence." This skill is rated much higher in the two Asian cultures than in the other two cultures. For American and Brazilian managers, planning skills and judgment and intelligence are rated as more highly desired negotiator characteristics than they were in the two Asian cultures. But there are also differences even between the two Asian cultures. The Japanese placed the highest importance on "dedication to the job," whereas "persistence and determination" ranked number one with the Taiwanese.

THE SITUATION SURROUNDING THE NEGOTIATIONS The second major variable affecting negotiation outcomes is the set of situational circumstances. Probably the most important are the location of the negotiations, the physical arrangements, the emphasis on speed and time, and the composition of the negotiating teams.

Location. Typically, there is a strong tendency to want to negotiate on your own turf or at neutral sites, especially for critical negotiations. The so-called "home court advantage" seems to be universal; everyone feels more comfortable and confident and has greater access to information and resources when negotiating at home. For international negotiations, negotiations conducted in a manager's own offices or even in his or her home country can be a psychological advantage.

Characteristics of locations, however, can vary by culture. For example, in the United States almost all negotiations occur in a formal setting, such as an office or conference room. In contrast, in Japan and Mexico, where relationship building is crucial, major parts of the process are likely to occur in an informal or nonwork setting, such as a restaurant or on a golf course. In Korea, the final contract produced by the negotiations is likely to be signed in a formal and public setting rather than in someone's office.

Physical Arrangements. The usual American approach to setting up a room for negotiations is to place the two parties on opposite sides of a table, facing each other, which emphasizes their competing interests. Other arrangements obviously are possible, though, including seating the two parties at right angles or along the same side "facing the problem" or at a round table where everyone is part of the total problem-solving effort.[45]

Emphasis on Speed and Time. Americans typically avoid wasting time. They want to "get right to the point" or "get down to business." Other cultures are different. In Mexico or China, for example, the norm is to invest considerable time in relationship building and other activities not directly related to the central negotiation process. Consequently, in such cultures, speed is sacrificed, and the effectiveness and efficiency of subsequent negotiations often hinge on how well the relationships between the parties have developed.

The Composition of the Negotiating Teams. The composition and size of teams representing the two parties in negotiations can also influence negotiations. For example, the more people involved at the negotiation table, the more preparation that needs to be done to ensure that the team presents a united front. The composition of the team in terms of decision-making authority is also important. If individuals at the table have authority to make binding decisions, the negotiations are generally more efficient than if they do not.

Team composition can vary significantly by culture. In countries that are sensitive to status differences and ranks (for example, Singapore, India, Venezuela, Japan), it is much more important for the members of one team to be similar in status, position, age, and authority to the team with which they are negotiating. This is less important in other countries (like New Zealand, Canada, United States). The size of negotiating teams also can differ markedly by culture. In the United States, where go-it-alone heroes are admired, team sizes are ordinarily much smaller than in more collectivist-oriented cultures such as those of Taiwan, China, and Japan. The problem is that the resulting mismatches in size can communicate unintended messages. The Taiwanese, for example, might interpret a single negotiator or a small team as a sign that the other party does not consider the negotiations to be important. Similarly, Americans might interpret the presence of a large team from a Taiwanese firm as an attempt to intimidate them with numbers.

THE NEGOTIATION PROCESS The third, and probably most crucial, variable determining the outcome of negotiations is the negotiating process itself. The five common stages in this process, which are basically the same across all cultures,[46] are described next and shown in Exhibit 12.13. They are also illustrated in the A Manager's Challenge, "American-Japanese Negotiations," which explores the five stages as they apply to two particular cultures—Japan and the United States.

Stage 1: Planning and Preparation. This stage involves laying the foundations through advance planning and analysis prior to any face-to-face interactions. At this stage, individuals or teams conduct background research, gather relevant information, and plan their strategy and tactics. Preliminary decisions are made about what the objectives will be and what can and cannot be conceded during the course of the negotiations.

Stage 2: Relationship-Building Between Negotiating Parties. This stage is commonly referred to as "nontask time," in which each side attempts to establish comfortable working relationships with the other side. As we pointed out earlier, Americans are inclined to make this stage briefer and believe such activities are relatively unimportant. On the other hand, negotiators from some other cultures such as Latin America, the Middle East and Asia believe exactly the opposite. Research suggests three types of behaviors during this stage: developing trust, developing personal rapport, and establishing long-term association.[47]

Stage 3: Information Exchange. In this stage, each party attempts to learn about the needs and demands of their counterparts. Managers from the United States often attempt to hurry through these activities with an attitude of "you tell me what you want, and I will tell you what I want."[48] In contrast, managers from Asian cultures take a much more indirect, more drawn out, and more thorough approach to acquiring and exchanging information. Arabic and Latin American managers appear to follow a similar approach, except that the latter are even more leisurely in their use of time at this stage.[49]

Stage 4: Persuasion Attempts. This stage focuses on attempts to modify the position of the other party and to influence that side to accept the negotiator's desired set of exchanges (for example, an exchange of a certain price for a certain quantity or quality of goods or services). American managers usually treat this as the most important stage. They are assertive and straightforward in an effort to get what they want. Sometimes this can involve the use of

EXHIBIT 12.13

The Five Stages in the Negotiating Process

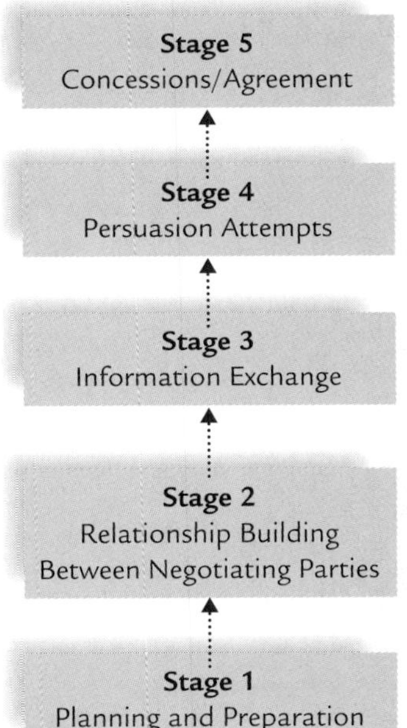

A MANAGER'S CHALLENGE
Globalization

American-Japanese Negotiations: An Intricate Dance

The United States and Japan are major trading partners. Given the critical economic (as well as political and military) relationship between the two countries, opportunities for negotiations occur frequently. However, the two countries differ substantially in their approaches to negotiations.

If you think of negotiations as a dance, then the Americans and the Japanese move to quite different beats. As a consequence, toes can get stepped on. Based on the five fundamental processes of negotiations, the importance that each culture puts on each stage and how much time each tends to spend at each stage can be mapped. As the accompanying diagram illustrates, the differences in patterns make for an awkward dance.

Members of both cultures spend time preparing for the negotiations, but the Japanese spend slightly more time. However, the two cultures differ dramatically at Stage 2: Americans put relatively little value on, and do not spend much time on, developing relationships. The Japanese are just the opposite. They spend more time on, and more highly value, the exchange of information than Americans do.

Both cultures place significant value on persuasion and on the conclusion of negotiations. However, the two critical timing differences are that by the time Americans want to be well into the persuasion stage (Stage 4), the Japanese are just wanting to end the relationship-building stage (Stage 2). As the diagram also demonstrates, the Japanese tend to take more time overall for negotiations.

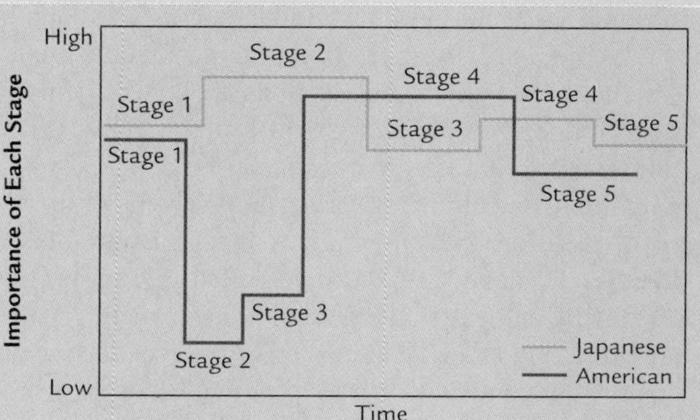

At the conclusion of negotiations, when negotiating with each other, Americans typically rely on long and extremely detailed contracts that explicitly spell out the obligations of each party and the penalties for noncompliance. In Japan, on the other hand, written agreements are often quite short and only describe the general intentions and obligations of the two parties. The last paragraph of these agreements in Japan may simply state that if disagreements arise, both parties will try to resolve them in good faith.

Even though the two cultures share the same basic sequence of negotiation stages, misunderstandings can easily develop. This is due to the fact that—unless adjustments are made on one side or the other, or by both parties—they differ in the importance attached to each stage and how long each stage typically lasts.

warnings or threats to try to force the other party to agree.[50] Managers from Arabic countries tend to show tactics similar to those of Americans at the persuasion stage, but they are less inclined to hurry. Negotiators from Asian cultures take a slow, careful approach but do not tend to be directly assertive until later in the negotiations. Managers from Latin American cultures tend to use a mixture of approaches during this stage by showing a moderate degree of assertiveness but also a willingness to use the tactic of "calculated delay" when this seems advisable.[51]

Stage 5: Concessions/Agreement. At this final point, if reasonable progress has been made, compromises and concessions are made that permit each party to take away something of value. Since American managers tend to begin the negotiation process with positions fairly close to what they will finally accept, they do not have much leeway for concessions.[52] Managers from Arabic and Latin American countries seem to open negotiations from more extreme positions, which permit them to offer concessions late in the process. Managers from Asian countries often employ "normative appeals" (such as "it's your obligation") to try to get the other party to offer concessions.[53]

Managerial Challenges from the Front Line

The Rest of the Story

After one particularly stressful communication incident, Bridgette Chambers sought out one of her mentors in the company for advice. "She looked me in the eye and said that I did not quite do the job [of communicating successfully] that I thought I was doing," said Chambers about her mentor. "She confirmed that while I got results, I left a wake behind me that may have been, in the long run, as costly as missing my targets. The feedback she gave me was like a knife."

Using that as a learning experience, Chambers has become more alert and sensitive to the kind of responses she can create with her direct communication style. Even when she has to communicate the details of uncomfortable changes to those who will be affected, she has learned to turn the potentially difficult situations into positive and productive opportunities that contribute to successful achievement of mutual objectives. Consequently, Chambers has continued to achieve corporate results while receiving numerous accolades and awards for her leadership efforts and communication endeavors.

Summary

- Since communication involves the transfer of information, meaning, and understanding, it is an essential component of managerial effectiveness and crucial for implementing effective leadership.
- The basic communication process involves senders who encode messages and transmit them by some medium, and receivers who decode and interpret the messages. Typically, there also will be some kind of feedback (including the possibility of an apparent absence of feedback) sent by the receiver back to the sender. Throughout the process there may be some level of "noise" or distraction that interferes between senders and receivers.
- Communication can either be verbal or nonverbal, and can differ in degree of "richness"—or capacity to facilitate shared meaning—of the medium used.
- Different features of the organizational context directly impact the effectiveness of communication. These features include the direction of the communication (downward, upward, and lateral), the channels used (formal and informal), and the prevailing patterns of communication networks that exist in the organization.
- Serious barriers to effective communication include: interpersonal barriers, such as emotion or differing frames of reference; organizational barriers, such as differences between the sender and receiver and their hierarchical levels or unit affiliations; and cultural barriers, such as ethnocentrism and language differences.
- Although many communication barriers are almost impossible to eliminate completely, steps can be taken to reduce their impact. Individuals can work to improve both their message sending and, especially, their listening skills. Organizations can become more aware and responsive to communication issues—such as those related to cross-cultural communications—and the need to improve their communication procedures.
- An increasingly important type of communication for managers, especially the higher they rise in their organization, is negotiation, the process of meeting with another party to arrive at an agreement. The negotiation process typically involves five key stages: planning and preparation, relationship building, information exchange, and persuasion attempts. As with any communication process, missteps can and often do occur in any or all of these stages.

Key Terms

Review Questions

1. What is communication?
2. What are the basic elements of the communication model?
3. Which mode of communication is the most flexible? The least flexible? Why?
4. What is meant by "media richness"
5. What are the typical differences in content of upward, downward, and lateral communication within organizations?
6. What is a communication network?
7. How are selective perception and frames of reference related?
8. What are the principal differences between high-context and low-context cultures relative to communication?
9. Discuss four ways to improve your listening skills.
10. What can organizations do to improve communication within them?
11. In negotiation, what is the difference between an "interest" and a "position"?
12. What are four helpful principles for effective negotiation?

Assessing Your Capabilities

How Good Are My Listening Skills?

Using the following scale, circle the number that best indicates the extent to which you agree or disagree with each statement.

Statement					
1. I frequently attempt to listen to several conversations at the same time.	1 Strongly Agree	2 Agree	3 Neither Agree nor Disagree	4 Disagree	5 Strongly Disagree
2. I like people to give me only the facts and then let me make my own interpretation.	1 Strongly Agree	2 Agree	3 Neither Agree nor Disagree	4 Disagree	5 Strongly Disagree
3. I sometimes pretend to pay attention to people.	1 Strongly Agree	2 Agree	3 Neither Agree nor Disagree	4 Disagree	5 Strongly Disagree
4. I consider myself a good judge of nonverbal communications.	1 Strongly Agree	2 Agree	3 Neither Agree nor Disagree	4 Disagree	5 Strongly Disagree
5. I usually know what another person is going to say before he or she says it.	1 Strongly Agree	2 Agree	3 Neither Agree nor Disagree	4 Disagree	5 Strongly Disagree
6. I usually end conversations that don't interest me by diverting my attention from the speaker.	1 Strongly Agree	2 Agree	3 Neither Agree nor Disagree	4 Disagree	5 Strongly Disagree
7. I frequently nod, frown, or provide other nonverbal cues to let the speaker know how I feel about what he or she is saying.	1 Strongly Agree	2 Agree	3 Neither Agree nor Disagree	4 Disagree	5 Strongly Disagree
8. I usually respond immediately when someone has finished talking.	1 Strongly Agree	2 Agree	3 Neither Agree nor Disagree	4 Disagree	5 Strongly Disagree

9. I evaluate what is being said while it is being said.	1 Strongly Agree	2 Agree	3 Neither Agree nor Disagree	4 Disagree	5 Strongly Disagree
10. I usually formulate a response while the other person is still talking.	1 Strongly Agree	2 Agree	3 Neither Agree nor Disagree	4 Disagree	5 Strongly Disagree
11. The speaker's "delivery" style frequently keeps me from listening to content.	1 Strongly Agree	2 Agree	3 Neither Agree nor Disagree	4 Disagree	5 Strongly Disagree
12. I usually ask people to clarify what they have said rather than guess at the meaning.	1 Strongly Agree	2 Agree	3 Neither Agree nor Disagree	4 Disagree	5 Strongly Disagree
13. I make a concerted effort to understand other people's points of view.	1 Strongly Agree	2 Agree	3 Neither Agree nor Disagree	4 Disagree	5 Strongly Disagree
14. I frequently hear what I expect to hear rather than what is said.	1 Strongly Agree	2 Agree	3 Neither Agree nor Disagree	4 Disagree	5 Strongly Disagree
15. Most people feel that I have understood their point of view when we disagree.	1 Strongly Agree	2 Agree	3 Neither Agree nor Disagree	4 Disagree	5 Strongly Disagree

Scoring

To obtain your score

1. Total your responses to questions 1–3, 5–11, and 14. Enter total here:_________
2. Reverse score (5 becomes 1; 4 becomes 2, etc.) questions 4, 12, 13, and 15. Enter total here:_________

Your overall score is the total of both partial scores. TOTAL:_________

Analysis and Interpretation

Effective communicators have developed good listening skills. This instrument is designed to provide you with some insights into your listening skills.

Scores range from 15 to 75. The higher your score the better listener you are. While any cutoffs are essentially arbitrary, if you score 60 or above, your listening skills are fairly well honed. Scores of 40 or less indicate you need to make a serious effort at improving your listening skills.

Good sources to help you improve your listening skills include:

- M. Helgessen, *Active Listening: Building Skills for Understanding* (New York: Cambridge University Press, 1994).
- M. Burley-Allen, *Listening: The Forgotten Skill* (Hoboken, NJ: Wiley, 1995).
- J. E. Sullivan, *The Good Listener* (Notre Dame, IN: Ave Maria Press, 2000).

Source: Prentice Hall's Self Assessment Library, ed. S. P. Robbins and T. A. Judge.

Team Exercise

Modeling the Might of Media Richness

This is a fun exercise that demonstrates vividly the importance of choosing the right medium for your communication needs. Your instructor will divide you into teams of teachers, learners, and observers.

Each teacher will attempt to instruct his or her learner partner in a complex task. Each team will use different levels of media richness in their instructions.

Following the demonstration exercise, the class will discuss the following questions:

1. Which method appears to have worked best?
2. Was the fastest method also the most successful?
3. What elements contributed to the success or failure of the instruction?
4. How does this exercise relate to media richness theory?
5. Give examples of unsuccessful media choices you have encountered. What was right or wrong in these situations? Were there harmful outcomes from the choice of an inappropriate medium?
6. How can you apply what you have learned to your workplace interactions?

Source: Adapted by Grace McLaughlin (2007) from discussions with other attendees at the Organizational Behavior Teaching Conference 2002. Used with permission.

Closing Case How One Company Tackled a Major Communication Problem

Paul Iams founded The Iams Company in Dayton, Ohio, in 1946, in an effort to improve the quality of food fed to pets. Procter & Gamble saw so much profit potential in pet food that it bought Iams in 1999. Today, the company's 2,000-plus employees produce premium dry and canned foods for dogs and cats at six manufacturing sites in the United States and the Netherlands, although the main office is still located in Dayton. Iams-branded dog and cat food products are sold through supermarkets, drug stores, pet stores, feed outlets, and other retail locations. A second Iams brand, Eukanuba, is sold only through veterinary offices.

In 1982, Clay Mathile, an Iams employee since 1970, bought the company from the founder. Within three years, Iams—still a private company—was ringing up $50 million in annual sales with a 200-person workforce. It was at that time that human resources managers decided to conduct the company's first survey of employee attitudes. The employees were generally positive. However, managers were troubled by the unexpectedly strong agreement to this statement: "We do not get enough information about how well our work group and company are doing."

Digging deeper into the survey results, Mathile and his managers realized that Iams employees were asking for more frequent and more detailed communication regarding both their particular facility's performance and the company's performance overall. Even though Iams was not publicly held, employees were paid bonuses based on sales and profits and were, therefore, keenly interested in following the company's progress. As a result, Mathile and his team began thinking about a formal process to share key information more often with employees, supervisors, and plant managers, addressing these internal audiences as if they owned company stock. Just as important, the process had to allow information to flow upward as well as downward so managers could take the pulse of the organization and, at the most basic level, determine whether employees understood the messages.

Taking a cue from the quarterly reports that public companies issue to stockholders, senior managers began traveling to meet with groups of employees every three months. Each Iams factory or office shuts down for a few hours during the quarter so that the employees and supervisors can hear top managers talk about the company's current financial situation as well as safety accomplishments and future plans. In addition, senior managers make a point of welcoming new employees and explaining Iams's mission and strategy. Then, each facility's top managers discuss local goals and results and acknowledge promotions and other achievements. Finally, a manager from headquarters reports on developments in one department, such as new employee benefits or upcoming product introductions.

At the end of each meeting, senior managers and local facility managers stand in front of the room and field audience questions. Over the years, employees have asked about a wide range of topics, such as the impact of Iams' overseas expansion on its U.S. facilities and even individual problems with health care benefits. If none of the managers can answer a particular question, one takes responsibility for researching the issue, responding to the questioner, and posting the answer for the entire facility

"It is a two-way street," says John Meyer, who helped implement the meeting process when he was senior vice president at Iams. "The leadership looks for feedback and ideas from every level of the company and employees are kept well-informed, focused on company goals, and motivated to follow through." Employees find out every quarter whether their facility and the entire company is on track toward the year's goals, rather than being surprised when they receive their year-end bonus checks. They also appreciate being praised for their accomplishments and having an open forum in which they can interact directly with top local and corporate managers, instead of filtering comments and questions through an intermediary such as the human resources staff.

This tradition of quarterly meetings continued under the leadership of Jeff Ansell, who became president after Procter & Gamble acquired Iams. Senior managers fan out to visit its worldwide facilities every three months. Managers in certain departments also use technology to share information with a far-flung employee base. For instance, managers used to bring the North American sales force together for twice-yearly new product briefings. In between, they scheduled telephone conference calls as needed to discuss upcoming product introductions.

With the advent of videoconferencing technology, however, sales managers can now see and talk with the entire sales team at any time. Displaying new products and prototypes, transmitting detailed product data, and facilitating group discussions is easier and cheaper than ever before because participants simply gather in the nearest company conference room to prepare for a division-wide sales meeting. Moreover, with online chats, e-mail, and other Web-based tools, managers can assess what the sales force needs to know and reinforce key data when necessary. "[Online] functions such as surveys and quizzes drive the information home," comments Scott George, who manages enterprise systems for Iams.

Taking communication a step further, Iams appointed Kersee, a golden retriever, as vice president of canine communication. Kersee sampled the company's products and greeted employees and visitors in the Dayton headquarters. Once Kersee's formal instruction was completed, her trainer even sent Iams's employees a list of the 30-odd commands the dog knows. Although Kersee has now retired, her position has been taken over by Euka, a labanese who performs all Kersee's former duties and helps in fund-raising activities.

So, the fundamental issue is: Has all this attention to communication been worth it to the organization? What are the potential long-term costs and benefits?

Questions

1. What effects, if any, do Iams's quarterly meetings of employees and senior-level managers have on the quality and extent of day-to-day communication between lower-level managers and their immediate subordinates? How will it help or hinder that communication?
2. How has the richness of the media used by Iams managers changed over the years? How do you think these changes have affected senders and receivers?
3. Do the communication benefits of holding company-wide quarterly meetings outweigh the costs of halting operations so employees can attend and having executives travel in person to different locations for the meetings? Explain your answer.
4. Analyze the communication network structure at Iams. Who is involved? At what levels(s)? In what ways?
5. Does this case suggest any linkages between the type and extent of managerial communication, on the one hand, and employees' trust in management and their motivation to perform?

Sources: J. Neff, "P&G Claims Iams Is Top Dog in Pet Food," *Advertising Age*, March 10, 2003, 4–5; J. Meyer, "Strategic Communication Enhances Organizational Performance," *Human Resource Planning* (June 2002): 7+; J. Neff, "It's a Dog-Eat-Dog World," *Food Processing*, June 2001, 49+; E. Goodridge, "Users Tap Collaborative Functions of E-Learning Apps," *InformationWeek*, December 10, 2001, 34; C. Wood, "Founding Father: Paul Iams Combined Science, Business and Compassion for Companion Animals," *The Pet Professional*, 2005, www.petprofessional.com; www.pg.cpm/annualreports/2005.

Part Four

Controlling

13

Operations Management

Learning Objectives

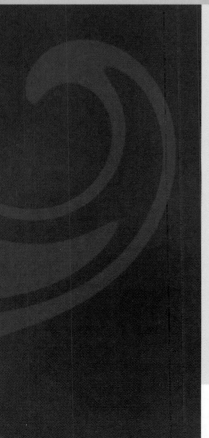

After studying this chapter, you should be able to:

Define *operations management* and explain its importance within service and manufacturing firms.

Describe key techniques and tools for enhancing product and service quality.

Explain common means of ensuring appropriate product quantity.

Discuss tools for managing the appropriate timing of inventory and finished product.

Describe methods for enhancing productivity and efficiency.

Explain the principle roles of effective supply chain management in the operations of organizations.

Managerial Challenges from the Front Line

Name: Michelle Jackson

Position: Marketing Manager, International Intermodal Operations, BNSF Railway Company

Alma mater: University of Oklahoma

Outside work activities: Big Brothers and Big Sisters member; Fort Worth Sister Cities member, National Black MBA Association member, working out at the gym, traveling, and spending time with family and friends

First Job out of school: Waitress at Casa Bonita restaurant in Tulsa, Oklahoma

Business book reading now: *In Business As in Life—You Don't Get What You Deserve, You Get What You Negotiate*, by Chester L. Karrass

Heroes: My father for being successful by overcoming life's obstacles and remaining an honest, faithful, and humble man. And my mother for having the biggest heart that anyone could have

Motto to live by: "Do today, what others put off to tomorrow"

What drives me: Knowing that I added value in either a person's life or on a project

Management style: Democratic style; allow others to give input and be a part of the decision-making process

Few people appreciate just how much of the U.S. economy (or most other countries as well) depends on the effective operation of railroads. Nearly half of all freight in the United States in terms of weight is moved by rail. The value of all the goods moved by rail is nearly 17 percent of the value of all imports into and exports out of the United States. Some industries are especially dependent on rail transportation. For example, about 70 percent of all coal and automobile shipments are done by rail. Therefore, if railroad operations do not go well, it affects not just the railroad company but the entire economy. This was clearly felt when the economy started recovering after the 2000–2001 recession. As consumer spending increased and imports from places in Asia, especially China, exploded, the demand on railways in the West stretched, and in some cases exceeded, rail capacity.

Michelle Jackson sits at the nexus of this challenge. The customers for whom Jackson works are international ocean liners that ship intermodal containers to and from the West Coast. In an age where manufacturers want parts delivered at just the right time (not too early or late) and consumers want products when they're hot, bottlenecks and the resulting delivery delays cause headaches for everyone. But building new capacity cannot be done overnight. Acquiring the rights to land, satisfying environmental impact demands, constructing new rail lines, and the like are costly and time-intensive activities.

Jackson and other operations managers at BNSF faced several options to reduce bottlenecks and thereby increase operational efficiency. They could add more capacity by simply increasing the length of the trains and adding more locomotives to pull the longer trains. They could increase capacity by adding more trains, which would require purchasing more locomotives and cars. However, adding more trains would require hiring and training new conductors, engineers, and other personnel. Also, if they increase capacity along the lines, they would also have to think about managing congestion that would likely result at the terminals and transshipment points where cars are taken from one train and shifted to another for their onward journey. They could, through better tracking and other technologies, increase the efficiency and movement of existing trains.

In the end, the actions need to not only add to the total volume that can be moved along the lines but also the quality of the service. This service includes both the speed of delivery (how long it takes to get freight shipped from point A to point B) and the reliability of delivery (how accurate the targeted delivery date is relative to actual delivery). Moving higher volumes with worse service quality would likely *not* lead to overall higher levels of customer satisfaction.

The Nature and Importance of Operations Management

operations management
a specialized field of management associated with the conversion or transformation of resources into products and services

Operations management is a specialized field of management focused on the conversion of resources into products and services. In the past, the focus was largely on manufacturing, and the term *production and operations management (POM)* was commonly used. With the lines between what is strictly a manufacturing firm versus what is strictly a service firm now blurred and with a greater portion of economic activity being devoted to services, the term *operations management (OM)* is a more generic one describing the activities related to producing both products and services. Because of the historic focus of operations management on manufacturing, some people incorrectly assume that the tools and techniques of operations management do not apply to service firms or service activities. However, as we will illustrate throughout the chapter, fundamentally all organizations have to deal with the same issues within operations whether they are transforming resources into physical products or intangible services. For example, by implementing a number of traditional operations management concepts, Jefferson Pilot Financial (now Lincoln Financial Group) reduced by 70 percent the time it took to process an insurance application and issue a policy. The company also reduced by 40 percent the number of policies that had to be reissued due to errors and reduced its total labor costs per application by 25 percent.[1]

Equally important to emphasize at the outset of this chapter is the strategic role of operations. Just as people incorrectly think that operations management is only about making products, some also incorrectly think that operations management is just a specialized function without organizational or strategic importance. Nothing could be further from the truth. All organizations survive and thrive in large measure to the extent that they produce a service or product with the quality, in the quantity, and at a time that customers desire. For an organization to survive very long, it must do this while maintaining a positive profit margin between its costs and the revenue it receives. This is true regardless of the specific strategy the firm pursues. Whether a firm is charging a premium or discount price relative to competitors, it still needs to ensure that the costs associated with operations help the company maintain a positive profit margin and that the outcome of the operations function enhances customer satisfaction and revenues.

In this context, managers working in operations typically have four related overall objectives. First, they are concerned about and manage activities designed to ensure that the services and products produced for customers have the appropriate quality. Second, operations managers have to also use tools and techniques to ensure that the right quantities of the products and services are produced. Third, operations managers must use a number of techniques to ensure that the products and services get to the customer at the right time. Finally, operations managers must also focus on delivering the three previous objectives at the best possible cost. As we will explore in this chapter, each of the first three objectives can have direct cost implications. However, there are a number of other factors that operations managers need to look after in order to ensure that the right quality, quantity, and timing objectives are met at the best possible cost. We will explore these factors as well.

Managing Quality

Ford Motor Company's advertising slogan, "Quality is Job One," points out how important the concept of quality can be to an organization. However, the firm's less than stellar performance in achieving this objective against Toyota illustrates that it's not slogans but actual delivery of quality that matters to customers and influences a firm's financial performance, such as sales and market share. Toyota's quality has consistently been rated among the highest of all automobile manufacturers and this has, in part, contributed to Toyota's surpassing Ford as the number two seller of automobiles in the world.

quality
the reliability, durability, serviceability, and dependability of products and services; also defined as fitness for use

A popular definition of **quality** is "fitness for use," which is a measure of how well a product or service performs its intended purpose, including how reliable it is or conversely how often it breaks down and how easy it is to service or repair when it does break down. Although this might sound as though it applies most directly to products, the elements also apply to services. For example, if we consider the service element of the front desk of a hotel, all the factors mentioned previously can be directly applied. The quality of this service would be high if when people check in, the front desk clerk can consistently locate their reservation and assign a room quickly (efficiency), ensure that features of the room requested by customers match those of the room assigned (effectiveness), and do both these things in a professional and friendly manner.

Increased quality has several key outcomes for the business. In the hotel example, higher service quality in terms of efficiency can influence at least two critical outcomes. First, greater *efficiency* can lead to lower costs because a given clerk could check in more customers, and, therefore, the hotel would need fewer clerks. Second, greater efficiency (that is, the speed of checking in guests) could also have a positive impact on the satisfaction of customers and their likelihood of becoming repeat customers. Higher quality in terms of *effectiveness* could also affect both current costs and future revenues. First, if the room assigned matches the room requested, this then lowers the costs associated with "fixing" mismatches. Second, the greater the match between the room requested and room assigned, the higher the customers' likely satisfaction and their probability of coming back in the future.

Exhibit 13.1 provides a general illustration of the potential outcomes of higher quality in operations. As we noted, higher quality can often enhance customer satisfaction, which in turn can lead to higher repeat business and, therefore, more revenue. If the quality and resulting satisfaction are high enough, it can even lead to customers' recommending the product to others or what marketers often call "positive word of mouth revenue." The most

EXHIBIT 13.1

The Economic Impact of Higher Quality

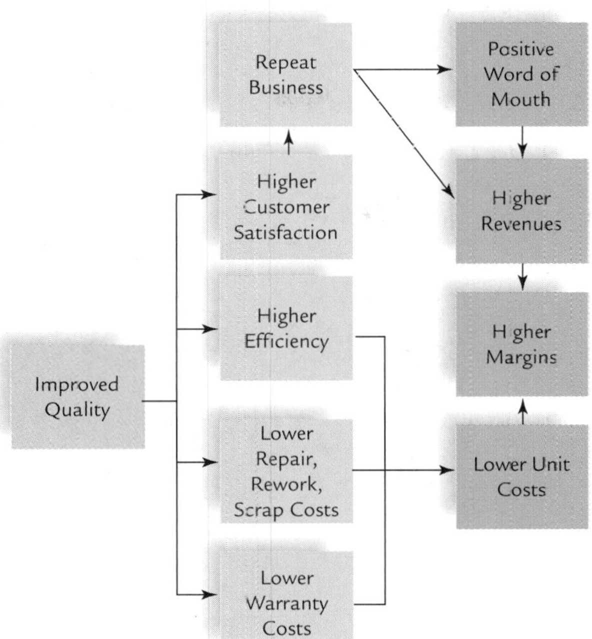

important assessment of quality is in the eye of the customer.[2] In summary, higher quality can lower costs through higher efficiency, lower repair costs, and lower warranty costs (that is, making good on warranty guarantees relative to a product's features or performance) and can increase revenues through higher customer satisfaction via repeat business and positive word of mouth.

Given the potential benefits of higher quality, how can it be enhanced? To address this question in the following sections, we first examine an overall philosophy known as **total quality management (TQM)**, and then look at other specific tools and techniques for enhancing quality.

total quality management (TQM)
a management approach and philosophy that involves a commitment from all levels of employees to continually strive to make improvements and satisfy customers

Total Quality Management

TQM is considered a management philosophy because it encompasses a commitment from employees at all levels to continually strive to make improvements and satisfy customers. In essence, TQM must be part of the organization's culture in order for a true commitment to quality to be realized. In contrast to traditional quality control efforts where a separate team of experts inspect products or services for defects or errors after completion, TQM emphasizes "quality at the source," that is, quality inspection at all stages of production or service output. Quality at the source includes engaging in quantitative techniques, such as statistical process control, as well as nonquantitative techniques, such as employee empowerment.

statistical process control (SPC)
a quantitative tool to aid in making decisions concerning how well a process is performing

Statistical process control (SPC) provides an objective tool to make decisions concerning how well a process is performing. Although all companies ideally should have a goal of zero defects, or 100 percent customer satisfaction, in reality, slight deviations cannot be completely eliminated. Thus, organizations try to minimize their occurrence. To track and highlight results and identify unacceptable deviations, most operations managers taking an SPC approach to quality use various forms of a process control chart. Control charts are typically developed for any quality-related characteristic that may cause defective products or services. Examples of quality-related characteristics include the temperature of fast-food items and the number of complaints from hospital patients.

The development of a control chart requires taking a sample, computing the average measurement, and establishing the upper and lower control limits. The control limits provide an acceptable range for measurements. Any measurements outside the range are considered unacceptable and cause for investigation. The most important use for control charts is to provide a basis for taking action to determine the causes of good or poor performance.

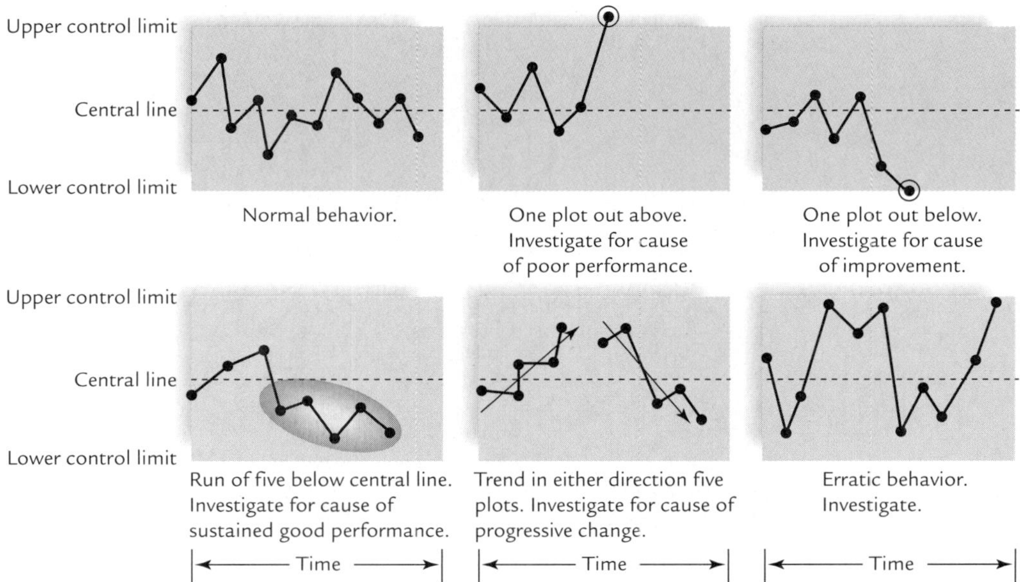

EXHIBIT 13.2

Quality Control Charts

continuous process improvement
incremental and breakthrough improvements in the way an organization does business; also known as business process reengineering and *kaizen*

Exhibit 13.2 provides examples of control charts and what actions should be taken based on the measurements.

Continuous process improvement, also known as business process reengineering and ***kaizen*** in Japan, refers to both incremental and breakthrough improvements in the way an organization does business. The fundamental notion of process reengineering is that form influences function. In other words, the way a process is designed influences how well or poorly it functions, which in turn has an important influence on key outcomes. A common approach to process reengineering has five key elements:

1. Objective: This step focuses on determining what a process is to achieve. For example, a loan application process should result in determining whether or not a loan should be given to an individual.
2. Design: This step examines the critical sequences and seeks to maximize the objective while minimizing the number, complexity, and time required in the process.
3. Capabilities: This step determines the required capabilities for executing the design.
4. Infrastructure: This step focuses on the information and other infrastructure needed for supporting the design and capabilities to meet the objective.
5. Metrics: Finally, this step determines the key metrics that help monitor and determine how well the redesign is doing in meeting the objectives.

For example, Clorox worked on redesigning its "order to cash" process (the process of getting a customer's order through to receiving cash for the fulfillment of the order). Over a four-year period from 2002 to 2006, Clorox's late shipments fell by 70 percent, old receivables fell by 67 percent, and perfect orders (orders that hit every key target metric along the process) rose from 19 percent to 70 percent.[3] In contrast to reengineering but in the same spirit of continuous improvement, *kaizen* seeks to improve all aspects of a process. For example, at the Toyota Manufacturing plant in Georgetown, Kentucky, an employee brought in a Bass Boat seat and placed it at his station on the line. A seated position made the installation of parts under the steering wheel much easier and faster. According to the criteria for the Malcolm Baldrige National Quality Award, several types of continuous improvements are possible, including:

1. Enhancing value to customers through new and improved products and services
2. Reducing errors, defects, and waste
3. Improving responsiveness and cycle time performance
4. Improving productivity and effectiveness in the use of all resources

5. Improving the company's performance and leadership position in fulfilling its public responsibilities and serving as a role model in corporate citizenship

Six Sigma is a disciplined, data-driven approach for eliminating defects and enhancing quality with an orientation toward the impact such improvements will have on the customer.[4] Statistically Six Sigma is represented by a 99.99966 percent reliability, or not producing more than 3.4 defects per million opportunities. A defect is not a product that doesn't work or a service that fails but any result that is outside of customer specifications. As a consequence, the focus is not just on hitting a target average, but reducing the variance around that target. For example, suppose you had a customer delivery target of 6 days after an order was placed. Having the actual delivery result of 3, 6, 4, 7, 8, 2, 5, 6, 8, 10, and 11 days would result in an average of 6 days. However, this would not even achieve One Sigma (that is, 69 percent reliability). Six Sigma is focused on not just achieving the desired average but having virtually no deviation away from or variance around that target.

Within Six Sigma, quality is improved through the use of two submethodologies: DMAIC and DMADV. The DMAIC process (define, measure, analyze, improve, control) is focused on existing processes that fall below the specification and how to improve them. The DMADV process (define, measure, analyze, design, verify) is focused on the development of new processes. According to the Six Sigma Academy, the highest level experts in Six Sigma (called "Black Belts") save companies approximately $230,000 per project and can complete four to six projects per year. General Electric estimated it saved $10 billion during the first five years of implementing its Six Sigma quality initiative.[5]

Although Six Sigma initiatives have focused largely on manufacturing environments, the principles can be applied with equal relevance and impact to service environments.[6] For example, Yale-New Haven Hospital determined that bloodstream infections (BSI) contributed to increased costs, with each BSI incident costing the hospital approximately $3,000. The hospital also found that there was a significant relationship between patients being catheterized and developing bloodstream infections. Upon further analysis, the hospital's Six Sigma team found large variations in how catheters were inserted, changed, and maintained. This led to several improvements being made, including using a new antiseptic when preparing a site, double gloving for staff when performing the procedure, and the development of standardized and preassembled catheterization kits. After the changes were made, BSI incidents fell from 12 per month to 3.[7]

Employee empowerment, defined in Chapter 9, is seen as being critical to the TQM philosophy. This is because however necessary the statistical monitoring and control of quality is, in the end, fixing quality problems and thereby achieving high quality requires action on the part of managers and their subordinates. The TQM philosophy is that organizations need to empower their employees so that they will take pride in and have a sense of responsibility for their individual output, as well as the output of the entire organization. By involving employees, organizations engage the expertise of those people who directly produce the product or provide the service. These individuals are the experts in their areas and should have input on how to improve the quality of the organization's product or service. In addition to employee involvement, a successful TQM philosophy requires a group of committed top managers who can effectively communicate the TQM vision and provide the strong leadership needed to implement the changes required. And, most importantly, a strong focus on the customer's needs and expectations is paramount.

The goal of exceeding customer expectations was the primary reason why Athens Insurance Center (AIC) implemented a TQM program. Part of its TQM effort helped to identify a need to cross-train its agents so that when customers called, they would be assisted immediately instead of having to wait for a particular agent. For AIC, the appeal of TQM was that "it attacks the flaws in the systems and procedures—not people." AIC reported that its TQM efforts helped instill a stronger sense of ownership and pride in their employees, which, in turn, improved customer satisfaction.

TQM efforts can also be found in nonbusiness settings such as schools. "Koalaty Kid," a program sponsored by the American Society for Quality, emphasizes TQM and continuous improvement in elementary schools worldwide. At Kingsley Elementary in Kingsport, Tennessee, writing was identified in the Kingsley School Improvement Plan as the academic subject most in need of quality improvement. Dr. Sandra Ramsey, the principal of the school, reported that after implementing a plan to improve the quality of instruction provided by the school's teachers, students achieved a 58 percent improvement in their writing over the course of a two-year period. On the student side, the quality improvement plan involved, among other things, recording and charting students' individual grades and recognizing students for their writing accomplishments in school announcements and during school assemblies.[8]

Quantity and Capacity Planning

Few people would debate that the right quality of a service or product is important. That said, customers also care about the right quantity. One of the principle means that operations managers use to ensure that the right quantity of product or service is produced is via **capacity planning**—determining how much a firm should be able to produce of a product or service.

capacity planning
the process of determining how much a firm should be able to produce or service

design capacity
the maximum capacity at which a facility can run under ideal conditions

effective capacity
the percent of design capacity a facility is actually expected to maintain

Although organizations would like to be able to operate at maximum capacity at all times, no organization could possibly sustain itself at this rate. Rather than run at its **design capacity**, which is the maximum capacity that can be attained under *ideal* conditions, organizations usually run at their effective capacities instead. The **effective capacity** is the percent of design capacity actually expected, and it can be expressed as a simple formula:

$$\text{Effective Capacity} = \text{Expected Capacity/Design Capacity}$$

Organizations may need to add capacity to meet increased demand; however, it is important to consider a number of different factors including the timing, amount, and types of capacity to add. For example, if a hospital plans to increase its number of beds, it will likely have to increase its number of nurses as well. The wrong type of capacity additions might even lead to a financial disaster. For example, airlines that increase their passenger capacity by purchasing large jumbo jets may become less competitive than ones that lease the same capacity, especially if periods of increased demand are temporary. This is partly why outsourcing, or contracting with external vendors to supply products or services to cover capacity shortages, is increasingly popular.

Capacity planning for operations managers is tricky business—especially when it comes to corn production. Due to government subsidies, the demand for corn used to produce ethanol for cars in the United States rose sevenfold between 2001 and 2006. But it's hard to predict whether the upward trend in both demand and supply will continue.

Changes in demand can create challenges for determining the needed capacity. Sometimes fads lead to a capacity dilemma. Consider the accompanying A Manager's Challenge and the demand for corn. Whether you are a manager of a farm trying to determine how many acres of corn to plant or whether to purchase more land or you are an operations manager in a company considering adding ethanol-refining capacity by building new plants or expanding existing ones, clearly, determining whether the increased demand for corn is a fad or a longer lasting trend is tricky for either farmers or distillers in the ethanol industry.

Materials requirement planning (MRP) is a system of "getting the right materials to the right place at the right time."[9] An MRP system is a sophisticated computer system that uses information from a company's master production schedule and inventory database. The system produces schedules that identify the required raw materials, parts, and assemblies the firm needs during each specified time period. Firms that implement an MRP

materials requirement planning (MRP)
a sophisticated computer system, derived from the master production schedule and an inventory database, whose output provides schedules that identify the required raw materials, parts, and assemblies needed during each specified time period

A MANAGER'S CHALLENGE

Change

Corn: Fad or Fundamental Change?

The demand for corn for use in the production of ethanol for cars in the United States alone rose from 2 million tons in 2001 to 14 million tons in 2006. But projecting future demand is tricky business.

One factor that makes it difficult is that while crop-based fuel production was in the past dependent on government subsidies, it is now driven by the price of oil. As world oil prices doubled from 2003 through 2006, the price of ethanol rose to the point where its price in 2006 was double its cost of production. This made its conversion into fuel for cars highly profitable.

This is partly why between October 25, 2005, and October 24, 2006, an astounding 54 new ethanol distilleries in the United States were constructed, with virtually all of them coming on line by the end of 2007 at the rate of one every week. This new capacity will allow 79 million tons of corn to be processed into ethanol—nearly double the industry's capacity (41 million tons) in 2005.

This added demand was one of the reasons why there was a 73-million-ton shortfall of corn processed in 2006, and prices rose from $2 per bushel to $3.74 (an 87 percent increase). However, because they need to rotate their crops, farmers cannot simply convert all their existing acres to corn production. It was estimated that in 2007, farmers would increase the number of acres they devoted to growing corn by 15 percent. Consequently, the chances of the ethanol industry doubling or tripling corn output in any one year are not good. Whether you are an operations manager on a farm or at an ethanol company, the challenge of determining the stability of demand and, therefore, the amount of capacity needed is complicated. Will oil demand stay high and supply lag, keeping prices high? Will consumers continue to view ethanol as a "green" alternative? What will happen if instead of ethanol, consumers begin demanding hybrid cars that run on regular gasoline and rely on electric powered engines? How should the spreading shortages of irrigation water and the prospect of even more intense heat waves as the earth's temperature rises be factored into the decision?

For the operations managers in ethanol distilleries, how might a clash between U.S. motorists and 854 million of the world's people who are chronically hungry and malnourished to the point that 24,000 of them, mostly children, die of starvation each day play out? On the other hand, what if the federal government continues to worry about growing U.S. dependence on imported oil and creates laws, regulations, and policies that continue to support the production and use of ethanol? Being caught short of capacity competitively can be just as damaging as being caught long on capacity.

Sources: Earth Policy Institute, November 3, 2006, www.earth-policy.org/Updates/2006/Update60.htm; J. Napsha, "Corn Prices May Cause a Small Ripple in Western PA," *Pittsburg Tribune-Review*, March 31, 2007; A. Speed and D. Pitt, Associated Press Writers, March 30, 2007, "Ethanol Demand Boosts Corn Planting," http://news.yahoo.com/s/ap/20070331/ap_on_bi_ge/planting_report.

system can often reduce their inventory, price their products more competitively, and better respond to customers' demands. Controlling their inventory levels allows organizations to be more profitable. The reason is simple: Companies have to spend money to acquire inventory. The more inventory there is in the system and the longer it sits idle, the more money the firm has tied up in nonperforming (that is, nonearning) assets. The two of the most basic approaches to inventory management that companies can use to enhance profitability are the economic order quantity (EOQ) model and ABC analysis.

economic order quantity (EOQ)
used to help managers determine the most economical quantity of products to order so that total inventory costs are minimized

The **economic order quantity (EOQ)** model was developed in the early 1900s and, thus, has enjoyed a rather long history in the field of operations management. The model is used to help managers determine the most economical quantity of products to order so that total inventory costs are minimized. The actual formula is as follows:

$$EOQ = \sqrt{(2 \times AD \times OC)/(HC)}$$

where

EOQ = economic order quantity (quantity to be ordered)
AD = annual demand
OC = restocking or ordering cost
HC = annual holding or carrying costs per unit

Suppose you were a retailer, and for one of your lines of suits your annual demand was 200 suits. Your ordering costs would be $50. The total unit cost of each suit was $200, and the holding, or carrying costs, related to maintaining each suit in your store until it is sold were 10 percent of the unit cost. Thus, your holding cost per suit would be $20. In this case, the economic order quantity would be 32 units (suits). So, as you can see, although the unit cost of an item is typically straightforward, true ordering costs can be harder to determine. Some research suggests that managers often underestimate the true costs of reordering, in part because they fail to consider such noncash costs as vetting vendors or processing requests for proposals (RFPs).[10] Exhibit 13.3 provides a general visual illustration of the fundamental aspects of EOQ.

Because the two major costs, ordering costs and annual carrying costs, vary inversely, there are always tradeoffs to make. For instance, a company might be able to get a discount for ordering large quantities less often, but its cost to store the items would likely be higher.

ABC analysis
an inventory management system that categorizes items to provide information concerning which items require the most control

Whereas the EOQ model helps managers make decisions about when and how much of a product to order, **ABC analysis** provides information about which inventory items require the most attention. In most companies, a small percentage (15 percent to 30 percent) of their inventory accounts for the greatest percentage (70 percent to 80 percent) of their inventory dollar volume. For this reason, companies are better off putting more effort into controlling and monitoring these high-dollar-volume items compared with the lower-dollar-volume items. For example, to prevent the theft of high-priced items, many

EXHIBIT 13.3

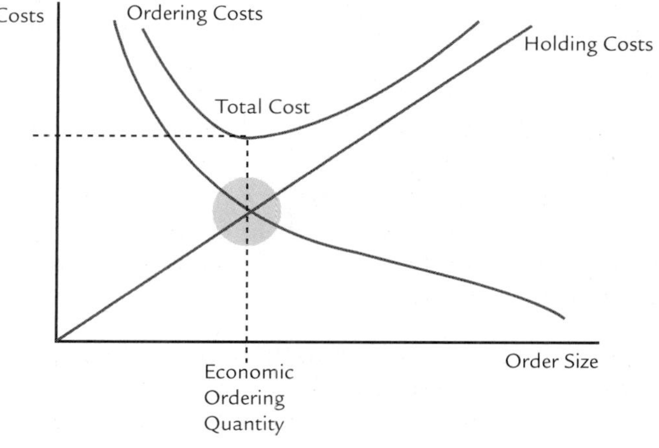

retail stores put special security tags on them. These items are likely categorized as "A" items. ABC analysis provides a way to classify inventory items into three value categories (A, B, and C):

1. A items typically account for the top 15 percent of the firm's dollar volume.
2. B items typically account for the next 35 percent of the firm's dollar volume.
3. C items typically account for the remaining 50 percent of the firm's dollar volume.

For a typical office supply company that sells computer equipment, office furniture, and miscellaneous supplies such as paper clips, it is likely that fax machines would be classified as an A item, whereas desks would be classified as B items, and paper clips would be classified as C items. Based on these categorizations, the firm would want to spend more time keeping better records of the computer equipment compared with the miscellaneous office supplies. The high dollar volume associated with A items occurs because either the items are low priced and have high usage rates (a high number of sales) or the items are high priced and have low usage rates (a low number of sales). In comparison, items classified as C result from either low demand, or sales, or low prices that result in a low dollar volume. Critical items that need a great deal of attention are likely to be categorized as A items regardless of the actual dollar volume of sales they generate. This would help ensure that sufficient inventory levels are kept on hand at all times. For example, hospitals would never want to run out of certain life-saving pharmaceuticals; thus, they would likely categorize these medications as A items to help ensure that sufficient levels are always on hand.

The Timing of Products and Services

Even if operations managers take the appropriate actions to produce the right quality and right quantity of products and services, they still have to ensure that the timing of the flow of inventory and delivery of products and services meet customers' requirements.[11] Not getting products and services to customers when they want them (often termed *stock outs*) can be as or more costly as having too much stock. Researchers have found that between 20 percent to 40 percent of customers who face a stock out leave the store and go to a competitor's store. Of those who continue shopping, 2 percent to 7 percent will leave the store without purchasing a substitute product.[12] The same researchers noted that 72 percent of all stock outs were due to poor operations management rather than unpredictable demand. A Manager's Challenge on the retailer Zara shows how operations managers there have contributed to the company's overall success.

Likewise, carrying excess inventory can also be costly.[13] For example, in the late 1990s when the PC division of Hewlett-Packard (HP) was struggling to compete with Dell, a thorough review of the division's internal costs showed excess inventories were its main cost drivers. The cost of the inventory equaled the division's entire operating income.[14] These costs can come from product-return costs and unsold components becoming obsolete and devalued. Managing these issues is especially important in industries in which customers' preferences can change frequently (such as retailing) or when technology advances and new product introductions are quick and frequent, making inventory like perishable fruit.[15] For example, in 2001, Cisco wrote off an incredible $2.5 billion in raw materials. Because the market was dynamic and rewarded Cisco for quickly meeting demand, the company, along with its suppliers, stockpiled inventory to meet rush orders. But when demand declined, there was too much "perishable" stock in their system.[16]

Just-in-time (JIT) systems refer to inventory management and control systems that ensure the timely delivery of a product or service and related inputs. The objective is to produce the product or service only as needed with only the necessary materials, equipment, and employee time that will add value to the product or service.

just-in-time (JIT) systems inventory management and control systems that have the objective of reducing waste throughout the production and delivery of a product or service; in manufacturing, also known as lean production or value-added manufacturing

The benefits of implementing JIT include:

- Reducing inventory levels to only the parts or supplies that are needed at the time and, thus, lowering the holding or carrying cost of inventory
- Improving productivity and quality by reducing labor and equipment time

A MANAGER'S CHALLENGE

Technology

Zara Managers Focus on Rapid Fulfillment

Zara is one of the key clothing brands within a larger company called Inditex. Zara operates more than 1,000 stores in over 60 countries. In the fashion business, where flamboyant designs and eccentric designers grab much of the headlines, you wouldn't expect operations managers to contribute so much to a leading fashion retailer's success. However, in an industry in which customers' preferences for color, texture, cut, and other elements can change multiple times a year, operations timing is critical. Zara excels at this. Its operations managers have designed, redesigned, and improved the company's system. The firm can now design, produce, deliver, and put on display in a store a new piece of clothing in just 15 days! Because customers can get the look and feel of clothes when they are in style, Zara gets full retail price on 85 percent of its products and has to put on sale only 15 percent of its products. In contrast, the average in the industry is closer to a 60:40 ratio. Getting a higher price also helps contribute to a profit margin that is typically 40 percent higher than the industry average.

To keep the sense that Zara is always on the cutting edge, designers for the company create more than 40,000 new items annually of which about 25 percent are selected for actual production. To encourage customers to buy items when they are in the store, the stock on display is kept purposely low. This way, customers think, "This shirt fits me and is in the right color and style but there are only two on the rack, so if I don't buy it now, it might not be here later." To make this possible, Zara operations managers have to ensure that they have a system that can both keep track of what is selling and resupply items quickly.

This requires the timely and constant exchange of information among the company's design, production, transportation, and retail managers. To ensure that this happens easily, Zara owns and operates all of its design, and most of its production and transportation operations. Designs are communicated directly to cutting machines at the factories for faster production. This close cooperation also allows Zara's managers to do novel things such as putting the price tags on clothes at the factory rather than at stores. Consequently, clothes can go directly from the delivery truck to the store shelves with no delay. This reduces the inventory that Zara stores have to carry, or store, by about 50 percent compared to other retailers such as the GAP or Benetton. The practice also financially benefits the company because Zara stores can be much smaller, pay less rent, and still carry as much merchandise on the floor as its competitors. Alternately, the money saved allows a Zara store to pay a higher amount of rent but set up shop in a more expensive location—a location that attracts more affluent customers or has better customer traffic. In either case, Zara ends up with much higher sales per square foot of retail space it rents.

Zara is the flagship brand of the Spanish based firm, Inditex, Europe's fastest-growing apparel retailer. To be sure, Zara's clothing designs are on the cutting edge. But so are the company's operations. In a mere 15 days, the firm can design, produce, deliver, and display a new piece of clothing in its stores.

Although having the right designs, the right quality, and the right material are all critical in the fashion clothing business, Zara's operations managers ensure that the product gets to the customer in a timely manner. These people ensure that as shoppers' preferences change, Zara can react faster and satisfy the customer better than its competitors can.

Sources: D. Kiley, "Is Zara All That?" *Business Week*, December 28, 2004; K. Ferdows, M. Lewis, and J. A. D. Machuca, "Rapid-Fire Fulfillment," *Harvard Business Review* (November 2004); "Zara: A Spanish Success Story," CNN.com, June 15, 2001, http://edition.cnn.com/BUSINESS/programs/yourbusiness/stories2001/zara.

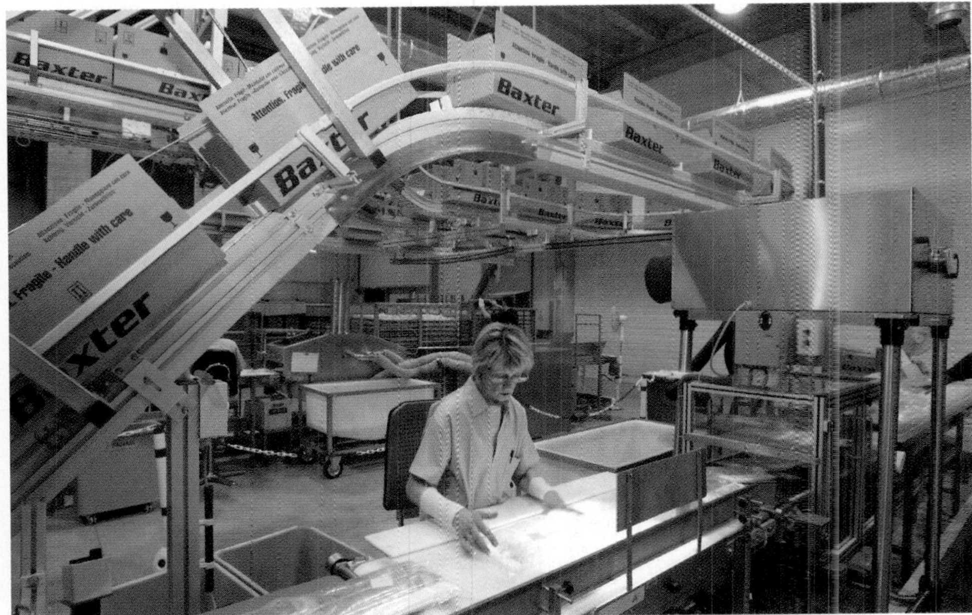

Just one year after a division of Baxter Healthcare Corporation implemented a JIT system and other quality initiatives, the division's defects fell by approximately one-third, and the number of days of inventory on hand fell by approximately two-thirds.

- Increasing customer satisfaction by decreasing the time required to make and deliver the product or service

A number of companies that have implemented JIT have found great success. An excellent example is the Converters/Customer Sterile Business Group of Baxter Healthcare Corporation, a producer of single-use supplies, such as disposable drapes and gowns for health care employees and facilities. Just one year after the division implemented a JIT system and other quality initiatives, defects fell by 32 percent and the number of days of inventory on hand fell by 66 percent. An unanticipated benefit that came from involving employees in the design and implementation of the system was a 37 percent decrease in employee turnover.

For the components to arrive just as they are needed and for the product or service to arrive as close to the time the customer needs it as possible, a high degree of integration of the components and their supply relative to the finished product or service is required. When there is a high level of repetitiveness and standardization of the production of a service or product and its related components, a JIT system tends to work well.[17] However, a JIT system is not as useful to organizations that make customized, one-of-a-kind products or services.

Gantt charts are named after Henry Gantt, their inventor, who was a pioneer of the scientific management era. These charts are nonmathematical graphical representations of projects. They are useful for determining what specific activities should be included to complete a project on time. They are especially important because they help managers monitor the progress of projects and are most often used for projects that have a manageable number of activities (approximately 25 or fewer). This technique helps ensure that projects related to production and the production process itself delivers the designed quality and quantity to the customer at the targeted time. Projects that are much larger often require a more sophisticated technique known as PERT/CPM, which we discuss next.

Gantt charts
nonmathematical graphical representations of projects used by managers to help monitor the progress of projects

The **program evaluation and review technique (PERT)** and the **critical path method (CPM)** are both useful tools for scheduling, monitoring, and controlling the timing of large, complex projects such as the expansion of a freeway system or the construction of a bridge. Due to the complexity of such projects, a number of PERT/CPM software packages have been developed. Although Gantt charts and PERT/CPM are similar in that they both require a complete list of the specific activities involved and time estimates for each, PERT/CPM goes one step further in terms of controlling the timing. Specifically, the PERT/CPM technique requires the project manager to determine which activities must

PERT/CPM
program evaluation and review technique (PERT)/critical path method (CPM) is a technique for scheduling and controlling large, complex projects

precede others and which must follow. These relationships help to determine the critical path through the network of activities. This path represents the *longest* time path for the project and the activities on the path that will delay the entire project if any one of them is delayed. For example, laying the foundation for a house would be considered a critical activity because it precedes a number of other activities, such as framing the house. Delays in laying the foundation then delay the construction of the entire house.

PERT/CPM software can also help operation managers reschedule the noncritical activities of a project, or those that can be delayed without causing the entire project to fall behind schedule. The software can even help the process get back on schedule. For example, laying the foundation for a house is a critical activity, but installing the cabinets is not. However, even though the cabinets typically come later in the building sequence, rather than having carpenters sit idle while waiting for the foundation to be poured, an operations manager might have them proceed with building the cabinets. This would both use otherwise idle workers and allow the cabinets to be installed as soon as the house is framed and sheetrocked.

Cost Reduction and Productivity

As we discussed earlier, making products of the appropriate quality, quantity, and timing can all contribute to lower costs. Nonetheless, there are additional issues that operations managers need to understand and deal with. Productivity and cost reductions are two of the most important of these issues.[18] We group them together here because one often leads to the other.

Managers are focusing on productivity and reducing costs to a greater extent, partly as a result of the greater levels of competition in the world today. The globalization of business is giving customers more choices and information about those choices. This creates less pricing power for companies. As a consequence, they have to increase their productivity and reduce their costs in order to maintain their profit margins. The simple formula for productivity is:

$$\text{Productivity} = \text{Output/Input}$$

productivity
measurement of how well an organization uses its inputs in producing its outputs

Thus, **productivity** measures how well an organization is using its resources (inputs) to produce goods and services (outputs). A useful productivity measure for a restaurant would be *the number of meals served per server*. For an automobile assembly plant, a useful productivity measure would be *the number of labor hours used to produce a car*. Productivity measures such as these can be used for two main comparative purposes. First, a firm can use the measures to compare itself with similar firms, and second, a firm can track productivity measures over time to identify trends. Most operations managers need to be concerned with both the productivity of people and the firm's assets.

Labor productivity applies to both service and manufacturing firms. If we take the case of two manufacturing firms (Toyota and GM), one of the most important measures of productivity is the labor hours required to build one complete vehicle. In 2003, GM's North American operations' hours per vehicle (HPV) built was 34.3. Over the next three years, GM managers worked hard to improve on that, and by 2006, had reduced its HPV to 33.19. In 2003, Toyota's North American operations had an HPV of 32.1. Over the next three years, Toyota's managers in North America also worked to improve their productivity, and by 2006, had reduced their operations' HPV to 29.40. This difference in productivity is one of the reasons why Toyota made money during the time period while GM lost money. In the case of services, Exhibit 13.4 provides a comparison of productivity in the postal and telecommunication industries for France, Germany, Netherlands, Canada, and the United States.[19]

work standard
the amount of time it takes a trained employee to complete a specific activity or process

Managers who are responsible for determining what a firm's productivity measures are and how improvements in them can be made often have to figure out how to measure the productivity of an employee or a group of employees. One of the common methods is via a work standard. A **work standard** is the amount of time it should take for a trained employee to complete a specific activity or process. Developing work standards involves

EXHIBIT 13.4

Service Productivity Differences by Country

	Pieces of Mail Delivered per Person Employed	Number of Calls Made per Person Employed
France	37.5	17.4
Germany	21.1	19.1
Netherlands	51.5	22.3
Canada	92.4	122.6
United States	100.0	100.0

using work measurement techniques. Two popular work measurement techniques are time and motion studies[20] and work sampling.

For time and motion studies, the first step is to review each activity in detail so that unnecessary steps are eliminated. The motto "work smart, not hard" applies here. Only after each process has been carefully reviewed should standard times be developed. Stopwatches are often used to ensure accuracy. In the past, many companies used outside employees to watch and time the employees actually doing the work. More recently, teams of coworkers have begun timing their own work groups. This has been the case for New United Motor Manufacturing Inc. (NUMMI), a GM-Toyota joint venture. At NUMMI, team members look for the safest, most efficient and effective way to complete each process at a sustainable pace while timing each other with stopwatches. This involvement has led to a greater acceptance of NUMMI's work standards and an increased interest in improving processes. This was one of the means by which NUMMI increased its productivity to the point that in 2006, its HPV reached 21.78.

Work sampling is also a popular way of determining time standards, or, more commonly, the percentage of time spent on each activity during a working day or shift. This method is not as accurate as time and motion studies for setting standards for repetitive, well-defined jobs, but it works well with nonrepetitive jobs. It involves sampling the activities performed by an employee or a group of employees at random times throughout a work shift. The assumption is that the percentage of time the specific activities were observed during the observation period is the same as the percentage of time actually spent on the activity. The key to an effective work sampling study is to create an observation sheet that lists all the possible activities an employee might perform. A trained observer then marks each activity observed during predetermined random times.

To determine the percentage of time spent on a particular activity, the total number of occurrences for each activity is divided by the total number of occurrences for all activities. For example, if a nurse is observed preparing medications 10 times out of 100 observations, then the percentage of time spent on this activity would be 10 percent (10/100). Work sampling can help identify areas that need improvement. If, for example, patients complained that they rarely saw their nurses, then work sampling could help determine the percentage of time spent directly with a patient. If this time were below the goal set, then changes in processes and/or staffing levels would likely be needed. These changes, in turn, would improve the quality of patient care. As this illustrates, productivity and quality often are directly related.

Similar principles apply to asset productivity, or utilization. It is helpful to look at asset productivity separately because of the relationships that exist between asset utilization, economies of scale, and unit costs. Economies of scale occur when the per unit cost of production falls as a firm's output increases. This is commonly achieved when a company has certain fixed costs that really don't change regardless of how many units of services or products it produces. The per unit allocation of these fixed costs and, therefore, the total cost per unit go down as more units are produced. For example, a very high proportion of the costs for a hotel are fixed. Whether 10 percent or 100 percent of the rooms are occupied, the furniture, construction, heating, tax, administrative, and other costs do not change very much. Therefore, as occupancy goes up, the allocated unit cost per occupied room comes down.

The nature of the production process can directly affect a firm's economies of scale. Simplified, there are four major classifications of production processes. *Continuous flow production* is characterized by inputs that are transformed into outputs in an uninterrupted stream. This type of process is common in chemical plants, refineries, integrated steel mills, and the like. Typically, the setup costs of these operations are high as are the costs of changeovers (changes in the product being produced). *Assembly line processes* are characterized by a series of workstations at which individual steps in the assembly of a product are carried out by workers or machines as the product is moved along. Cars, computers, and cameras are all examples of products that are typically made via assembly line processes. *Small batch processes* are used to produce exactly that—small batches of products or services. For example, many university classes are small batch processes. A group of students (for example, 30) attend a particular class for a predetermined amount of time, and inputs are added (hopefully knowledge). By putting together a four-year string of these small batch processes, a student emerges at the end with a degree and hopefully possesses the characteristics for which "customers" (employers) are looking. Finally, *job shops* are characterized by production processes that focus on the creation of small groups of products (as small as one) with features that are typically different from one job to the next. For example, most of the high-end tailors on Savile Row in London making "bespoke" suits would be considered job shops. These tailors produce custom-made suits for individual customers.

As Exhibit 13.5 illustrates, typically there is a tradeoff between the flexibility, or customization, offered by each of the four basic production types and its ability to capture economies of scale and thereby reduce the unit cost as greater units are produced.

However, it is important to understand that economies of scale are not the only means of capturing lower costs through higher volumes. There are also *learning effects*. Learning effects occur when the firm gets more experienced at making a product and develops greater insight about how to do the task more efficiently. This, in turn, increases productivity and lowers unit costs. For example, if we return to the case of the bespoke suit tailor on Savile Row, there are essentially very few economies of scale to be captured in this business. Just because a particular shop makes more suits than another does not mean that its production costs will come down. For example, most shops take 50 to 70 different measurements of one customer in order to tailor the suit to that particular customer. The time and associated cost of taking these measurements is the same for 1 suit as it is for 100 suits, except for the learning effects for the tailor. That is, when a tailor is new on the job, it might take him or her 60 minutes to conduct the 60 separate measurements. After having done the 60 measurements on 100 different clients, the learning effect might allow the tailor to now do those same 60 measurements in 30 minutes instead of 60 minutes.

EXHIBIT 13.5

Production Types and Trade Offs

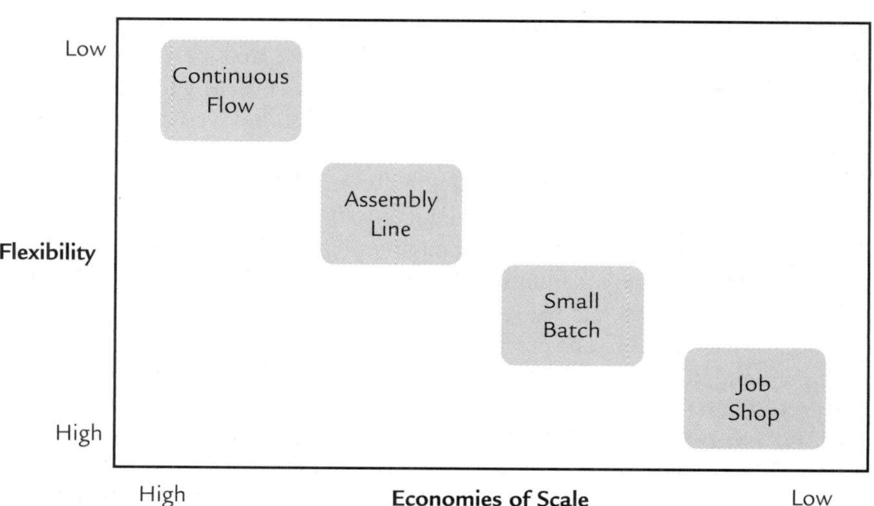

Many operations managers would like to capture *both* the economies of scale associated with continuous flow and assembly line production systems and the flexibility and customization benefits of small batch and job shop systems. This pursuit has led to an effort to develop **flexible manufacturing systems (FMS)**. A flexible manufacturing system is a system that has a higher degree of ability to adjust to both anticipated and unanticipated changes. This flexibility generally falls into one of two categories: station flexibility and routing flexibility. Station flexibility is either the ability to change the order of the firm's operations or the ability of a given worker or machine at a particular point in the production process to adjust quickly so as to produce different products.

flexible manufacturing system (FMS)
automation of a production line by controlling and guiding all machinery by computer

Routing flexibility is the ability to use different people or multiple machines to perform the same operation on a part, as well as the overall production system's ability to absorb large-scale changes, such as changes in volume, capacity, or capabilities. Typically, computers and other automation tools centrally control the whole FMS.

Automotive companies have been big proponents of flexible manufacturing systems, especially after seeing the productivity and revenue benefits achieved by Toyota—arguably the pioneer in this area. The cost of setting up an assembly plant for producing a car is staggering, typically exceeding $500 million and often approaching $1 billion. Moreover, the construction of such a plant often takes 2 to 3 years. Despite managers' best efforts to estimate the demand for a product produced as a result of such a massive investment, many unpredictable factors can influence actual demand. In the case of Toyota, these factors might include changes in the car preferences of customers or increases in gas prices. Therefore, being able to build more than one type of vehicle at a given plant and easily and quickly shift to making particular models based on changes in demand can significantly improve a company's costs and revenues. A Manager's Challenge describes Chrysler's attempt to implement a flexible manufacturing system and the benefits the company hopes to capture as a result.

Computer-aided design (CAD) and **computer-aided engineering (CAE)** are computerized processes for designing new products, making modifications to existing products, and testing prototypes or models of products that can operate separately from a flexible manufacturing system or can be an important part of its design and ongoing operations. In either case, they represent important technologies for reducing costs in large part because they replace the manual and time-consuming process of drafting. The main goals of these systems are to improve the quality of the designs and to reduce the time required to produce the designs. These two objectives, in turn, reduce the costs involved in manufacturing a product because potential problems can be detected at the design stage. CAD and CAE systems also allow designs to be stored and transferred so they can be revised more easily.

computer-aided design (CAD)/computer-aided engineering (CAE)
computerized systems used to design new products, make modifications to existing ones, and test prototypes

A more sophisticated form of CAD/CAE is called rapid prototyping, which uses a technique known as stereolithography to build three-dimensional models out of plastic. United Technology was able to use this technology to build a one-sixth model of its Comanche helicopter used for radar testing. The use of CAD, CAE, and stereolithography provided the information needed for designers to work quickly to perfect the helicopter's precise design specifications.

Once a product is designed via a computer, the next logical step is to allow the computer to manufacture it. **Computer-aided manufacturing (CAM)** refers to the use of computers to direct manufacturing processes. The CAM system can be programmed to guide equipment to perform various manufacturing processes, such as drilling a hole of a specified size, pouring a liquid mixture into a mold, and cutting materials at a certain speed. CAM is most beneficial when the manufacturing process is complex and when frequent design changes are made. The use of a combined CAD/CAE/CAM system can help eliminate duplication between a company's design and manufacturing groups, which not only saves time and money but also improves internal communication among employees within the organization.

computer-aided manufacturing (CAM)
computerized systems used to direct manufacturing processes

Designing for manufacturing (DFM) refers to the process of designing products to both maximize their functionality for customers and to maximize their ease of production and minimize their associated costs. Designing for manufacturing often means reducing

designing for manufacturing (DFM)
designing products for ease of manufacturing so that quality is built into the design process

A MANAGER'S CHALLENGE

Technology

Gaining Flexibility at Chrysler

Chrysler invested over $500 million in its Sterling Heights, Michigan, assembly plant in order to expand the company's flexible manufacturing strategy. The investment will allow the plant to produce the all-new 2008 Chrysler Sebring Convertible and the 2008 Dodge Avenger sedan alongside the Chrysler Sebring sedan.

The investment included a number of technological changes. For example, $278 million of the $500 million Chrysler invested in the FMS was used to overhaul the plant's body and paint shop and assembly areas. This included new tooling and about 620 new welding and material handling robots. Now in the body shop, only the robots' end effectors, or "hands," need to be changed in order to build a different car model. This change can now be done within the time it takes to cycle from one vehicle to the next.

"The assembly operation now has the capability to build multiple upper bodies and multiple vehicle families or architectures, which gives us the flexibility to add new models or 'cross-load' models from other plants in order to better meet the dynamics of the market," said Fred Goedtel, the vice president of Chrysler's Small/Premium/Family Vehicle Assembly division. "In addition, the Sterling Stamping Plant can weld and assemble more than one product on the same line."

The investment allows the plant to produce a higher-quality product faster, and for a lower cost. It also allows managers to efficiently build a lower volume of certain vehicles demanded by niche market segments. Managers can also quickly shift production volumes between different models within a single plant or among multiple plants to match changes in customer demand.

In addition to technology, a new workplace organizational model was implemented to increase the flexibility of the plant's workforce. Employees were trained extensively and encouraged to become involved in all facets in the design and processing of the work stations. "We are seeing a great deal of success at the Sterling Heights facility due to the commitment of our plant employees," said Frank Ewasyshyn, Chrysler's executive vice president of manufacturing. "Their willingness to support and foster a small-team workplace model has delivered a successful launch."

By investing more than $500 million in its Sterling Heights, Mich., plant, Chrysler has been able to produce multiple vehicles faster and at a lower cost. Managers at the plant can quickly shift the production volumes of different vehicles to respond to changes in the demand for them. To further improve the plant's flexibility, employees were trained extensively and encouraged to become involved in all production and design facets.

Sources: "Two Detroit-Area Chrysler Group Plants to Receive Half-Billion Dollars in Upgrades," Press Release, March 22, 2007, accessed March 30, 2007, at www.daimlerchrysler.com/dccom/0-5-7153-1-477538-1-0-0-0-0-0-3882-7145-0-0-0-0-0-0-1.html; "Flexible Manufacturing Retool Delivers New Convertible," March 30, 2007, accessed April 2, 2007, at www.justauto.com/article.aspx?id=90905; "Chrysler Group's Sterling Heights Assembly Plant Produces All-New 2008 Chrysler Sebring Convertible," March 30, 2007, accessed April 2, 2007, at www.theautochannel.com/news/2007/03/30/041715.html.

the number of parts required in a product. This often requires that a firm's various groups, such as its design or research and development groups, closely coordinate with, for example, its engineering and operations groups. For example, McDonnell Douglas Corporation has used DFM in its military and commercial divisions. Specifically, the firm captured a

EXHIBIT 13.6

Instrument-Panel Improvements Achieved via DFM

	Previous Instrument Panel	**DFM Instrument Panel**
Part count	74 pieces	9 pieces
Fabrication time	305 hours	20 hours
Assembly time	149 hours	8 hours
Installation time	153 hours	153 hours
Total time	697 hours	181 hours
Weight	3.00 kilograms	2.74 kilograms
Cost	74% reduction	

significant amount of savings from its F-18 fighter jet program. On one specific aspect of the program, managers reduced the number of parts by 84 percent, lowered costs by 73 percent, reduced the jet's weight by 11 percent, and increased assembly speed by 89 percent. In converting the F/A-18 C/D into F/A-18 E/F, managers reduced parts from 1,744 to 1,048. In the commercial division, by designing the MD-11 cargo liner with customer specifications and manufacturing needs in mind, managers achieved cost savings per aircraft of $86,000. In just changing and simplifying one bulkhead, managers saved $4,000 per plane. In general the part count reduction done by McDonnell Douglas has been in the range from 36 percent to 96 percent on several of its aircraft component assemblies. Based on this, for its Longbow prototype helicopters, executives created an Integrated Product Development (IPD) team to conduct the redesign. The IPD team consisted of individuals from McDonnell Douglas' engineering, manufacturing, procurement, product support, and quality groups as well as its suppliers and others to work together to develop a product design. Initially, the team applied DFM to a limited number of items within the "crewstation." Specifically, the team focused on the pilot's instrument panel. The preexisting panel consisted of 74 parts, weighed 3 kilograms, required 305 hours to fabricate, and 149 hours to assemble. Using DFM, Exhibit 13.6 summarizes the results of the team's efforts.[21]

Managing the Supply Chain

The supply chain refers to the coordinated system of resources, information, activities, people, and organizations involved in moving a product or service from raw materials to components and into a finished product or service delivered to the end customer.[22] As a consequence, many of the activities we have already covered in this chapter related to managing the supply chain. We provide a separate discussion of this area of operations management in part because the increasing technical aspects of managing the entire supply chain and the global scope of the chain for a growing number of organizations makes an integrated discussion throughout the chapter just too complex.[23] Also, increasingly managers have to match how they manage their supply chain to the nature of the business strategy and the dynamics and complexity of the market.[24] As the complexity of managing supply chains increased, so has its potential strategic importance.[25]

Consider the complexity of the supply chain and all the coordination involved in making a Dell laptop computer. Exhibit 13.7 provides a list of the key activities, locations, and organizations involved from the time you might call in an order to the time you receive the computer at your home.[26]

Such far-flung and complicated supply chains would not be very efficient without the technological advances in information systems.[27] Operations managers can track component

EXHIBIT 13.7

Dell's Supply Chain

Activity or Component	Organization(s)	Location
Phone order	Dell	25 centers around the world, including the United States, the Philippines, and India
Assembly	Dell	Limerick, Ireland; Xiamen, China; Eldorado do Sul, Brazil; Nashville, Tennessee; Austin, Texas; Penang, Malaysia
Notebook design	Dell	United States
	(ODM) Original Design Manufacturer	Taiwan
Microprocessor	Intel	Philippines, Costa Rica, Malaysia, China
Memory	Samsung	Korea
	Nanya	Taiwan
	Infineon	Germany
	Elpida	Japan
Graphics card	MSI	Taiwan
	Foxconn	China
Cooling fan	CCI	Taiwan
	Auras	Taiwan
Motherboard	Samsung	Korea
	Quanta	Taiwanese (China factory)
	Compal	Taiwan
	Wistron	Taiwan
Keyboard	Alps	Japanese (China factory)
	Sunrex	Taiwanese (China factory)
	Darfon	Taiwanese (China factory)
LCD display	Samsung	Korea
	LG Philips	Korea
	Toshiba	Japan
	Chi Mei Optoelectronics	Taiwan
	Hannstar Display	Taiwan
	AU Optronics	Taiwan
Wireless card	Agere	United States (China factory)
	Arrow	United States (Malaysia factory)
	Askey	Taiwan
	Gemtek	Taiwan
	USI	China
Modem	Asustek	Taiwanese (China factory)
	Liteon	Taiwanese (China factory)
	Foxconn	China
Battery	Motorola	United States (Malaysia factory)
	SDI	Korea
	Simplo	Taiwan
Hard drive	Segate	United States (Singapore factory)
	Hitachi	Japanese (Thailand factory)
	Fujitsu	Japanese (Thailand factory)
	Toshiba	Japanese (Philippines factory)

EXHIBIT 13.7

(Continued)

Activity or Component	Organization(s)	Location
CD/DVD drive	Samsung	Korean (Indonesia or Philippine factory)
	NEC	Japanese (China or Malaysia factory)
	Teac	Japanese (Indonesia, China, or Malaysia factory)
Power adapter	Delta	Thailand
	Liteon	Taiwan
	Samsung	Korea
	Mobility	United States (China factory)
Power cord	Volex	United Kingdom (China, Malaysia, or India factory)
Memory stick	M-System	Israel
	Smart Modular	United States (Malaysia factory)

parts throughout the entire chain. The increasing use of *electronic data interchange* (EDI), or the integration and, in many cases, real-time exchange of supply chain information allows supply chain managers at Dell to manage such complicated relationships and processes. Sometimes the integration is so deep that customers like Dell are able to determine that they can meet an up-tick in demand for computers with certain features by instructing their suppliers to use some spare capacity in one of the supplier's plants. In other words, Dell is able to see its suppliers' currently used and spare capacity almost as easily as it can its own.

The emergence of the Internet and standard protocols is not only increasing the ease of these exchanges but lowering the costs as well.[28] Prior to the Internet, companies had to invest in and commit to expensive and restrictive proprietary software systems. Web-based systems allow these interchanges to be put into practice in short order and with little expense. One consequence of this is that small companies that previously would not have had the size or global presence to link into supply chains, such as Dell's, can now become partners much quicker if they are able to demonstrate superior quality, reliability, and cost.

These factors create a dynamic tension between suppliers and customers.[29] On the one hand, the higher integration tends to create incentives for customers such as Dell to take a more "partnership" approach with its suppliers. In other words, the tighter Dell is integrated with its suppliers and the more it is dependent on them, the more its operations managers need to work closely with suppliers and the more they tend to need to take a longer-term perspective to the relationship and build trust between the partners.[30] On the other hand, the fact that Web-based technologies lower the entry barriers for new suppliers and lower the switching costs to new suppliers for Dell, the more Dell managers want to not get too wedded to their current suppliers and want to leave themselves open to new suppliers. In addition, there is always the threat that suppliers of core components can decide to put their own supply chain together and become a competitor to their former customer. BenQ of Taiwan did just that to Siemens in its mobile phone business and eventually bought the business in 2005.[31] Thus, there is a dynamic tension between taking a transactional and adversarial orientation on the one hand and a partnership orientation on the other.[32] Exhibit 13.8 provides a comparison of the two basic orientations along a number of different dimensions.

Today, the ever increasing technical complexity of standard consumer goods, combined with the ever increasing size and depth of the global market has meant that the link between consumer and vendor is usually only the final link in a long and complex chain or network of exchanges. Although many companies and corporations today operate not just on a national or regional scale but also on a global scale, none are of a size that enables

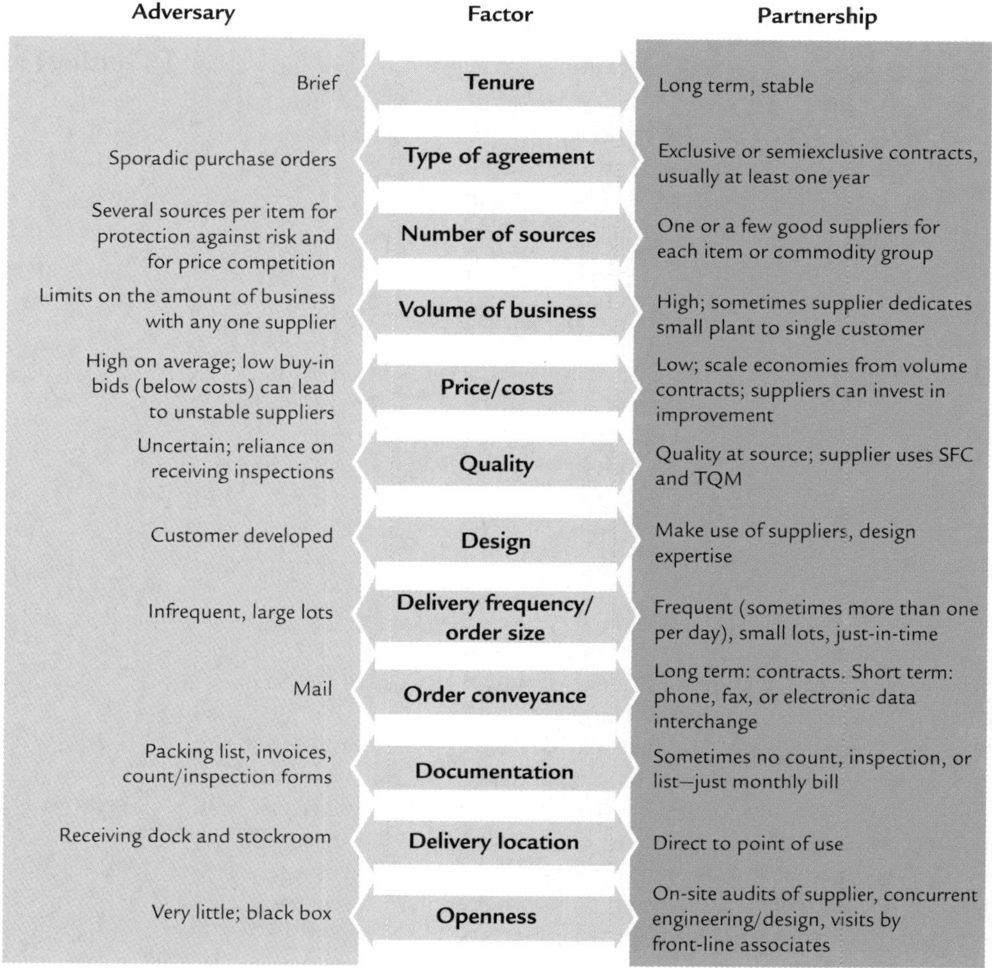

Adversary
Factor
Partnership
Brief
Tenure
Long term, stable
Sporadic purchase orders
Type of agreement
Exclusive or semiexclusive contracts, usually at least one year
Several sources per item for protection against risk and for price competition
Number of sources
One or a few good suppliers for each item or commodity group
Limits on the amount of business with any one supplier
Volume of business
High; sometimes supplier dedicates small plant to single customer
High on average; low buy-in bids (below costs) can lead to unstable suppliers
Price/costs
Low; scale economies from volume contracts; suppliers can invest in improvement
Uncertain; reliance on receiving inspections
Quality
Quality at source; supplier uses SFC and TQM
Customer developed
Design
Make use of suppliers, design expertise
Infrequent, large lots
Delivery frequency/ order size
Frequent (sometimes more than one per day), small lots, just-in-time
Mail
Order conveyance
Long term: contracts. Short term: phone, fax, or electronic data interchange
Packing list, invoices, count/inspection forms
Documentation
Sometimes no count, inspection, or list—just monthly bill
Receiving dock and stockroom
Delivery location
Direct to point of use
Very little; black box
Openness
On-site audits of supplier, concurrent engineering/design, visits by front-line associates

EXHIBIT 13.8

Supplier Relationships

Source: Adapted from Richard J. Schonberger and Edward M. Knod Jr., *Operations Management*, 5th ed., p. 276, Richard D. Irwin, copyright 1994. Reproduced with permission of The McGraw-Hill Companies.

them to control the entire supply chain. Virtually no company controls every link in the chain, from raw material extraction to consumer.

Most of the exchanges in the supply chain are made between different companies. All of them generally seek to maximize their revenues within their areas of expertise. However, most have little knowledge or interest in the remaining players in the supply chain, except those to which they are directly linked. If not managed carefully, the supply chain becomes a chain of competitors without an overall aim. This can result in a less-attractive final product being offered to the consumer due to a combination of increased costs and decreased service levels. Consumer sales eventually decrease, and, as a result, all the links (companies) in the supply chain lose revenue.

Getting raw materials in and transformed into finished products and services for customers has long been the goal of operations managers. Increasingly, though, operations managers have begun focusing on the "reverse supply chain." The reverse supply chain relates to the activities needed to retrieve a used product from a customer and either reuse it or dispose of it. Some of these activities are being forced on to companies due to legislation and regulation. For example, from 2003 onward, tire companies in Europe were required to arrange for one recycled tire for every new tire they sold. As a result, reverse supply chain managers have to focus on at least five key activities: (1) acquiring the used products, (2) managing the reverse logistics to get the products to the company, (3) inspecting the product, (4) determining the disposition (destruction or reuse), and (5) distributing and selling refurbished products.[33]

Managerial Challenges from the Front Line

The Rest of the Story

Michelle Jackson relates that BNSF's operations managers undertook several actions to add capacity and increase service quality. To add capacity, they both increased the length of trains as well as added trains. To add new trains, they needed to not only buy the equipment (locomotives and cars) but also hire and train the needed personnel. To cope with the larger number of trains in the system, operations managers had to add rail capacity. Rather than building new lines, BNSF operations managers instead chose to increase rail capacity by "double" and in some places "triple tracking" the company's Transcon line. The Transcon line is BNSF's main track route from Southern California to Chicago. Double and triple tracking involves laying down a second or third track next to the main one to accommodate additional volume.

Although this helps increase capacity, it can create added congestion at BNSF's terminals and other transshipment points. As a result, BNSF's operations managers determined that they would also need to add more parking spaces at terminals for railcars that were being switched from one train to another as well as more cranes to lift the containers and change them from one train and track to another. Another initiative involved diverting some of the traffic to less-used ports such as those in Portland, Oregon, and Tacoma, Washington. Yet another initiative involved using fuel trucks to gas up BNSF's locomotives directly at the ports. As a result, the trains don't have to travel to nearby rail yards to fill up before leaving for their destinations.

However, despite these efforts, some changes in the delivery schedules were also required. To ensure that the promised delivery dates matched actual ones, at peak times of the year, managers simply had to quote longer shipping times. Jackson also had to convince her customers to change their shipping patterns somewhat to relieve congestion. "We held meetings with our shippers to tell them about the changes," she says. "None of them were happy, but they knew something had to be done to ease congestion." While not ideal, the changes seemed to make a difference. Today, there are fewer bottlenecks than there were in years past, and Jackson's customers are happier as a result. Apparently investors are happy with how BNSF does business too: In about five years, the value of the company's shares has more than tripled!

Summary

- Operations management is a specialized field of management that focuses on efficiently converting resources into products and services and getting them to consumers on time. It is strategically important because it can directly affect both the costs and revenues and, therefore, the margins of a company.
- By taking steps to ensure customers receive the quality and quantity of products or services when they want them, operations managers can improve the repeat business from customers and even the firm's revenues through positive word of mouth.
- Total quality management (TQM) is a general philosophy of enhancing quality at its source. Specific tools for enabling the desired benefits of this philosophy include statistical process control (SPC), continuous improvement (*kaizen*), and Six Sigma. SPC focuses on setting tolerances around targets, tracking performance, and eliminating unacceptable deviations. Continuous improvement techniques focus not just on hitting targets and eliminating deviations but also on increasing performance and extending

targets. Six Sigma is a systematic approach ensuring that all of the firm's activities contribute to meeting customers' specifications with a 99.99966 percent reliability.

- Capacity planning, materials requirement planning (MRP), the economic order quantity (EOQ), and ABC analysis are tools and techniques that help operations managers ensure that the right quantity of products and services are available for customers. Capacity planning involves determining how much a firm should be able to produce of a product or service. MRP focuses on ensuring that the required resources to make the product or service are available. EOQ is a technique for determining the most efficient and effective quantity of an input to order. Finally, ABC is a technique for ensuring that operations managers focus their time on the inputs that have the highest impact on the company's production efforts and customer satisfaction.
- Just-in-time (JIT), Gantt charts, the program evaluation and review technique (PERT), and the critical path method (CPM) are common techniques for ensuring that the delivery of products and projects associated with the production of products are timely. JIT focuses on the management of inventory for the timely delivery of a product or service and related inputs. Gantt charts are used to lay out activities and their timing in order to meet deadlines. PERT and CPM are techniques that not only lay out the sequencing and timing of activities but specify which activities are critical and could cause delays.
- Operations managers need to look for ways to capture economies of scale and learning effects as well as flexibility and the ability to customize products. Developing productivity measures involves determining work standards. Capturing both cost reductions and customization advantages likely will require managers to understand flexible manufacturing, CAD, CAE, and CAM tools, as well as DFM approaches.
- Because of the growing complexity and globalization of supply chains, managers in this area have to focus on coordinating resources, information, activities, people, and organizations involved in moving a product or service from raw materials to a finished product or service delivered to the end customer.

Key Terms

ABC analysis 378
capacity planning 376
computer-aided design (CAD) 385
computer-aided engineering (CAE) 385
computer-aided manufacturing (CAM) 385
continuous process improvement 374
critical path method (CPM) 381
design capacity 376
designing for manufacturing (DFM) 385
economic order quantity (EOQ) 378
effective capacity 376
flexible manufacturing systems (FMS) 385
Gantt charts 381
Just-in-time (JIT) systems 379
materials requirement planning (MRP) 377
operations management 371
productivity 382
program evaluation and review technique (PERT) 381
quality 372
statistical process control (SPC) 373
total quality management (TQM) 373
work standard 382

Review Questions

1. What is operations management and why is it strategically important for all firms, regardless of their focus on or mix of products and services?
2. What are the key similarities and differences between SPC (statistical process control) and *kaizen*?
3. What are the two main Six Sigma techniques, and what is each intended to target?
4. What is EOQ and why is it a useful tool for managers in operations?
5. What are the key similarities and differences between Gantt charts and PERT/CPM techniques?
6. What is JIT, and what are its principal benefits?
7. Contrast and compare economies of scale and learning effects.
8. What is DFM, and what are its common benefits?
9. Explain the key functions of effective supply chain management and the two key tensions.

Team Exercise

Charting the End of Semester

Toward the end of each semester, students often find that there is not enough time to get things done that they need to. This is especially true during the fall semester when final exams are approaching and holiday shopping, wrapping, mailing, travel arranging, and other activities need to be done. Devise a Gantt chart listing all the possible activities and target deadlines. Use PERT and CPM concepts to arrange the activities in key sequences and to identify critical paths. If you followed the resulting plan, how different would your academic and personal results compare to what they are now?

Closing Case Cranston Nissan

Steve Jackson, general manager of Cranston Nissan, slowly sifted through his usual Monday morning stack of mail. The following letter was one he would not soon forget.

Dear Mr. Jackson:

I am writing this letter so that you will be aware of a nightmare I experienced recently regarding the repair of my 300ZX in your body shop and subsequently in your service department. I will detail the events in chronological order.

August 28

I dropped the car off for repair of rust damage in the following areas:

Roof—along the top of the windshield area
Left rocker panel—under driver's door
Left quarter panel—near end of bumper
Rear body panel—under license plate

I was told it would take three or four days.

September 1

I called to inquire about the status of the car, since this was the fifth day the car was in the shop. I was told that I could pick up the car anytime after 2 P.M. My wife and I arrived at 5 P.M. The car was still not ready. In the meantime, I paid the bill for $443.17 and waited. At 6 P.M. the car was driven up dripping wet (presumably from a wash to make it look good). I got into the car and noticed the courtesy light in the driver's door would not turn off when the door was closed. I asked for help, and Jim Boyd, body shop manager, could not figure out what was wrong. His solution was to remove the bulb and have me return after the Labor Day holiday to have the mechanic look at it. I agreed and began to drive off. However, the voice warning, "Left door is open," repeatedly sounded. Without leaving the premises I returned to Mr. Boyd, advising him to retain the car until it was fixed—there was no way I could drive the car with that repeated recording. Mr. Boyd then suggested I call back the next day (Saturday) to see if the mechanic could find the problem. I must emphasize, I brought the car to the body shop on August 28 in perfect mechanical working condition—the repair work was for body rust. This point will become important as the story unfolds.

September 2

I called Jim Boyd at 10:30 A.M. and was told that the car had not been looked at yet. He promised to call back before the shop closed for the holiday, but he never did. I later learned that he did not call because "there was nothing to report." The car sat in the shop Saturday, Sunday, and Monday.

September 5

I called Jim Boyd to check on the status of the car. It was 4 P.M., and Mr. Boyd told me nothing had been done, but that it should be ready by the next day. At this point it was becoming obvious that my car did not have priority in the service department.

September 6

I called Jim Boyd again (about 4 P.M.) and was told that work had halted on the car because the service department needed authorization and they didn't know how much it would run. At the hint that I would have to pay for this mess I became very upset and demanded that the car be brought immediately to the mechanical condition it was in when it was dropped off on August 28. At this point Ted Simon, service department manager, was summoned, and he assured me that if the problem was caused by some action of the body shop, I would not be financially responsible. I had not driven the car since I dropped it off, and I could not fathom the evidence anyone could produce to prove otherwise.

September 7

Again late in the day, I called Mr. Simon, who said that Larry (in the service department) knew about the problem and switched me over to him. Larry said that they had narrowed it down to a wire that passed several spots where body work was performed. He said the work was very time consuming and that the car should be ready sometime tomorrow.

September 8
I called Mr. Simon to check on the status of the car once more. He told me that the wiring problem was fixed, but now the speedometer didn't work. The short in the wires was caused by the body work. Larry got on the phone and said I could pick up the car, but they would send the car out to a subcontractor on Monday to repair the speedometer. He said that when the mechanic test-drove the car he noticed the speedometer pinned itself at the top end, and Larry thought that someone must have done something while searching for the other problem. I asked him if there would be charges for this, and he said there would not. My wife and I arrived to pick up the car at 5 P.M. I clarified the next steps with Larry and was again assured that the speedometer would be repaired at no charge to me.

The car was brought to me, and as I walked up to it I noticed that the rubber molding beneath the driver's door was hanging down. I asked for some help, and Mr. Simon came out to look at it. He said it must have been left that way after the search process for the bad wire. He took the car back into the shop to screw it on. When it finally came out again, he said that he would replace the molding because it was actually damaged.

When I arrived home, I discovered that the anti-theft light on the dash would not stop blinking when the doors were closed. Attempting to activate the security system did not help. The only way I could get the light to stop flashing was to remove the fuse. In other words, now my security system was damaged. Needless to say, I was very upset.

September 11
On Sunday evening I dropped off the car and left a note with my keys in the "early bird" slot. The note listed the two items that needed to be done from the agreement of last Friday—the molding and the speedometer. In addition, I mentioned the security system problem and suggested that "somebody must have forgotten to hook something back up while looking for the wire problem." On Monday I received a call from someone in the service department (I think his name was John), who said that the problem in the security system was in two places—the hatchback lock and "some wires in the driver's door." The lock would cost me $76, and the cost of the rest was unknown. The verbal estimate was for a total of $110. I asked him why he did not consider this problem a derivative of the other problems. He said that the body shop and the mechanic who worked on the wire problem said they could see no way that they could have caused this to happen.

I told the fellow on the phone to forget fixing the security system because I was not going to pay for it. At this point I just wanted the car back home, thinking I could address the problem later with someone such as yourself. I told him to have the speedometer fixed and again asked about charges for it. I was assured there would be none.

September 13
The service department called to say I could pick up the car anytime before 8 P.M. He also said that the molding had to be ordered because it was not in stock. The need for the part was known on September 8, and NOW the part must be ordered. This will cause me another trip to the shop.

When I went to the service department to pick up the car, I was presented a bill for $126. I asked what the bill was for, and I was shown an itemized list that included speedometer repair and searching for the security problem. I said my understanding was that there would be no charge. Somebody at the service desk was apprised of the problem and released the car to me with the understanding that the service manager would review the situation the next day.

My car was brought around to me by the same person who brought it to me September 8. As I got into the driver's seat, I noticed there was no rear view mirror—it was lying in the passenger's seat, broken off from its mounting. I was too shocked to even get mad. I got out of the car and asked how something like this could happen without anyone noticing. Jim Boyd said someone probably did not want to own up to it. He requisitioned a part and repaired the mirror mounting.

Mr. Jackson, I realize this is a long letter, but I have been so frustrated and upset over the past three weeks that I had to be sure that you understood the basis for that frustration. I am hoping you can look into this matter and let me know what you think.

Sincerely,

Sam Monahan
555 South Main, Turnerville

Managerial Challenges from the Front Line

Name: Bradley S. Carter

Position: Strategic Accounts—Construction, East Coast Regional Sales Manager, Fastenal

Alma mater: Austin Peay State University

Outside work activities: Model aviation

First job out of school: Sales Representative, Fastenal

Business book reading now: *Good to Great* by Jim Collins

Hero: Popeye

Motto to live by: "Excuses only satisfy you."

What drives me: Self-achievement, influence in positive change, developing people

Management style: "Determine your own destiny; I'll provide the tools."

Brad Carter has always been busy. Even while attending college, he worked a full-time job as an assistant manager at a local grocery store chain. After obtaining his bachelor's degree, Carter took a position as a sales representative servicing hardware stores with the retail division of a firm called Fastenal. Within a year or so, he transferred to the National Accounts division of Fastenal, again as a sales representative. A year later he was promoted to the position of regional manager in the Carolinas, where he was given the assignment to develop sales growth. From that position, he was promoted to his present job as regional manager for the East Coast in the company's Strategic Accounts group, which focuses on the construction industry. He is responsible for a team of six that produces over $12 million in sales per year.

When Fastenal first created the national accounts division, the company used Microsoft Excel as a rudimentary way of tracking sales. Excel was used because it was both simple and low cost, and it enabled managers to monitor customer contact times and sales representatives' activity. However, as Carter's team grew in size and more customers were added, the whole operation increased in complexity. Brad was confronted with a problem: It was becoming more difficult to track sales call activity in a precise way that matched each individual account with a particular sales representative. This meant that the process of combining and managing sales information was becoming increasingly cumbersome and time-consuming. He had a choice: Continue to hold down monitoring costs by staying with the basic Excel file format or invest in a more expensive and sophisticated customer retention software program that would involve additional—and potentially costly—training of the sales representatives, some of whom had limited computer know-how.

Managerial control problems occur in almost all types of organizations—whether they are large and complex or small and simple. Exercising effective control is a universal and exceedingly important managerial challenge, as Brad Carter found out.

Probably the most critical part of this challenge, for individual managers as well as for organizations, is where to draw the line between too much control and too little control. Most of us can think of examples from our own work or other group experiences: We have probably encountered the downside of excessive control by the actions of individuals, supervisors, or by organizations through their rules and regulations. At the extreme, overcontrol conjures up images of "Big Brother," creating a situation in which you cannot make a move without first obtaining permission from someone higher up in the organizational structure.[1] More typically, too much control can result in resentment and squelched motivation.

At the other extreme, too little control can expose an organization and its managers to very costly risks. In milder forms, undercontrol contributes to sloppy operations and failure to use resources efficiently and effectively. Errors can increase, and the organization may not know where or when problems are occurring and, particularly, how to fix them. In severe cases, the potential consequences can be catastrophic for the organization, as they were for the now-infamous Enron Corporation.

Exercising control, then, presents not only major challenges for managers but also difficult dilemmas. The issue gets further complicated by the fact that, as we will discuss later, there are different types of control. A certain type of control may be quite effective in one situation but very ineffective or even damaging in other circumstances. The bottom line is that managers, no matter where they are in an organization or at what level, will have to deal with fundamental questions of control.

To explore the issue of control, we first look at the role that control plays in organizations and the way it relates to other managerial functions, such as strategy formulation and planning. Next, the four basic elements of the control process—establishing standards, measuring performance, comparing performance against standards, and evaluating results (and, if necessary, taking action)—are reviewed. Following this is a discussion of the different levels of control (strategic, tactical, and operational) and the various forms of control. The chapter concludes with an examination of factors that can influence the effectiveness of controls, such as their focus, amount, and the cost of implementing them. How these factors lead to crucial managerial choices is also explored.

The Control Function of Management

On the face of it, the word *control* sounds negative. It can mean restraints, constraints, or checks. This clearly connotes restricted freedom of action—an idea that many people, especially in some cultures, may find troublesome. Certainly, within the context of organizations, **control** involves regulation of activities and behaviors (see Exhibit 14.1). To control, in an organizational setting, means to adjust or bring about conformity to specifications or objectives that have been set. In this sense, then, the control responsibilities of managers are bound to restrict someone's freedom. A manager cannot control without restricting. However, whether this is good or bad depends on the consequences of the control and whose perspectives are being considered.

control
regulation of activities and behaviors within organizations; adjustment or conformity to specifications or objectives

Some amount of control in organizations is unavoidable. The very essence of organizations is that individuals give up total independence so that common goals and objectives may be accomplished. As one organizational scholar put it, "The coordination and

EXHIBIT 14.1

The Control Function in Management

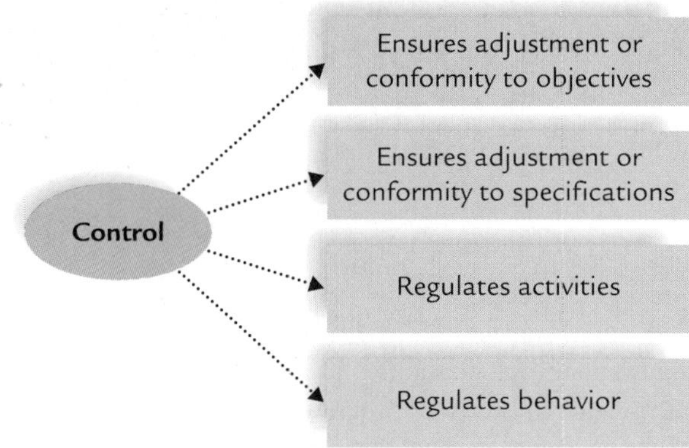

order created out of the diverse interests and potentially diffuse behaviors of members is largely a function of control."[2] Thus, control is a fundamental characteristic of organized activity. Managers should always keep in mind, however, that control is a means for achieving a goal—and is not the goal itself (as the A Manager's Challenge, "Steak Right" illustrates).

The managerial function of control comes at the end of a chain of the other major functions of planning, organizing, and leading. (That is why a chapter on control is almost always found toward the end of most management textbooks.) If those prior functions are carried out well, generating positive responses to controls will be much easier. Conversely, if major problems exist in planning, organizing, and leading, almost no amount of attention to control is likely to work very well. In this sense, effective control is a managerial function that depends heavily on the other functions that precede it. When these preceding functions work well, control tends to work well. When they don't, control can become a major headache for a manager.

Control can also be thought of as a "causal" variable because the results of control efforts can inform and improve the planning process of the organization. Control is thus part of a feedback loop into planning and organizing (see Exhibit 14.2) that can help managers adapt to changing circumstances and conditions. When either the internal or external organizational environment changes, good control systems let managers know if the current ways of operating are still meeting the organization's objectives. For example, some years ago, certain sales agents within a major life insurance company tried to increase their revenues and their personal bonuses based on larger sales through "churning." The churning involved persuading customers who had long-standing policies with built-up cash value to take out new, bigger policies on the promise that these new policies would not cost them more. Customers were not told that the cash values of their old policies were being used to pay the higher costs of the new policies. So, although the customers were not laying out any more cash in monthly premiums than they did before, the new policies were, indeed, costing them. An external audit at one point warned senior managers about the problem. Unfortunately for the insurance company, however, while this control provided

EXHIBIT 14.2

Control's Feedback Loop

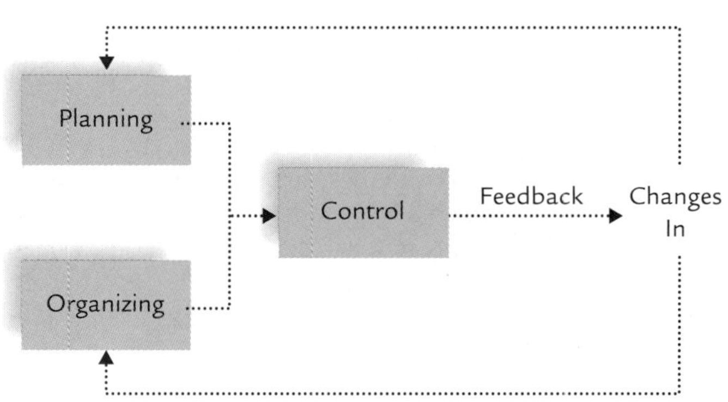

A MANAGER'S CHALLENGE

Change

Steak Right

For fine restaurants, cooking is an art, not a science. The reputation of the food at these restaurants is usually a function of the chef's creativity. So the ideas of standardization and tight control are generally alien to upscale restaurants.

This is not the case with Morton's Restaurant Group, a company that operates more than 70 expensive steak houses and runs many aspects of them with McDonald's-type precision. Morton's chairman emeritus, Allen J. Bernstein, firmly believes that tight controls have been the key to his firm's financial success. By the late 1990s, the company had quadrupled the number of its restaurants and increased its net income as well.

Then, the external environment changed. An economic slump—coupled with businesses spending less on travel and entertainment—hurt Morton's revenues and profits. In addition, the expansion of high-end steak restaurants such as Ruth's Chris Steak House and Smith & Wollensky had intensified the competitive environment in many markets in which Morton's operated. Morton's was under pressure to make changes that would reduce costs. Nonetheless, it kept its customers loyal and attracted new fans by refusing to compromise its strict controls on food preparation and presentation.

The Morton's Steak House chain adheres to strict portion regulation and entrée presentation coupled with an effective cost control and inventory tracking system. The company is said to be able to track a single lost steak.

Morton's controls start with the "bible." This phone-book-thick illustrated binder prescribes, ingredient by ingredient, the preparation of the 500 items coming from the kitchen. The binder exactly specifies everything from the sauces to a medium rare porterhouse steak. The presentation of the food is also not open to individual interpretation. Color photographs line the wall of every Morton's kitchen. Evaluating the presentation of a dish then becomes a relatively easy matter. Either the dish to be served looks like the photograph, or it doesn't.

The push for control is so stringent that each restaurant has a food and beverage controller who spends 12 hours a day tracking the movement of every item. Even the potatoes must meet rigorous standards. "I weigh every potato," says Andrew Moger, a food and beverage controller in the Manhattan Morton's. "They have to be at least a pound apiece."

The adherence to portion regulation and presentation is coupled with an effective cost control and inventory tracking system. Morton's is said to be able to track a single lost steak, which is no small matter with such valuable inventory.

The result is a consistent atmosphere and a dependable menu that brings loyal customers back again and again. "I like knowing what to expect," says one regular customer who brings clients to Morton's for business entertaining. "You never worry about the food or service. When business is involved, you can't trust things to chance."

Morton's consistency through tough times paid off when a mad-cow disease scare hit the industry early in 2004. The company's sales didn't suffer, and its revenues actually climbed. Its consistency produced by the highly developed control system has also made it a desirable tenant in the buildings in which it rents space.

"Landlords want to use us as an anchor," explained Bernstein. "We're in demand because developers can get other tenants if we're there. Of course, they want their new

Morton's to be like the old ones in every way." And—regardless of changes in the external business environment or increased competitive pressures—the steak house intends to be just that. Even a change in the company's top manager hasn't changed the controls at Morton's. Although Bernstein retired in 2005, Morton's continues its stringent control policies under his successor, Thomas J. Baldwin.

Sources: C. Hymowitz, "Managers Are Starting to Loosen Budgets as Optimism Grows," *Wall Street Journal,* January 6, 2004, B1; R. Smith, "Castle Harlan Completes Acquisition of Morton's," *Feedstuffs,* August 12, 2002, 6; G. Collins, "A Big Mac Strategy at Porterhouse Prices," *New York Times,* August 13, 1996, C1, C4; "Morton's Restaurant Group, Inc., Investment Conference," *Press Release,* March 6, 2007, www.mortons.com; "Morton's Restaurant Group's Spectacular Italian Restaurant, Trivi, Opens in Las Vegas," Press Release, February 5, 2007, www.mortons.com.

an early warning signal, managers did not do enough to follow up and investigate, and the company was hit by a raft of lawsuits.[3]

The Basic Control Process

The basic elements of the control process in an organizational setting are simple and straightforward (see Exhibit 14.3):

1. Establish standards
2. Measure performance
3. Compare performance against standards
4. Evaluate results (of the comparison) and, if necessary, take action

Each of these basic components involves important managerial attention and decisions.

Establish Standards

Specifying what management expects is absolutely critical at each step of the control process. This starts at the top of the organization and, ideally, should eventually involve every level of employee. First and foremost, those at the highest levels should be able to articulate a vision and formulate broad strategic goals for the organization. For instance, the motto of Dart Transit Company, a long-haul company that for 70 years has operated with a network of independent truckers, is "to exceed the expectations of our customers."[4] From this example, it is easy to see how particular **standards**, or targets of performance, might be developed. Without a strategic vision and goals for the overall organization, managers in various parts of the organization will find it difficult to develop meaningful and agreed-upon performance yardsticks.

standards
targets of performance

EXHIBIT 14.3

The Basic Elements in the Control Process

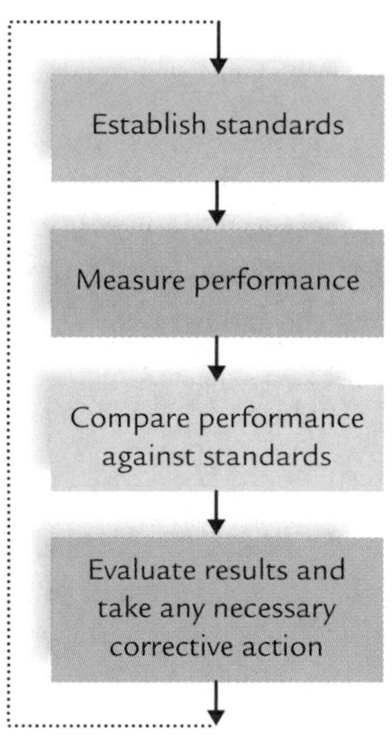

The establishment of standards—wherever they exist throughout the organization—requires as much specificity as possible. The reason for this is that measuring performance against standards cannot readily be accomplished if the standards are vague. A standard of "efficiently responds to customer complaints," for example, does not provide usable guidelines for determining whether the standard has been met. A standard of "responds, on average, to three customer complaints per hour" would permit an objective measurement of performance.

However, for some aspects of performance, especially in higher-level and more complex jobs, such as those in research laboratories, it is often not possible nor even desirable to set up easily quantified standards (such as number of discoveries per year). In these kinds of positions, the most important elements of performance may be the most difficult to measure, such as the probable long-term impact of a given discovery. Moreover, as in the example in the preceding paragraph, the quality of response to customer complaints may be more important than the rate of response. However, quality is often more difficult to measure. As shown in Exhibit 14.4, the more abstract the standard, the greater the possibility of confusion in measuring performance, and the greater the problem of gaining the acceptance of those measurements by members whose performance is being assessed.

If anyone knows how to put on the "ritz," it's Ritz-Carlton employees in the company's 60 hotels located in 20 countries. Each Ritz employee gets over 100 hours of customer service training annually. A daily "SQI" (Service Quality Indicator) in every hotel is displayed on TV screens for hotel personnel to see. The SQI monitors production and service processes up to the minute so problems are apparent and can be immediately remedied.

Other issues also can arise in the establishment of standards (see Exhibit 14.5). One issue revolves around who should set the standards. In general, research has shown that in setting standards participation by those who will be affected is beneficial in two respects.[5] First, because they have had some opportunity to influence the standards being set, those affected are more likely to be committed to meeting them. Second, involving those who have to meet the standards often results in a useful exchange of information and expertise that, in turn, results in more appropriate standards.

Another issue is the degree of difficulty of the standards themselves. As we saw in the chapter on motivation, the research on goal setting points to the conclusion that difficult but achievable goals seem to result in the highest levels of performance.[6] Similar views have been expressed regarding goals in the budgetary process. Thus, "the ideal budget is one that is challenging but attainable."[7] Achievable budget standards are regarded as desirable because they reduce the motivation to manipulate data or to focus only on short-term actions at the expense of long-term objectives. Such budgets also have the potential for

EXHIBIT 14.4

The Effect of Specificity of Standards on Performance Measurement

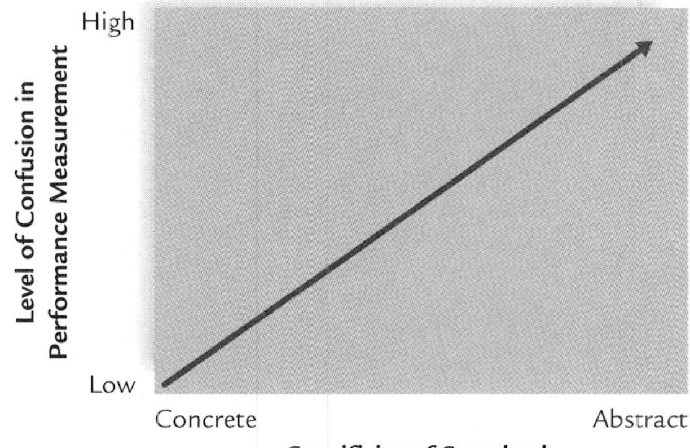

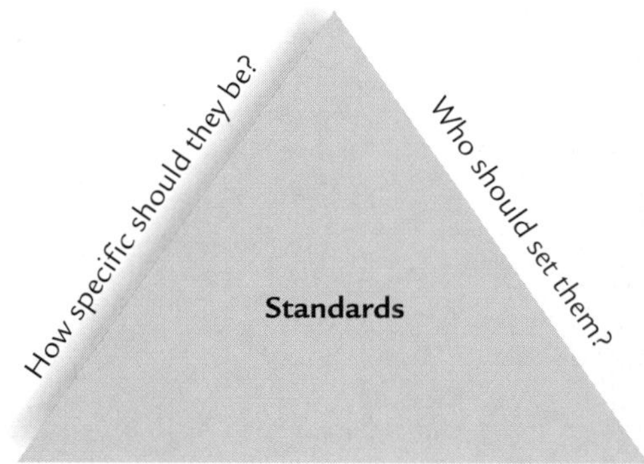

EXHIBIT 14.5

Issues in Establishing Standards

increasing morale and generating a "winning atmosphere."[8] This assumes, as noted, that the budgetary targets are not only attainable but also reasonably difficult. Here, again, where to draw the line between goals that are too challenging and those that are not challenging enough is itself another type of managerial challenge.

An interesting side note on the topic of budgets is that some companies have rejected the use of budgets, and the wrangling over what the data indicate. In the absence of budgets, they use alternative financial and nonfinancial goals and measures. Companies that have rejected budgets require employees to measure themselves against the performance of competitors and against internal peer groups. Because employees do not know whether they have succeeded until they can look back on the results of a given period, they must make sure that they beat the competition. A key feature of many companies that have rejected budgets is the use of rolling forecasts, which are created every few months and typically cover five to eight quarters.[9]

Measure Performance

The second step in the basic control process is the measurement of performance—the actions of people and equipment that the organization wants to monitor (see Exhibit 14.6). If specific and concrete standards have been set, measurement is facilitated and there is more likely to be agreement on how performance is to be measured.

When readily quantifiable criteria do not exist, however, it becomes especially important to obtain as much consensus as possible about the way in which performance is to be assessed. To use an analogy, when true-false or multiple-choice tests are used in a class, the score a student receives is seldom contested (even though the quality of the questions often is). On the other hand, the score given to the answers on tests composed of essay questions is frequently the cause of disputes between students and their teachers. The more an instructor and the class members can agree in advance about the qualities of good answers and on how the essay questions will be graded, the more likely that the measurement process will be accepted. This occurs even though that process is clearly subjective. Similarly, in work situations, gaining an up-front commitment to the performance measurement methods—what are often called key performance indicators (KPIs)[10]—is critical and will reduce later complaints about what those measurements showed and what they mean to individuals and to the organization.

Most jobs involve multiple activities. Thus, it is important for the measurements taken to be comprehensive. If only some aspects of performance are measured, the results can be

EXHIBIT 14.6

Issues in the Measurement of Performance

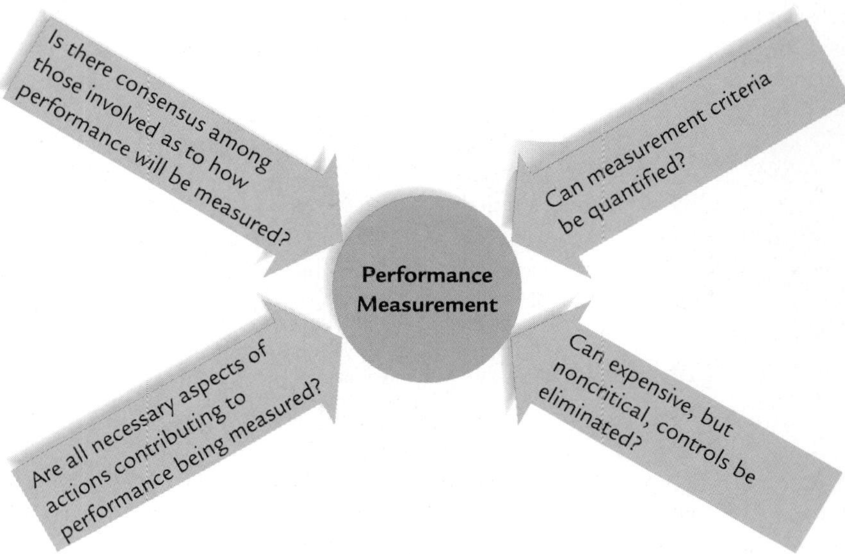

misleading; they can skew the data that are used for the next two steps in the control process, especially taking action to change the performance. Companies such as Kodak, Motorola, Rolls Royce, and General Electric use a comprehensive control technology called "stage-gate" throughout the life of a project. Each project is divided into several stages with "gates" between them. Collectively, the gates act as comprehensive quality control checks that have to be passed before the gate will open, allowing the project to move on to the next stage. This allows management, at each gate, to review the progress of the project and decide whether it merits continued funding.[11] A potential danger, though, is that promising new products might be killed too soon by over-eager, stage-gate keepers.

Finally, even though measurement should be comprehensive, not everything that possibly could be measured should be measured. Measurement has a cost, and the usefulness of the information obtained may not justify the costs. The issue here is one of criticality, that is, what is measured should be highly relevant to the goals of the organization. Activities that are necessary but that do not provide relevant indicators of progress toward goals do not justify the expense to measure them. What is easy to measure may not be what is most important to control (as we also noted in Chapter 8).

Compare Performance Against Standards

Comparing performance results against previously set standards is the third step in the control process. Just as performance measurement is strongly influenced by the standards, so are comparisons affected by the kinds of measurements available. If key measurements have not already been built into the system, it is usually not possible to go back and reconstruct them for purposes of comparison. Sometimes managers realize too late that appropriate comparisons cannot be made.

When several dimensions of performance have been measured, this step in the process can involve multiple comparisons. If those comparisons all point in the same direction, interpretation is relatively straightforward. However, the picture of performance that emerges from a set of comparisons may be inconsistent or contradictory. That is, some comparisons may show good adherence to standards and targets, and others may reveal problems. So managers need to know how to interpret the patterns of comparisons and to draw appropriate conclusions. A single negative comparison may outweigh a number of positive comparisons, or vice versa.

For example, after a major restructuring, Safeway found that its sales per grocery store had nearly tripled, and its sales per employee had also risen by 70 percent. Overall profits were up, but customer satisfaction scores were down. What were managers to make of this? In Safeway's case, sales per store and per employee as well as overall profits were up because it had sold off or closed its least profitable stores (many of which were operating at a loss). All of this might paint a very positive picture. However, the fact that customer satisfaction was down was potentially a bad sign. Grocery stores make money through volume. Therefore, if dissatisfied customers were to start spending less at Safeway and more at competitors, positive results could deteriorate rapidly. Consequently, for any grocery or other type of retail store chain, placing too much emphasis on per-store sales compared with customer satisfaction could be a control mistake.

In this step, managers need to compare expected performance with actual performance. These comparisons often involve both subjective estimates as well as objective ones. However, even if the comparison involves only objective, quantitative numbers, judgment is still needed. For example, suppose Safeway's customer satisfaction numbers were down from 5.5 to 5.2. Anyone can compute that customer satisfaction had declined by 0.3. However, the key question is, "Is this drop significant?" The answer to this question requires managerial judgment.

Evaluate Results and Take Action

The fourth step, evaluate results and take action, is arguably the most difficult managerial task in the entire control process. The results that emerge from the performance comparisons may or may not require action. Managers need to consider whether any single comparison or a pattern of comparisons requires action to be taken. If actual performance deviates from expected performance, how much of a difference is required before something is done about that difference? That question has no single answer. It requires evaluation of the importance and magnitude of the deviation.

An analogy illustrates what is involved in this type of judgment. In industrialized countries, the directors of the national banking system—the Board of Governors of the Federal Reserve System, in the case of the United States—periodically receive the most current data about the national economy, including the unemployment rate, the consumer price index, the index of consumer confidence, the rate of new starts in home building, and the like. These data are compared against predetermined benchmarks, and then a decision must be made about whether to take action (for example, to increase interest rates). The problem for the board, as for any manager in an organization, is to determine which data are most important and how much of a change is significant. However, the issue is even more complicated. Managers must determine whether a slight change in the same direction for all of the indicators is more or less important than a major change in just one indicator. As any macroeconomist would testify regarding the national economy, this type of judgment is not easy.

The other basic judgment that must be made in this fourth step is what action to take if the pattern and size of deviations from expected performance are determined to be significant. Managers need knowledge about the causes of the deviation as well as about the potential actions that are possible.

The evaluation and action step of control requires managers to have strong diagnostic skills as well as a certain level of expertise. Sometimes, the causes of a problem may be easily recognized, but the decisions about which actions to take to correct them may be extremely difficult. Conversely, the most effective actions may be well-known, if only the causes could be clearly identified.

If a manager discovers major negative differences between performance and standards, some type of action is clearly needed because failure to act can lead to more severe problems in the future. However, if the deviations are major but positive, the necessity for action is usually much less (see Exhibit 14.7). Such positive differences, though, may provide valuable insights about unexpected opportunities that should be pursued. For example, a major maker of baby food discovered stronger-than-expected sales of its new line of toddler foods in Florida. Further investigation revealed that the increased sales were not due to a higher-than-expected number of toddlers; rather, they were due to older customers with teeth problems who bought the product because it was easier to chew. This led to a whole new line of packaged foods targeted at this particular consumer segment.

To help maintain positive performance, employees who are doing better than expected can be given increased recognition and rewards to reinforce their excellent performance. Likewise, sales that exceed their forecast may mean that production should be increased or the product line should be extended. Costs that are below target may suggest an efficient

EXHIBIT 14.7

Outcomes of Performance Measurement

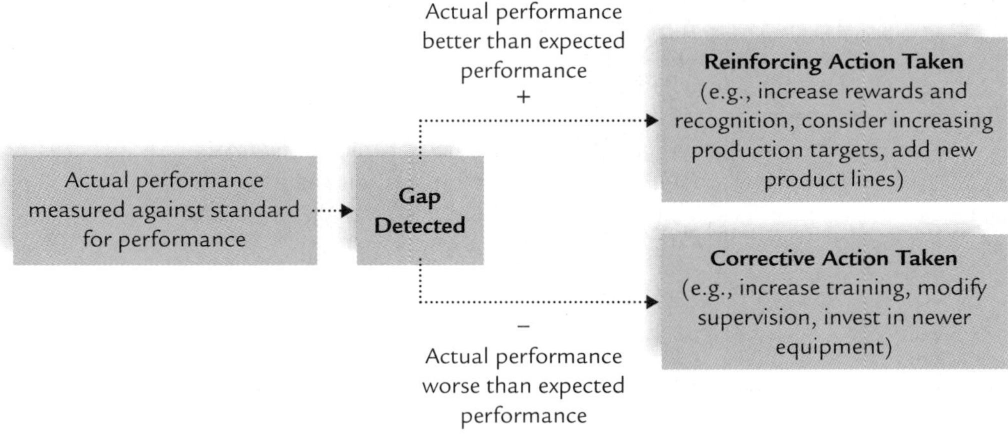

practice that could be duplicated for other employees to follow to reduce the costs even further. In short, it is as important to evaluate surprises on the upside as it is on the downside.

One other issue is involved in determining what action managers should take in the case of significant deviations from standards (either in the positive or negative direction). This is the judgment about whether the standards are correct and the performance is the problem, or whether the performance is appropriate but the standards are too difficult or too easy. That is why a broken-line feedback arrow is shown from "Evaluate Results" to "Establish Standards" in Exhibit 14.3, indicating that the standards may need to be adjusted.

Over time, standards are sometimes modified as experience is gained and the feasibility of existing standards is better understood. If a great deal of effort and care has been used in setting the standards and participation in setting them was broad, then the issue is probably likely to be one of performance. If, though, the standards have been set hastily or without appropriate input from the relevant parties, then performance may not be the problem. This kind of issue points out once again the tight interconnection of the four basic steps of the control process.

Scope of Control in the Organization

Even though the four steps of the control process are similar wherever they occur in organizations, the scope of what is being controlled can vary widely. This, in turn, affects how the steps are actually put into use. A bank provides a simple illustration. The bank manager may need to assess whether she has an adequate level of deposits relative to outstanding loans. The scope is quite broad because the outcome of this assessment could affect the entire organization. If the ratio is too low, the bank may need to reduce its level of lending or try to get more deposits. On the other hand, the manager may also need to evaluate the ratio of human bank tellers to automatic teller machines at each branch. In this case, the scope is much narrower because the issue only involves a small part of the bank's total set of activities. In the former instance we would label the scope as "strategic," and in the latter instance it would be regarded as an "operational" control issue. These represent two of the three major categories of control scope. The third, and intermediate level between strategic and operational, is a category typically called "tactical." (Refer back to Chapter 6 for a discussion of these three categories.)

In the remainder of this section, we look at the issues involved in each of these three types of control classified by the breadth of their scope. However, it is useful to remember that no hard-and-fast boundaries separate the three types (see Exhibit 14.8). The differences between strategic and tactical control issues often are blurred, and likewise, it is not always clear whether a control issue should be considered tactical or operational. Nevertheless, the three categories help remind managers where they should focus their attention.

strategic control
assessment and regulation of how the organization as a whole fits its external environment and meets its long-range objectives and goals

Strategic Control

As discussed in Chapter 5, strategy refers to the direction for the organization as a whole. It is linked to the mission of the organization and to the basic plans for achieving that mission. Thus, **strategic control** is focused on how the organization as a whole fits its external

EXHIBIT 14.8

Types and Scope of Control

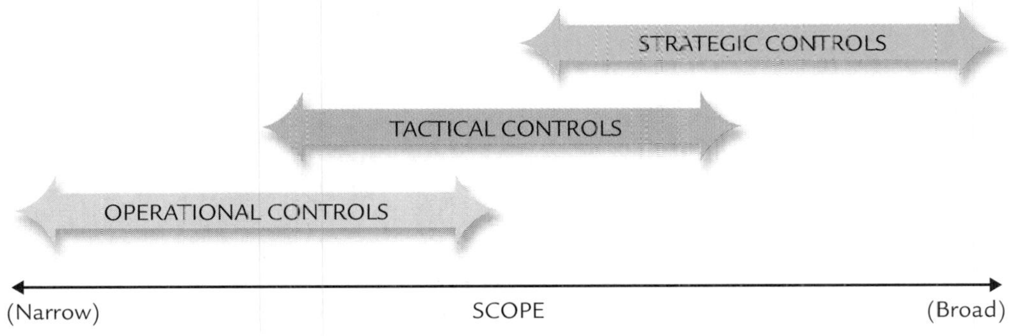

environment and meets its long-range objectives and goals.[12] Strategic control systems, where they exist, are designed to determine how well those types of objectives and goals are being met.

A particular challenge in formulating strategic controls is the fact that strategic goals are broad and, especially, long term. This means that such goals typically are more abstract than goals for particular units. Consequently, setting strategic standards and measuring strategic performance can be especially challenging. For this reason, research has shown that only a relatively small number of firms in both Europe and the United States have yet set what could be termed strategic control systems.[13] The numbers will undoubtedly increase in the future, but important obstacles interfere with establishing such systems.

A significant factor that affects whether strategic control systems can be set up, and whether they will be effective, is the unpredictability of the external environments in which many organizations operate and from which they obtain resources. This also makes it difficult to develop standards and measures that are relevant for more than short periods of time. It is particularly problematic for firms to try to develop useful criteria for assessing the long-term performance of individual managers.[14]

The environmental conditions of large companies affect how much leeway each division or unit is given to determine its own competitive strategies for dealing with its particular markets.[15] The issue is essentially one of how much strategic control systems should be centralized versus decentralized, and how much variation should be allowed by unit. Such a decision involves not only matters of strategy but also of organization structure (Chapter 7).

Sometimes, because of changes in the external environment, companies find they have to reverse course on their overall strategic approach to controls. Thus, McDonald's had to restructure its U.S. operations to reinstate controls it had abandoned in the mid-1990s. Why? Because it was suffering a decreased earnings trend. To deal with this, the company began controlling not only its ingredients but also shaping the experience customers have in its restaurants. It has gone back to more inspections of every store and the use of mystery shoppers, both in the United States and abroad. It is also making more use of extensive customer surveys.[16]

Research indicates, however, that "the efficiencies of managing through centralized control may be greater . . . when the operating environments of divisions in multidivisional organizations are relatively stable and predictable" (see Exhibit 14.9).[17] When there is more uncertainty in the environment, centralized control becomes less efficient. In other words, in relatively turbulent environments, it is difficult for centralized strategic control systems to keep up with events. Consequently, more responsibility for control must be delegated to major units. When the environment is changing rapidly, as it is for many companies these days, too much reliance on organization-wide strategic goals and standards of performance that are set too far in advance can interfere with the needed speed and flexibility of the various operating units to respond effectively to the environment, especially in complex organizations with many types of units.[18]

EXHIBIT 14.9

Degree of Centralization of Control in Relation to Environmental Stability

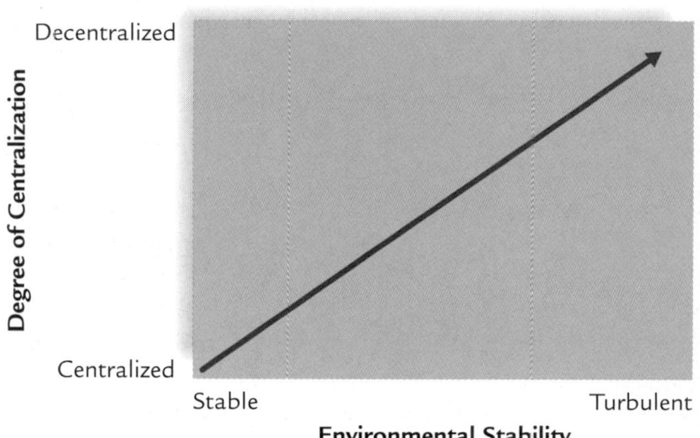

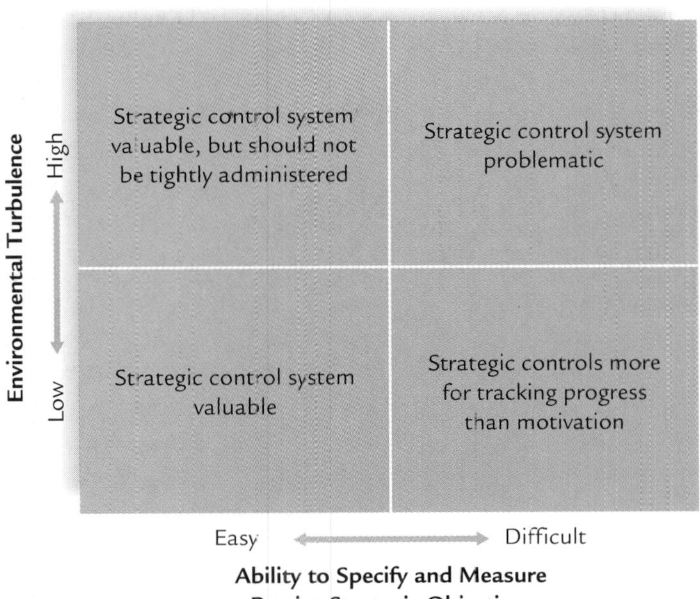

EXHIBIT 14.10

Approaches to Strategic Control

Source: M. Goold and John J. Quinn, "The Paradox of Strategic Controls," *Strategic Management Journal* 11, no. 1 (1990), pp. 43–57 (p. 55).

As Exhibit 14.10 shows, both the degree to which it is possible to measure precisely how well performance conforms with strategic goals and the degree of turbulence or uncertainty in the environment can affect the value of having strategic control systems.[19] They are most likely to be useful when measurement is easy and operating environments are relatively calm, as in the case of the cement industry, for example. Although this industry basically follows the ups and downs of the construction industry, the factors that significantly affect these movements are relatively well known. For instance, changes in interest rates have a significant impact on building booms and busts. As rates go down and money is cheaper to borrow, construction increases. As rates go up and money becomes more expensive to borrow, construction decreases. Thus, for a concrete firm, strategic controls such as being number one in sales in a region can be relatively useful.

Conversely, strategic controls are probably least useful when exact measurement is difficult and the environment is fluctuating rapidly. As recently as five years ago, putting up a Web site for a company involved contracting with a vendor that specialized in the unique and various languages used on the Internet. Companies providing such services have seen their world change dramatically. New languages and tools have emerged so that almost anyone with a little skill and knowledge can create a professional-looking Web site. In such a turbulent environment, strategic goals do not last long. Therefore, strategic controls are of more limited value in these types of organizations.

Strategic control is especially challenging in international organizations. Even with advances in communication and transportation technology, Sydney is still a long way from Paris, so to speak. Consequently, maintaining strategic control across a worldwide organization that crosses cultural, economic, social, political, and religious borders as well as 13 different time zones is significantly more difficult than it is for a purely domestic organization.

Tactical Control

Tactical control focuses on the implementation of strategy. Thus, this level of control forms the heart and, one might say, the soul of an organization's total set of controls. Tactical control involves the fundamental control arrangements of the organization, those with which its members have to live day to day. Four of the most important types of tactical control systems are financial controls, budgets, the supervisory structure, and human resource policies and procedures.

tactical control
assessment and regulation of the day-to-day functions of the organization and its major units in the implementation of its strategy

The first two types of control, financial and budgetary, contain elements of both strategic and tactical control systems. To the extent they focus on the entire organization, they

EXHIBIT 14.11

Characteristics of Strategic and Tactical Controls

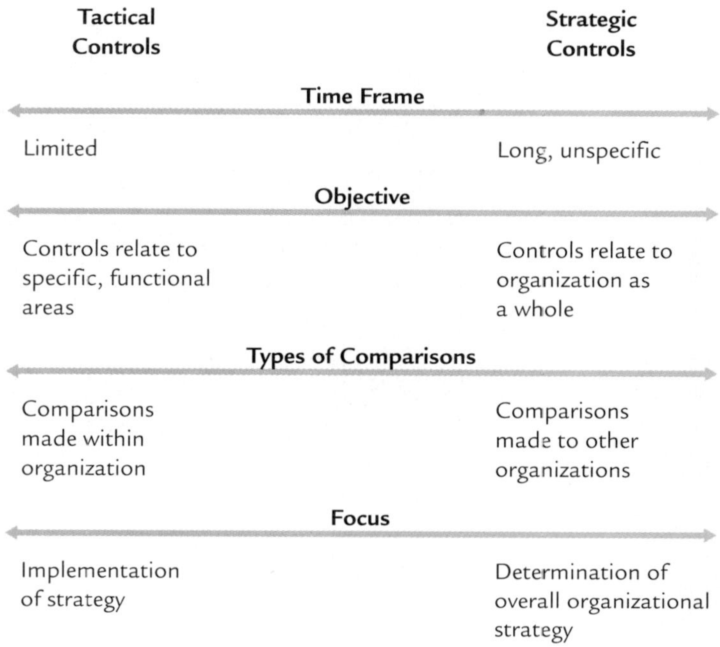

tend to be more toward the strategic end of the continuum (see Exhibit 14.11), and the more they focus on specific units within an overall organization, they tend to be toward the tactical end. We have chosen to discuss them in this section since they most often focus on organizational units, but keep in mind that they, especially financial controls, can also be used as well for some strategic control considerations.

FINANCIAL CONTROLS Financial controls include several important quantitative ratios involving key financial statistics.[20] Although these statistics are always generated at the organization-wide level as well as at the organizational-unit level, they are especially useful at the unit level as a form of tactical control.

The data used for the most important financial controls involve a basic cost-benefit analysis. For example, ratios relevant to the profitability of a given unit are constructed from revenue data (benefit) in relation to given amounts of investment (cost). The ratio is called return on investment (ROI), or alternatively, return on equity (ROE), and compares the amount of net profit before taxes (the numerator of the ratio) to the total amount of assets invested (the denominator). Thus, a unit that earns a profit of $500,000 in a given year from invested assets of $10 million would have an ROI of 0.05 for that year. If another unit generated that same amount of profit on invested assets of only $5 million, its ROI would be 0.10. This unit's financial performance would be superior because it generated an equal benefit for less cost.

Other financial ratios that are commonly used to assess unit performance include, in addition to profitability ratios, those related to liquidity (current assets in relation to current liabilities), which provides an indication of how well the unit can meet its short-term cash requirements; leverage (a firm's total debt to its total assets), which provides an indication of a company's ability to meet its long-term financial obligations; and efficiency or activity (for example, the amount of sales in a given period relative to the cost of inventory used to generate those sales), measuring how efficiently assets are used.

Exhibit 14.12 shows examples of these four types of ratios for two organizations in the retail industry for the year 2006. As seen in the exhibit, The Limited had a lower ROI than The GAP that year, somewhat less liquidity, a less favorable leverage ratio, and a slightly less efficient use of inventory. If these had been two units within the same larger organization, one would say that for this year The GAP unit was doing better overall insofar as its financial performance was concerned.

RATIO	FORMULA	COMPANY			
		The Gap Inc. 2006 (In $ millions)		The Limited Inc. 2006 (In $ millions)	
Profit					
Return on Investment	Net Profit Before Taxes / Total Asset	1,793 / 8,821	0.20	957 / 5,346	0.15
Liquidity					
Current Ratio	Current Assets / Current Liabilities	5,239 / 1,942	2.70	2,784 / 1,575	1.77
Leverage					
Debt to Asset	Total Debt / Total Assets	3,396 / 8,821	.038	3,875 / 5,346	0.61
Activity					
Inventory Turnover	Sales / Inventory	16,023 / 1,696	9.45	9,699 / 1,160	8.36

EXHIBIT 14.12

Examples of Company Financial Ratios

The important point here, regarding the various financial ratios, is not the detailed steps that need to be taken to calculate the ratios. Rather, it is that when the ratios are calculated, they can be used to compare one organization, or one unit, to another. It is this comparative nature of the ratios that provides managers with the information they need to take action during the control process. The numbers used to calculate a ratio, such as inventory turnover, for example, will show whether the ratio is relatively unfavorable, and if so, an examination of the two components used in the ratio will also indicate whether the problem seems to be in the amount of sales (too low), or in the amount of inventory (too high), or both. In other words, financial ratios are a very useful diagnostic control tool for managers.

Another financial measure is sometimes used for control purposes in business organizations. That measure is called the **break-even point (B-E P)**. Essentially, the B-E P is where the selling price of a unit of a product (or service) minus its variable costs exceeds the fixed costs for that unit. The lower the fixed costs, the fewer the units of goods or services that need to be sold for a break-even point to be reached. Likewise, the lower the variable costs, the higher the profit per unit and, therefore, the fewer the units that need to be sold to reach that point. Break-even analysis, then, provides a way for managers to gauge whether new products or services have a potential to turn a profit. Managers can, therefore, exercise control *before* new ventures are undertaken. Even more important, for ongoing operations, a break-even point analysis focuses managers' attention on reducing or controlling the two categories of costs—fixed and variable—to take the pressure off the need to sell larger volumes.

break-even point (B-E P) amount of a product that must be sold to cover a firm's fixed and variable costs

The airline industry provides an example of where a break-even point analysis can illustrate comparisons between two organizations, or business units. Many of the larger airlines have set up separate subsidiary airlines. For example, American Eagle was set up by American Airlines to handle its short-haul commuter routes. These commuter airlines can operate on relatively small volumes of passenger traffic because their costs—like lower wage bases for their pilots—produce lower break-even points. Similarly, certain independent airlines—if they are especially efficient—can charge very low fares on many of their routes and still make a profit. Southwest Airline is another example. Southwest avoided the cost of passengers' meals by serving only snacks long before other airlines did. It also kept its highly flexible point-to-point route system, instead of adopting the hub-and-spoke system of most major airlines.[21]

Although a B-E P analysis can provide extremely useful information for managers for control purposes, such an analysis also has limitations. Looking strictly at the numbers of a B-E P analysis may discourage certain decisions that could ultimately result in very profitable activities that do not initially appear to be profitable. Also, it is not always easy to allocate costs between fixed and variable categories, and it is sometimes difficult to project costs accurately, especially variable costs. Like other financial controls, a break-even point analysis can be an aid to exercising effective control, but it is not by itself a guarantee of wise decisions. What it does, however, is highlight the potential advantages to be gained by controlling specific types of costs.

budgetary control
a type of tactical control based on responsibility for meeting financial targets and evaluating how well those targets have been met

BUDGETARY CONTROLS Budgets are used in almost every organization (as we discussed in Chapter 6), and, like financial controls, can sometimes be considered elements of a strategic system. **Budgetary controls**, however, are more usefully viewed as a significant form of tactical control because they focus on how well strategies are being implemented. In contrast to purely strategic control, budgetary controls:

- Typically cover a relatively limited time frame (usually 12-month or 3-month periods).
- Focus exclusively on one type of objective (financial).
- Usually cannot be used to compare a total organization's progress relative to its competitors.[22]

Anyone occupying a managerial position both is controlled by budgets and uses budgets to control others. A budget is a commitment to a forecast to make an agreed-upon outcome happen.[23] Thus, it is more than a forecast, which is simply a prediction. A budget is designed to influence behavior so that forecasts or plans for expenditures and (where relevant) revenues can be achieved. It "controls" by assigning responsibility for meeting financial targets and for evaluating how well those targets have been met. It would be difficult indeed to maintain an organization if none of its members were held accountable for limits on expenditures.

When using budgets as a form of control, managers face several important issues, as shown in Exhibit 14.13. One is the question of whether to use a fixed budget for a specific period, usually 12 months, and stick with those numbers, or to revise it midway during the period based on changes in operating conditions. Ace Hardware, for example, adopted a rolling planning and budgetary process. With the previous annual process, the conditions on which Ace's budget were based were frequently out of date by the time the budget was finalized.[24] A rolling budgetary process with relatively frequent revisions has the advantage of being more current and, therefore, more accurate; however, it also can take more managerial time and effort.

Another budget issue is whether compensation bonuses should be based on the achievement of budgetary targets. This sounds good, but it has the great disadvantage of encouraging budget game playing. Why? Because the person being evaluated has an incentive to provide high cost and low revenue estimates when the budget is first developed. By creating "budgetary slack" with relatively easy targets, the person has a higher probability of hitting the targets and earning a bonus. Thus, managers who supervise the preparation of budgets need to be alert to how a bonus system of this type can distort estimates and thus undermine control. Managers also need to make sure that they don't inadvertently create a short-term focus on the part of subordinates attempting to meet budgetary targets at the expense of more important, longer-term organizational goals.[25]

A third budgetary control issue involves the question of whether those responsible for meeting specified targets should be evaluated only on expenditures and revenues over which they have direct control, or whether they should be evaluated on a final "net" figure based on all costs and revenues for a given unit. The former results in a more direct link between managerial behavior and budgetary responsibility, but the latter is the ultimate "bottom line," especially for publicly held corporations. For example, as a manager of a sales unit, you might have strong control over the revenues that your unit generates and the money spent on travel expenses. When these travel expenses are subtracted from sales, your unit might look very good. However, if your unit also uses marketing and promotion materials to get these sales, they may need to be factored into the overall assessment. Otherwise, you may overspend on marketing and promotion activities.

EXHIBIT 14.13

Issues in Budgetary Control

Issue	Questions
Rolling budgets and revision	Should the budget period be for 12 months followed by another 12-month budget a year later, or should a calendar quarter be added each time a new calendar quarter begins? Should the budget remain fixed for the budget period or should it be revised periodically during the period?
Fixed or flexible budgets	Should performance be evaluated against the original budget or against a budget that incorporates the actual activity level of the business?
Bonuses based on budgets	Should incentive compensation, if any, be based on actual versus budgeted performance, or on actual performance against some other standard?
Evaluation criteria	Should the budget used to evaluate performance include only those items over which the evaluated manager has control, or should it include all unit costs and revenues appropriate to the managerial unit?
Tightness of the budget	What degree of "stretch" should there be in the budget?

Source: Adapted from N. C. Churchill, "Budget Choices: Planning vs. Control," *Harvard Business Review 62*, no. 4 (1984), pp. 150–64 (p. 151).

The final, and perhaps most important, managerial control issue regarding budgets is how tight or loose to make them. Should a budget require those charged with meeting it to make an extra "stretch"? As we have said before, research indicates that the best performance results from goals that are challenging but achievable. Since budgets represent goals, this conclusion seems highly relevant to the issue of budgetary control.

SUPERVISORY STRUCTURE CONTROLS The basic **supervisory structure** of an organization is probably the most widespread tactical control system that a typical employee encounters. The amount and form of such control, as well as how employees react to it, varies considerably from organization to organization[26] but almost always exists in some form. In organizations of any size, there is always someone or some group to which an employee or manager reports. (Recall the discussion of span of control in Chapter 7.) Even in the least bureaucratic types of work organizations, such as research laboratories and nonprofit enterprises, some sort of reporting structure almost always regulates the activities of each member. However, such supervisory control structures, like other controls, can fail.

supervisory structure
a type of tactical control based on reporting levels in an organization

This was demonstrated several years ago at the Ohio division of the American Cancer Society. Up until then, the organization had enjoyed a great deal of success. However, in 2000, the society's board of directors announced that its chief administrative officer had embezzled $7.5 million over a period of approximately three years. This had occurred even though a new CEO had checked all security arrangements when he started a few years before. The administrative officer had used a variety of schemes to steal the funds, such as billing for imaginary services, charging personal home repairs and expenditures to the organization, and transferring money to secret accounts in Europe. The board and top managers were shocked to find out that all their controls had failed in this instance. The administrative officer had never received a background check (which would have revealed

EXHIBIT 14.14

Opportunities for Control in the Human Resource Function

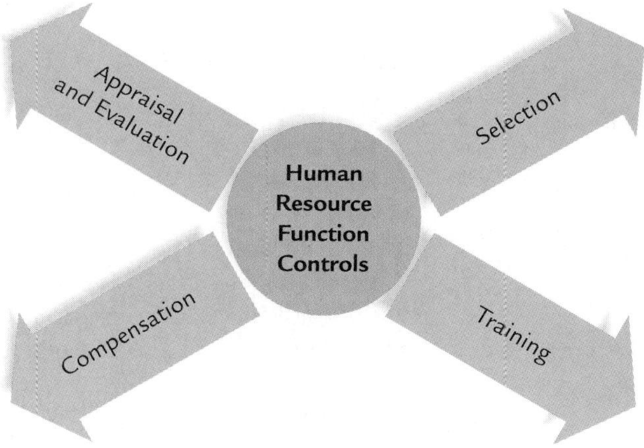

previous problems), was the only person authorized to sign large-amount checks, and, especially, had received no direct supervision of his day-to-day activities.[27]

human resource policies and procedures
a type of tactical control based on the organization's overall approach to utilizing its human resources

HUMAN RESOURCE CONTROLS **Human resource policies and procedures** are a fourth major type of tactical control that affects everyone working in an organization. We have discussed these in detail in Chapter 8, but what is important to stress about them here is that they provide a number of different opportunities for control (see Exhibit 14.14):

- Selection procedures can specify the range of abilities and knowledge that will be brought into the organization.[28]
- Training can improve people's skills and performance levels so that they meet standards.
- Appraisal and evaluation methods can reinforce desired behavior and discourage undesirable levels of performance.
- Compensation can be used to motivate employees and increase their efforts in particular directions.

An example of using human resource procedures to reinforce desired behavior occurred when Standard Life of Scotland, one of the largest insurance companies in Europe, changed its performance evaluation and reward systems to a "contribution management system." The new system focused on the importance (not just the number) of an employee's accomplishments, his or her effort to develop the competencies needed to accomplish critical tasks, and the employee's contribution to customer satisfaction and the overall performance of the business. The change in approach required employees to be highly involved in goal setting, training plans, and reward determinations. As a result of these changes in human resource procedures, the company has gone from being one of the lowest ranked with regard to performance and customer satisfaction to one of the highest within the United Kingdom. It was also voted "company of the year" five years running in its industry.[29]

Because the effects of human resource policies and procedures are so extensive, they are a very powerful means of control. When used with skill and deftness, they are a significant aid to the achievement of organizational objectives, as the Standard Life of Scotland example illustrates. When used ineptly, and with heavy-handedness, however, they can hinder organizational progress.

CONTRASTING APPROACHES TO USING TACTICAL CONTROLS The ways in which tactical control systems are implemented say a great deal about an organization—what it is like to work there and how effective the control is. These control systems characterize an organization and are a critical part of its identity. For these reasons, it is important to specify and discuss the two fundamental approaches to tactical control: (a) imposed, or bureaucratic, control and (b) elicited, or commitment or clan, control (see Exhibit 14.15).[30] Most organizations use a combination of these two approaches but also tend to emphasize one over the other.

Type of Control	Social Requirements[a]	Control Approach	Informational Requirements
Bureaucracy	• Norm of reciprocity • Legitimate authority	• Adherence to rules and regulations • Formal and impersonal • Emphasis on detecting deviance • Imposed on the individual	• Rules
Clan	• Norm of reciprocity • Legitimate authority • Shared values, beliefs	• Stresses group consensus on goals and their measurement • Mutual assistance in meeting performance standards • Uses deviations as guidelines in diagnosing problems • Control comes from the individuals or groups	• Traditions

[a]Social requirements are the basic agreements between people that, at a minimum, are necessary for a form of control to be employed.

Source: Adapted from William G. Ouchi, "A Conceptual Framework for the Design of Organizational Control Mechanisms," *Management Science* 25, no. 9 (1980), pp. 833–47 (p. 838)

EXHIBIT 14.15 Control in Bureaucracy and Clan Structures

Bureaucratic control stresses adherence to rules and regulations and a formal, impersonal administration of control systems. For instance, ExxonMobil has a thick operating manual for refinery managers. It specifies everything from which types of capital budget requests need which type of approval to equipment maintenance schedules. This approach highlights rational planning and orderliness. It heavily emphasizes detecting deviance from standards. The *failure* to follow standard operating manuals in this type of bureaucratic control was illustrated several years ago in an incident where high winds blew parts of a scaffold off the John Hancock Center building in Chicago, killing four people.[31] Regardless of whether this type of control is effective or not, its foremost feature, in a control sense, is that control is *imposed* on the person, group, or activity. From an employee's perspective, "others" do the controlling.

bureaucratic control
an approach to tactical control that stresses adherence to rules and regulations and is imposed by others

Commitment, or **clan, control** stresses obtaining consensus on what goals should be pursued and then developing a shared sense of responsibility and self-control for achieving those goals.[32] It is called a "clan" approach to control because of the emphasis on generating shared and deeply held values, as in a set of close relatives, and on mutual assistance in meeting performance standards. Unlike the bureaucratic approach, the clan approach tends to treat deviations from standards more as a basis for diagnosis than for taking corrective action. Its foremost feature, in a control sense, is that control is viewed as being *elicited from,* rather than imposed on, the person, group, or activity. From an employee's perspective, the employee or his or her group, rather than others, does the controlling.

commitment (clan) control
an approach to tactical control that emphasizes consensus and shared responsibility for meeting goals

You might wonder why every organization doesn't use a commitment approach. It sounds as if it would function better for both the organization and those who work in it. However, things are not that simple. Creating a genuine clanlike atmosphere among employees, especially in large organizations, is extremely difficult. It takes time and also considerable managerial effort. It may not succeed, or, more likely, succeed only partially. If a true clanlike, high-commitment culture is not created, an organization cannot rely on self-control by individuals or groups to exercise sufficient control. However distasteful it may sound, some amount of bureaucratic managerial control seems necessary for most complex organizations.

Even from the perspective of the organization member or employee, self-imposed clan control may not be as satisfying as it would seem at first glance. A detailed study of a small manufacturing company illustrates the point.[33] This company converted its traditional hierarchical structure, which emphasized a high degree of supervisory control, to a structure that was built around self-managing work teams. In the first phase of the transition, the teams spent a good deal of time developing consensus on what constituted, both collectively and individually, good work for the teams and good patterns of behavior that would translate those standards into action. In the second phase, the teams developed strong norms regarding expected behavior. Experienced team members expected new workers to buy into the teams' values and act according to their norms.

Under the old system, supervisors tolerated some slackness among the workers. But in the team system, the members exercised their newfound authority with much less patience. The clan approach to control tended to formalize the teams' norms and create ironclad, self-imposed rules. The researcher studying this company stated, "The teams had now created, in effect, a nearly perfect form of control. . . an essentially total system of control almost impossible to resist. . . . The team members had become their own masters and their own slaves." For these teams, clan control had become an "iron cage," as the researcher put it.

The previous example serves to emphasize the point that no single approach to managerial control will work well in all situations. It also shows that whatever approach is chosen will have its own unique problems as well as advantages.

Operational Control

operational control
assessment and regulation of the specific activities and methods an organization uses to produce goods and services

precontrol
a type of operational control that focuses on the quality, quantity, and characteristics of the inputs into the production process

concurrent control
a type of operational control that evaluates the conversion of inputs to outputs while it is happening

postcontrol
a type of operational control that checks quality after production of goods or services outputs

Operational control, as the name implies, regulates the activities or methods an organization uses to produce the goods and services it supplies to customers and clients. It is control applied to the transformation of inputs into outputs, such as the actions that produce a car, administer therapy to an ill patient, cook and serve a restaurant meal, send a satellite into the sky, or write computer software. In short, operational control "is where the rubber meets the road."

The overall management of operations involves a number of critical and often technical issues. Here, we focus specifically on an overview of the control process relating to operations. Operational control can be analyzed by relating it to the three basic elements involved in any type of service or goods production: inputs, transformation, and outputs (Exhibit 14.16).[34] These three elements can be related to the location of control in the production process: before transformation occurs, or **precontrol**; during transformation, or **concurrent control**; and after transformation takes place, or **postcontrol**.

PRECONTROL OF OPERATIONS This form of operational control focuses on the quality, quantity, and characteristics of the inputs into the production process—for example, the purity of steel, the grade of beef, the number of passengers, the age of patients, the test scores of entering students, the aptitudes of job applicants. Such precontrol is illustrated by the actions of a company called South West Trading, which manufactures yarns made from bamboo, corn, and soybeans. It controls its raw materials at the point of origin and utilizes the services of United Parcel Service (UPS) to combine orders from various factories into one container for shipment.[35]

The more stringent the control over the quality of inputs, the less need for control at the later two stages. The higher the quality of army recruits, for example, the easier it is to train them to be competent soldiers. However, there is a cost involved in exacting precontrol

EXHIBIT 14.16

Operational Controls

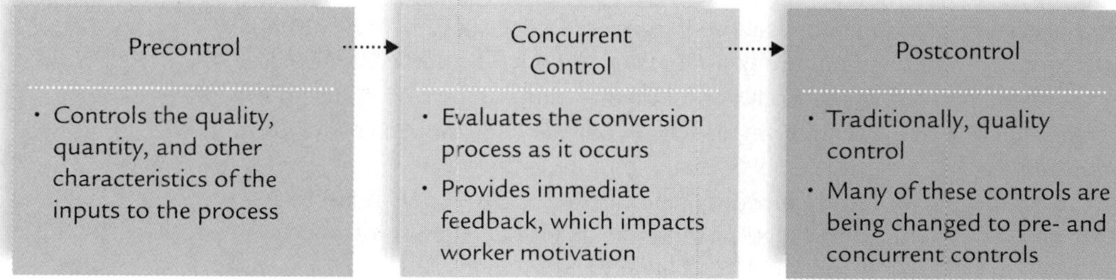

Precontrol
• Controls the quality, quantity, and other characteristics of the inputs to the process
Concurrent Control
• Evaluates the conversion process as it occurs
• Provides immediate feedback, which impacts worker motivation
Postcontrol
• Traditionally, quality control
• Many of these controls are being changed to pre- and concurrent controls

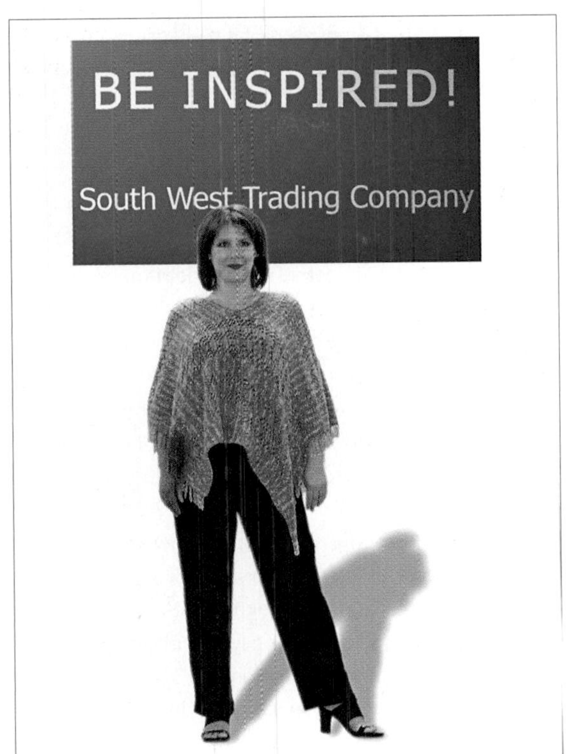

South West Trading, which manufactures yarns made from bamboo, corn, and soybeans, focuses on operational precontrol—that is, the strict control of inputs into the production process. The firm controls its raw materials beginning with their point of origin and utilizes the services of United Parcel Service (UPS) to combine orders from various factories into one container for shipment.

standards. Higher-quality inputs typically cost more, and the effort to ensure that the quality is high also increases costs. Nevertheless, those costs in many cases may be well justified. In other words, customers may be willing to pay more for better products and services.

CONCURRENT CONTROL OF OPERATIONS Concurrent control involves real-time assessment of the quality of the transformation process, that is, evaluation of the conversion of inputs to outputs while it is happening. For example, Koch Pipeline Company uses concurrent information provided by its central computers that model 125,000 data points from its pipeline networks. This system allows the monitoring safety managers to spot leaks within seconds and to prevent catastrophic incidents before they can occur. The result of this concurrent control is that pipeline accident incidents fell by 94 percent between 1995 and 2005.[36] Another good illustration of concurrent control in action in different types of organizational settings is presented in A Manager's Challenge on the use of RFID technology.

Other typical examples of concurrent control are the monitoring of a customer service representative's performance while handling a telephone inquiry or the inspection of fruit while a batch of it is proceeding along a conveyer belt. This type of control is designed to provide immediate feedback so that operations can be changed rapidly to decrease errors or increase quality. To have effective concurrent control procedures, however, managers must give considerable attention in advance to how such systems are designed and implemented. Also, managers need to be aware that this kind of control can have strong impacts on the motivation of those carrying out the operations since the feedback is so immediate and often very direct.

POSTCONTROL OF OPERATIONS Postcontrol was the traditional form of control in manufacturing—checking quality *after* a product (TV sets, shoes, furniture, and so forth) was produced. Thus, companies typically have had quality control inspectors or whole departments that checked the rate of defective products and then decided what to do if those rates were too high. For example, Toyota inspects each car coming off the assembly line on a basic list of criteria. It also randomly inspects cars based on a significantly longer and more detailed list of quality criteria. In recent years, quality control at many companies has been greatly diminished in favor of pre- and concurrent controls instead. The adage has been: "*Build* quality into the product, rather than inspect quality into the product."[37] Also, the

A MANAGER'S CHALLENGE

Technology

RFID: The Ultimate Tracker?

Technological devices over the years have always been of major assistance to the control systems of organizations of all types—business companies, government agencies, and health care institutions, just to name a few. Recent years have seen the development of a technological method that holds great promise for reducing costs of control and, especially, for increasing accuracy. It is radio-frequency identification (RFID). RFID is an automatic identification method that uses tags or transponders to send data that can be remotely retrieved and stored. RFID tags with silicon chips containing antennas are small enough to be inserted into—or attached to—a person, animal, or product for identification purposes using the emitted radio waves. Larger transponders are used currently in everyday activities, such as the automatic identification of cars on toll roads.

A major hurdle that had to be overcome before RFID could be more widely used, particularly by global companies, was the lack of an agreed-upon set of standards for passive RFID tags (tags with no internal power source). If standards could not be agreed on, efficiencies would be reduced and costs increased. However, this problem was mostly resolved when a number of countries—including China, which is the world's largest exporter—agreed on a standard in 2006.

As with any technology, especially relatively new ones, there are always plusses and minuses. On the positive side: RFID opens up many new approaches for managers and organizations to enhance their control actions. For example, two major retail chains, Wal-Mart and Marks & Spencer, have been especially active in the adoption of this technology. Wal-Mart has applied it to the issue of how to avoid the perennial "out-of-stock" problem that plagues all stores of any size. Shortly after trying out RFID technology, the firm was able to reduce the incidences of the problem by 13 percent in its inventory of mid-price items. A few years later, that percentage reduction was 62 percent and is still improving. Wal-Mart has also used RFID tags to track high-cost items in its stores to prevent them from being shoplifted. Likewise, Marks & Spencer uses the technology to help manage inventory turnover by precisely tracking its merchandise. As a Marks & Spencer executive explained: "Most people think that the benefits of RFID are around cost reduction and speed, but the main benefit is control. Sending the right product in the right quantity to the right depot at the right time is far more important."

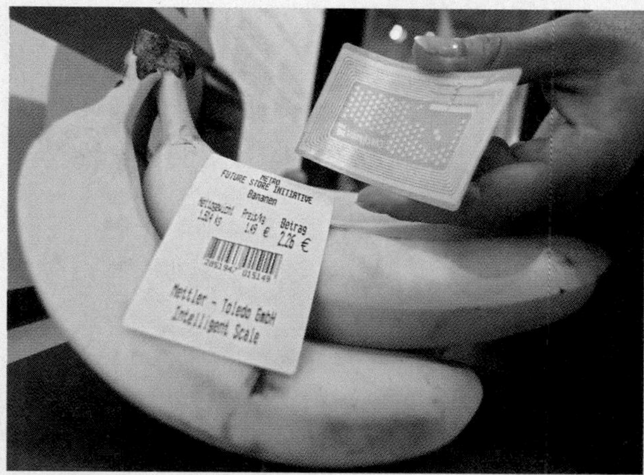

Radio-Frequency Identification tags like the one shown here are allowing Wal-Mart and other firms to track the movement of their inventory with greater precision.

In the health care industry, RFID is being increasingly used. Specifically, the tagging procedure has been used to control the flow of pharmaceuticals from their point of origin through their dispensation to patients. As in retail stores, the technology has been used in hospitals to keep track of, and reduce the theft of, high-cost drugs and other items. Additionally, RFID has been used to keep track of patients and the location of personnel within the hospital.

On the downside, three major concerns associated with RFID technology have slowed down its more wide-scale adoption. The first of these, as we mentioned, was the lack of agreed-upon standards. To some extent, this problem has been solved. A second deterrent has been the high costs related to purchasing the tags and their sophisticated readers. Experience has shown, however, that if the initial investment can be made, the subsequent results of RFID have more than justified the costs. Finally, and perhaps the most difficult problem to solve, has been the public's concerns with privacy: It is one thing to track the movement of goods, and quite another thing to track the movement and activities of individual people. This "Big Brother is watching you" issue is likely to be a continuing topic of discussion in the coming years.

Sources: B. Trebilcock, "RFID: 6 Key Trends," *Modern Materials Handling* 61, no. 13 (2006): 43–46; W. McKnight, "RFID for the Information Management Professional, Part 2," *DM Review* 11, no. 13 (2006): 41; W. Hadfield, "RFID Tags Overtake Barcodes in M&S Food Business Supply Chain," *Computer Weekly*, March 28, 2006, 5; D. Power, "RFID Aids Inventory Control at Wal-Mart," *Women's Wear Daily* 191, no. 113 (2006): 27; R. A. Perrin and M. B. McAndrew, "RFID: The New Strategy in Healthcare IT," *Healthcare Purchasing News* 30, no. 10 (2006): 13–19; J. Silva, "RFID Tracking Gets 'Thumbs Down' from Government Panel," *Wireless News*, November 27, 2006, 3–4; "EC's Reding: RFID Policy Must Address Privacy Fears," *Telecommunications Reports*, November 1, 2006, 22.

more contemporary approach to operational control has been to shift control responsibilities to operations personnel and away from separate evaluators at the end of the process.

Control-Effectiveness Factors

Regardless of good intentions, control systems in organizations can break down completely or at least not work very well. There can be many reasons for this, but alert managers can take the initiative to lessen the possibility of this occurring. The effectiveness of control is very much under their control. Again, there are no automatic prescriptions or rules of thumb for managing the control process well. Instead, managers can use certain potential sources of influence to increase the probability of success. In this section, we look at some of the key factors that make controls effective (see Exhibit 14.17).

The Focus of Control

The decision about where to focus control in an organization involves critical choices based on which actions and outcomes should receive the greatest attention. In other words, the focus of control refers not only to *what* is to be controlled but also to *where* control should be located in the organizational structure. This means paying careful attention to which people or positions in the structure have responsibility for different types and areas of control and how broad or narrow is their scope of responsibility. Control responsibility that is too broad can lead to omissions, and responsibility that is too concentrated can result in bottlenecks and decision delays. On the one hand, if too many different people are assigned responsibility for quality control of a complex set of equipment, each may assume that one of the others has taken care of a particular problem, and, as a consequence, some aspect of control gets left undone. On the other hand, if only one person is charged with inspecting all the pieces of equipment, that person may get overloaded, with the result that some critical detail gets inadvertently overlooked. Either way, effective control could be compromised.

The guiding principle for focusing control is that it should be closely linked to the strategic goals and, particularly, the planning process of the organization. For example, Nordstrom's strategic focus is customer service. As a consequence, while the company would probably not be wise to ignore inventory controls, the focus would need to be on how to maintain a high level of customer satisfaction.

EXHIBIT 14.17

Key Factors in Determining the Effectiveness of Controls

Key Factor	Concerns
Focus of control	• What will be controlled? • Where should controls be located in the organizational structure? • Who is responsible for which controls?
Amount of control	• Is there a balance between over- and undercontrol?
Quality of information collected by the controls	• Is the information useful? • Is the information accurate? • Is the information timely? • Is the information objective?
Flexibility of controls	• Are the controls able to respond to varying conditions?
Favorable cost-benefit ratio	• Is the information being gathered worth the cost of gathering it?
Source of control	• Is control imposed by others? • Is control decided by those who are affected?

To be most effective, planning should be part of the control process, and control should be part of the planning process. Priorities should be set regarding what should be intensely monitored and controlled and what should be given less attention. As software firms have found out, for example, little is to be gained from requiring star programmers to come to work on a precise schedule, given that the real objective is to produce innovative software. It is worth considerable control effort in that kind of organization, however, to make sure that the software that is written is as absolutely error-free as possible.

balanced scorecard
an integrated and "balanced" set of measures for four critical areas or perspectives: financial, customers, internal business, and innovation and learning

One approach to determining the focus of control that has become popular in recent years is the **balanced scorecard**. Advocates of this approach argue that historically there has been an "over-focus" on financial ratios and budgetary controls and a corresponding neglect of other important areas of measurement of a company's performance.[38] To remedy this, the developers of the balanced scorecard approach proposed an integrated and "balanced" set of measures for four critical areas ("perspectives" as they called them):[39]

1. The (traditional) financial perspective: How do shareholders perceive the company?
2. The customer perspective: How do customers perceive the company?
3. The internal business perspective: Does the company excel in its internal business operations and procedures?
4. The innovation and learning perspective: How well is the company doing at innovating, improving, and creating value?

Balanced-scorecard proponents argue that financial perspective approaches primarily pay attention to the past and that the other three categories are much more future oriented. In effect, a presumed advantage of the balanced scorecard is that it requires managers to link measures of organizational success more closely to strategic objectives. It also encourages managers to assess whether success in one area may be coming at the expense of poor performance in another area(s). It is intended, therefore, to bring greater focus and concentration on a total set of the most important areas of evaluation and control.

Many companies—perhaps as many as 60 percent of large U.S. firms—appear to have adopted some form of the balanced-scorecard approach.[40] Executives at ExxonMobil and Cigna Insurance, for example, believe the balanced-scorecard approach has helped to improve overall corporate performance. Nonetheless, some questions have been raised about the approach. One is whether or not there are only four major areas to measure and whether these areas are the "correct" ones. A missing area, for example, is how employees perceive the organization. For example, is it doing a good job of attracting and retaining talent? Also, should a company concentrate on only one or two of the areas or some other sort of mix?[41] Still another issue—which is common to any system or overall approach to control measurement—is how difficult it is to design and implement the types of measures called for in this comprehensive approach.[42] Regardless, it is clear that the balanced scorecard has introduced a significant and innovative approach to control—one that focuses on more than just financial numbers.

The Amount of Control to Apply

As we discussed at the beginning of this chapter, one of the greatest control challenges for any organization or manager is to determine the amount of control to apply—a choice that can mean the difference between the life and death of an organization. A Manager's Challenge illustrates such a situation: A company that almost went out of existence not only because of deliberate flouting of controls by the top executive, but also because there had been too little control virtually throughout the organization for an extended period of time.

Effective control involves finding a balance between overcontrol and undercontrol. Often, less-experienced managers tend to apply more control than is necessary in their eagerness to demonstrate that they are "in charge." This, in turn, can produce unintended resentment and resistance. Thus, new managers need to be aware of this tendency and moderate it.

A MANAGER'S CHALLENGE

Ethics

Collapse of Control—or Worse?

Sometimes, the breakdown of controls in an organization can be deliberate on someone's part, and sometimes it can be inadvertent. In the case of the software company CA (formerly, Computer Associates) in the last few years, it seems to have been both. The "deliberate" aspect was confirmed by the guilty plea of former CEO Sanjay Kumar in April 2006, and his subsequent sentencing in November of that year to 12 years in federal prison.

What were the charges against Kumar that constituted deliberate flouting of the organization's control systems? Among them were falsely reporting revenues to the U.S. Securities and Exchange Commission (SEC) over at least a three-year period. These revenues, from licensing agreements, were reported in a given quarter, despite the fact that some of the deals were not formally closed until at least the following quarter, a practice referred to colloquially as a "35-day month." This was done in order to make the company's revenue picture look more impressive than it actually was, which of course helped its stock price. Additionally, Kumar had conspired with other company officials to backdate contracts and other documents. All of this was further compounded by the fact that he then "obstructed justice" by lying about these activities to the SEC and the FBI.

Clearly, unethical behavior was involved in Kumar's actions. However, the company also had major control problems that were unrelated to the fraudulent activities described previously. A truly great irony at CA was the fact that although it was a company that specialized in providing extremely complex software systems in areas such as database management and storage to over 95 percent of the *Fortune* 500 companies, it had never installed sophisticated business software in its own company! A classic example of "do as I say (sell to you), but not as I do!"

The lack of adequate control systems in its own operations resulted in at least two accounting restatements, a late filing of an SEC 10-K form, and a botched sales commission program. The latter had been developed by the CEO who followed Kumar. The program was designed to alter the reward basis for commissions in order to create better and longer-term relationships with customers. However, the revised commission plan turned out to be very complex and overwhelmed the company's archaic computer systems. So much so that as one report put it, "[15 people in the finance department] were assigned the unenviable task of individually calculating each commission for the company's 4,000 salespeople." Or, as one former CA executive said: "A lot of the [company's] systems were internally developed and had not been updated . . . so it was very much a spaghetti code of an application. And no one could believe any of the data."

Overall, the new CEO, John Swainson, recruited from IBM in 2004, has taken a number of steps to improve CA's operations and controls, as well as its ethical climate. However, as he indicated in late 2005, "It took a long time for the company to get screwed up, [and] it will take a long time to get it 'unscrewed' up." It seems, however, that in the following several years at least some progress had been made in that direction. Nevertheless, making up for prior ethical lapses (by others) and inadequate control systems is not an easy managerial task.

Sources: N. Varchaver, S. Kaufman, and D. Burke, "Long Island Confidential," *Fortune*, November 27, 2006, 172–186; W. Atkinson, "CA's Procurement Overhaul Focuses on Global Expertise," April 6, 2006, www.purchasing.com, 17–20; "Ex CA CEO Gets Prison," *Network World*, November 6, 2006, www.networkworld.com, "CA Makes Headway," *Business Week Online*, February 5, 2007; A. N. Stuart, "Sins of Commission," *CFO* 22, no. 9 (2006): 20; R. J. Newman, "Debugging CA," *U. S. News & World Report*, 2006, EE12.

If this were not a big enough challenge by itself, it is compounded in multinational corporations. In those organizations, perceptions of what is too much oversight can vary considerably from one country and culture to another. For example, tight monitoring of a manager's time and movements is more accepted in countries such as Thailand; however, managers in Australia are likely to react quite strongly and negatively to tight monitoring.

When managers have more experience, they have a better basis for gauging the minimum levels of control that will get the job done without incurring unjustified risks. Even seasoned managers often find it difficult to judge correctly the degree of control required, and problems of undercontrol can crop up where least expected. No predetermined "right" amounts of control apply to all work situations. The best guideline for a manager to follow is to view the amount of control as something that, within limits, can be adjusted. Additionally, the undesirable consequences of excessive control and the dangers of too little control need to be made part of careful assessments of performance requirements and not inadvertently or casually overlooked. As we have already mentioned, involving those who will be directly influenced by the control measures in setting the amount of control increases the chances that an appropriate level of control is set from the outset. Furthermore, if adjustments need to be made, this initial involvement will likely reduce the resistance to needed changes.

The Quality of Information

Effective control requires using knowledge that is based on accurate data, a situation that Brad Carter faced in deciding whether to invest in new customer retention software; that is, it requires good information. Four characteristics that determine the quality of information are usefulness, accuracy, timeliness, and objectivity.

USEFULNESS Not all data collected for control purposes are equally useful in managerial operations and decisions. Sometimes data that were once useful continue to be collected, even though the original purposes for obtaining that information have disappeared. Such a situation existed some years ago in a division of a major manufacturing company. Because of major changes in the operating environment at one of its units, the company decided to find out which accounting reports, if any, were actually helpful to managers. Did the information contained in the reports actually assist managers to do their jobs better? The answer was a resounding "no." Investigation indicated the accounting department thought it was gathering data that two separate groups could use: corporate managers and plant managers. Yet, it turned out that the information being disseminated was of assistance only to the first group. As a result, the accounting department worked with operations managers in the plants to develop control reports that would help them do their particular jobs more effectively.[43]

ACCURACY Data or numbers that are inaccurate or misleading not only fail to provide a good basis for control steps but also breed cynicism among those whose performance is being measured. Since control actions, especially those designed to change behavior that does not meet agreed-upon standards, can have such powerful effects, it is vital that substantial effort be put into obtaining data that are absolutely valid. Otherwise, no information is better than inaccurate information.

TIMELINESS Even accurate data, if they arrive too late, are not useful. This is true for any organizational actions but especially so for purposes of control. In the fast-paced world of global business, data that are out of date are of virtually no use. For effective control, information must arrive on time to those who can take action and make any required changes. In everyday life, for example, information that arrives to truck drivers 10 minutes after the wrong route has been taken is not very useful. Effective control systems require speed.

OBJECTIVITY Objectivity, especially as it relates to control, is something of a two-edged sword. Almost everyone would agree that objective facts are better than subjective, and possibly biased, opinions. However, for some kinds of performances, objective data may not be possible to obtain or even may be misleading. In a diving competition, the exact height that a diver jumps off a springboard may be much less important than the subjective opinion of an experienced judge about the form of the dive. Similarly, in organizations, some of the most easily measured activities, and, therefore, the most easily controlled, may be relatively insignificant for the achievement of major, strategic goals. All other factors being equal, objective information would be preferred, but in many situations, those other factors may not be equal, and thoughtful judgments rather than unimportant "facts" may provide the best basis for action decisions.

For example, in a customer service call center, it is relatively easy to gather objective data on the length of time a customer service agent spends on the phone with each caller. However, comparing the number of callers served by each agent may not tell you the most important thing—how well each customer was served. If the number of calls answered becomes the key performance measure, customer service agents may begin to provide poor service in order to get customers off the phone quickly and move on to the next customer, thereby maximizing the number of calls they take in a day. In this case, it is clear that the objective data (the number of calls taken) may not be the most important data (that is, how well the customer is served). To measure customer service effectively may require having a supervisor randomly listen in on service calls or going to the cost and effort of trying to measure customer satisfaction by polling customers who have called in to the service center.

Flexibility

For control to be effective, its procedures must respond to changing conditions. Organizations and managers get accustomed to control procedures that are already in place. It is a human tendency to stay the course when things appear to be going well. But that tendency can defeat effective control. Well-designed control systems should be able to account for changing circumstances and adjust accordingly. Rigidity of control systems usually is not a feature to be prized. Flexibility is.[44]

Favorable Cost-Benefit Ratio

The designs of some control systems look good on paper, but they prove to be impractical or costly to use. To be effective, the benefits of controls must outweigh both the direct financial costs and the indirect costs of inconvenience and awkwardness in implementation. Elaborate, complicated control systems immediately raise the issue of whether they will be worth the expense involved. Sometimes, the simplest systems are nearly as effective. Consider again the customer service call center example. Obtaining satisfaction ratings directly from customers may cost significantly more and not provide much better information than feedback that well-trained supervisors can provide.

Some situations, however, require that intricate and complex controls be implemented because not doing so could be disastrous. Nuclear power plants, military weapons units, and federal air traffic control agencies need to invest heavily in control systems that ensure an exceedingly high degree of reliability. Consequently, they have to make costly investments—in, for example, continual training, back-up staffing, and very expensive equipment—to control operations and reduce the possibility of a catastrophic accident to absolute minimum levels.[45] In such cases, high control costs are obviously justified.

Sources

The source of control often affects the willingness of organization members to work cooperatively with the system. As we discussed earlier, in recent years many organizations have changed from bureaucratic control to control that relies more on members' monitoring their own or their team's performance. Thus, the source of control is shifted, and the change may increase positive reactions because employees have more trust in a process over which they have some influence.

Similarly, controls that provide information from equipment or instruments often seem less resented and more fair than controls involving what can be viewed as the sometimes arbitrary actions of supervisors. For any type of control, the source has a great deal to do with the acceptability of the system. Acceptability, in turn, affects how well control systems work in practice and not just in theory.

Managerial Challenges from the Front Line

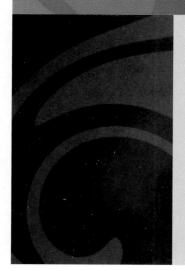

The Rest of the Story

Brad Carter decided that it was worth it to invest in the new customer retention software. The software was installed across the board on all the sales representatives' computers, and an additional investment was also made to train each of the representatives to use it. Along with the installation of this new tracking aid, the sales representatives were given explicit targets of how many customer contacts they should make each week. Furthermore, they were told that the actual number of contacts that were made would be compared against the target number on a monthly basis.

With the new software, the number of actual customer contacts could be precisely tracked both by Carter as a manager and by each salesperson. As a result of this enhanced method of accountability, sales soon increased by 60 percent, more than repaying the investments made in the new system.

Summary

- The word *control* often has negative connotations. However, control has an essential role in the overall process of management. It involves the regulation of activities and behavior to determine the degree of conformity to an organization's objectives. In other words, without controls there is very little coordination that can take place within an organization. Control is a necessary function that follows, but complements, the other major functions of management: planning, organizing, and leading.
- There are four basic elements of any control process in organizations: establishing standards, measuring performance, comparing performance against standards, and evaluating the results of the comparisons and taking any necessary follow-up action. Each of these elements of the control function has its own problems and issues, such as: how stringent the standards should be, what aspects of performance should be measured, whether comparisons against standards should be judged on an overall basis or a standard-by-standard basis, and whether any deviations from standards are major enough to cause a change in policies or procedures.
- A significant dimension of control in organizations is the breadth of scope of controls. Generally, the degree of scope falls under three major categories: strategic, or very broad controls addressed to long-range goals; tactical, or controls that are intermediate in breadth and that focus on the implementation of strategy; and operational, or very concrete controls that assess and regulate specific activities or methods against very well-defined immediate objectives.
- Strategic controls are very broad, and, thus, it is often difficult to measure their effectiveness. They can also be affected by unexpected changes in the organization's external environment, This can cause problems when it comes to setting standards that are applicable across extended periods of time. Generally, the greater the degree of environmental uncertainty, the more decentralized an organization's control system will be.
- Tactical controls are intermediate in scope. They are typically the fundamental part of the overall set of controls that apply to specific units of the organization in connection with the implementation of strategy. Some of the major types of tactical controls are financial controls, budgetary controls, supervisory structure controls, and human resource controls. Two general orientations to how tactical controls are applied in practice are: a rules-and-regulation, or bureaucratic-oriented, approach; and a commitment, or clan, type of self-control approach.

- Operational controls relate to the transformation of organizational inputs into outputs. Operational controls can be applied at three different stages of a process: before the transformation takes place (precontrols), during the actual transformation (concurrent controls), or after the transformation is completed (postcontrols). In recent years, organizations have attempted to place more emphasis on pre- and concurrent controls instead of relying only on postcontrols.
- A number of factors, such as the focus of control, the quality of information, and the flexibility of controls, can determine the effectiveness of control systems. A particularly difficult issue for organizations that can impact control effectiveness is to decide on the amount of control. An error in either direction—either too little or too much control—can lead to potentially severe consequences.

Key Terms

balanced scorecard 420
break-even point (B-E P) 411
budgetary controls 412
bureaucratic control 415
commitment, or clan, control 415
concurrent control 416
control 399
human resource policies and procedures 414
operational control 416
postcontrol 416
precontrol 416
standards 402
strategic control 407
supervisory structure 413
tactical control 409

Review Questions

1. What is meant by *control* in organizations?
2. How is the control function linked to other managerial functions?
3. Who is responsible for setting standards?
4. What are key issues managers must consider when establishing standards?
5. When measuring performance, can nonquantifiable data be helpful? How?
6. What is the limiting factor in comparing performance against standards?
7. Compare strategic, tactical, and operational control. Why are the boundaries between each not always clear?
8. Describe four managerial control issues involving budgets.
9. What is the fundamental difference between bureaucratic control and commitment (clan) control?
10. What is the relationship between pre-, concurrent, and postcontrols of operations? Which type is best?
11. What are the advantages and the problems involved in using a balanced-scorecard approach?
12. What factors determine the usefulness of information to the control process?

Assessing Your Capabilities

How Willing Am I to Delegate?

Using the following scale, circle the number that best indicates the extent to which you agree or disagree with each statement. If you have not worked in a supervisory role, consider a supervisor you have had. Evaluate that individual on these questions. Then, consider how you reacted to the type of control used by your supervisor. You can also apply this to student groups or teams where you have been in charge.

1. I'd delegate more, but the jobs I delegate never seem to get done the way I want them to be done.	1 Strongly Agree	2 Agree	3 Neither Agree nor Disagree	4 Disagree	5 Strongly Disagree
2. I don't feel I have the time to delegate properly.	1 Strongly Agree	2 Agree	3 Neither Agree nor Disagree	4 Disagree	5 Strongly Disagree
3. I carefully check on subordinates' work without letting them know I'm doing it, so I can correct their mistakes if necessary before they cause too many problems.	1 Strongly Agree	2 Agree	3 Neither Agree nor Disagree	4 Disagree	5 Strongly Disagree

Managerial Challenges from the Front Line

Name: Albert Torres

Position: Director of Information Technology and Research and Development at Pay Plus Benefits

Alma mater: Washington State University

Outside work activities: The political process where I hope to make a difference

First job out of school: Tech Support, Microsoft Corporation

Business book reading now: *Blue Ocean Strategy* by W. Chan Kim and Renée Mauborgne

Hero: My parents are my heroes, the older I get the more I admire them.

Motto to live by: "Try not to become a man of success, but rather try to become a man of value." Albert Einstein

What drives me: Personal responsibility

Management style: I manage projects, systems, and ideas. We select people who enjoy freedom and accept personal responsibility.

Pet peeve: Indecisiveness

According to National Hockey League champion and Hall of Famer, Wayne Gretzky, "A good hockey player plays where the puck is. A great hockey player plays where the puck is going to be." This was also the change philosophy and perspective of Albert Torres.

Albert Torres, shown here with his wife and business partner, Bianca Torres, is the director of information technology and research and development at Pay Plus Benefits, Inc., a company that provides outsourcing services to other companies, especially in the area of payroll and benefit administration. For example, instead of having its own call center to answer employee questions on benefits, a client would outsource this activity to Pay Plus Benefits.

Though still growing and making money, Pay Plus Benefits's internal costs were increasing, and as a consequence, its profit margin was decreasing. Torres' role as the director of information technology and research and development was to make a change that would, in his words, "reduce operational costs and increase our service offering to attract new clients."

Torres decided that the needed change should focus on automating some of the call center services by creating a Web-based self-service portal the client employees could access. If Torres pursued this anticipatory change, he would have to overcome some likely resistance and help his people see the need for change. First, since Pay Plus Benefits was still making money and not in crisis, employees in Torres's unit would likely not automatically see a need for change in general. Second, according to Torres, "This was something totally new to us, and while we had an excellent software programming team, this project presented many new challenges and unknown variables."

In the end, to manage the change Torres would have to determine what to focus the change on, how much change to make, how to overcome likely resistance, and how fast to push the change. Major miscalculations on his part could easily cause the change initiative to fail, which, in turn, could accelerate the crisis (and its likely costs) that he was trying to avoid. In any case, it didn't seem to him that the external pressures driving the change were going to go away so the need to "get this change right" was, in Torres's mind, fairly important for him as a manager.

As the real case of Albert Torres illustrates, organizations never stay the same because the world around them never stays the same. From ancient times forward, all organizations have had to foster the capacity to change.[1] Making changes and managing that process have been essential to the vitality of all organizations throughout history but arguably are more important today than ever. However, managing the change process is no easy task. While the need to change is often obvious, making successful changes presents formidable managerial challenges. For example:

- How much change is enough?
- How fast should change take place?
- How should the need for continual changes be balanced against the need for a minimum level of stability and continuity?
- Who should be the major players in change processes, and what should their roles be?
- Who, exactly, is likely to benefit and who could be harmed by particular changes?

How these and other similar questions are answered will determine the fate of attempted changes in any organization.

Throughout this book, we have emphasized understanding change as a major theme because it is so critical to managerial success. In this, our final chapter, we focus specifically on bringing about change in organizational settings. As a result, in this chapter we address specific means and methods used in changing the overall organization as well as units within it. This chapter presumes a basic knowledge of the other topics covered in this book. This knowledge will be helpful in analyzing the significant issues involved in organizational development and transformation.

Organizational contexts, because of their complexity, provide managers with many opportunities as well as challenges for making changes. Sometimes the changes that need to be made are unplanned and unpleasant. For example, to reduce its expenses quickly, GM was forced to lay off 30,000 employees in 2006.[2] Other changes, like that undertaken by Albert Torres, involve more planning and are designed to change fundamental aspects of the organization so that sudden, drastic changes, like layoffs, will not be necessary.

The first parts of this chapter examine general issues and principles relating to organizational development and transformation. We first review why organizations change—focusing on the forces that can cause changes. Particular attention is given to analyzing internal and external forces of change as well as recognizing and diagnosing those forces. The specific areas of change a company might undertake—its technology, shared values and culture, strategy, structure, systems, and staff—are considered next. These sections, in turn, provide a background for an examination of managerial choices regarding the preparation, implementation, and evaluation of the change process.

We conclude the chapter with an analysis of three major, typically organization-wide, approaches to planned change frequently used in contemporary organizations. These include the organizational development (OD) approach, process redesign (also known as reengineering), and the development of the learning organization. We will look at how these approaches are used, and at their relative strengths and weaknesses.

What Causes Organizations to Change?

The causes of organizational change originate from both external and internal forces, and a manager must be alert to all of them (see Exhibit 15.1). Sometimes those causes arise almost totally from factors outside of the organization, such as economic or business conditions, technological developments, demographic shifts, and the like. At other times, the forces of change arise inside the organization. These forces include changes initiated by managers and employees. Often, the causes of change are a combination of both external and internal forces.

Forces Outside the Organization

A major driver of organizational change is the external environment in which the organization exists. A whole host of forces outside the organization can bring about changes inside it. Here, we discuss several of the most important.

ECONOMIC CONDITIONS Obvious forces for change affecting business organizations are developments in the economic environment. If the economy weakens, then many companies are likely to reduce their workforces or at least limit hiring, prune low-profit product lines, and the like. DuPont Textiles and Interiors (a subsidiary of DuPont) is a good

EXHIBIT 15.1

Forces for Change

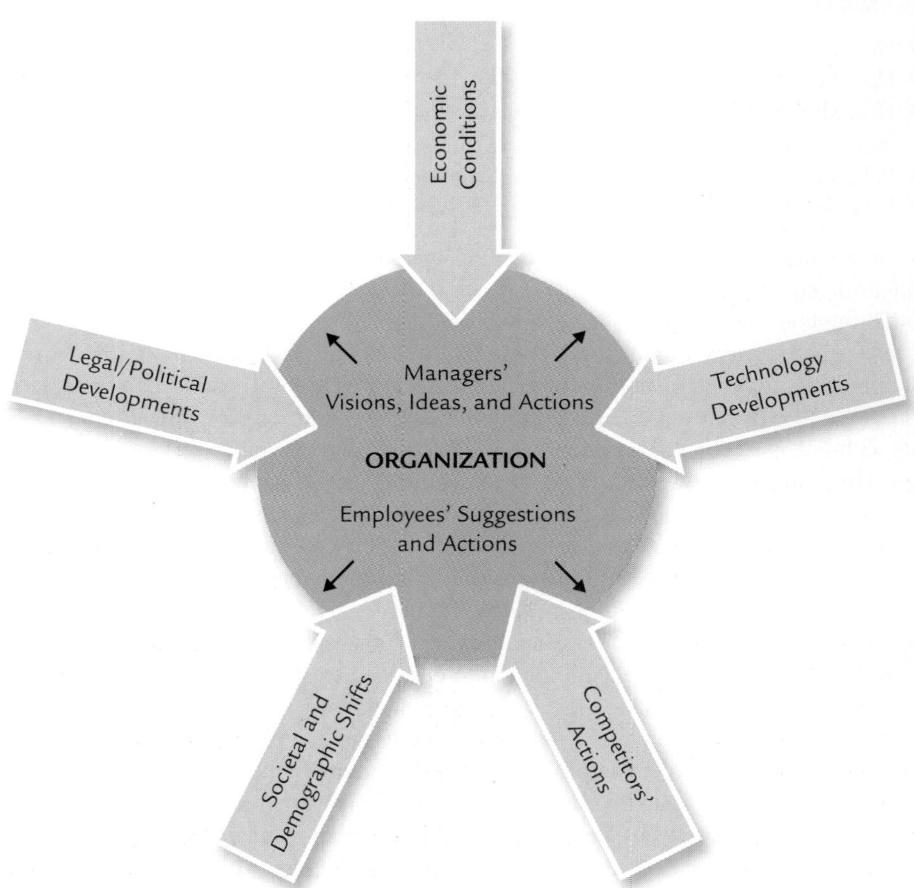

example. The company shut down two plants and laid off 10 percent of its workforce during the 2000–2003 U.S. recession.[3] Conversely, if the economy is vibrant and expanding, many firms consider adding new services or products, creating new units or divisions, increasing their geographic areas of operations, and undertaking similar growth changes. For example, foreign companies, such as DuPont, nearly doubled their investments in China as the country's economy boomed from 2003 to 2006.[4]

Analogous to these business-world examples, many nonbusiness organizations, especially governmental agencies, contract or expand in relation to economic conditions because external forces directly impact their budgets. For example, the various projects planned by the National Aeronautics and Space Administration (NASA) have been put on slower timetables because of severe budget cuts during slowdowns in the economy that directly affected government revenues via taxes.[5]

COMPETITORS' ACTIONS Regardless of the state of the economy, most businesses and many other organizations are likely to be extremely sensitive to moves made by their direct competitors, especially those in response to changes in the market or customers' preferences. The actions of other significant players in the immediate environment often can trigger changes inside a given organization, even when that organization would prefer not to make any changes. For example, in response to competitors' moves, Mellon Bank decided to get out of the traditional, low-yield retail banking business and is now concentrating on managing mutual funds and performing settlement services, which are more high-growth and high-fee businesses. Mellon later expanded into Europe when the U.S. money management market appeared to be oversupplied.[6] Actions by competitors in the deregulated Mexican insurance market led Metropolitan Life to acquire major Mexican subsidiaries (Aseguradora Hidalgo and Seguros Genesis) in order not to be shut out of that market.[7]

TECHNOLOGICAL DEVELOPMENTS Changes in technology developed outside of an organization frequently require it to respond, whether it wants to or not. Technological advances offer both opportunities and threats to organizations. If managers are slow to respond to technological changes, the consequences can be dire. A Manager's Challenge illustrates how a company that dominated its industry for more than 200 years nearly disappeared because of technological changes to which it did not respond appropriately. The company is Encyclopædia Britannica. As you read this example, why do you think managers in the company were so slow to respond? What might they have done differently and how would it have affected the outcome? Keeping in mind that hindsight is 20/20, what arguments would you have made for change before the fateful events left the company with too few options?

LEGAL AND POLITICAL DEVELOPMENTS When governments make new laws or courts issue new interpretations of those laws, managers need to respond, even when the solutions or types of changes that should be made are not obvious. In the United States, the passage of Title IX of the 1964 Civil Rights Law required universities to provide equal resources and opportunities to male and female students (in relation to their proportions in the student body). Directors of intercollegiate athletics at U.S. universities eventually realized that this would have major implications for their area of activities. Because of tight budgets, however, these particular managers, the athletic directors, found it difficult to add enough women's sports to equalize the proportion of men to women athletes. Nevertheless, some managers handled this situation much better than others and made the changes more quickly and with less conflict within their organizations. Clearly, however, the external force of law in this instance caused changes that would likely not have come about for any other reason. Also, in this example, the political climate added a force to the legal enactment that hastened the need to make these changes.

SOCIETAL AND DEMOGRAPHIC SHIFTS Other types of external forces for change can take longer to develop and be more subtle and difficult to detect, such as changing societal attitudes toward various products, services, and practices. Many employers around the

A MANAGER'S CHALLENGE

Technology

Two Centuries of Dominance End for Encyclopædia Britannica

Written in the 1700s, Encyclopædia Britannica arguably invented the category in which it competes. For more than 200 years Encyclopædia Britannica was considered the most authoritative encyclopedia in the market, and in the 1970s, a full set of the books sold for as much as $2,000. Then in the mid-1980s a little known company called Microsoft (only 10 years old at the time) approached Britannica to discuss a potential collaboration but was turned down flat. Why would a company with such a stellar brand and reputation that had been successful for more than 200 years team up with a new, unknown company that had no reputation as a publisher?

Rebuffed, Microsoft used content from *Funk & Wagnall's Standard Encyclopedia* to create what is now known as *Encarta*. Executives at Britannica could only smile as the desperation of one of its more lowly esteemed competitors drove it into the arms of such a strange and immature bedfellow as Microsoft. This view was only reinforced as Britannica's sales grew, hitting $650 million in 1990.

However, just three years later in 1993, Microsoft began bundling *Encarta* with its Office suite of products. Although *Encarta's* content was not nearly as good as Britannica's, it was essentially free. Britannica's sales dropped like a rock. Determined to survive, Britannica executives decided to come out with a CD-ROM version of the product, but all the information could not fit on one disk. It came on three disks, making it inconvenient for customers because depending on what information you wanted, you had to make sure you put in the correct disk. On top of that, Britannica executives priced their CD offering at $995. The hope was that such a high price for three CDs would encourage customers to continue to buy the company's nicely bound volumes.

The plan did not work, and in 1994, executives decided to launch an online version of its famed encyclopedia. However, they priced a user's subscription at $2,000. Again, the hope was that such a high-priced online subscription would encourage customers to continue to buy traditional book sets. But sales at Britannica plummeted yet further. In 1996, only 20,000 hard copy versions were sold compared with 117,000 in 1990.

Up to this point, the tale of Britannica is a sad one. The company's revenues had shrunk by more than 80 percent in just 2 percent of the company's lifespan. However, in the end, Britannica's fate was sealed not by Microsoft but by another organization, called Wikipedia. The ironic point of this tale is that virtually all the information we have conveyed about Encyclopædia Britannica can be found at www.wikipedia.org—a free, online encyclopedia that relies on literally tens of thousands of writers, who voluntarily contribute to the site for free.

Beginning in the 1990s, Microsoft's Encarta software, followed by Wikipedia, the Web-based encyclopedia, practically rendered obsolete Encyclopædia Britannica—a firm that had dominated its industry since the 1700s.

Neither Britannica, as it struggled just to stay alive, nor Microsoft, as it continued to bundle *Encarta* with its Office suite of products, envisioned this online form of encyclopedia. When Wikipedia was launched in 2001, who would have predicted that by 2007, Wikipedia would have 4.6 million articles consisting of 1.4 billion words across 200 languages or would have 1.5 million articles in English totaling over 500 million words? To put this in perspective, Wikipedia's English articles are three times larger than the largest Encyclopædia Britannica set. Who could have seen this blinding pace of change? The speed at which Wikipedia is being updated is so fast that even if you read all the *new and edited* material seven days a week, 24 hours a day, you could not keep up.

Sources: Adopted from J. S. Black and H. B. Gregersen, *Leading Strategic Change* (Upper Saddle River, NJ: Financial Times Prentice Hall, 2007); "Encyclopædia Britannica," accessed January 20, 2007 at http://en.wikipedia.org/wiki/Encyclopedia_britannica; B. Helm, "Vote of Confidence for Wikipedia," *Business Week*, December 15, 2005.

The percentage of people over the age 60 is increasing rapidly in the United States and other developed countries. A potential shortage of workers and changing demand for products are just two of the side effects managers are likely to struggle with because of this demographic shift.

United States, as well as many restaurants and bars, for example, recently have had to change their practices regarding indoor smoking. In response to both tighter legal restrictions and changing levels of public tolerance to smoking in confined areas, these organizations have had to pay attention to an area of employee-customer behavior they had long ignored.[8]

Shifting demographic patterns, such as the aging of populations in the United States and Japan in recent years, are another type of slow-moving external force. For example, the U.S. Bureau of the Census projects that between 2010 and 2020, the number of people in the United States over age 60 will jump by over 30 percent, whereas almost all other age groups will stay roughly the same in numbers.[9] Such alterations in the age makeup of society will, for example, challenge retailing and other consumer-oriented firms to change their product mixes and take new approaches to sales and marketing. These kinds of demographic shifts do not take place overnight, but they can exert a powerful force nevertheless.

Forces Inside the Organization

As with external factors, many potential forces inside the organization can cause changes to take place. Two of the most important are (1) managerial decisions and (2) employee preferences and pressures.

MANAGERIAL DECISIONS Managers at any level of an organization operate under certain constraints that limit what they can change. However, in many instances they have considerable authority to make changes in their particular parts of the enterprise. Even in flatter organizational structures, the higher up managers are in an organization, the more leeway they typically have to institute changes. Managers are often reluctant, though, to use their power for this purpose. Some experts argue that managers tend to *underutilize* their power to make changes.[10] The risk is that an attempted change will be unsuccessful, and the manager will end up with less power than before. This is why in the next section we discuss one of the most critical leadership issues facing you as a manager: accurately evaluating the need for change.

EMPLOYEE PREFERENCES AND SUGGESTIONS Managers are not the only source of change inside organizations. Lower-level employees often are an excellent source of innovative suggestions for change. For example, a few years ago the Children's Hospital and Health Care Center in San Diego, California, decided that because of poor communication between the center's managers and staff, low morale, and job dissatisfaction, more input from employees was needed. The center proceeded to institute monthly meetings. During the meetings, each supervisor was required to report ideas and suggestions from a set of employees not reporting to them. As a result of these suggestions, changes were made throughout the organization that led to higher levels of job satisfaction and improved manager-employee communications.[11]

In extreme instances, employees can exert overt pressure for changes. For example, workers at the Port of Los Angeles opposed the introduction of new cargo handling technologies. Their "work slow down" efforts basically stopped traffic into the Port of Los Angeles for several weeks and caused losses approaching $2 billion, which demanded management's attention.[12]

Managers need to distinguish between employee pressures that address legitimate needs for change and pressures that attempt to obstruct or intimidate. Making such judgments wisely and responding appropriately are essential managerial skills, as discussed in the next section. Regardless of the extent to which managers have that skill, however, employees can be a stimulus for change that frequently cannot, and should not, be ignored.

Determining Where Organizational Changes Should Occur

When managers decide that change is needed, or when they realize that they have no choice but to make changes, one of the first issues they face is: What to change? While not exhaustive, a reasonably comprehensive set of areas to consider include, technology, shared values and culture, strategy, structure, system, and staff. Any change will almost certainly involve at least one of these areas of focus, and the larger the change the more likely several areas will be involved. (See Exhibit 15.2.) The "Manager's Challenge" regarding Sony that is presented at the end of this section is a good example of change that involves multiple areas of focus. Particularly complex and comprehensive changes—"transformational changes"—will involve all six (see Exhibit 15.3).

EXHIBIT 15.2

Focus of Organizational Changes

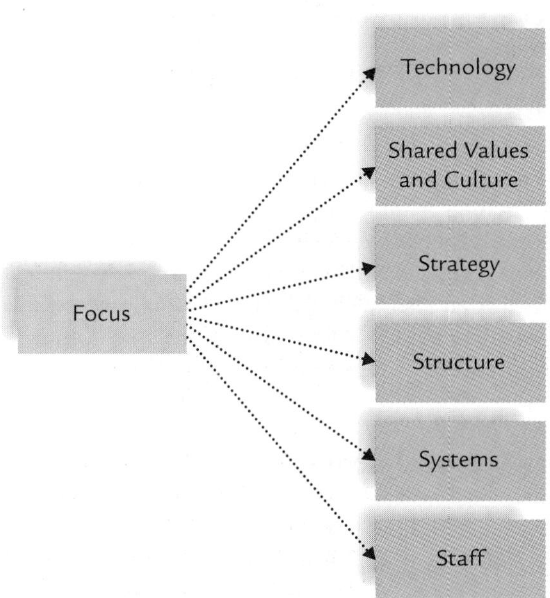

EXHIBIT 15.3

Some Specific Examples of Focus of Change

Focus	Examples
Strategy	• Change from niche market to general market focus • Change focus from individual customer to large corporate customer
Structure	• Change from a geographic to a customer structure • Implement an international division
Systems	• Replace batch with continuous flow manufacturing • Change from last in-first out to first in-first out inventory valuation
Technology	• Update computer systems • Use holography in product design
Shared Values and Culture	• Implement diversity awareness program • Institute participatory decision making throughout organization
Staff	• Encourage cooperation through cross-training program • Increase number and availability of training workshops for lower-level employees

Strategy

Changes in many of these external forces mean that managers must alter the strategy of their organizations.[13] For example, if your competitors introduce a popular new product to the market, you may have no choice but to change your organization's strategy in response.[14] Top managers more than lower-level managers are typically charged with determining an organization's strategy. Lower-level managers are more involved in implementing that strategy.[15]

Announcing a change in strategy is vastly different from actually bringing about such a change, though. For example, a few years ago, Honda sought to convert itself from "a local company in Japan, with a global viewpoint, into a global company with a local viewpoint." In other words, Honda's new strategy was to be as flexible as a small local company while developing and using all the strengths of a large, global company. To support the strategy, the organization developed a global product supply network, a new flexible manufacturing system, and a global standard layout. This was no easy task. Today, however, Honda is noted for its flexible manufacturing capabilities. Its major North American production facilities can assemble nearly any vehicle it sells, depending on what consumers on that continent are demanding.[16]

Structure

Changing the structural makeup of organizations is sometimes one of the most valuable tools managers have to create other desired changes. Many structural changes like reorganizing the firm on a product rather than a geographic basis or consolidating a company's major divisions can affect how different units interact and how information flows in the organization. Nokia, which has offices on multiple continents, had formerly been organized on a geographic basis, but reorganized by product. Now each division operates with its own strategy and profit-and-loss responsibility.[17]

Other structural changes can be made at the intermediate level. They can include combining or dividing departments or changing locations and reporting relationships within or among business units. Still other structural changes can be made at very micro levels, such as forming new project groups or altering the composition of particular jobs or positions. For example, several years ago, the Mayo Clinic formed a group of 13 examining physicians and 17 staff members as part of the clinic's new Executive Health Program. Today, the group oversees the annual physical examinations of over 4,500 U.S. corporate executives.[18]

As with changes in strategy, changes in structure are not especially difficult to pull off initially, but making them generate the desired effects can be particularly challenging for managers. Research shows that almost no other event in an organization can create as much political maneuvering as potential, or rumored, reorganization changes.[19] The ambiguity of the effects of such changes, coupled with their potential importance for the jobs of those who may be directly affected, causes high levels of anxiety and frequent politicking by employees.

Systems

Another major object of change can involve the firm's system of formal processes or procedures. These changes involve the sequence and manner in which work activities are carried out. For example, Intel has changed its procedure for opening new plants. Its new procedure for opening new plants is to exactly duplicate each and every one—even, for example, down to the color of the gloves workers wear.[20]

Changes in a firm's processes and procedures often come about because of prior changes in the organization's strategy or structure have been made. The purchase of new equipment, for instance, would be a primary change, and the adoption of new procedures because of this equipment would be the secondary change. Molecular profiling equipment has allowed the pharmaceutical firm Merck to dramatically change its systems for developing new drugs.[21]

Technology

For many organizations—from the corner dry cleaner to the largest multinational—the most obvious and most frequent object of change is technology. This has always been the case in manufacturing and capital-intensive companies, where replacing and upgrading equipment and technology have been the keys to organizational survival and an ability to keep ahead of the competition. In recent years, however, virtually all types of firms, government agencies, and nonbusiness organizations have been paying increasing attention to improving and expanding their information technology.[22] For example, Emerson (formerly Emerson Electronics) began using a new Internet program, Emerson Express, to consolidate its smaller shipments into full-truck shipments. It's now saving the company approximately $11 million a year. To implement this technology-driven change, each of the company's 50-plus autonomous divisions sends information concerning upcoming individual shipments to a central location where they can be consolidated.[23]

Usually a change in technology will have ripple effects on other parts of the organization that can be a real challenge for managers. New equipment, for example, can result in entirely different patterns of work relationships among employees, and that, in turn, can create considerable confusion. If these effects are significant or persistent, they can take a toll on the improvements the firm is trying to make. Therefore, focusing solely on technology as a source of change isn't always the answer.

Shared Values and Culture

The shared values and culture of the organization are another major focus for change. Changing an organization's culture can be as potent as making major changes in the firm's strategy or technology. Despite its potential, however, changing an organization's embedded traditions and accepted ways of doing things can be extremely difficult. For example, when China Development Industrial Bank bought Grand Cathay Brokerage of Taiwan, over 100 of Grand Cathay's key employees left within the first year as a result of the new culture that had been imposed. As one departing employee put it, "Grand Cathay had a very democratic culture. When policies were made, we were always invited to give feedback. Our opinions mattered. But the new management has a very autocratic style."[24]

A MANAGER'S CHALLENGE

Change

Saving Sony

Sony is famous the world over for its Walkman music player, PlayStation game console, TVs, and other electronic gadgets. Unfortunately, success rarely lasts forever: From 2000 to 2003, Sony's hot-under-the-collar shareholders watched the value of their shares drop from $150 to $25. It was enough to force some major changes at the company.

In 2005, Howard Stringer became the first non-Japanese head of the company in its history and one of the few to ever lead any major Japanese company. Stringer was born in Wales in 1942 but moved to the United States in 1965. He joined Sony in 1997 as the head of Sony America, turning around the performance in that unit by establishing higher levels of integration and cooperation across its electronics, game, and entertainment units.

However, after taking over as CEO of the global enterprise, Stringer determined that Sony's problems were both broad and deep. It was facing mounting financial losses and increasing pressure from relatively new products, such as Samsung's LCD and plasma televisions and Apple's category-killer iPod. To compete, Stringer decided Sony had to streamline its businesses into five groups focusing more on electronics, televisions, digital imaging, DVD recorders, and portable audio. That would entail closing 11 plants and laying off 10,000 employees.

The cost of the restructuring? An estimated $1.8 billion. Because of the changes, Sony reported that it expected to incur a financial loss of about $90 million on sales of about $65.1 billion in 2005. Previously it had been expected to post a profit of $90 million. Some people inside and outside Sony were skeptical of the change because past efforts to transform the company had failed. "We have made promises before, but we failed to execute them," Stringer said.

Stringer was determined to make the change a success. A key part of the initiative involved giving Sony's Electronics division central decision-making authority over key areas. Previously each unit had its own planning, human resources, finance, and sales functions and operated with considerable autonomy. Stringer believed the new structure would streamline and speed up decision making across Sony's product lines. It would also permit uniform software development across the lines so Sony's products would operate seamlessly with one another. This would, of course, also eliminate design and product redundancies and optimize the firm's R&D spending.

Stringer also hoped the change in structure would help change Sony's corporate culture. Sony had a tradition of engineering the best products. This approach had worked wonders for years. However, the development of Apple's iPod highlighted the fact that consumers were not just interested in technical superiority but the easy use of products. And some of Sony's products had become too complicated for customers to operate.

The change plan also affected specific technologies. For example, Sony executives declared that television was of the utmost importance to the company. The firm would scrap the production of cathode ray tube (CRT) television sets and focus on LCD and rear-projection TVs and technology. Furthermore, Sony would focus on self-luminous flat-panel organic light-emitting diode (OLED) displays, on high-definition technology Blu-ray, and mobile technologies.

"Our target is for the Sony Group to achieve consolidated sales of over 8 trillion yen and an operating profit margin of 5 percent (electronics 4 percent) by the end of fiscal year 2007."

Sources: Sony Consolidated Financial Statements, 2006 and Sony Press Release, 2005, accessed at www.sony.net/SonyInfo/News/Press/200509/05-050E/index.html.

Putting the firm's new values into a mission statement is easy enough. However, making them part of the basic fabric of the organization is exceedingly difficult and can take a long time. More likely than not, it is easier and less costly for managers to attempt to change other factors, such as the firm's strategy or structure. Nevertheless, a firm's culture does represent a significant, if difficult, target for making fundamental changes.

Staff

Finally, people—both individuals and groups—can be the focus of major changes. Essentially, changes that focus on people involve one or more of the following four elements:

- Who the people are.
- What their attitudes and expectations are.
- How they interact interpersonally.
- How they are trained or developed.

In the first instance, change can be brought about by adding, subtracting, or interchanging people. Bringing in a new supervisor or transferring a difficult employee from one unit to another are examples of change focusing on the selection and placement of people.

The second element, people's attitudes and expectations, can sometimes be modified without excessive effort or cost by the manager. For example, providing people with new information or a new way to look at problems, issues, or events can potentially create significant changes in their behavior. There are no guarantees that this will occur, however.[25]

Attempting to change how staff members relate to one another—such as by being more cooperative and supportive of their coworkers—represents a third, people-oriented change focus.

The fourth and often most lasting people-change approach involves directly enhancing their knowledge, skills, and abilities—typically through education, training, and personal development activities. This can improve the performance of individuals, groups, and even larger units, regardless of any other changes a manager might initiate.

As with other types of changes, efforts to change people can be costly and time consuming. Managers need to weigh these costs against the potential benefits, such as having a more capable, creative, and innovative workforce, better morale, and, perhaps, lower turnover.

Evaluating the Need for Change

Is change always necessary? To answer that question, you should undertake two critical steps. One is to recognize the possible need for change and to correctly assess the strength of that need. The other is to accurately diagnose the problems and issues that the change or changes should address. Misjudgments at either step can lead to severe problems, if not outright disaster.[26] Jumping in to make changes before taking *both* these steps is a recipe for almost certain failure.

Recognizing and Assessing the Need for Change

As we have stressed earlier, making changes is definitely not a cost-free activity (see Exhibit 15.4). This puts a premium on not making changes if the costs will outweigh the potential benefits. It also means that it is crucial to make an accurate assessment of the strength of the forces behind the need for change.

PROACTIVE RECOGNITION Effective managers, no matter where they are in the organization's structure, are those who can recognize the need for change at the earliest possible time. To do this, they must have systems and methods in place to monitor the environment in which they and their units operate. They need to be able to detect trends before they become obvious warning signs.[27]

Collecting this information can be done in a number of ways. Sophisticated information systems can be used. So can gathering the information via more mundane activities such as spotting trends or anomalies in sales reports and actively seeking out the opinions of one's clients, customers, and employees. Starbucks, the coffee house giant, tries to spot trends by proactively studying various ways to retain its current customers and attract the next generation of young coffee drinkers. The company even hypnotized a group of 20-plus-year-old volunteers to try to find out what they *really* think about Starbucks. As a result of these assessments, the company established Starbucks Express. Starbucks Express allows customers to e-mail their orders to the stores they patronize. The stores then have their coffee waiting for them in personalized cups when they arrive.[28]

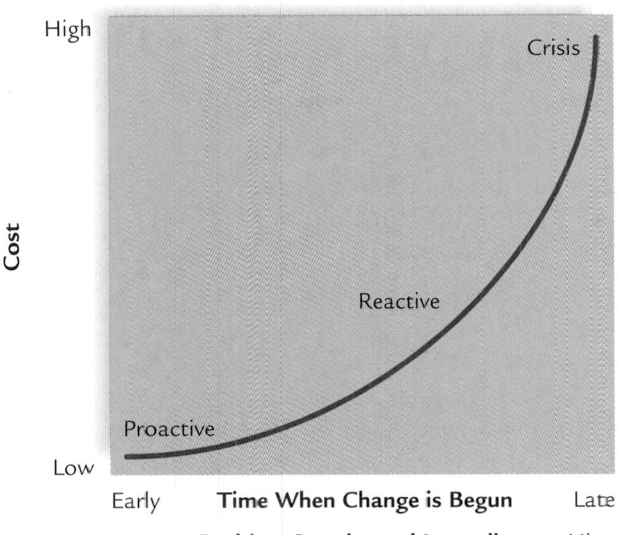

EXHIBIT 15.4

Relative Cost of Change

REACTIVE RECOGNITION Not *all* needs for change can be identified in advance, regardless of how much proactive recognition is attempted. Invariably, some developments in the internal or external environment will take place so quickly, or reach critical mass so unexpectedly, that managers must react to them in real time rather than plan for them in advance.[29] America Online (AOL) faced this kind of situation in 2006 AOL's core customers—Internet subscribers—were canceling their service and getting free e-mail accounts from competitors, such as Google. As a consequence, AOL made many of its services free and changed its strategy from generating revenues via consumer subscriptions to sales via advertising on its site.[30]

Diagnosing Problems

The recognition that change needs to take place is only a starting point. Much like a physician identifying the source of a symptom in a patient, the next step is to make an accurate diagnosis of what is causing the problem so that changes can be made to deal with it effectively. Initiating changes that do not improve the underlying problems is sometimes worse than making no changes at all. Thus, managers need to avoid premature conclusions about causes. Instead, they should obtain information from a variety of sources, if possible; compare the information to uncover consistent patterns or trends; and, most important, attempt to determine what are the most likely causes. The end result of a comprehensive analysis of this type should be an accurate, valid diagnosis of what, and who, needs to change.

First National Bank of Chicago carried out this type of diagnosis several years ago when the bank decided that within its small business loans department, processing costs were too high and turnaround times too slow. Before instituting a change, however, officials attended a roundtable discussion on small business lending sponsored by a local consulting firm. The bank also conducted surveys with its customers about proposed process changes and obtained information on the practices of its competitors. The diagnosis revealed that rather than treating them like it did its large business customers, First National needed to treat its small business customers much the same way it treated individual consumers seeking loans.[31]

The Change Process

One of the most enduring, simple, and yet comprehensive frameworks of the change process was proposed by psychologist Kurt Lewin over 50 years ago.[32] He argued that change (personal, team, or organizational change) went through three distinctive phases: unfreezing, movement, and refreezing.

EXHIBIT 15.5

Change Failure Framework

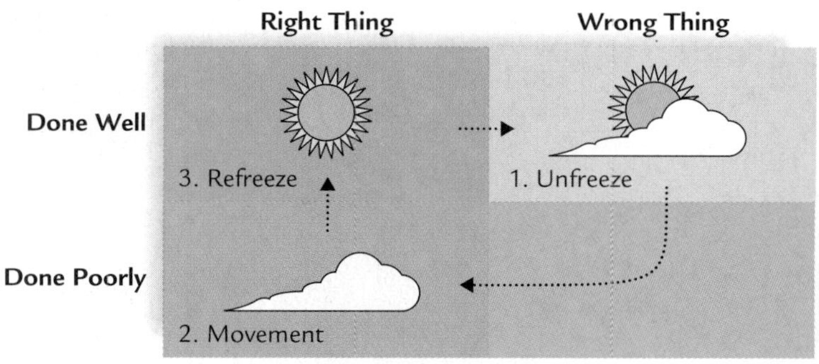

Phase 1—Unfreezing

Most change is preceded by something. Usually, that "something" is success. In other words, individuals, teams, or companies usually have a history of doing the right thing and doing it well before a change is needed (see Exhibit 15.5). In general, the longer a previous "right thing" has proven itself successful, the more likely people are to want to hang on to it.[33] Change is typically stimulated when something is anticipated to change or actually changes in the environment (external or internal). Simplistically, the change in the context causes the previous right thing for the past to become the wrong thing for the future.

For example, suppose you had the pattern of making decisions on your own without seeking input from subordinates. This pattern worked for you for many years, in part because the decisions you faced as a manager were fairly routine. You had all the knowledge you needed to make the decisions without seeking the input of others. Your individual decision-making approach was right, and you were good at it.

Then something happens. The nature of your company's customers changes. They require much more sophisticated products. These new products involve technologies that are new to you. You now need to involve others more in decision making because you don't have all the information or answers yourself. The environment has shifted and what used to be the right thing—individual decision making—is now the wrong thing. However, you are still very good at it.

A similar pattern can happen at the organizational level. For example, for more than a decade NEC, a large Japanese electronics firm, was one of the leading makers of computer displays. NEC's displays were based on the cathode ray tube (CRT) technology of TVs. At the time, Lucky Goldstar (LG), a Korean electronics firm using LCD technology, was not a major player in computer displays.

But NEC's long history of success made it difficult for its executives to see the advantages of LCD technology or the threat posed by LG. By the time they did see a need for change, they were left with virtually no options but to drop out of the computer display market and let LG rise to become one of the largest suppliers in the world.

Several factors can cause people to not see or resist seeing the initial need for change and create problems for the unfreezing state of change, including:

- ***Inertia.*** Simply being comfortable with their present ways of doing things. Without significant incentive to change or high-perceived risks for not changing, people simply find it easier to do things the way they always have rather than to operate or behave differently.
- ***Mistrust.*** Mistrust of those communicating the need for change by those affected by the proposed change can be a significant barrier to unfreezing.
- ***Lack of Information.*** Lack of adequate information about both the need for the change and what its effects are likely to be can be a third powerful force of resistance.

Fundamentally, the unfreezing process involves recognizing that what was right for the past is wrong for the future and why. However, even if you recognize the need for change, Lewin argued that unless we undo or unfreeze these old patterns, it is difficult to change to something new. To better appreciate Lewin's notion, you might think about an ice sculpture. Suppose you wanted to change an ice sculpture of a bird into a sculpture of a fish. You could try to chip away at the old bird and fashion the new fish, but it's a difficult process. Instead, what would happen if you unfroze or melted the bird sculpture? You could then use the water to create a new bock of ice from which you could carve a fish. Trying to simply carve a fish out of the original bird sculpture is perhaps possible but not very efficient or effective.

This was part of the problem for managers at NEC. Since the technology for producing flat-panel screens is completely different than that used in CRTs, you have to let go of the old technology in order to get your mind around the new technology. In NEC's case, both senior executives as well as managers in the R&D area resisted letting go of the old. Some of the strongest champions of the new technology were younger scientists, but in a very hierarchical organization such as NEC, they were unable to get older managers to unfreeze their notions about what customers wanted in a computer screen—which was for it to provide good resolution but take up less space.

Phase 2—Movement

Unfortunately, even if people accept that the old right thing is now the wrong thing, they may still resist moving or changing. Specific sources of resistance to the movement stage of the change process include the following:

- ***Lack of Clarity.*** If the new right thing or the target of change is not clear to people, they are likely to resist movement toward it. Why? Because to them it is like shooting in the dark.
- ***Lack of Capabilities.*** As we discussed in the chapter on motivation (Chapter 10), if people believe they lack the capabilities needed to implement the change, they may resist movement (even if they see the need for change).
- ***Lack of Sufficient Incentives.*** If those affected by the change believe that the anticipated negative consequences of the change outweigh the positive consequences, resistance to movement is almost guaranteed.

As Exhibit 15.5 illustrates, change typically requires people to go from doing the wrong thing well to doing the right thing poorly. For example, if you have made decisions on an individual basis for many years, even if you recognize the need to make decisions in a more participative manner by involving others, you are not likely to be great at participative decision making at first. Research has demonstrated that one of the biggest determinants of resistance during the movement stage of the change process is the level of uncertainty associated with the change.[34] The greater the uncertainty of what will happen, generally the greater the resistance to move or change. Moreover, in general, there is a relationship between the magnitude of the change and the level of uncertainty.[35] If the magnitude of the change increases, so too will the level of uncertainty. Both, in turn, will likely lead to higher levels of resistance by employees. As a consequence, you will have to do more planning and preparation in order to make the change a success. In the end, unless people are confident that they can go from doing the new right thing poorly to doing it well, they will fail to move.[36]

Phase 3—Refreezing

But suppose you are successful getting people to see the need to unfreeze and you are also able to get them moving toward the desired change, what are the odds that the change will last? To appreciate why Lewin stressed this third stage of change, you only need to think about the percentage of people who start a new diet or exercise program and subsequently stick with it past the first few weeks. Less than one in four people sustain this type of personal change. If it is hard to sustain change in ourselves, we can appreciate the managerial challenge, which is to sustain change in others.

PULL OF PAST COMPETENCIES Lewin contended that the "pull" of old, successful patterns was strong and that simply making the move from the old to the new was not enough to ensure lasting success.[37] This was in part because, whatever the "old" pattern, it existed in the first place because it was positively rewarded. In other words, most people have the communication patterns, a leadership style, a decision-making approach or companies have a specific strategy, structure, or culture because they worked in the past. In this sense, you can think of past patterns as having a kind of gravity that will pull us back to them unless a greater force is in place to keep us moving forward.

This is why Lewin stressed the refreezing stage of the change process. However, when most people hear the term *refreezing*, they usually get images of things frozen solid and unmovable. By *refreezing*, Lewin did not intend to imply that the new state should be static with no movement. He did not mean for the term to imply that once change is made that there should be no monitoring or adjusting. Instead, the term was designed to reflect the notion that after a change is made, forces need to be put in place to keep people and behaviors from giving in to the gravitational pull of the past and reverting back to old patterns.

As a consequence, refreezing involves monitoring the change to see if it is producing the anticipated and desired results. To the extent the change is succeeding, the refreezing phase should involve reinforcing the change so that it becomes more established.[38] This is important because as Lewin recognized, and research has confirmed, without reinforcement people will return to past habits and patterns.[39]

NONIMMEDIATE RESULTS This is especially true if the results from the change are slow in coming, which is the case with change initiatives of moderate or greater magnitude. This is in part why people have difficulty changing their diet or exercise habits. They want the envisioned changes in their fitness or appearance, but when those results are slow in coming, people often return to the old habits. The inconvenient truth is that most significant change does not produce instant, positive consequences. As a consequence, managers that only pay attention to the first two phases of change tend to find that the overall change initiative fails to deliver the desired results because of problems in the third phase.

Overcoming Resistance to Change

With the overall framework of unfreeze, move, and refreeze, practicing managers want to know how they can overcome common challenges and successfully lead and manage change in themselves and others. That's precisely what this section addresses.

Overcoming Resistance to Unfreeze

As we stated, if people cannot see the need for change, the entire change process doesn't even get going. Most needed changes for an individual, team, or organization are stimulated by some anticipated or existing change outside that person, team, or organization. For example a needed change in an individual's behavior might stem from a change in the organization's strategy. A change in the organization's strategy might stem from an anticipated change in technology. As a consequence, one of the keys to unfreezing is helping people see what has changed in the larger context that requires a change from them. Getting this contrast clear between how things were before and why the past approach was successful and how things are different going forward and why what worked in the past may not in the future is a critical first step in managing change. Consider the case faced by Tom Alexander of Hewlett-Packard, illustrated in A Manager's Challenge. What do you think of the way that Tom tried to illustrate the contrast between how HP made printers in the past and what was needed by consumers in the future? What do you think of the outcome? Would you have taken the same approach?

This process of illustrating the contrast can involve communicating to people the reason for the change or getting those affected by the change to analyze the stimulus for the change. Because involvement and participation generally take more time, managers often have to take time pressures into account in order to determine what level of involvement is appropriate. As we discussed in Chapter 4, "Decision Making", if there is time and participants have the needed information and capabilities, involving them can often increase their level of buy in and reduce their resistance to the change.

A MANAGER'S CHALLENGE

Change

Changing the Crown Jewels at HP

Hewlett-Packard (HP) is a well-known technology company. One of its most important businesses is printers. Printers account for about two-thirds of its profits. As recently as 2004, HP's printer division accounted for almost *all* of the firm's market value because its two other major divisions (services and computers) were generally losing money. In short, printers were the crown jewels of HP.

Beginning in the late 1990s, however, HP managers saw their strong position begin to slip away, especially the position of its low-end products. Specifically, Lexmark, a key competitor, introduced good quality printers that sold for a retail price of under \$100. Soon Lexmark saw its share of the market double to 14 percent.

In response to this change in the environment, the head of HP's printer division, Vyomesh Joshi, determined that HP had to change. Joshi determined that HP needed to build a new line of printers, including a printer that HP could manufacture for \$49 or \$30 cheaper than its least expensive printer at the time. This would then allow the printer to retail for under \$100. He also challenged his group to go from "concept to shelf" (idea to putting the printer on retailer's shelves) in three years rather than the normal four.

Most HP managers said they thought building a printer for \$49 instead of \$79 was impossible. Tom Alexander, a key project manager, knew he needed to "explode their complacency." In a team meeting, he created a high contrast that helped people see the need for change and unfreeze the past.

After listening to people say how impossible the task of building a significantly less expensive printer was, Alexander grabbed an HP printer, put it on the floor, and stood on it—all 200 pounds of him. In that instant, the people in the room broke through the failure to see barrier and got the message. HP printers were overengineered. They did not need to be engineered and constructed to be as sturdy as stepping stools. The extra engineering, material, and manufacturing costs were significant, making it impossible to bring down the cost and be competitive with Lexmark.

In the 1990s, Lexmark chewed away at the profits of Hewlett Packard, the dominant player in the printer business. HP's managers initially had a hard time convincing employees that the firm needed to design smaller, less-expensive copiers like the one shown here.

In the end, HP managers delivered a line of 14 inkjet printers and 7 "all-in-one" printers based on just two cost-efficient platforms. The new line was produced on time and at the desired cost. It also included a printer that cost HP \$49 to make and retailed for under \$100. Following their introduction, HP sold \$5.6 billion worth of the new printers (a 12 percent year-over-year increase) at a profit margin of 16.5 percent (a 14 percent increase in profitability). HP took 70 percent of the market share, and much of it came from Lexmark.[40]

Overcoming Resistance to Move

Even though unfreezing is a necessary step in the change process, it is not a sufficient one. More to the point, even if managers are successful in getting others to see the need for change, they still may encounter resistance in the moving stage of the change process. As we discussed, one of the prime sources of resistance to move is lack of clarity about what people are moving toward. Thus, one of the first means of overcoming the failure to move is to educate people as to what the desired change is. For example, if you want to change from an individual decision-making style, you need to not only recognize the need to change, but you have to see and understand the new, participative approach. You may have to educate yourself as to how effectively to involve others in gathering and processing information. Until the new destination is clear, you are likely to stay where you are.

However, simply making the alternative or new destination clear may not be sufficient to get the desired movement or change. For example, suppose you are the manager of a group of customer service representatives. You have helped your team see the changes in customers' expectations and, therefore, the need to switch from focusing on how many customers you can service in a given time period to how delighted you can make customers with the service you provide. You clearly describe the new destination of customer service. You explain that the objective is to be sure that you understand the customer's questions and then answer the questions without having to pass the customer on to someone else. But even if people now see the need to change and can clearly envision the new destination, they may fail to move.

In addition to helping your people see the new destination, you have to make sure they have the needed capabilities (information, tools, resources, and skills). This typically requires an assessment of what is required and what exists. Based on this gap analysis, as the manager of the customer service representatives, you would need to help your subordinates bridge the gap through training, tools, or other resources.[41]

Finally, the call representatives need to perceive that the anticipated benefits of the change will outweigh any negative outcomes. Simply communicating how the change will directly affect them in a positive way can often increase support and reduce resistance during the movement stage. For example, you might highlight how the installation of new equipment will make their work easier, or how the additional training will add to their repertoire of skills and general future employability. At other times, providing incentives might involve conferring benefits directly to those affected. This could include, for example, either nonmonetary incentives, such as praise, or the use of some form of monetary incentives, such as increased compensation for increased customer satisfaction.

Overcoming the Failure to Finish

Suppose you have been able to get your team to see the need for change and have gotten them moving toward the change. How can you ensure that movement continues and avoid the failure-to-finish problem? How can you, in Lewin's terms, refreeze the change and ensure that it lasts?

As we discussed earlier, the pull of past patterns and the lack of early, natural positive consequences often causes change not to last. Refreezing is not an instant process because instant expertise in a new behavior is almost never possible. For example, improvement in customer service versus call processing comes gradually. Early attempts by your customer service representatives to answer customers' questions and not transfer them to another department are likely to produce less-than-stellar results at first. Early on when call representatives' proficiency at the new approach is low, customers might even ask to be transferred: "Well, if you can't answer my question, then connect me with someone who can." Initial low proficiency at customer service will produce negative consequences that, in general, tend to drive out the desired behavior. Consequently, one of the key things managers need to do to refreeze change is compensate for the early negative consequences that naturally follow from low proficiency.

This compensatory action to provide positive reinforcement of desired efforts even when results are below the target is the subject of a number of authors and studies. This is often referred to as "celebrating early wins." Whether this or another term is used, the idea is the same: When people engage in change, they need early and consistent reinforcement to overcome the gravitational pull of past patterns and build momentum in moving toward establishing new patterns.[42] Managers are likely to need to celebrate and reinforce early correct efforts and not just desired outcomes. As we previously described, proficiency at new activities does not come instantly and so neither do the positive consequences naturally associated with high proficiency. Therefore, early on managers need to reinforce the desired behaviors so that they get repeated and eventually lead to higher proficiency, which, in turn, will lead to a higher frequency of desired results.

However, even if managers use reinforcement to sustain early efforts and help push the change into the early portion of the refreezing stage, it may not be sufficient to move completely through it. This is, in part, because typically progress and improvement are made in small enough increments that without feedback, people can underestimate their progress. If they underestimate sufficiently, they can feel like they are making no progress and give up on the change. Thus, in addition to reinforcing early and desired efforts, managers also need to provide feedback on progress—both to individuals as well as groups. Many of the principles of feedback and performance management that we discussed earlier in the chapter on human resources apply to this aspect of managing change. Exhibit 15.6 provides a general description of these various methods for dealing with resistance to change and summarizes their advantages and disadvantages.

EXHIBIT 15.6 Possible Methods for Dealing with Resistance to Change

Approach	Commonly Used In Situations—	Advantages	Disadvantages
Negotiation and Agreement (e.g., use formal or informal processes to gain advanced agreement to change before implementation)	In which someone or some group will clearly lose out in a change, and in which that group has considerable power to resist	Sometimes major resistance can be reduced or avoided	Can be expensive in many cases if it alerts other groups to want to negotiate too
Participation and Involvement (e.g., involve affected employees in planning the change)	In which the initiators do not have all the information they need to design the change, and in which others have considerable power to resist	People who participate are more likely to be committed to implementing change, and any relevant information they have will be integrated into the change plan	Can be both time-consuming and awkward if participants design an inappropriate change
Communication and Education (e.g., provide increased information to employees concerning the short- and long-term effects of the change)	In which there is a lack of information or inaccurate information and analysis	Once persuaded, people will often help with the implementation of the change	Can be very time-consuming if many people are involved
Facilitation and Support (e.g., offer seminars in stress management, personal development, anger resolution, etc.)	In which people are resisting because of problems in adjusting to the changes	No other approach works as well with problems of adapting to changes	Can be expensive, and still fail
Explicit and Implicit Coercion (e.g., use position power to order change)	In which speed is essential, and the change initiators possess considerable power	It is speedy and can overcome many kinds of resistance	Can be risky if it leaves people angry at the initiators and lowers trust in them

Source: Adapted and reprinted by permission of *Harvard Business Review*. An exhibit from "Methods for Dealing with Resistance to Change" by John P. Kotter and Leonard A. Schlesinger (March/April 1979), p. 111.

EXHIBIT 15.7

The Change Process

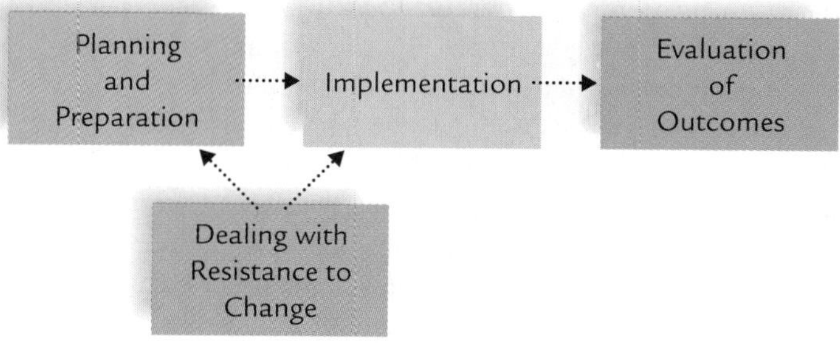

Managing Change

So far in this chapter, we have focused on the background and context of change in organizations: That is, the forces and targets of change, the process of change, and, especially, managers' roles in understanding, assessing, and evaluating the need for change. Now, we turn to the processes of managing change, including planning and preparing for it, implementing it, and evaluating its outcomes (see Exhibit 15.7).

Planning and Preparing for Change

Once a manager or a group of managers have been convinced that change is necessary and that an accurate diagnosis has been made of the causes requiring change, preparation for the changes can begin. Exhibit 15.8 shows the issues related to this planning.

force field analysis
uses the concept of equilibrium, a condition that occurs when the forces for change, the "driving forces," are balanced by forces opposing change, the "restraining forces," and results in a relatively steady state.

FORCE FIELD ANALYSIS One very useful way of looking at the change challenge is what is called a **force field analysis**, as Lewin proposed some years ago. This analysis, as depicted in Exhibit 15.9, uses the concept of equilibrium, a condition that occurs when the "driving forces" of change are roughly balanced by the "restraining forces" of change. Such a condition results in a relatively steady state that is disrupted only when the driving forces for innovation become stronger than the restraining forces for inertia (the two forces are sometimes called the "in" forces.[43]) If we apply this analysis to typical organizational changes, we see that managers basically face two choices: add more force for change, such as putting more pressure on subordinates to conform to new procedures; or reduce the resistance forces, such as convincing informal leaders that they will benefit from the change. The basic problem with increasing the driving forces is that this often results in increasing the opposing forces. Therefore, Lewin's analysis suggests that weakening restraints may be the more effective way to bring about change.

With this general framework in mind, managers still have a variety of key decisions and judgments to make relative to planning and implementing a change. Sadly, there are no

EXHIBIT 15.8

Planning Choices for Change

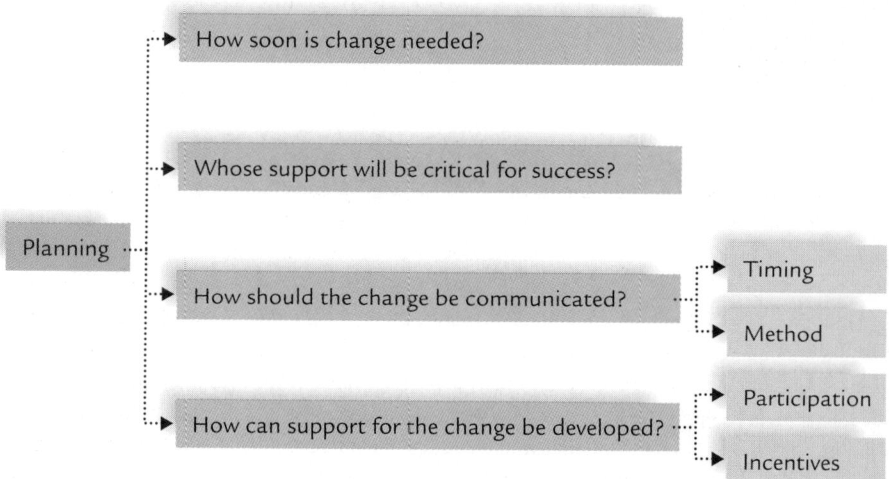

EXHIBIT 15.9

Force Field Analysis

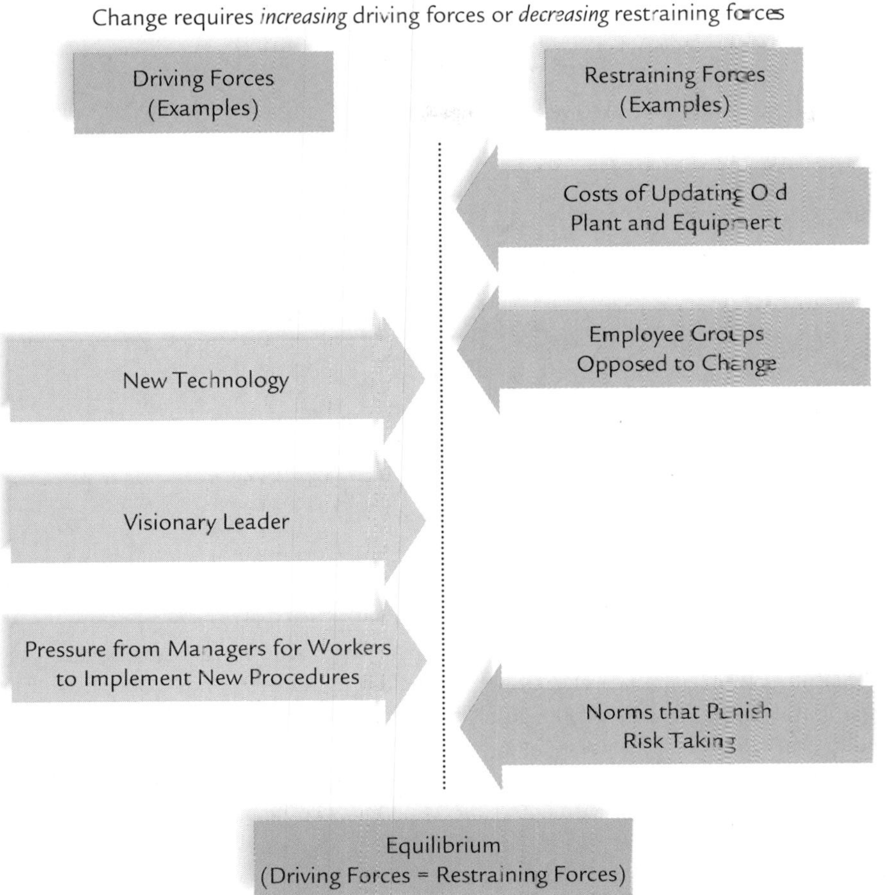

magic formulas to map out exactly what choices should be made under which conditions. However, deliberately thinking about the choices rather than just falling victim to one's own biases, tendencies, fears, preferences, and the like increases the chances that you will make a better judgment and decision.

TIMING Managers are often tempted to initiate something quickly, especially if the need for change seems exceptionally strong. Whether rapid implementation is a good idea or not represents a difficult judgment call. Acting too quickly can lead to changes that are not well planned and that often fail because they lack sufficient support. On the other hand, waiting too long to make necessary changes can also be a recipe for failure. In late 2005, David Gunn, then CEO of Amtrak, was ousted by the company's board of directors precisely because, according to its chairman, "the railroad needed immediate changes and Gunn resisted those changes."[44] It is clear that the timing of changes can be critical to their success.

BUILDING SUPPORT Whereas in the previous section we focused on overcoming resistance in general, this aspect of managing change is focused on building support. Developing this foundation requires especially careful analysis. First, it involves determining who are more likely to be in favor of the change. Second, it involves analyzing who has power or influence over others. The ideal people to build early support with are those who come out high on both criteria of agreeability and influence (see Exhibit 15.10). This group is often referred to as a **leading coalition**, a group of early supporters who are both favorably inclined toward the change and can exercise influence over others toward the change. People who have high influence over others but may not be agreeable to the change at first can be potential supporters if they listen to and can be influenced by the "high agreeable, high influence" group. People who have high agreeability but low influence over others can

leading coalition
a group of supporters who are favorably inclined toward change and can influence others toward change

EXHIBIT 15.10

Matrix of Agreeability and Influence

Agreeability	Low Influence	High Influence
High	**Potential Key Supporters** (if numbers are large)	**Most Important Supporters**
Low	**Least Important Supporters**	**Potential Key Supporters** (if they listen to "most important supporters")

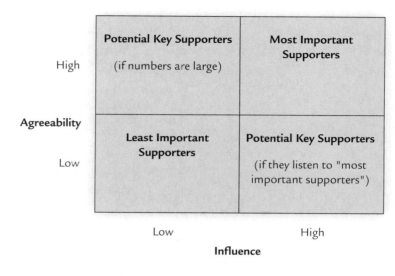

be potential supporters if there are many of them; their sheer numbers can provide support and momentum for the change.

COMMUNICATION In conjunction with the analysis of who is agreeable and influential, it is often important to have a plan of communicating with them. For example, during the reorganization of Cookson Group, a multibillion-dollar conglomerate of international manufacturing companies, the headquarters' treasury unit was given the job of reviewing and revising the funding and capital investment policies and practices at each company. The unit found that the key to making the change work was to begin by meeting with senior managers in each company to convince them of the benefits to be gained by centralizing the firm's capital investment procedures.[45]

PARTICIPATION During the planning stage, obtaining the participation of those who are agreeable and influential can help strengthen their support. Plans can often be improved and commitment gained through such participation. The use of participation is not cost free. As we mentioned in the previous section, it takes time and effort. Also, participation can backfire if participants' suggestions diverge widely from managers' goals. Furthermore, if those asked to participate sense that their input is not really wanted and that a manager is only "going through the motions," this can quickly lead to a feeling of being "manipulated." In such cases, participation typically erodes rather than builds support for change.

INCENTIVES Giving leading coalition members incentives to make the change also can help build support for it. For example, offering a set of lead call representatives a bonus based on customer satisfaction scores rather than the number of calls they answer may be a way to motivate them to engage in new behavior. Here, managers should take care because providing incentives may make the beneficiaries feel as if they are being "bought off." Thus, the use of incentives for change, especially monetary incentives, can potentially boomerang by increasing the skepticism and cynicism of managers' motives for the changes.

Implementation Choices

Where planning for change leaves off and implementation of change begins is often difficult to specify because the process is, or should be, more or less continuous. Regardless of where that boundary is, however, implementing change involves several critical choices for managers (see Exhibit 15.11). Three of the most important are discussed here.

CHOICE OF FOCUS Earlier in this chapter, we identified six types, or focuses, of change: strategy, structure, systems, technology, shared values, and staff. To initiate the change process, one or more of these focuses need to be selected. The choice depends in large part on

EXHIBIT 15.11

Implementation Choices

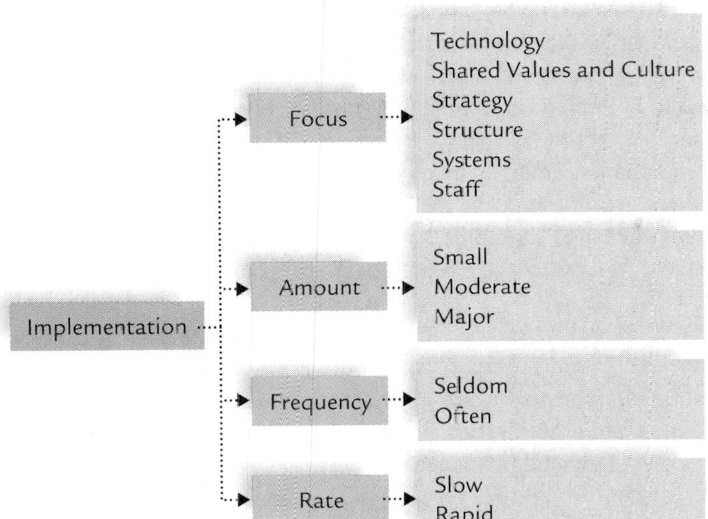

the objectives to be accomplished, which, in turn, are linked to the problems identified in the assessment of the need to change. If the major problem is outdated equipment, then, obviously, changing the technology will be the focus of choice. However, if the problem is one of sluggish growth in sales compared with competitors, then the choice of focus is not so self-evident. It could be that the organization is not sufficiently market oriented, which could indicate a need for change in strategy and culture of the organization. That is exactly what took place in Poland beginning in 2003 when its telecommunication markets were opened up to international competition. For decades, Poland's telecommunications leader, Telekomunikacja Polska S.A. (TP), had enjoyed monopolistic control over the country's telecommunications market. Legislation passed in May 2000 opened local markets to competition in 2002 and opened international markets in 2003. This liberalization of the markets prompted TP to transition its technology-focused organization into a more customer-oriented culture.

CHOICE OF AMOUNT Even after managers have decided what approaches to take and have started to implement those choices, they must also confront another, but related, set of issues: How much change should take place? That is, how comprehensive should the change be, and what parts of the unit or the whole organization should be affected? These questions have no easy answers.

When change is too little, the benefits are not likely to outweigh the costs involved. For example, 3M Corporation tried for several years to fix its magnetic data storage business problems through minor cost-cutting changes. After 10 years of escalating losses, the firm finally divested itself of this part of the company.[46] Even modest changes can take a great amount of effort and cause disruptions that are almost as great as if the change were much more sizable. Thus, managers must decide whether implementing minimal changes are worth these costs or simply wait until the problems are large enough to justify the substantial investments that will be required. The argument in favor of making minimal changes, however, is that even though the immediate cost–benefit ratio may not be favorable, changes postponed until later will be much more expensive; therefore, the longer-term benefits can easily prove the worth of making small changes early. The old adage of "pay me now, or pay me later" comes to mind here.

Changes can be too massive as well as too small. Although managers are sometimes tempted to make big changes, they often overlook the potential costs. For example, large scale changes can be confusing and difficult to coordinate because they affect multiple parts of the organization but affect them in different ways. Very large changes are sometimes what are called for, especially when major changes are occurring in the unit's or organization's environment. Changes such as these can also help "galvanize the troops" by inspiring their best efforts. However, as we already discussed, any change can cause resistance, and big changes can cause immense resistance. Thus, too great a change, in effect, can create more chaos and more problems than existed initially. When this happens, no change at all would have been better than the change that was attempted but failed.

The lesson for managers is that they must take great care in deciding how much change they should implement.[47] Potential problems exist in making changes so small that they either don't justify the costs or they produce minimal effects. Similarly, there can be other kinds of dangers in making changes that are too large. In particular instances, however, one of these extremes may be the best alternative. The general guideline, therefore, is that the amount of change should fit the severity of the problems, and this should be determined by a sound analysis of the strength of the need for change.

CHOICE OF FREQUENCY Another aspect of change that needs to be considered is the frequency of changes. Because today's competitive pressures are shifting more frequently, changes must be implemented much more often than in the past. In some sense, change is a more or less constant condition. However, this can become mentally and physically exhausting for the organization's members. Imagine, for example, that you are a member of a sales department in a large, geographically dispersed company. Now suppose your company decides that the firm's sales data should be centralized, so a new information system linking all of the sales regions is installed. Next, the company reorganizes the sales department by geographic region rather than by type of product as well as institutes a team sales structure. Each of these changes, by itself, might improve customer satisfaction and employee performance. However, if they all occur within a short space of time, you might not have time to completely adjust to any one of them. Therefore, the frequency of changes must be considered along with their size.

CHOICE OF RATE Just as the amount and frequency of change are important, so is the rate of change. If the pace of change is too slow, conditions that created the need for it in the first place might again shift significantly. Also, change that is too slow can frustrate many people who want to see at least some early and tangible results in return for their efforts. For instance, suppose a company spends several months putting together new work teams and training employees in decision-making techniques, group processes, conflict resolution, and computerized tracking techniques. Then, however, suppose it delayed installing the new equipment and software. Employees would likely be frustrated by not being able to put their new knowledge and skills to immediate use.

Change that is too rapid can also cause major problems. Whether the change is primarily technological, structural, procedural, or some other focus, people need to adapt to the rate. Rates that are excessively fast can exceed the typical person's ability to cope and increase resentment and resistance. It has even been suggested that in situations of rapid change, the work experience may be so stressful and so damaging to a person's self-identity as to trigger violent behavior.[48]

Managers sometimes deliberately and appropriately make rapid changes. One obvious case is when the forces for change are so overwhelming that swift change is essential. Furthermore, managers sometimes institute a fast rate of change precisely to determine who can keep up and who cannot. In such circumstances, a rapid rate may be a viable change tactic—if the manager has carefully considered what is to be accomplished and what the potential negative consequences or costs might be. In many other cases, however, managers have not adequately assessed the possible costs and benefits and may have simply implemented an abrupt change because of their eagerness to see results quickly.

As with choices about the amount of change, managers often face clear options about the rate of change they can choose. However, there is one major difference. When dealing with the rate of change, managers can make midcourse corrections more easily than they can when it comes to the amount of change. (It is very difficult, for example, to suddenly convert a large change into a small change.) If the initial pace has started slowly, managers can increase it if this appears desirable. Likewise, a change that has started out rapidly can be slowed, allowing for adaptation to catch up with events. Thus, just as the rate of speed of a car can be increased or decreased depending on road conditions, so can the rate of change in organizational settings. Just as in a car, if the rate is changed too often or too drastically, it can be very uncomfortable for those required to adapt. This, in turn, can reduce confidence in the person responsible for the changes.

Evaluating Change Outcomes

Once change has been carried out, whether throughout the entire organization or within one unit, managers need to evaluate the outcomes. If the effects of changes are not appraised in some manner, managers have no way of knowing whether additional changes are needed and also whether the particular approaches implemented should be used again in similar circumstances. To carry out the evaluation process, three things must be done: data must be collected, the results of the data must be compared against the change's goals, and ultimately the results must be communicated to those affected by it. (See Exhibit 15.12)

DATA COLLECTION The data that can be collected to evaluate the outcomes of change essentially come in two forms: objective, or quantitative, data and subjective, or attitude, data. Both types can be useful to the manager who has implemented change, and often it will be necessary to tap several sources of each type. For example, after introducing new information technology, a manager could evaluate its effectiveness by measuring changes in output per employee, the speed of response to customers, and the attitudes of employees and clients who deal with them.

It is important to keep in mind that the collection of different sets of data, such as these, to measure change outcomes may well require significant costs. Therefore, not every type of data that could be collected should be collected. As with other organizational actions, the benefits should be weighed against the costs. The point, though, is that significant sources of data should not be overlooked, and the more types of data that can be collected, the more likely the analysis of the effects will be informative. Also, in most cases, data should be collected at periodic intervals to measure the lasting power of the change. A recent survey showed that two-thirds of companies are using some form of scorecard software to measure everything from financial progress to customer satisfaction. These scorecards can be customized to reflect only the measures the company wishes to track. Then, by targeting the distribution of this kind of data, a company can ensure, for example, that managers from marketing, finance, and research and development are all discussing the same measures in meetings.[49]

COMPARING THE OUTCOMES AGAINST THE CHANGE'S GOALS Collecting data is only a first step in evaluating outcomes. The next step is comparing the outcomes against the goals and various benchmarks, or standards, set in advance of the change. Without those standards, interpreting the data will be almost meaningless. To know that sales increased by 3 percent isn't enough unless the result can be compared with some explicit goal, such as a 5 percent increase. In other words, absolute results are not as informative as relative results. Goals and benchmarks that have been specified in advance of change efforts provide the basis for making meaningful relative comparisons.

COMMUNICATING THE RESULTS OF THE CHANGE The final step in evaluating change outcomes is communicating the findings to those who are involved with or affected by the change. As we discussed earlier in the chapter, this is one of the keys to ensure that the

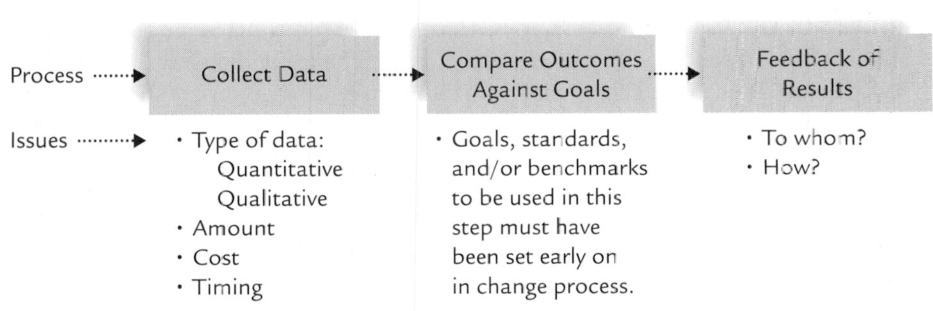

EXHIBIT 15.12

Evaluating Change Outcomes

change lasts (the refreeze stage in Lewin's model). Managers seldom, if ever, neglect to provide this information to their superiors. Their subordinates are another story. This may be short-sighted. Not providing feedback can frustrate employees. They may even question a manager's motives for not supplying it, thereby creating an element of distrust and hampering successful changes in the future.

Specific Approaches to Planned Change

Throughout the earlier parts of this chapter, we have presented general issues and principles relating to organizational change and renewal. Here, in this final section, we look at three specific, usually organization-wide, approaches to planned change. The first is *organizational development*, which is an approach with a strong behavioral and people orientation. The second is the more engineering-based approach called *process redesign* (or *reengineering*). The final part of this section describes what is almost more a particular framework or perspective than a change approach as such, namely, *organizational learning*.

The Organizational Development (OD) Approach to Change

organizational development (OD)
approach to organizational change that has a strong behavioral and people orientation, emphasizing planned, strategic, long-range efforts focusing on people and their interrelationships in organizations

T-groups
groups of individuals participating in organizational development sessions away from the workplace; also called basic skills training groups

The essence of an **organizational development (OD)** approach to change is its emphasis on planned, strategic, long-range efforts focusing on people and their interrelationships in organizations.[50] Although "organizational development" may seem like a general term that could be applied to almost any aspect of the topic of organizational change, as we noted at the beginning of this chapter, it refers to a specific approach to bringing change to organizations. It grew out of behavioral science research aimed at improving the communication and quality of interactions among individuals in groups. Researchers put together groups of individuals in sessions away from the workplace in what were termed basic skill training groups, or, as they came to be called for short, **T-groups**.[51] The T-group orientation over time broadened into a focus on interpersonal relationships throughout the larger organization, and hence the attention to *organizational*, not just group, development.

VALUES AND ASSUMPTIONS The early formulation of what eventually evolved into the OD approach placed particular importance on certain values and assumptions, and they have remained at the heart of this approach to change to this day.[52] One set of these values related to the people in organizations: First and foremost is the assumption that "people are the cornerstone of success in any organizational endeavor."[53] A second value or assumption is that most people want opportunities for personal growth and enhancement of their capabilities. Another basic belief that underlies this approach is that people's emotions are as important as their thoughts. Therefore, the open expression of these emotions can be critical in facilitating real change.

The fundamental assumption about organizations in the OD approach is that they are systems composed of interdependent parts. Thus, a change in one part can affect other parts.[54] Another assumption is that the way organizations are designed and structured will influence the interpersonal relationships among the people within them. In other words, the behavior of people in organizational settings is at least partly caused by the conditions they encounter there—and these conditions can be changed.

BASIC APPROACH TO THE PROCESS OF CHANGE The basic OD approach to organizational change fundamentally follows the three stages of change outlined earlier in the chapter: Unfreezing, movement (changing), and refreezing.[55] Thus, in an OD approach to change, the initial challenge is to critically examine existing behavioral patterns by getting people not to take them for granted but to question them and look at their effects.

change agents
individuals who are responsible for implementing change efforts; they can be either internal or external to the organization

In the traditional OD approach, both the first and second steps—unfreezing and movement—call for the use of **change agents**, individuals specifically responsible for managing change efforts.[56] These people can be either internal change agents, that is, from inside the organization—often from the human resource area—or they can be external change agents from outside the organization. In either case, the OD change agent is someone who is not a member of the particular groups or units directly involved. Frequently, this person is a consultant, someone with expertise in helping groups see the need for and make changes.

The changes themselves are achieved by the use of one or more **interventions**, that is, "sets of structured activities," or action steps, designed to improve the organization.[57] Some of these interventions, such as fact finding, begin in the unfreezing stage, and others, such as team building and coaching or counseling, take place in the changing stage. Exhibit 15.13 shows several of the more common types of interventions.

interventions
sets of structured activities or action steps designed to improve organizations

The priority in the second change stage is on exploring new forms of behavior and relationships. Particularly important at this point is an emphasis on behavioral processes, such as leader–group relations, decision making, intergroup cooperation, and the like. This **behavioral process orientation** is a key distinguishing feature of the OD approach to organizational change.

behavioral process orientation
key distinguishing feature of the OD approach to organizational change that focuses on new forms of behavior and new relationships

Merely engaging in new and different ways of behaving, relating, and interacting is not enough for changes to have lasting effects. This is the reason for the third stage, refreezing. As we discussed earlier in this chapter, the intent of this third stage is to make sure that the changes "stick" and that behavior and relationships don't easily return to their former—less effective—states. However, since the time of the original formulation of the three-stage change process many years ago, the goal of refreezing has been broadened into the objective of **organizational renewal**. The idea behind organizational renewal recognizes that in a fast-changing, competitive world, new habits and patterns rapidly become outdated. Therefore, the emphasis has shifted from simply locking changes into place and instead to developing a *capacity* for renewal, that is, the flexibility to change more or less continually.

organizational renewal
a concept of organizational change that proposes a goal of flexibility and capability for continual change

EXHIBIT 15.13 Types of OD Interventions

Intervention	Objective	Examples
Diagnostic Activities	To determine the current state of the organization or the parameters of a problem	Interviews Questionnaires Surveys Meetings
Individual Enhancement Activities	To improve understanding of and relationships with others in the organization	Sensitivity training (T-groups) Behavior modeling Life and career planning
Team Building	To improve team operation, abilities, cohesiveness	Diagnostic meetings Role analysis Responsibility charting
Intergroup Activities	To improve cooperation between groups	Intergroup team building
Technostructural or Structural Activities	To find solutions to problems through the application of technological and structural changes	Job enrichment Management by objective New technology introduction
Process Consultation	To disseminate information concerning the future diagnosis and management of human processes in organizations including communication, leadership, problem solving and decision making, and intra- and intergroup relationships	Agenda setting Feedback and observation Coaching and counseling Structural change suggestions

Source: Adapted from Wendell L. French and Cecil H. Bell Jr., *Organization Development: Behavioral Science Interventions for Organizational Improvement*, 5th ed. (Upper Saddle River, NJ: Prentice Hall, 1995), p. 165.

In recent years, the OD approach to change, which formerly was almost a rigid set of procedures, has evolved into a more general approach—one that emphasizes line managers as potential change agents. Also, many OD intervention methods, such as team-building, have now become day-to-day activities for firms. Other comprehensive approaches to change have attracted increasing attention in the last decade or so. Two of these are process redesign and organizational learning, discussed next.

Process Redesign (Reengineering)

process redesign (reengineering)
involves a fundamental redesign of business processes to achieve dramatic improvements

Process redesign, or **reengineering**, involves redesigning a firm's processes to achieve dramatic improvements.[58] Technology, especially information technology, usually plays a central role in such reengineering efforts. However, the human and managerial issues related to process redesign are also extremely crucial. (See Exhibit 15.14).

Reengineering first appeared in the late 1980s, and seemed to peak in popularity in the mid-1990s.[59] The approach is based on two key principles: Many companies have business processes that are inefficient and structures that involve more people than necessary. The goal is to reduce costs, shorten cycle times, and improve quality.[60] IBM was one of the first companies to take a reengineering approach. In the 1990s, the company shortened its credit approval process from two weeks to just two hours with no increase in staff.

The most successful process redesign efforts appear to have both breadth and depth.[61] Breadth of reengineering involves redesigning a set of processes rather than a single process. Depth of reengineering involves changing a host of core elements, such as the roles and responsibilities, structure, incentives, and shared values, within an organization.

But breadth and depth are not enough for a reengineering effort to succeed. Key executives in the organization must also make a major commitment to it. For example, they must supply the necessary resources to implement the activities and demonstrate that they are personally involved in the effort. Like any comprehensive change approach, reengineering requires enormous energy, planning, a coordinated effort, persistence, and attention to detail. Otherwise, it is likely to fail.

Even under the best circumstances, however, reengineering does not always produce effective changes. This has led to some disillusionment with the approach.[62] For one, the amount of effort it requires has not always been commensurate with the results obtained. One European commercial bank, for example, saw its reengineering effort yield only a 5 percent cost reduction rather than an anticipated 23 percent reduction.[63] A second reason that some managers have become disenchanted with the approach is that it can cause continual disorder, or, as some managers call it, "mass chaos."[64]

As the history of companies' attempts to implement process redesign illustrates, it is an approach or organizational renewal that is not exactly embraced by many of those who have to take part in it. One of the coauthors of the book (Michael Hammer), who was most influential in popularizing this approach, has stated that the people aspects of reengineering were not always given enough attention. "I was insufficiently appreciative of the human dimension. I've learned that's critical."[65] Nevertheless, despite its problems, at least some CEOs and other corporate leaders appear to remain positive about the potential of this comprehensive approach to change.[66]

EXHIBIT 15.14

Issues in Process Redesign

Objectives	Coverage	Potential Drawbacks
• Reduce costs • Shorten cycle times • Improve quality	• Breadth • Depth	• Requires high level of persistence and involvement of top management • Effort may be greater than results • High chaos factor • High levels of resistance

Organizational Learning

Although the concept has been around for some time, it was not until relatively recently that **organizational learning** has become a major approach to organizational change and renewal.[67] A firm that is good at organizational learning is said to be "skilled at creating, acquiring, and transferring knowledge, and at modifying its behavior to reflect new knowledge and insights."[68] Such an organization would be called a *learning organization*.

organizational learning exhibited by an organization that is skilled at creating, acquiring, and transferring knowledge, and at modifying its behavior to reflect new knowledge and insights

Several factors have been shown to facilitate learning by organizations:

- Employees with well-developed core competencies.
- An organizational culture that supports continuous improvement.
- The capability (such as managerial expertise) to implement necessary changes.[69]

Managers and organizations cannot simply decide, or declare, that learning should take place. The elements listed previously need to be in place as a starting point if organizational learning is going to lead to any real benefits. Then, a number of activities need to take place to implement fully an ongoing learning process in organizations. Five of the more important ones are explained here.[70]

A SYSTEMATIC, ORGANIZED, AND CONSISTENT APPROACH TO PROBLEM SOLVING Rather than relying on assumptions or guesswork to solve problems and make decisions, learning organizations systematically and continually collect data related to them.

EXPERIMENTATION TO OBTAIN NEW KNOWLEDGE Learning organizations experiment with new methods and procedures to expand their knowledge and gain fresh insights. They engage in a steady series of small experiments to keep acquiring new knowledge consistently and to help employees become accustomed to change. Corning, Allegheny Ludlum, and Nucor Steel are companies that constantly try new methods and processes to improve their productivity.

DRAWING ON PAST EXPERIENCES Enterprises with strong learning cultures pay particular attention to past failures as well as successes. For example, because of problems with the development of its 737 and 747 planes, Boeing initiated a three-year project to compare the development of these planes to the earlier, more reliable 707 and 727 planes. This project resulted in a booklet of "lessons learned," which was then used in the development and manufacture of 757s and 767s.

A strong learning culture at Seattle-based Boeing motivated the company to compare the development of its different plane models and improve its designs and manufacturing processes.

EXHIBIT 15.15

Commonly Benchmarked Business Practices

Business Process
Employee development training
Billing
Information systems technology
Customer service
Process improvement management
Facility management
Human Resources
Project management

benchmarking
identification, analysis, and comparison of the best practices of competitors against an organization's own practices

focus groups
small groups involved in intense discussions of the positive and negative features of products or services

LEARNING FROM THE BEST PRACTICES AND IDEAS OF OTHERS Learning organizations and their managers consistently scan their environments for information and knowledge from a variety of external sources, including their competitors, customers, and even other industries. One increasingly common form of this is **benchmarking**, where the best practices of competitors are identified, analyzed, and compared against one's own practices.[71] Exhibit 15.15 shows some of the business processes that are commonly being benchmarked by companies today. Xerox, Corning, the U.S. Army, and the U.S. Social Security Administration are among the major U.S. organizations that heavily make use of benchmarking.

Other ways of generating this kind of learning include putting together **focus groups** of customers that spend time in small groups for intense discussions of the positive and negative features of products or services.

TRANSFERRING AND SHARING KNOWLEDGE Learning organizations also ensure that the knowledge they gain is disseminated throughout their organizations. This can include such activities as distributing reports, developing demonstration projects, initiating training and education programs, and rotating or transferring those with the knowledge. General Motors, for example, developed a series of plant tours to introduce new workers to the distinctive procedures being used at its facilities. The tours were developed not only for hourly employees but also for upper and middle managers, with each tour concentrating on issues most relevant to the targeted group.[72]

As an approach to change, an organizational learning perspective has much to offer. It emphasizes paying constant attention to potentially needed changes, and it embodies the goal of renewal—of pushing organizations to continually reinvent themselves through the purposeful and persistent acquisition of new knowledge. One of the best ways to keep abreast of changing environments is for managers to focus intently on instilling a learning culture within their work groups.

Managerial Challenges from the Front Line

The Rest of the Story

As Albert Torres anticipated, some people at Pay Plus Benefits did not see the need for change. To overcome this, Torres tried to unfreeze things by involving several key people in his department in discussions about increasing health care costs and how they were lowering Pay Plus Benefits's pricing power, which, in combination, were putting downward pressure on the firm's internal profit margins.

According to Torres, "We educated our team on the reasons behind our vision of the future and where we wanted to position our company relative to that future. [We stressed] a good hockey player plays where the puck is. A great hockey player plays where the puck is going to be. We believed that the days of calling your human resource and payroll departments for general questions, reports, and transactions were going to be obsolete in the wake of a new 24-by-7, self-service Web-portal model for managers and employees."

Torres also realized that although the entire project was outside of employees' direct experience and looked like it might be beyond their capabilities, if broken down into small pieces, it was not. He said that by focusing on "the big picture," moving through Pay Plus Benefits's known options, and ultimately reaching the scope of each employee's work detail by functional area or department, he was able to give people the confidence to achieve the change and move the company forward.

The project was so successful that not only was Pay Plus Benefits able to offer the new Web-based self-service portal to its existing clients, but it was able to license the product to competitors for them to offer to their clients. As desired, the project lowered Pay Plus Benefits's operating costs while maintaining or improving service to clients and their employees. The change didn't cost Torres nearly as much to write the code and produce the self-service portal as it would have to hire call center representatives to answer by phone questions from client companies' employees. At the same time, the new product generated new revenues without increasing Pay Plus Benefits's internal costs much.

In short, change is about helping people you manage answer three basic questions: (1) What's wrong with just staying put? (2) Where do we want to go instead? (3) How are we going to get there? Without convincing answers to these essential questions, most people are unlikely to change. The stimulating thing about managing change, however, is that no two situations are identical, nor are the people who are involved in, or affected by, the change.

Summary

- The forces for change are primarily external or internal. Key external forces include economic conditions, competitors, technology, legal and political contexts, and societal and demographic trends.
- Change can be focused on or directed to one or more of the following key targets: strategy, structure, systems, technology, culture, and staff.
- In analyzing and evaluating the need for change, managers may take a proactive, reactive, or crisis approach. In any case, it is critical to diagnose the real problem so that the changes actually improve the situation the organization faces.
- The three major stages in the process of change include unfreezing, moving, and refreezing.
- Resistance to change in each stage is common. In the unfreezing stage, inertia, mistrust, and lack of information are often common causes of resistance. During the movement stage, lack of clarity regarding the change, lack of capabilities, and lack of sufficient incentives are core sources of resistance. During the refreezing stage, the pull of past competencies and the nonimmediate nature of results both can contribute to resistance and ultimately the failure of change.
- Four key actions can help managers overcome the resistance to change: First, it is usually critical to help people understand the rationale for the change. Second, it is vital that people clearly understand the change and know what they will do differently. Third, if people are to make the desired changes, they need the capabilities to implement the change, including knowledge, information, skills, and other resources. Finally, managers must ensure that they reinforce early correct efforts and not just desired results.

- Managing change involves a number of key choices that managers need to make. In the planning stage, managers need to decide on the timing of the change, build a leading coalition, determine how to communicate the plan, the levels of participation, and types of incentives. Before implementing the change, managers must determine the focus, amount, frequency, and rate of change.
- Making changes is time consuming and costly. Therefore, ensuring that the benefits outweigh the costs is critical. This process typically involves gathering data, comparing it to goals, and then providing feedback to involved parties on the progress.
- Organizational development (OD) is a large-scale change that focuses on interventions designed to change people's behaviors. These interventions are led by a designated change agent or group of agents.
- Process redesign, or reengineering, is a general change approach that focuses on improving an organization's work processes (and thereby productivity) by changing what people do and how they do it. Changes in how work is done often involve changes in or additions of technology.
- Organizational learning is more of a general framework for continual organizational change. Companies that are good at it have a systematic approach to problem solving, experiment, learn from the past as well as others, and share that knowledge broadly within their organizations.

Key Terms

behavioral process orientation 455
benchmarking 458
change agents 454
focus groups 458
force field analysis 448
interventions 455
leading coalition 449
organizational development (OD) 454
organizational learning 457
organizational renewal 455
process redesign (reengineering) 456
T-groups 454

Review Questions

1. List the forces that act from outside an organization to bring about change within it.
2. What are an organization's internal forces for change?
3. What components within an organization can be changed? (Hint: The chapter discusses six of them.)
4. What is the key to changing an organization's culture?
5. Is it more difficult to change an organization's strategy or its culture? Why?
6. What is meant by proactive and reactive change?
7. What are the three major stages in the change process?
8. What are the key sources of resistance in each major stage of the change process?
9. What are some of the considerations managers face when planning change?
10. What are the key considerations and choices in implementing change?
11. What are the two key criteria in determining targeted supporters for change?
12. Why is it important to be careful in choosing the amount and rate of change? What are the benefits and drawbacks involved in large- and small-scale change? In rapid or slow change?
13. List the drawbacks to using incentives to gain cooperation during a change.
14. What are some of the ways managers can overcome employees' resistance to change?
15. What is meant by force field analysis?
16. In evaluating the outcome of a planned change, what types of data are used?
17. What are the three steps in evaluating the outcome of a planned change?
18. What is the emphasis of the OD approach to change?
19. What are the key steps in the OD approach to change?
20. What is a change agent? Where do they come from?
21. What is the difference between the breadth and the depth of reengineering?
22. Describe a learning organization.
23. How could you tell when you are encountering a learning organization?

Assessing Your Capabilities

Select a change initiative to assess. It is best to select a change initiative that you are currently facing or will soon face. However, you can also choose a past change that you were part of. Once you have the change initiative in mind, simply follow the step-by-step assessment instructions.

For each of the following statements, indicate the extent to which you agree or disagree by circling the appropriate number to the right. In responding to each item, use as a reference group those people who will be most directly and significantly impacted by the change initiative you have in mind. The reference group might be as small as a team or as large as all the employees in an organization. Whatever is the case, simply use that group as your reference as you respond to the following statements.

See the Need						
1. The contrast between where we are and where we need to be is clear.	1 Strongly Disagree	2 Disagree	3 Somewhat Disagree	4 Somewhat Agree	5 Agree	6 Strongly Agree
2. The reason for the needed change is clear to those most affected by it.	1 Strongly Disagree	2 Disagree	3 Somewhat Disagree	4 Somewhat Agree	5 Agree	6 Strongly Agree
3. How things will be after the change is clear—people can envision the destination.	1 Strongly Disagree	2 Disagree	3 Somewhat Disagree	4 Somewhat Agree	5 Agree	6 Strongly Agree
Make the Move						
4. A powerful and capable team to lead the change is in place.	1 Strongly Disagree	2 Disagree	3 Somewhat Disagree	4 Somewhat Agree	5 Agree	6 Strongly Agree
5. Those who need to change understand the path forward.	1 Strongly Disagree	2 Disagree	3 Somewhat Disagree	4 Somewhat Agree	5 Agree	6 Strongly Agree
6. Those who need to change have the tools, resources, and capabilities to make the required changes.	1 Strongly Disagree	2 Disagree	3 Somewhat Disagree	4 Somewhat Agree	5 Agree	6 Strongly Agree
Reinforce the Finish						
7. Capable champions are in place who will reinforce early efforts and successes.	1 Strongly Disagree	2 Disagree	3 Somewhat Disagree	4 Somewhat Agree	5 Agree	6 Strongly Agree
8. Systems are in place to chart and communicate progress to individuals and groups.	1 Strongly Disagree	2 Disagree	3 Somewhat Disagree	4 Somewhat Agree	5 Agree	6 Strongly Agree
9. Key systems (e.g., rewards, performance appraisal, training, etc.) have been aligned to support (not work against) the required changes.	1 Strongly Disagree	2 Disagree	3 Somewhat Disagree	4 Somewhat Agree	5 Agree	6 Strongly Agree

Now record your totals for each section by simply adding your scores:

See	(Q1 + Q2 + Q3) =	________
Move	(Q4 + Q5 + Q6) =	________
Finish	(Q7 + Q8 + Q9) =	________

Now add all three scores together:

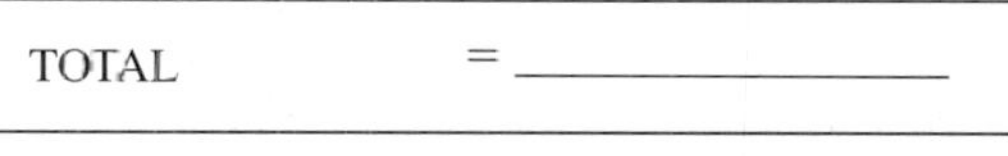
TOTAL = ________

Use the following table for a rough interpretation of your scores:

	3–8 points Bad News	8–12 points Not Good News	13–15 points Good News	16–18 points Great News
See	Change initiatives with these scores tend to fail on the launch pad. If they do get off the pad, they tend to come crashing back to earth.	Change initiatives with these scores tend to get started but then fizzle and fade.	Scores in this range often indicate enough fuel to get off the launch pad, but the change may lose momentum breaking through the first barrier.	Scores in this range often indicate enough fuel to get off the launch pad and make it successfully through the first barrier.
Move	Change initiatives with these scores (if they make it through the first barrier) slam to a stop at the second.	Change initiatives with these scores (if they make it through the first barrier), sputter but usually die before making it through the second barrier.	Scores in this range often signal enough momentum to push the envelope of the second barrier but tend to break through only for small to moderate change initiatives.	Scores in this range usually lead to success in breaking through the second barrier.
Finish	Scores in this range occur even when scores for See and Move are high. Unfortunately, with scores in this range the change initiative still is likely to be among the 70% that ultimately fail.	Scores in this range suggest that while the change might achieve initial success, it will fall far short of its goal and has a high chance of ultimate failure.	If the scores for See and Move were high, there's hope, but if they were only good, this is likely to be the end—with the designation in sight but just out of reach.	While nothing is guaranteed, scores in this range in combination with strong See and Move scores put you in the elite group whose change initiative likely succeeds.
TOTAL	**9–24 points Bad News** The odds of your change initiative succeeding are as good as a motorcycle breaking through a thick, concrete wall.	**25–37 points Not Good News** You may feel like you've got the odds of success on your side, but you don't. You have a 70% chance of failure.	**38–47 points Good News** You're close enough that if there's time you can strengthen some aspects of the change initiative and still succeed.	**48–54 points Great News** With total scores in this range, the odds are on your side. You have a better than 70% chance of success.

Team Exercise

Leading Change at GenCom

Divide into groups of three to five members each. Each group should take one of two perspectives. One group should take the perspective of the review committee while the other group should take the perspective of the general employees. Each group should read the following short scenario and then prepare for a dialog. Use the questions at the end to help guide your preparations. (Note: The objective is to bring out the dynamic of change and key issues, not for either side to fabricate data, past experiences, etc. in order to win their point.)

Two years ago GenCom gave its production review committee responsibility for developing and implementing procedures to improve manufacturing productivity. Jerry, the manager of GenCom's engineering department, is the co-chair of the committee along with Gene, GenCom's production manager. They and the three other committee members jointly decide on any major productivity changes.

A monthly meeting of the production review committee had already begun when Gene hurried in. "Have you seen these production figures?" he asked. "They are incredible—just look at the increase in productivity in this department!"

Jerry was surprised at Gene's enthusiasm and said, "Wait a minute. Just what are you talking about that has you so excited?"

Gene realized the other members of the committee hadn't yet seen the new report and quickly handed copies of it around. He then took a deep breath and started explaining. "Several months ago, I told Kim, the manager of extract processing, that I was somewhat disappointed by the latest productivity figures and wished someone could figure out a way to improve them. I didn't think about that statement until just this morning when Kim walked into my office and handed me this report. It seems she has had her team working on the problem for the last four months. They collected information on productivity levels at other similar companies and carefully studied the procedures of the most successful. They worked with several of the ideas in their group, testing the ideas separately and in combination and with new additions until they found a method that seemed to work. Wow! I'll say it seems to work. Just look at those figures. I think we ought to immediately implement their idea in all the production units. Just think of the profit improvements that would result from across-the-board performance improvements matching these."

Jerry and the other members of the committee were pleased with the report and decided to accept Gene's recommendation for a company-wide application of the new procedures developed by Kim's team. They had all been anxious to find a new initiative that would really work since their last two change attempts had been unsuccessful. Both previous initiatives had been scrapped rather quickly. The first one had not worked because the plant didn't have the right type of equipment and infrastructure to support it. The second had failed because of high levels of resistance from employees. However, after discussion, the committee members were convinced that this new approach would definitely work, and they decided to implement it throughout all relevant units. After all, it had worked out exceedingly well in Kim's department.

However, before the review committee could formulate its plan, the firm's employees heard both about the result in Kim's department and rumors that the committee was considering another "flavor of the month" change based on what happened for a short period of time in Kim's department.

1. As a member of the review committee, analyze the forces for and against this change (force field analysis). Based on this, what early actions might you take?
2. What would be the basic elements and choices in your change plan?
3. As an employee, why might you resist this change? What might make you less resistant to the change?

Closing Case Leading Change at LSP

Leading Signal Processing (LSP—a disguised name but a real company) produces diagnostic instruments primarily for the health care industry. Over most of its history, its leading-edge products, based on state-of-the-art analog signal technology, were used by scientific and hospital researchers in diagnostic tests and cellular and blood chemical analysis.

After years of success, the company's CEO noticed digital signal processing emerging as a potential new technological platform, though initially it seemed unable to rival LSP's analog technology at the moment. He also recognized a shift in customers and end users. In the past, MDs and PhDs had performed diagnostics and analyses in research labs and hospitals; now technicians in clinics were increasingly performing these tests. Many of LSP's largest customers were likely to be slow to make this transition, but midsize and small customers were more likely to quickly change over and save money. In addition, the market was moving away from separate tests and analyses toward integrated systems and analyses.

Although LSP's CEO recognized that these environmental shifts would require the company to change, many of the firm's scientists—analog technology experts—resisted, seeing digital technology as a threat to their jobs. The more the CEO talked about environmental shifts, the harder these scientists worked on customized analog products for customers, especially big customers. This was, in part, because it took years to become an accomplished analog scientist, and analog and digital science were like Greek and Chinese—knowing Greek did you very little good in mastering Chinese and vice versa. Moving from the top of the analog learning curve to the bottom of the digital learning curve was very unappealing, especially to the more senior and influential scientists in the company.

The CEO also realized that the trend toward integrated systems would require LSP's workforce to collaborate using both cross-product and cross-functional teams composed of employees from research, development, marketing, and manufacturing. Such teamwork was rare within LSP. Each department did its own thing, and the R&D department was clearly the most important. From their perspective, the company had succeeded in the past because their products were so leading edge that they essentially sold themselves; marketing and sales were simply "order takers."

As a few competitors brought new digital products to market, LSP's research scientists scoffed at their initially lower reliability and inferior performance. Although the manager of the R&D group was more favorably inclined to the changes, he was only 6 to 12 months away from retirement. And his most senior signal processing scientist, Dr. Lee, was completely opposed to the changes. This was critical because Dr. Lee was without question the most brilliant of all the scientists and his innovations in analog signal processing were used in virtually all of LSP's current products. Most of the more junior scientists had been exposed to digital signal processing in their studies, but many of them had joined LSP in part because of Dr. Lee's fame and reputation.

The head of marketing thought that small- and medium-sized clinics, labs, and other enterprises constituted a large and growing set of potential customers LSP was not currently tapped into. He was fully in favor of digital technology and felt it "represented the only way the company was really going to grow."

The head of manufacturing was more neutral on digital technology and the potential changes it implied. Production was working fairly well at the moment. And although LSP's manufacturing costs were slightly higher than other firms' manufacturing costs, the leading edge nature of its products allowed it to enjoy pricing premiums that offset the higher costs.

The CEO wondered what he should do and how he should approach this challenge. If he waited too long to make a move, LSP might lose its reputation as a technology leader. He might also see his traditional customer base decline relative to the total size and nature of the market and its segments. On the other hand, he was up against some very powerful resistors. Dr. Lee had visibility to and credibility with the CEO's boss—the board of directors. In the past, Dr. Lee had made several presentations to the board on technical matters, and his recommendations had generally proven correct. Would the board listen to the CEO or Dr. Lee?

Questions

1. What is your analysis relative to a potential leading coalition?
2. At the three different stages of change, what are the likely sources of resistance?
3. Why is Dr. Lee so opposed to the potential change? Can anything be done to reduce his resistance?
4. What would your general recommendations be relative to building a leading coalition, communication plan, levels of participation, and types of incentives?
5. What would your general recommendations be relative to the focus, amount, frequency, and rate of change?

General Motors: How Pioneering Managers Struggled to Organize a New Industry

When the American auto industry came into being just after the beginning of the twentieth century, new car manufacturers soon faced emerging problems, among them how to organize the work and lines of communication. For each of these companies to survive the tumultuous changes of the new century, including rapid growth, changes in technology, and market shifts, executives had to find a rational way to manage the workforce as well as the structure of the organization. One such top manager was Alfred P. Sloan, Jr., who served as CEO of General Motors from 1923 to 1946.

General Motors was founded in 1908. It is important to keep in mind that management theories, as they related to the new industrial era, were in their infancy then. By the early 1920s, when Sloan took over at General Motors, many manufacturers had adopted an approach called "scientific management" (discussed later in this appendix), which was designed to organize factory floor tasks. But usable and systematic approaches to management that dealt with the total organization had yet to evolve to any extent. Thus, Sloan and his colleagues struggled to find a solution.

Sloan recalled that, at General Motors, "It was . . . management by crony, with the divisions operating on a horse-trading basis." In the first few years immediately following the end of World War I, divisions were competing against each other for available funds, which were often allocated based on top managers' preferences rather than unbiased evaluation. "The important thing was that no one knew how much was being contributed—plus or minus—by each division to the common good of the corporation. And since, therefore, no one knew, or could prove, where the efficiencies and inefficiencies lay, there was no objective basis for the allocation of new investment," observed Sloan.

Sloan recognized that the organization had to change. "I became convinced that the corporation could not continue to grow and survive unless it was better organized, and it was apparent that no one was giving that subject the attention it needed." With Sloan's support, late in 1920, General Motors new President Pierre du Pont and new executive committee began to implement "a highly rational and objective mode of operation." Using the findings from an "Organizational Study" conducted by Sloan, they developed a new policy, which Sloan ultimately called a "trend toward a happy medium to industrial organization." General Motors to new policy was designed so that the organization could evolve in a strong yet flexible manner. The policy included decisions about the amount of responsibility that individual divisions would retain—and "thus initiated for the modern General Motors," Sloan wrote in 1964, "the trend toward a happy medium in industrial organization between the extremes of pure centralization and pure decentralization." Finding that "happy medium" is still a managerial problem that faces many organizations, including General Motors, even today, some 85 years later!

Source: Alfred P. Sloan, Jr., *My Years with General Motors* (New York: Doubleday & Company, Inc., 1964), pp. 27, 42, 48, 52, 65; "General Motors History" at the GM Web site, accessed at http://www.gm.com, November 3, 1998.

As this opening story about the trials and tribulations of General Motors at the beginning of the 1920s demonstrates, industrial and other leaders throughout the twentieth century struggled with how to approach the challenge of managing their organizations. In this task, they were assisted by various writers and scholars who contributed ideas and theories about this complex topic. Some of those more important thinkers and their ideas are covered in this appendix.

It is important to keep in mind a basic proposition: To understand the present, you must know something about the past. A review of the history of management thought, especially during the twentieth century, can help us to gain a better understanding of different approaches to management—how those approaches have changed over the years and why they are the way they are now. Although, as we will see, there have been ideas about management since antiquity, so-called "modern" management is only roughly 100 years old.

We begin with a brief look at the earlier origins of organized and systematic thinking about management, especially those that arose from the Industrial Revolution in England and later in the United States. Then we trace the development of the scientific management approach, classical management theory, and neoclassical theory. Later in the appendix, three more contemporary approaches are discussed: behavioral, decision-making, and integrative approaches. To give you some perspective, Exhibit A.1 provides a timeline of the developments in management thought that places them in the historical context of other events that were occurring at the same approximate period of time. The exhibit emphasizes the point that conditions and events in society and industry existing in a given time period strongly influence the type of management theories and approaches being proposed.

EXHIBIT A.1 History of Events and Managerial Thought and Practice Through the End of the Twentieth Century

Date	General Events	Industrial Events	Management Thought/Practice
700–0 B.C.	First written laws of Athens Mayan civilization Greek civilization Rise of Rome	Canal between Nile and Red Sea Sundials, water clocks Mediterranean trade Great Wall of China (215 B.C.)	Sun Tzu, *The Art of War* (4th century B.C.)
A.D. 1–1450	London founded (A.D. 43) Fall of the Roman Empire (455—Vandals sack Rome) Dark Ages in Europe Mohammed (570–632) Oxford University founded (1167) Black Death decimates European population (1347–1349)	Applicants for public office in China required to take examinations (606) Postal and news services in the Caliph's empire (945) Trade between Asia and Western Europe via Venice (983) Coal mining begins in Newcastle, England (1233)	

(*continues*)

EXHIBIT A.1 (Continued)

Date	General Events	Industrial Events	Management Thought/Practice
A.D. 1–1450		Guild system Standardization of measurements in England Bankruptcy of Florentine banking houses (1345)	
1450–1700	Renaissance in Europe The Spanish Inquisition (1478–1834) Columbus lands in the Americas (1492) Age of Exploration Slave trade begins in Europe and Americas Plague in Europe (1563) New York City founded (1626) Harvard College founded (1636) Great Fire of London (1666) Newton's theories (1687)	Printing press (1455) Regular postal service in Europe (Vienna to Brussels to Madrid) (1500) Beginning of textile industry in England (1641) Hudson Bay Company founded (1670) Mitsui family trading and banking house in Japan founded (1673)	Machiavelli, *The Prince* (1513)
1700–1800	Yale University founded (1701) American Revolution (1776) French Revolution (1789)	Bernoulli's work on hydrodynamics (1738) Benjamin Franklin invents the lightning conductor (1752) First iron mill in England (1754) Industrial Revolution begins London Stock Exchange founded (1773) Steam engine (1775) New York Stock Exchange founded (1790) Whitney invents the cotton gin (1793) First telegraph, Paris-Lille (1794)	Smith, *An Inquiry into the Nature and Causes of the Wealth of Nations* (1776) Malthus, *Essay on the Principle of Evolution* (1798)
1800–1900	Century of Steam Luddite riots in England (1811) Trade union movement Darwin, *On the Origin of the Species by Natural Selection* (1859) American Civil War (1861–1865) Transcontinental railroad (1869) First U.S. business school: Wharton at the University of Pennsylvania (1881) Nobel Prizes established (1896)	First battery (1800) Robert Owen institutes social reforms at the Lanarck Mills (1800) Steam locomotive (1814) First typewriter patented (1830) Faraday works with electromagnetism (1831) British Factory Act provides system for factory inspection (1833) Morse demonstrates electric telegraph (1837) Standard Oil Company founded by John D. Rockefeller (1870) Telephone invented (1876)	Babbage, *On the Economy of Machinery and Manufacturers* (1832) Cournot, *Researches into the Mathematical Principles of the Theory of Wealth* (1838) Engels, *The Condition of the Working Class in England* (1845) Marx and Engels, *The Communist Manifesto* (1848) Towne, *Engineer as Economist* (1886)

EXHIBIT A.1 (Continued)

Date	General Events	Industrial Events	Management Thought/Practice
1800–1900		Phonograph invented (1877) Introduction of electric lights (1880) AT&T formed (1885) Eastman produces box camera (1888)	
1900–1920	Century of electricity First MBA program established at the Tuck School, Dartmouth College (1900) Wright brothers flight (1903) Einstein's special theory of relativity (1905) World War I (1914–1918) Russian revolution (1917)	U.S. Steel organized (1901) Ford Motor Company founded (1903) General Motors formed (1908) Weekends become popular (1910) Woolworth Co. founded (1912) Ford introduces assembly line (1913) Airmail service established from New York to Washington, D.C. (1918)	Taylor, *The Principles of Scientific Management* (1911) Fayol, *Administration Industrielle et Générale* (1916) The Gilbreths, *Applied Motion Study* (1917)
1920s	Lindbergh flies across Atlantic (1927) Stock market crash (1929)	Sloan reorganizes General Motors into multidivisional structure Beginning of chain stores	Mary Parker Follett, *Creative Experience* (1924) Hawthorne studies (1924–1932)
1930s	The Great Depression Social Security Act (1935)	First supermarkets Sit-down strikes Industrial Unionism as a challenge to managerial control	Mooney and Reiley, *Onward Industry* (1931) Mayo, *The Human Problems of Industrial Civilization* (1933) Barnard, *The Functions of the Executive* (1938) Roethlisberger and Dickson, *Management & the Worker* (1939)
1940s	World War II (1939–1945) Atomic age begins (1945) First session of the United Nations (1946) Partition of Palestine, creation of State of Israel (1947)	Commercialization of television ENIAC—Birth of general purpose computing (1946) Xerography process invented (1946) First supersonic flight (1947) Transistor invented at Bell Labs (1947) Creation of the World Bank and IMF	Weber, *Theory of Social and Economic Organization* (trans. 1947) Simon, *Administrative Behavior: A Study of Decision-Making Processes in Administrative Organization* (1947) Lewin, *Resolving Social Conflicts* (1948)
1950s	Korean War Colonial independence movements Suburbanization U.S. Interstate Highway System USSR launches Sputnik (1957) European Common Market (1958)	Color television introduced in U.S. (1951) Electric power produced from atomic energy (1951) Transatlantic cable telephone service (1956) AFL merges with CIO (1955)	Maslow, *Motivation and Personality* (1954) Drucker, *The Practice of Management* (1954) Argyris, *Personality and Organization* (1957) March and Simon, *Organizations* (1958) Herzberg et al., *The Motivation to Work* (1959)

(*continues*)

EXHIBIT A.1 (Continued)

Date	General Events	Industrial Events	Management Thought/Practice
1960s	Civil Rights Movement Women's Movement Vietnam War Campus protests Assassinations of John Kennedy, Robert Kennedy, Martin Luther King, Jr. Berlin Wall constructed (1961) Cuban missile crisis (1962) Rachel Carson, *Silent Spring* (1962) Nobel prize for discovery of structure of DNA to Watson, Crick, and Wilkins (1962) Six Day War in Middle East (1967) First moon landing (July 20, 1969)	Conglomerates emerge as organizational form "Military-Industrial Complex" Jet travel Franchising Environmental Protection Agency Equal opportunity legislation	McGregor, *The Human Side of Enterprise* (1960) Likert, *New Patterns of Management* (1961) Chandler, *Strategy and Structure* (1962) Cyert and March, *A Behavioral Theory of the Firm* (1963) Sun Tzu, *The Art of War* (trans. 1963) Lawrence and Lorsch, *Organizations and the Environment* (1967)
1970s	U.S. withdraws from Vietnam Western trade opened with China Oil embargo Airline deregulation	Dow Jones Index at 631 (1970) Birth of Apple Computer Handheld calculators Fiber optics	Major growth in number of MBA graduates Quality circles Mintzberg, *The Nature of Managerial Work* (1973)
1980s	Deregulation Berlin Wall falls (1989)	Breakup of AT&T Major growth in personal computing Wal-Mart	M. Porter, *Competitive Strategy* (1980) Ouchi, *Theory Z: How American Business Can Meet the Japanese Challenge* (1981) Peters and Waterman, *In Search of Excellence* (1982) M. Porter, *Competitive Advantage* (1985) Just-in-time inventory systems
1990s	Soviet Union dissolves NAFTA European Union near reality	Internet Electronic commerce Microsoft Corporation dominance in software	Corporate downsizing Rightsizing Empowerment Reengineering Corporate governance issues Total quality management (TQM) Outsourcing Learning organizations Increasing emphasis on teams

The appendix concludes with a look at the status of management thought as the twenty-first century unfolds. As you read the appendix, keep in mind two key questions to enhance your understanding: (1) What preceded the development of a particular way of thinking about management? (2) What was the world—in particular, the world of work—like at the time the theory or approach emerged?

The Origins of Managerial Thought

The topic of how to manage organizations did not receive systematic and widescale attention until virtually the start of the twentieth century. However, writers have been commenting on, and even analyzing, managerial issues throughout the past 3,000 years. As we will see in the next few pages, a scattering of writers and recorded examples from a small number of organizations in different places in the civilized world did leave their mark on management thought and practice before the beginning of the twentieth century.

Pre-Industrial Revolution Influences

As the box, "Even Ancient Civilizations Faced Managerial Challenges," shows, as far back as roughly 1000 B.C., perceptive officials in China were writing about how to manage and control organized human activity. Five hundred or so years later, approximately the fourth century B.C., an illustrious Chinese military leader of the time, Sun Tzu, wrote about his views of principles of leadership (e.g., the need for the leader to promote unity within an organization), ideas that many consider are still relevant to today's organizations.[1]

Other civilizations, such as those of ancient Egypt and, later, Rome, were able to organize large numbers of people to carry out coordinated activities that required a form of what today we would call "management." The Egyptians built pyramids as far back as 2700 B.C., and the Romans in the early centuries A.D., and even before, were able to develop highly organized and well-led armies that exercised control over wide areas of territory. Thus, although relatively little was written systematically at the time about how these feats of organization and leadership were carried out, the results demonstrated that management was being successfully practiced in terms of achieving goals and objectives.

In the late Middle Ages (fifteenth and sixteenth centuries), city-states in Europe such as Venice and Florence were managing certain activities with procedures that today we would consider "modern." For example, Venice had a large shipyard at that time that, in effect, adopted such managerial control procedures as the standardization of parts, inventory control, and analysis of costs of materials.[2] Also in this era, Machiavelli (in 1513) published his famous treatise—*The Prince*—on opportunistic and, some would say, crafty techniques for leaders of state to rule their subjects.

Although all of these and other developments relevant to management thought and practice took place before the eighteenth century, it was not until the middle of that century that the issue of how to manage organizations started to become a more prominent concern. Until that time, most organizations (with a few exceptions such as those noted, the Catholic Church, and military organizations), were still relatively small and simple in structure. For this reason, it had been unnecessary to give serious thought to the way jobs were carried out, work divided among people, and their efforts coordinated. All this was about to change around 1750 when the Industrial Revolution began in England. (This period of societal transformation was not called by that name at the time but was given that label by historians many decades later.) It would take some years, however, before that "revolution" would spread to other places, including the Western hemisphere and Asia.

Even Ancient Civilizations Faced Managerial Challenges

Although this appendix primarily focuses on the history of management thought and practice dating from the eighteenth century, we can turn even further back in time to gain an understanding of how organizations function. Four thousand years ago, Chinese rulers faced the same challenge that today's managers face: how to organize people (including different levels of officials) in order to complete tasks and achieve goals. Until 250 B.C., China was made up of many states of differing sizes, populations, and natural resources. In fact, China resembled a modern, large, multidivisional corporation. Then, between 250 B.C. and 206 B.C., China became a centralized empire with tight control from the top, a structure that is not totally unfamiliar in some of today's large companies.

What methods did Chinese rulers develop over centuries to meet the challenge of governing such a large country, and how do they relate to today's methods? *The Officials of Chou*, developed either by King Ching of Chou or the Duke of Chou sometime around 1100 B.C., outlines in great detail many of the features that management experts now think of as tenets of a true bureaucracy, including clear, specific job descriptions for officials at every level; explicitly stated rights, powers, and obligations of senior officials; division of labor based on specialization (and, ultimately, technical competence in those areas); clear hierarchy of authority; clearly defined work procedures; and promotion or advancement based on merit (technical competence). King Ching also outlined several important "rules of good management," including personal qualities such as carefulness and economy, the quest for self-improvement, the necessity of making bold decisions as well as conforming to rules, and the importance of promoting subordinates. All of these characteristics probably sound quite familiar, as if they might be found in an employee's or manager's handbook for a large, contemporary corporation.

Leadership style also played an important part in the governing of ancient China. In addition to the rules of good management, high-level officials were encouraged to be benevolent in their methods of governing because this behavior would, in the end, engender support from the people. E Yin, who was prime minister around 1750 B.C., wrote, "Do not slight the concerns of the people: Think of their difficulties. . . . Be careful to think about the end at the beginning. When you hear words against which your mind sets itself, you must inquire whether these words are not right. When you hear words that agree with your own thinking, you must ask whether these words are not wrong." Being able to communicate effectively with subordinates and citizens and win their support was crucial to the survival of a leader's power—and perhaps his life. China's social system was clan based, and many of the clans had their own armies. Apparently, a number of rulers were overthrown simply because their behavior and style of governing were unacceptable to the clans.

With their global reach and capacity for instantaneous communication, today's corporations may not appear to resemble ancient China's agrarian civilization. But it is clear that even four thousand years ago, rulers searched for efficient, effective ways to manage people. In some respects, they came up with answers that sound very familiar today.

Source: V. P. Rindova and W. H. Starbuck, "Ancient Chinese Theories of Civilization," *Journal of Management Inquiry* 6, no. 2 (June 1997), 144–59; copyright 1997 Sage Publications, Inc.

The Industrial Revolution in England

The fundamental changes that took place in human work performance in the latter half of the 1700s received that impetus from one key source: advances in technology, especially those related to mechanized power. Up to that time, work was accomplished almost solely through human or animal effort, sometimes supplemented by wind or water power. Consequently, work was organized around the family and was located typically within each family's dwelling. The nature of this system—subsequently labeled the "domestic system" by historians[3]—made it difficult to perform more complex work, to produce more complex products, and especially to turn out goods in high volumes.

The beginning of the end of the domestic production system was signaled by the introduction of power-driven machinery, especially the steam engine. Although the now-famous inventor James Watt produced the first functional steam engine in 1765, it was another 20 years before it was put into general use.[4] From then on the steam engine, and what it could do, rapidly altered the ways many types of goods were produced. Its development was perhaps the single most important step in the rise of the factory system. The steam engine made it possible to increase vastly the volume of production; however, increased production also required more materials and hence more capital. To put those resources to more efficient use, in turn, required more people working together in one location. This meant, in effect, bringing people to the work rather than bringing work to the people. Hence, the factory seemed to answer the emerging question of how to take the greatest advantage of the potential of steam power for increased productivity.

Once factories were established at the end of the 1700s in England, it became clear that although they solved one problem, they created another: how best to coordinate workers' efforts for maximum efficiency. One approach was to divide up the work so that each person performed a limited number of tasks; in other words, specialized tasks. This idea, which came to be called **division of labor,** was especially championed by one of the founders of modern economics, Adam Smith. In 1776, about the time the Revolutionary War was beginning in America, Smith published his seminal work, *The Wealth of Nations*. That book (consisting of several volumes) contained a very clear description of the advantages of the division of labor:

division of labor
the division of work so that each person performs a limited number of tasks (specialized tasks); first used early in the Industrial Revolution

> *This great increase of the quantity of work which, in consequence of the division of labour, the same number of people are capable of performing, is owing to three different circumstances: first, to the increase of dexterity in every particular workman; secondly, to the saving of the time which is commonly lost in passing from one species of work to another; and lastly, to the invention of a great number of machines which facilitate and abridge labour, and enable one man to do the work of many.*[5]

Interestingly, some people today forget that Smith also had great insight in anticipating the potential *dis*advantages of the implementation of the division of labor idea, especially as it related to the workers who would be involved:

> *The man whose whole life is spent in performing a few simple operations . . . naturally loses, therefore, the habit of [mental] exertion, and generally becomes stupid and ignorant as it is possible for a human creature to become. . . . His dexterity at his own particular trade seems . . . to be acquired at the expense of his intellectual, social, and martial virtues.*[6]

In addition to the issues of how to divide up the work efficiently, the other problem relating to factories was how to coordinate the efforts of all of the workers—in other words, how to manage them. There were a number of aspects to the management problem. The owners of early factories and their immediate family were also the managers. As factories grew in size, however, it became impossible for family members to supervise all the workers. This meant that other people had to be hired for supervision. But who was to do this?

At the beginning of the Industrial Revolution, there were no trained supervisors or managers, because this task had never existed before. The early nonfamily supervisors were usually "illiterate workers promoted from the ranks because they evidenced a greater degree of technical skills or had the ability to keep discipline."[7] As management historian Daniel Wren has summed up the situation: "The transformation of England from an agrarian to an industrial society meant that there was no managerial class or, in modern terms, no professional managers. First, there was no common body of knowledge about how to manage. . . . Second, there was no common code of management behavior, no universal set of expectations about how a manager should act."[8]

The need for attention to the process that would come to be known as "management" became more acute as England entered the nineteenth century and the Industrial Revolution became more widespread and affected more people. Several prominent individuals, typically entrepreneurs or factory owners themselves, in the early 1800s in England and Scotland did consider how best to organize the activities of factories and direct the work of the people employed in them. Some of these earliest management thinkers, such as Robert Owen and Charles Babbage, even published their ideas in books. Consequently, they can be thought of as the first "management writers" of modern times, but their impact was relatively limited. Book reading in that era was not widespread, and the typical factory manager was busy coping with his own day-to-day problems, not worrying about other people's thoughts on how to run factories more efficiently. Also, much of this early writing focused on techniques applicable to specific firms rather than on general principles or theories about management. Formal writing about principles of management was still more than half a century away.[9]

The Industrial Revolution in America

The Industrial Revolution started in England, but it was in the New World in America that it flourished. One contributing factor to its success was the abundance of raw materials and natural resources, such as water, timber, and minerals. Another factor was the general absence of old traditions to slow the adoption of new methods. Also, American manufacturers gained an advantage from early trial and error of their English counterparts, some of whom migrated to the United States and brought their most successful methods with them.

Three types of industrial enterprises in the first half of the nineteenth century accounted for most of the improvements in managing enterprises in the United States: textile manufacturing, arms manufacturing, and railroads.[10] As one historian has noted, "The American Industrial Revolution began in textiles."[11] Textile manufacturing was the principal industrial activity that benefited most from a large number of people working together in one location. Manufacturers of arms and weapons, on the other hand, were the key developers of interchangeable parts. In doing so, they advanced the practice of using division of labor and high degrees of employee specialization and significantly increased the ability of a manufacturer to turn out products requiring precision work.

In the railroads, however, the first systematic thinking emerged about how to *manage* a company more effectively. The critical challenge to railroads, from a management standpoint, was quite different from that faced by manufacturers. Railroads had to organize, coordinate, and supervise multiple operations in widely dispersed geographical locations. Although armies and the Catholic Church had been coping with such problems for many years, those organizations had unique sources of discipline and control unavailable to private-sector industrial organizations. In the decades just before and after the Civil War, several far-sighted individuals connected with railroads began to propose specific methods to deal with organizational problems. One such person was David McCallum, general superintendent of the Erie Railroad in the 1850s. McCallum instituted a number of procedures and policies that we now take for granted, but for the time they were quite innovative. He developed organizational charts, regular reports from lower and middle managers, formal job descriptions, and promotions based on merit.[12] The issue of how best to run railroads efficiently and safely set the stage for more formal, systematic approaches to managerial activities. We turn next to a review of the insights and ideas of those who contributed such systematic approaches, the pioneers of modern management theory.

Pioneers: The Scientific Management Approach

The rapid growth in the number and size of factories following the end of the American Civil War in 1865 resulted in increased attention to the issue of how to improve industrial efficiency. By the 1880s, professional engineers were beginning to address this problem directly. A paper delivered in 1886 in Chicago at a meeting of the American Society of Mechanical Engineers is regarded as the beginning of "modern" management in the United States.[13] This paper, titled "The Engineer as Economist," was presented by engineer Henry R. Towne, who was the co-founder of the Yale Lock Company. The significance of Towne's paper is that it represented one of the first formal calls for serious attention to the business aspects of engineering activities. Specifically, Towne urged engineers to consider that "the matter of shop management is of equal importance with that of engineering as affecting the successful conduct of most, if not all, of our great industrial establishments, and . . . the *management of works* [Towne's italics] has become a matter of such great and far-reaching importance as perhaps to justify its classification . . . as one of the modern arts."[14]

Frederick W. Taylor (1856–1915)

Towne's call was not immediately heeded by most of his engineering colleagues. However, at roughly the same time period (i.e., the 1880s), an engineer working at the Midvale Steel Company in Philadelphia was thinking along somewhat the same lines. His name was Frederick Winslow Taylor, and he was to become one of the most famous people in the Western world in the early years of the twentieth century.

To put Taylor's ideas into perspective, it is necessary to take a brief look at what the United States was like around the turn of the century. At that time, the typical education level of an industrial worker was less than the sixth grade, and there were only about 15,000 college graduates per year in a population of over 58 million. (Compare education levels over 100 years later in the early years of the new century, when the respective numbers are 1.3 million degrees conferred and a population of about 290 million. The ratio of college graduates per year to the total population has thus changed from .03 percent to .4 percent.) It is crucial to keep such facts in mind when considering what Taylor proposed and why he advocated the ideas and procedures he did.

Taylor began his life's work as a common laborer and as an apprentice tool and die maker. Thus, hard-earned, on-the-job experience in blue-collar jobs provided his initial ideas and motivation about how to improve the efficiency of industrial plants. Taylor developed a strong belief that only through rigorous scientific experimentation could better methods be developed. He was particularly keen on time study and analysis of workers' individual tasks—a truly innovative concept for its day. As noted management author Peter Drucker has written, "Taylor was the first man in history who actually studied work seriously."[15] In some respects, the emphasis on gathering factual data about tasks and jobs might be regarded as Taylor's greatest contribution to the advancement of the practice of management.

scientific management approach developed by Frederick Winslow Taylor focusing on basic principles for improving performance, such as studying jobs by using objective measurements in order to determine the one best way, selecting the best persons for the job, training them in the most efficient methods, and providing sufficient monetary incentive to those performing the work

TAYLOR'S PRINCIPLES OF SCIENTIFIC MANAGEMENT Even though most of Taylor's fact-finding studies concentrated on the hourly employee and the first level of supervision, his total approach as it evolved and expanded over the years came to be called **scientific management**. The essence of Taylor's scientific management approach focused on a few

Frederick Winslow Taylor, 1856–1915

Frederick Winslow Taylor was born in 1856 in Germantown, Pennsylvania. His father was a prosperous lawyer, and Taylor grew up in an affluent family. Taylor's family was of Puritan descent, arriving in the United States in 1629 at Plymouth, Massachusetts. This ancestry instilled in Taylor many Puritan values, including the need to search for the truth, to avoid waste of any type, and to judge by observation of the facts. These values in part drove Taylor's search for the "one best way" even in his youth. For example, while just a boy, Taylor searched for the one best way to play croquet and the best way to make a cross-country walk covering the greatest distance with the least fatigue.

Although he enrolled in Harvard Law School to follow his father's footsteps, he had to withdraw because of poor health and eyesight. After leaving Harvard, Taylor started as an apprentice at Enterprise Hydraulic Works of Philadelphia and finished his apprenticeship in 1878 at the age of 22. During this time he developed an appreciation for workers' points of view and saw problems with worker "soldiering" (i.e., loafing), poor quality of management, and poor relations between workers and management.

In 1878 Taylor moved to Midvale Steel (Pennsylvania) and worked as a common laborer. Within six years he moved from laborer to clerk, to machinist, to gang boss of machinists, to foreman of the machine stop, to master mechanic, to chief engineer. While working full-time at Midvale, Taylor also enrolled in a home study course from Stevens Institute of Technology in New Jersey. He attended classes only to take examinations. Two-and-a-half years after enrolling, Taylor graduated in 1883 with a degree in mechanical engineering.

Source: F. B. Copley, *Frederick W. Taylor: Father of Scientific Management*, 2 vols. (New York: Harper & Row, 1923).

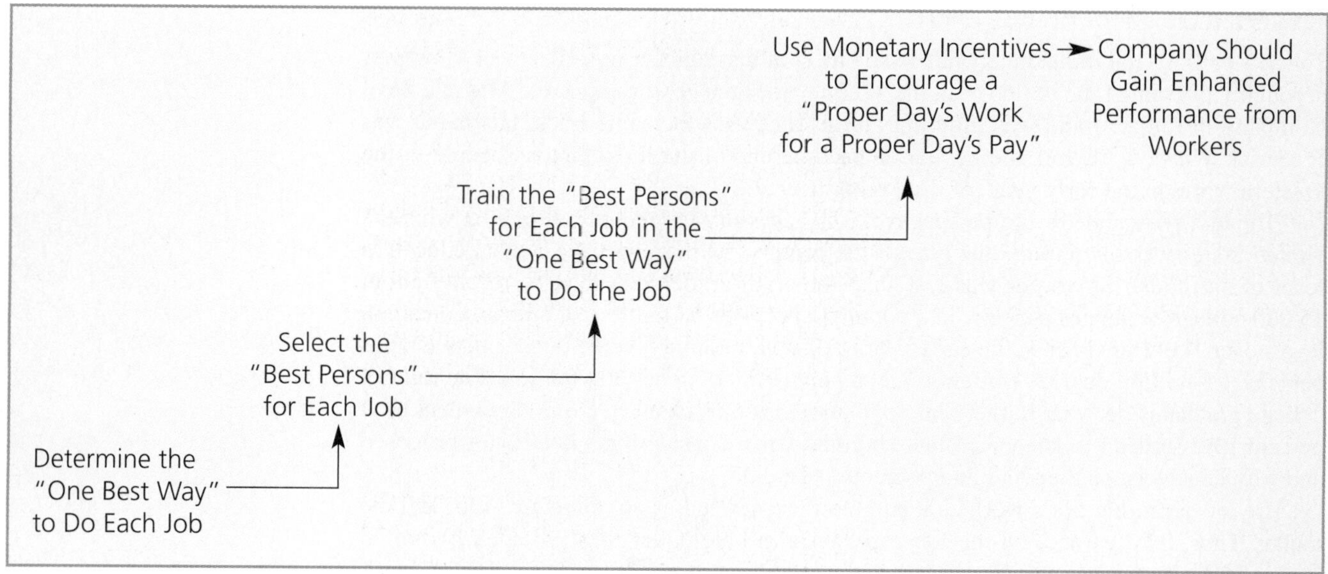

EXHIBIT A.2 Basic Elements of Scientific Management

key principles that gradually evolved over years of extensive study of task and supervisory practices and how they could be combined for improved performance. The basic elements of scientific management (shown in Exhibit A.2) were the following:

- ***Determine the one best way to do each job through precise, objective measurement:*** Taylor's entire approach was fundamentally based on meticulously studying and measuring the efforts involved in performing each task and movement that constituted a job, and then determining from the data the single best way to carry out the total set of procedures.
- ***Select the "best persons" for the job:*** For many of the blue-collar jobs Taylor investigated, such as loading pig iron, the best person meant the strongest person with the strongest desire to do a good job. For other jobs not involving sheer strength, this meant the person with the most aptitude for a particular set of tasks.
- ***Train the "best person" in the most efficient methods of performing the task(s)—the one best way:*** Taylor stressed that it was management's—not the worker's—responsibility to study the task and determine scientifically the optimal way to perform it. This might mean retraining workers who had already been performing the task.
- ***Provide sufficient monetary incentive to the workers to perform the task correctly and meet a defined hourly or daily target rate of output (a "proper day's work"):*** Taylor believed that it was only fair for workers to share directly in the rewards of higher levels of output that would result when correct methods were used and when the prescribed rate of performance was achieved. These rewards were to be in the form of sharply higher take-home wages for individuals who met or exceeded the standards, compared with the wages of workers who produced at slower rates and did not meet assigned targets.

TAYLOR'S IMPACT By the time Taylor's major work, *The Principles of Scientific Management*, was published in 1911, he already had attained considerable notoriety, both within the business world as well as in the wider society. Companies were beginning to explore ways to implement versions of Taylor's approach in order to increase the performance level of their operations. At the same time, however, some of the labor unions of the day were becoming more concerned and vocal about the possible exploitation of workers if Taylor's methods were used widely. Even the U.S. Congress took note of Taylor, when hearings were held in 1911 and 1912 by the House Labor Committee. The committee examined Taylor's views on how scientific management was affecting the ordinary worker, among other matters.

The major criticism of Taylor and his overall approach (see Exhibit A.3) was that his methods not only placed undue pressure on workers but also disproportionately rewarded management compared with employees. Taylor himself maintained that companies and their workers should have a joint and mutual interest in improving output through scientific management principles and that increased levels of efficiency and production would benefit both parties.[16] He also argued that he was not anti-union, but that unions would become unnecessary if management fairly shared productivity gains with workers. What constitutes an equitable sharing of gains (including protection against layoffs caused by increased rates of production) has never been resolved, and, thus, organized labor has always remained extremely wary of many features of scientific management.

In later years, some behavioral scientists criticized Taylor and the scientific management approach on several grounds (as shown in Exhibit A.3), including the following: (1) scientific management was an oversimplified approach to motivation that emphasized the importance of wage incentives; (2) it paid insufficient attention to other, especially social, factors that affect employee behavior in work settings; (3) it was an authoritarian, management-dominated approach; (4) it placed too much emphasis on specialization of tasks and jobs; and (5) Taylor failed to give credit to those who helped develop the ideas and procedures commonly identified with "scientific management."[17] Some of these criticisms have been challenged by other management scholars, and, thus, the validity of the criticisms is still disputed.

Nevertheless, several facts ought to be kept in mind about Taylor and the impact of his contributions:

1. ***The influence of his times:*** Just as we all are products of our own times, so was Taylor. He was strongly influenced by many factors at the turn of the century (e.g., the average education level of the workforce) that have changed considerably in the intervening 90-plus years. Were today's conditions present then, he undoubtedly would have modified some of his views.
2. ***Order out of chaos:*** Taylor spent a great amount of effort, as we have noted earlier, on systematically studying jobs and work. As a result of his research and demonstrations, he helped persuade managers to abandon a haphazard approach to planning and organizing work and instead to base it on facts, especially at the hourly worker's level and the first level of supervision.

EXHIBIT A.3 Contributions and Criticisms of Scientific Management

CONTRIBUTIONS	• Emphasized the Gathering of Factual Data Concerning Jobs and Tasks • Persuaded Managers to Abandon Haphazard Approaches to Planning and Organizing Work • Stressed the Role of Management in Organizing Work, Training Workers, and Instituting Incentives	
CRITICISMS	FROM ORGANIZED LABOR	FROM BEHAVIORAL SCIENTISTS
	• Too Much Pressure to Perform Placed on the Workers • Unfair Division of Rewards Between Management and Labor	• Presents an Oversimplified Approach to Worker Motivation • Pays Insufficient Attention to Social Factors in the Workplace that Affect Worker Behavior • Too Authoritarian in Approach • Demands Excessive Specialization of Jobs and Tasks

3. ***Managerial responsibilities:*** Taylor continually stressed that it was management's responsibility to organize the work, train the workers, and institute an effective incentive system. In his own words, he wanted to bring about "a complete mental revolution," not only on the part of the workers but also, and particularly, "on the part of those on the management's side—the foreman, the superintendent, the owner of the business, the board of directors—a complete mental revolution as to their duties toward their fellow workers in the management, toward their workmen, and toward all of their daily problems."[18] This, perhaps, was Taylor's most enduring legacy to the development of management thought.

Other Leaders of Scientific Management

Although Frederick Taylor was the acknowledged founder and central figure in the scientific management movement, several others played important roles in advancing and extending the general approach to fact-based and orderly processes for managing industrial organizations. Three of those, whom we briefly mention here, were Henry L. Gantt and Frank and Lillian Gilbreth.

H. L. GANTT (1861–1919) Gantt was a young engineering colleague of Taylor's at the Midvale Steel Company at the end of the 1880s, but by the early 1900s he was well launched in his own career as one of the first bona fide management consultants. He was heavily influenced in his early career by Taylor's views, but he subsequently became known chiefly for developing graphic methods to aid in organizing and coordinating multiple tasks in complex production jobs. While serving as a volunteer consultant to the U.S. government during World War I, he perfected a type of bar chart that showed the order in which tasks had to be initiated and the time allotted for each. Versions of this graphic display, now called Gantt charts, have been widely used and were the direct forerunner of modern-day Program Evaluation and Review Techniques (PERT) methods. The importance of Gantt's graphic approach was that it reinforced the need for systematic planning in order to sequence tasks efficiently and for more direct control over the time allotted to them, which, in turn, directly lowered costs and increased performance.

FRANK AND LILLIAN GILBRETH (1868–1924 AND 1878–1972) This husband-and-wife team were strong advocates of Taylor's general approach, but they were able to add their own unique contributions. Frank Gilbreth was a contractor who became intensely interested in studying how various construction tasks could be performed more efficiently and with reduced fatigue for the worker. Using the recently invented motion picture camera, he developed techniques to analyze each motion that went into performing a task, such as bricklaying. Eventually, Gilbreth was able to categorize any motion into one of 17 basic types (which he called "Therbligs," a reversal—with *t* and *h* transposed—of the spelling of *Gilbreth*). In theory, this categorization of motions made it possible to develop the most effective combination for performing any physical task. Lillian Gilbreth was one of the first doctoral-level industrial psychologists in the United States. In her early career, she worked closely with her husband on his analytical studies of motions. She concentrated on the "mental" tasks facing management and on how psychological principles could further the application of a scientific management approach that would benefit both worker and manager. Lillian Gilbreth (who died in 1972 at the age of 93) achieved many "firsts" (e.g., she was the first woman member of both the Society of Industrial Engineers and the Society of Mechanical Engineers) and in later years her peers called her "the first lady of management."[19] Not the least of the two Gilbreths' many joint accomplishments was their success in raising 12 children, the story of which was immortalized in a book, *Cheaper by the Dozen*, and a movie (1950) of the same name. The Gilbreths, thus, applied scientific management principles in the home as well as in their extensive investigations of industrial jobs. It was in the latter area, however, where their individual and combined efforts had worldwide impact.

Pioneers: Classical Management Theory

While Taylor and various associates were spreading the gospel of scientific management in the United States and Europe in the first two decades of the twentieth century, others also were beginning to think seriously and insightfully about how to manage organizations. Four of those who had the greatest impact on subsequent management thought and practice will be discussed here. Two of them essentially worked and wrote individually, and the other two jointly authored a book. One was French, one was German, and the other two were Americans (see Exhibit A.4). Their ideas, together with some of the emerging concepts identified with the scientific management approach, have come to be called "classical management theory."

Classical management theory focuses on the study of the principles and functions of management and the authority structures of organizations. In some cases, the term *administrative theory* could be used interchangeably with *management theory*. The term *classical management theory* was never attached to this broad set of ideas during the era in which they appeared (from roughly 1900 to the early 1930s). It has only been more recently applied. The ideas and thoughts are considered classical because they had some relatively enduring qualities and served as a springboard for others' thinking and action. As we will see later in this appendix, they even served as a model against which newer and quite different theories and approaches were contrasted.

classical management theory
ideas concerning the management of organizations arising from pioneers such as Taylor, Fayol, Weber, and Mooney and Reiley, together with emerging concepts identified with the scientific management approach

Henri Fayol (1841–1925)

Henri Fayol was a French mining engineer who rose rapidly in his company to become president at age 37. Under his leadership, his company became a large, integrated mining, iron, and steel organization, which took raw materials and transformed them into finished product. Fayol's relatively early and extended exposure to the top management position of a sizable firm gave him an opportunity to reflect on what was required to manage the total enterprise. Using his experience to good advantage, Fayol put some of his ideas on management into written form, culminating with the publication of his most famous work in 1916, a monograph entitled *Administration Industrielle et Générale* ("General and Industrial Management").

Fayol's publication had lasting impact for two reasons. First, his attempt to define management as consisting of five key elements was a major advance.[20] His approach was analytical and focused attention on management as a legitimate, specialized set of activities, and it identified what those activities were: planning (in French, "prévoyance"), organizing, command, coordination, and control. These "elements," as Fayol termed them, have subsequently been called (in English) **functions of management**, and in slightly

functions of management
basic elements of management as originally identified by Henri Fayol, consisting of planning, organizing, command, coordination, and control

EXHIBIT A.4 Contributors to Classical Management Theory

	HENRI FAYOL (FRENCH)	MAX WEBER (GERMAN)	J. D. MOONEY AND A. C. REILEY (AMERICAN)
WROTE	*General and Industrial Management*	*The Theory of Social and Economic Organization*	*Onward Industry!*
STATED/DEFINED	• Five Functions of Management • 14 Principles of Management	• Three Basic Types of Authority Relationships • Bureaucracy	• Four Basic Principles of Management
(COMMENT)	Focused on middle and upper management activities in multi-unit organizations	Writings aimed more for scholars than practicing managers, but ultimately influenced society as a whole	Fayol and Weber had not yet been published in America, so the similarity of Mooney and Reiley's descriptions of management was used to argue the universality of management principles

modified form, they have prevailed to the present day. The alert reader will recognize that Fayol's list of elements is quite similar to the major sections of this text and nearly all other contemporary management texts. The most common current version of the list collapses the functions to four (allocating coordination activities across the other four functions) and changing the term *command* to *influencing* or *leading*. In short, even with the passage of about 90 years since the publication of *Administration Industrielle et Générale*, few improvements have been made on Fayol's "classic" list of management functions.

The other reason Fayol's work received a great deal of attention in later years was that it also presented a list of 14 management "principles," or, more accurately, guidelines that he found effective and thought could be used to improve the performance of a wide variety of organizations. Some of the more important of these (paraphrased) were: division of labor (specialization of work); unity of command (each person in the organization should receive orders from only one other person); unity of direction (all persons in a part of the organization must govern their actions by the same, single plan); and "scalar chain" (there must be a clear line of authority from the bottom to the top of the organization). (See Exhibit A.5 for the complete list of Fayol's principles). These principles have been challenged in recent years, but they appeared at a time when business and industrial activity was quite different from that of today and the context (government, society, technology, etc.) in which such activity took place was profoundly different.

The importance of Fayol's contributions was not fully recognized in the English-speaking world until later translations appeared (e.g., in 1949), but the originality of his ideas and the clarity and systematized way in which they were presented endure. Also, it should be noted that Fayol's focus, in contrast to much of Taylor's work, was directed toward the middle and upper levels of managerial activities of multi-unit enterprises rather than toward shop floor supervision and the management of individual factories. In that sense, Fayol's ideas were consistent with Taylor's, but they covered new ground—ground that would be especially relevant to the types of firms and corporations prominent in the last half of the twentieth century.

Max Weber (1864–1920)

Although Max Weber lived at approximately the same time as did Taylor and Fayol, he neither influenced them nor was influenced by them. Weber was a German academic and scholar who never managed an organization, or even part of one, but who was one of history's most perceptive organizational observers. As one of the early forerunners of modern sociology, Weber was an organization theorist and not a management theorist per se. We mention him here, however, because by the mid-twentieth century he had become extremely influential in how leading thinkers viewed the management process in organizations—industrial or otherwise.

Weber's most significant work dealing with organizations, *The Theory of Social and Economic Organization*, although originally published in 1922 after his death, was not translated into English until 1947. He was a product of the German culture and society of his era, and this background no doubt had a strong bearing on the kinds of intellectual issues he chose to analyze. With respect to organizations, those issues centered on the concept of authority, especially the questions of "Why do individuals obey commands?" and "Why do people do as they are told?"[21] He theorized that three basic types of authority relationships or structures could be used to classify organizations:

1. ***Traditional authority:*** authority exercised on the basis of custom or past practice. According to Weber, its weakness as a source of authority in organizations was that it emphasizes precedent for its own sake rather than making the best possible decisions.
2. ***Charismatic authority:*** based on "devotion to the specific and exceptional sanctity, heroism, or exemplary character of an individual person."[22] The weakness of charismatic authority, as stressed by Weber, is that it does not provide a basis for succession of authority relationships when the charismatic leader leaves the scene, and hence this threatens the continuity of the organization.

1. Division of Work	Divide work into specialized tasks and functions, each assigned to specific individuals.
2. Authority	Authority must be accompanied by responsibility.
3. Discipline	Sanctions are necessary to minimize or prevent the recurrence of behavior that violates agreed-upon expectations.
4. Unity of Command	"For any action whatsoever, an employee should receive orders from one superior only."
5. Unity of Direction	There should be "one head and one plan for a group of activities having the same objective."
6. Subordination	"The interest of one employee or group of employees should not prevail over that of the [organization]."
7. Remuneration	". . . should be fair and, as far as s possible, afford satisfaction both to personnel and firm (employee and employer)."
8. Centralization	The amount of centralization or decentralization necessary to a firm is a function both of the size of the firm and the ability of the manager(s). Organizational effectiveness is increased by determining the optimal level of centralization.
9. Scalar Chain	"The scalar chain is the chain of supervisors ranging from the ultimate authority to the lowest ranks. The line of authority is the route followed—via every link in the chain—by all communications which start from or go to the ultimate authority."
10. Order	There must be order in both material and personnel. For material: "things [must] be in their place suitably arranged . . . so as to facilitate all activities." For personnel: "Perfect order requires . . . that the place be suitable for the employee and the employee for the place . . . the right man in the right place."
11. Equity	To encourage employee loyalty and performance, employers must treat employees fairly, combining kindness and justice, but not excluding forcefulness or sternness.
12. Stability of Tenure of Personnel	It requires time for an employee to develop the skills necessary to perform his or her work well. Therefore, successful companies are those with low turnover (high stability of tenure) of personnel. "Instability of tenure is at one and the same time cause and effect of bad [management]."
13. Initiative	"At all levels of the organizational ladder zeal and energy on the part of employees are augmented by initiative [the thinking out and implementation of plans]. The initiative of all, added to that of the manager, and supplementing it if need be, represents a great source of strength for businesses."
14. Esprit de Corps	"Union is strength. Harmony union among the personnel of a concern is great strength in that concern. Effort, then, should be made to establish it."

Source: Adapted from H. Fayol, *General and Industrial Management* (London: Pitman, 1949), chapter 4. (Translation by C. Storrs from 1916 French edition, *Administration Industrielle et Générale*.)

EXHIBIT A.5 Fayol's 14 Principles of Management

3. ***Rational-legal authority:*** authority exercised to achieve specifically designated goals and based on the legal right of the person in a particular office (*buro* in German) to issue commands. In Weber's analysis, this type of authority is best suited for larger, complex organizations because it emphasizes obedience to orders issued by someone—*whoever that person is*—fulfilling an official position and acting on the basis of powers conferred on that position (and not to a particular person). This basis for authority overcomes, in Weber's view, the disadvantages of the other two forms of authority.

Weber went on to describe the type of organization that would result if the use of rational-legal authority were maximized: namely, a "bureaucracy." In describing bureaucracies, Weber was not necessarily advocating that every organization should become one, only that if this type of authority were put into place throughout an organization, it would have certain features; for example:

- An explicit set of rules to govern official actions
- Clearly defined duties for each office (i.e., position)
- Competence and technical qualifications as the basis for selection of officeholders
- Comprehensive training for people occupying particular positions

In assessing the impact of Weber and his writings on the history of management thought, several points should be made. To begin with, it should be reiterated that Weber has affected society's views about the management of organizations by influencing scholars rather than by directly addressing managers. Nevertheless, although Weber wrote independently of others who concentrated specifically on ways to improve the performance of managerial activities, his analysis of the advantages of bureaucratic organization was consistent with the prescriptions for managers provided by Taylor and Fayol. It is also necessary to keep in mind that Weber's concept of a bureaucracy was that of a form of organization based on a specified type of authority and not the caricature of a sluggish, rule-strangled organization that the term has come to mean in recent years. If Weber were alive today, he would probably think of that type of organization as a sort of bureaucracy run amok and not at all what he envisioned.

J. D. Mooney (1884–1957) and A. C. Reiley (1869–1947)

The final set of classical management theorists to be discussed here are two American executives, James D. Mooney and Allan C. Reiley. Both were upper-level managers within the General Motors Corporation, with a particular interest in the historical evolution of organizational principles. In the depths of the Great Depression (in 1931), they published a book that had the bold title of *Onward Industry!* This book, which gained considerable visibility for its authors, attempted to demonstrate how all great organizations of the past and present tended to follow several fundamental principles, principles we now refer to as the center of the classical approach to management:

1. The *coordinative principle:* the need to obtain a high degree of coordination of actions toward a common purpose.
2. The *scalar principle:* the need to designate the precise delegation of authority from the top to the bottom of the organization.
3. The *functional principle*: the need to achieve a tight grouping of specialized functions or duties.
4. The *staff principle:* the need to provide managers in the direct chain of command (the line) with ideas and information from specialized experts (the staff), and the related need to distinguish clearly between the two types of positions.

Although Mooney and Reiley apparently had never read the works of either Henri Fayol or Max Weber (since they had not yet been translated into English), their managerial and organizational principles were remarkably similar to those that these two theorists had developed in other countries and cultures some two decades earlier. Some management writers later took this to be evidence for the universality of management principles.

The Impact of Classical Management Theory

As we said at the beginning of this section, the term *classical management theory* is a label that has been applied in recent years to the collection of ideas put forth by people such as Fayol, Weber, Mooney and Reiley, and others in the first 35 years of the twentieth century. Those ideas do not constitute "theory" in the strict scientific use of that word. Rather, they are a loose set of concepts and principles that have provided a coherent and, above all, rational way to think about how organizations should be structured and managed. Because this cluster of ideas—along with those of Taylor and the scientific management approach—amounted to such an advance in thinking, they were indeed influential. They provided guidance for those who wanted to develop and operate effective and efficient organizations. Furthermore, and this should not be overlooked, many of these notions have persisted to this day in one form or another. Anyone who has ever worked in a company, a government office, or in almost any organization cannot help but notice how often and how widespread is the attempted application of many of the so-called principles of classical management theory even 90 years after they were first proposed.

Despite the progress in management thinking that classical management theorists represent, there were (and are) major problems with their basic approach. To obtain a sense of some of those problems, we need only to consider the underlying assumptions, which are summarized in Exhibit A.6. First and foremost, as summarized in Exhibit A.7, the underlying assumptions implied an extremely limited view of the role of people in organizations. Second, and also quite important, the classical management approach was essentially a static view of how organizations should be managed and did not deal sufficiently with the effects of changing conditions. Classical theory implicitly assumed that all organizations should be managed in "the one best way." As with its close cousin, scientific management (often classified as a classical theory), it was clearly a product of its times, even though this fact was not apparent to those who proposed its principles nor especially to those who to this day still believe that what worked in 1925 will still work just as well in 2025!

EXHIBIT A.6

Assumptions Underlying Classical Management Theory

1. "Efficiency of an undertaking is measured solely in terms of productivity."
2. "Human beings can be assumed to act rationally."
3. "[Employees] are unable to work out the relationships of their positions without detailed guidance from their supervisors."
4. "Unless clear limits to jobs are defined and enforced, [employees] will tend to be confused . . ."
5. "Human beings prefer the security of a definite task and do not value the freedom of determining their own approaches to problems . . ."
6. "It is possible to predict and establish clear-cut patterns of future activities and the relationships among activities."
7. "Management involves primarily the formal and official activities of individuals."
8. "The activities of [employees] should be viewed on an objective and impersonal basis . . ."
9. "Workers are motivated by economic needs . . ."
10. "People do not like to work, and therefore, close-supervision and accountability should be emphasized."
11. "Coordination will not be achieved unless it is planned and directed from above."
12. "Authority has its source at the top of a hierarchy and is delegated downward."
13. "Simple tasks are easier to master and thus lead toward higher productivity by concentrating on a narrow scope of activity."
14. "Managerial functions . . . have universal characteristics and can be performed in a given manner regardless of the environment and qualities of the personnel involved."

Source: J. L. Massie, "Management Theory," in *Handbook of Organizations*, ed. J. G. March (Chicago: Rand McNally, 1965). Reprinted with permission of J. G. March.

CONTRIBUTIONS	• Provided a coherent and Rational Way to Think about the Structure and Management of Organizations • Provided Directions for Managers Attempting to Increase Effectiveness and Efficiency in Their Organizations • Many of the Principles Have Persisted in One Form or Another to the Present
CRITICISMS	• Assumed an Extremely Narrow View of the Role of People in Organizations • Assumed There is "One Best Way" to Manage Businesses • Assumed (implicitly) a Static Role for the Business Environment

EXHIBIT A.7 Contributions and Criticisms of Classical Management Theory

Neoclassical Administrative Theory

By the beginning of the 1920s, the world of work was changing. The size and complexity of organizations were increasing, as shown in the General Motors example that opened this appendix, and the skills, abilities, and expectations of employees were also becoming more complex. These changes made it obvious that the traditional approach to managing was not adequate nor always appropriate. Revisions in the ways of thinking about how to manage organized work activity began in the 1920s and continued to the 1940s. As might be expected, the new thinking drew from the accepted wisdom of basic management principles, even though it went beyond those principles in interesting new directions. Because these ideas had at least some links to past thinking, this approach is now often called neoclassical management theory. **Neoclassical management theory** continued to emphasize the study and analysis of managerial functions and organizational structures but expanded to include situational and social considerations such as communication and cooperation. Two individuals closely associated with this label were Mary Parker Follett and Chester Barnard, as shown in Exhibit A.8.

neoclassical management theory
thinking about organized work activity and how to manage that drew from classical theory in its emphasis on study and analysis of the workplace but expanded to include situational and social considerations (i.e., communication and cooperation)

Mary Parker Follett (1868–1933)

Lillian Gilbreth was not the only prominent woman who contributed to management thought in the early part of the twentieth century. Mary Parker Follett was a writer, lecturer, and independent consultant who early in life became interested in political philosophy but

EXHIBIT A.8 Contributors to Neoclassical Management Theory

	MARY PARKER FOLLETT	CHESTER BARNARD
WROTE	*Creative Experience*	*The Functions of the Executive*
AGREED WITH CLASSICAL THEORISTS ON	• Importance of Detailed Analysis of Work Settings • Coordination of Work Activities	• Importance of Detailed Analysis of Work Settings
EMPHASIZED	• Cooperation Between Managers and Subordinates • Integration of Interests of Organization and Employees • The Use of the Type of Authority Appropriate to the Situation	• A View of Organizations as Cooperative Social Systems • The Need for Managers to Obtain Voluntary Cooperation from Their Workers • The "Zone of Indifference" • The Need for Efficient Organizational Communication
(COMMENT)	Forerunner of many modern ideas of management, particularly the contingency approach	Views on authority were innovative and anticipated later behavioralist thinking

who later turned her attention to the management of organizations. She was especially influential in the 1920s.

In many respects, Follett's thinking was consistent with Taylor's and the scientific management movement in that she placed great importance on detailed study and analysis of the work setting and on the necessity for careful coordination of activities. However, she also emphasized the need to generate a spirit of cooperation between managers and their subordinates and to integrate the interests of the organization and its employees. In this regard, her ideas differed from the typical views of many contemporary advocates of scientific management. Also, in contrast to Weber's analysis, Follett focused not on the formal powers conferred on an office but rather on the dictates of the **law of the situation**, that is, the authority—based on a person's knowledge and experience—that seems appropriate to the circumstances. This type of thinking anticipated by some 40 years a prominent modern approach to management, the contingency approach, which is discussed later in this appendix. In summary, although Mary Parker Follett and her ideas are often classified as being associated with classical management theory, she was someone who was a clear forerunner of much of modern management thought that has dominated the last half of the twentieth century. Thus, we have placed her here in the neoclassical category of management thinkers.

law of the situation
Mary Parker Follett's emphasis on the need to generate a spirit of cooperation between managers and their subordinates with a focus on the authority (based on a person's knowledge and experience) that seems appropriate to the circumstances

Chester Barnard (1886–1961)

A long-time executive at AT&T and ultimately president of then New Jersey Bell Telephone company, Chester Barnard spent a considerable amount of time and thought in formulating his unique and detailed ideas regarding the nature of organizations and the role of their managers and leaders. This effort resulted in a highly regarded book published in 1938, *The Functions of the Executive*, that has had considerable influence on the field of management ever since.

Barnard, as did most classical management theorists, provided a very systematic but nonempirical (nondata) analysis of the tasks of management. In this sense, the starting point for his analysis could be considered somewhat similar to classical theorists. However, Barnard differed sharply from the standard classical approach by viewing organizations as cooperative social systems. As it was for Mary Parker Follett, cooperation was at the center of Barnard's thinking about the nature of organizations. He believed that all organizations, no matter what type, required (1) willingness to cooperate, (2) common purpose, and (3) communication. In particular, he stressed the need for managers in organizations to obtain the voluntary cooperation of those they lead. Additionally, his strong focus on the need for communication as an essential ingredient in any organization was also a ground-breaking notion for its day.

Mary Parker Follett, 1868–1933

Mary Parker Follett was born in Boston, Massachusetts. Although a contemporary of Taylor, Follett was much more a philosopher than manager. She was educated at what is today called Radcliffe College. Her early interests in John Fichte (1762–1814), a German philosopher who espoused a nationalism in which freedom of the individual had to be subordinated to the group, led her to write the book *The New State*. In this book, Follett argued that an individual could find his or her true self only through group orientation.

She began to be more of a business philosopher in 1924 after she published *Creative Experience*. This book was widely read by businessmen of the day. In 1924 and 1925, Follett gave a series of lectures in New York that were sponsored by the Bureau of Personnel Administration. The lectures were well received and led Follett to focus most of her later writings and lectures on principles of business organization and administration.

Source: H. C. Metcalf and L. Urwick, *Dynamic Administration: The Collected Papers of Mary Parker Follett* (New York: Harper & Row, 1940).

In his discussion of the concept of authority, however, Barnard probably achieved his greatest influence on others. He argued that the source of a manager's authority depends on the acceptance of his or her orders by the subordinate. This was a truly radical idea for its time, because until then traditional management theory had always insisted that the source of authority was solely determined by the position of the manager and that the higher the position, the greater the authority possessed by the person occupying it. Barnard elaborated on his perspective by defining what he called the "zone of indifference" (which others later labeled the "zone of acceptance"). This zone consisted of orders that would be accepted by the subordinate without question. Barnard did believe (in line with classical theory) that this zone was wider the higher the position of the order giver, but he also contended that the leadership skills and abilities of the manager were critical to broaden the scope of orders that a subordinate would accept without dispute or resistance. His thinking, thus, foreshadowed later behavioral approaches to the process of management.

Behavioral Approaches

Early management theorists, especially Frederick Taylor and the proponents of a scientific management approach, did not entirely ignore the human component of organizations. Rather, they viewed the human dimension of organizations in very specific and limited ways. Scientific management and classical management approaches placed great emphasis on initial selection of workers for jobs and in effect, on individual capabilities, such as differences in physical agility or strength. They also believed that worker motivation stemmed almost solely from the financial incentives offered by hourly and piecework wages linked directly to the amount of output. What was not given much, if any, attention in these approaches were the following:

- Capacities of employees for further development after they are hired for particular jobs
- Other sources of employee motivation in addition to financial rewards
- The impact of relationships among employees and with their supervisors

While it is easy to say with the benefit of hindsight that even the earliest management theorists ought to have paid more attention to these factors, remember that the level of education

Chester Barnard, 1886–1961

Chester Barnard was born to a farming family in Malden, Massachusetts. Through his talent and hard work, he earned a scholarship to Harvard University, where he studied economics. While a student, Barnard supplemented his income by tuning pianos and running a small dance band. He completed his studies in three years but was not granted a degree because even though he had passed a certain course with distinction, he had been too busy to take the laboratory section.

Barnard left Harvard in 1909 and joined the Statistics Department of American Telephone and Telegraph. He worked hard and applied both the formal learning he had received at Harvard and the knowledge he gained from his own studies. Despite being a "Harvard drop-out," Barnard was a scholar who read Vilfredo Pareto in French and Kurt Lewis and Max Weber in German. In 1927 he was named president of New Jersey Bell.

Barnard also spent considerable time and energy working in voluntary organizations. He helped David Lilienthal establish the policies of the U.S. Atomic Energy Commission. He worked with the United States Service Organization and served as its president for three years. He also served as the president of the Rockefeller Foundation for four years.

After 10 years as president of New Jersey Bell, Barnard gave a series of lectures at the Lowell Institute in Boston. An expansion of the lectures was published in Barnard's famous book, *Functions of the Executive*, published by Harvard University Press in 1938.

Source: W. B. Wolf, *How to Understand Management: An Introduction to Chester J. Barnard* (Los Angeles: Lucas Bro. Publishers, 1968).

of the average person was much lower then than now and that the social and cultural conditions that existed in those times resulted in different employee and management expectations compared with those of today. Put another way, traditional ways of operating were much different then, and those traditions exerted a powerful influence on management theories of that era.

The neoclassical theorists, such as Mary Parker Follett and Chester Barnard, with their strong focus on the need for cooperation in organizations, did begin to bring the human element more to the forefront in discussions of how enterprises should be managed. Nevertheless, it took the dramatic findings of a years-long set of research studies, the Hawthorne studies, to focus a spotlight on how the human factor impacted work performance at the shop floor level. These findings led to a whole new approach called the human relations approach.

The Human Relations Approach

human relations approach approach springing from the findings of the Hawthorne studies that focused on the importance of relationships among people in the workplace.

Hawthorne studies a series of research studies at the Hawthorne plant of the Western Electric Company that focused a spotlight on the importance of the human factor in productivity

The **human relations approach** to management did not suddenly emerge full blown. Instead, it evolved as the findings from the **Hawthorne studies** began to achieve prominence toward the end of the 1930s, with the publication of the famous book, *Management and the Worker*, by Roethlisberger and Dickson in 1939. This series of investigations started in the mid-1920s at the Hawthorne plant of the Western Electric Company (a manufacturing subsidiary of the American Telephone and Telegraph Company [AT&T] at the time) outside Chicago. They were directed initially by researchers from the Massachusetts Institute of Technology.[23] However, as time went by, the research program became more associated with two well-known Harvard professors, the Australian social scientist Elton Mayo and a management professor by the name of Fritz Roethlisberger.

The first studies at the Hawthorne plant, as befitting the times, were designed to determine the effects of changes in the physical working environment, namely lighting, on productivity. However, when the early findings were analyzed by the researchers, it became apparent that what seemed to be causing the largest effects on worker performance was not the amount of light in the workplace, but rather the relations among the workers and between them and their supervisors. (Analyses of the data carried out some years later suggested that changes in the wage incentive system at the time also may have played a role in determining changes in worker output in some of the test conditions.)[24]

These initial results led to other studies over the next half-dozen years at Hawthorne (in the late 1920s and early 1930s) that were designed to gather more detailed data on the nature of these relationships among workers and supervisors and on how they affected employee output. The additional studies included observations under researcher-controlled conditions about how a group of workers could act together to exert considerable influence on the performance of individual members of the group. The researchers also carried out extensive interviewing of employees regarding their attitudes toward their work. The overall findings from the series of studies that spanned some eight years were then summarized in the 1939 Roethlisberger and Dickson book. Among other prominent outcomes of the Hawthorne studies, incidentally, was the demonstration of the apparent effect on worker behavior of having that behavior observed and given special attention. That phenomenon became known as the *Hawthorne effect*.

Although the Hawthorne studies have received criticism for inadequacies in research design and in the way in which some of the data were analyzed, the highly publicized findings did strongly impact many managers.[25] In effect, as management historians have put it, "the Hawthorne studies . . . introduced a new way of thinking about the people factor."[26] It became evident that if those who ran factories or companies were interested in improving productivity, more attention—than had been the case in most organizations up to that time—would have to be paid to the way in which the people relationships were handled, thus, leading to the origin of the term *human relations approach*. Simply instructing employees on how to operate machines or equipment and providing them with a wage incentive for doing so was not sufficient.

Those advocating more attention to human relations concentrated particularly on the role of the first-line supervisor and his (since in those days it usually was a "he") interactions with subordinates. The advice was to treat subordinates not as impersonal cogs in a machine but as individual human beings with feelings and emotions and needs other than just financial. This approach also stressed that it was the task of upper management to provide the necessary support and backing for the first-level supervisors, or foremen, in the time and effort they devoted to improving relations. The logic involved was that if workers felt better about their relationships with their supervisor and their working conditions, they would have a greater desire to produce more—or, at least, have less of a desire to try to restrict output.

The Human Resources Approach

The human relations movement flourished in the 1940s and 1950s, as many organizations attempted to implement a more human and humane approach to their treatment of employees. Again, it must be emphasized that the assumption—sometimes explicit but often implicit—was that improved worker satisfaction would result in better performance. By the 1960s, as a result of continuing research carried out in a variety of work circumstances, the human relations approach was shown to be incomplete at best and highly misleading at worst. In effect, the findings from these studies demonstrated that there was seldom a direct connection between satisfaction and performance and that, furthermore, from a psychological perspective, it should not be presumed that more satisfied workers necessarily will be more productive workers. Such results, coupled with additional analyses, led to new behavioral formulations relevant to the management process. One of these, called the human resources approach, provides a distinct contrast to the human relations approach and puts particular emphasis on starting from a different set of managerial assumptions concerning people. Exhibit A.9 shows the basic differences between these two approaches.

human resources approach approach involving a basic belief that people possess and want to make greater use of their talents and capabilities and that if allowed to do so, performance and satisfaction will increase

In essence, the core of the **human resources approach** to management thinking—led by such scholars as Douglas McGregor, Rensis Likert, and Chris Argyris—stresses a fundamental belief that most people possess and want to use more talent and capabilities in their work than may be readily apparent from their past or present job assignments. If so, it becomes management's primary role to develop these untapped human resources through increased opportunities for self-direction and self-control. The logic is that if human resources are better used, performance will be enhanced. Increased satisfaction, if it occurs, becomes the by-product rather than the cause of this improved performance. Direct evidence for the effectiveness of the human resources approach is not easy to obtain, but this general orientation toward the human component of organization underlies the basic behavioral approach to management in a large number of organizations as the new century begins.

Decision-Making Approaches

The behavioral approaches just described emphasize the motivation of individuals to excel at their jobs. Although it is hard to deny the importance of such perspectives, other processes taking place in organizations also have considerable consequences for their overall effectiveness. One of the most crucial is decision making. Good decisions can

EXHIBIT A.9 Differences Between Human Relations and Human Resources Approaches to Management

HUMAN RELATIONS APPROACH PROPOSED:

HUMAN RESOURCES APPROACH PROPOSED:

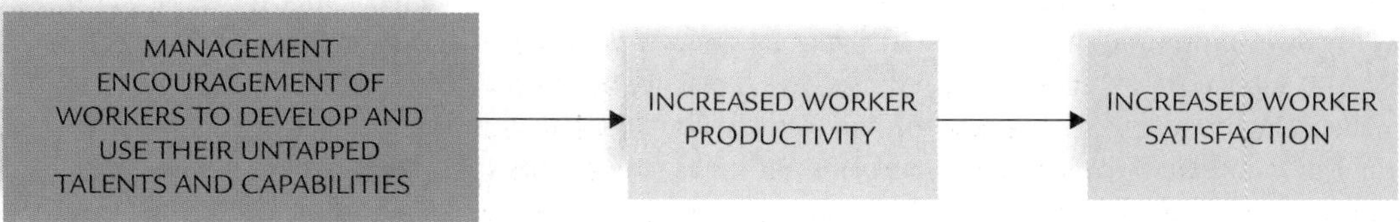

mobilize many people, and bad decisions can undercut and even jeopardize the continued existence of the organization. Despite the importance of decision making for the fate of organizations, it was not until after World War II that this process received concerted attention from management theorists. When this did happen, two lines of inquiry developed, one more behavioral and one more mathematical. We will look at both briefly here but only in terms of their historical significance.

Behavioral Decision-Making Approach

The emphasis on decision making as a critical element in the management process is generally credited to Herbert Simon, a Nobel Laureate in economics, who originally received his doctoral training in political science. Early in his academic career, Simon turned his attention to the concept of "economic man," the notion that individuals are totally rational and that in their decisions they can evaluate all alternative courses of action and their consequences and then select that one that has the best chance of maximizing goal attainment (e.g., profit). Simon was particularly interested in how this concept worked in practice in real organizational settings. His analyses led him to develop an alternative model, "administrative man." In contrast to economic man, administrative man—managers in real-life organizations—does not have information on all possible alternative courses of action and also does not have complete information on the probabilities of various consequences arising from particular actions. Simon did not dispute the idea that managers attempt to make rational decisions, but he proposed that such thinking is constrained by human limitations and results in what he called **bounded rationality.** Because of their "bounded," or constrained, rationality, according to Simon, managers do not search indefinitely for the best alternative (i.e., goal maximization) but rather make a decision that "satisfices." **Satisficing** is a decision that results in an acceptable course of action, although not necessarily the best course. Satisficing is necessary, in actual situations, according to Simon, because managers almost always must operate under conditions of uncertainty rather than certainty.

bounded rationality
Herbert Simon's concept that managers attempt to make rational decisions, but their thinking is constrained by human limitations

satisficing
decisions that result in an acceptable course of action rather than the best alternative, or goal maximization

Although Simon's ideas probably have had more direct effect on academics who study management than on managers themselves, they nevertheless have been extremely influential, as attested to by the Nobel award. His 1940s writing on decision making led to additional important work on this topic in the 1950s and 1960s by himself and his colleagues at Carnegie Mellon University, James March and Richard Cyert. The latter two scholars authored an important book in the early 1960s, *A Behavioral Theory of the Firm*, which provided an all-encompassing view of organizations from a decision-making perspective.

Quantitative Decision-Making Approaches

Quantitative, or mathematical, approaches to managerial problems, especially problems requiring specific decisions, did not emerge until after World War II. Using techniques that had been developed during wartime, a new field of study was developed called **management science**, or **operations research**. Each of these terms caused some confusion, the former because of its similarity to the term *scientific management* and the latter because it did not convey precise meaning. Nevertheless, the field (which we will refer to as *management science*) grew rapidly in popularity for its ability to provide precise solutions to decision problems involving many variables and complicated connections among those variables. In effect, management science techniques such as linear programming (a mathematical procedure for determining the optimal combination of resources under specific constraining conditions) and various mathematical modeling procedures provided valuable tools to managers to assist in planning and forecasting activities. Along with **simulation** techniques, where various potential combinations of variables can be mathematically manipulated in advance of actual decisions to determine the possible effects of changes in one or more variables, such mathematical modeling approaches have greatly improved the quality of managerial analyses of complicated decisions. However, such techniques do not in themselves provide comprehensive theories of management and hence have not had the same impact as some of the other major conceptual approaches to management covered earlier in this appendix. Nevertheless, their introduction did bring a much stronger analytical approach to some management tasks.

management science (operations research)
quantitative or mathematical approaches to managerial problems, especially those requiring specific decisions

simulation
a set of techniques in which various potential combinations of variables can be mathematically manipulated in advance of actual decisions to determine the possible effects of changes in one or more variables

Integrative Approaches

integrative approaches
recent approaches to management that include systems theory and contingency approaches and emphasize a consideration of a wide range of factors

The final set of approaches to management that we consider in this appendix are more recent and can loosely be labeled **integrative approaches**, that is, approaches that attempt to combine a number of different variables or elements into a more wholistic approach to the broad process of management. Since they are so relatively recent, it is questionable whether they should be included in a chapter on the *history* of management thought. But we include them to provide background on current management thinking and to show how historical approaches have been modified to the present. Also, you will encounter them, in one form or another, throughout this book, and, therefore, we only introduce them briefly here. The two that are most encompassing and that most widely affect contemporary management thinking are systems theory and contingency approaches.

Systems Theory

system
an interconnected set of elements that have orderly interactions that form a unitary whole

systems theory
the processes involved in how "inputs" get transformed by the organization into "outputs"

What has been called General Systems Theory (GST) was developed as early as the 1920s and was especially used in biology ("living systems") and engineering ("mechanical systems"), among other scientific areas of endeavor.[27] This approach was not applied to organizations until the 1960s, but since then it has been a prominent form of organizational analysis with considerable implications for understanding the process of management. A **system** refers to an interconnected set of elements that have orderly interactions that form a unitary whole. Thus, **systems theory** in the organizational context refers to the process involved in how "inputs" get transformed by the organization into "outputs," as illustrated in Exhibit A.10. Organizational inputs are generally considered to be of three major types: financial, material, and human resources. These inputs are combined and modified by technological and managerial actions into the two major types of organizational outputs, goods and services. Thus, from this perspective, management can be viewed as a type of transformation process, with the manager's role being one of converting a collection of resources into useful output. Understanding how all of these elements relate to each other and effectively integrating units and processes provide two major challenges for managers.

closed system
a system in which there is no interaction of the elements with the outside environment

open system
a system in which there is interaction of the elements with the outside environment

Systems theory also distinguishes between **closed systems** and **open systems** as shown in Exhibit A.11. In the former, there is no interaction of the elements of the system with the outside environment, and in the latter there is. Therefore, organizations can be considered open systems that constantly interact with their environment, importing resources from it into the organization and exporting goods and services back out into the outside world. Since traditional management theory often seemed to treat organizations as if they were more or less closed systems, it tended to overlook many of the important impacts that relations with the outside environment could have on functions inside the company or plant. Viewing organizations as open systems, on the other hand, provides an appropriate, and necessary, perspective for any manager operating in the rapidly changing world of the twenty-first century.

EXHIBIT A.10 Systems Theory Applied to Organizations: An Example

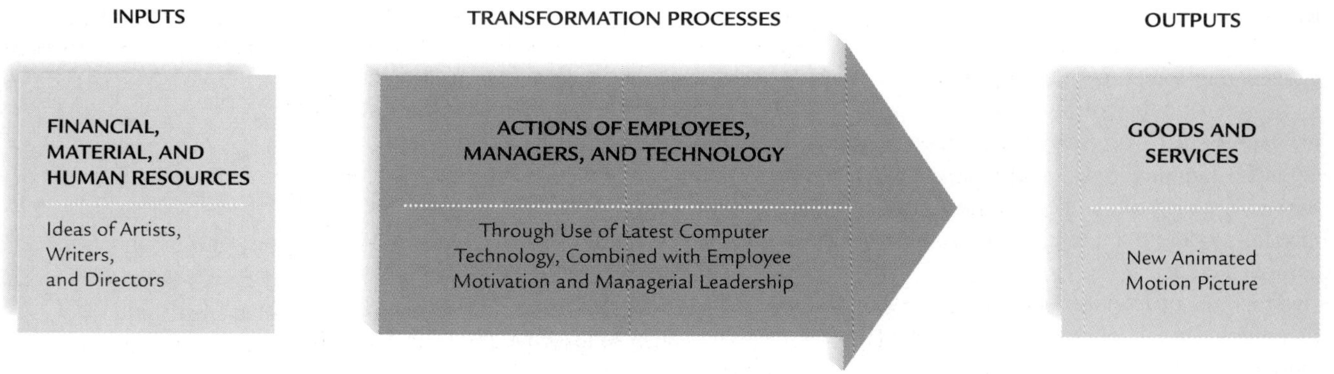

INPUTS	TRANSFORMATION PROCESSES	OUTPUTS
FINANCIAL, MATERIAL, AND HUMAN RESOURCES	ACTIONS OF EMPLOYEES, MANAGERS, AND TECHNOLOGY	GOODS AND SERVICES
Ideas of Artists, Writers, and Directors	Through Use of Latest Computer Technology, Combined with Employee Motivation and Managerial Leadership	New Animated Motion Picture

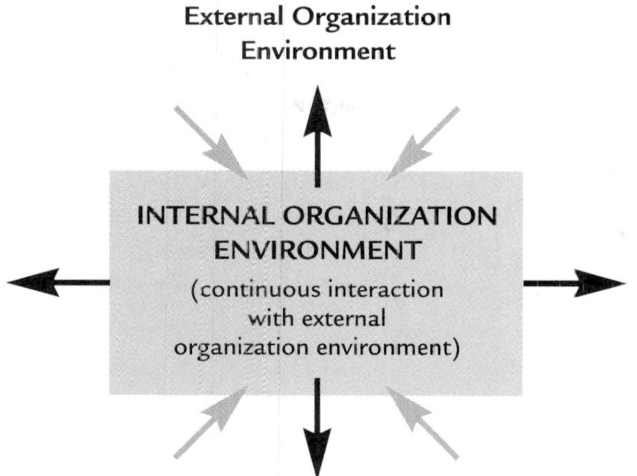

EXHIBIT A.11

Open System

Contingency Approaches

A cornerstone of scientific management and classical management theories was that there was *one best way* of doing a job, including the various functions of management. If an employee or manager performed tasks in any other way, the outcome, according to those theories, would be a reduction in effectiveness. Furthermore, these approaches specified what should characterize this one best way as it related to managerial jobs and roles: namely, unity of command, clear hierarchy of authority, precise specification of job duties, and so forth. The central theme of the "one best way" persisted for decades after the idea was first proposed by Taylor and others.

What was challenged over the years, particularly in the 1940s and 1950s, was the nature of what the one best way should be. That is, in some organizations a version of a human relations approach replaced the traditional way of operating. Thus, for such firms and agencies there was an effort to substitute a more responsive and employee-centered approach that stressed increasing employee satisfaction and morale and providing more flexible rules and regulations. It was almost as if some organizations had made 180-degree turns in their attempts to do things differently. Sometimes this change met with success, but often companies and other organizations found that they had simply exchanged one type of problem (employee dissatisfaction) for another type (casual or sloppy performance).

By the end of the 1960s, interesting research findings were emerging that suggested that perhaps what was being overlooked was how well different approaches to management (e.g., the highly structured traditional approach versus the flexible, employee-centered approach) worked in different sets of organizational circumstances.[28] In effect, the findings tended to indicate that the highly structured approach (sometimes called the **mechanistic approach**) was better suited to stable external environments, highly repetitive tasks, and employees with limited technical or professional expertise. On the other hand, the flexible approach (often labeled the **organic approach**) seemed better suited for rapidly changing and complex environments, nonrepetitive tasks, and employees with considerable training and competence. Collectively, the research findings led many management scholars to the view that the most effective type of management would be a **contingency approach** that took into account the circumstances that existed, especially the nature of the organization's environment, its technology, the tasks to be performed within the organization, and the types of individual members—with their particular capabilities—the organization could attract and retain.

In its narrower sense, then, the term *contingency approach* refers to a choice between more traditional forms of organizational structure and methods of management and more flexible and less specified structure and methods. This choice, as it relates to the process of management, is well summed up in the often-quoted statement of the former manager of the Los Angeles Dodgers, Tommy Lasorda: "Management is like holding a dove: squeeze it too hard and it dies; hold it too loose and it flies away."

mechanistic approach
highly structured traditional management approach, which may be better suited to stable external environments, highly repetitive tasks, and employees with limited technical or professional expertise

organic approach
a flexible, employee-centered management approach that seems better suited for rapidly changing and complex environments, nonrepetitive tasks, and employees with considerable training and competence

contingency approach
a management theory that emphasizes matching a structured or flexible management style to the organization's environment, its technology, the tasks to be performed, and the types of employees

In its broader sense, the contingency approach simply means that there are no general principles of management that can be applicable to *all* situations. What is best will depend on a whole host of variables, many of them beyond the manager's direct control, but most of which should be considered in deciding how to proceed. Interestingly, in management theory, we have gone from one extreme—"one best way"—to another extreme—"it all depends." Although this latter stance does not appear on the surface to provide much obvious guidance, it is clearly more suited to the current era of exceedingly rapid and often discontinuous change. It also puts the burden squarely where it belongs: on managers themselves to develop their diagnostic and analytical skills to provide effective approaches for changing circumstances.

Looking Back and Looking Forward

The history of management thought and practice up to this point in time can be compared to a flowing river. In the centuries before 1900, there was only a relatively tiny stream of ideas about how to manage organizations of any size and complexity. Like small brooks forming the source of a river, the ideas of ancient writers made their individual contributions to the development of management thought, but it was not until other events occurred, in this case the Industrial Revolution, that a major river was formed.

The needs of expanding industrial societies provided the setting and the impetus for concentrated attention on the subject of management. Even within the fertile context, however, it took the exceptional efforts and dedication of a relatively small number of people, such as Taylor, Follett, the Gilbreths, and Barnard, to increase the flow of ideas. They not only increased the size of the river, but they also changed its course, while always being strongly affected by events and circumstances of the times in which they lived. They brought greater rationality to a former haphazard process and, over time, a broader and more complex view of what the process of management was all about. It took the Hawthorne studies and the publication of their findings in the late 1930s, however, to bring additional clarity to the river of management ideas by emphasizing the centrality of the people component of organizations and the importance of the human relations that existed within them.

In the years following World War II, the management river broadened out considerably with the input of such major tributaries as the behavioral, decision-making, systems, and contingency theory approaches to management. Each of these sets of ideas added to those that preceded them and often opened up whole new ways of thinking about managerial issues. Now, here at the start of the new century, the river of management history has, in effect, arrived at a sort of delta, with a very large spread of ideas and practices. With all of the influences of significant forces for change in the external environment—such as leapfrog advances in information technology, the increasing diversity of workforces, the expanding globalization of business, and the intensifying use of "voice" (i.e., speaking up) by employees and society at large—it makes it extremely difficult to chart the future of management.

It is useful to take an overview of where management thought is currently. One conclusion that can be stated unequivocally: There is no single, grand theory or all-encompassing approach that dominates the thinking about management. Rather, as we have seen in the preceding sections, there are a variety of perspectives that have been developed in recent years that have shaped how both academic scholars and practicing managers view the challenge of managing organizations effectively. Many of these more recently developed frameworks discussed in the past few pages have been based on rigorous research and related analysis; that is, they have been based on attempts to develop a science of management (not to be confused with "scientific management" or "management science"). Such research and analysis are continuing at a brisk pace and could lead to new insights and major innovations within the next decade or so.

To reiterate, the reality today is that the competitive world of organizations, especially business organizations, is so complex and so fast-changing that no single, overall theory or approach to management can be expected to provide *the* way of thinking about this topic. Managers, and those who expect to be managers in the future, need to draw their ideas from many different sources and be able to take into account—but critically evaluate—multiple approaches to managing. That would seem to be the clear message and challenge in the years ahead.

References

Chapter 1

1. G. Davenport (trans. 1976). *Herakleitos and Diogenes*. Pt. 1, Fragment 23.
2. T. Reay, K. Golden-Biddle, and K. Germann, "Legitimizing a New Role: Small Wins and Microprocesses of Change," *Academy of Management Journal* 49 (2006): 977–996.
3. M. A. Hitt, B. W. Keats, and S. M. DeMarie, "Navigating in the New Competitive Landscape: Building Strategic Flexibility and Competitive Advantage in the 21st Century," *Academy of Management Executive* 12, no. 4 (1998): 22–42.
4. Ibid.
5. T. L. Friedman, *The World Is Flat* (New York: Farrar, Straus and Giroux, 2005).
6. M. A. Hitt, V. Franklin, and H. Zhu, "Culture, Institutions and International Strategy," *Journal of International Management* 12 (2006): 222–234.
7. Y. Luo and O. Shenkar, "The Multinational Corporation as a Multilingual Community: Language and Organization in a Global Context," *Journal of International Business Studies* 37 (2006): 321–339.
8. K. Meyer, "Globalfocusing: From Domestic Conglomerates to Global Specialists," *Journal of Management Studies* 43 (2006): 1109–1144.
9. D. G. Sirmon, M. A. Hitt, and R. D. Ireland, "Managing Firm Resources in Dynamic Environments to Create Value: Looking Inside the Black Box," *Academy of Management Review* 32 (2007): 273–292.
10. S. Thornhill, "Knowledge, Innovation and Firm Performance in High- and Low-Technology Regimes," *Journal of Business Venturing* 21 (2006): 687–703.
11. J. Salk and M. A. Lyles, "Gratitude, Nostalgia and What Now? Knowledge Acquisition and Learning a Decade Later," *Journal of International Business Studies* 38 (2007): 19–26.
12. D. Tan and J. T. Mahoney, "Why a Multinational Firm Chooses Expatriates: Integrating Resource-based, Agency and Transaction Costs Perspectives," *Journal of Management Studies* 43 (2006): 457–484.
13. A. K. Gupta, K. G. Smith, and C. E. Shalley, "The Interplay Between Exploration and Exploitation," *Academy of Management Journal* 49 (2006): 693–706; D. Lavie, "Capability Reconfiguration: An Analysis of Incumbent Responses to Technological Change," *Academy of Management Review* 31 (2006): 153–174.
14. A. M. Mulcahy, From Survival to Success: Leading in Turbulent Times, speech in the U.S. Chamber of Commerce Leadership Series, Washington, D.C., www.uschamber.com, April 2, 2003.
15. R. E. Ployhart, "Staffing in the 21st Century: New Challenges and Strategic Opportunities," *Journal of Management* 32 (2006): 868–897.
16. M. A. Hitt, L. Bierman, K. Uhlenbruck, and K. Shimizu, "The Importance of Resources in the Internationalization of Professional Service Firms: The Good, the Bad and the Ugly," *Academy of Management Journal* 49 (2006): 1137–1157.
17. M. A. Hitt, R. D. Ireland, and R. E. Hoskisson, *Strategic Management: Competitiveness and Globalization* (Cincinnati, OH: Southwestern Publishing Co., 2007).
18. A. S. DeNisi, M. A. Hitt, and S. E. Jackson, "The Knowledge-Based Approach to Sustainable Competitive Advantage," in S. E. Jackson, M. A. Hitt, and A. S. DeNisi (eds.), *Managing Knowledge for Sustained Competitive Advantage* (San Francisco, CA: Jossey-Bass, 2003).
19. S. L. Newbert, "Empirical Research on the Resource-Based View of the Firm: An Assessment and Suggestions for Future Research," *Strategic Management Journal* 28 (2007): 121–146.
20. Sirmon, Hitt, and Ireland, "Managing Firm Resources in Dynamic Environments to Create Value."
21. G. Edmondson, C. Palmeri, B. Grow, and C. Tierney, "BMW: Will Panke's High-Speed Approach Hurt the Brand?" *Business Week*, June 9, 2003, 57–60.
22. R. A. Baron, "Opportunity Recognition as Pattern Recognition: How Entrepreneurs 'Connect the Dots' to Identify New Business Opportunities," *Academy of Management Perspectives* 20 (2006): 104–119; J. M. Howell, C. M. Shea, and C. A. Higgins, "Champions of Product Innovations: Defining, Developing, and Validating a Measure of Champion Behavior," *Journal of Business Venturing* 20 (2005): 641–661.
23. M. A. Hitt, R. D. Ireland, S. M. Camp, and D. S. Sexton, *Strategic Entrepreneurship: Creating a New Mindset* (Oxford, UK: Blackwell Publishing, 2002).
24. R. McGrath and I. MacMillan, *The Entrepreneurial Mindset* (Boston: Harvard Business School Press, 2000).
25. R. D. Ireland, M. A. Hitt, and D. G. Sirmon, "A Model of Strategic Entrepreneurship: The Construct and Its Dimensions," *Journal of Management* 29 (2003): 963–989.
26. Ibid.
27. V. P. Rindova and W. H. Starbuck, "Ancient Chinese Theories of Control," *Journal of Management Inquiry* 6 (1997): 144–159.
28. D. A. Wren and R. G. Greenwood, *Management Innovators: The People and Ideas That Have Shaped Modern Business* (New York: Oxford University Press, 1998).
29. S. Wagner-Tsukamoto, "An Institutional Economic Reconstruction of Scientific Management: On the Lost Theoretical Logic of Taylorism," *Academy of Management Review* 32 (2007): 105–117.
30. Ibid.
31. S. J. Carroll and D. J. Gillen, "Are Classical Management Functions Useful in Describing Managerial Jobs and Behavior," *Academy of Management Review* 12 (1987): 39–51.
32. V. F. Misangyi, H. Elms, T. Greckhamer, and J. A. LePine, "A New Perspective on a Fundamental Debate: A Multilevel Approach to Industry, Corporate and Business Unit Effects," *Strategic Management Journal* 27 (2006): 571–590.

33. S. Brown and K. Blackmon, "Aligning Manufacturing Strategy and Business-Level Competitive Strategy in New Competitive Environments: The Case for Strategic Resonance," *Journal of Management Studies* 42 (2005): 793–815.
34. G. Dowell, "Product Line Strategies of New Entrants in an Established Industry: Evidence from the U.S. Bicycle Industry," *Strategic Management Journal* 27 (2006): 959–979.
35. S. Shane and F. Delmar, "Planning for the Market: Business Planning Before Marketing and the Continuation of Organizing Efforts," *Journal of Business Venturing* 19 (2004): 767–785.
36. J. L. Morrow, D. G. Sirmon, M. A. Hitt, and T. R. Holcomb, "Creating Value in the Face of Declining Performance: Firm Strategies and Organizational Recovery," *Strategic Management Journal* 28 (2007): 271–283.
37. M. Lindgren and J. Packendorff, "What's New in New Forms of Organizing? On the Construction of Gender in Project-based Work," *Journal of Management Studies* 43 (2006): 841–866.
38. G. Hoetker, "Do Modular Products Lead to Modular Organizations?" *Strategic Management Journal* 27 (2006): 501–518.
39. S. Karim, "Modularity in Organizational Structure: The Reconfiguration of Internally Developed and Acquired Business Units," *Strategic Management Journal* 27 (2006): 799–823.
40. A. W. Harzing, "Geographical Distance and the Role and Management of Subsidiaries: The Case of Subsidiaries Down-Under," *Asia-Pacific Journal of Management* 23 (2006): 167–185.
41. B. Erdogan, R. C. Liden, and M. L. Kraimer, "Justice and Leader-Member Exchange: The Moderating Role of Organizational Culture," *Academy of Management Journal* 49 (2006): 395–406.
42. D. S. Elenkov and I. M. Manev, "Top Management Leadership and Influence on Innovation: The Role of Sociocultural Context," *Journal of Management* 31 (2005): 381–402; R. T. Sparrowe, B. W. Soetjipto, and M. L. Kraimer, "Do Leaders' Influence Tactics Relate to Members' Helping Behaviors? It Depends on the Quality of the Relationship," *Academy of Management Journal* 49 (2006): 1194–1208.
43. R. F. Piccolo and J. A. Colquitt, "Transformational Leadership and Job Behaviors: The Mediating Role of Core Job Characteristics," *Academy of Management Journal* 49 (2006): 327–340.
44. P. Steel and C. L Konig, "Integrating Theories of Motivation," *Academy of Management Review* 31 (2006): 889–913.
45. P. Balkundi and D. A. Harrison, "Ties, Leaders and Time in Teams: Strong Inference About Network Structure's Effects on Team Viability and Performance," *Academy of Management Journal* 49 (2006): 49–68; A. Srivastava, K. M. Bartol, and E. A. Locke, "Empowering Leadership in Management Teams: Effects on Knowledge Sharing, Efficacy and Performance," *Academy of Management Journal* 49 (2006): 1239–1251.
46. T. R. Tyler and S. L. Blader, "Can Business Effectively Regulate Employee Conduct? The Antecedents of Rule Following in Work Settings," *Academy of Management Journal* 49 (2006): 1143–1158.
47. B. E. Litzky, K. A. Eddleston, and D. L. Kidder, "The Good, the Bad, and the Misguided," *Academy of Management Perspectives* 20 (2006): 91–103.
48. H. Mintzberg, "The Manager's Job: Folklore and Fact," *Harvard Business Review* 5, no. 4 (1975): 49–61.
49. G. K. Lee, "The Significance of Network Resources in the Race to Enter Emerging Product Markets: The Convergence of Telephony Communications and Computer Networking, 1989–2001," *Strategic Management Journal* 28 (2007): 17–37.
50. J. H. Dyer and N. W. Hatch, "Relation-specific Capabilities and Barriers to Knowledge Transfers: Creating Advantage Through Network Relationships," *Strategic Management Journal* 27 (2006): 701–719.
51. T. Talaulicar, J. Grundei, and A. V. Werder, "Strategic Decision Making in Start-ups: The Effect of Top Management Team Organization and Processes on Speed and Comprehensiveness," *Journal of Business Venturing* 20: 519–541.
52. E. Dane and M. G. Pratt, "Exploring Intuition and Its Role in Managerial Decision Making," *Academy of Management Review* 32 (2007): 33–54.
53. R. Stewart, "A Model for Understanding Managerial Jobs and Behavior," *Academy of Management Review* 7 (1982): 7–13.
54. M. W. McCall and M. M. Lombardo, *Off the Track* (Greensboro, NC: Center for Creative Leadership, 1983).

Chapter 2

1. P. Hosking, "Citigroup Agree to Pay," *Timesonline,* June 29, 2005.
2. M. Friedman, "The Social Responsibility of Business Is to Increase Its Profits," *New York Magazine,* September 13, 1970, 32–33, 122, 126.
3. A. Smith, *An Inquiry into the Nature and Causes of the Wealth of Nations,* ed. R H. Campbell and A. S. Skinner (Oxford, UK: Clarendon Press, 1976).
4. Friedman, "The Social Responsibility of Business Is to Increase Its Profits," 32; C. E. Bagley, "The Ethical Leader's Decision Tree," *Harvard Business Review* 81, no. 2 (2003): 18–19.
5. J. Schmeltzer, "Taco Bell Sales Hurt by E. Coli Outbreak," *Chicago Tribune,* December 15, 2006.
6. S. K. May, G. Cheney, and J. Roper, eds., *The Debate over Corporate Social Responsibility*, (Oxford University Press, 2007); P. Kotler and N. Lee, *Corporate Social Responsibility* (Hoboken, NJ: John Wiley & Sons, 2005).
7. J. Joha, L. Serbet, and A. Sundaram, "Cross-Border Liability of Multinational Enterprises: Border Taxes and Capital Structure," *Financial Management* (Winter 1991): 54–67; C. Handy, "What's a Business For?" *Harvard Business Review* 80, no. 12 (2003): 49–55.
8. Joha, Serbet, and Sundaram, "Cross-Border Liability of Multinational Enterprises: Border Taxes and Capital Structure."
9. A. McWilliams and D. Siegel, "Corporate Social Responsibility and Financial Performance: Correlation or Misspecification?" *Strategic Management Journal* 21

(2000): 603–609; B. Ruf, K. Muralidhar, R. Brown, J. Janney, and K. Paul. "An Empirical Investigation of the Relationship Between Change in Corporate Social Performance and Financial Performance: A Stakeholder Theory Perspective," *Journal of Business Ethics* 32, no. 2 (2001): 143–156; C. Sanchez, "Value Shift: Why Companies Must Merge Social and Financial Imperatives to Achieve Superior Performance," *Academy of Management Executive* 17, no. 2 (2000): 142–144; J. Griffin and J. F. Mahon, "The Corporate Social Performance and Corporate Financial Performance Debate: Twenty-five Years of Incomparable Research," *Business and Society* 36 (1997): 5–31.

10. McWilliams and Siegel, "Corporate Social Responsibility and Financial Performance: Correlation or Misspecification?"; B. Ruf, K. Muralidhar, R. Brown, J. Janney, and K. Paul, "An Empirical Investigation of the Relationship Between Change in Corporate Social Performance and Financial Performance: A Stakeholder Theory Perspective"; Sanchez, "Value Shift: Why Companies Must Merge Social and Financial Imperatives to Achieve Superior Performance"; Griffin and Mahon, "The Corporate Social Performance and Corporate Financial Performance Debate: Twenty-five Years of Incomparable Research."
11. M. E. Porter and M. R. Kramer, "Strategy and Society: The Link Between Competitive Advantage and Corporate Social Responsibility," *Harvard Business Review* (December 2006): 78–93; M. E. Porter and M. R. Kramer, "The Competitive Advantage and Corporate Philanthropy," *Harvard Business Review* (December 2002); D. Grayson and A. Hodges, *Corporate Social Opportunity* (Austin, TX: Greenleaf, 2004).
12. M. A. Hitt, R. D. Ireland, and R. E. Hoskisson, *Strategic Management: Competitiveness and Globalization* (Cincinnati, OH: South-Western Publishing, 2005).
13. J. B. Cullen, K. Parboteeah, and M. Hoegl, "Cross-National Differences in Managers' Willingness to Justify Ethically Suspect Behaviors: A Test of Institutional Anomie Theory," *Academy of Management Journal* 47, no. 3 (2004): 411–421.
14. D. Peterson, A. Rhoads, and B. C. Vaught, "Ethical Beliefs of Business Professionals: A Study of Gender, Age, and External Factors," *Journal of Business Ethics* 31, no. 3 (2001): 225–232; E. Marnburg, "The Questionable Use of Moral Development Theory in Studies of Business Ethics: Discussion and Empirical Findings," *Journal of Business Ethics* 32, no. 4 (2001): 275–283.
15. J. Tsalikis, B. Seaton, and P. Tomaras, "A New Perspective on Cross-Cultural Ethical Evaluations: The Use of Conjoint Analysis," *Journal of Business Ethics* 35, no. 4 (February 2002): 281–292; L. Thorne and S. B. Saunders, "The Socio-Cultural Embeddedness of Individuals' Ethical Reasoning in Organizations (Cross-Cultural Ethics)," *Journal of Business Ethics* 35, no. (February 2002): 1–14; J. B. Hamilton III and S. B. Knouse, "Multinational Enterprise Decision Principles for Dealing with Cross Cultural Ethical Conflicts," *Journal of Business Ethics* 31, no. 1 (May 2001): 77–94; C. J. Robertson and W. F. Crittenden, "Mapping Moral Philosophies: Strategic Implications for Multinational Firms," *Strategic Management Journal* 24, no. 4 (2003): 385–392.
16. Cullen, Parboteeah, and Hoegl, "Cross-National Differences in Managers' Willingness to Justify Ethically Suspect Behaviors: A Test of Institutional Anomie Theory"; Thorne and Saunders, "The Socio-Cultural Embeddedness of Individuals' Ethical Reasoning in Organizations (Cross-Cultural Ethics)"; A. J. Dubinsky, M. A. Jolson, M. Kotabe, and C. U. Lim, "A Cross-National Investigation of Industrial Salespeople's Ethical Perceptions," *Journal of International Business Studies* (Fourth Quarter 1991): 651–669; J. K. Giacobbe-Miller, D. J. Miller, W. Zhang, and V. I. Victorov, "Country and Organization-level Adaptation to Foreign Workplace Ideologies: A Comparative Study of Distributive Justice Values in China, Russia and the United States," *Journal of International Business Studies* 34, no. 4 (2003): 389–406.
17. A. J. Dubinsky, M. A. Jolson, M. Kotabe, and C. U. Lim, "A Cross-National Investigation of Industrial Salespeople's Ethical Perceptions," *Journal of International Business Studies* 4 (1991): 651–669.
18. A. Kolk and R. Van Tulder, "Ethics in International Business," *Journal of World Business* (February 2004) 49–61; J. Tsui and C. Windsor, "Some Cross-Cultural Evidence of Ethical Reasoning," *Journal of Business Ethics* 31 (2001): 143–150; Robertson and Crittenden, "Mapping Moral Philosophies: Strategic Implications for Multinational Firms."
19. L. Stroh, M. E. Mendenhall, J. S. Black, and H. B. Gregersen, *International Assignments: An Integration of Research and Practice* (Hillsdale, NJ: Erlbaum, 2005).
20. C. Hess and K. Hey, "Good Doesn't Always Mean Right," *Across the Board* 38, no. 4 (2001): 61–64; A Chia and L. S. Mee, "The Effects of Issue Characteristics on the Recognition of Moral Issues," *Journal of Business Ethics* 27 (2000): 255–269; A Gaudine and L. Thorne, "Emotion and Ethical Decision Making in Organizations," *Journal of Business Ethics* 31, no. 2 (2001): 175–187.
21. J. Rawls, *A Theory of Justice* (Cambridge, MA: Harvard University Press, 1971); J. Greenberg, "A Taxonomy of Organizational Justice Theories," *Academy of Management Review* 12 (1987): 9–22; Giacobbe-Miller, Miller, Zhang, and Victorov, "Country and Organization-level Adaptation to Foreign Workplace Ideologies: A Comparative Study of Distributive Justice Values in China, Russia and the United States."
22. T. Donaldson and T. W. Dunfee, "Toward a Unified Conception of Business Ethics," *Academy of Management Review* 19 (1994): 252–84; J. A. Colquitt, R. Noe, and C. L. Jackson, "Justice in Teams: Antecedents and Consequences of Procedural Justice Climate," *Personnel Psychology* 55, no. 1 (2002): 83–109.
23. R. Pillai, E. Williams, and J. J. Tan. "Are the Scales Tipped in Favor of Procedural or Distributive Justice? An Investigation of the U.S., India, Germany, and Hong Kong (China)," *International Journal of Conflict Management* 12, no. 4 (2001): 312–332; D. Fields, M. Pang, and C. Chiu, "Distributive and Procedural Justice as Predictors of Employee Outcomes in Hong Kong," *Journal of Organizational Behavior* 21, no. 5 (2000): 547–562; Y. Cohen-Charash and E. Spector, "The Role of Justice in Organizations: A Meta-Analysis," *Organizational Behavior and Human Decision Processes* 86, no. 2 (2001): 278–321; J. A. Colquitt,

D. E. Conlon, M. J. Wesson, C. Porter, and Y. K. Ng, "Justice at the Millennium: A Meta-Analytic Review of 25 Years of Organizational Justice Research," *Journal of Applied Psychology* 86, no. 3 (2001): 424–445; S. L. Blader, C. C. Chang, and T. R. Tyler, "Procedural Justice and Retaliation in Organizations: Comparing Cross-Nationally the Importance of Fair Group Processes," *International Journal of Conflict Management* 12, no. 4 (2001): 295–311; J. Greenberg, "Who Stole the Money, and When? Individual and Situational Determinants of Employee Theft," *Organizational Behavior and Human Decision Processes* 89, no. 1 (2002): 985–1003; B. J. Tepper and E. C. Taylor, "Relationships Among Supervisors' and Subordinates' Procedural Justice Perceptions and Organizational Citizenship Behaviors," *Academy of Management Journal* 46, no. 1 (2003): 97–105.

24. J. Dietz, S. L. Robinson, R. Folger, R. A. Baron, and M. Schultz, "The Impact of Community Violence and an Organization's Procedural Justice Climate on Workplace Aggression," *Academy of Management Journal* 46, no. 3 (2003): 317–326.
25. J. M. Jones, "Ethical Decision Making by Individuals in Organizations: An Issue-Contingent Model," *Academy of Management Review* 16 (1991): 366–395.
26. Ibid.
27. J. Paolillo and S. J. Vitell, "An Empirical Investigation of the Influence of Selected Personal, Organizational and Moral Intensity Factors on Ethical Decision Making," *Journal of Business Ethics* 35, no. 1 (2002): 65–74.
28. A. Chia and L. S. Mee, "The Effects of Issue Characteristics on the Recognition of Moral Issues," *Journal of Business Ethics* 27, no. 3 (2000): 255–269.
29. D. Carlson, K. M. Kacmar, and L. L. Wadsworth, "The Impact of Moral Intensity Dimensions on Ethical Decision Making: Assessing the Relevance of Orientation," *Journal of Managerial Issues* 14, no. 1 (2002): 15–30; J. M. Dukerich, M. J. Waller, E. George, and G. Huber, "Moral Intensity and Managerial Problem Solving," *Journal of Business Ethics* 24, no. 1 (2000): 29–38.
30. J. Katz, "Study: Ethical Misconduct Rising," *Industry Week*, October 20, 2005.
31. S. Ring and A. Van De Ven, "Developmental Process of Cooperative Interorganizational Relationships," *Academy of Management Review* 19 (1994): 90–118.
32. D. Robin, M. Giallourakis, F. R. David, and T. Moritz, "A Different Look at Codes of Ethics," *Business Horizons* (January–February 1989): 66–73.
33. C. C. Langlois and B. B. Schlegelmilch, "Do Corporate Codes of Ethics Reflect National Character? Evidence from Europe and the United States," *Journal of International Business Studies* (Fourth Quarter 1991): 519–539.
34. G. Wood, "A Cross-Cultural Comparison of the Content of Codes of Ethics: USA, Canada, and Australia," *Journal of Business Ethics* 25, no. 4 (2000): 281–298.
35. Robin, et al., "A Different Look at Codes of Ethics."
36. Ibid.
37. B. Ettorre, "Ethics Inc.: The Buck Stops Here," *HR Focus* (June 1992): 11.
38. L. White and L. W. Lam, "A Proposed Infrastructural Model for the Establishment of Organizational Ethical Systems," *Journal of Business Ethics* 28, no. 1 (2000): 35–42; S. A. DiPiazza. "Ethics in Action," *Executive Excellence* 19, no. 1 (2002): 15–16.
39. C. Verschoor, "To Talk About Ethics, We Must Train on Ethics," *Strategic Finance* 81, no. 10 (2000): 24, 26; T. Donaldson, "Editor's Comments: Taking Ethics Seriously—A Mission Now More Possible," *Academy of Management Review* 28, no. 3 (2003): 363–366.
40. "Stronger Than Ever," *LM Today,* (January 2004): 8; K. Shelton, "The Dilbert Dilemma," *Executive Excellence*, (November 2003): 2; R. Carey, "The Ethics Challenge," *Successful Meetings* 47, no. 5 (1998): 57–58.
41. A. Pomeroy, "Whistleblowing: When It Works—and Why," *Academy of Management Perspectives* 20, no. 3 (2006): 128–130; M. McClearn, "A Snitch in Time," *Canadian Business,* June 18, 2004, 60–67; M. Miceli and J. Near, *Blowing the Whistle* (Lexington, MA: Lexington Books, 1992).
42. Miceli and Near, *Blowing the Whistle*.
43. C. Daniels, "It's a Living Hell," *Fortune*, April 15, 2002, 367–368.
44. M. Miceli and J. Near, "The Relationships Among Beliefs, Organizational Position, and Whistle Blowing Status: A Discriminant Analysis," *Academy of Management Journal* 27 (1984): 687–705.
45. M. Miceli and J. Near, "Whistle Blowing: Reaping the Benefits," *Academy of Management Executive* 8 (1994): 65–71.
46. Miceli and Near, *Blowing the Whistle.*
47. R. Sims and J. Brinkmann, "Leaders as Moral Role Models: The Case of John Gutfreund at Salomon Brothers," *Journal of Business Ethics* 35, no. 4 (2002): 327–339; R. Galford and A. S. Drapeau, "The Enemies of Trust," *Harvard Business Review* 81, no. 2 (2003): 88–95; L. R. Offermann and A. B. Malamut, "When Leaders Harass: The Impact of Target Perceptions of Organizational Leadership and Climate on Harassment Reporting and Outcomes," *Journal of Applied Psychology* 87, no. 5 (2002): 885–893.
48. *Columbia Journalism Review*, 39, no. 4 (November–December 2000): 13.
49. M. Zuckerman, "Policing the Corporate Suites," U.S. *News & World Report*, January 19, 2004, 72; *Modern Healthcare* 28, no. 16 (April 20, 1998): 54–56.

Chapter 3

1. M. A. Hitt, R. D. Ireland, and R. E. Hoskisson, *Strategic Management: Competitiveness and Globalization* (Cincinnati, OH: Thomson/South-Western Publishing, 2007); P. Williamson and M. Zeng, "Strategies for Competing in a Changed China," *MIT Sloan Management Review* 45, no. 4 (2004): 85–91.
2. T. L. Friedman, *The World Is Flat* (New York: Farrar, Straus and Giroux, 2005).
3. M. Mandel, "Can Anyone Steer This Economy?" *BusinessWeek*, November 20, 2006, 56–62.
4. M. A. Hitt, H. Li, and W. Worthington, "Emerging Markets as Learning Laboratories: Learning Behaviors of Local Firms and Foreign Entrants in Different Institutional Contexts," *Management and Organization Review* 1 (2005): 353–380.

5. Friedman, *The World Is Flat*.
6. Ibid.
7. D. Wilson and R. Purushothaman, "Dreaming with BRICs: The Path to 2050". Goldman Sachs Global Economics Paper No. 9, 2003.
8. R. D. Ireland, M. A. Hitt, S. M. Camp, and D. S. Sexton, "Integrating Entrepreneurship and Strategic Management Actions to Create Firm Wealth," *Academy of Management Executive* 46, no. 34 (2001): 49–63.
9. C. Fishman, "No Satisfaction," *Fast Company,* December 2006, 82–92.
10. Wal-Mart International Fact Sheet, www.walmartfacts.com, November 2006.
11. M. A. Hitt, R. M. Holmes, T. Miller, and M. P. Salmador, Modeling country institutional profiles: The dynamics of institutional environments. Paper presented at the Strategic Management Society Conference, November, Vienna, Austria, 2006.
12. S. Chetty, K. Eriksson, and J. Lindbergh. "The Effect of Specificity of Experience on a Firm's Perceived Importance of Institutional Knowledge in an Ongoing Business," *Journal of International Business Studies* 37 (2006): 699–712.
13. R. Hoskisson, L. Eden, C.M. Lau, and M. Wright, "Strategy in Emerging Economies," *Academy of Management Journal* (Special Research Forum on Strategies in Emerging Economies) 433 (2000): 249–67.
14. J. Dunning, "Reevaluating the Benefits of Foreign Direct Investment," *Transnational Corporations* 34 (1994): 23–51.
15. *Business Week*, "The Jury Is Out," December 8, 2006, 106.
16. S. Labaton, "S.E.C. Eases Regulations on Business," *New York Times*, December 14, 2006, www.nytimes.com.
17. M. A. Hitt, M. T. Dacin, E. Levitas, J.-L. Arregle, and A. Borza, "Partner Selection in Developed and Emerging Market Contexts: Resource-based and Organizational Learning Perspectives," *Academy of Management Journal* 434 (2000): 4349–4467.
18. T. Isobe, S.Makino, and D.B. Montgomery, "Resource Commitment, Entry Timing, and Market Performance of Foreign Direct Investments in Emerging Economies: The Case of Japanese International Joint Ventures in China," *Academy of Management Journal* 43 (2000): 468–484.
19. S. M. Lee, "South Korea: From the Land of Morning Calm to ICT Hotbed," *Academy of Management Executive 17* (2003): 7–18.
20. Hitt, Holmes, Miller, Salmador, "Modeling Country Institutional Profiles."
21. S. Chetty, K. Eriksson, and J. Lindbergh, "The Effect of Specificity of Experience on a Firm's Perceived Importance of Institutional Knowledge in an Ongoing Business," *Journal of International Business Studies* 37 (2006): 699–712.
22. C. C. Kwok and S. Tadesse, "The MNC as an Agent of Change for Host-Country Institutions: FDI and Corruption," *Journal of International Business Studies* 37 (2006): 767–785.
23. A. Cuervo-Cazurra, "Who Cares About Corruption?" *Journal of International Business Studies* 37 (2006): 807–822.
24. K. Leung, R. S. Bhagat, N. R. Buchan, M. Erez, and C. B. Gibson, "Culture and International Business: Recent Advances and Their Implications for the Future," *Journal of International Business Studies* 36 (2005): 357–378.
25. P. C. Earley, "Leading Cultural Research in the Future: A Matter of Paradigms and Taste," *Journal of International Business Studies* 37 (2006): 922–931.
26. R. Steers and J. S. Black, *Organization Behavior* (New York: HarperCollins, 1994).
27. G. Hofstede, *Culture's Consequences* (Beverly Hills, CA: Sage, 1980); G. Hofstede, *Cultures and Organizations* (Berkshire, U.K.: McGraw-Hill, 1994); R. J. House, P. J. Hanges, et al., *Culture, Leadership and Organizations: The Globe Study of 62 Societies* (Thousand Oaks, CA: Sage, 2004).
28. D. A. Waldman, A. S. de Luque, N. Washburn, R. J. House, et al, "Cultural and Leadership Predictors of Corporate Social Responsibility Values of Top Management: A GLOBE Study of 15 Countries," *Journal of International Business Studies* 37 (2006): 823–837.
29. Hitt Ireland, and Hoskisson, *Strategic Management.*
30. H. J. Sapienza, E. Autio, G. George, and S. Zahra, "A Capabilities Perspective on the Effects of Early Internationalization on Firm Survival and Growth," *Academy of Management Review* 31 (2006): 914–933.
31. E. Maitland, E. L. Rose, and S. Nicholas, "How Firms Grow: Clustering as a Dynamic Model of Internationalization," *Journal of International Business Studies,* 36 (2005): 435–451.
32. Hitt, Ireland, and Hoskisson, *Strategic Management.*
33. N. Zamiska and V. O'Connell, "Philip Morris in Talks to Make Marlboro in China," *Wall Street Journal,* April 21, 2005, B1–B2.
34. J. S. Harrison, M. A. Hitt, R. E. Hoskisson, and R. D. Ireland, "Resource Complementarity in Business Combinations: Extending the Logic to Organizational Alliances," *Journal of Management* 27 (2001): 679–690.
35. J. J. Reuer and M. Zollo, "Termination Outcomes of Research Alliances," *Research Policy* 34 (1) (2005): 101–115.
36. R. D. Ireland, M. A. Hitt, and D. Vaidyanath, "Alliance Management as a Source of Competitive Advantage," *Journal of Management* 28 (2002): 413–446.
37. Chetty, Eriksson, and Lindbergh, "The Effect of Specificity on Experience . . ."
38. Hitt, Dacin, Levitas, Arregle, and Borza, "Partner Selection in Developed and Emerging Market Contexts . . ."
39. M. A. Hitt, D. Ahlstrom, M. T. Dacin, E. Levitas, and L. Svobodina, "The Institutional Effects on Strategic Alliance Partner Selection in Transition Economies: China Versus Russia," *Organization Science* 15 (2004): 173–185.
40. K. Shimizu, M. A. Hitt, D. Vaidyanath, and V. Pisano, "Theoretical Foundations of Cross-border Mergers and Acquisitions: A Review of Current Research and Recommendations for the Future," *Journal of International Management* 10 (2004): 307–353.
41. J. Levine, "Europe: Gold Mines and Quicksand," *Forbes,* April 12, 2004, 76.
42. H. G. Barkema, J. H. J. Bell, and J. M. Pennings, "Foreign Entry, Cultural Barriers and Learning," *Strategic Management Journal* 17 (1996): 151–166.

43. M. A. Hitt, V. Franklin, and H. Zhu, "Culture, Institutions and International Strategy," *Journal of International Management* 12 (2006): 222–234.
44. U. Weitzel and S. Berns, "Cross-border Takeovers, Corruption, and Related Aspects of Governance," *Journal of International Business Studies* 37 (2006): 786–806.
45. A. W. Harzing, "Acquisitions Versus Greenfield Investments: International Strategy and Management of Entry Modes," *Strategic Management Journal* 23 (2002): 211–227.
46. B. Elango, "The Influence of Plant Characteristics on the Entry Mode Choice of Overseas Firms," *Journal of Operations Management* 23 (2005): 65–79.
47. B. Stanley, "United Parcel Service to Open a Hub in Shanghai," *Wall Street Journal*, July 8, 2005, B2; B. Stanley, "FedEx Plans Hub in Guangzhou: Facility to Begin Operation in 2008 as Cargo Industry Tries to Claim Turf in Asia," *Asian Wall Street Journal*, July 14, 2005, A3.
48. D. Lee, "EBay to Enlist a Partner in China," *Los Angeles Times,* December 20, 2006, www.latimes.com; K. Hafner and B. Stone, "EBay Is Expected to Close Its Auction Site in China," *New York Times,* December 19, 2006, www.nytimes.com.
49. Hitt, Ireland, and Hoskisson, *Strategic Management.*
50. A.-W. Harzing and A. Sorge, "The Relative Impact of Country of Origin and Universal Contingencies in Internationalization Strategies and Corporate Control in Multinational Enterprises: Worldwide and European Perspectives," *Organization Studies* 24 (2003): 187–214.
51. G. Jones, "Control, Performance and Knowledge Transfers in Large Multinationals: Unilever in the United States, 1945–1980," *Business History Review* 76 (2002): 435–478.
52. J. P. Millikin and D. Fu, "The Global Leadership of Carlos Ghosn at Nissan," *Thunderbird International Business Review* 47, no. 1 (2005): 121–137.
53. E. Hall, *Beyond Culture* (Garden City, NY: Doubleday, 1976); S. A. Zahra, R. D. Ireland, and M.A. Hitt, "International Expansion by New Venture Firms: International Diversity, Mode of Entry, Technological Learning and Performance," *Academy of Management Journal* 43 (2000): 925–950.
54. D. L. Shapiro, S. A. Furst, G. M. Spreitzer, and M. A. Von Glinow, "Transnational Teams in the Electronic Age: Are Team Identity and High Performance at Risk?" *Journal of Organizational Behavior* 23 (2002): 455–467.
55. Y. Shin, "A Person–Environment Fit Model for Virtual Organizations," *Journal of Management,* 30 (2004): 725–743.
56. S. L. Jarvenpaa and D. E. Leidner, "Communication and Trust in Virtual Teams," *Organization Science,* 10 (1999): 791–815.
57. M. A. Hitt, C. C. Miller, and A. Colella, *Organizational Behavior: A Strategic Approach* (Hoboken, NJ: John Wiley & Sons, 2006).
58. M. A. Hitt, L. Tihanyi, T. Miller, and B. Connelly, "International Diversification: Antecedents, Outcomes and Moderators," *Journal of Management* 32 (2006): 831–867.
59. K. E. Meyer, "Global Focus in: From Domestic Conglomerates to Global Specialist," *Journal of Management Studies* 43 (2006): 1109–1144.
60. M. Javidan, R. M. Steers, and M. A. Hitt (eds.), *The Global Mindset. Advances in International Management,* Volume 19 (Amsterdam: Elsevier Science, 2007).
61. G. Colvin, "Lafley and Immelt: In Search of Billions," *Fortune,* December 11, 2006, 70–72.
62. J. Sheth, "Clash of Cultures or Fusion of Cultures? Implications for International Business," *Journal of International Management* 12 (2006): 218–221.

Chapter 4

1. W. Edwards, R. Miles, and D. von Winterfeldt, eds., *Advances in Decision Analysis: From Foundations to Applications* (Cambridge: Cambridge University Press, 2007); J. F. Yates, E. S. Veinott, and A. L. Patalano, "Hard Decisions, Bad Decisions: On Decision Quality and Decision Aiding," in *Emerging Perspectives on Judgment and Decision Research*, eds. S. L. Schneider and J. Shanteau (Cambridge: Cambridge University Press, 2003), 13–63; G. R. Ungson and D. N. Braunstein, *Decision Making* (Boston: Kent, 1982).
2. D. Miller and M. Star, *The Structure of Human Decisions* (Upper Saddle River, NJ: Prentice Hall, 1967).
3. A. M. Isen and A. A. Labroo, "Some Ways in Which Positive Affect Facilitates Decision Making and Judgment," in *Emerging Perspectives on Judgment and Decision Research*, eds. S. L. Schneider and J. Shanteau (New York: Cambridge University Press, 2003), 365–393; D. Kahneman, "A Perspective on Judgment and Choice," *American Psychologist* 58 (2003): 697–720; J. E. Dutton and S. E. Jackson, "Categorizing Strategic Issues: Links to Organizational Action," *Academy of Management Review* 12 (1987), 76–90; A. Drach-Zahavy and M. Erez, "Challenge Versus Threat Effects on the Goal-Performance Relationship," *Organizational Behavior and Human Decision Processes* 88, no. 2 (2002): 667–682.
4. H. A. Simon, *The New Science of Management Decisions* (Upper Saddle River, NJ: Prentice Hall, 1977); J. Parking, "Organizational Decision Making and the Project Manager," *International Journal of Project Management* 14, no. 5 (1996), 257–263.
5. D. C. Ganster, "Executive Job Demands: Suggestions from a Stress and Decision-Making Perspective," *Academy of Management Review* 30 (2005): 492–502.
6. H. A. Simon, *Administrative Behavior* (New York: The Free Press, 1957).
7. J. G. March and H. A. Simon, *Organizations* (New York: Wiley, 1958), 140–141.
8. R. Pieters, H. Baumgartner, and R. Bagozzi, "Biased Memory for Prior Decision Making: Evidence from a Longitudinal Field Study," *Organizational Behavior and Human Decision Processes* 99 no. 1 (2006): 34–48; F. Phillips, "The Distortion of Criteria After Decision-Making," *Organizational Behavior and Human Decision Processes* 88 no. 2 (2002): 769–784.
9. P. Soelberg, "Unprogrammed Decision Making," *Industrial Management* (1967): 19–29; D. Cray, G. H. Haines, and G. R. Mallory "Programmed Strategic Decision Making," *British Journal of Management* 5, no. 3 (1994): 191–204.
10. G. Loveman, "Diamonds in the Data Mine," *Harvard Business Review* 81 no. 5 (2003): 109–113; E. Bonabeau,

"Don't Trust Your Gut," *Harvard Business Review* 81 no. 5 (2003): 116–123.

11. E. Dane and M. G. Pratt, "Exploring Intuition and Its Role in Managerial Decision Making," *Academy of Management Review* 32 (2007): 33–54; J. Johnson, et al. "Vigilant and Hypervigilant Decision Making," *Journal of Applied Psychology* 82, no. 4 (1997): 614–622; Bonabeau "Don't Trust Your Gut."
12. D. A. Rettinger; and R. Hastie, "Content Effects on Decision Making," *Organizational Behavior and Human Decision Processes* 85, no. 2 (2001): 336–359.
13. March and Simon, *Organizations.*
14. M. Bazerman, *Judgment in Managerial Decision Making* (Hoboken, NJ: John Wiley & Sons, 2005); T. R. Mitchell and J. R. Larson, *People in Organizations* (New York: McGraw-Hill, 1987).
15. T. A. Louie, "Hindsight Bias and Outcome-Consistent Thoughts when Observing and Making Service Provider Decisions," *Organizational Behavior and Human Decision Processes* 98 no. 1 (2005): 88–95.
16. S. Venkatraman, J. A. Aloysius, and F. D. Davis, "Multiple Prospect Framing and Decision Behavior: The Mediational Roles of Perceived Riskiness and Perceived Ambiguity," *Organizational Behavior and Human Decision Processes* 101, no. 1 (2006): 59–73.
17. B. J. Weber and G. B. Chapman, "The Combined Effects of Risk and Time on Choice: Does Uncertainty Eliminate the Immediacy Effect? Does Delay Eliminate the Certainty Effect?" *Organizational Behavior and Human Decision Processes* 96, no. 2 (2005): 104–118.
18. I. Janis, *Victims of Groupthink* (Boston: Houghton Mifflin, 1972); M. E. Turner and A. R. Pratkamis, "Twenty-five Years of Groupthink Theory and Research: Lessons from the Evaluation of a Theory," *Organizational Behavior and Human Decision Processes* 73 nos. 2, 3 (1998): 105–115; J. K. Esser; "Alive and Well After 25 Years: A Review of Groupthink Research," *Organizational Behavior and Human Decision Processes* 73 nos. 2, 3 (1998): 116–141.
19. S. Schulz-Hardt, M. Jochims, and D. Frey, "Productive Conflict in Group Decision Making: Genuine and Contrived Dissent as Strategies to Counteract Biased Information Seeking," *Organizational Behavior and Human Decision Processes* 88, no. 2 (2002): 563–586.
20. B. M. Staw, "The Escalation of Commitment to a Course of Action," *Academy of Management Review* 6 (1981): 577–587; G. Whyte, "Escalating Commitment in Individual and Group Decision Making: A Prospect Theory Approach," *Organizational Behavior and Human Decision Processes* 54, no. 3 (1993): 430–455; G. Whyte, A. M. Saks, and S. Hook, "When Success Breeds Failure," *Journal of Organizational Behavior* 18, no. 5 (1997): 415–432; D. R. Bobocel and J. P. Meyer, "Escalating Commitment to a Failing Course of Action," *Journal of Applied Psychology* 79, no. 3 (1994): 360–363; J. Ross and M. Straw, "Organizational Escalation and Exit: Lessons from the Shoreham Nuclear Power Plant," *Academy of Management Journal* 36, no. 4 (1993): 701–732.
21. G. McNamara, H. Moon, and P. Bromiley, "Banking on Commitment: Intended and Unintended Consequences of an Organization's Attempt to Attenuate Escalation of Commitment," *Academy of Management Journal* 45, no. 2 (2002): 443–452.
22. Staw, "The Escalation of Commitment to a Course of Action," 578.
23. S. E. Seibert, S. R. Silver, W. A. Randolph, "Taking Empowerment to the Next Level: A Multiple-Level Model of Empowerment, Performance, and Satisfaction," *Academy of Management Journal* 47, no. 3 (2004): 332–349; R. C. Liden, S. J. Wayne, and R. T. Sparrowe, "An Examination of the Mediating Role of Psychological Empowerment on the Relations Between the Job, Interpersonal Relationships, and Work Outcomes," *Journal of Applied Psychology* 85 (2000): 407–416; N. Margulies and J. S. Black, "Perspectives on the Implementation of Participative Approaches," *Human Resource Management* 26, no. 3 (1987): 385–412.
24. J. S. Black and H. B. Gregersen, "Participative Decision Making: An Integration of Multiple Perspectives," *Human Relations* 50 (1997): 859–878.
25. V. Vroom and P. Yetton, *Leadership and Decision Making* (Pittsburgh: University of Pittsburgh Press, 1973); V. Vroom and A. Jago, *The New Leadership: Managing Participation in Organizations* (Upper Saddle River, NJ: Prentice Hall, 1988)
26. R. Ebert and T. Mitchell, *Organizational Decision Processes Concepts and Analysis* (New York: Crane, Russak, 1975).
27. S. S. K. Lam, X.-P. Chen, and J. Schaubroeck, "Participative Decision Making and Employee Performance in Different Cultures: The Moderating Effects of Allocentrism, Idiocentrism and Efficacy," *Academy of Management Journal* 45, no. 5 (2002): 905–914.
28. R. Hof, "Why Once Ambitious Computer Firm Quit," *Peninsula Times Tribune,* September 29, 1984, B1.
29. K. Eisenhardt and L. J. Bourgeois, "Making Fast Strategic Decisions in High Velocity Environments," *Academy of Management Journal* 32 (1989): 543–576; S. L. Brown and K. M. Eisenhardt, *Competing on the Edge: Strategy as Structured Chaos* (Boston: Harvard Business School Press, 1998); J. R. Hough and M. A. White, "Environmental Dynamism and Strategic Decision-Making Rationality: An Examination at the Decision Level," *Strategic Management Journal* 24, no. 5 (2003): 481–489.
30. M. Bazerman, *Judgment in Managerial Decision Making* (Hoboken, NJ: John Wiley & Sons, 2005); W. Edwards, R. Miles, and D. von Winterfeldt, eds., *Advances in Decision Analysis: From Foundations to Applications* (Cambridge: Cambridge University Press, 2007); C. Schwenk and H. Thomas, "Formulating the Mess: The Role of Decision Aids in Problem Formulation," *Omega* 11 (1983): 239–252.
31. P. L. Roth, "Group Approaches to the Schmidt-Hunter Global Estimation Procedure," *Organizational Behavior and Human Decision Processes* 59, no. 3 (1994): 428–451; A. Van deVen and A. Delbecq, "The Effectiveness of Nominal, Delphi, and Interacting Group Decision Making Processes," *Academy of Management Journal* 17 (1974): 607–626.
32. B. B. Baltes, M. W. Dickson, M. P. Sherman, C. C. Bauer, and J. S. LaGanke "Computer-Mediated Communication and Group Decision Making: A Meta-Analysis." *Organizational Behavior and Human Decision Processes* 87,

no. 1 (2002): 156–179; Bonabeau, "Don't Trust Your Gut."
33. M. Wells, "Lord of the Skies" *Fortune*, October 14, 2002.
34. J. Levere, "Low-fare Airlines Aims to Build on Attitude and Hostility," *New York Times*, December 1, 2000.
35. K. Dawson, "Workforce Optimization Helps Airline Improve Service Levels by 38%," CommWeb.com, October 21, 2002.
36. Ibid.
37. Baltes, Dickson, Sherman, Bauer, and LaGanke, "Computer-Mediated Communication and Group Decision Making: A Meta-Analysis."
38. March and Simon, *Organizations*.

Chapter 5

1. C. Fishman, "The Wal-Mart Effect and a Decent Society: Who Knew Shopping Was so Important?" *Academy of Management Perspectives* 20, no. 3 (2006): 6–25.
2. M. A. Hitt, R. D. Ireland, and R. E. Hoskisson, *Strategic Management: Competitiveness and Globalization* (Cincinnati, OH: South-Western Publishing Company, 2007).
3. M. A. Hitt, C. C. Miller, and A. Colella, *Organizational Behavior: A Strategic Approach* (Hoboken, NJ: John Wiley & Sons, 2006).
4. Hitt, Ireland and Hoskisson, *Strategic Management*; R. Adner and P. Zemsky, "A Demand-based Perspective on Sustainable Competitive Advantage," *Strategic Management Journal* 27 (2006): 215–239; D. Lavie, "The Competitive Advantage of Interconnected Firms: An Extension of the Resource-based View," *Academy of Management Review* 31(2006): 638–658; D. Miller, "An Asymmetry-based View of Advantage: Towards an Attainable Sustainability," *Strategic Management Journal* 24, no. 10 (2003), 961–976.
5. S. L. Newbert, "Empirical Research on the Resource-based View of the Firm: An Assessment and Suggestions for Future Research," *Strategic Management Journal* 28 (2007): 121–146; D. G. Sirmon, M. A. Hitt, and R. D. Ireland, "Managing Firm Resources in Dynamic Environments to Create Value: Looking Inside the Black Box," *Academy of Management Review* 32 (2007): 273–292; J. Barney, "Firm Resources and Sustained Competitive Advantage," *Journal of Management* 17 (1991): 99–120.
6. Hitt, Ireland, and Hoskisson, *Strategic Management.*
7. M. B. Lieberman and N. S. Asaba, "Why Do Firms Imitate Each Other?" *Academy of Management Review* 31 (2006): 368–385; D. M. De Carolis, "Competencies and Imitability in the Pharmaceutical Industry: An Analysis of Their Relationship with Firm Performance," *Journal of Management* 29 (2003): 27–50.
8. S. K. McEvily and B. Chakravarthy, "The Persistence of Knowledge-based Advantage: An Empirical Test for Product Performance and Technological Knowledge," *Strategic Management Journal* 23, no. 4 (2002): 285–305; A. Andal and G. S. Yip, "Advantage Amnesia," *Business Strategy Review* 13, no. 1 (2002): 1–11; A. Afuah, "Mapping Technological Capabilities into Product Markets and Competitive Advantage: The Case of Cholesterol Drugs," *Strategic Management Journal* 23, no. 2 (2002): 171–181.
9. D. J. Collis and C. A. Montgomery, "Competing on Resources: Strategy in the 1990s," *Harvard Business Review* (July–August 1995): 119–128.
10. Sirmon, Hitt, and Ireland, "Managing Resources in Dynamic Environments to Create Value."
11. M. A. Hitt, R. D. Ireland, and R. E. Hoskisson, *Understanding Business Strategy* (Cincinnati, OH: Thomson South-Western, 2006).
12. G. Hamel and C. K. Prahalad, *Competing for the Future* (Boston, MA: Harvard Business Press, 1994).
13. R. Emmerich, "What's in a Vision?" *CMA Management* 75, no. 8 (2001): 10.
14. J. Collins and J. Porras, "Building Your Company's Vision," *Harvard Business Review* 74, no. 5 (1996): 65–77; C. Rarick and J. Vitton, "Mission Statements Make Sense," *Journal of Business Strategy* 16, no. 1 (1995): 11–12.
15. K. Andrews, *The Concept of Corporate Strategy* (Homewood, IL: Richard Irwin, 1971); J. A. Aragon-Correa and S. Sharma, "A Contingent Resource-based View of Proactive Corporate Environmental Strategy," *Academy of Management Review* 2 (2003): 71–88; S. A. Zahra and A. P. Nielsen, "Sources of Capabilities Integration and Technology Commercialization," *Strategic Management Journal* 23 (2002): 377–398; V. K. Garg, B. K. Walters, and R. I. Priem, "Chief Executive Scanning Emphases Environmental Dynamism and Manufacturing Firm Performance," *Strategic Management Journal* 24, (2003): 725–744.
16. E. Zajac, M. S. Kraatz, and R. Bresser, "Modeling the Dynamics of Strategic Fit: A Normative Approach to Strategic Change," *Strategic Management Journal* 21 (2000): 429–453.
17. M. E. Porter, *Competitive Advantage* (New York: Free Press, 1985).
18. www.cdc.gov, accessed on May 10, 2002; M. Moynihan, *Global Consumer Demographics* (New York: Business International, 1991).
19. *Statistical Handbook of Japan*, Statistics Bureau and Statistical Research and Training Institute, www.stat.go.jp/english/data/handbook, accessed February 11, 2006; S. Moffett, "For Ailing Japan, Longevity Takes Bite Out of Economy," *Wall Street Journal,* February 11, 2003, 1.
20. A. Sagie and Z. Aycan, "A Cross-cultural Analysis of Participative Decision-making in Organizations," *Human Relations* 56, no. 4 (2003): 453–473.
21. S. P. Seithi and P. Steidlmeier, "The Evolution of Business' Role in Society," *Business and Society Review* 94 (Summer 1995): 9–12; L. L. Martins, K. A. Eddleston, and J. E. Veiga, "Moderators of the Relationship Between Work-Family Conflict and Career Satisfaction," *Academy of Management Journal* 45, no. 2 (2002): 399–409.
22. A. Serwer, "The Next #1," *Fortune*, April 4, 2002; B. Caldwell, "Wal-Mart Ups the Pace," *Informationweek* 609 (1996): 37–51.
23. Personal communication with Dofasco senior management, 2003.
24. M. D. Ensley, C. L. Pearce, and K. M. Hmieleski, "The Moderating Effect of Environmental Dynamism on the Relationship Between Entrepreneur Leadership and New Venture Performance," *Journal of Business Venturing*, 21 (2006): 243–263.
25. "Glass Fibers Make Smokestacks Cleaner," *Machine Design* 67, no. 18 (1995): 123.
26. J. E. Oxley and B. Yeung, "E-Commerce Readiness: Institutional Environment and International Competitiveness,"

Journal of International Business Studies 32, no. 4 (2001): 705–723.

27. C. M. Lau, D. K. Tse, and N. Zhou, "Institutional Forces and Organizational Culture in China: Effects on Change Schemas, Firm Commitment and Job Satisfaction," *Journal of International Business Studies* 33, no. 3 (2002): 533–550.
28. M. Porter, *Competitive Strategy: Techniques for Analyzing Industries and Competitors* (New York: Free Press, 1980).
29. W. S. DeSarbo, R. Grewal, and J. Wind, "Who Competes Against Whom? A Demand-based Perspective for Identifying and Representing Asymmetric Competition," *Strategic Management Journal,* 27 (2006): 101–129; S. Slater and E. Olson. "A Fresh Look at Industry and Market Analysis," *Business Horizons* 45, no. 1 (2002): 15–22.
30. R. L. Priem, "A Consumer View of Value Creation," *Academy of Management Review*, 32 (2007): 219–235.
31. R. D. Ireland, M. A. Hitt, and D. Vaidyanath, "Alliance Management as a Source of Competitive Advantage," *Journal of Management* 28 (2002): 413–446.
32. Porter, *Competitive Advantage.*
33. D. Lavie, "Capability Reconfiguration: An Analysis of Incumbent Responses to Technological Change," *Academy of Management Review* 31 (2006): 153–174.
34. D. Bovet and J. Martha, "From Supply Chain to Value Net," *Journal of Business Strategy* 21, no. 4 (2000): 24–28; D. Bovet and J. Martha, "Value Nets: Reinventing the Rusty Supply Chain for Competitive Advantage," *Strategy and Leadership* 28, no. 4 (2000): 21–26; A. Afuah, "How Much Do Your Competitors' Capabilities Matter in the Face of Technological Change?" *Strategic Management Journal* 21, no. 3 (2000): 387–404.
35. A. Afuah, "How Much Do Your Competitors' Capabilities Matter in the Face of Technological Change?"; J. Stock, T. Speh, and H. Shear, "Many Happy (Product) Returns," *Harvard Business Review* 80, no. 7 (2002): 16–17; J. Hagel III, "Leveraged Growth: Expanding Sales Without Sacrificing Profits," *Harvard Business Review* 80, no. 10 (2002): 68–77; V. Shankar and B. L. Bayus, "Network Effects and Competition: An Empirical Analysis of the Home Video Game Industry," *Strategic Management Journal* 24, no. 4 (2003): 375–384.
36. J. Barney, "Looking Inside for Competitive Advantage," *Academy of Management Executive* 9, no. 4 (1995): 49–61; B. S. Teng and J. L. Cummings, "Trade-offs in Managing Resources and Capabilities," *Academy of Management Executive* 16, no. 2 (2002): 81–91; D. G. Hoopes, T. L. Madsen, and G. Walker, "Guest Editors' Introduction to the Special Issue: Why Is There a Resource-based View? Toward a Theory of Competitive Heterogeneity," *Strategic Management Journal* 24, (2003): 889–902.
37. Sirmon, Hitt, and Ireland, "Managing Resources in Dynamic Environments to Create Value."
38. P. Deng, "Investing for Strategic Resources and Its Rationale: The Case of Outward FDI from Chinese Companies," *Business Horizons* 50, no. 1 (2007): 71–81.
39. M. A. Hitt, L. Bierman, K. Uhlenbruck, and K. Shimizu, "The Importance of Resources in the Internationalization of Professional Service Firms: The Good, the Bad and the Ugly," *Academy of Management Journal* 49 (2006): 1137–1157; M. A. Hitt, L. Bierman, K. Shimizu, and R. Kochhar, "Direct and Moderating Effects of Human Capital on Strategy and Performance in Human Service Firms: A Resource-based Perspective," *Academy of Management Journal* 44 (2001): 13–28.
40. D. Tan and J. T. Mahoney, "Why a Multinational Firm Chooses Expatriates: Integrating Resource-based, Agency and Transaction Costs Perspectives," *Journal of Management Studies* 43 (2006): 457–484.
41. A. A. Marcus and M. H. Anderson, "A General Dynamic Capability: Does It Propogate Business and Social Competencies in the Retail Food Industry?" *Journal of Management Studies* 43 (2006): 19–46; R. Adner and C. E. Helfat, "Corporate Effects and Dynamic Managerial Capabilities," *Strategic Management Journal* 24 (2003): 1011–1025; K. Eisenhardt and J. Martin, "Dynamic Capabilities: What Are They?" *Strategic Management Journal* 21, (2000): 1105–1121;
42. H. J. Sapienza, "A Capabilities Perspective on the Effects of Early Internationalization on Firm Survival and Growth," *Academy of Management Review* 31 (2006): 914–933.
43. C. K. Prahalad and G. Hamel, "The Core Competence of the Corporation," *Harvard Business Review* 68, no. 3 (1990): 79–91.
44. J. Younker, "Organization Direction-Setting," *Tapping the Network Journal* 2, no. 2 (1991): 20–23; W. Schiemann, "Strategy, Culture, Communication: Three Keys to Success," *Executive Excellence* 6, no. 8 (1989): 11–12.
45. S. C. Abraham, *Strategic Planning: a Practical Guide for Competitive Success* (Cincinnati, OH: Thomson South-Western, 2007).
46. Hitt, Ireland, and Hoskisson, *Strategic Management.*
47. S. Brown and K. Blackmon, "Aligning Manufacturing Strategy and Business-level Competitive Strategy in New Competitive Environments: The Case for Strategic Resonance," *Journal of Management Studies* 42: 793–815.
48. V. F. Misangyi, H. Elms, T. Greckhamer, and J. A. LePine, "A New Perspective on a Fundamental Debate: A Multi-level Approach to Industry, Corporate and Business Unit Effects," *Strategic Management Journal* 27 (2006): 571–590.
49. Porter, *Competitive Advantage*; M. Partridge and L. Perren, "Developing Strategic Direction: Can Generic Strategies Help?" *Management Accounting-London* 72, no. 5 (1994): 28–29.
50. "Cemex Launches E-tail Website, Opens New Customer Service Center," *Caribbean Business* (November 20, 2003): 54; R. Sudip, "Cementing Global Success," *Direct Investor* (March 2003): 12–14; www.cemex.com, accessed July 4, 2002; J. Watson, "Cemex Buys Puerto Rican Company for Stronger Hold of Caribbean Market," *AP Worldstream,* June 12, 2002; J. Moreno, "Mexican Cement Giant's Deal Laid Solid Foundation for Entering U.S. Market," *Houston Chronicle,* April 10, 2001; "The Cemex Way," *Economist,* June 16, 2001: 75–76.
51. Hitt, Miller, and Colella, *Organizational Behavior.*
52. A. K. Gupta, K. G. Smith, and C. E. Shalley, "The Interplay Between Exploration and Exploitation," *Academy of Management Journal* 49 (2006): 693–706.
53. L. Nachum and C. Wymbs, "Product Differentiation, External Economies and MNE Locations Choices: M&As in Global Cities," *Journal of International Business Studies* 36 (2005): 415–434.

54. S. Voelpel, M. Leibold, E. Tekie, and G. von Krogh, "Escaping the Red Queen Effect in Competitive Strategy: Sense-testing Business Models," *European Management Journal* 23 (2005): 37–49.
55. D. Lee, "Hyundai's Hard Road," *Los Angeles Times,* February 4, 2007, www.latimes.com.
56. J. A. Pearce, "How Companies Can Preserve Market Dominance After Patents Expire," *Long Range Planning* 39 (2006): 71–87.
57. G. Hamel, "Innovate Now!" *Fast Company,* December 2002, www.fastcompany.com.
58. M. A. Hitt, R. D. Ireland, S. M. Camp, and D. L. Sexton, *Strategic Entrepreneurship: Integrating a New Mindset* (Oxford, UK: Blackwell Publishing).
59. G. Colvin, "Lafley and Immelt: In Search of Billions," *Fortune*, December 11, 2006, 70–82.
60. O. Sorenson, S. McEvily, C. R. Ren, and R. Roy, "Niche Width Revisited: Organizational Scope Behavior and Performance," *Strategic Management Journal* 27: 915–936.
61. G. Dowell, "Product Line Strategies of New Entrants in an Established Industry: Evidence from the U.S. Bicycle Industry," *Strategic Management Journal* 27 (2006): 959–979.
62. Hitt, Ireland, and Hoskisson, *Strategic Management.*
63. L. Fuentelsaz and J. Gomez, "Multipoint Competition, Strategic Similarity and Entry into Geographic Markets," *Strategic Management Journal* 27 (2006): 477–499.
64. Ibid.
65. T. L. Friedman, *The World Is Flat* (New York: Farrar, Straus & Giroux, 2005).
66. B. Quinn, *Intelligent Enterprise* (New York: Free Press, 1992); C. B. Dobni and G. Luffman, "Determining the Scope and Impact of Market Orientation Profiles on Strategy Implementation and Performance," *Strategic Management Journal* 24, no. 6 (2003): 577+; L. G. Love, R. L. Priem, and G. T. Lumpkin, "Explicitly Articulated Strategy and Firm Performance Under Alternative Levels of Centralization," *Journal of Management* 28, no. 5 (2002): 611–627.
67. U. Weitzel and S. Berns, "Cross-border Takeovers, Corruption and Related Aspects of Governance," *Journal of International Business Studies* 37 (2006): 786–806.
68. K. Uhlenbruck, M. A. Hitt, and M. Semadeni, "Market Value Effects of Acquisitions Involving Internet Firms: A Resource-based Analysis," *Strategic Management Journal* 27 (2006): 899–913; M. B. Heeley, D. R. King, and J. G. Covin, "Effects of Firm R&D Investment and Environment on Acquisition Likelihood," *Journal of Management Studies* 43 (2006): 1513–1535.
69. J. J. Reuer and R. Ragozzino, "Agency Hazards and Alliance Portfolios," *Strategic Management Journal* 27 (2006): 27–43.
70. J. H. Dyer and N. W. Hatch, "Relations-specific Capabilities and Barriers to Knowledge Transfers: Creating Advantage Through Network Relationships," *Strategic Management Journal* 27 (2006): 701–719; R. J. Arend, "SME-Supplier Alliance Activity in Manufacturing: Contingent Benefits and Perceptions," *Strategic Management Journal* 27: 741–763; F. T. Rothaermel, M. A. Hitt, and L. A. Jobe, "Balancing Vertical Integration and Strategic Outsourcing: Effects on Product Portfolio, Product Success and Firm Performance," *Strategic Management Journal* 27: 1033–1056.

Chapter 6

1. R. Adner and P. Zemsky, "A Demand-based Perspective on Sustainable Competitive Advantage," *Strategic Management Journal* 27 (2006): 215–239; J. A. Pearce, III, "How Companies Can Preserve Market Dominance After Patents Expire," *Long Range Planning* 39 (2006): 71–87.
2. M. A. Hitt, L. Bierman, K. Uhlenbruck, and K. Shimizu, "The Importance of Resources in the Internationalization of Professional Service Firms: The Good, the Bad and the Ugly," *Academy of Management Journal* 49 (2006): 1137–1157; M. A. Hitt, L. Bierman, K. Shimizu, and R. Kochhar, "Direct and Moderating Effects of Human Capital on Strategy and Performance in Human Service Firms: A Resource-based Perspective," *Academy of Management Journal* 44 (2001): 13–28.
3. G. Colvin, "On the Hot Seat," *Fortune,* December 11, 2006, 75–82.
4. M. A. Hitt, R. D. Ireland, and R. E. Hoskisson, *Strategic Management: Competitiveness and Globalization* (Cincinnati, OH: South-Western Publishing Co., 2007).
5. G. S. Yip, A. M. Rugman, and A. Kudina, "International Success of British Companies," *Long Range Planning* 39 (2006): 241–264.
6. H. E. Hodges and T. W. Kent, "Impact of Planning and Control Sophistication in Small Business," *Journal of Small Business Strategy* 17 (2006/2007): 75–87.
7. Colvin, "On the Hot Seat," 79.
8. J. A. Pearce, K. Robbins, and R. Robinson, "The Impact of Grand Planning Formality on Financial Performance," *Strategic Management Journal* 8 (1987):125–34.
9. V. F. Misangyi, H. Elms, T. Greckhamer, and J. A. LePine, "A New Perspective on a Fundamental Debate: A Multi-level Approach to Industry, Corporate and Business Unit Effects," *Strategic Management Journal* 27: 571–590.
10. R. Van Wingerden, "Managing Change," *International Journal of Technology Management* 21, nos. 5, 6 (2001): 487–95.
11. O. Sorenson, S. McEvily, C. R. Ren, and R. Roy, "Niche Width Revisted: Organizational Scope, Behavior and Performance," *Strategic Management Journal* 27 (2006): 915–936.
12. D. Rheault, "Freshening Up Strategic Planning: More than Fill-in-the-Blanks," *Journal of Business Strategy* 24, no. 6 (2003): 33–38; B. Walters, I. Clarke, S. Henley, and M. Shandiz, "Strategic Decision-Making Among Top Executives in Acute-Care Hospitals," *Health Marketing Quarterly* 19, no. 1 (2001): 43–59.
13. G. Dowell, "Product Line Strategies of New Entrants in an Established Industry: Evidence from the U.S. Bicycle Industry," *Strategic Management Journal* 27 (2006): 959–979.
14. J. E. Mathieu and W. Schulze, "The Influence of Team Knowledge and Formal Plans on Episodic Team Process-Performance Relationships," *Academy of Management Journal* 49 (2006): 605–619.
15. J. Carnillus, "Reinventing Strategic Planning," *Strategy and Leadership* (May–June 1996): 6–12.

16. *Best Buy 2006 Annual Report.*
17. M. A. Peteraf and M. E. Bergen, "Scanning Dynamic Competitive Landscapes: A Market-based and Resource-based Framework," *Strategic Management Journal* 24 (2003): 1027–1041; M. D. Watkins and M. H. Bazerman, "Predictable Surprises: The Disasters You Should Have Seen Coming," *Harvard Business Review* 81, no. 3 (2003): 72–80.
18. E. A. Boyd and I. O. Bilegan, "Revenue Management and E-commerce," *Management Science* 49 (2003): 1363–1386; M. Spann and B. Skiera, "Internet-based Virtual Stock Markets for Business Forecasting," *Management Science* 49 (2003): 1310–1326.
19. J. A. Zuniga-Vicente and J. D. Vicente-Lorente, "Strategic Moves and Organizational Survival in Turbulent Environments: The Case of Spanish Banks (1983–1997)," *Journal of Management Studies* 43 (2006): 485–519.
20. A. S. Cui, D. A. Griffith, S. T. Cavusgil, and M. Dabic, "The Influence of Market and Cultural Environmental Factors on Technology Transfer Between Foreign MNCs and Local Subsidiaries: A Croatian Illustration," *Journal of World Business* 41 (2006): 100–111.
21. M. Hileman, "Future Operations Planning Will Measure Plan Achievability," *Oil and Gas Journal* (March 18, 2002): 84–87.
22. D. Cameron, "KB Home in Stock-Options Investigation," *Financial Times*, January 29, 2007.
23. "Benchmarking Strategies," *Brand Strategy* (December/January 2004): 3; D. J. Smith, Y. Hwang, B. K. W. Pei, and J. H. Reneau, "The Performance Effects of Congruence Between Product Competitive Strategies and Purchasing Management Design," *Management Science* 48 (2002): 866–885.
24. C. Barker, C. Thunhurst, and D. Ross, "An Approach to Setting Priorities in Health Planning," *Journal of Management in Medicine* 12, no. 2 (1998): 92; A. Bhid, "The Questions Every Entrepreneur Must Ask," *Harvard Business Review* 74, no. 6 (1997): 120–130.
25. A. Locke and G. P. Latharn, *A Theory of Goal Setting and Task Performance* (Upper Saddle River, NJ: Prentice Hall, 1990); A. Lederer and A. Mendelow, "Information Systems Planning and the Challenge of Shifting Priorities," *Information and Management* 24, no. 6 (1993): 319–328.
26. J. Barney, *Gaining and Sustaining a Competitive Advantage* (Upper Saddle River, NJ: Pearson Prentice Hall, 2007).
27. J. P. Morgan, "EVA Measures Competitiveness," *Purchasing*, September 4, 2003, 16–18; R. Kaplan and D. Norton, "Strategic Learning and the Balanced Score Card," *Strategy and Leadership* 24, no. 5 (1996):18–24; I. Morgan and J. Rao, "Aligning Service Strategy Through Super-Measure Management," *Academy of Management Executive* 16, no. 4 (2002): 121–131; L. Airnan-Smith and S. G. Green, "Implementing New Manufacturing Technology: The Related Effects of Technology Characteristics and User Learning Activities," *Academy of Management Journal* 45 (2002): 421–430; L. G. Love, R. L. Priem, and G. T. Lumpkin, "Explicitly Articulated Strategy and Firm Performance Under Alternative Levels of Centralization," *Journal of Management* 28 (2002): 611–627.
28. C. Lawton and J. S. Lublin, "Dell's Founder Returns as CEO as Rollins Quits," *Wall Street Journal*, January 31, 2007.
29. I. Rivenbark and M. Frost, "Strategic Planning for Success," *HR Magazine*, July 2003, 120–121.
30. S. Mallya, S. Banerjee, and W. G. Bistline, "A Decision Support System for Production/Distribution Planning in Continuous Manufacturing," *Decision Sciences* 32 (2001): 545–556; P. Cowling and M. Johansson, "Using Real Time Information for Effective Dynamic Scheduling," *European Journal of Operational Research* 139 (2002): 230–244.
31. R. Wiltbank, N. Dew, S. Read, and S. D. Saravathy, "What to Do Next? The Case for Non-Predictive Strategy," *Strategic Management Journal* 27 (2006): 981–998; E. Harrison, "Strategic Control at the CEO Level," *Long Range Planning* 24, no. 6 (1991): 78–87.
32. M. A. Hitt, C. C. Miller, and A. Colella, *Organizational Behavior: A Strategic Approach* (Hoboken, NJ: John Wiley & Sons, 2006).
33. C. S. Katsikeas, S. Samiee, and M. Theodosiou, "Strategy Fit and Performance: Consequences of International Marketing Standardization," *Strategic Management Journal* 27 (2006): 867–890.
34. S. M. Kim and J. T. Mahoney, "Mutual Commitment to Support Exchange: Relation-Specific IT System as a Substitute for Managerial Hierarchy," *Strategic Management Journal* 27 (2006): 401–423.
35. W. R. Guffey and B. J. Nienhaus, "Determinants of Employee Support for the Strategic Plan of a Business Unit," *S.A.M. Advanced Management Journal* (Spring 2002): 23–30.
36. J. Balogun, "Managing Change: Steering a Course Between Intended Strategies and Unanticipated Outcomes," *Long Range Planning* 39 (2006): 29–49.
37. F. T. Rothaermel, M. A. Hitt, and L. A. Jobe, "Balancing Vertical Integration and Strategic Outsourcing: Effects on Product Portfolio, Product Success, and Firm Performance," *Strategic Management Journal* 27 (2006): 1033–1056.
38. J. White, "Almost Nothing New Under the Sun: Why the Work of Budgeting Remains Incremental," *Public Budgeting and Finance* 14, no. 1 (1994): 113–134.
39. W. Llewellyn, "A Review of the Budgeting System," *Assessment* 1, no. 5 (1994): 47–50.
40. Hitt, Miller, and Colella, *Organizational Behavior;* Locke and Latham, "A Theory of Goal Setting and Task Performance."
41. Hitt, Miller, and Colella, *Organizational Behavior.*
42. G. P. Latham, *Work Motivation: History, Theory, Research and Practice* (Thousand Oaks, CA: Sage Publications); A. Drach-Zahavy and M. Erez, "Challenge Versus Threat Effects on the Goal-Performance Relationship," *Organizational Behavior and Human Decision Processes* 88 (2002): 667–682.

Chapter 7

1. W. D. Sine, H. Mitsuhashi, and D. A. Kirsch, "Revisiting Burns and Stalker: Formal Structure and New Venture Performance in Emerging Economic Sectors," *Academy of Management Journal* 49 (2006): 121–132.

2. C. W. L. Hill, M. A. Hitt, and R. E. Hoskisson, "Cooperative Versus Competitive Structures in Related and Unrelated Diversified Firms," *Organization Science* 3 (1992): 501–521.
3. B. W. Keats and M.A. Hitt, "A Causal Model of Linkages Among Environmental Dimensions, Macro Organizational Characteristics and Performance," *Academy of Management Journal* 31 (1988): 570–598.
4. M. A. Hitt, R. D. Ireland, and R. E. Hoskisson, *Strategic Management: Competitiveness and Globalization* (Cincinnati, OH: South-Western Publishing Co., 2007).
5. H. Mintzberg, *The Structuring of Organizations* (Upper Saddle River, NJ: Prentice Hall, 1979).
6. B. Keats and H. O'Neill, "Organizational Structure: Looking Through a Strategy Lens," eds. M. A. Hitt, R. E. Freeman, and J. S. Harrison, *Handbook of Strategic Management* (Oxford, UK: Blackwell Publishers, 2001), 520–542.
7. P. Lawrence and J. W. Lorsch, *Organization and Environment* (Boston: Harvard University Press, 1967); J. R. Galbraith, *Designing Complex Organizations* (Reading, MA: Addison Wesley, 1977).
8. Ibid.
9. D. Miller and C. Droge, "Psychological and Traditional Determinants of Structure," *Administrative Science Quarterly* 31 (1986): 539–560; L. L. Levesque, J. Wilson, and R. Douglas, "Cognitive Divergence and Shared Mental Models in Software Development Project Teams," *Journal of Organizational Behavior* 22 (2001): 135–144.
10. P. Puranam, H. Singh, and M. Zollo, "Organizing for Innovation: Managing the Coordination-Autonomy Dilemma in Technology Acquisitions," *Academy of Management Journal* 49 (2006): 263–280.
11. Lawrence and Lorsch, *Organization and Environment*; Galbraith, *Designing Complex Organizations*; M. A. Schilling and H. K. Steensma, "The Use of Modular Organizational Forms: An Industry-level Analysis," *Academy of Management Journal* 44 (2001): 1149–1168; O. Sorenson, "Interdependence and Adaptability: Organizational Learning and the Long-Term Effect of Integration," *Management Science* 49 (2003): 446–463.
12. Puranam, Singh, and Zollo, "Organizing for Innovation."
13. A. W. Richter, M. A. West, and R. van Dick, "Boundary Spanners' Identification, Intergroup Contact and Effective Intergroup Relations," *Academy of Management Journal* 49 (2006): 1252–1269.
14. R. Steers and J. S. Black, *Organizational Behavior* (New York: HarperCollins, 1993); R. H. Hall, *Organizations: Structures, Process, and Outcomes*, 5th ed. (Upper Saddle River, NJ: Prentice Hall, 1991); Sorenson, "Interdependence and Adaptability," 446–463.
15. R. Cyert and J. March, *The Behavioral Theory of the Firm* (Upper Saddle River, NJ: Prentice Hall, 1963); J. R. Galbraith, "Organization Design: An Information Processing View," *Interfaces* 4, no. 3 (1974): 28–36; Hall, *Organizations*; J. Birkinshaw, R. Nobel, and J. Ridderstrale, "Knowledge as a Contingency Variable: Do the Characteristics of Knowledge Predict Organization Structure?" *Organization Science* 13 (2002): 274–289; R. J. Trent and R. M. Monczka, "Pursuing Competitive Advantage Through Integrated Global Sourcing," *Academy of Management Executive* 16, no. 2 (2002): 66–80.
16. E. E. Klein, "Using Information Technology to Eliminate Layers of Bureaucracy," *National Public Accountant* 46 (June 2001): 46–48.
17. Sine, Mitsuhashi, and Kirsch, "Revisiting Burns and Stalker: Formal Structure and New Venture Performance in Emerging Economic Sectors."
18. D. Nadler and M. Tushman, *Competing by Design: The Power of Organizational Architecture* (New York: Oxford University Press, 1997).
19. AES Corporation, *AES Corporation 2005 Annual Report*, www.aes.com, March 3, 2007.
20. Y. Rhy-song and T. Sagafi-nejad, "Organizational Characteristics of American and Japanese Firms in Taiwan," *Academy of Management Proceedings* (1987): 111–115.
21. S. H. Park and Y. Luo, "Guanxi and Organizational Dynamics: Organizational Networking in Chinese Firms," *Strategic Management Journal* 22 (2001): 455–477.
22. C. A. Bartlett and S. Ghoshal, "Organizing for Worldwide Effectiveness: The Transnational Solution," *California Management Review* 29 (Fall 1988): 54–74; D. H. Doty, W. H. Glick, and G. P. Huber, "Fit, Effectiveness, and Equifinality: A Test of Two Configurational Theories," *Academy of Management Journal* 36 (1993): 1196–1250.
23. J. R. Lincoln, M. Hanada, and K. McBride, "Organizational Structures in Japanese and U.S. Manufacturing," *Administrative Science Quarterly* 31 (1986), 338–364.
24. J. Schachter, "When Hope Turns to Frustration: The Americanization of Mitsubishi Has Had Little Success," *Los Angeles Times*, July 10, 1988, 1.
25. Sony, Company Bios, www.sony.com, March 3, 2007.
26. E. Wang, "Linking Organizational Context with Structure," *Omega* 29 (2001): 429–443.
27. A. A. King, M. J. Lenox, and A. Terlaak, "The Strategic Use of Decentralized Institutions: Exploring Certification with the ISO 14001 Management Standard," *Academy of Management Journal* 48 (2005): 1091–1106.
28. S. C. Abraham, *Strategic Planning: A Practical Guide for Competitive Success* (Cincinnati, OH: Thomson South-Western, 2006).
29. G. Hoetker, "Do Modular Products Lead to Modular Organizations?" *Strategic Management Journal* 27 (2006): 501–518.
30. A.-W. Harzing, "Geographical Distance and the Role and Management of Subsidiaries: The Case of Subsidiaries Down-Under," *Asia-Pacific Journal of Management* 23 (2006): 167–185.
31. S. Karim, "Modularity in Organizational Structure: The Reconfiguration of Internally Developed and Acquired Business Units," *Strategic Management Journal* 27 (2006): 799–823.
32. EDS, Recent Contract Awards, www.eds.com, March 3, 2007.
33. J. Sandberg, "How Long Can India Keep Office Politics Out of Outsourcing?" *Wall Street Journal*, February 27, 2007, www.wsj.com.
34. D. Colker, "India Outsources to U.S.," *Los Angeles Times*, March 3, 2007, www.latimes.com.

35. A. Deutschman, "Open Wide: The Traditional Business Organization Meets Democracy," *Fast Company*, March 2007, 40–41.
36. D. G. Sirmon, M. A. Hitt, and R. D. Ireland, "Managing Firm Resources in Dynamic Environments to Create Value: Looking Inside the Black Box," *Academy of Management Review* 32 (2007): 273–292; Y. Luo, "Market-seeking MNEs in an Emerging Market: How Parent-Subsidiary Links Shape Overseas Success," *Journal of International Business Studies* 34 (2003): 290–309.
37. M. Badri, D. Davis, and D. Davis, "Operations Strategy, Environmental Uncertainty and Performance: A Path Analytic Model of Industries in Developing Countries," *Omega* 28, no. 2 (2000), 155–173; M. Van Gelderen, M. Frese, and R. Thurik, "Strategies, Uncertainty and Performance of Small Business Startups," *Small Business Economics* 15, no. 3 (2000), 165–181; V. K. Garg, B. A. Walters, and R. L. Priem, "Chief Executive Scanning Emphases, Environmental Dynamism, and Manufacturing Firm Performance," *Strategic Management Journal* 24, no. 8 (2003), 725–744
38. R. Engdahl, R. Keating, and K. Aupperle, "Strategy and Structure: Chicken or Egg? (Reconsideration of Chandler's Paradigm for Economic Success)," *Organization Development Journal* 18, no. 4 (2000): 21–33; D. E. W. Marginson, "Management Control Systems and Their Effects on Strategy Formation at Middle Management Levels: Evidence from a U.K. Organization," *Strategic Management Journal* 23 (2002): 1019–1031; J. Smith David, Y. Hwang, B. K. W. Pei, and J. H. Reneau, "The Performance Effects of Congruence Between Product Competitive Strategies and Purchasing Management Design," *Management Science* 48 (2002): 866–885; M. Goold and A. Campbell, "Do You Have a Well-designed Organization?" *Harvard Business Review* 80, no. 3 (2002): 117–124.
39. S. F. Slater, E. M. Olson, and G. T. M. Hult, "The Moderating Influence of Strategic Orientation on the Strategy Formation Capability-Performance Relationship," *Strategic Management Journal* 27 (2006): 1221–1231.
40. Hitt, Ireland, and Hoskisson, *Strategic Management*.
41. J. Stopford and L. Wells, *Managing the Multination Enterprise* (New York: Basic Books, 1972).
42. J. Daniels, R. Pitts, and M. Tretter, "Strategy and Structure of U.S. Multinationals: An Exploratory Study," *Academy of Management Journal* 27 (1984): 292–307.
43. J. Wolf and W. Egelhoff, "Reexamination and Extension of International Strategy-Structure Theory," *Strategic Management Journal* 23 (2002), 181–189.
44. M. A. Hitt, L. Tihanyi, T. Miller, and B. Connelly, "International Diversification: Antecedents, Outcomes and Moderators," *Journal of Management* 32 (2006): 831–867; M. W. Peng and A. Delios, "What Determines the Scope of the Firm over Time and Around the World? An Asia Pacific Perspective," *Asia Pacific Journal of Management* 23 (2006): 385–405.
45. Wolf and Egelhoff, "Reexamination and Extension of International Strategy-Structure Theory."
46. C. Bartlett and S. Ghoshal, *Managing Across Borders* (Boston: Harvard Business School Press, 1989); P. Ghemawat, "The Forgotten Strategy," *Harvard Business Review* 81, no. 11 (2003), 76–84.

Chapter 8

1. S. A. Snell, M. A. Shadur, and P. M. Wright, "Human Resources Strategy: The Era of Our Ways," in *Handbook of Strategic Management*, eds. M. A. Hitt, R. E. Freeman, and J. S. Harrison (Oxford, UK: Blackwell Publishing, 2001).
2. M. A. Hitt and R. D. Ireland, "The Essence of Strategic Leadership: Managing Human and Social Capital," *Journal of Leadership & Organization Studies* 9 (2002): 3–14.
3. D. Urich and W. Brockbank, *HR Value Proposition* (Boston, Harvard Business School Press, 2005); P. M. Wright, B. B. Dunford, and S. A. Snell, "Human Resources and the Resource-based View of the Firm," *Journal of Management* 27 (2001): 701–721.
4. M. W. McCall and M. M. Lombardo, *Off the Track: Why and How Successful Executives Get Derailed* (Greensboro, NC: Center for Creative Leadership, 1983).
5. J. H. Gittell, *The Southwest Airlines Way* (New York: McGraw–Hill, 2003).
6. D. Urich and W. Brockbank, *HR Value Proposition* (Boston: Harvard Business School Press, 2005); D. Ulrich, *Human Resource Champions* (Boston: Harvard Business School Press, 1997).
7. S. C. Kang, S. S. Morris, and S. A. Snell, "Relational Archetypes, Organizational Learning, and Value Creation: Extending The Human Resource Architecture," *Academy of Management Review* 32, no. 1 (2007): 236–256; R. W. Rowden, "Potential Roles of the Human Resource Management Professional in the Strategic Planning Process," *S.A.M. Advanced Management Journal* 64, no. 3 (1999): 22–27.
8. C. J. Collins and K. G. Smith, "Knowledge Exchange and Combination: The Role of Human Resource Practices in the Performance of High-Technology Firms," *Academy of Management Journal* 49, no. 3 (2006): 544–560; M. A. Huselid, S. Jackson, and R. Schuler, "Technical and Strategic Human Resource Management Effectiveness as Determinants of Firm Performance," *Academy of Management Journal* 40 (1997): 171–188; K. S. Law, D. K. Tse, and N. Zhou, "Does Human Resource Management Matter in a Transitional Economy? China as an Example," *Journal of International Business Studies* 34, no. 3 (2003): 255–265; S. L. Rynes, K. G. Brown, and A. E. Colbert, "Seven Common Misconceptions About Human Resource Practices: Research Findings Versus Practitioner Beliefs," *The Academy of Management Executive* 16, no. 3 (2002): 92–102; R. Batt, "Managing Customer Services: Human Resource Practices, QUIT rates, and Sales Growth," *Academy of Management Journal* 45, no. 3 (2002): 587–597.
9. M. Subramaniam and M. A. Youndt, "The Influence of Intellectual Capital on the Types of Innovative Capabilities," *Academy of Management Journal* 48, no. 3 (2005): 450–463; J. Pfeffer, *Competitive Advantage Through People: Unleashing the Power of the Workforce* (Boston: Harvard Business School Press, 1994).
10. R. E. Ployhart, "Staffing in the 21st Century: New Challenges and Strategic Opportunities," *Journal of Management* 32, no. 6 (2006): 868–897.
11. S. Bates. "Growing Pains Are Cited in Study of HR Outsourcing," *HRMagazine* 47, no. 8 (2002): 10;

D. P. Lepak, and S. A. Snell, "Examining the Human Resource Architecture: The Relationships Among Human Capital, Employment, and Human Resource Configurations," *Journal of Management* 28, no. 4 (2002): 517–543.

12. W. Wiggenhorn, "Motorola U: When Training Becomes an Education," *Harvard Business Review* (July–August 1990): 71–83; Lepak and Snell, "Examining the Human Resource Architecture."
13. M. O'Daniel, "Online Assistance for Job Seekers," *New Strait Times,* November 11, 2003; L. Goff, "Job Surfing," *ComputerWorld* 30, no. 36 (1996): 81; M. K. McGee, "Job Hunting on the Internet," *Informationweek* 576 (1996): 98.
14. J. A. Breaugh and M. Starke, "Research on Employee Recruitment: So Many Studies, So Many Remaining Questions," *Journal of Management* 26, no. 3 (2000): 405–434.
15. L. M. Berry, *Employee Selection* (New York: Wadsworth Publishing Company, 2002); D. Terpstra, "The Search for Effective Methods," *HR Focus* 73, no. 5 (1996): 16–17.
16. L. Stroh, M. E. Mendenhall, J. Stewart Black, and H. B. Gregersen, *International Assignments: An Integration of Research and Practice* (Hillsdale, NJ: Lawrence Erlbaum, 2005); J. S. Black, H. B. Gregersen, M. E. Mendenhall, and L. Stroh, *Global People Through International Assignments* (Reading, MA: Addison–Wesley, 1999).
17. J. Conway, R. Jako, and D. Goodman, "A Meta-Analysis of Interrater and Internal Consistency Reliability of Selection Interviews," *Journal of Applied Psychology* 80, no. 5 (1995): 565–579; M. McDaniel, D. Whetzel, F. Schmidt, and S. Maurer, "The Validity of Employment Interviews: A Comprehensive Review and Meta-Analysis," *Journal of Applied Psychology* 79, no. 4 (1994): 599–616.
18. G. Dessler, *Human Resource Management*, 8th ed. (Upper Saddle River, NJ: Prentice Hall, 2000), Chapter 6.
19. L. Rudner, "Pre-Employment Testing and Employee Productivity," *Public Management* 21, no. 2 (1992): 133–50; P. Lowry, "The Assessment Center: Effects of Varying Consensus Procedures," *Public Personnel Management* 21, no. 2 (1992): 171–183; T. Payne, N. Anderson, and T. Smith, "Assessment Centres: Selection Systems and Cost-Effectiveness," *Personnel Review* 21, no. 4 (1992): 48–56; D. J. Schleicher, D. V. Day, B. Mayes,and R. E. Riggio, "A New Frame for Frame-of-Reference Training: Enhancing the Construct Validity of Assessment Centers," *Journal of Applied Psychology* 87, no. 4 (2002): 735–746; F. Lievens, "Trying to Understand the Different Pieces of the Construct Validity Puzzle of Assessment Centers: An Examination of Assessor and Assessee Effects," *Journal of Applied Psychology* 87, no. 4 (2002): 675–686; W. Arthur Jr., E. A. Day,T. L. McNelly, and P. S. Edens, "A Meta-Analysis of the Criterion–related Validity of Assessment Center Dimensions," *Personnel Psychology* 56, no. 1 (2003):125–154; D. J. Woehr, and W. Arthur Jr., "The Construct-related Validity of Assessment Center Ratings: A Review and Meta-Analysis of the Role of Methodological Factors," *Journal of Management* 29, no. 2 (2003): 231; K. Dayan, R. Kasten,and S. Fox, "Entry-level Police Candidate Assessment Center: An Efficient Tool for a Hammer to Kill a Fly?" *Personnel Psychology* 55, no. 4 (2002): 827–849.
20. R. Bentley, "Candidates Face Alternative Testing," *Computer Weekly,* November 18, 2003, 54; S. Adler, "Personality Tests for Salesforce Selection," *Review of Business* 16, no. 1 (1994): 27–31.
21. M. McCullough, "Can Integrity Testing Improve Market Conduct?" *LIMRA's Marketfacts* 15, no. 2 (1996): 15–16; H. J. Bernardin and D. Cooke, "Validity of an Honesty Test in Predicting Theft Among Convenience Store Employees," *Academy of Management Journal* 36, no. 50 (1993): 1097.
22. B. Murphy, W. Barlow, and D. Hatch, "Employer-Mandated Physicals for Over-70 Employees Violate the ADEA," *Personnel Journal* 72, no. 6 (1993): 24; R. Ledman and D. Brown, "The Americans with Disabilities Act," *SAM Advanced Management Journal* 58, no. 2 (1993): 17–20.
23. C. Fisher, "Organizational Socialization: An Integrative Review," in K. Rowland and J. Ferris (eds.), *Research in Personnel and Human Resource Management* 4 (1986): 101–145.
24. T. J. Fogarty. "Socialization and Organizational Outcomes in Large Public Accounting Firms," *Journal of Managerial Issues* 12, no. 1 (2000): 13–33; M. K. Ahuja, and J. E. Galvin, "Socialization in Virtual Groups," *Journal of Management* 29, no. 2 (2003): 161; E. W. Morrison, "Newcomers' Relationships: The Role of Social Network Ties During Socialization," *Academy of Management Journal* 45, no. 6 (2002): 1149–1160.
25. B. Jacobson and B. Kaye, "Service Means Success," *Training and Development* 45, no. 5 (1991): 53–58; J. Brechlin and A. Rossett, "Orienting New Employees," *Training* 28, no. 4 (1991): 45–51.
26. W. P. Anthony, P. L. Perrewe, and K. M. Kacmar, *Strategic Human Resource Management* (Fort Worth, TX: Harcourt Brace Jovanovich, 1993).
27. L. W. Porter and L. E. McKibbin, *Management Education and Development* (New York: McGraw-Hill, 1988); A. Kristof–Brown, M. R. Barrick, and M. Franke, "Applicant Impression Management: Dispositional Influences and Consequences for Recruiter Perceptions of Fit and Similarity," *Journal of Management* 28, no. 1 (2002): 27–46.
28. J. De Kok, "The Impact of Firm-provided Training on Production," *International Small Business Journal* 20, no. 3 (2002): 271–295.
29. J. K. Eskildsen and J. J. Dahlgaard. "A Causal Model for Employee Satisfaction," *Total Quality Management* 11, no. 8 (2000): 1081–1094; J. L. Pierce, "Employee Affective Responses to Work Unit Structure and Job Design: A Test of an Intervening Variable," *Journal of Management* 5 (1979): 193–211.
30. M. Hammer and J. Champy, *Reengineering the Corporation* (New York: HarperCollins, 1993); D. A. Buchanan, "Demands, Instabilities, Manipulations, Careers: The Lived Experience of Driving Change," *Human Relations* 56, no. 6 (2003): 663.
31. J. D. Elicker, P. E. Levy, and R. J. Hall, "The Role of Leader-Member Exchange in the Performance Appraisal Process,"*Journal of Management* 32 (2006): 531–551; R. D. Bretz Jr., G. T. Milkovich, and W. Read, "The

Current State of Performance Appraisal Research and Practice: Concerns, Directions, and Implications," *Journal of Management* 18 (1992): 321–352.

32. S. L. Rynes, K. G. Brown, and A. E. Colbert, "Seven Common Misconceptions About Human Resource Practices: Research Findings Versus Practitioner Beliefs," *Academy of Management Executive* 16, no. 3 (2002): 92–103; T. Redman, E. Snape, and G. McElwee, "Appraising Employee Performance: A Vital Organizational Activity?" *Education and Training* 35, no. 2 (1993): 3–10; Bretz, Milkovitch, and Read. "The Current State of Performance Appraisal Research and Practice."
33. R. Cardy and G. Dobbins. *Performance Appraisal* (Cincinnati, OH: South-Western Publishing. 1994).
34. J. Greenberg, C. E. Ashton-James, and N. M. Ashkanasy, "Social Comparison Processes in Organizations," *Organizational Behavior and Human Decision Processes* 102, no. 1 (2007): 22–41; L. Gomez-Mejia, "Evaluating Employee Performance: Does the Appraisal Instrument Make a Difference?" *Journal of Organizational Behavior Management* 9, no. 2 (1988): 155–172.
35. M. Hosoda, E. F. Stone-Romero, and G. Coats, "The Effects of Physical Attractiveness on Job-related Outcomes: A Meta-Analysis of Experimental Studies," *Personnel Psychology* 56, no. 2 (2003): 431; T. J. Watson, "Ethical Choice in Managerial Work: The Scope for Moral Choices in an Ethically Irrational World," *Human Relations* 56, no. 2 (2003): 167–185; C. Rarick and G. Baxter, "Behaviorally Anchored Rating Scales: An Effective Performance Appraisal Approach," *Advanced Management Journal* 5l, no. 1 (1986): 36–39; D. Naffziger, "BARS, RJPs, and Recruiting," *Personnel Administrator* 30, no. 8 (1985): 85–96.
36. K. Clark, "Judgment Day," *U.S. News & World Report,* 134, no. 2 (2003): 31; D. Bohl, "Minisurvey: 360 Degree Appraisals Yield Superior Results," *Compensation and Benefits Review* 28, no. 5 (1996): 16–19.
37. L. K. Johnson "The Ratings Game: Retooling 360s for Better Performance," *Harvard Management Update* 8, no. 1 (January 2004); M. S. Brutus and M. Derayeh, "Multisource Assessment Programs in Organizations: An Insider's Perspective," *Human Resource Development Quarterly* 13, no. 2 (2002): 187–202; M. Vinson, "The Pros and Cons of 360 Degree Feedback," *Training and Development* 50, no. 4 (1996): 11–12.
38. J. Lawrie, "Steps Toward an Objective Appraisal," *Supervisory Management* 34, no. 5 (1989): 17–24.
39. "Changing with the Times," *IRS Employment Review,* February 21, 2003, Issue 770, 14–17; J. Kanin–Lovers and M. Cameron, "Broad banding—A Step Forward or a Step Backward?" *Journal of Compensation and Benefits* 9, no. 5 (1994): 39–42.
40. K. M. Kuhn and M. D. Yockey "Variable Pay as a Risky Choice: Determinants of the Relative Attractiveness of Incentive Plans," *Organizational Behavior and Human Decision Processes,*90, no. 2 (2003): 323–341; L. Stroh, J. Brett, J. Baumann, and A. Reilly, "Agency Theory and Variable Pay Compensation Strategies," *Academy of Management Journal* 39, no. 3 (1996): 51–67.
41. J. Herman, "Beating the Midlife Career Crisis," *Fortune* 128, no. 5, 1993, 52–62.
42. L. Stroh, M. E. Mendenhall, J. S. Black, and H. B. Gregersen, *International Assignments: An Integration of Research and Practice* (Hillsdale, NJ: Lawrence Erlbaum, 2005); A. M. Chaker, "Luring Moms Back to Work," *Wall Street Journal* 242, no. 127 (2003): D1-2; A. Leibowitz and J. Merman, "Explaining Changes in Married Mothers' Employment Over Time," *Demography* 32, no. 3 (1995): 365–78; S. Werner, "Recent Developments in International Management Research: A Review of 20 Top Management Journals," *Journal of Management* 28, no. 3 (2002): 277–305.
43. J. S. Black and H. B. Gregersen, *So You're Going Overseas: A Handbook for Personal and Professional Success* (San Diego, CA: Global Business Publishers, 1999).
44. J. Brockner, G. Spreitzer, A. Mishra, and W. Hochwarter, "Perceived Control as an Antidote to the Negative Effects of Layoffs on Survivors' Organizational Commitment and Job Performance," *Administrative Science Quarterly* 49 (2004): 75–100; W. F. Cascio, "Downsizing: What Do We Know? What Have We Learned?" *Academy of Management Executive* 3, no. 1(1997): 95–104.
45. H. S. Farber and B. Western. "Accounting for the Decline of Unions in the Private Sector, 1973–1998," *Journal of Labor Research* 22, no. 3 (2001): 459–485.
46. U.S. Department of Labor, www.dol.gov/wb/stats, accessed on January 10, 2007.
47. "Leaders of the Pack," *Fortune*, October 16, 2006, 189.
48. P. Feltes, R. K. Robinson, and R L. Fink, "American Female Expatriate and the Civil Rights Act of 1991: Balancing Legal and Business Interests," *Business Horizons* (March–April 1993): 82–86.
49. N. Adler, "Expecting International Success: Female Managers Overseas," *Columbia Journal of World Business* 19 (1987): 79–85.
50. Personal communication with human resource executive at Delta Airlines.
51. E. P. Gray, "The National Origin of BFOQ Under Title VII," *Employee Relations Law Journal* 11, no. 2 (1985): 311–321.
52. K. Williams and C. O'Reilly, "Forty Years of Diversity Research: A Review," in *Research in Organizational Behavior*, ed. B. M. Staw and L. L. Cummings (Greenwich, CT: JAI, 1981 Press), 77–140; D. Van Knippenberg, C. De Dreu, and A. C. Homan, "Work Group Diversity and Group Performance: An Integrative Model and Research Agenda," *Journal of Applied Psychology* 89, no. 6 (2004): 1008–1022; L. H. Pelled, K. M. Eisenhardt, and K. R. Xin, "Exploring the Black Box: An Analysis of Work Group Diversity, Conflict, and Performance," *Administrative Science Quarterly* 44, (1999): 1–28.
53. O. C. Richard, T. Barnet, S. Dwyer, and K. Cadwick, "Cultural Diversity in Management, Firm Performance, and the Moderating Role of Entrepreneurial Orientation Dimensions," *Academy of Management Journal* 47 (2004): 255–265.

Chapter 9

1. R. M. Stogdill, "Historical Trends in Leadership Theory and Research," *Journal of Contemporary Business* 3, no. 4 (1974): 1–17 (p. 2).

2. R. Levering and M. Moskowitz, *The 100 Best Companies to Work for in America,* Rev. ed. (New York: Plume, 1993); R. Galford and A. S. Drapeau, "The Enemies of Trust," *Harvard Business Review* 81, no. 2 (2003): 88–95; A. C. Edmondson and S. E. Cha "When Company Values Backfire," *Harvard Business Review* 80, no. 11 (2002): 18–19; T. Simons, "The High Cost of Lost Trust," *Harvard Business Review* 80, no. 9 (2002): 18–19.
3. D. Katz and R. L. Kahn, *The Social Psychology of Organizations*, 2nd ed. (New York: Wiley, 1978); S. D. Dionne, F. J. Yammarino, L. E. Atwater, and L. R. James, "Neutralizing Substitutes for Leadership Theory: Leadership Effects and Common-Source Bias," *Journal of Applied Psychology* 87, no. 3 (2002): 454–464.
4. S. Finkelstein, "Seven Habits of Spectacularly Unsuccessful People," *Strategy Review* 14, no. 4 (2003): 39–51; N. Nohria, W. Joyce, and B. Roberson, "What Really Works," *Harvard Business Review* 81, no. 7 (2003): 42–52; W. G. Bennis and B. Nanus, *Leaders: Strategies for Taking Charge,* 2nd ed. (New York: Harper Business, 1997); J. P. Kotter, "What Leaders Really Do," *Harvard Business Review* 68, no. 3 (1990): 103–111; A. Zaleznik, "Managers and Leaders: Are They Different?" *Harvard Business Review* 70, no. 2 (1992): 126–135.
5. R. J. House, ed., *Culture, Leadership, and Organizations: The GLOBE Study of 62 Societies* (Thousand Oaks, CA: Sage Publications, 2004); M. W. Dickson, D. N. Den Hartog, and J. K. Mitchelson, "Research on Leadership in a Cross-Cultural Context: Making Progress and Raising New Questions," *The Leadership Quarterly* 14 (2003): 729–768.
6. Westwood and Chan, *Headship and Leadership.*
7. S. Ronen, *Comparative and Multinational Management* (New York: Wiley, 1986), 191.
8. Westwood and Chan, *Headship and Leadership.*
9. E. Ogliastri, C. McMillen, C. Altschul, M. E. Arias, C. Bustamante, C. Davila, P. Dorfman, M. Ferreira, C. Finmen, and S. Martinez, "Cultura y Liderazgo Organizacional en America Latina: El Estudio GLOBE (Culture and Organizational Leadership in Latin America: The GLOBE Study)," *Revista Latinoamericana de Administración* (1999).
10. Dickson, Den Hartog, and Mitchelson, "Research on Leadership in a Cross-Cultural Context: Making Progress and Raising New Questions"; P. W. Dorfman and J. P. Howell, "Leadership in Western and Asian Countries: Commonalities and Differences in Effective Leadership Processes Across Cultures," *The Leadership Quarterly* 8 (1997): 233–274.
11. M. Javidan, et al., "In the Eye of the Beholder: Cross Cultural Lessons in Leadership from Project GLOBE," *Academy of Management Perspectives* 20 (2006): 67–90; P. Dorfman, P. J. Hanges, and F. C. Brodbeck, "Leadership and Cultural Variation: The Identification of Culturally Endorsed Leadership Profiles," ed. R. J. House, P. J. Hanges, M. Javidan, P. Dorfman and V. Gupta, *Leadership, Culture, and Organizations: The GLOBE Study of 62 Societies* (Thousand Oaks, CA: Sage Publications, Inc., 2004), 667–718.
12. B. Powell, R. Tomlinson, E. Nee, J. Fox, et al., "25 Rising Stars," *Fortune*, 2001, 140–164.
13. J. Pfeffer, *Managing with Power: Politics and Influence in Organizations* (Boston, MA: Harvard Business School Press, 1992), 45.
14. D. A. Whetten and K. S. Cameron, *Developing Management Skills*, 4th ed. (Reading, MA: Addison–Wesley, 1998), 229.
15. G. E. G. Catlin, *Systematic Politics* (Toronto: University of Toronto Press, 1962), 71.
16. M. Davids, "Where Style Meets Substance," *Journal of Business Strategy* 16 (1995): 48–52+.
17. Pfeffer. *Managing with Power.*
18. W. G. Bennis and B. Nanus, *The Strategies for Taking Charge,* 1st ed. (New York: Harper and Row, 1985), 6.
19. B. M. Bass, *Leadership, Psychology, and Organizational Behavior* (New York: Harper, 1960); A. Etzioni, *A Comparative Analysis of Complex Organizations: On Power, Involvement, and Their Correlates* (New York: Free Press of Glencoe, 1961); G. A. Yukl, *Leadership in Organizations,* 3rd ed. (Upper Saddle River, NJ: Prentice Hall, 1994).
20. J. R. P. French and B. Raven, *The Bases of Social Power*, in *Studies in Social Power*, ed. D. Cartwright (Ann Arbor, MI: Institute for Social Research, 1959), 150–167.
21. D. Mechanic, "Sources of Power of Lower Participants in Complex Organizations," *Administrative Science Quarterly* 7 (1962): 349–364.
22. B. Breen, "Trickle-up Leadership," *Fast Company, 52,* 2001, 70.
23. Pfeffer, *Managing with Power*, 46; N. Nicholson, "How to Motivate Your Problem People," *Harvard Business Review* 81, no. 1 (2003): 56–65; M. Mongeau, "Moving Mountains," *Harvard Business Review* 81, no. 1 (2003): 41–47
24. D. Kipnis, S. M. Schmidt, and I. Wilkinson, "Intra–organizational Influence Tactics: Explorations in Getting One's Way," *Journal of Applied Psychology* 65 (1980): 440–452; L. W. Porter, R. W. Allen, and H. L. Angle, "The Politics of Upward Influence in Organizations," in *Research in Organizational Behavior* 3, ed. L. L. Cummings and B. M. Staw (Greenwich, CT: JAI Press, 1981), 109–139; G. Yukl and C. M. Falbe, "Influence Tactics and Objectives in Upward, Downward and Lateral Influence Attempts," *Journal of Applied Psychology* 75 (1990): 132–140; G. Yukl, R. Lepsinger and T. Lucia, "Preliminary Report on the Development and Validation of the Influence Behavior Questionnaire," in *The Impact of Leadership*, ed. K. Clark and M. Clark (Greensboro, NC: Center for Creative Leadership, 1992); G. Yukl and J. B. Tracey, "Consequences of Influence Tactics Used with Subordinates, Peers, and the Boss," *Journal of Applied Psychology* 77 (1992): 525–535; M. D. Mumford, et al. "Leading creative people: Orchestrating expertise and relationships." *The Leadership Quarterly. 13*(2002), 705–815.
25. Bennis and Nanus, *Leaders*; R. M. Kanter, "Frontiers for Strategic Human Resource Planning and Management," *Human Resource Management* 1 no. 2 (1983): 9–21; J. A. Conger, "Leadership: The Art of Empowering Others," *Academy of Management Executive* 3 (1989): 17–24; J. A. Conger and R. N. Kanungo, "The Empowerment Process: Integrating Theory and Practice," *Academy of Management Review* 13 (1988): 471–482; P. G. Foster-Fishman and C. B. Keys, "The Inverted Pyramid: How a

Well Meaning Attempt to Initiate Employee Empowerment Ran Afoul of the Culture of a Public Bureaucracy," *Academy of Management Journal,* Best Papers Proceedings (1995): 364–368; G. M. Spreitzer, "Psychological Empowerment in the Workplace: Dimensions, Measurement, and Validation," *Academy of Management Journal* 38 (1995): 1442–1465; G. M. Spreitzer, "Social Structural Characteristics of Psychological Empowerment," *Academy of Management Journal* 39 (1996): 483–504; N. M. Tichy and M. A. Devanna, "The Transformational Leader," *Training and Development* 40, no. 7 (1986): 27–32.

26. N. Moskowitz and R. Levering, "Great Companies in Europe: Novo Nordisk," *Fortune,* 2002, 60–61; www.novonordisk-us.com, accessed March 2007.
27. Bennis and Nanus, *Leaders*; R. M. Kanter, "Frontiers for Strategic Human Resource Planning and Management"; Conger and Kanungo, "The Empowerment Process"; Tichy and Devanna, "The Transformational Leader"; R. Kark, B. Shamir, and G. Chen, "The Two Faces of Transformational Leadership: Empowerment and Dependency," *Journal of Applied Psychology* 88, no. 2 (2003): 246–255; N. Turner, J. Barling, O. Epitropaki, V. Butcher, and C. Milner, "Transformational Leadership and Moral Reasoning," *Journal of Applied Psychology* 87, no. 2 (2002): 304–311; T. Dvir, D. Eden, B. J. Avolio, and B. Shamir, "Impact of Transformational Leadership on Follower Development and Performance: A Field Experiment," *Academy of Management Journal* 45, no. 4 (2002): 735–744.
28. R. M. Stogdill, "Personal Factors Associated with Leadership: A Survey of the Literature," *Journal of Psychology* 25 (1948): 35–71.
29. R. G. Lord, C. L. De Vader, and G. M. Alliger, "A Meta-Analysis of the Relation Between Personality Traits and Leadership Perceptions: An Application of Validity Generalization Procedures," *Journal of Applied Psychology* 71 (1986): 402–441; S. A. Kirkpatrick and E. A. Locke, "Leadership: Do Traits Matter?" *Academy of Management Executive* 5, no. 2 (1991): 48–60; Yukl, *Leadership in Organizations*; R. M. Kramer, "The Harder They Fall," *Harvard Business Review* 81, no. 10 (2003): 58–66.
30. Kirkpatrick and Locke, *Leadership*; Yukl, *Leadership in Organizations*; D. V. Day, D. J. Schleicher, A. L. Unckless, and N. J. Hiller, "Research Reports—Self-monitoring Personality at Work: A Meta-Analytic Investigation of Construct Validity," *Journal of Applied Psychology* 87, no. 2 (2002): 390–401.
31. J. B. Miner, "Twenty Years of Research on Role-Motivation Theory of Managerial Effectiveness," *Personnel Psychology* 31 (1978): 739–760; F. E. Berman and J. B. Miner, "Motivation to Manage at the Top Executive Level: A Test of the Hierarchic Role-Motivation Theory," *Personnel Psychology* 38 (1985): 377–391.
32. Bennis and Nanus, *Leaders*; J. M. Kouzes and B. Z. Posner, *The Leadership Challenge: How to Get Extraordinary Things Done in Organizations* (San Francisco: Jossey-Bass, 1987).
33. A. Bandura, *Social Foundations of Thought and Action: A Social Cognitive Theory* (Upper Saddle River, NJ: Prentice Hall, 1986); B. M. Bass, *Handbook of Leadership: A Survey of Theory and Research* (New York: Free Press, 1990); D. C. McClelland and R. E. Boyatzis, "Leadership Motive Pattern and Long-Term Success in Management," *Journal of Applied Psychology* 67 (1982): 737–743; A. Howard and D. W. Bray, *Managerial Lives in Transition: Advancing Age and Changing Times* (New York: Guilford Press, 1988).
34. Kouznes and Posner, *The Leadership Challenge.*
35. J. R. O'Neil, *The Paradox of Success: When Winning at Work Means Losing at Life. A Book of Renewal for Leaders* (New York: G. P. Putnam and Sons, 1994); M. Maccoby, "Narcissistic Leaders: The Incredible Pros, the Inevitable Cons," *Harvard Business Review* 82, no. 1 (2004): 92–100.
36. Bass, *Handbook of Leadership*; Bennis and Nanus, *Leaders*; Howard and Bray, *Managerial Lives in Transition*; C. D. McCauley and M. M. Lombardo, "Benchmarks: An Instrument for Diagnosing Managerial Strengths and Weaknesses," in *Measures of Leadership,* ed. K. E. Clark and M. B. Clark (West Orange, NJ: Leadership Library of America, Inc., 1990), 535–545; D. Goleman, R. Boyatzis, and A. McKee, *Primal Leadership: Realizing the Power of Emotional Intelligence* (Boston: Harvard Business School Press, 2002); D. L. Coutu, "Putting Leaders on the Couch: A Conversation with Manfred F. R. Kets de Vries," *Harvard Business Review* 82, no. 1 (2004): 64–71.
37. R. I. Westwood and A. Chan, "Headship and Leadership," in *Organizational Behavior: Southeast Asian Perspectives,* ed. R. I. Westwood (Hong Kong: Longman, 1992), 118–143.
38. M. Weber, *The Theory of Social and Economic Organization,* trans. A. M. Henderson and T. Parson, ed. with an introduction by T. Parsons (New York: Free Press, 1948).
39. S. Callan, "Charismatic Leadership in Contemporary Management Debates"; M. Frese, S. Beimel, and S. Schoenborn, "Action Training for Charismatic Leadership: Two Evaluations of Studies of a Commercial Training Module on Inspirational Communication of a Vision," *Personnel Psychology* 56, no. 3 (2003): 671–697; R. Khurana, "The Curse of the Superstar CEO," *Harvard Business Review* 80, no. 9 (2002): 60–66; S. W. Lester, B. M. Meglino, and M. A. Korsgaard, "The Antecedents and Consequences of Group Potency: A Longitudinal Investigation of Newly Formed Work Groups," *Academy of Management Journal* 45, no. 2 (2002): 352–368; D. De Cremer and D. van Knippenberg, "How Do Leaders Promote Cooperation? The Effects of Charisma and Procedural Fairness," *Journal of Applied Psychology* 87, no. 5 (2002): 858; J-C. Pastor, J. R. Meindl, and M. C. Mayo, "A Network Effects Model of Charisma Attributions," *Academy of Management Journal* 45, no. 2 (2002): 410–420; B. R. Agle, N. J. Nagarajan, J. A. Sonnenfeld, and D. Srinivasan, "Does CEO Charisma Matter? An Empirical Analysis of the Relationships Among Organizational Performance, Environmental Uncertainty, and Top Management Team Perceptions of CEO Charisma," *Academy of Management Journal* 49, no. 1 (2006):161–174; J. E. Bono and R. Ilies, "Charisma, Positive Emotions and Mood Contagion," *Leadership Quarterly* 17, no. 4 (2006): 317–334; M. E. Brown and L. K. Trevino, "Socialized Charismatic Leadership, Values Congruence, and Deviance in Work Groups," *Journal of Applied Psychology* 91, no. 4 (2006): 954–962; A. H. B. de Hoogh, D. N. den Hartog,

P. L. Koopman, H. Thierry, P. T. van den Berg, J. G. van der Weide, et al. "Leader Motives, Charismatic Leadership, and Subordinates' Work Attitude in the Profit and Voluntary Sector," *Leadership Quarterly* 16, no. 1 (2005): 17–38; K. S. Groves, "Linking Leader Skills, Follower Attitudes, and Contextual Variables via an Integrated Model of Charismatic Leadership," *Journal of Management* 31, no. 2 (2005): 255–277; J. J. Sosik, "The Role of Personal Values in the Charismatic Leadership of Corporate Managers: A Model and Preliminary Field Study," *Leadership Quarterly* 16, no. 2 (2005): 221–244.

40. House, *A 1976 Theory of Charismatic Leadership.*
41. M. E. Brown and L. K. Trevino, "Socialized Charismatic Leadership, Values Congruence, and Deviance in Work Groups," *Journal of Applied Psychology* 91, no. 4 (2006): 954–962.
42. C. Macrae, I. Ryder, J. Yan, J. Caswell, T. Kitchin, T. Power, M. McQuarrie, and S. Anholt, "Can Brand Leadership Recover Local Trust and Global Responsibility?" *Journal of Brand Management* 10, nos. 4–5 (2003): 268–279; R. L. Veninga, "Five Ways to Rebuild Trust," *Executive Excellence* 18, no. 10 (2001): 13–14.
43. J. E. Bono and R. Ilies, "Charisma, Positive Emotions and Mood Contagion," *Leadership Quarterly* 17, no. 4 (2006): 317–334; K. S. Groves, "Linking Leader Skills, Follower Attitudes, and Contextual Variables via an Integrated Model of Charismatic Leadership," *Journal of Management* 31, no. 2 (2005): 255–277; J. J. Sosik, "The Role of Personal Values in the Charismatic Leadership of Corporate Managers: A Model and Preliminary Field Study," *Leadership Quarterly* 16, no. 2 (2005): 221–244.
44. L. Lee, "Tricks of E*Trade: In His Drive to Create a Net Powerhouse, Christos Costakos Is Building a Culture That's Edgy, a Bit Bizarre—and Often Brilliant," *Business Week,* 2000, EB18.
45. Goleman, Boyatzis, and McKee, *Primal Leadership: Realizing the Power of Emotional Intelligence*; D. Goleman, "What Makes a Leader?" *Harvard Business Review* 76, no. 6 (1998): 92–103; J. D. Mayer and P. Salovey, "Emotional Intelligence and the Construction and Regulation of Feelings," *Applied and Preventive Psychology* 4 (1995): 197–208; J. D. Mayer, D. Goleman, C. Barrett, S. Gutstein, et al., "Leading by Feel," *Harvard Business Review* 82, no. 1 (2004): 27–37; D. Goleman, "What Makes a Leader?" *Harvard Business Review* 82, no. 1 (2004): 82–91; J. E. Dutton, P. J. Frost, M. C. Worline, J. M. Lilius, and J. M. Kanov, "Leading in Times of Trauma," *Harvard Business Review* 80, no. 1 (2002): 54–61.
46. Goleman, "What Makes a Leader?"
47. J. E. Barbuto Jr., S. M. Fritz, and D. Marx, "A Field Examination of Two Measures of Work Motivation as Predictors of Leaders' Influence Tactics," *Journal of Social Psychology* 132 (2002): 601–616; R. S. Rubin, D. Munz, and W. H. Bommer, "Leading from Within: The Effects of Emotion Recognition and Personality on Transformational Leadership Behavior," *Academy of Management Journal* 48 (2005): 845–858.
48. D. Goleman, *Emotional Intelligence* (New York: Bantam Books, 1995).
49. Goleman, Boyatzis, and McKee, *Primal Leadership: Realizing the Power of Emotional Intelligence.*
50. D. Goleman, *Social Intelligence: The New Science of Human Relationships* (New York: Bantam Books, 2006).
51. J. Misumi and M.E. Peterson, "The Performance-Maintenance (PM) Theory of Leadership: Review of a Japanese Research Program," *Administrative Science Quarterly* 30 (1985): 198–223; R. T. Lewis, "New York Times Company President and Chief Executive Officer Russell Lewis on 'The CEO's Lot Is Not a Happy One . . .' (with apologies to Gilbert and Sullivan)," *Academy of Management Executive* 16, no. 4 (2002): 37–42.
52. E. A. Eagly and B. T. Johnson, "Gender and Leadership Style: A Meta-Analysis," *Psychological Bulletin* 108 (1990): 235–256; J. B. Rosener, "Ways Women Lead," *Harvard Business Review* 68, no. 6 (1990): 119–125; G. N. Powell, "One More Time: Do Female and Male Managers Differ?" *Academy of Management Executive* 4, no. 3 (1990): 68–75; D. J. Campbell, W. Bommer, and E. Yeo, "Perceptions of Appropriate Leadership Style: Participation Versus Consultation Across Two Cultures," *Asia Pacific Journal of Management* 10, no. 1 (1993): 1–9; G. Morse, "The Emancipated Organization," *Harvard Business Review* 80, no. 9 (2002): 20–21; A. H. Eagley and L. L. Carli, "The Female Leadership Advantage: An Evaluation of the Evidence," *The Leadership Quarterly* 14 (2003): 807–834; R. P. Vecchio, "In Search of Gender Advantage," *The Leadership Quarterly* 14 (2003): 835–850; A. H. Eagly and L. L. Carli, "Finding Gender Advantage and Disadvantage: Systematic Research Integration is the Solution," *The Leadership Quarterly* 14 (2003): 851–859.
53. "Sex and Leadership Styles: A Meta-Analysis of Research Published in the 1990s," *Psychological Reports* 94, no. 1 (2004): 3–18.
54. R. R. Blake and J. S. Mouton, *The Management Grid* (Houston: Gulf Publishing, 1964); M. Wood, "The Fallacy of Misplaced Leadership," *Journal of Management Studies* 42, no. 6 (2005): 1101–1121.
55. Burns, *Leadership.*
56. B. M. Bass, "Leadership: Good, Better, Best," *Organizational Dynamics* 13, no. 3 (1985): 26–40; B. M. Bass and B. J. Avolio, "Developing Transformational Leadership: 1992 and Beyond," *Journal of European Industrial Training* 14, no. 5 (1992): 21–27.
57. Bass, *Leadership.*
58. B. M. Bass, D. I. Jung, B. J. Avolio, and Y. Berson, "Predicting Unit Performance by Assessing Transformational and Transactional Leadership," *Journal of Applied Psychology* 88, no. 2 (2003): 207–218; B. J. Avolio, "Re-examining the Components of Transformational and Transactional Leadership Using the Multifactor Leadership Questionnaire," *Journal of Occupational and Organizational Psychology* 72 (1999): 441–463.
59. C. L. Hoyt and J. Blascovich, "Transformational and Transactional Leadership in Virtual and Physical Environments," *Small Group Research* 34, no. 6 (2003): 678–716; N. M. Tichy and M. A. Devanna, "The Transformational Leader," *Training and Development* 40, no. 7 (1986): 27–32; G. A. Yukl, *Leadership in Organizations,* 3rd ed. (Upper Saddle River, NJ: Prentice Hall, 1994).
60. Bennis and Nanus, *Leaders.*
61. Yukl, *Leadership in Organizations.*

62. B. J. Avolio and W. L. Gardner, "Authentic Leadership Development: Getting to the Root of Positive Forms of Leadership," *Leadership Quarterly* 16, no. 3 (2005): 315–338. W. L. Gardner, B. J. Avolio, F. Luthans, D. R. May, and F. Walumbwa, "'Can You See the Real Me?' A Self-based Model of Authentic Leader and Follower Development," *Leadership Quarterly* 16, no. 3 (2005): 343–372; R. Ilies, F. P. Morgeson, and J. D. Nahrgang, "Authentic Leadership and Eudaemonic Well-being: Understanding Leader-Follower Outcomes," *Leadership Quarterly* 16, no. 3 (2005): 373–394.
63. P. N. Hineline, "The Several Meanings of 'Positive,'" *Journal of Organizational Behavior Management* 12, nos. 1–2 (2005): 55–66.
64. E. P. Hollander, "The Essential Interdependence of Leadership and Followership," *Current Directions in Psychological Science* 1, no. 2 (1992): 71–75; R. Stewart, *Choices for the Manager* (Upper Saddle River, NJ: Prentice Hall, 1982); Cited in: E. P. Hollanader, "Leadership, Followership, Self and Others," *Leadership Quarterly* 3, no. 1 (1992): 43–54; L. R. Offermann, "When Followers Become Toxic," *Harvard Business Review* 82, no. 1 (2004): 54–60; B. van Knippenberg and D. van Knippenberg, "Leader Self-sacrifice and Leadership Effectiveness: The Moderating Influence of Leader Prototypicality," *Journal of Applied Psychology* 90, no. 1 (2005): 25–37.
65. S. Motsch, "Think Gray," *Incentive* 169, no. 4 (1995): 59–60; N. Shope Griffin, "Personalize Your Management Development," *Harvard Business Review* 81, no. 3 (2003): 113–119.
66. R. E. Kelly, "In Praise of Followers," *Harvard Business Review* 66, no. 6 (1988): 142–149.
67. R. G. Lord and K. H. Maher, "Alternative Information-Processing Models and Their Implications for Theory, Research, and Practice," *Academy of Management Review* 15 (1990): 9–28.
68. B. J. Calder, "An Attribution Theory of Leadership," in *New Directions in Organizational Behavior,* ed. B. M. Staw and G. R. Salancik (Chicago: St. Clair, 1997); Lord, De Vader and Alliger, "A Meta–Analysis of the Relation Between Personality Traits and Leadership Perceptions"; A. C. Edmondson and S. E. Cha, "When Company Values Backfire," *Harvard Business Review* 80, no. 11 (2002): 18–19; B. Schyns, "The Role of Implicit Leadership Theories in the Performance Appraisals and Promotion Recommendations of Leaders," *Equal Opportunities International* 25, no. 3 (2006): 188–199.
69. Calder, "An Attribution Theory of Leadership"; J. Pfeffer, "The Ambiguity of Leadership," *Academy of Management Review* 2 (1977): 104–112.
70. P. Hersey, *Situational Selling* (Escondido, CA: Center for Leadership Studies, 1985); P. Hersey, K. Blanchard, and D. Johnson, *Management of Organizational Behavior: Leading Human Resources,* 8th ed. (Upper Saddle River, NJ: Prentice Hall, 2001).
71. G. B. Graen, R. C. Liden, and W. Hoel, "Role of Leadership in the Employee Withdrawal Process," *Journal of Applied Psychology* 67 (1982): 868–872; G. B. Graen, T. A. Scandura, and M. R. Grae, "A Field Experimental Test of the Moderating Effects of Growth Need Strength on Productivity," *Journal of Applied Psychology* 3 (1986): 484–491.
72. F. Dansereau, G. Graen, et al., "A Vertical Dyad Linkage Approach to Leadership Within Formal Organizations," *Organizational Behavior and Human Performance* 13, no. 1 (1975): 46–78; G. Grae and J. F. Cashman, "A Role-making Model of Leadership in Formal Organizations—A Developmental Approach," *Organization and Administrative Sciences* 6, nos. 2–3 (1975): 143–165; J. F. Cashman, F. Dansereau, G. Graen, and W. J. Haga, "Organizational Understructure and Leadership: A Longitudinal Investigation of the Managerial Role-making Process," *Organizational Behavior and Human Performance* 15 (1976): 278–296; G. B. Graen and M. Uhl-Bien, "Relationship-based Approach to Leadership: Development of Leader-Member Exchange (LMX) Theory of Leadership over 25 Years: Applying a Multi-domain Perspective," *The Leadership Quarterly, Special Issue: Leadership* 6 (1995): 219–247; M. Uhl-Bien and G. B. Graen, "Leadership Making in Self-managing Professional Work Teams: An Empirical Investigation," in *The Impact of Leadership,* ed. K. E. Clark, M. B. Clark, and D. P. Campbell (West Orange, NJ: Leadership Library of America, 1993). 379–387.
73. T. N. Bauer and S. G. Green, "Development of Leader-Member Exchange: A Longitudinal Test," *Academy of Management Journal* 39 (1996): 1538–1567; C. R. Gerstner and D. V. Day, "Meta-Analytic Review of Leader-Member Exchange Theory: Correlates and Construct Issues,' *Journal of Applied Psychology* 82 (1997): 827–844; Graen, et al. "Role of Leadership in the Employee Withdrawal Process"; Graen, Scandura, and Graen, "A Field Experimental Test of the Moderating Effects of Growth Need Strength on Productivity"; T. A. Scandura and G. B. Graen, "Moderating Effects of Initial Leader-Member Exchange Status on the Effects of a Leadership Intervention," *Journal of Applied Psychology* 69 (1984): 428–436.
74. Bauer and Green, "Development of Leader-Member Exchange"; D. A. Hofmann, S. J. Gerras, and F. P. Morgeson, "Climate as a Moderator of the Relationship Between Leader-Member Exchange and Content Specific Citizenship: Safety Climate as an Exemplar," *Journal of Applied Psychology* 88, no. 1 (2003): 170.
75. Graen and Uhl-Bien, "Relationship-based Approach to Leadership"; Uhl-Bien and Graen, "Leadership Making in Self-managing Professional Work Teams"; R. T. Sparrowe and R. C. Liden, "Process and Structure in Leader-Member Exchange," *Academy of Management Review* 22 (1997): 522–552; W. C. H. Prentice, "Understanding Leadership," *Harvard Business Review* 82, no. 1 (2004): 102–109; S. J. Wayne, L. M. Shore, W. H. Bommer, and L. E. Tetrick "The Role of Fair Treatment and Rewards in Perceptions of Organizational Support and Leader-Member Exchange," *Journal of Applied Psychology* 87, no. 3 (2002): 590–598.
76. W. Hui, et al., "Leaders-Member Exchange as a Mediator of the Relationship Between Transformational Leadership and Follower Performance and Organizational Citizenship Behavior," *Academy of Management Journal* 48 (2005): 420–432.

77. A. N. Turner and P. R. Lawrence, *Industrial Jobs and the Worker: An Investigation of Response to Task Attributes* (Boston: Harvard University, Division of Research, Graduate School of business Administration, 1965); R. W. Griffin, *Task Design: An Integrative Approach* (Glenview, IL: Scott, Foresman, 1982); J. R. Hackman and G. R. Oldham, *Work Redesign* (Reading, MA: Addison-Wesley, 1980).
78. L. W. Porter and G. B. McLaughlin, "Leadership and the Organizational Context: Like the Weather?" *The Leadership Quarterly* 17 (2006): 559–576.
79. L. R. Anderson and F. E. Fiedler, "The Effect of Participatory and Supervisory Leadership on Group Creativity," *Journal of Applied Psychology* 48 (1964): 227–236; F. E. Fiedler, *A Theory of Leadership Effectiveness* (New York: McGraw-Hill, 1967); M. M. Chemers and F. E. Fiedler, "The Effectiveness of Leadership Training: A Reply to Argyris," *American Psychologist* 33 (1978): 391–394.
80. M. G. Evans, "The Effects of Supervisory Behavior on the Path-Goal Relationship," *Organizational Behavior and Human Performance* 5 (1970): 277–298; R. J. House, "A Path-Goal Theory of Leader Effectiveness," *Administrative Science Quarterly* 16 (1971): 321–329; R. J. House and G. Dessler, "The Path-Goal Theory of Leadership: Some Post Hoc and A Priori Tests," in *Contingency Approaches to Leadership,* ed. J. Hunt and L. Larson (Carbondale, IL: Southern Illinois Press, 1974), 81–97; R. J. House and T. R. Mitchell, "Path-Goal Theory of Leadership," *Journal of Contemporary Business* 3, no. 4 (1974): 81–97.
81. House, "A Path-Goal Theory of Leader Effectiveness," 324.
82. S. Kerr and J. M. Jermier, "Substitutes for Leadership: Their Meaning and Measurement," *Organizational Behavior and Human Performance* 22 (1978): 375–403; J. P. Howell, D. E. Bowen, P. W. Dorfman, S. Kerr, et al., "Substitutes for Leadership: Effective Alternatives to Ineffective Leadership," *Organizational Dynamics* 19 (1990): 20–38; J. P. Howell and P. W. Dorfmann, "Substitutes for Leadership: Test of a Construct," *Academy of Management Journal* 24 (1981): 714–28; P. M. Podsakoff, S. B. MacKenzie, and W. H. Bommer, "Transformational Leader Behaviors and Substitutes for Leadership as Determinants of Employee Satisfaction, Commitment, Trust, and Organizational Citizenship Behaviors," *Journal of Management* 22 (1996): 259–298; S. B. MacKenzie, P. M. Podsakoff, and R. Fetter, "The Impact of Organizational Citizenship Behavior on Evaluations of Salesperson Performance," *Journal of Marketing* 57 (1993): 70–80; P. M. Podsakoff, B. P. Nichoff, S. B. MacKenzie, and M. L. Williams, "Do Substitutes for Leadership Really Substitute for Leadership? An Empirical Examination of Kerr and Jermier's Situational Leadership Model," *Organizational Behavior and Human Decision Processes* 54 (1993): 1–44.

Chapter 10

1. D. Brady, "Yes, Winning Is Still the Only Thing," *BusinessWeek,* 2006, 52–55.
2. G. P. Latham and C. C. Pinder, "Work Motivation Theory and Research at the Dawn of the Twenty-First Century," *Annual Review of Psychology* 56 (2005): 485–516.
3. G. Hofstede, "Culture and Organizations," *International Studies of Management and Organization* 10, no. 4 (1980): 15–41; C. Sue-Chan and M. Ong, "Goal Assignment and Performance: Assessing the Mediating Roles of Goal Commitment and Self-efficacy and the Moderating Role of Power Distance," *Organizational Behavior and Human Decision Processes* 89, no. 2 (2002): 1140–1161; P. E. Spector, C. L. Cooper, J. I. Sanchez, M. O'Driscoll, and K. Sparks, "Locus of Control and Well-being at Work: How Generalizable Are Western Findings," *Academy of Management Journal* 45, no. 2 (2002): 453–466.
4. A. H. Maslow, *Motivation and Personality,* 2nd ed. (New York: Harper & Row, 1970).
5. R. Jacob, "Secure Jobs Trump Higher Pay," *Fortune*, 1995, 24.
6. K. Schoenberger, P. J. McDonnell, and S. Hubler, "Thais Found in Sweatshop Are Released," *Los Angeles Times*, August 21, 1995, A1+.
7. C. P. Alderfer, "An Empirical Test for a New Theory of Human Needs," *Organizational Behavior and Human Performance* 4 (1969): 142–175; C. P. Alderfer, *Existence, Relatedness and Growth: Human Need in Organizational Settings* (New York: The Free Press, 1972); H. Levinson, "Management by Whose Objectives?" *Harvard Business Review* 81, no. 1 (2003): 107–116.
8. F. Ferris, "Unlocking Employee Productivity," *American Printer* 2, no. 5 (1995): 30–34.
9. D. C. McClelland, *Human Motivation* (Glenview, IL: Scott, Foresman, 1985); D. C. McClelland and R. E. Boyatzis, "Leadership Motive Pattern and Long-Term Success in Management," *Journal of Applied Psychology* 67 (1982): 734–743; D. C. McClelland and D. G. Winter, *Motivating Economic Achievement* (New York: The Free Press, 1969).
10. S. H. Schwartz and W. Blisky, "Toward a Universal Psychological Structure of Human Values," *Journal of Personality and Social Psychology* 53 (1987): 550–562; S. H. Schwartz and W. T. Bilsky, "Toward a Theory of the Universal Content and Structure of Values: Extensions and Cross-cultural Replications," *Journal of Personality and Social Psychology* 58 (1990): 878–881.
11. M. Erez and P. C. Earley, *Culture, Self-Identity, and Work* (New York: Oxford University Press, 1993), 102.
12. J. W. Connor and G. A. DeVos, "Cultural Influences on Achievement Motivation and Orientation: Towards Work in Japanese and American Youth," in *Influences of Social Structure, Labor Markets, and Culture*, ed. D. Stern and D. Eichorn (Hillsdale, NJ: Lawrence Erlbaum Associates, 1989), 291–326.
13. A. Sagie, D. Elizur, and H. Yamauchi, "The Structure and Strength of Achievement Motivation: A Cross-cultural Comparison," *Journal of Organizational Behavior* 17 (1996): 431–444; K. P. Parboteeah and J. B. Cullen, "Social Institutions and Work Centrality: Explorations Beyond National Culture," *Organization Science* 14, no. 2 (2003): 137–148; K. S. Law, D. K. Tse, and N. Zhou, "Does Human Resource Management Matter in a Transitional Economy? China as an Example," *Journal of International Business Studies* 34, no. 3 (2003): 255–265.
14. F. Herzberg, *Work and the Nature of Man* (Cleveland: Worth Publishing, 1966); F. Herzberg, "One More Time:

How Do You Motivate Employees?" *Harvard Business Review* 46 (1968): 54–62; F. Herzberg, B. Mausner, and B. B. Snyderman, *The Motivation to Work* (New York: Wiley, 1959).

15. J. E. LaBelle, "The Paradox of Safety Hopes and Rewards," *Professional Safety* 50, no. 12 (2005): 37–42.
16. M. Murray, "Giant Task: GE's Immelt Starts Renovations on the House That Jack Built—Under Intense Spotlight, CEO Focuses on Core Operations That Welch Had Trimmed—Opening the Books a Bit Wider," *Wall Street Journal,* February 6, 2003, A1.
17. R. W. Griffin, *Task Design: An Integrative Approach* (Glenview, IL: Scott, Foresman, 1982); J. L. Pierce and R. B. Dunham, "Task Design: A Literature Review," *Academy of Management Review* 1 (1976): 83–97.
18. J. R. Hackman and G. R. Oldham, *Work Redesign* (Reading, MA: Addison-Wesley, 1980).
19. J. O'Toole and E. E. Lawler III, *The New American Workplace* (New York: Palgrave MacMillan, 2005), 55–56.
20. J. S. Adams, "Towards an Understanding of Inequity," *Journal of Abnormal and Social Psychology* 67 (1963): 422–436; J. S. Adams, "Inequity in Social Exchange," in *Advances in Experimental Social Psychology*, ed. L. Berkowitz (New York: Academic Press, 1965), vol. 2, 267–299; R. T. Mowday, "Equity Theory Predictions of Behavior in Organizations," in *Motivation and Leadership at Work.* 6th ed., ed. R. M. Steers. L. W. Porter, and G. A Bigley (New York: McGraw-Hill. 1996); J. D. Shaw, N. Gupta, and J. E. Delery, "Pay Dispersion and Workforce Performance: Moderating Effects of Incentives and Interdepence," *Strategic Management Journal* 23, no. 6 (2002): 491–512; C. C. Chen, J. Choi, and S-C Chi, "Making Justice Sense of Local-Expatriate Compensation Disparity: Mitigation by Local Referents, Ideological Explanations, and Interpersonal Sensitivity in China-Foreign Joint Ventures," *Academy of Management Journal* 45, no. 5 (2003): 807–817.
21. C. C. Pinder, *Work Motivation in Organizational Behavior* (Upper Saddle River, NJ: Prentice Hall, 1998), 287.
22. V. H. Vroom, *Work and Motivation* (New York: Wiley, 1964).
23. "Integrate Corporate Culture and Employee Engagement," *Strategic HR Review* 4, no. 6 (2005): 5.
24. J. Caisson, "Jump Start Motivation," *Incentive* 175, no. 5 (2001): 77, 88; A. Erez and M. A. Isen, "The Influence of Positive Affect on the Components of Expectancy Motivation," *Journal of Applied Psychology* 87, no. 6 (2002): 1055–1067.
25. K. Hafner, "New Incentive for Google Employees: Awards Worth Millions," *New York Times,* February 1, 2005, section C, column 2, 10.
26. D. Addison, "Tailored Recognition at Lloyds TSB Asset Finance," *Strategic HR Review* 4, no. 6 (2005): 8–9.
27. A. D. Stajkovic and F. Luthans, "Social Cognitive Theory and Self-efficacy: Going Beyond Traditional Motivational and Behavioral Approaches," *Organizational Dynamics* 26, no. 4 (1998): 62–74; T. A. Wright, "What Every Manager Should Know: Does Personality Help Drive Employee Motivation?" *Academy of Management Executive* 17, no. 2 (1998): 131–133.
28. A. D. Stajkovic and F. Luthans, "Social Cognitive Theory and Self-efficacy: Implications for Motivation Theory and Practice," in *Motivation and Work Behavior,* ed. L. W. Porter, G. A. Bigley, and R. M. Steers (New York: McGraw-Hill, 2003); A. Bandura and E. A. Locke, "Negative Self-efficacy and Goal Effects Revisited," *Journal of Applied Psychology* 88, no. 1 (2003): 87–99.
29. M. Erez, "Goal Setting," in *Blackwell Encyclopedic Dictionary of Organizational Behavior,* ed. N. Nicholson (Cambridge, MA: Blackwell Business Publishing, 1995), 193–194; E. A. Locke, "The Motivation Sequence, the Motivation Hub, and the Motivation Core," *Organizational Behavior and Human Decision Processes* 50 (1991): 288–299; E. A. Locke and G. P. Latham, *A Theory of Goal Setting and Task Performance* (Upper Saddle River, NJ: Prentice Hall, 1990); W. Q. Judge, G. E. Fryxell, and R. S. Dooley, "The New Task of R&D Management: Creating Goal-Directed Communities for Innovation," *California Management Review* 39, no. 3 (1997): 72–85; T. A. Wright, "What Every Manager Should Know: Does Personality Help Drive Employee Motivation?" *Academy of Management Executive* 17, no. 2 (2003): 131–133.
30. E. A. Locke and G. P. Latham, "Goal Setting Theory: An Introduction," in *Motivation and Leadership at Work,* 6th ed., ed. R. M. Steers, L. W. Porter, and G. A. Bigley (New York: McGraw Hill, 1996).
31. R. Ilies and T. A. Judge, "Goal Regulation Across Time: The Effects of Feedback and Affect," *Journal of Applied Psychology* 90 (2005): 453–467.
32. Erez, *Goal Setting;* A. Drach-Zachavy and M. Erez, "Challenge Versus Threat Effects on the Goal-Performance Relationship," *Organizational Behavior and Human Decision Processes* 88, no. 2 (2002): 667–682; T. W. Britt, "Black Hawk Down at Work," *Harvard Business Review* 81, no. 1 (2003): 16; N. Nicholson, "How to Motivate Your Problem People," *Harvard Business Review* 81, no. 1 (2003): 56–58.
33. Ibid.
34. L. Helliker, "Pressure at Pier 1: Beating Sales Numbers of Year Earlier Is a Storewide Obsession," *Wall Street Journal,* December 7, 1995, B1.
35. M. Erez and P. C. Early, "Comparative Analysis of Goal-Setting Strategies Across Cultures," *Journal of Applied Psychology* 72 (1987): 658–665; S. S. K. Lam, X-P Chen, and J. Schaunbroeck, "Participative Decision Making and Employee Performance in Different Cultures: The Moderating Effects of Allocentrism/Idiocentrism and Efficacy," *Academy of Management Journal* 45, no. 5 (2002): 905–914.
36. Erez and Early, *Culture, Self-Identity, and Work,* 107.
37. J. L. Komaki, T. Coombs, and S. Schepman, "Motivational Implications of Reinforcement Theory," in *Motivation and Leadership at Work,* 6th ed., ed. R. M. Steers, L. W. Porter, and G. A. Bigley (New York: McGraw Hill, 1996).
38. S. Kerr, "On the Folly of Rewarding A While Hoping for B," *Academy of Management Journal* 18 (1975): 769–783.
39. Labelle, op. cit.
40. S. Kerr, *Ultimate Rewards* (Boston, MA: Harvard Business School Press, 1997).
41. Komaki, Coombs, and Schepman, *Motivational Implications of Reinforcement Theory.*

42. Ibid.
43. H. C. Triandis, "Collectivism vs. Individualism: A Reconceptualization of a Basic Concept in Cross-Cultural Social Psychology," in *Cross-Cultural Studies of Personality, Attitudes, and Cognition,* ed. G. K. Verma, Y. C. Bagley (London: Macmillan, 1988), 60–95; Erez and Earley, *Culture, Self-Identity, and Work.*
44. S. E. Seashore, *Group Cohesiveness in the Industrial Work Group* (Ann Arbor, MI: Survey Research Center, Institute for Social Research, University of Michigan, 1954).
45. D. Krackhardt and L. W. Porter, "When Friends Leave: A Structural Analysis of the Relationship Between Turnover and Stayers Attitudes," *Administrative Science Quarterly* 30 (1985): 242–261.
46. L. Chang, "Amway, Once Barred in China, Now Finds Business Booming," *Wall Street Journal*, March 12, 2003, B1.
47. D. Coats, "One in Four British Workers Feel Failed by Their Managers," *British Journal of Administrative Management* 51 (2006): 7.
48. F. Dansereau Jr., G. Graen, and W. J. Haga, "A Vertical Dyad Linkage Approach to Leadership Within Formal Organizations: A Longitudinal Investigation of the Role Making Process," *Organizational Behavior and Human Performance* 13 (1975): 46–78; G. B. Graen and J. F. Cashman, "A Role Making Model of Leadership in Formal Organizations: A Developmental Approach," in *Leadership Frontiers,* ed. J. G. Hunt and L. L. Larson (Kent, OH: Kent State University Press, 1975), 143–165; M. Mongeau, "Moving Mountains," *Harvard Business Review* 81, no. 1 (2003): 41–47.
49. D. Mechanic, *Students Under Stress: A Study in the Social Psychology of Adaptation* (New York: Free Press of Glencoe, 1962).
50. C. O'Reilly, "Corporations, Culture, and Commitment: Motivation and Social Control in Organizations," *California Management Review* 31, no. 4 (1989): 12.
51. E. Schonfeld, "Have the Urge to Merge? You'd Better Think Twice," *Fortune,* 1997, 114–116.
52. Erez and Earley, *Culture, Self-Identity, and Work*; Locke, *The Motivation Sequence, the Motivation Hub, and the Motivation Core.*
53. F. Elashmawi and R. R. Harris, *Multicultural Management: New Skills for Global Success* (Houston, TX: Gulf Publishing, 1993), Table 6.2, 144; G. Morse, "Why We Misread Motives," *Harvard Business Review* 81, no. 1 (2003): 18.
54. H. C. Triandis, R. Brislin, and C. H. Hui, "Cross-Cultural Training Across the Individualism-Collectivism Divide," *International Journal of Intercultural Relations* 12 (1988): 269–289.
55. K. Leung and M. H. Bond, "How Chinese and Americans Reward Task-related Contributions: A Preliminary Study," *Psychologia: An International Journal for Psychology in the Orient* 25, no. 1 (1982): 32–39; M. H. Bond, K. Leung, and K. C. Wan, "How Does Cultural Collectivism Operate? The Impact of Task and Maintenance Contributions on Reward Distribution," *Journal of Cross-Cultural Psychology* 47 (1982): 793–804; K. Leung and H. Park, "Effects of Interactional Goal on Choice of Allocation Rule: A Cross-National Study," *Organizational Behavior and Human Decision Processes* 37 (1986): 111–120; K. I. Kim, H. Park, and N. Suzuki, "Reward Allocations in the United States, Japan, and Korea: A Comparison of Individualistic and Collectivistic Cultures," *Academy of Management Journal* 33 (1990): 188–198; C. C. Chen, J. Choi, and S-C Chi, "Making Justice Sense of Local-Expatriate Compensation Disparity: Mitigation by Local Referents, Ideological Explanations, and Interpersonal Sensitivity in China-Foreign Joint Ventures," *Academy of Management Journal* 45, no. 5 (2003): 807–817.
56. M. Weber, *The Protestant Work Ethic and the Spirit of Capitalism*, trans. T. Parsons (New York: Scribner, 1958); R. Wuthnow, "Religion and Economic Life," in *The Handbook of Economic Sociology*, ed. N. J. Smelser and R. Swedbert (Princeton: Princeton University Press, 1994), 620–646.
57. G. W. England and I. Harpaz, "Some Methodological and Analytic Considerations in Cross-National Comparative Research," *Journal of International Business Studies* 14, no. 2 (1983): 49–59.
58. I. Harpaz and H. Fu, "Work Centrality in Germany, Israel, Japan, and the United States," *Journal of Cross-Cultural Research* 31 (1997): 171–200.
59. S. P. Eisner, "Managing Generation Y," *SAM Advanced Management Journal* 70, no. 4 (2005): 4–15; R. L. Lord and P. A. Farrington, "Age-Related Differences in the Motivation of Knowledge Workers," *Engineering Management Journal* 18, no. 3 (2006): 20–26.
60. D. Finegold and S. Mohrman, "What Do Employees Really Want: The Perception vs. the Reality." Paper presented at the World Economics Forum Annual Meeting, Davos, Switzerland, 2001.

Chapter 11

1. H. J. Leavitt, "The Old Days, Hot Groups, and Managers' Lib," *Administrative Science Quarterly* 41 (1996): 288–300; L. I. Glassop, "The Organizational Benefit of Teams," *Human Relations* 55, no. 2 (2002): 225–249.
2. E. A. Locke, D. Tirnauer, Q. Roberson, B. Goldman, M. E. Latham, and E. Weldon, "The Importance of the Individual in an Age of Groupism," in *Groups at Work: Theory and Research*, ed. M. Turner (Mahwah, NJ: Erlbaum, 2001), 501–528.
3. B. I. Kirkman and D. L. Shapiro, "The Impact of Cultural Values on Employee Resistance to Teams: Toward a Model of Globalized Self-managing Work Team Effectiveness," *Academy of Management Review* 22 (1997): 730–757; S. S. K. Lam, X-P. Chen, and J. Schaubroeck, "Participative Decision Making and Employee Performance in Different Cultures: The Moderating Effects of Allocentrism/ Idiocentrism and Efficacy," *Academy of Management Journal* 45, no. 5 (2002): 905–914; D. C. Thomas and K. Au, "The Effect of Cultural Differences on Behavioral Responses to Low Job Satisfaction" *Journal of International Business Studies* 33, no. 2 (2002): 309–326; L. I. Glassop, "The Organizational Benefit of Teams," *Human Relations* 55 (2002): 225–249.
4. P. Sellers, "Get Over Yourself," *Fortune*, 2001, 76–88.

5. E. Sundstrom, K. P. de Meuse, and D. Futrell, "Work Teams: Applications and Effectiveness," *American Psychologist* 45, no. 2 (1990): 120–133.
6. M. Cotrill, "Give Your Work Teams Time and Training," *Academy of Management Executive* 11, no. 3 (1997): 87–89; R. D. Banker, J. M. Field, R. G. Schroeder, and K. K. Sinha, "Impact of Work Teams on Manufacturing Performance: A Longitudinal Field Study," *Academy of Management Journal* 39 (1996): 867–890.
7. "Ball Aerospace Hi-rise Camera Returns Stunning Mars Images," *Imaging Update* 17, no. 11 (November 2006): 6–7.
8. M. Weinstein, "Coming Up Short? Join the Club," *Training* 43, no. 4 (2006): 14.
9. J. McGregor, "I Can't Believe They Took the Whole Team," *Business Week Online*, December 18, 2006, www.businessweek.com/magazine/content/06_51/b4014075.htm?chan=search.
10. J. R. Hackman, "The Design of Work Teams," in *Handbook of Organizational Behavior*, ed. J. W. Lorsch (Upper Saddle River, NJ: Prentice Hall, 1987), 315–342.
11. S. Caminiti, "What Team Leaders Need to Know," *Fortune*, 1995, 93–100.
12. Banker et al., "Impact of the Work Teams on Manufacturing Performance."
13. C. D. Cramton, "The Mutual Knowledge Problem and Its Consequences for Dispersed Collaboration," *Organization Science* 12 (2001): 346–367; C. D. Cramton, "Finding Common Ground in Dispersed Collaboration," *Organizational Dynamics* 4 (2002): 356–371; M. K. Ahuja and J. A. Galvin, "Socialization in Virtual Groups," *Journal of Management* 29, no. 2 (2003): 161–186.
14. Cramton, "Finding Common Ground in Dispersed Collaboration"; Ahuja and Galvin, "Socialization in Virtual Groups."
15. B. E. Ashforth and F. Mael, "Social Identity Theory and the Organization," *Academy of Management Review* 14 (1989): 20–39; Bettenhausen, "Five Years of Group Research: What We Have Learned and What Needs to Be Addressed."
16. J. S. Heinem and E. Jacobsen, "A Model of Task Group Development in Complex Organizations and a Strategy of Implementation," *Academy of Management Review* 1, no. 4 (1976): 98–111; B. W. Tuckman and M. A. Jensen, "Stages of Small-Group Development Revisited," *Group and Organization Studies* 2 (1977): 419–427; R. L. Moreland and J. N. Levine, "Group Dynamics over Time: Development and Socialization in Small Groups," in *The Social Psychology of Time: New Perspectives*, ed. J. M. McGrath (Newbury Park, CA: Sage, 1988), 151–181; Sundstrom et al., "Work Teams"; Bettenhausen, "Five Years of Group Research"; A. Chang, P. Bordia, and J. Duck, "Punctuated Equilibrium and Linear Progression: Toward a New Understanding of Group Development," *Academy of Management Journal* 46, no. 1 (2003): 106–117.
17. B. W. Tuckman, "Development Sequence in Small Groups," *Psychological Bulletin* 63 (1965): 384–399; Tuckman and Jensen, "Stages of Small Group Development Revisited."
18. Sundstron et al., "Work Teams," 127.
19. J. M. Perdue, "A Global Success Story," *Oil and Gas Investor. Supplement: ExxonMobil's Hoover/Diana–A Deepwater Pioneer* (2002): 16–19.
20. A. De Marco, "Teamwork Pays Off for Ross and Sterling Winthrop," *Facilities Design and Management* 12, no. 12 (1993): 38–41.
21. Sundstron et al., "Work Teams," 126; B. B. Baltes, M. W. Dickson, M. P. Sherman, C. C. Bauer, and J. S. LaGanke, "Computer-Mediated Communication and Group Decision Making: A Meta-Analysis," *Organizational Behavior and Human Decision Processes* 87, no. 1 (2002): 156–179.
22. B. Mullen, C. Symons, L. Hu, and E. Salas, "Group Size, Leadership Behavior, and Subordinate Satisfaction," *Journal of General Psychology* 116, no. 2 (1989): 155–170.
23. B. Mullen, D. A. Johnson, and S. D. Drake, "Organizational Productivity as a Function of Group Composition: A Self-Attention Perspective," *Journal of Social Psychology* 127 (1987): 143–50; L. Fried, "Team Size and Productivity in Systems Development," *Information Systems Management* 8, no. 3 (1991): 27.
24. B. Latane, K. Williams, and S. Harkings, "Social Loafing," *Psychology Today* 13, no. 5 (1979): 104–110; P. C. Earley, "Social Loafing and Collectivism: A Comparison of the United States and the People's Republic of China," *Administrative Science Quarterly* 34 (1989): 565–581; S. M. Murphy, S. J. Wayne, R. C. Liden, and B. Erdogan, "Understanding Social Loafing: The Role of Justice Perceptions and Exchange Relationships," *Human Relations* 56, no. 1 (2003): 61–84; X-P Chen and D. G. Bachrach, "Tolerance of Free-Riding: The Effects of Defection Size, Defection Pattern, and Social Orientation in a Repeated Public Goods Dilemma," *Organizational Behavior and Human Decision Processes* 90, no. 1 (2003): 139–147; H. Goren, R. Kurzban, and A. Rapoport, "Social Loafing vs. Social Enhancement: Public Goods Provisioning in Real-Time with Irrevocable Commitments," *Organizational Behavior and Human Decision Processes* 90, no. 2 (2003): 277–290.
25. K. L. Bettenhausen, "Five Years of Group Research: What We Have Learned and What Needs to Be Addressed," *Journal of Management* 17 (1991): 345–381; H. Weggem and S. A. Haslam, "Improving Work Motivation and Performance in Brainstorming Groups: The Effects of Three Group Goal-Setting Strategies," *European Journal of Work and Organizational Psychology*, 14 (2005): 400–430; L. Chidambaram and L. L. Tung, "Is Out of Sight, Out of Mind? An Empirical Study of Social Loafing in Technology-Supported Groups," *Information Systems Research*, 16, no. 2 (2005): 149–168; S. G. Scott and W. O. Einstein, "Strategic Performance Appraisal in Team-based Organizations: One Size Does Not Fit All," *Academy of Management Executive* 15, no. 2 (2001): 107–116.
26. K. D. Williams, S. A. Nica, L. D. Baca, and B. Latane, "Social Loafing and Swimming: Effects of Identifiability on Individual and Relay Performance of Intercollegiate Swimmers," *Basic and Applied Social Psychology* 10 (1989): 73–81.
27. W. K. Gabrenya, Y. Wang, and B. Latane, "Social Loafing on an Optimizing Task: Cross-Cultural Differences Among Chinese and Americans," *Journal of Cross-Cultural Psychology* 16 (1985): 223–242.
28. M. E. Shaw, *Group Dynamics: The Psychology of Small Group Behavior*, 3rd ed. (New York: McGraw-Hill, 1981).

29. B. Davis, "Michelin Unit Attempts to Satisfy Dealer Complaints," *Rubber and Plastics News* 36, no. 12 (2007): 22.
30. R. E. Silverman, "For Charlie Kim, Company of Friends Proves a Lonely Place," *Wall Street Journal*, February 1, 2001, A1+.
31. L. H. Pelled, "Demographic Diversity, Conflict, and Work Group Outcomes: An Intervening Process Theory" *Administrative Science Quarterly* 7 (1996): 615–631; L. H. Pelled, K. M. Eisenhardt, and X. R. Xin, "Exploring the Black Box: An Analysis of Work Group Diversity, Conflict, and Performance," *Administrative Science Quarterly* 44 (1999): 1–28; K. Jehn, G. B. Northcraft, and M. A. Neale, "Why Differences Make a Difference: A Field Study of Diversity, Conflict, and Performance in Workgroups," *Administrative Science Quarterly* 44 (1999): 741–763.
32. S. Caudron, "Keeping Team Conflict Alive," *Training & Development* 52, no. 9 (1998): 48–52; G. S. Van der Vegt and O. Janssen, "Joint Impact of Interdependence and Group Diversity on Innovation," *Journal of Management* 29, no. 5 (2003): 729–751.
33. S. G. Cohen, "What Makes Teams Work: Group Effectiveness Research from the Shop Floor to the Executive Suite," *Journal of Management* 23 (1997): 239–290; J. T. Polzer, L. P. Milton, and W. B. Swann Jr., "Capitalizing on Diversity: Interpersonal Congruence in Small Work Groups," *Administrative Science Quarterly* 47, no. 2 (2002): 296–324; G. S. Van der Vegt and O. Janssen, "Joint Impact of Interdependence and Group Diversity on Innovation," *Journal of Management* 29, no. 5 (2003): 729–751; Pelled, "Demographic Diversity, Conflict, and Work Group Outcomes: An Intervening Process Theory"; Pelled et al., "Exploring the Black Box: An Analysis of Work Group Diversity, Conflict, and Performance"; J. A. Chatman and F. J. Flynn, "The Influence of Demographic Heterogeneity on the Emergence and Consequences of Cooperative Norms in Work Teams," *Academy of Management Journal* 44 (2001): 956–974; D. A. Harrison, K. H. Price, and M. P. Bell, "Beyond Relational Demography: Time and the Effects Of Surface- and Deep-Level Diversity on Work Group Cohesion," *Academy of Management Journal* 41 (1998): 96–107; Jehn et al. Why Differences Make A Difference: A Field Study of Diversity, Conflict, and Performance in Workgroups; J. S. Bunderson and K. M. Sutcliffe, "Comparing Alternative Conceptualizations of Functional Diversity in Management Teams: Process and Performance Effects," *Academy of Management Journal* 45, no. 5 (2002): 875–893; D. A. Harrison, K. H. Price, J. H. Gavin, and A. T. Florey, "Time, Teams, and Task Performance: Changing Effects of Surface- and Deep-Level Diversity on Group Functioning," *Academy of Management Journal*, 45, no. 5 (2002): 1029–1045.
34. Harrison et al., "Beyond Relational Demography: Time and the Effects of Surface- and Deep-Level Diversity on Work Group Cohesion."
35. J. Gordon, M. Hequet, C. Lee, M. Picard, et al., "Workplace Blues," *Training* 33, no. 2 (1996): 16.
36. M. S. Abramson, "First Teams," *Government Executive* 18, no. 5 (1996): 53–58; L. F. Brajkovich, "Executive Commentary," *Academy of Management Executive* 17, no. 1 (2003): 110–111; L. Thompson, "Improving the Creativity of Organizational Work Groups," *Academy of Management Executive* 17, no. 1 (2003): 96–97; G. S. Van der Vegt and O. Janssen, "Joint Impact of Interdependence and Group Diversity on Innovation," *Journal of Management* 29, no. 5 (2003): 729–751; R. Sethi, D. C. Smith, and C. W. Park, "How to Kill a Team's Creativity," *Harvard Business Review* 80, no. 8 (2002): 16–17.
37. C. C. Manz and H. P. Sims Jr., "Leading Workers to Lead Themselves: The External Leadership of Self-Managing Work Teams," *Administrative Science Quarterly* 32 (1987): 106–129.
38. C. Fishman, "Creative Tension," *Fast Company*, 2000, 359–366.
39. Shaw, *Group Dynamics*; M. C. Thomas-Hunt, T. Y. Ogden, and M. A. Neale, "Who's Really Sharing? Effects of Social and Expert Status on Knowledge Exchange Within Groups," *Management Science* 49, no. 4 (2003): 464–477; T. R. Tyler and S. L. Blader, "Autonomous vs. Comparative Status: Must We Be Better Than Others to Feel Good About Ourselves?" *Organizational Behavior and Human Decision Processes* 89, no. 1 (2002): 813–838; P. M. Valcour, "Managerial Behavior in a Multiplex Role System," *Human Relations* 55, no. 10 (2002): 1163–1188.
40. J. E. Driskell and E. Salas, "Group Decision Making Under Stress," *Journal of Applied Psychology* 76 (1991): 473–78.
41. Shaw, *Group Dynamics*.
42. E. White, "Culture Shock: Learning Customs of a New Office," *Wall Street Journal*, November 28, 2006, B6.
43. Ibid.
44. D. C. Feldman, "The Development and Enforcement of Group Norms," *Academy of Management Review* 9 (1984): 47–53.
45. Caminiti, "What Team Leaders Need to Know."
46. Shaw, *Group Dynamics*; see also: N. Nicholson, ed., *Encyclopedic Dictionary of Organizational Behavior* (Oxford, UK: Blackwell, 1995), 199.
47. Cohen, "What Makes Teams Work: Group Effectiveness Research from the Shop Floor to the Executive Suite."
48. D. Druckman and J. A. Swets, eds., *Enhancing Human Performance: Issues, Theories and Techniques* (National Research Council, Washington, D. C.: National Academy Press, 1988).
49. R. R. Hirschfeld, M. H. Jordan, H. S. Feild, W. F. Giles, and A. A. Armenakis, "Teams' Female Representation and Perceived Potency as Inputs to Team Outcomes in a Predominantly Male Field Setting," *Personnel Psychology* 58, no. 4 (2005): 893–924.
50. Ibid.
51. Shaw, *Group Dynamics;* Sethi, Smith, and Park, "How to Kill a Team's Creativity."
52. Ibid, 218; Sethi, Smith, and Park, "How to Kill a Team's Creativity."
53. D. M. Landers, M. O. Wilkinson, B. D. Hatfield, and H. Barber, "Causality and the Cohesion-Performance Relationship," *Journal of Sport Psychology*, 4, no. 2 (1982): 170–183; J. A. LePine, J. R. Hollenbeck, D. R. Ilgen, J. A. Colquitt, and A. Ellis, "Gender Composition, Situational Strength, and Team Decision-Making Accuracy: A Criterion Decomposition Approach," *Organizational*

Behavior and Human Decision Processes, 88, no. 1 (2002): 445–475.

54. M. H. Safizadeh, "The Case of Workgroups in Manufacturing Operations," *California Management Review* 33, no. 4 (1991): 61–82; A. Erez, J. A. Lepine, and H. Elms, "Effects of Rotated Leadership and Peer Evaluation on the Functioning and Effectiveness of Self-Managed Teams: A Quasi-Experiment," *Personnel Psychology* 55, no. 4 (2002): 929–948; L. I. Glassop, "The Organizational Benefit of Teams," *Human Relations* 55, no. 2 (2002): 225–249.
55. J. O'Toole and E. E. Lawler III, *The New American Workplace* (New York: Palgrave-McMillan, 2006).
56. Kirkman and Shapiro, "The Impact of Cultural Values on Employee Resistance to Teams."
57. R. Gildersleeve, "dj Orthopedics Adopts 'Lean' Product Developments Processes to Win," *Visions* 30, no. 3 (2006): 45.
58. K. Lovelace, D. L. Shapiro, and L. R. Weingart, "Maximizing Cross-Functional New Product Teams' Innovativeness and Constraint Adherence: A Conflict Communications Perspective," *Academy of Management Journal* 44 (2001): 779–793.
59. A. R. Jassawalla and H. C. Sashittal, "Building Collaborative Cross-Functional New Product Teams," *Academy of Management Executive* 13, no. 3 (1999): 50–63; J. S. Bunderson and K. M. Sutcliffe, "Comparing Alternative Conceptualizations of Functional Diversity in Management Teams: Process and Performance Effects," *Academy of Management Journal* 45, no. 5 (2002): 875–893; Sethi, Smith, and Park, "How to Kill a Team's Creativity."
60. J. J. Distefano and M. L. Maznevski, "Creating Value with Diverse Teams in Global Management," *Organizational Dynamics* 29 (2000): 45–63.
61. K. M. Chudoba, E. Wynn, M. Lu, and M. B. Watson-Manheim, "How Virtual Are We? Measuring Virtuality and Understanding Its Impact in a Global Organization," *Information Systems Journal* 15, no. 4 (2005): 279–306.
62. B. L. Kirkman, B. Rosen et al., "Five Challenges to Virtual Team Success: Lessons from Sabre Inc." *Academy of Management Executive* 16 (2002): 67–79.
63. P. M. Beranek, J. Broder et al., "Management of Virtual Project Teams: Guidelines for Team Leaders," *Communication of AIS* 16 (2005): 247–259.
64. S. Dani, N. Burns et al., "The Implications of Organizational Culture and Trust in the Working of Virtual Teams," *Proceedings of the Institution of Mechanical Engineers* 220 (2006): 951–960; J. Goodbody, "Critical Success Factors for Global Virtual Teams," *Strategic Communication Management* 9, no. 2 (2005): 18–21.
65. J. A. Cannon-Bowers and E. Salas, "Teamwork Competencies: The Interaction of Team Member Knowledge, Skills, and Attitudes," in *Workforce Readiness: Competencies and Assessment*, ed. H. F. O'Neil Jr. (Mahwah, NJ: Lawrence Erlbaum Associates, 1997), 151–174; J. A. Cannon-Bowers and E. Salas, "A Framework for Developing Team Performance Measures in Training," in *Team Performance Assessment and Measurement: Theory, Methods, and Applications*, ed. M. T. Brannick, E. Salas, and C. Prince (Mahwah, NJ: Lawrence Erlbaum Associates, 1997); J. A. Cannon-Bowers, S. I. Tannenbauam, E. Salas, and C. E. Volpe, "Defining Competencies and Establishing Team Training Requirements," in *Team Effectiveness and Decision Making in Organizations*, ed. R. A. Guzzo, E. Salas, and Associates (San Francisco: Jossey-Bass Publishers, 1995); E. Salas, T. L. Dickinson, S. A. Converse, and S. I. Tannenbaum, "Toward an Understanding of Team Performance and Training," in *Teams: Their Training and Performance*, ed. R. Swezey and E. Salas (Norwood, NJ: Ablex, 1992), 3–29; G. A. Okhuysen and K. M. Eisenhardt, "Integrating Knowledge in Groups: How Formal Interventions Enable Flexibility," *Organization Science* 13, no. 4 (2002): 370–386.
66. P. J. Jordan and A. C. Troth, "Managing Emotions During Team Problem Solving," *Human Performance* 17, no. 2 (2004): 195–218.
67. J. A. Cannon-Bowers et al., "Defining Competencies and Establishing Team Training Requirements."
68. S. Caudron, "Keeping Team Conflict Alive," *Training and Development* 52, no. 9 (1998): 48–52.
69. A. C. Amason, W. A. Hochwater, K. R. Thompson, and A. W. Harrison, "Conflict: An Important Dimension in Successful Management Teams," *Organizational Dynamics* 24, no. 2 (1995): 20–35; S. Schulz-Hardt, M. Jochims, and D. Frey, "Productive Conflict in Group Decision Making: Genuine and Contrived Dissent as Strategies to Counteract Biased Information Seeking," *Organizational Behavior and Human Decision Processes* 88, no. 2 (2002): 563–586.
70. K. A. Jehn, "A Multimethod Examination of the Benefits and Detriments of Intragroup Conflict," *Administrative Science Quarterly* 40 (1995): 256–282; Schulz-Hardt, Jochims, and Frey, "Productive Conflict in Group Decision Making: Genuine and Contrived Dissent as Strategies to Counteract Biased Information Seeking."
71. Amason et al., "Conflict"; K. M. Eisenhardt, J. L. Kahwajy, and L. J. Bourgeois III, "Conflict and Strategic Choice: How Top Management Teams Disagree," *California Management Review* 39, no. 2 (1997): 42–62; K. A. Jehn and E. A. Mannix, "The Dynamic Nature of Conflict: A Longitudinal Study of Intragroup Conflict and Group Performance," *Academy of Management Journal* 44 (2001): 238–251; T. L. Simons and R. S. Peterson, "Task Conflict and Relationship Conflict in Top Management Teams: The Pivotal Role of Intragroup Trust," *Journal of Applied Psychology* 85 (2000): 102–111; Pelled, Eisenhardt, and Xin, "Exploring the Black Box: An Analysis of Work Group Diversity, Conflict, and Performance."
72. Jehn, "A Multimethod Examination of the Benefits and Detriments of Intragroup Conflict."
73. C. K. W. DeDreu and L. R. Weingart, "Task Versus Relationship Conflict, Team Performance, and Team Member Satisfaction: A Meta-Analysis," *Journal of Applied Psychology* 88 (2003): 741–749.
74. Amason et al., "Conflict."
75. Ibid; Jehn, "A Multimethod Examination of the Benefits and Detriments of Intragroup Conflict."
76. Pelled, Eisenhardt, and Xin, "Exploring the Black Box: An Analysis of Work Group Diversity, Conflict, and Performance."

77. Pelled, "Demographic Diversity, Conflict, and Work Group Outcomes."
78. Jehn, Gregory, and Neale, "Why Differences Make A Difference: A Field Study of Diversity," 81.
79. Amason et al., "Conflict."
80. Eisenhardt et al., "Conflict and Strategic Choice."
81. Jehn et al., "Why Differences Make a Difference."
82. Jenn and Mannix, "The Dynamic Nature of Conflict."
83. M. Hoegl, K. Wienkauf, et al. "Interteam Coordination, Project Commitment and Teamwork in Multiteam R&D Projects: A Longitudinal Study," *Organization Science* 15, no. 1 (2004): 38–55.
84. D. R. Forsyth, *An Introduction to Group Dynamics* (Monterey, CA: Brooks/Cole Publishing, 1983).
85. G. A. Neuman and J. Wright, "Team Effectiveness: Beyond Skills and Cognitive Ability," *Journal of Applied Psychology* 84 (1999): 376–389; D. E. Hyatt and T. M. Ruddy, "An Examination of the Relationship Between Work Group Characteristics and Performance: Once More into the Breech," *Personnel Psychology* 50 (1997): 553–585; M. A. Campion, E. M. Papper, and G. J. Medsker, "Relations Between Work Team Characteristics and Effectiveness: A Replication and Extension," *Personnel Psychology* 49 (1996): 429–452; Cohen and Bailey, "What Makes Teams Work."
86. J. Fitz-Enz, "Measuring Team Effectiveness," *HR Focus* 74, no. 8 (1997): 3.
87. J. R. Hackman, ed., *Groups That Work (and Those That Don't): Creating Conditions for Effective Teamwork* (San Fransisco: Jossey-Bass, 1990).
88. Hackman, *Groups That Work.*
89. Campion et al., "Relations Between Work Team Characteristics and Effectiveness"; Hyatt and Ruddy, "An Examination of the Relationship Between Work Group Characteristics and Performance."
90. R. Wageman and G. Baker, "Incentives and Cooperation: The Joint Effects of Task and Reward Interdependence on Group Performance," *Journal of Organizational Behavior* 18, no. 2 (1997): 139–158.
91. Banker et al., "Impact of Work Teams on Manufacturing Performance"; Cottrill, "Give Your Teams Time and Training."
92. Abramson, "First Teams."
93. J. R. Hackman and R. Wageman, "A Theory of Team Coaching," *Academy of Management Review* 30 (2005): 269–287.
94. Cohen and Bailey, "What Makes Teams Work."
95. G. L. Hallam, "Seven Common Beliefs About Teams: Are They True?" *Leadership in Action* 17, no. 3 (1997): 1–4.

Chapter 12

1. S. Bing, "Business as a Second Language," *Fortune* (1998): 57–58.
2. K. Krone, F. M. Jablin, and L. L. Putnam, "Communication Theory and Organizational Communication: Multiple Perspectives," in *Handbook of Organizational Communication: An Interdisciplinary Perspective*, ed. F. M. Jablin, L. L. Putnam, K. H. Roberts, and L. W. Porter (Newbury Park, CA: Sage Publications, 1987).
3. H. C. Triandis, *Culture and Social Behavior* (New York: McGraw-Hill, 1994); B. A. Bechky, "Sharing Meaning Across Occupational Communities: The Transformation of Understanding on a Production Floor," *Organization Science* 14, no. 3 (2003): 312; M. Becerra and A. K. Gupta, "Perceived Trustworthiness Within the Organization: The Moderating Impact of Communication Frequency on Trustor and Trustee Effects," *Organization Science* 14, no. 1 (2003): 32–44.
4. R. L. Daft and R. H. Lengel, "Information Richness: A New Approach to Managerial Behavior and Organization Design," in *Research in Organizational Behavior*, ed. L. L. Cummings and B. Staw (Greenwich CT: JAI, 1984), 191–223; R. L. Daft and R. H. Lengel, "Organizational Information Requirements, Media Richness and Structural Design," *Management Science* 32 (1986): 554–572; K. Miller, *Organizational Communication: Approaches and Processes*, 2nd ed. (Belmont, CA: Wadsworth, 1999).
5. L. K. Trevino, R. L. Daft, and R. H. Lengel, "Understanding Managers Media Concerns," in *Organizations and Communication Technology*, ed. J. Fulk and C. Steinfeile (Newbury Park: Sage, 1990); "How to Create Communications Materials Employees Will Actually Use," *Harvard Business Review* 80, no. 1 (2002): 102.
6. S. Salmon and T. A. Joiner, "Toward an Understanding Communication Channel Preferences for the Receipt of Management Information," *Journal of American Academy of Business* 7, no. 2 (2005): 56–62.
7. J. Yates and W. J. Orlikowski, "Genres of Organizational Communication: A Structurational Approach to Studying Communication and Media," *Academy of Management Review* 17 (1992): 299–326.
8. L. W. Porter, E. E. Lawler III, and J. R. Hackman, *Behavior in Organizations* (New York: McGraw-Hill, 1975).
9. K. Davis, "The Care and Cultivation of the Corporate Grapevine," *Dun's Review* 102, no. 1 (1973): 44–47.
10. C. Dellarocas, "The Digitization of Word of Mouth: Promise and Challenges of Online Feedback Mechanisms," *Management Science* 49, no. 10 (2003): 1407–1424.
11. "BASF Launches SM/PO Venture," *Chemical Market Reporter* 262, no. 11 (2002): 23.
12. "He said, she said," *Communications* 46 (2003): 9, 11; H. Ibarra, "Homophily and Differential Returns: Sex Differences in Network Structure and Access in an Advertising Firm," *Administrative Science Quarterly* 37 (1992): 422–447; H. Ibarra, "Personal Networks of Women and Minorities in Management: A Conceptual Framework," *Academy of Management Review* 18 (1993): 56–87; H. Ibarra, "Race, Opportunity, and Diversity of Social Circles in Managerial Networks," *Academy of Management Journal* 38 (1995): 673–703; K. A. Mollica, B. Gray, and L. K. Trevino, "Racial Homophily and Its Persistence in Newcomers' Social Networks," *Organization Science* 14, no. 2 (2003): 123–136.
13. J. M. Beyer, P. Cattopadhyay, E. George, W. H. Glick, et al., "The Selective Perception of Managers Revisited," *Academy of Management Journal* 40 (2003): 716–737.
14. A. Tversky and D. Kahneman, "Rational Choice and the Framing of Decisions," *Journal of Business* 59 (1986):

S251–78; "Nothing Serious? Candidates' Use of Humour in Management Training," *Human Relations* 55, no. 4 (2002): 387–406.

15. C. M. Jones, "Shifting Sands: Women, Men, and Communication," *Journal of Communication* 49 (1999): 148–155.
16. C. R. Rogers and F. J. Roethlisberger, "Barriers and Gateways to Communication," *Harvard Business Review* 69, no. 6 (1991): 105–111; L. Perlow and S. Williams, "Is Silence Killing Your Company?" *Harvard Business Review* 81, no. 5 (2003): 52–58.
17. R. Wilkinson, "Do You Speak Obscuranta?" *Supervision* 49, no. 9 (1988): 3–5; C. Argyris, "Four Steps to Chaos," *Harvard Business Review* 81, no. 10 (2003): 140.
18. R. Harrison, *Beyond Words: An Introduction to Nonverbal Communication* (Upper Saddle River, NJ: Prentice Hall, 1974); A. Kristof-Brown, M. R. Barrick, and M. Franke, "Applicant Impression Management: Dispositional Influences and Consequences for Recruiter Perceptions of Fit and Similarity," *Journal of Management* 28, no. 1 (2002): 27–46; H. A. Elfenbein and N. Ambady, "Predicting Workplace Outcomes from the Ability to Eavesdrop on Feelings," *Journal of Applied Psychology* 87, no. 5 (2002): 963–971.
19. J. A. Mausehund, S. A. Timm, and A. S. King, "Diversity Training: Effects of an Intervention Treatment on Nonverbal Awareness," *Business Communication Quarterly* 58, no. 1 (1995): 27–30.
20. S. Gibson, "Understanding the Indian 'Yes'," *eWeek* 23, no. 10 (2006): 32.
21. A. Mlynek, "Say Goodbye to Shy," *Canadian Business* 79, no. 18, September 11, 2006, 125–128.
22. J. H. Robinson, "Professional Communication in Korea: Playing Things by Eye," *IEEE Transactions on Professional Communication* 39, no. 3 (1996): 129–134; G. E. Kersten, S. T. Koeszegi, and R. Vetschera, "The Effects of Culture in Computer-Mediated Negotiations," *Journal of Information Technology Theory and Application* 5, no. 2 (2003): 1–28.
23. T. E. McNamara and K. Hayashi, "Culture and Management: Japan and the West Towards a Transnational Corporate Culture," *Management Japan* 27, no. 2 (1994): 3–13.
24. S. Okazaki and J. Alonso, "Right Messages for the Right Site: On-line Creative Strategies by Japanese Multinational Corporations," *Journal of Marketing Communications* 9, no. 4 (2003): 221–240; M. Rosch and K. G. Segler, "Communication with Japanese," *Management International Review* 27, no. 4 (1987): 56–67.
25. C. Gouttefarde, "Host National Culture Shock: What Management Can Do," *European Business Review* 92, no. 4 (1992): 1–3.
26. H. Triandis, "Cross-Cultural Contributions to Theory in Social Psychology," in *Reading on Communication with Strangers*, ed. W. B. Gudykunst and Y. Y. Kim (New York: McGraw-Hill, 1992), 75; R. S. Marshall and D. M. Boush, "Dynamic Decision-Making: A Cross-Cultural Comparison of U.S. and Peruvian Export Managers," *Journal of International Business Studies* 32, no. 4 (2001): 873–893; T. R. Tyler and S. L. Blader, "Autonomous vs. Comparative Status: Must We Be Better Than Others to Feel Good About Ourselves?" *Organizational Behavior and Human Decision Processes* 89, no. 1 (2002): 813–838; L. Huff and L. Kelley, "Levels of Organizational Trust in Individualist Versus Collectivist Societies: A Seven-Nation Study," *Organization Science* 14, no. 1 (2003): 81–90; A. C. Lewis and S. J. Sherman, "Hiring You Makes Me Look Bad: Social-Identity Based Reversal of the Ingroup Favoritism Effect," *Organizational Behavior and Human Decision Processes* 90, no. 2 (2003): 262–276.
27. S. Carlson, "International Transmission of Information and the Business Firm," *Annals of the American Academy of Political and Social Science* 412 (1974): 55–63; Marshall and Boush, "Dynamic Decision-Making: A Cross-Cultural Comparison of U.S. and Peruvian Export Managers"; Y. Luo, "Building Trust in Cross-Cultural Collaborations: Toward a Contingency Perspective," *Journal of Management* 28, no. 5 (2002): 669–694.
28. J. Main, "How 21 Men Got Global in 35 Days," *Fortune* (1989): 71–79.
29. C. Peter, P. Scott, and J. Calvert, "Chinese Business Face: Communication Behaviors and Teaching Approaches," *Business Communication Quarterly* 66, no. 4 (2003): 19–23; R. S. Burnett, "Ni Zao: Good Morning, China," *Business Horizons* 33, no. 6 (1990): 65–71.
30. S. Silverstein, "Employers Project More Jobs for MBAs in 2006," News Release. Accessed March 28, 2006, at: www.gmac.com/gmac/NewsCenter/PressReleases/EmployersProjectMoreJobsforMBAsin2006.htm.
31. R. Alsop, "MBA Survey: Something Old, Something New," WSJOnline. Accessed September 20, 2006, at http://online.wsj.com/article/SB115860376846766495.html.
32. Ibid.
33. W. E. Kraus, "The 'Cool Hand Luke' Theory of Project Communication," *AACE International Transactions* (2006): 91–94.
34. A. March, "Babbling Interviewer Disease," *Business 2.0* (2006): 54.
35. T. D. Lewis and G. H. Graham, "Six Ways to Improve Your Communication Skills," *Internal Auditor* (1988): 25.
36. G. M. Barton, "Manage Words Effectively," *Personnel Journal* 69, no. 1 (1990): 32–40.
37. L. W. Porter and L. E. McKibbin, *Management Education and Development: Drift or Thrust into the 21st Century* (New York: McGraw-Hill, 1988).
38. S. L. Silk, "Making Your Speech Memorable," *Association Management* 46, no. 1 (1994): L59–L62.
39. A. DeMeyer, "Tech Talk: How Managers Are Stimulating Global R&D Communication," *Sloan Management Review* 32, no. 3 (1991): 49–58.
40. R. Fisher and W. Ury, *Getting to Yes* (London: Simon & Schuster, 1987); K. A. Wade-Benzoni, A. J. Hoffman, L. L. Thompson, D. A. Moore, et al. "Barriers to Resolution in Ideologically Based Negotiations: The Role of Values and Institutions," *Academy of Management Review* 27, no. 1 (2002): 41–57.
41. Ibid.
42. Ibid, 54.
43. N. J. Adler, *International Dimensions of Organizational Behavior*, 2nd ed (Boston: PWS-Kent, 1991), 185.
44. J. L. Graham and R. A. Herberger Jr., "Negotiators Abroad Don't Shoot from the Hip," *Harvard Business Review* 83, no. 4 (1983): 160–168.

45. Fisher and Ury, *Getting to Yes*.
46. M. Lee, "10 Myths About Multicultural Customers," *Selling* (November 2003): 10–12; K. Kumar, S. Noneth, and C. Yauger, "Cultural Approaches to the Process of Business Negotiation: Understanding Cross-Cultural Differences in Negotiating Behaviors," in *International Research in the Business Disciplines*, ed. C. L. Swanson (Greenwich, CT: JAI Press, 1993), 79–90; B. M. Hawrysh and J. L. Zaichkowsky, "Cultural Approaches to Negotiations: Understanding the Japanese," *International Marketing Review* 7, no. 2 (1990): 28–42.
47. Kumar et al., "Cultural Approaches to the Process of Business Negotiations."
48. Graham and Herberger, "Negotiators Abroad Don't Shoot from the Hip."
49. Kumar et al., "Cultural Approaches to the Process of Business Negotiations."
50. N. Woliansky, "We Do (Do Not) Accept Your Offer," *Management Review* 78, no. 12 (1989): 54–55; Kumar et al., "Cultural Approaches to the Process of Business Negotiations."
51. Graham and Herberger, "Negotiators Abroad Don't Shoot from the Hip."
52. J. L. Graham and N. J. Adler, "Cross-Cultural Interaction: The International Comparison Fallacy?" *Journal of International Business Studies* 20 (1989): 515–537; C. Barnum and N. Wolniasky, "Why Americans Fail at Overseas Negotiations," *Management Review* 78, no. 10 (1989): 55–57.
53. Kumar et al., "Cultural Approaches to the Process of Business Negotiations."

Chapter 13

1. C. K. Swank, "The Lean Service Machine," *Harvard Business Review* (October 2003).
2. B. Mitra and P. N. Golder, "Quality Is in the Eye of the Beholder," *Harvard Business Review* (April 2007).
3. M. Hammer, "The Process Audit," *Harvard Business Review* (April 2007).
4. M. J. Harry and R. Schroeder, *Six Sigma: The Breakthrough Management Strategy Revolutionizing the World's Top Corporations* (New York: Currency, 2000).
5. iSixSigma.com, "Six Sigma—What Is Six Sigma?" accessed April 1, 2007, at www.isixsigma.com/sixsigma/six_sigma.asp.
6. M. L. George, *Lean Six Sigma for Services* (New York: McGraw-Hill, 2003).
7. R. Snee, "Can Six Sigma Boot Your Company's Growth?" *Harvard Business Review* (June 2004).
8. Accessed April 5, 2007, at www.asq.org/edu/kkid/highlights.html.
9. S. C. Aggarwal, "MRP, JIT, OPT, FMS?" *Harvard Business Review* (September–October 1985).
10. Z. Degraeve and F. Roodhooft, "A Smarter Way to Buy," *Harvard Business Review* (June 2001).
11. J. F. Kros, M. Falasca, S. S. Nadler, "Impact of Just-in-Time Inventory Systems on OEM Suppliers," *Industrial Management and Data Systems* 106, no. 2, 2006: 224–241.
12. D. Corsten and T. Gruen, "Stock Outs Cause Walkouts," *Harvard Business Review* (May 2004).
13. R. Crandall and R. Crandall, "Managing Excess Inventories," *Academy of Management Executive* 17, no. 3 (2003): 99–113.
14. G. Callioni, X. de Montgros, R. Slagmulder, L. N. Van Wessenhove, and L. Wright, "Inventory-Driven Costs," *Harvard Business Review* (March 2005).
15. F. Abernathy, J. Dunlop, J. H. Hammond, and D. Weil, "Control Your Inventory in a World of Lean Retailing," *Harvard Business Review* (November–December 2000).
16. V. G. Narayanan and A. Raman, "Aligning Incentives in the Supply Chain," *Harvard Business Review* (November 2004).
17. P. H. Zipkin, "Does Manufacturing Need a JIT Revolution?" *Harvard Business Review* (January–February 1991): 4–11.
18. M. J. Benner and M. L. Tushman, "Exploitation, Exploration, and Process Management: The Productivity Dilemma Revisited," *Academy of Management Review* 28, no. 2 (2003): 238–256.
19. B. Vanark, E. Monnikhof, and C. Nannomulder, "Productivity in Services: An International Comparative Perspective," *Canadian Journal of Economics (Revue Canadienne d'Economique)* 32, no. 2 (1999).
20. P. S. Adler, "Time-and-Motion Regained," *Harvard Business Review* (January–February 1993).
21. A. Herrea, Design for Manufacturing and Assembly Application on the Design of the Ah64d Helicopter, paper presented at the 12th International Forum on DFMA, June 1997, Newport, RI.
22. S. Chopra and P. Meindl, *Supply Chain Management: Strategy, Planning, and Operation* (Upper Saddle River, NJ: Prentice Hall, 2001); S. Croom, P. Romano, and M. Giannakis, "Supply Chain Management: An Analytical Framework for Critical Literature Review," *European Journal of Purchasing and Supply Management* 6 (2000): 67–83.
23. M. C. Cooper, D. M. Lambert, and J. D. Pagh, "Supply Chain Management: More Than a New Name for Logistics," *The International Journal of Logistics Management* 8, no. 1 (1997): 1–14.
24. M. L. Fischer, "What Is the Right Supply Chain for Your Product?" *Harvard Business Review* (March–April 1997).
25. M. T. Frohlich and R. Westbrook, "Arcs of Integration: An International Study of Supply Chain Strategies," *Journal of Operations Management* 19 (2001): 185–200.
26. T. Friedman, *The World Is Flat* (New York: Penguin Group, 2005).
27. P. J. McGoldrick and P. M. Barton, "High-Tech Ways to Keep Cupboards Full," *Harvard Business Review* (March 2007).
28. R. A. Lancioni, M. F. Smith, and T. A. Oliva, "The Role of the Internet in Supply Chain Management," *Industrial Marketing Management* 29 (2000): 45–56.
29. R. Krishnan, X. Martin, and N. G. Noorderhaven, "When Does Trust Matter to Alliance Performance?" *Academy of Management Journal* 49 (2006): 894–917; J. T. Mentzer, S. Min, and Z. G. Zacharia, "The Nature of Interfirm Partnering in Supply Chain Management," *Journal of Retailing* 76, no. 4 (2000): 549–568; J. H. Bantham, K. G. Celuch, and C. J. Kasouf, "A Perspective of Partnerships Based on Interdependence and Dialectal Theory," *Journal of Business Research* 56 (2003): 265–227.

30. J. K. Liker and T. Y. Choi, "Build Deeper Supplier Relationships," *Harvard Business Review* (December 2004).
31. B. Arrunada and X. H. Vazques, "When Your Contract Manufacturer Becomes Your Competitor," *Harvard Business Review* (September 2006).
32. H. Ma and L. Ojala, "Benchmarking the Collaboration in the Supply Chain," *International Journal of Services and Operations Management* 2, no. 4 (2006): 367–387; M. Bengtsson and S. Kock, "'Coopetition' in Business Networks—To Compete and Cooperate Simultaneously," *Industrial Marketing Management* 29, no. 5 (2000): 411–426; T. M. Simatupang and R. Sridharan, "The Collaboration Index: A Measure for Supply Chain Collaboration," *International Journal of Physical Distribution and Logistics Management* 35, no. 1 (2005): 44–62.
33. V. D. R. Guide and L. N. Van Wassenhove, "The Reverse Supply Chain," *Harvard Business Review* (February 2002).

Chapter 14

1. G. Orwell, *1984: A Novel* (New York: New American Library, 1950); D. E. W. Marginson, "Management Control Systems and Their Effects on Strategy Formation at Middle-Management Levels: Evidence from a U.K. Organization," *Strategic Management Journal* 23, no. 11 (2002): 1019–1031; M. Goold and A. Campbell, "Do You Have a Well-Designed Organization?" *Harvard Business Review* 80, no. 3 (2002): 117–124; W. Nasrallah, R. Levitt, and P. Glynn, "Interaction Value Analysis: When Structured Communication Benefits Organizations," *Organization Science* 14, no. 5 (2003): 541–557.
2. A. S. Tannenbaum, ed., *Control in Organizations* (New York: McGraw-Hill, 1968); Marginson, "Management Control Systems and Their Effects on Strategy Formation at Middle-Management Levels: Evidence from a U.K. Organization"; Campbell, "Do You Have a Well-Designed Organization?"; Nasrallah, Levitt, and Glynn, "Interaction Value Analysis: When Structured Communication Benefits Organizations."
3. L. Seism, "Prudential auditor gave early warning signals about sales abuses," *Wall Street Journal* (August 7, 1997): A1, A4.
4. Dart Transit Vision Statement, accessed November 30, 2002, at www.dartadvantage.com/vision.html.
5. B. Govrindarajan, "Impact of Participation in the Budgetary Process on Managerial Attitudes and Performance: Universalistic and Contingency Perspectives," *Decision Sciences* 7 (1986): 496–516.
6. E. A. Lock, "The Ubiquity of the Technique of Goal Setting in Theories of and Approaches to Employee Motivation," *Academy of Management Review* 3 (1978): 594–601; A. Drach-Zachavy and M. Erez, "Challenge Versus Threat Effects on the Goal-Performance Relationship," *Organizational Behavior and Human Decision Processes* 88, no. 2 (2002): 667–682.
7. R. N. Anthony and J. S. Reece, *Accounting Principles,* 7th ed. (Chicago: Richard D. Irwin, 1995).
8. Ibid.
9. J. Hope and R. Fraser, "Who Needs Budgets?" *Harvard Business Review* 81, no. 2 (2003): 108–115.
10. "Measuring the Immeasurable," *Strategic HR Review* 4, no. 5 (2005): 7.
11. F. D. Buggie, "Set the 'Fuzzy Front End' in Concrete," *Research Technology Management* 45, no. 4 (2002): 11–14; R. G. Cooper, "Managing Technology Development Projects," *Research Technology Management* 49, no. 6 (2006): 23–31; J. E. Ettlie and J. M. Elsenbach, "Modified Stage-Gate Regimes in New Product Development," *Journal of Product Innovation Management* 24, no. 1 (2007): 20–33.
12. Y. Li, L. Li, et al. "Linking Management Control System with Product Development and Process Decisions to Cope with Environment Complexity," *International Journal of Production Research* 43, no. 12 (2005): 2577–2591.
13. Marginson, "Management Control Systems and Their Effects on Strategy Formation at Middle-Management Levels: Evidence from a U.K. Organization"; M. Goold and J. J. Quinn, "The Paradox of Strategic Controls," *Strategic Management Journal* 11 (1990): 43–57.
14. J. Hogan and B. Holland, "Using Theory to Evaluate Personality and Job-Performance Relations: A Socioanalytic Perspective," *Journal of Applied Psychology* 88, no. 1 (2003): 100; P. Lorange and D. C. Murphy, "Strategy and Human Resources: Concepts and Practice," *Human Resource Management* 22, nos. 1–2 (1983): 111–135.
15. J. A. Alexander, "Adaptive Change in Corporate Control Practices," *Academy of Management Journal* 34 (1991): 162–193; V. Govindarajan and J. Fisher, "Strategy, Control Systems, and Resource Sharing: Effects on Business-Unit Performance," *Academy of Management Journal* 33 (1990): 259–285.
16. A. Zuber, "McD Restructures to Beef Up Performance," *Nation's Restaurant News* 35, no. 44 (2001): 1, 6; K. Benner, "Consumer Confidential: Get Paid to Shop," CNNMoney.com, November 29, 2005, http://money.cnn.com/2005/11/29/pf/secret_shop/index.htm.
17. Alexander, "Adaptive Change in Corporate Control Practices," 181.
18. G. Hamel and L. Valikangas, "The Quest for Resilience," *Harvard Business Review* 81, no. 9 (2003): 52–63; Goold and Quinn, "The Paradox of Strategic Controls."
19. Ibid, figure 2, 55.
20. Op cit. Li, et al., "Linking Management Control System with Product Development and Process Decisions to Cope with Environment Complexity."
21. L. Strauss, "Come Fly with Me," *Barron's* 82, no. 33 (2002): T8.
22. Goold and Quinn, "The Paradox of Strategic Controls."
23. N. C. Churchill, "Budget Choice: Planning vs. Control," *Harvard Business Review* 62, no. 4 (1984): 150–164.
24. R. Whiting, "Crystal-Ball Glance into Fiscal Future," *Information Week,* July 22, 2002, 37.
25. W. A. Van der Stede, "The Relationship Between Two Consequences of Budgetary Controls: Budgetary Slack Creation and Managerial Short-Term Orientation," *Accounting, Organizations and Society* 25 (2000): 609–622.

26. C. Bendersky, C. Morill, et al., "Fair Control: Complementarities Between Types of Managerial Controls and Employees' Fairness Evaluations," *Academy of Management Proceedings* (2006): F1–F6.
27. M. Gallagher and V. S. Radcliffe, "Internal Controls in Nonprofit Organizations: The Case of the American Cancer Society, Ohio Division," *Nonprofit Management and Leadership* 12, no. 3 (2002): 313–325.
28. P. Kibort, "Raising the Bar of Safety for Your Medical Staff," *Physician Executive* 22, no. 1 (2007): 48–51.
29. D. Brown, "Using Competencies and Rewards to Enhance Business Performance and Customer Service at the Standard Life Assurance Company," *Compensation and Benefits Review* 33, no. 4 (2001): 14–24.
30. J. R. Barker, "Tightening the Iron Cage: Concertive Control in Self-Managing Teams," *Administrative Science Quarterly* 38 (1993): 408–437; Goold and Quinn, "The Paradox of Strategic Controls"; W. G. Ouichi, "A Conceptual Framework for the Design of Organizational Control Mechanisms," *Management Science* 25 (1979): 833–848; W. G. Ouichi, "Markets, Bureaucracies, and Clans," *Administrative Science Quarterly* 25 (1980): 129–141; R. E. Walton, "From Control to Commitment in the Workplace," *Harvard Business Review* 63, no. 2 (1985): 76–84.
31. "Experts Say Improper Rigging Caused Hancock Accident," *ENR: Engineering News-Record*, 257, no. 16 (2006): 13.
32. T. R. Tyler and S. L. Blader, "Can Businesses Effectively Regulate Employee Conduct? The Antecedents of Rule Following in Work Settings," *Academy of Management Journal* 4 (2005): 1143–1158.
33. Barker, "Tightening the Iron Cage: Concertive Control in Self-Managing Teams."
34. W. H. Newman, *Constructive Control: Design and Use of Control Systems* (Upper Saddle River, NJ: Prentice Hall, 1975).
35. J. Sloane, "Small Companies That Play Big," *Fortune Small Business,* 2006, 26–38.
36. "Koch Pipeline Reaches Safety Milestone," *Pipeline and Gas Journal* 223, no. 12 (2006): 2–4.
37. R. N. Anthony, J. Dearden, and V. Govindarajan, *Management Control Systems*, 8th ed. (Burr Ridge, IL: Richard D. Irwin, 1995).
38. R. S. Kaplan and D. P. Norton, "The Balanced Scorecard—Measures That Drive Performance," *Harvard Business Review* 70, no. 1 (1992): 71–80; A. Neely and M. Bourne, "Why Measurement Initiatives Fail," *Quality Focus* 4, no. 4 (2000): 3–6.
39. Kaplan and Norton, "The Balanced Scorecard—Measures That Drive Performance."
40. Neely and Bourne, "Why Measurement Initiatives Fail"; E. M. Olson and S. F. Slater, "The Balanced Scorecard, Competitive Strategy, and Performance," *Business Horizons* 45, no. 3 (2002): 11–16.
41. Olson and Slater, "The Balanced Scorecard, Competitive Strategy, and Performance."
42. Neely and Bourne, "Why Measurement Initiatives Fail."
43. G. F. Hanks, M. A. Freid, and J. Huber, "Shifting Gears at Borg-Warner Automotive," *Management Accounting* 75, no. 8 (1994): 25–29.
44. G. A. Bigley and K. H. Roberts, "The Incident Command System: High-Reliability Organizing for Complex and Volatile Task Environments," *Academy of Management Journal* 44 (2001): 1281–1299.
45. K. H. Roberts, "Managing High Reliability Organizations," *California Management Review* 32, no. 4 (1990): 101–113.

Chapter 15

1. P. F. Drucker, "The New Society of Organizations," *Harvard Business Review* 70, no. 5 (1992): 95–104; C. K. Wagner, "Managing Change in Business: Views from the Ancient Past," *Business Horizons* 38 (1995): 812; G. Hamel and L. Valikangas, "The Quest for Resilience," *Harvard Business Review* 81, no. 9 (2003): 52–63; H. Tsoukas and R. Chia, "On Organizational Becoming: Rethinking Organizational Change," *Organization Science* 13, no. 5 (2002): 567–582.
2. S. Shankland, "EMC Layoffs to Cut Deeper Than Forecast," CNETNews.com, January 5, 2007; C. Isdore, "GM's Big Shakeup," CNNMoney.com, November 21, 2005.
3. E. Walzer, "Eye on Fiber: DuPont Trims Its Textile Subsidiary," *Sporting Goods Business* 35, no. 6 (2002): 56.
4. U.S.-China Business Council, "Foreign Investment in China," accessed January 15, 2007, at www.uschina.org/statistics/2005foreigninvestment.html.
5. C. Covault, "Kennedy Cutbacks Could Risk Capability," *Aviation Week and Space Technology* 145, no. 10 (1996): 53.
6. Mellon, Press Release, accessed 2006 at www.mellon.com/pressreleases/2006/pdf/pr101806.pdf; A. Capon, "Peddling Mellon in Europe," *Institutional Investor-International Edition*, November 2003, 77; J. McTague, "New and Improving," *Barron's* 2002, 19–20.
7. C. Fox, "Reducing Risk," *Business Mexico* 12, no. 11 (2002): 38–41.
8. CDC, "State Smoking Restrictions for Private-Sector Worksites, Restaurants, and Bars—United States, 1998 and 2004," accessed January 17, 2007, at www.cdc.gov/mmwr/preview/mmwrhtml/mm5426a1.htm; "Workplace Smoking Ban Would Help Kick Habit," *Occupational Health* 54, no. 9 (2002): 7; L. Doss, "Operators Feel Del. Smoke Ban's Heat, Fear Law Will Filter Business," *Nation's Restaurant News* 36, no. 23 (2002): 8, 12; P. Frumpkin, "N.Y. County's Smoke Ban Sparks Downstate Furor," *Nation's Restaurant News* 36, no. 42 (2002): 4, 6.
9. U.S. Census Bureau, "Population Projections Program, Population Division," Washington, D.C: 20233 (301) 763–2428.
10. J. Pfeffer, "Understanding Power in Organizations," *California Management Review* 34, no. 2 (1992): 29–50.
11. E. J. Sobo and B. L. Sadler, "Improving Organizational Communication and Cohesion in a Health Care Setting Through Employee-Leadership Exchange," *Human Organization* 61, no. 3 (2002): 267–277.
12. E. Iritani and M. Dickerson, "Tallying Port Dispute's Costs," *Los Angeles Times*, November 25, 2002, B1.
13. A. D. Chandler, *Strategy and Structure: Chapters in the History of the Industrial Enterprise* (Cambridge, MA:

M.I.T. Press, 1962); T. L. Amburgey and T. Dacin, "As the Left Foot Follows the Right? The Dynamics of Strategic and Structural Change," *Academy of Management Journal* 37 (1994): 1427–1452; M. T. Hannan, L. Polos, and G. R. Carroll, "Cascading Organizational Change," *Organization Science* 14, no. 5 (2003): 463–482.

14. M. A. Hitt, R. D. Ireland, and R. E. Hoskisson, *Strategic Management: Competitiveness and Globalization* (Cincinnati, OH: South-Western Publishing Co, 2005).
15. D. A. Nadler and M. L. Tushman, "Beyond the Charismatic Leader: Leadership and Organizational Change," *California Management Review* 32, no. 2 (1990): 77–97; Hannan, Polos, and Carroll, "Cascading Organizational Change."
16. Honda, "Summary of 2006 Mid-Year CEO Speech," Press Release, 2006, accessed at http://world.honda.com/news/2006/c060517MidYearCEOSpeech; M. Wall, "Manufacturing Flexibility," *Automotive Industries* 183, no. 10 (2003): 44–46; T. Sonoda, "Honda: Global Manufacturing and Competitiveness," *Competitiveness Review* 12, no. 1 (2002): 7–13.
17. "Nokia Restructures for More 'Mobility,'" *Electronic News (North America)* 49, no. 39 (2003).
18. D. Tuller, "Get a Check Up," 2007, accessed at www.menatrisk.org/health/checkup.html; "Executive Program," accessed 2006 at www.mayoclinichealth managementresources.com/products/executiveprogram.cfm; L. A. Armour, "Me and the Mayo," *Fortune*, 2006, 86–89.
19. D. L. Madison, R. W. Allen, L. W. Porter, P. A. Renwick, et al. "Organizational Politics: An Exploration of Managers' Perceptions," *Human Relations* 33, no. 2 (1980): 79–100; M. C. Kernan and P. J. Hanges, "Survivor Reactions to Reorganization: Antecedents and Consequences of Procedural, Interpersonal, and Informational Justice," *Journal of Applied Psychology* 87, no. 5 (2002): 916–928.
20. D. Clark, "Inside Intel, It's All Copying," *Wall Street Journal*, October 28, 2002, B1.
21. A. Barrett and J. Carety, "Merck's New Alchemist," *Business Week*, December 16, 2002, 40.
22. R. Barkerville, *Business Agility and Information Technology Diffusion* (New York: Springer, 2005); N. Venkatraman, "IT-Enabled Business Transformation: From Automation to Business Scope Redefinition," *Sloan Management Review* 35, no. 2 (1994): 73–87.
23. P. Bradley, "Emerson Retools," *Logistics Management* 41, no. 6 (2002): 22–24.
24. J. Evans, "Grand Cathay's Assets Take a Walk," *Asiamoney* 13, no. 9 (2002): 49.
25. S. Ghoshal and C. A. Bartlett, "Rebuilding Behavioral Context: A Blueprint for Corporate Renewal," *Sloan Management Review* 37, no. 2 (1996): 23–36.
26. W. Weitzel and E. Johnson, "Decline in Organizations: A Literature Integration and Extension," *Administrative Science Quarterly* 34 (1989): 91–109.
27. B. Dumaine, "Times Are Good? Create a Crisis," *Fortune*, 1993, 123–130.
28. B. Nussbaum, "Learning to Be Like Apple, Nike, Starbucks, Nokia, P&G and Other Creative Companies," *Business Week*, April 7, 2006; I. Isidro, "10 Lessons Small Businesses Can Learn from Starbucks," PowerHomeBiz.com, accessed October 5, 2004, at www.powerhomebiz.com/vol144/starbucks.htm; S. Holmes, "Planet Starbucks," *Business Week*, September 9, 2002, 100–110.
29. M. L. Tushman, W. H. Newman, and E. Romanelli, "Convergence and Upheaval: Managing the Unsteady Pace of Organizational Evolution," *California Management Review* 29, no. 1 (1986): 29–44.
30. A. Jesdanum, "Effect of AOL Changes on Consumers," accessed August 3, 2006, at www.washingtonpost.com/wp-dyn/content/article/2006/08/03/AR2006080300302.html.
31. C. Fonicki, "Case Study: Improving the Efficiency of Small Business Lending at First National Bank of Chicago," *Commercial Lending Review* 11, no. 2 (1996): 51–60.
32. K. Lewin, "Frontiers in Group Dynamics," *Human Relations* 1 (1947): 5–41.
33. F. Gavetti and D. Levinthal, "Looking Forward and Looking Backward: Cognitive and Experiential Search," *Administrative Science Quarterly* 45 (2000): 113–137.
34. D. M. Macri, "A Grounded Theory for Resistance to Change in Small Organizations," *Journal of Organizational Change Management* 15 (2002): 292–309.
35. T. L. Saaty and L. G. Vargas, "Uncertainty and Rank Order in the Analytic Hierarchy Process," *European Journal of Operational Research* 32, no. 1 (1987): 108–118.
36. L. L. Paglis and S. G. Green, "Leadership Self-Efficacy and Managers' Motivation for Leading Change," *Journal of Organizational Behavior* 23 (2002): 215–235.
37. Lewin, "Frontiers in Group Dynamics"; M. L. McDonald and J. D. Westphal, "Getting by with the Advice of Friends: CEOs' Advice Networks and Firms' Strategic Responses to Poor Performance," *Administrative Science Quarterly* 48, no. 1 (2003): 1–32.
38. Lewin, "Frontiers in Group Dynamics."
39. R. Cacioppe, "Using Team-Individual Reward and Recognition Strategies to Drive Organizational Success," *Leadership and Organization Development Journal* 20 (1999): 322–331.
40. B. Dobbin, "Kodak Enters Inkjet-Printer Market," Star-Telegram.com, February 6, 2007; N. Watson, "What's Wrong with this Printer?" *Fortune*, 2003, 120C–120.
41. D. Blankenship, "Preparing Employees for Change," *Baylor Business Review* 13, no. 2 (1995): 14+; M. Cortsjens and J. Merrihue, "Optimal Marketing," *Harvard Business Review* 81, no. 10 (2003): 114–122.
42. J. Covington and M. L. Chase, "Eight Steps to Sustainable Change," *Industrial Management* 44, no. 6 (2002): 8–11.
43. K. Lewin, *Field Theory in Social Science; Selected Theoretical Papers* (New York: Harper, 1951).
44. K. L. Alexander, "Amtrak Fires President Days After Bad Report," *Washington Post*, accessed November 10, 2005, at www.washingtonpost.com/wp-dyn/content/article/2005/11/09/ AR2005110900643.html.
45. M. MacCallan, "Re-engineering Treasury at Cookson Group," *TMA Journal* 16, no. 4 (1996): 45–51.
46. T. A. Stewart, "3M Fights Back," *Fortune*, 1996, 94–99.
47. C. R. Leana, "Stability and Change as Simultaneous Experiences in Organizational Life," *Academy of Management Review* 25 (2000): 753–762; Q. N. Huy, "Emotional Balancing of Organizational Continuity and Radical Change: The Contribution of Middle Managers," *Administrative Science Quarterly* 47, no. 1 (2002): 31–69.

48. V. Baxter and A. Margavio, "Assaultive Violence in the U.S. Post Office," *Work and Occupations* 23 (1996): 277–296.
49. B. K. Spiker and E. Lesser, "We Have Met the Enemy," *Journal of Business Strategy* 16, no. 2 (1995): 17–21.
50. J. Kurtzman, "Is Your Company Off Course: Now You Can Find Out Why," *Fortune*, 1997, 58–60.
51. W. L. French, C. H. Bell Jr., and R. A. Zawicki, *Organizational Development and Transformation: Managing Effective Change*, 4th ed. (Burr Ridge, IL: Richard D. Irwin, 1994).
52. Ibid.
53. R. Beckhard, *Organization Development: Strategies and Models* (Reading, MA: Addison-Wesley, 1969); R. D. Smither, J. M. Houston, and S. D. McIntire, *Organization Development: Strategies for Changing Environments* (New York: HarperCollins, 1996); B. Pitman, "Leading for Value," *Harvard Business Review* 81, no. 4 (2003): 41–46.
54. Smither et al., *Organization Development: Strategies for Changing Environments*.
55. Ibid.
56. K. Lewin, "Frontiers in Group Dynamics," *Human Relations* 1 (1947): 5–41; A. Clardy, "Learning to Change: A Guide for Organization Change Agents," *Personnel Psychology* 56, no. 3 (2003): 785–788.
57. Smither et al., *Organization Development: Strategies for Changing Environments;* N. J. Foss, "Selective Intervention and Internal Hybrids: Interpreting and Learning from the Rise and Decline of the Oticon Spaghetti Organization," *Organization Science* 14, no. 3 (2003): 331+.
58. W. L. French and C. H. Bell Jr., *Organization Development: Behavioral Science Interventions for Organizational Improvement*, 5th ed (Upper Saddle River, NJ: Prentice Hall, 1995), 156; M. J. Benner and M. L. Tushman, "Exploitation, Exploration, and Process Management: The Productivity Dilemma Revisited," *Academy of Management Review* 28, no. 2 (2003): 238–256; M. J. Benner and M. Tushman, "Process Management and Technological Innovation: A Longitudinal Study of the Photography and Paint Industries," *Administrative Science Quarterly* 47, no. 4 (2002): 676–706.
59. D. A. Garvin, "Leveraging Processes for Strategic Advantage," *Harvard Business Review* 73, no. 5 (1995): 76–79; M. Hammer and J. Champy, "Reengineering the Corporation," *Small Business Reports* 18, no. 11 (1993): 65–69.
60. D. Rigby, "Management Tools and Techniques: A Survey," *California Management Review* 43, no. 2 (2001): 139–161.
61. Ibid.
62. G. Hall, J. Rosenthal, and J. Wade, "How to Make Reengineering Really Work," *Harvard Business Review* 71, no. 6 (1993): 119–131.
63. J. B. White, "Next Big Thing: Reengineering Gurus Take Steps to Remodel Their Stalling Vehicles," *Wall Street Journal*, November 26, 1996, A1, A10; Rigby, "Management Tools and Techniques: A Survey"; D. Elmuti and Y. Kathawala, "Business Reengineering: Revolutionary Management Tool, or Fading Fad?" *Business Forum* 25, nos. 1–2 (2000): 29–36.
64. Hall and Rosenthal, "How to Make Reengineering Really Work"; M. J. Benner and M. L. Tushman, "Exploitation, Exploration, and Process Management: The Productivity Dilemma Revisited," *Academy of Management Review* 28, no. 2 (2003): 238–256.
65. Elmuti and Kathawala, "Business Reengineering: Revolutionary Management Tool, or Fading Fad?"; M. C. Kernan and P. J. Hanges, "Survivor Reactions to Reorganization: Antecedents and Consequences of Procedural, Interpersonal, and Informational Justice," *Journal of Applied Psychology* 87, no. 5 (2002): 916–928; D. A. Buchanan, "Demands, Instabilities, Manipulations, Careers: The Lived Experience of Driving Change," *Human Relations* 56, no. 6 (2003): 663–684.
66. White, "Next Big Thing: Reengineering Gurus Take Steps to Remodel Their Stalling Vehicles"; M. J. Benner and M. Tushman, "Process Management and Technological Innovation: A Longitudinal Study of the Photography and Paint Industries," *Administrative Science Quarterly* 47, no. 4 (2002): 676–706; Q. N. Huy, "Emotional Balancing of Organizational Continuity and Radical Change: The Contribution of Middle Managers," *Administrative Science Quarterly* 47, no. 1 (2002): 631–691; A. E. Akgun, G. S. Lynn, and J. C. Byrne, "Organizational Learning: A Socio-Cognitive Framework," *Human Relations* 56, no. 7 (2003): 839–868.
67. D. M. Rousseau, "Organizational Behavior in the New Organizational Era," *Annual Review of Psychology* 48 (1997): 515–546; C. Argyris and D. A. Schoen, *Organizational Learning II: Theory, Method, and Practice* (Reading, MA: Addison-Wesley, 1996); D. A. Garvin, "Building a Learning Organization," *Harvard Business Review* 71, no. 4 (1993): 78–91; E. C. Nevis, A. J. DiBella, and J. A. Gould, "Understanding Organizations as Learning Systems," *Sloan Management Review* 36, no. 2 (1995): 73–85; F. A. Schein, "How Can Organizations Learn Faster? The Challenge of Entering the Green Room," *Sloan Management Review* 34, no. 2 (1993): 85–92; P. M. Senge, "The Leader's New Work: Building Learning Organizations," *Sloan Management Review* 32, no. 1 (1990): 7–23; P. M. Senge, *The Fifth Discipline* (New York: Doubleday, 1990); S. F. Slater, "Leaning to Change," *Business Horizons* 38, no. 6 (1995): 13–20.
68. A. D. Ellinger, A. E. Ellinger, Y. Bayin, and S. W. Howton, "The Relationship Between the Learning Organization Concept and Firms' Financial Performance: An Empirical Assessment," *Human Resource Development Quarterly* 13, no. 1 (2002): 5–21.
69. Garvin, "Building a Learning Organization," 80.
70. Nevis et al., "Understanding Organizations as Learning Systems."
71. J. Levinson, "Benchmarking Compliance Performance," *Environmental Quality Management* 6, no. 4 (1997): 49–60.
72. Nummi, "Tours," accessed December 10, 2002, at www.nummi.com/tours.html.

Appendix

1. C. A. Rarick, "Ancient Chinese Advice for Modern Business Strategists," *SAM Advanced Management Journal* 61 (1996): 38–43; H. W. Vroman, "Sun Tzu and the Art of Business," *Academy of Management Executive* 11 (1997):

129–130; C. H. Wee, "Fighting Talk," *People Management* 3, no. 21 (1997): 40–44; Y. Y. Wong, T. E. Haher, and G. Lee, "The Strategy of an Ancient Warrior: An Inspiration for International Managers," *Multinational Business Review* 6 (1998): 83–93.

2. C. S. George, *The History of Management Thought* (Upper Saddle River, NJ: Prentice Hall, 1972).
3. Ibid.
4. D. Wren, *The History of Management Thought*, 5th ed. (New York: Wiley, 2005): 41.
5. Ibid., 34. From Adam Smith, *An Inquiry Into the Nature and Causes of the Wealth of Nations*, Great Books of the Western World, vol. 39 (Chicago: Encyclopædia Britannica, 1952; originally published in 1776).
6. Wren, *The History of Management Thought*, 36. From Smith, *An Inquiry Into the Nature and Causes of the Wealth of Nations*.
7. Wren, *The History of Management Thought*, 50.
8. Ibid., 50–51.
9. George, *The History of Management Thought*.
10. Wren, *The History of Management Thought* (see especially Chapter 5).
11. Ibid., p. 77.
12. George, *The History of Management Thought*, p. 83; Wren, *The History of Management Thought*, 77.
13. D. A. Wren, ed. and J. A. Pearce II, assoc. ed., *Papers Dedicated to the Development of Modern Management: Celebrating 100 Years of Modern Management: 50th Anniversary of the Academy of Management* ([S.I.]: Academy of Management, 1986).
14. From *Transactions* 7 (1886), pp. 428–432, published by the American Society of Mechanical Engineers. Reprinted in Wren, *Papers Dedicated to the Development of Modern Management*, 3–4.
15. P. F. Drucker, "The Coming Rediscovery of Scientific Management," *Conference Board Record* 13, no. 6 (1976): 26.
16. Edwin A. Locke, "The Ideas of Frederick W. Taylor: An Evaluation," *Academy of Management Review* 7, no. 1 (1982): 15.
17. Charles D. Wrege and Amede Perroni, "Taylor's Pig Tale—A Historical Analysis of Frederick W. Taylor's Pig-Iron Experiment," *Academy of Management Journal* 17, no. 1 (1974): 6–27; Locke, "The Ideas of Frederick W. Taylor," 18–19.
18. U.S. House of Representatives, Labor Committee, "Hearings on House Resolution 8662, A Bill to Prevent the Use of Stop Watch or Other Time-Measuring Devices on Government Work and the Payment of Premiums or Bonuses to Government Employees," (Washington, DC: Government Printing Office, 1994), 1387. Quoted in Wren, *The History of Management Thought*, 127.
19. Ronald G. Greenwood, Regina A. Greenwood, and Jay A. Severance, "Lillian M. Gilbreth, First Lady of Management," in Jeffrey C. Susbauer, ed., *Academy of Management Proceedings*, San Francicso, 1978, 2. Cited in Wren, *The History of Management Thought*, p. 143.
20. D. S. Pugh, D. J. Hickson, and C. R. Hinings, *Writers on Organizations* (Beverly Hills, CA: Sage, 1985), 64.
21. Ibid., 15.
22. A. M. Henderson and T. Parsons, eds. and trans. *Max Weber: The Theory of Social and Economic Organization* (New York: Free Press, 1947), 328.
23. R. G. Greenwood and C. D. Wregge, "The Hawthorne Studies," in Wren, *Papers Dedicated to the Development of Modern Management*.
24. Ibid.
25. A. Carey, "The Hawthorne Studies: A Radical Criticism," *American Sociological Review* 32 (1967): 403–16.
26. Greenwood and Wregge, "The Hawthorne Studies."
27. Ludwig von Bertalanffy, "General Systems Theory: A New Approach to the Unity of Science," *Human Biology* 23 (1951): 302–361.
28. Tom Burns and G. M. Stalker, *The Management of Innovation* (London: Tavistock Publishers, 1961); Joan Woodward, *Industrial Organization: Theory and Practice* (London: Oxford University Press, 1965); and Paul R. Lawrence and Jay W. Lorsch, *Organization and Environment: Managing Differentiation and Integration* (Homewood, IL: Richard D. Irwin, 1967).

Glossary

360-degree feedback performance appraisal system in which information is gathered from supervisors, co-workers, subordinates, and sometimes suppliers and customers

ABC analysis an inventory management system that categorizes items to provide information concerning which items require the most control

above-average returns profits that are above the average for a comparable set of firms

acquired needs theory motivation theory that focuses on learned needs—such as those for achievement, power, and affiliation—that become enduring tendencies

affirmative action programs hiring and training programs intended to correct past inequalities for certain categories of people based on gender, race and ethnicity, age, or religion

approved budget the budget specifies what the manager is actually authorized to spend money on and how much

at-risk compensation pay that varies depending on specified conditions, including the profitability of the company; hitting particular budget, revenue, or cost savings targets for a unit; or meeting specified individual performance targets

balanced scorecard an integrated and "balanced" set of measures for four critical areas or perspectives: financial, customers, internal business, and innovation and learning

behavioral process orientation key distinguishing feature of the OD approach to organizational change that focuses on new forms of behavior and new relationships

behaviorally anchored rating scales (BARS) a performance appraisal system in which the rater places detailed employee characteristics on a rating scale

benchmarking investigating the best results obtained by your competitors and noncompetitors and the practices that led to those results

bona fide occupational qualifications (BFOQ) qualifications that have a direct and material impact on job performance and outcomes

bounded rationality Herbert Simon's concept that managers attempt to make rational decisions, but their thinking is constrained by human limitations

bounded rationality model (administrative model) a model that assumes that people usually settle for acceptable rather than maximum options because the decisions they confront typically demand greater information-processing capabilities than they possess

brainstorming a process of generating many creative solutions without evaluating their merit

break-even point (B-E P) amount of a product that must be sold to cover a firm's fixed and variable costs

broad band systems pay structures in which the range of pay is large and covers a wide variety of jobs

budget a tool used to quantify and allocate resources to specific activities

budgetary control a type of tactical control based on responsibility for meeting financial targets and evaluating how well those targets have been met

bureaucratic control an approach to tactical control that stresses adherence to rules and regulations and is imposed by others

cafeteria-style plans benefit plans in which employees have a set number of "benefit dollars" that they can use to purchase benefits that fit their particular needs

capacity planning the process of determining how much a firm should be able to produce or service

capital expenditure budget a tool that specifies the amount of money to spend on specific items that have long-term use and require significant amounts of money

career paths sets and sequences of positions and experiences

centralized organizations organizations that restrict decision making to fewer individuals, usually at the top of the organization

change agents individuals who are responsible for implementing change efforts; they can be either internal or external to the organization

charismatic leader leadership by someone who has influence over others based on individual inspirational qualities rather than formal power

classical management theory ideas concerning the management of organizations arising from pioneers such as Taylor, Fayol, Weber, and Mooney and Reiley, together with emerging concepts identified with the scientific management approach

closed system a system in which there is no interaction of the elements with the outside environment

code of ethical conduct a formal settlement that outlines types of behavior that are and are not acceptable

coercive power a type of position power based on a person's authority to administer punishments, either by withholding something that is desired or by giving out something that is not desired

cognitive differentiation the extent to which people in different units within an organization think about different things or about similar things differently

cohesion the degree to which members are motivated to remain in the group

collaboration part of negotiation in which parties work together to attack and solve a problem

collectivism the extent to which identity is a function of the group(s) to which an individual belongs (e.g., families, firm members, community members, etc.) and the extent to which group members are expected to look after each other

command (supervisory) group a group whose members consist of a supervisor or manager and all those who report to that person

commitment (clan) control an approach to tactical control that emphasizes consensus and shared responsibility for meeting goals

committee a group that is either permanent or temporary (ad hoc) whose members meet only occasionally and otherwise report to different permanent supervisors in an organization's structure

communication the process of transferring information, meaning, and understanding from sender to receiver

communication networks identifiable patterns of communication within and between organizations, whether using formal or informal channels

compensatory justice if distributive and procedural justice fail, those hurt by the inequitable distribution of rewards are compensated

competitive advantage the ability of a firm to win consistently over the long term in a competitive situation

computer-aided design (CAD)/computer-aided engineering (CAE) computerized systems used to design new products, make modifications to existing ones, and test prototypes

computer-aided manufacturing (CAM) computerized systems used to direct manufacturing processes

concentration of effect the extent to which consequences are focused on a few individuals or dispersed across many

concurrent control a type of operational control that evaluates the conversion of inputs to outputs while it is happening

conformity close adherence to the group's norms by the individual members

content theories motivation theories that focus on what needs a person is trying to satisfy and on what features of the work environment seem to satisfy those needs

contingency approach a management theory that emphasizes matching a structured or flexible management style to the organization's environment, its technology, the tasks to be performed, and the types of employees

contingency plans plans that identify key factors that could affect the desired results and specify what actions will be taken if key events change

continuous process improvement incremental and breakthrough improvements in the way an organization does business; also known as business process reengineering and *kaizen*

control regulation of activities and behaviors within organizations; adjustment or conformity to specifications or objectives

controlling regulating the work of those for whom a manager is responsible

core competence focuses on an interrelated set of activities that can deliver competitive advantage in the short term and into the future

cost leadership strategy a strategy that involves being the lowest-cost producer of a product or provider of a service while charging only slightly less than industry average prices

critical incidents recording of specific incidents in which the employee's behavior and performance were above or below expectations

cross-border acquisitions acquisitions of local firms made by foreign firms to enter a new international market

cross-functional job rotation opportunities for employees to work in different functional areas and gain additional expertise

cross-functional teams employees from different departments, such as finance, marketing, operations, and human resources, who work together in problem solving

cultural context the degree to which a situation influences behavior or perception of the appropriateness of behaviors

cultural distance the overall difference between two cultures' basic characteristics such as language, level of economic development, and traditions and customs

culture a learned set of assumptions, values, and beliefs that members of a group have accepted and that affect human behavior

customer segment a group of customers who have similar preferences or place similar value on product features

decentralized organizations organizations that tend to push decision-making authority down to the lowest level possible

decision making a process of specifying the nature of a particular problem or opportunity and selecting among available alternatives to solve a problem or capture an opportunity

decoding the act of interpreting a message

delphi technique a decision-making technique that never allows decision participants to meet face-to-face but identifies a problem and offers solutions using a questionnaire

design capacity the maximum capacity at which a facility can run under ideal conditions

designing for manufacturing (DFM) designing products for ease of manufacturing so that quality is built into the design process

devil's advocate a group member whose role is to challenge the majority position

dialectical inquiry a process to improve decision making by assigning a group member (or members) the role of questioning the underlying assumptions associated with the formulation of the problem

differentiation the extent to which tasks are divided into subtasks and performed by individuals with specialized skills

directing the process of attempting to influence other people to attain an organization's objectives

distributive justice the equitable distribution of rewards and punishment, based on performance

downward communication messages sent from higher organizational levels to lower levels

dual-career couples couples in which both partners work full-time in professional, managerial, or administrative jobs

economic order quantity used to help managers determine the most economical quantity of products to order so that total inventory costs are minimized

effective capacity the percent of design capacity a facility is actually expected to maintain

effective leadership influence that assists a group or organization to meet its goals and objectives and perform successfully

efficiency perspective the concept that a manager's responsibility is to maximize profits for the owners of the business

emotional intelligence involves an awareness of others' feelings; and a sensitivity to one's own emotions and the ability to control them

empathy the ability to put yourself in someone else's place and to understand his or her feelings, situations, and motives

empowerment sharing of power with others, especially by those with high amounts of position power

encoding the act of constructing a message

entry barriers the obstacles that make it difficult for firms to enter a particular type of business (industry).

environmental complexity the breadth and depth of differences and similarities in an organization's external environment

equity theory a motivation theory proposing that individuals will compare their circumstances with those of others and that such comparisons may motivate certain kinds of behavior

escalating commitment the tendency to exhibit greater levels of commitment to a decision as time passes and investments are made in the decision, even after significant evidence emerges indicating that the original decision was incorrect

ethical dilemmas having to make a choice between two competing but arguably valid options

ethical lapses decisions that are contrary to an individual's stated beliefs and policies of the company

ethnocentrism the belief in the superiority and importance of one's own group

expectancy theory motivation theory that focuses on the thought processes people use when choosing among alternative courses of action with their anticipated consequences

expense budget a budget that includes all primary activities on which a unit or organization plans to spend money and the amount allocated for the upcoming year

expert power a type of personal power based on specialized knowledge not readily available to many people

exporting manufacturing products in a firm's home country and shipping them to a foreign market

externalities indirect or unintended consequences imposed on society that may not be understood or anticipated

extinction the absence of positive consequences for behavior, lessening the likelihood of that behavior in the future

flat organization structure a structure that has fewer layers in its hierarchy than a tall organization

flexible manufacturing system (FMS) automation of a production line by controlling and guiding all machinery by computer

focus groups small groups involved in intense discussions of the positive and negative features of products or services

focus strategy a strategy that targets a particular market segment. The strategy may be a focused cost leadership strategy or a focused differentiation strategy

focused differentiation strategy a strategy to gain a competitive advantage by making a product or service different from those of your competitors

force field analysis uses the concept of equilibrium, a condition that occurs when the forces for change, the "driving forces," are balanced by forces opposing change, the "restraining forces," and results in a relatively steady state.

Foreign Corrupt Practices Act (FCPA) a law prohibiting employees of U.S. firms from corrupting the actions of foreign officials, politicians, or candidates for office

formal communication channels routes that are authorized, planned, and regulated by the organization and that are directly connected to its official structure

formal group a group that is designated, created, and sanctioned by the organization to carry out its basic work and to fulfill its overall mission

formalization the official and defined structures and systems related to the decision making, communication, and control in an organization

formulation a process involving identifying a problem or opportunity, acquiring information, developing desired performance expectations, and diagnosing the causes and relationships among factors affecting the problem or opportunity

frames of reference existing sets of attitudes that provide quick ways of interpreting complex messages

functions of management basic elements of management as originally identified by Henri Fayol, consisting of planning, organizing, command, coordination, and control

Gantt charts nonmathematical graphical representations of projects used by managers to help monitor the progress of projects

gatekeepers individuals who are at the communication interface between separate organizations or between different units within an organization

gender focus the extent to which people in a country value masculine or feminine traits

general environment sociocultural, technological, economic, political-legal, and global forces that can influence the effectiveness of an organization's strategy

glass ceiling an invisible barrier that prevents women from promotion to the highest executive ranks

global approach integrating the firm's activities on a coordinated, worldwide basis

global mind-set a set of cognitive attributes that allows an individual (e.g., manager) to influence individuals, groups, and organizations from diverse sociocultural and institutional environments

globalization the flow of goods and services, capital (money), and knowledge across country borders

globally focused organization an organization that invests the primary authority for major strategic decisions in the home office

goal-setting theory assumes that human action is directed by conscious goals and intentions

Gresham's law of planning the tendency for managers to let programmed activities overshadow nonprogrammed activities

group a set of people, limited in number (usually from 3 to 20), who have some degree of mutual interaction and shared objectives

groupthink a mode of thinking in which pursuit of agreement among members becomes so dominant that it overrides a realistic appraisal of alternative courses of action

Hawthorne studies a series of research studies at the Hawthorne plant of the Western Electric Company that focused a spotlight on the importance of the human factor in productivity

Hersey and Blanchard's "Situational Leadership Model" a model that states that different types of appropriate leadership are "contingent" on some other variable, in this case "followers' readiness to learn new tasks"

heuristic a rule that guides the search for alternatives into areas that have a high probability for yielding success

high-context cultures cultures where people pay close attention to the situation and its various elements

human relations approach approach springing from the findings of the Hawthorne studies that focused on the importance of relationships among people in the workplace

human resource policies and procedures a type of tactical control based on the organization's overall approach to utilizing its human resources

human resources approach approach involving a basic belief that people possess and want to make greater use of their talents and capabilities and that if allowed to do so, performance and satisfaction will increase

incentive plans systems that tie some compensation to performance

incremental budgeting approach a budgeting approach whereby managers use the approved budget of the previous year and then present arguments for why the upcoming year's budget should be more or less

individualism the extent to which people's identities are self-oriented and people are expected to take care of themselves and their immediate families

industry and competitor forces five environmental forces (Porter's Five Forces) that can significantly influence the performance of organizations in an industry

influence tactics specific behaviors used to affect the behavior and attitudes of other people

informal communication channels routes that are not prespecified by the organization but that develop through typical and customary activities of people at work

informal group a group whose members interact voluntarily

informal organization the unofficial but influential means of communication, decision making, and control that are part of the habitual way things get done in an organization

in-group the group to which an individual belongs

institutional environment the country's rules, policies, and enforcement processes that influence individuals' and organizations' behaviors that operate within the country boundaries

integrated differentiation cost leadership strategy a set of actions designed to differentiate the firm's product in the marketplace while simultaneously maintaining a low-cost position relative to its competitors.

integration the extent to which various parts of an organization cooperate and interact with each other

integrative approaches recent approaches to management that include systems theory and contingency approaches and emphasize a consideration of a wide range of factors

interdependence the degree to which one unit or one person depends on another to accomplish a task

intergroup conflict differences that occur between groups

interventions sets of structured activities or action steps designed to improve organizations

intragroup conflict differences that occur within groups

intuitive decision making the primarily subconscious process of identifying a decision and selecting a preferred alternative

job analysis determination of the scope and depth of jobs and the requisite skills, abilities, and knowledge that people need to perform their jobs successfully

job characteristics model approach that focuses on the motivational attributes of jobs by emphasizing three sets of variables: core job characteristics, critical psychological states, and outcomes

job design the structuring or restructuring of key job components

job enrichment increasing the complexity of a job to provide a greater sense of responsibility, accomplishment, and achievement

job posting an internal recruiting method whereby a job, its pay, level, description, and qualifications are posted or announced to all current employees

job sharing situation in which two people share the same job by each working part-time

justice approach focuses on how equitably the costs and benefits of actions are distributed

just-in-time (JIT) systems inventory management and control systems that have the objective of reducing waste throughout the production and delivery of a product or service; in manufacturing, also known as lean production or value-added manufacturing

lateral communication messages sent across essentially equivalent levels of an organization

law of the situation Mary Parker Follett's emphasis on the need to generate a spirit of cooperation between managers and their subordinates with a focus on the authority (based on a person's knowledge and experience) that seems appropriate to the circumstances

leading coalition a group of supporters who are favorably inclined toward change and can influence others toward change

legitimate power (or formal authority) a type of position power granted to a person by the organization

liaisons individuals designated to act as a "bridge" or connection between different areas of a company

licensing arrangements establishing how to allow a local firm in the new market to manufacture and distribute a firm's product

line of authority specifies who reports to whom

local approach differentiating the firm's activities country by country

low-context cultures cultures where contextual variables have much less impact on the determination of appropriate behaviors

magnitude of the consequences the anticipated level of impact of the outcome of a given action

management the process of assembling and using sets of resources in a goal-directed manner to accomplish tasks in an organizational setting

management science (operations research) quantitative or mathematical approaches to managerial problems, especially those requiring specific decisions

managerial ethics the study of morality and standards of business conduct

Maslow's need hierarchy theory states that people will first attempt to fulfill basic needs, such as physiological and safety needs, before making efforts to satisfy other needs, such as social and esteem needs

materials requirement planning (MRP) a sophisticated computer system, derived from the master production schedule and an inventory database, whose output provides schedules that identify the required raw materials, parts, and assemblies needed during each specified time period

mechanistic approach highly structured traditional management approach, which may be better suited to stable external environments, highly repetitive tasks, and employees with limited technical or professional expertise

media richness different media are classified as rich or lean based on their capacity to facilitate shared meaning

medium the method or means of transmission of a message

mission statement a statement that articulates the fundamental purpose of the organization; the statement often contains several components

moral intensity the degree to which people see an issue as an ethical one

moral rights approach focuses on examination of the moral standing of actions independent of their consequences

motivation set of forces that energize, direct, and sustain behavior

multiple advocacy a process to improve decision making by assigning several group members to represent the opinions of various constituencies that might have an interest in the decision

multipoint competition strategy a strategy that involves competing with firms across markets by using strengths in one market to overcome weaknesses in another market

negative reinforcements undesirable consequences that, by being removed or avoided following a behavior, increase the likelihood of that behavior being repeated in the future

negotiation the process of conferring to arrive at an agreement between different parties, each with its own interests and preferences

negotiation "interests" a party's or parties' concerns and desires—in other words, what they want

negotiation "positions" a party's or parties' stance regarding their interests

neoclassical management theory thinking about organized work activity and how to manage that drew from classical theory in its emphasis on study and analysis of the workplace but expanded to include situational and social considerations (i.e., communication and cooperation)

network structures formal or informal relationships among units or organizations (for example, along the firm's value chain)

networking a process of developing regular patterns of communication with particular individuals or groups to send and receive information

neutralizers of leadership aspects of the organization or work situation that can hinder the exercise of leadership

noise interference with the transmission or decoding of a message

nominal group technique a process of having group members record their proposed solutions, summarize all proposed solutions, and independently rank solutions until a clearly favored solution emerges

nonprogrammed decision a decision about a problem that is either poorly defined or novel

norms a group's shared standards that guide the behavior of its individual members

objectives the end states or targets that a company's managers aim for

open system a system in which there is interaction of the elements with the outside environment

operational control assessment and regulation of the specific activities and methods an organization uses to produce goods and services

operational plans plans that translate tactical plans into specific goals and actions for small units of the organization and focus on the near term

operations management a specialized field of management associated with the conversion or transformation of resources into products and services

opportunity a chance to achieve a more desirable state than the current one

organic approach a flexible, employee centered management approach that seems better suited for rapidly changing and complex environments, nonrepetitive tasks, and employees with considerable training and competence

organizational charts illustrate relationships among a firm's units and the lines of authority among supervisors and subordinates

organizational design the process of assessing an organization's strategy and environmental demands and then determining the appropriate organizational structures

organizational development (OD) approach to organizational change that has a strong behavioral and people orientation, emphasizing planned, strategic, long-range efforts focusing on people and their interrelationships in organizations

organizational learning exhibited by an organization that is skilled at creating, acquiring, and transferring knowledge, and at modifying its behavior to reflect new knowledge and insights

organizational renewal a concept of organizational change that proposes a goal of flexibility and capability for continual change

organizational structure the sum of the ways an organization divides its labor into distinct tasks and then coordinates them

organizations interconnected sets of individuals and groups who attempt to accomplish common goals through differentiated functions and their coordination

organizing systematically integrating resources to accomplish tasks

outsourcing the practice of contracting out a significant activity within the organization to an independent party

path-goal theory of leadership a contingency theory of leadership that focuses on the leader's role in increasing subordinate satisfaction and effort by increasing personal payoffs for goal attainment and making the path to these payoffs easier.

pay structure a range of pay for a particular position or classification of positions

perception a way one sees a situation based on experiences, personality, and current needs

perceptual distortion highlighting the positive features of the implicit favorite over the alternative

personal power power based on a person's individual characteristics

PERT/CPM program evaluation and review technique (PERT)/critical path method (CPM) is a technique for scheduling and controlling large, complex projects

planning a decision-making process that focuses on the future of an organization and how it will achieve its goals

plans the means by which managers hope to hit the desired targets

pooled interdependence when several groups are largely independent in their functions but collectively contribute to a common output

position power power based on a person's position and rank in an organization

positive reinforcements desirable consequences that, by being given or supplied following a behavior, increase the likelihood of that behavior being repeated in the future

postcontrol a type of operational control that checks quality after production of goods or services outputs

power the capacity or ability to influence

power distance the extent to which people accept power and authority differences among people

precontrol a type of operational control that focuses on the quality, quantity, and characteristics of the inputs into the production process

primary activities activities that are directly involved in the creation of a product or service and getting it into the hands of the customer, and keeping it there

probability of effect the moral intensity of an issue rises and falls depending on how likely people think the consequences are

problem a gap between existing and desired performance

procedural justice ensuring that those affected by managerial decisions consent to the decision-making process and that the process is administered impartially

process costs increasing costs of coordination as group size increases

process redesign (reengineering) involves a fundamental redesign of business processes to achieve dramatic improvements

process theories motivation theories dealing with the way different variables combine to influence the amount of effort people put forth

productivity measurement of how well an organization uses its inputs in producing its outputs

profit center a unit or product line in which the related expenses are deducted from the revenue generated

programmed decision a standard response to a simple or routine problem

project/task force a temporary group put together by an organization for a particular purpose

proposed budget a budget that outlines how much money an organization needs; it is submitted to a superior or budget review committee

prospective rationality a belief that future courses of action are rational and correct

proximity the physical, psychological, and emotional closeness the decision maker feels to those affected by the decision

punishments undesirable consequences given following behavior to decrease the likelihood it will be repeated

quality the reliability, durability, serviceability, and dependability of products and services; also defined as fitness for use

rational model (classical model) a seven-step model of decision making that represents the earliest attempt to model decision processes

reciprocal interdependence when two or more groups depend on one another for inputs

reengineering fundamental rethinking and radical redesign of business processes to achieve dramatic improvements in critical, contemporary measures of performance, such as cost, quality, service, or speed

referent power a type of personal power gained when people are attracted to, or identify with, that person

region–country focus when the primary authority to determine competitive strategy rests with the management of the international subsidiary based in a region of the world or a specific country

relationship conflict interpersonal differences among group members

retrospective decision model (implicit favorite model) a decision-making model that focuses on how decision makers attempt to rationalize their choices after they are made

reward power a type of position power based on a person's authority to give out rewards

role ambiguity a situation in which the expected behaviors for a group member are not clearly defined

role conflict a situation in which a member of a group faces two or more contrasting sets of expectations

satisficing the tendency for decision makers to accept the first alternative that meets their minimally acceptable requirements rather than pushing them further for an alternative that produces the best results

scientific management appraoch developed by Frederick Winslow Taylor focusing on basic principles for improving performance, such as studying jobs by uisng objective measurements in order to determine the one best way, selecting the best persons for the job, training them in the most efficient methods, and providing sufficient monetary incentive to those performing the work

selective perception the process of screening out some parts of an intended message because they contradict our beliefs or desires

self-efficacy an individual's confidence about his or her abilities to mobilize motivation, cognitive resources, and courses of action needed to successfully execute a specific task within a given context

self-managing (autonomous) workgroup a group that has no formally appointed supervisor but is similar to command groups in that the members coordinate their organizational work as if they all reported to the same formally appointed supervisor; members usually appoint their own informal team leader

sequential interdependence when the outputs of one group become the inputs of another group

simulation a set of techniques in which various potential combinations of variables can be mathematically manipulated in advance of actual decisions to determine the possible effects of changes in one or more variables

social cognitive theory a process theory that, in part, describes how to increase an individual's sense of self-efficacy, thus increasing motivation

social consensus the extent to which members of a society agree that an act is either good or bad

social intelligence the ability to "read" other people and their intentions and adjust one's own behavior in response

social loafing the phenomenon of reduced effort per person in large groups

sociocultural forces forces consisting primarily of the demographics and the cultural characteristics of the societies in which an organization operates

solution a process involving generating alternatives, selecting the preferred solution, and implementing the decided course of action

span of control the number of employees reporting to a given supervisor

stakeholders individuals or groups who have an interest in and are affected by the actions of an organization

standard operating procedure (SOP) established procedure for action used for programmed decisions that specifies exactly what should be done

standards targets of performance

statistical process control (SPC) a quantitative tool to aid in making decisions concerning how well a process is performing

status the standing or prestige that a person has in a group, which can be based on a number of factors such as perceived leadership abilities, seniority, or special skills

stereotyping the tendency to oversimplify and generalize about groups of people

strategic alliances cooperative arrangements between two firms in which they agree to share resources to accomplish a mutually desirable goal

strategic control assessment and regulation of how the organization as a whole fits its external environment and meets its long-range objectives and goals

strategic corporate social responsibility perspective a three-criteria model that can help managers focus on social areas where there is the highest possibility of creating shared value for the business and society

strategic objectives objectives that turn the strategic intent and mission of a firm into concrete and measurable goals

strategic plans plans that focus on the broad future of the organization and incorporate both external environmental demands and internal resources into managers' actions

strategic scope the scope of a firm's strategy or breadth of focus

strategic vision provides a view of the firm over the long term and what it should achieve in the future

structured debate a process to improve problem formulation that includes the processes of devil's advocate, multiple advocacy, and dialectical inquiry

structured interview one in which interviewers ask a standard set of questions of all candidates about qualifications and capabilities related to job performance

subjectively expected utility (SEU) model a model of decision making that asserts that managers choose the alternative that they subjectively believe maximizes the desired outcome

substitution whether or not the customer's need that you fulfill can be met by alternative means

superior value products and services that produce value for customers that is superior to the value provided by competitors

supervisory structure a type of tactical control based on reporting levels in an organization

support activities activities that facilitate the creation of a product or service and its transfer to the customer

swift trust the rapid development of trust in teams with positive and reciprocal communications about the team's task activities

SWOT analysis an analysis of the firm's strengths, weaknesses, opportunities, and threats (SWOT) to its continued operation

system an interconnected set of elements that have orderly interactions that form a unitary whole

systems theory the processes involved in how "inputs" transformed by the organization into "outputs"

tactical control assessment and regulation of the day-to-day functions of the organization and its major units in the implementation of its strategy

tactical plans plans that translate strategic plans into specific goals for specific parts of the organization

tall organization structure a structure that has multiple layers or is high in terms of vertical differentiation

task conflict conflict that focuses on differences in ideas and courses of action in addressing the issues facing a group

task differentiation differentiation by what employees do

team a type of group that has additional characteristics: a high degree of interdependent, coordinated interaction and a strong sense of members' personal responsibility for achieving specified group outcomes

temporal immediacy a function of the interval between the time the action occurs and the onset of its consequences

T-groups groups of individuals participating in organizational development sessions away from the workplace; also called basic skills training groups

total quality management (TQM) a management approach and philosophy that involves a commitment from all levels of employees to continually strive to make improvements and satisfy customers

traits relatively enduring characteristics of a person

transactional leadership leadership that focuses on motivating followers' self-interests by exchanging rewards for their compliance; emphasis is on having subordinates implement procedures correctly and make needed, but relatively routine, changes

transformational leadership leadership that motivates followers to ignore self-interests and work for the larger good of the organization to achieve significant accomplishments; emphasis is on articulating a vision that will convince subordinates to make major changes

transnational organization an organization that strives to be simultaneously centralized and decentralized

two-factor theory motivation theory that focuses on the presumed different effects of intrinsic job factors (motivation) and extrinsic situational factors (hygiene factors)

uncertainty the extent to which organizations cannot accurately forecast future input, throughput, and output factors

uncertainty avoidance when cultures differ in the extent to which they need things to be clear or ambiguous

unity of command the notion that an employee should have one and only one boss

universal approach choosing a course of action that you believe can apply to all people under all situations

upward communication messages sent from lower organizational levels to higher levels

utilitarian approach focuses on the consequences of an action

valid selection technique a screening process that differentiates those who would be successful in a job from those who would not

value chain the set of key activities that directly produce or support the production of a firm's products and service offered to customers.

values fundamentally important behaviors, activities, and outcomes

virtual teams teams that rely on electronically mediated communication

whistle-blower an employee who discloses illegal or unethical conduct on the part of others in the organization

wholly owned subsidiaries direct investments to establish a business in a foreign market in which the local firm owns and controls 100 percent of the business

work centrality the degree of general importance that working has in the life of an individual at a point in time

work standard the amount of time it takes a trained employee to complete a specific activity or process

zero-based budgeting approach a budgeting approach that assumes that all funding allocations must be justified from zero each year

Name Index

Subject Index

Photo Credits

Chapter 1 p. 4 Courtesy of Blaine Halvorson, Junk Food Clothing; p. 8 Ben Baker, Redux Pictures; p. 9 PhotoDisc/ Getty Images; p. 25 Les Stone, The Image Works

Chapter 2 p. 28 Half Price Books; p. 33 Don Ryan, AP Wide World Photos; p. 44 Peter Charlesworth, OnAsia; p. 50 AP Wide World Photos

Chapter 3 p. 58 Steve Radewych; p. 62 Getty Images, Inc.; p. 70 Daniel Acker/Bloomberg News, Landov LLC; p. 71 Bob Riha, Jr., AP Wide World Photos; p. 72 Adrian Sherratt, Alamy.com

Chapter 4 p. 84 Lead Dog Productions; p. 87 United Parcel Service; p. 96 (left) Nokia; p. 96 (right) Nokian Footwear Ltd.; p. 102 Courtesy of Computer History Museum

Chapter 5 p. 114 Babcock Graduate School of Management; p. 117 Francois Mori, AP Wide World Photos; p. 120 Richard Michael Pruitt/Dallas Morning News, Corbis/Sygma; p. 127 Noah Berger/Bloomberg News, Landov LLC; p. 132 Pascal Sittle/REA, Redux Pictures

Chapter 6 p. 144 Matt Kinkaid, President DMSK Inc.; p. 146 Mike Simons, Getty Images, Inc.; p. 149 Tim Boyle, Getty Images, Inc.; p. 156 Elaine Thompson, AP Wide World Photos

Chapter 7 p. 168 Luiz Freire; p. 181 © Jerry McCrea/Star Ledger, CORBIS-NY, All Rights Reserved; p. 188 John Froschauer, AP Wide World Photos; p. 199 Ron Helfin, AP Wide World Photos

Chapter 8 p. 204 Jean Jacques Beaussart; p. 207 Phil Huber, Black Star; p. 210 Keith Brofsky, Getty Images, Inc.—PhotoDisc; p. 219 Janet Hostetter, AP Wide World Photos; p. 232 Jeff Zaruba, Zaruba Photography

Chapter 9 p. 242 Courtesy of Taylor Ridout, The Shoppes at Brownstone Village; p. 247 Kistone Photography; p. 256 George Burns, AP Wide World Photos; p. 263 Kim Kulish, Corbis/Bettmann

Chapter 10 p. 276 Courtesy of Elizabeth Hayes, America Online; p. 280 Ann States, Ann States Photography; p. 283 Paul S. Howell, Getty Images, Inc.—Liaison

Chapter 11 p. 308 Courtesy of Stephen Ortiz, Prairie Band Casino & Resort; p. 316 AP Wide World Photos; p. 318 Corbis Royalty Free; p. 319 Simon Brooke-Webb, Logica CMG; p. 328 Jon Feingersh, Corbis Zefa Collection

Chapter 12 p. 340 Bridgette Chambers; p. 345 James Callaghan, Alamy.com; p. 346 Colin Young-Wolff, PhotoEdit, Inc.; p. 352 Barbara Filet, FILET PHOTO-GRAPHICS; p. 355 Getty Images, Inc.

Chapter 13 p. 370 Courtesy of Michelle Jackson, BNSF Railway Company; p. 376 Andy Sachs, Getty Images, Inc.; p. 380 Miguel Riopa/AFP, Getty Images, Inc.; p. 381 Fred Guerdin/Reporters, Redux Pictures, Inc.; p. 386 Bill Pugliano, Getty Images

Chapter 14 p. 398 Bradley Scott Carter; p. 401 Rachel Weill, Getty Images, Inc.; p. 403 Toshifumi Kitamura/ AFP, Getty Images, Inc.; p. 417 Courtesy of Jonelle Raffino, South West Trading Company, www.soysilk.com; p. 418 David Hecker/AFP, Getty Images, Inc.

Chapter 15 p. 430 Albert Torres; p. 434 Myrleen Ferguson, PhotoEdit, Inc.; p. 435 Simone van den Berg, Shutterstock; p. 444 Hewlett Packard Development Company, L.P.; p. 457 Museum of Flight, Corbis/ Bettmann